PIECES OF

THE

PERSONALITY

PUZZLE

READINGS IN THEORY AND RESEARCH

David C. Funder

UNIVERSITY OF CALIFORNIA, RIVERSIDE

Daniel J. Ozer

UNIVERSITY OF CALIFORNIA, RIVERSIDE

W · W · NORTON & COMPANY

NEW YORK · LONDON

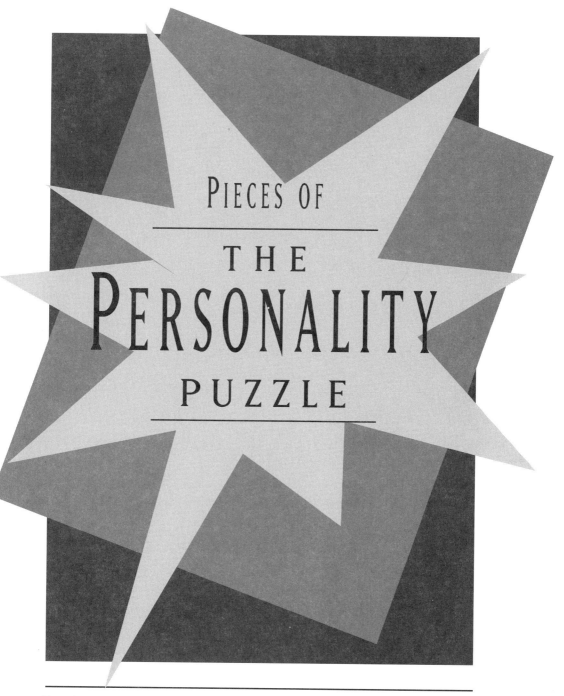

PIECES OF

THE

PERSONALITY

PUZZLE

READINGS IN THEORY AND RESEARCH

ISBN 0-393-97048-5 (pbk.)

W. W. Norton & Company, Inc., 500 Fifth Avenue, New York, N.Y. 10110
http://www.wwnorton.com

W. W. Norton & Company Ltd, 10 Coptic Street, London WC1A 1PU

1 2 3 4 5 6 7 8 9 0

CONTENTS

PREFACE   xi

Part I

Research Methods   1

McAdams, Dan P.	WHAT DO WE KNOW WHEN WE KNOW A PERSON? 3	
Craik, Kenneth H.	PERSONALITY RESEARCH METHODS: AN HISTORICAL PERSPECTIVE 15	
Block, Jack	STUDYING PERSONALITY THE LONG WAY 33	
Horowitz, Leonard	THE CONCEPT OF CORRELATION 41	
Rosenthal, Robert, and Rubin, Donald B.	A SIMPLE, GENERAL-PURPOSE DISPLAY OF MAGNITUDE OF EXPERIMENTAL EFFECT 47	
Cronbach, Lee J., and Meehl, Paul E.	CONSTRUCT VALIDITY IN PSYCHOLOGICAL TESTS 51	
Campbell, Donald T., and Fiske, Donald W.	CONVERGENT AND DISCRIMINANT VALIDATION BY THE MULTITRAIT-MULTIMETHOD MATRIX 60	
Abelson, Robert	MAKING CLAIMS WITH STATISTICS 69	

Part II

The Trait Approach to Personality 81

O'Connor, Edwin — FROM *THE LAST HURRAH* 83

Allport, Gordon W. — WHAT IS A TRAIT OF PERSONALITY? 85

Sanford, R. Nevitt, Adorno, T. W., Frenkel-Brunswik, Else, and Levinson, Daniel J. — THE MEASUREMENT OF IMPLICIT ANTIDEMOCRATIC TRENDS 89

Mischel, Walter — CONSISTENCY AND SPECIFICITY IN BEHAVIOR 101

Block, Jack — SOME REASONS FOR THE APPARENT INCONSISTENCY OF PERSONALITY 115

Kenrick, Douglas T., and Funder, David C. — PROFITING FROM CONTROVERSY: LESSONS FROM THE PERSON-SITUATION DEBATE 118

Snyder, Mark — SELF-MONITORING OF EXPRESSIVE BEHAVIOR 135

Shedler, Jonathan, and Block, Jack — ADOLESCENT DRUG USE AND PSYCHOLOGICAL HEALTH: A LONGITUDINAL INQUIRY 144

Costa, Jr., Paul, and McCrae, Robert R. — FOUR WAYS FIVE FACTORS ARE BASIC 163

Part III

Biological Approaches to Personality 173

Wells, Samuel R. — THE TEMPERAMENTS 175

Dabbs, Jr., James N., Carr, Timothy S., Frady, Robert L., and Riad, Jasmin K. — TESTOSTERONE, CRIME, AND MISBEHAVIOR AMONG 692 MALE PRISON INMATES 182

Zuckerman, Marvin — GOOD AND BAD HUMORS: BIOCHEMICAL BASES OF PERSONALITY AND ITS DISORDERS 191

Bouchard, Jr., Thomas J. — GENES, ENVIRONMENT, AND PERSONALITY 201

Plomin, Robert — ENVIRONMENT AND GENES: DETERMINANTS OF BEHAVIOR 206

Buss, David M., Larsen, Randy J., Westen, Drew, and Semmelroth, Jennifer — SEX DIFFERENCES IN JEALOUSY: EVOLUTION, PHYSIOLOGY, AND PSYCHOLOGY 210

Wilson, Margo I., and Daly, Martin — MALE SEXUAL PROPRIETARINESS AND VIOLENCE AGAINST WIVES 217

Bem, Daryl J. — EXOTIC BECOMES EROTIC: A DEVELOPMENTAL THEORY OF SEXUAL ORIENTATION 225

Part IV

Psychoanalytic Approaches to Personality 245

Freud, Sigmund — LECTURE XXXI: THE DISSECTION OF THE PSYCHICAL PERSONALITY 247

Freud, Sigmund — LECTURE III: PARAPRAXES 256

Jung, Carl — PSYCHOLOGICAL TYPES 265

Adler, Alfred — LOVE AND MARRIAGE 270

Horney, Karen — THE DISTRUST BETWEEN THE SEXES 277

Erikson, Erik — EIGHT STAGES OF MAN 283

Silverman, Lloyd H., and Weinberger, Joel — MOMMY AND I ARE ONE: IMPLICATIONS FOR PSYCHOTHERAPY 292

Steinem, Gloria — WOMB ENVY, TESTYRIA, AND BREAST CASTRATION ANXIETY: WHAT IF FREUD WERE FEMALE? 303

Part V

Humanistic Approaches to Personality 311

Sartre, Jean-Paul — THE HUMANISM OF EXISTENTIALISM 313

Maslow, Abraham H. — EXISTENTIAL PSYCHOLOGY—WHAT'S IN IT FOR US? 321

Allport, Gordon W. — IS THE CONCEPT OF SELF NECESSARY? 326

Maslow, Abraham H.   A THEORY OF HUMAN MOTIVATION 333

Kelly, George   THE THREAT OF AGGRESSION 344

Rogers, Carl R.   A THEORY OF PERSONALITY AND BEHAVIOR 350

Csikszentmihalyi, Mihalyi   FROM *FLOW: THE PSYCHOLOGY OF OPTIMAL EXPERIENCE* 363

Part VI

Cross-cultural Approaches to Personality 375

Caughey, John L.   PERSONAL IDENTITY ON FÁÁNAKKAR 377

Yang, Kuo-shu, and Bond, Michael Harris   EXPLORING IMPLICIT PERSONALITY THEORIES WITH INDIGENOUS OR IMPORTED CONSTRUCTS: THE CHINESE CASE 383

Jones, Enrico E., and Thorne, Avril   REDISCOVERY OF THE SUBJECT: INTERCULTURAL APPROACHES TO CLINICAL ASSESSMENT 393

Markus, Hazel Rose, and Kitayama, Shinobu   A COLLECTIVE FEAR OF THE COLLECTIVE: IMPLICATIONS FOR SELVES AND THEORIES OF SELVES 404

Lodge, David   FROM *NICE WORK* 417

Triandis, Harry C.   THE SELF AND SOCIAL BEHAVIOR IN DIFFERING CULTURAL CONTEXTS 419

Part VII

Behaviorist, Social Learning, and Cognitive Approaches to Personality 435

Skinner, B. F.   WHY ORGANISMS BEHAVE 439

Skinner, B. F.   WHATEVER HAPPENED TO PSYCHOLOGY AS THE SCIENCE OF BEHAVIOR? 448

Rotter, Julian   AN INTRODUCTION TO SOCIAL LEARNING THEORY 454

Bandura, Albert   THE SELF SYSTEM IN RECIPROCAL DETERMINISM 463

Mischel, Walter   TOWARD A COGNITIVE SOCIAL LEARNING RECONCEPTUALIZATION OF PERSONALITY 476

Norem, Julie K. COGNITIVE STRATEGIES AS PERSONALITY: EFFECTIVENESS, SPECIFICITY, FLEXIBILITY, AND CHANGE 487

Dweck, Carol S., and Leggett, Ellen L. A SOCIAL-COGNITIVE APPROACH TO MOTIVATION AND PERSONALITY 498

AFTERWORD 511

Funder, David GLOBAL TRAITS: A NEO-ALLPORTIAN APPROACH TO PERSONALITY 513

REFERENCES FOR EDITORS' INTRODUCTORY NOTES 525

PREFACE

Theory and research in personality psychology address the ways in which people are different from one another, the relations between body and mind, how people think (consciously and unconsciously), what people want (consciously and unconsciously), and what people do. Personality is the broadest, most all-encompassing part of psychology.

This breadth of relevance is personality psychology's greatest attraction, but it also makes good work in this field difficult to do. Nearly all personality psychologists have therefore chosen to limit their approach in some way, by focusing on particular phenomena they deemed of special interest and more or less neglecting everything else (Funder, 1997). A group of psychologists who focus on the same basic phenomena could be said to be working within the same paradigm, or following the same basic approach.

The articles in this reader are organized by the basic approaches they follow. The first section presents articles that describe and discuss the research methods used by personality psychologists. The second section includes articles relevant to the trait approach, the approach that concentrates on the conceptualization and measurement of individual differences in personality. The third section presents articles that follow the biological approach, and attempt to connect the biology of the body and nervous system with the processes of emotion, thought, and behavior. The fourth section presents classic and modern research from the psychoanalytic approach, which considers (among other things) unconscious processes of the mind based, ultimately, on the writings of Sigmund Freud. The fifth section presents some examples from the humanistic approach, which focuses on experience, free will, and the meaning of life. Articles in the sixth section consider the constancy and variability of personality across different cultures. Finally, articles in the seventh section trace the way the behavioristic approach developed into social learning theory, and from there into modern social-cognitive approaches to personality. The reader will come almost full circle at that point, as we observe (in a brief afterword) that some of the issues considered by the social-cognitive approach concerning the nature and operation of individual differences are similar to those sometimes addressed by the trait approach.

There is no substitute for reading original work in a field to appreciate its content and its style. But assembling a reader such as this does entail certain difficulties, and requires some strategic choices. The editors chose, first of all, to be representative rather than exhaustive in our coverage of the domain of personality psychology. While we believe the most important areas of personality are represented by an exemplar or two in what follows, no topic is truly covered in depth. If you become seriously interested, we hope you will use the reference sections that follow each article as a guide to further reading.

A second choice was to search for articles most likely to be interesting to an audience that does *not* consist entirely of professionally trained psychologists. At the same time, we tried to ensure that many of the most prominent personality psychologists of this century were represented. In some cases, this meant we chose a prominent psychologist's most accessible—rather than by some definition most "important"—writing.

A third decision—made reluctantly—was to excerpt nearly all of these articles. Most of the articles that follow are, in their original form, much longer. We tried to be judicious in our editing. We removed passages that would be incomprehensible to a nonprofessional reader, digressions, and treatments of issues beside the main point of each article. We have marked all changes to the original text; three asterisks centered on a blank line mark the omission of a complete paragraph or section, while three asterisks run into the text indicate that sentences within that paragraph have been omitted.

Most articles have footnotes. Some of these are by the original authors (we have indicated which these are), but we deleted most author footnotes. We have added many footnotes of our own. These define bits of jargon, explain references to other research, and—when we couldn't help ourselves—provide editorial commentary.

Each section begins with an introduction that describes the articles to follow and lays out their sequence. Each article is preceded by a brief essay outlining what we see as its take-home message and some issues we believe the reader should consider.

Finally, this volume contains a few surprises. The reader will find two passages from novels, an excerpt from a 19th-century textbook in "physiognomy," and an article originally published in *Ms.* These were not written by psychologists, but we believe they are of interest and shed a kind of light on their topic not always provided by the professional literature.

The reader follows the same organization as Funder's (1997) textbook, *The Personality Puzzle*, and some of the research referred to in that book will be found here. However, one does not need to use that text to use this reader; the two books are largely independent, and this reader was designed to be useful in conjunction with almost any textbook—or even by itself. The reader includes representative writings in method, theory and research, the three staples of any good personality course.

Acknowledgments

Many individuals assisted this project in many ways. Useful suggestions were provided by Jana Spain of Highpoint University, Susan Krauss Whitbourne of the University of Massachusetts (Amherst), Andrew J. Tomarken of Vanderbilt University, and Brian C. Hayden of Brown University. Liz Suhay of W. W. Norton assembled the manuscript, gathered copyright permissions, and performed numerous other necessary tasks with speed and good humor. April Lange, our editor, patiently shepherded this book to completion and talked us out of several truly bad ideas. The original idea for a book of readings to accompany Funder's *Personality Puzzle* came from Don Fusting, a former Norton editor. We are grateful to all these individuals, and also to the authors who graciously and generously allowed us to edit and reproduce their work.

PART I

Research Methods

How do you find out something new, and learn something that nobody has ever known before? This is the question of "research methods," the strategies and techniques that are used to obtain new knowledge. The knowledge of interest for personality psychology is knowledge about people, so for this field the question of research methods translates into a concern with the ways in which one can learn more about a person. These include techniques for measuring an individual's personality traits as well as his or her thoughts, motivations, emotions, and goals.

Personality psychologists have a long tradition in being particularly interested in and sophisticated about research methods. Over the years, they have developed new sources of data, invented innovative statistical techniques, and even provided some important advances in the philosophy of science. The selections in this section address some critical issues that arise when considering the methods one might use to learn more about people.

The opening selection, by Dan McAdams, asks "what do we know when we know a person?" The article presents an introduction to and comparison of the various conceptual units—ranging from traits to the holistic meaning of life— that personality psychologists have used to describe and understand people.

The second selection, by Kenneth Craik, is a historical survey of the most important basic methods that personality psychologists have used to gather information about individuals. The article illustrates both the diversity of methods that have been tried and the uneven history of their development—some have been used continuously over the years; some were popular for a time and then died out; and others continue to come and go.

The third selection, by Jack Block, is an introduction to the longitudinal method of personality research. In this method, the same people are studied over a range of time—many years—sufficient to provide a window into some of the important ways in which they develop. Of course, this research is extraordinarily difficult to do, but Block argues for its importance and outlines some vital considerations for how it should be conducted.

The fourth selection, by Leonard Horowitz, is a brief introduction to a particular statistic that is unavoidable by any reader of personality research—the correlation coefficient. The fifth selection, by Robert Rosenthal and Donald Rubin, describes a useful technique for interpreting the size of a correlation coefficient. For example, if someone tells you they have obtained a correlation between a trait and behavior equal to .32, is this big or little? (For reasons Rosenthal and Rubin explain, the answer is "pretty big.")

The fifth and sixth selections are two of the unquestioned all-time classics of psychological methodology. They are absolutely required reading for any psychologist. The article by Cronbach and Meehl concerns "construct validity," or the issue of how one determines whether a test of personality (or any other attribute) really measures what it is supposed to. The article by Campbell and Fiske presents an important method, called the multitrait-multimethod matrix, for separating out the components of a measurement that reflect real properties of people, as opposed to properties of the instrument used to take the measurement.

The final selection is an excerpt from an important book by Robert Abelson. It argues that the topic of statistical data analysis is not a matter of formal proof or even mathematics. Rather, the essence of data analysis is understanding a set of observations and communicating this understanding to others. We consider this the most important lesson about research methodology that one can learn.

WHAT DO WE KNOW WHEN WE KNOW A PERSON?

Dan P. McAdams

Personality psychology is all about understanding individuals better. In this first selection, the personality psychologist Dan McAdams asks one of the fundamental questions about this enterprise, which is: when we learn about a person, what is it we learn? He begins by describing the kind of personality psychology that nonpsychologists (or psychologists when off duty) frequently practice: discussing an individual that one has just met. In such discussions, the individual is often considered at several different levels, ranging from surface descriptions of behavior to inferences about deeper motivations.

The challenge for professional personality psychologists, McAdams argues, is to become at least as sophisticated as amateur psychologists by taking into account aspects of individuals at multiple levels. In his own work, McAdams collects life stories and tries to understand individuals in holistic terms. He is a critic of the more dominant approach that characterizes individuals in terms of their personality traits. However, in this well-balanced article we see McAdams attempt to integrate the various levels of personality description into a complete portrait of what we know when we know a person.

From "What Do We Know When We Know a Person?" by D. P. McAdams (1995). In *Journal of Personality, 63,* 365–396. Copyright © 1996 by Duke University Press. Reprinted with permission.

One of the great social rituals in the lives of middle-class American families is "the drive home." The ritual comes in many different forms, but the idealized scene that I am now envisioning involves my wife and me leaving the dinner party sometime around midnight, getting into our car, and, finding nothing worth listening to on the radio, beginning our traditional post-party postmortem. Summoning up all of the personological wisdom and nuance I can muster at the moment, I may start off with something like, "He was really an ass." Or adopting the more "relational" mode that psychologists such as Gilligan (1982) insist comes more naturally to women than men, my wife may say something like, "I can't believe they stay married to each other." It's often easier to begin with the cheap shots. As the conversation develops, however, our attributions become more detailed and more interesting. We talk about people we liked as well as those we found offensive. There is often a single character who stands out from the party—the person we found most intriguing, perhaps; or the one who seemed most troubled; maybe the one we would like to get to know much better in the future. In the scene I am imagining, let us call that person "Lynn" and let us consider what my wife and I might say about her as we drive home in the dark.

I sat next to Lynn at dinner. For the first 15 minutes, she dominated the conversation at our end of the table with her account of her recent trip to Mexico where she was doing research for an article to appear in a national magazine. Most of the people at the party knew that Lynn is a free-lance writer whose projects have taken her around the world, and they asked her many questions about her work and her travels. Early on, I felt awkward and intimidated in Lynn's presence. I have never been to Mexico; I was not familiar with her articles; I felt I couldn't keep up with the fast tempo of her account, how she moved quickly from one exotic tale to another. Add to this the fact that she is a strikingly attractive woman, about 40 years old with jet black hair, dark eyes, a seemingly flawless complexion, clothing both flamboyant and tasteful, and one might be able to sympathize with my initial feeling that she was, in a sense, "just too much."

My wife formed a similar first impression earlier in the evening when she engaged Lynn in a lengthy conversation on the patio. But she ended up feeling much more positive about Lynn as they shared stories of their childhoods. My wife mentioned that she was born in Tokyo during the time her parents were Lutheran missionaries in Japan. Lynn remarked that she had great admiration for missionaries "because they really believe in something." Then she remarked: "I've never really believed in anything very strongly, nothing to get real passionate about. Neither did my parents, except for believing in us kids. They probably believed in us kids too much." My wife immediately warmed up to Lynn for this disarmingly intimate comment. It was not clear exactly what she meant,

but Lynn seemed more vulnerable now, and more mysterious.

I eventually warmed up to Lynn, too. As she and I talked about politics and our jobs, she seemed less brash and domineering than before. She seemed genuinely interested in my work as a personality psychologist who, among other things, collects people's life stories. She had been a psychology major in college. And lately she had been reading a great many popular psychology books on such things as Jungian archetypes, the "child within," and "addictions to love." As a serious researcher and theorist, I must confess that I have something of a visceral prejudice against many of these self-help, "New Age" books. Still, I resisted the urge to scoff at her reading list and ended up enjoying our conversation very much. I did notice, though, that Lynn filled her wine glass about twice as often as I did mine. She never made eye contact with her husband, who was sitting directly across the table from her, and twice she said something sarcastic in response to a story he was telling.

Over the course of the evening, my wife and I learned many other things about Lynn. On our drive home we noted the following:

1. Lynn was married once before and has two children by her first husband.
2. The children, now teenagers, currently live with her first husband rather than with her; she didn't say how often she sees them.
3. Lynn doesn't seem to like President Clinton and is very critical of his excessively "liberal" policies; but she admires his wife, Hillary, who arguably is more liberal in her views; we couldn't pin a label of conservative or liberal to Lynn because she seemed to contradict herself on political topics.
4. Lynn hates jogging and rarely exercises; she claims to eat a lot of "junk food"; she ate very little food at dinner.
5. Lynn says she is an atheist.
6. Over the course of the evening, Lynn's elegant demeanor and refined speech style seemed to give way to a certain crudeness;

shortly before we left, my wife heard her telling an off-color joke, and I noticed that she seemed to lapse into a street-smart Chicago dialect that one often associates with growing up in the toughest neighborhoods.

As we compared our notes on Lynn during the drive home, my wife and I realized that we learned a great deal about Lynn during the evening, and that we were eager to learn more. But what is it that we thought we now knew about her? And what would we need to know to know her better? In our social ritual, my wife and I were enjoying the rather playful exercise of trying to make sense of persons. In the professional enterprise of personality psychology, however, making sense of persons is or should be the very raison d'être of the discipline. From the time of Allport (1937) and Murray (1938), through the anxious days of the "situationist" critique (Bowers, 1973; Mischel, 1968), and up to the present, upbeat period wherein we celebrate traits[1] (John, 1990; Wiggins, 1996) while we offer a sparkling array of new methods and models for personality inquiry (see, for example, McAdams, 1994a; Ozer & Reise, 1994; Revelle, 1995), making sense of persons was and is fundamentally what personality psychologists are supposed to do, in the lab, in the office, even on the drive home. But how should we do it?

Making Sense of Persons

* * *

Since the time of Allport, Cattell, and Murray, personality psychologists have offered a number of different schemes for describing persons. For ex-

ample, McClelland (1951) proposed that an adequate account of personality requires assessments of stylistic traits (e.g., extraversion, friendliness), cognitive schemes (e.g., personal constructs, values, frames), and dynamic motives (e.g., the need for achievement, power motivation). In the wake of Mischel's (1968) critique of personality dispositions, many personality psychologists eschewed broadband constructs such as traits and motives in favor of more domain-specific variables, like "encoding strategies," "self-regulatory systems and plans," and other "cognitive social learning person variables" (Mischel, 1973). By contrast, the 1980s and 1990s have witnessed a strong comeback for the concept of the broad, dispositional trait, culminating in what many have argued is a consensus around the five-factor model of personality traits (Digman, 1990; Goldberg, 1993; McCrae & Costa, 1990). Personality psychologists such as A. H. Buss (1989) have essentially proclaimed that personality *is traits* and only traits. Others are less sanguine, however, about the ability of the Big Five trait taxonomy in particular and the concept of trait in general to provide all or even most of the right stuff for personality inquiry (Block, 1995; Briggs, 1989; Emmons, 1993; McAdams, 1992, 1994b; Pervin, 1994).

Despite the current popularity of the trait concept, I submit that I will never be able to render Lynn "knowable" by relying solely on a description of her personality traits. At the same time, a description that failed to consider traits would be equally inadequate. Trait descriptions are essential both for social rituals like the post-party postmortem and for adequate personological inquiry. A person cannot be known without knowing traits. But knowing traits is not enough. Persons should be described on at least *three separate* and, at best, *loosely related levels* of functioning. The three may be viewed as levels of comprehending *individuality* amidst otherness—how the person is similar to and different from *some* (but not all) other persons. Each level offers categories and frameworks for organizing *individual differences* among persons. Dispositional traits comprise the first level in this scheme—the level that deals pri-

---

[1]The reference here is to the "person-situation debate" that dominated personality psychology from 1968 to 1988. The debate was about whether the most important causes of behavior were properties of people or of the situations they find themselves in. The "situationist" viewpoint was that situations were more important. As McAdams notes, the eventual resolution of this controversy reaffirmed the importance—but not all-importance—of stable individual differences in personality (traits) as important determinants of behavior.

marily with what I have called (McAdams, 1992, 1994b) a "psychology of the stranger."

The Power of Traits

Dispositional traits are those relatively nonconditional, relatively decontextualized, generally linear, and implicitly comparative dimensions of personality that go by such titles as "extraversion," "dominance," and "neuroticism." One of the first things both I and my wife noticed about Lynn was her social dominance. She talked loudly and fast; she held people's attention when she described her adventures; she effectively controlled the conversation in the large group. Along with her striking appearance, social dominance appeared early on as one of her salient characteristics. Other behavioral signs also suggested an elevated rating on the trait of neuroticism, though these might also indicate the situationally specific anxiety she may have been experiencing in her relationship with the man who accompanied her to the party. According to contemporary norms for dinner parties of this kind, she seemed to drink a bit too much. Her moods shifted rather dramatically over the course of the evening. While she remained socially dominant, she seemed to become more and more nervous as the night wore on. The interjection of her off-color joke and the street dialect stretched slightly the bounds of propriety one expects on such occasions, though not to an alarming extent. In a summary way, then, one might describe Lynn, as she became known during the dinner party, as socially dominant, extraverted, entertaining, dramatic, moody, slightly anxious, intelligent, and introspective. These adjectives describe part of her dispositional signature.

How useful are these trait descriptions? Given that my wife's and my observations were limited to one behavioral setting (the party), we do not have enough systematic data to say how accurate our descriptions are. However, if further systematic observation were to bear out this initial description—say, Lynn were observed in many settings; say, peers rated her on trait dimensions;

say, she completed standard trait questionnaires such as the Personality Research Form (Jackson, 1974) or the NEO Personality Inventory (Costa & McCrae, 1985)—then trait descriptions like these, wherein the individual is rated on a series of linear and noncontingent behavior dimensions, prove very useful indeed.

* * *

The Problem with Traits

It is easy to criticize the concept of trait. Trait formulations proposed by Allport (1937), Cattell (1957), Guilford (1959), Eysenck (1967), Jackson (1974), Tellegen (1982), Hogan (1986), and advocates of the Big Five have been called superficial, reductionistic, atheoretical, and even imperialistic. Traits are mere labels, it is said again and again. Traits don't explain anything. Traits lack precision. Traits disregard the environment. Traits apply only to score distributions in groups, not to the individual person (e.g., Lamiell, 1987). I believe that there is some validity in some of these traditional claims but that traits nonetheless provide invaluable information about persons. I believe that many critics expect too much of traits. Yet, those trait enthusiasts (e.g., A. H. Buss, 1989; Digman, 1990; Goldberg, 1993) who equate personality with traits in general, and with the Big Five in particular, are also claiming too much.

Goldberg (1981) contended that the English language includes five clusters of trait-related terms—the Big Five—because personality characteristics encoded in these terms have proved especially salient in human interpersonal perception, especially when it comes to the perennial and evolutionary crucial task of sizing up a stranger. I think Goldberg was more right than many trait enthusiasts would like him to be. Reliable and valid trait ratings provide an excellent "first read" on a person by offering estimates of a person's relative standing on a delimited series of general and linear dimensions of proven social significance. This is indeed crucial information in the evaluation of strangers and others about whom we know very little. It is the kind of information that strangers quickly glean from one another as they size one another up and anticipate future interactions. It did not take long for me to conclude that Lynn was high on certain aspects of Extraversion and moderately high on Neuroticism. What makes trait information like this so valuable is that it is comparative and relatively nonconditional. A highly extraverted person is generally more extraverted than most other people (comparative) and tends to be extraverted in a wide variety of settings (nonconditional), although by no means in all.

Consider, furthermore, the phenomenology of traditional trait assessment in personality psychology. In rating one's own or another's traits on a typical paper-and-pencil measure, the rater/subject must adopt an observational stance in which the target of the rating becomes an object of comparison on a series of linear and only vaguely conditional dimensions (McAdams, 1994c). Thus, if I were to rate Lynn, or if Lynn were to rate herself, on the Extraversion-keyed personality item "I am not a cheerful optimist" (from the NEO), I (or Lynn) would be judging the extent of Lynn's own "cheerful optimism" in comparison to the cheerful optimism of people I (or she) know or have heard about, or perhaps even an assumed average level of cheerful optimism of the rest of humankind. Ratings like these must have a social referent if they are to be meaningful. The end result of my (or her) ratings is a determination of the extent to which Lynn is seen as more or less extraverted across a wide variety of situations, conditions, and contexts, and compared to other people in general. There is, therefore, no place in trait assessment for what Thorne (1989) calls the conditional patterns of personality (see also Wright & Mischel, 1987). Here are some examples of conditional patterns: "My dominance shows when my competence is threatened; I fall apart when people try to comfort me; I talk most when I am nervous" (Thorne, 1989, p. 149). But to make traits into conditional statements is to rob them of their power as nonconditional indicators of general trends.

The two most valuable features of trait description—its comparative and nonconditional qualities—double as its two greatest limitations as well.[2] As persons come to know one another better, they seek and obtain information that is both noncomparative and highly conditional, contingent, and contextualized. They move beyond the mind-set of comparing individuals on linear dimensions. In a sense, they move beyond traits to construct a more detailed and nuanced portrait of personality, so that the stranger can become more fully known. New information is then integrated with the trait profile to give a fuller picture. My wife and I began to move beyond traits on the drive home. As a first read, Lynn seemed socially dominant (Extraversion) and mildly neurotic (Neuroticism). I would also give her a high rating on Openness to Experience; I would say that Agreeableness was probably medium; I would say that Conscientiousness was low to medium, though I do not feel that I received much trait-relevant information on Conscientiousness. Beyond these traits, however, Lynn professed a confusing set of political beliefs: She claimed to be rather conservative but was a big fan of Hillary Clinton; she scorned government for meddling in citizens' private affairs and said she paid too much in taxes to support wasteful social programs, while at the same time she claimed to be a pacifist and to have great compassion for poor people and those who could not obtain health insurance. Beyond traits, Lynn claimed to be an atheist but expressed great admiration for missionaries. Beyond traits, Lynn appeared to be having problems in intimate relationships; she wished she could believe in something; she enjoyed her work as a freelance writer; she was a good listener one on one but not in the large group; she expressed strong interest in New Age psychology; she seemed to think her parents invested too much faith in her

---

[2]This observation provides an example of Funder's First Law, which states that great strengths are often great weaknesses and, surprisingly often, the opposite is also true (Funder, 1997).

and in her siblings. To know Lynn well, to know her more fully than one would know a stranger, one must be privy to information that does not fit trait categories, information that is exquisitely conditional and contextualized.

Going beyond Traits: Time, Place, and Role

There is a vast and largely unmapped domain in personality wherein reside such constructs as motives (McClelland, 1961), values (Rokeach, 1973), defense mechanisms (Cramer, 1991), coping styles (Lazarus, 1991), developmental issues and concerns (Erikson, 1963; Havighurst, 1972), personal strivings (Emmons, 1986), personal projects (Little, 1989), current concerns (Klinger, 1977), life tasks (Cantor & Kihlstrom, 1987), attachment styles (Hazan & Shaver, 1990), conditional patterns (Thorne, 1989), core conflictual relationship themes (Luborsky & Crits-Christoph, 1991), patterns of self-with-other, domain-specific skills and talents (Gardner, 1993), strategies and tactics (D. M. Buss, 1991), and many more personality variables that are both linked to behavior (Cantor, 1990) and important for the full description of the person (McAdams, 1994a). This assorted collection of constructs makes up a second level of personality, to which I give the generic and doubt-lessly inadequate label of *personal concerns*. Compared with dispositional traits, personal concerns are typically couched in motivational, developmental, or strategic terms. They speak to what people want, often during particular periods in their lives or within particular domains of action, and what life methods people use (strategies, plans, defenses, and so on) in order to get what they want or avoid getting what they don't want over time, in particular places, and/or with respect to particular roles.

What primarily differentiates, then, personal concerns from dispositional traits is the contextualization of the former within time, place, and/or role. Time is perhaps the most ubiquitous context. In their studies of the "intimacy life task"

among young adults, Cantor, Acker, and Cook-Flanagan (1992) focus on "those tasks that individuals see as personally important and time consuming at particular times in their lives" (p. 644). In their studies of generativity across the adult life span, McAdams, de St. Aubin, and Logan (1993) focus on a cluster of concern, belief, commitment, and action oriented toward providing for the well-being of the next generation, a cluster that appears to peak in salience around middle age. Intimacy and generativity must be contextualized in the temporal life span if they are to be properly understood. By contrast, the traits of Extraversion and Agreeableness are easily defined and understood outside of time. They are not linked to developmental stages, phases, or seasons.

The temporal context also distinguishes traits on the one hand from motives and goals on the other. Motives, goals, strivings, and plans are defined in terms of future ends. A person high in power motivation wants, desires, strives for power—having impact on others is the desired end state, the temporal goal (Winter, 1973). To have a strong motive, goal, striving, or plan is to orient oneself in a particular way in time. The same cannot be readily assumed with traits. Extraversion is not naturally conceived in goal-directed terms. It is not necessary for the viability of the concept of extraversion that an extraverted person strive to obtain a particular goal in time, although of course such a person may do so. Extraverted people simply *are* extraverted; whether they try to be or not is irrelevant. The case is even clearer for neuroticism, for the commonsense assumption here is that highly neurotic people do not strive to be neurotic over time. They simply are neurotic. While dispositional traits may have motivational properties (Allport, 1937; McCrae & Costa, 1996), traits do not exist in time in the same way that motives, strivings, goals, and plans are temporally contextualized. To put it another way, I cannot understand Lynn's life in time when I merely consider her dispositional traits. Developmental and motivational constructs, by contrast, begin to provide me with the temporal context, the life embedded in and evolving over time.

Contextualization of behavior in place was a major theme of the situationist critique in the 1970s (Frederiksen, 1972; Magnusson, 1971). The situationists argued that behavior is by and large local rather than general, subject to the norms and expectations of a given social place or space. Attempts to formulate taxonomies of situations have frequently involved delineating the physical and interpersonal features of certain kinds of prototypical behavioral settings and social environments, like "church," "football game," "classroom," and "party" (Cantor, Mischel, & Schwartz, 1982; Krahe, 1992; Moos, 1973). Certain domain-specific skills, competencies, attitudes, and schemas are examples of personality variables contextualized in place. For example, Lynn is both a very good listener in one-on-one conversations, especially when the topic concerns psychology, and an extremely effective storyteller in large groups, especially when she is talking about travel. When she is angry with her husband in a social setting, she drinks too much. The latter is an example of a conditional pattern (Thorne, 1989) or perhaps a very simple personal script. Some varieties of personal scripts and conditional patterns are contextualized in place and space: "When I am at home, I am unable to relax"; "When the weather is hot, I think about how miserable I was as a child, growing up in St. Louis"; "If I am lost in Chicago, I never ask for directions." To know a person well, it is not necessary to have information about all of the different personal scripts and conditional patterns that prevail in all of the different behavioral settings he or she will encounter. Instead, the personologist should seek information on the most salient settings and environments that make up the ecology of a person's life and investigate the most influential, most common, or most problematic personal scripts and conditional patterns that appear within that ecology (Demorest & Alexander, 1992).

Another major context in personality is social role. Certain strivings, tasks, strategies, defense mechanisms, competencies, values, interests, and styles may be role-specific. For example, Lynn may employ the defense mechanism of rationalization to cope with her anxiety about the setbacks she has experienced in her role as a mother. In her role as a writer, she may excel in expressing herself in a laconic, Hemingway-like style (role competence, skill) and she may strive to win certain journalistic awards or to make more money than her husband (motivation, striving). In the role of student/learner, she is fascinated with New Age psychology (interests). In the role of daughter, she manifests an insecure attachment style, especially with her mother, and this style seems to carry over to her relationships with men (role of lover/spouse) but not with women (role of friend). Ogilvie (Ogilvie & Ashmore, 1991) has developed a new approach to personality assessment that matches personality descriptors with significant persons in one's life, resulting in an organization of self-with-other constructs. It would appear that some of the more significant self-with-other constellations in a person's life are those associated with important social roles. Like social places, not all social roles are equally important in a person's life. Among the most salient in the lives of many American men and women are the roles of spouse/lover, son/daughter, parent, sibling, worker/provider, and citizen.

* * *

There is no compelling reason to believe that the language of nonconditional and decontextualized dispositions should work well to describe constructs that are situated in time, place, and role. Consistent with this supposition, Kaiser and Ozer (under review) found that personal goals, or what they term "motivational units," do not map onto the five-factor structure demonstrated for traits. Instead, their study suggests that the structure of personal goals may be more appropriately conceptualized in terms of various content domains (e.g., work, social). It seems reasonable, therefore, to begin with the assumption that an adequate description of a person should bring together contrasting and complementary attributional schemes, integrating dispositional insights with those obtained from personal concerns. To know Lynn well is to be able to describe her in ways that go significantly beyond the language of traits. This is not to suggest that Levels I and II are or must be completely unrelated to each other, that Lynn's extraversion, for example, has nothing to do with her personal career strivings. In personality psychology, linkages between constructs at these different levels should and will be investigated in research. But the linkages, if they indeed exist, should be established empirically rather than assumed by theorists to be true.

What Is Missing?

As we move from Level I to Level II, we move from the psychology of the stranger to a more detailed and nuanced description of a flesh-and-blood, in-the-world person, striving to do things over time, situated in place and role, expressing herself or himself in and through strategies, tactics, plans, and goals. In Lynn's case, we begin our very provisional sketch with nonconditional attributions suggesting a high level of extraversion and moderately high neuroticism and we move to more contingent statements suggesting that she seems insecurely attached to her parents and her husband, strives for power and recognition in her career, wants desperately to believe in something but as yet has not found it in religion or in spirituality, holds strong but seemingly contradictory beliefs about politics and public service, employs the defense of rationalization to cope with the frustration she feels in her role as mother, has interests that tend toward books and ideas rather than physical health and fitness, loves to travel, is a good listener one on one but not in groups, is a skilled writer, is a good storyteller, tells stories that are rambling and dramatic. If we were to continue a relationship with Lynn, we would learn more and more about her. We would find that some of our initial suppositions were naive, or even plain wrong. We would obtain much more information on her traits, enabling us to obtain a clearer and more accurate dispositional signature. We would learn more about the contextualized constructs of her personality, about how she functions in time, place, and role. Filling in more and more information in Levels I and II, we might get to know Lynn very well.

But I submit that, as Westerners living in this modern age, we would not know Lynn "well enough" until we moved beyond dispositional traits and personal concerns to a third level of personality. Relatedly, should Lynn think of herself only in Level I and Level II terms, then she, too, as a Western, middle-class adult living in the last years of the 20th century, would not know herself "well enough" to comprehend her own identity. The problem of identity is the problem of overall unity and purpose in human lives (McAdams, 1985). It is a problem that has come to preoccupy men and women in Western democracies during the past 200 years (Baumeister, 1986; Langbaum, 1982). It is not generally a problem for children, though there are some exceptions. It is probably not as salient a problem for many non-Western societies that put less of a premium on individualism and articulating the autonomous adult self, although it is a problem in many of these societies. It is not equally problematic for all contemporary American adults. Nonetheless, identity is likely to be a problem for Lynn, for virtually all people attending that dinner party or reading this article, and for most contemporary Americans and Western Europeans who at one time or another in their adult lives have found the question "Who am I?" to be worth asking, pondering, and worth working on.

Modern and postmodern democratic societies do not explicitly tell adults who they should be. At the same time, however, these societies insist that an adult should be someone who both fits in and is unique (Bellah, Madsen, Sullivan, Swidler, & Tipton, 1985). The self should be defined so that it is both separate and connected, individuated and integrated at the same time. These kinds of selves do not exist in prepackaged, readily assimilated form. They are not passed down from one generation to the next, as they were perhaps in simpler times. Rather, selves must be made or discovered as people become what they are to become in time. The selves that we make before we reach late adolescence and adulthood are, among other things, "lists" of characteristics to be found in Levels I and II of personality. My 8-year-old daughter, Amanda, sees herself as relatively shy (low Extraversion) and very caring and warm (high Agreeableness); she knows she is a good ice skater (domain-specific skill); she loves amusement parks (interests); and she has strong feelings of love and resentment toward her older sister (ambivalent attachment style, though she wouldn't call it that). I hazard to guess that these are a few items in a long list of things, including many that are not in the realm of personality proper ("I live in a white house"; "I go to Central School"), that make up Amanda's self-concept. A list of attributes from Levels I and II is not, however, an identity. Then again, Amanda is too young to have an identity because she is probably not able to experience unity and purpose as problematic in her life. Therefore, one can know Amanda very well by sticking to Levels I and II.

But not so for Lynn. As a contemporary adult, Lynn most likely can understand and appreciate, more or less, the problem of unity and purpose in her life. While the question of "Who am I?" may seem silly or obvious to Amanda, Lynn is likely to see the question as potentially problematic, challenging, interesting, ego-involving, and so on. For reasons that are no doubt physiological and cognitive, as well as social and cultural, it is in late adolescence and young adulthood that many contemporary Westerners come to believe that the self must or should be constructed and told in a manner that integrates the disparate roles they play, incorporates their many different values and skills, and organizes into a meaningful temporal pattern their reconstructed past, perceived present, and anticipated future (Breger, 1974; Erikson, 1959; McAdams, 1985). The challenge of identity demands that the Western adult construct a telling of the self that synthesizes synchronic and diachronic elements in such a way as to suggest that (a) despite its many facets the self is coherent and unified and (b) despite the many changes that attend the passage of time, the self of the past led up to or set the stage for the self of the present,

which in turn will lead up to or set the stage for the self of the future (McAdams, 1990, 1993).

What form does such a construction take? A growing number of theorists believe that the only conceivable form for a unified and purposeful telling of a life is the story (Bruner, 1990; Charme, 1984; Cohler, 1982, 1994; Hermans & Kempen, 1993; Howard, 1991; Kotre, 1984; Linde, 1990; MacIntyre, 1984; Polkinghorne, 1988). In my own theoretical and empirical work, I have argued that identity is itself an internalized and evolving life story, or personal myth (McAdams, 1984, 1985, 1990, 1993, 1996). Contemporary adults create identity in their lives to the extent that the self can be told in a coherent, followable, and vivifying narrative that integrates the person into society in a productive and generative way and provides the person with a purposeful self-history that explains how the self of yesterday became the self of today and will become the anticipated self of tomorrow. Level III in personality, therefore, is the level of identity as a life story. Without exploring this third level, the personologist can never understand how and to what extent the person is able to find unity, purpose, and meaning in life. Thus what is missing so far from our consideration of Lynn is her very identity.

Misunderstandings About Level III

Lynn's identity is an inner story, a narration of the self that she continues to author and revise over time to make sense, for herself and others, of her own life in time. It is a story, or perhaps a collection of related stories, that Lynn continues to fashion to specify who she is and how she fits into the adult world. Incorporating beginning, middle, and anticipated ending, Lynn's story tells how she came to be, where she has been and where she may be going, and who she will become (Hankiss, 1981). Lynn continues to create and revise the story across her adult years as she and her changing social world negotiate niches, places, opportunities, and positions within which she can live, and live meaningfully.

What is Lynn's story about? The dinner party

provided my wife and me with ample material to begin talking about Lynn's personality from the perspectives of Levels I and II. But life-story information is typically more difficult to obtain in a casual social setting. Even after strangers have sized each other up on dispositional traits and even after they have begun to learn a little bit about each others' goals, plans, defenses, strategies, and domain-specific skills, they typically have little to say about the other person's identity. By contrast, when people have been involved in long-term intensive relationships with each other, they may know a great deal about each others' stories, about how the friend or lover (or psychotherapy client) makes sense of his or her own life in narrative terms. They have shared many stories with each other; they have observed each other's behavior in many different situations; they have come to see how the other person sees life, indeed, how the other sees his or her own life organized with purpose in time.

Without that kind of intimate relationship with Lynn, my wife and I could say little of substance about how Lynn creates identity in her life. We left the party with but a few promising hints or leads as to what her story might be about. For example, we were both struck by her enigmatic comment about passionate belief. Why did she suggest that her parents believed too strongly in her and in her siblings? Shouldn't parents believe in their children? Has she disappointed her parents in a deep way, such that their initial belief in their children was proven untenable? Does her inability to believe passionately in things extend to her own children as well? It is perhaps odd that her ex-husband has custody of their children; how is this related to the narrative she has developed about her family and her beliefs? And what might one make of that last incident at the party, when Lynn seemed to lapse into a different mode of talking, indicative perhaps of a different persona, a different public self, maybe a different "character" or "imago" (McAdams, 1984) in her life story? One can imagine many different kinds of stories that Lynn might create to make sense of

her own life—adventure stories that incorporate her exotic travels and her considerable success; tragic stories that tell of failed love and lost children; stories in which the protagonist searches far and wide for something to believe in; stories in which early disappointments lead to cynicism, hard-heartedness, despair, or maybe even hope. We do not know Lynn well enough yet to know what kinds of stories she has been working on. Until we can talk with some authority both to her and about her in the narrative language of Level III, we cannot say that we know her well at all. On the drive home, my wife and I know Lynn a little better than we might know a stranger. Our desire to know her much better than we know her now is, in large part, our desire to know her story. And were we to get to know her better and come to feel a bond of intimacy with her, we would want her to know our stories, too (McAdams, 1989).

* * *

References

Allport, G. W. (1937). *Personality: A psychological interpretation.* New York: Holt, Rinehart & Winston.

Baumeister, R. F. (1986). *Identity: Cultural change and the struggle for self.* New York: Oxford University Press.

Bellah, R. N., Madsen, R., Sullivan, W. M., Swidler, A., & Tipton, S. M. (1985). *Habits of the heart.* Berkeley: University of California Press.

Block, J. (1995). A contrarian view of the five-factor approach to personality description. *Psychological Bulletin.*

Bowers, K. S. (1973). Situationism in psychology: An analysis and critique. *Psychological Review, 80,* 307–336.

Breger, L. (1974). *From instinct to identity: The development of personality.* Englewood Cliffs, NJ: Prentice-Hall.

Briggs, S. R. (1989). The optimal level of measurement for personality constructs. In D. M. Buss & N. Cantor (Eds.), *Personality psychology: Recent trends and emerging directions* (pp. 246–260). New York: Springer-Verlag.

Bruner, J. S. (1990). *Acts of meaning.* Cambridge, MA: Harvard University Press.

Buss, A. H. (1989). Personality as traits. *American Psychologist, 44,* 1378–1388.

Buss, D. M. (1991). Evolutionary personality psychology. In M. R. Rosenzweig & L. W. Porter (Eds.), *Annual review of psychology* (Vol. 42, pp. 459–491). Palo Alto, CA: Annual Reviews.

Buss, D. M., & Canton, N. (Eds.). (1989). *Personality psychology: Recent trends and emerging directions.* New York: Springer-Verlag.

Cantor, N. (1990). From thought to behavior: "Having" and "doing" in the study of personality and cognition. *American Psychologist, 45*, 735–750.

Cantor, N., Acker, M., & Cook-Flanagan, C. (1992). Conflict and preoccupation in the intimacy life task. *Journal of Personality and Social Psychology, 63*, 644–655.

Cantor, N., & Kihlstrom, J. F. (1987). *Personality and social intelligence.* Englewood Cliffs, NJ: Prentice-Hall.

Cantor, N., Mischel, W., & Schwartz, J. C. (1982). A prototype analysis of psychological situations. *Cognitive Psychology, 14*, 45–77.

Cattell, R. B. (1957). *Personality and motivation structure and measurement.* New York: Harcourt, Brace & World.

Charme, S. T. (1984). *Meaning and myth in the study of lives: A Sartrean perspective.* Philadelphia: University of Pennsylvania Press.

Cohler, B. J. (1982). Personal narrative and the life course. In P. Baltes & O. G. Brim, Jr. (Eds.), *Life span development and behavior* (Vol. 4, pp. 205–241). New York: Academic Press.

Cohler, B. J. (1994, June). *Studying older lives: Reciprocal acts of telling and listening.* Paper presented at annual meeting of the Society for Personology, Ann Arbor.

Costa, P. T., Jr., & McCrae, R. R. (1985). *The NEO Personality Inventory.* Odessa, FL: Psychological Assessment Resources.

Cramer, P. (1991). *The development of defense mechanisms.* New York: Springer-Verlag.

Demorest, A. P., & Alexander, I. E. (1992). Affective scripts as organizers of personal experience. *Journal of Personality, 60*, 645–663.

Digman, J. M. (1990). Personality structure: Emergence of the five-factor model. In M. R. Rosenzweig & L. W. Porter (Eds.), *Annual review of psychology* (Vol. 41, pp. 417–440). Palo Alto, CA: Annual Reviews.

Emmons, R. A. (1986). Personal strivings: An approach to personality and subjective well-being. *Journal of Personality and Social Psychology, 51*, 1058–1068.

Emmons, R. A. (1993). Current status of the motive concept. In K. H. Craik, R. Hogan, & R. N. Wolfe (Eds.), *Fifty years of personality psychology* (pp. 187–196). New York: Plenum.

Erikson, E. H. (1959). Identity and the life cycle: Selected papers. *Psychological Issues, 1*(1), 5–165.

Erikson, E. H. (1963). *Childhood and society* (2nd ed.). New York: Norton.

Eysenck, H. J. (1967). *The biological basis of personality.* Springfield, IL: Thomas.

Frederiksen, N. (1972). Toward a taxonomy of situations. *American Psychologist, 27*, 114–123.

Gardner, H. (1993). *Creating minds.* New York: Basic Books.

Gilligan, C. (1982). *In a different voice.* Cambridge, MA: Harvard University Press.

Goldberg, L. R. (1981). Language and individual differences: The search for universals in personality lexicons. In L. Wheeler (Ed.), *Review of personality and social psychology* (Vol. 2, pp. 141–166). Beverly Hills: Sage.

Goldberg, L. R. (1993). The structure of phenotypic personality traits. *American Psychologist, 48*, 26–34.

Guilford, J. P. (1959). *Personality.* New York: McGraw-Hill.

Hankiss, A. (1981). On the mythological rearranging of one's life history. In D. Bertaux (Ed.), *Biography and society: The life history approach in the social sciences* (pp. 203–209). Beverly Hills: Sage.

Havighurst, R. J. (1972). *Developmental tasks and education* (3rd ed.). New York: McKay.

Hazan, C., & Shaver, P. (1990). Love and work: An attachment-theoretical perspective. *Journal of Personality and Social Psychology, 59*, 270–280.

Hermans, H. J. M., & Kempen, H. J. G. (1993). *The dialogical self.* New York: Academic Press.

Hogan, R. (1986). *Hogan Personality Inventory manual.* Minneapolis: National Computer Systems.

Howard, G. S. (1991). Culture tales: A narrative approach to thinking, cross-cultural psychology, and psychotherapy. *American Psychologist, 46*, 187–197.

Jackson, D. N. (1974). *The Personality Research Form.* Port Huron, MI: Research Psychologists Press.

John, O. P. (1990). The "Big Five" factor taxonomy: Dimensions of personality in the natural language and in questionnaires. In L. Pervin (Ed.), *Handbook of personality theory and research* (pp. 66–100). New York: Guilford.

Kaiser, R. T., & Ozer, D. J. (under review). The structure of personal goals and their relation to personality traits. Manuscript under editorial review.

Klinger, E. (1977). *Meaning and void.* Minneapolis: University of Minnesota Press.

Kotre, J. (1984). *Outliving the self: Generativity and the interpretation of lives.* Baltimore: Johns Hopkins University Press.

Krahe, B. (1992). *Personality and social psychology: Toward a synthesis.* London: Sage.

Lamiell, J. T. (1987). *The psychology of personality: An epistemological inquiry.* New York: Columbia University Press.

Langbaum, R. (1982). *The mysteries of identity: A theme in modern literature.* Chicago: University of Chicago Press.

Lazarus, R. J. (1991). *Emotion and adaptation.* New York: Oxford University Press.

Linde, C. (1990). *Life stories: The creation of coherence* (Monograph No. IRL90-0001). Palo Alto, CA: Institute for Research on Learning.

Little, B. R. (1989). Personal projects analysis: Trivial pursuits, magnificent obsessions, and the search for coherence. In D. M. Buss & N. Cantor (Eds.), *Personality psychology: Recent trends and emerging directions* (pp. 15–31). New York: Springer-Verlag.

Loevinger, J. (1976). *Ego development.* San Francisco: Jossey-Bass.

Luborsky, L., & Crits-Christoph, P. (1991). *Understanding transference: The core conflictual relationship theme method.* New York: Basic Books.

MacIntyre, A. (1984). *After virtue.* Notre Dame: University of Notre Dame Press.

Magnusson, D. (1971). An analysis of situational dimensions. *Perceptual and Motor Skills, 32*, 851–867.

McAdams, D. P. (1984). Love, power, and images of the self. In C. Z. Malatesta & C. E. Izard (Eds.), *Emotion in adult development* (pp. 159–174). Beverly Hills: Sage.

McAdams, D. P. (1985). *Power, intimacy, and the life story: Personological inquiries into identity.* New York: Guilford.

McAdams, D. P. (1989). *Intimacy: The need to be close.* New York: Doubleday.

McAdams, D. P. (1990). Unity and purpose in human lives:

The emergence of identity as a life story. In A. I. Rabin, R. A. Zucker, R. A. Emmons, & S. Frank (Eds.), *Studying persons and lives* (pp. 148–200). New York: Springer.

McAdams, D. P. (1992). The five-factor model *in* personality: A critical appraisal. *Journal of Personality, 60,* 329–361.

McAdams, D. P. (1993). *The stories we live by: Personal myths and the making of the self.* New York: Morrow.

McAdams, D. P. (1994a). *The person: An introduction to personality psychology* (2nd ed.). Fort Worth: Harcourt Brace.

McAdams, D. P. (1994b). A psychology of the stranger. *Psychological Inquiry, 5,* 145–148.

McAdams, D. P. (1994c). Can personality change? Levels of stability and growth in personality across the life span. In T. F. Heatherton & J. L. Weinberger (Eds.), *Can personality change?* (pp. 299–314). Washington, DC: American Psychological Association.

McAdams, D. P. (1996). Narrating the self in adulthood. In J. Birren, G. Kenyon, J. E. Ruth, J. J. F. Schroots, & T. Svensson (Eds.), *Aging and biography: Explorations in adult development.* New York: Springer.

McAdams, D. P., de St. Aubin, E., & Logan, R. L. (1993). Generativity among young, midlife, and older adults. *Psychology and Aging, 8,* 221–230.

McClelland, D. C. (1951). *Personality.* New York: Holt, Rinehart & Winston.

McClelland, D. C. (1961). *The achieving society.* New York: D. Van Nostrand.

McCrae, R. R., & Costa, P. T., Jr. (1996). Toward a new generation of personality theories: Theoretical contexts for the five-factor model. In J. S. Wiggins (Ed.), *The five-factor model of personality.* New York: Guilford.

Mischel, W. (1968). *Personality and assessment.* New York: Wiley.

Mischel, W. (1973). Toward a cognitive social-learning reconceptualization of personality. *Psychological Review, 80,* 252–283.

Moos, R. H. (1973). Conceptualization of human environments. *American Psychologist, 28,* 652–665.

Murray, H. A. (1938). *Explorations in personality.* New York: Oxford University Press.

Ogilvie, D. M., & Ashmore, R. D. (1991). Self-with-other representation as units of analysis in self-concept research. In R. A. Curtis (Ed.), *The relational self: Theoretical convergences in psychoanalysis and social psychology* (pp. 282–314). New York: Guilford.

Ozer, D. J., & Reise, S. P. (1994). Personality assessment. In L. W. Porter & M. R. Rosenzweig (Eds.), *Annual review of psychology* (Vol. 45, pp. 357–388). Palo Alto, CA: Annual Reviews.

Pervin, L. (1994). A critical analysis of current trait theory. *Psychological Inquiry, 5,* 103–113.

Polkinghorne, D. (1988). *Narrative knowing and the human sciences.* Albany, NY: SUNY Press.

Revelle, W. (1995). Personality processes. In L. W. Porter & M. R. Rosenzweig (Eds.), *Annual review of psychology* (Vol. 46, pp. 295–328). Palo Alto, CA: Annual Reviews.

Rokeach, M. (1973). *The nature of human values.* New York: Free Press.

Tellegen, A. (1982). *Brief manual for the Differential Personality Questionnaire.* Unpublished manuscript, University of Minnesota.

Thorne, A. (1989). Conditional patterns, transference, and the coherence of personality across time. In D. M. Buss & N. Cantor (Eds.), *Personality psychology: Recent trends and emerging directions* (pp. 149–159). New York: Springer.

Wiggins, J. S. (Ed.). (1996). *The five-factor model of personality.* New York: Guilford.

Winter, D. G. (1973). *The power motive.* New York: Free Press.

Wright, J. C., & Mischel, W. (1987). A conditional approach to dispositional constructs: The local predictability of social behavior. *Journal of Personality and Social Psychology, 53,* 1159–1177.

PERSONALITY RESEARCH METHODS: AN HISTORICAL PERSPECTIVE

Kenneth H. Craik

Over its relatively brief history, personality psychology has employed a wide variety of methods. Some, such as personality questionnaires, have been used frequently, and others, such as observing individuals in their daily lives, have been used rarely. In the following selection, the personality psychologist Ken Craik presents a scholarly, historical survey of the methods that have been used by scientific personality psychology over the past 60 years. He points out that the use of different methods has been uneven, and that it is an interesting and challenging task to try to understand why some methods thrive, some fall permanently out of use, and others come and go.

This article provides a long list of references that would be useful for any reader interested in learning more about the methods of personality psychology. Craik also provides several—and in the editors' view, well-taken—suggestions for where personality psychology should go from here. Perhaps Craik's most important suggestion is that psychologists not forget the wide diversity of methods that exists, and that they try to use as many different methods as possible to avoid tunnel vision and attain a more complete understanding of personality.

*   *   *

In its recent past, the study of personality has journeyed through the doldrums, encountered challenges, and emerged with an uncertain sense of renewal. Although now seemingly revitalized, the state of the field continues to be unsettled in character and direction.[1] At such a time, formulation of an explicit and shared historical perspective upon our mode of inquiry and its scientific past secure in its fundamental assumptions and basic research directions. However, the field remains lively and capable of generating controversy. To see the kinds of issues that personality psychologists continue to debate, we recommend that the reader consult almost any issue of the journal *Psychological Inquiry*, available in most college libraries.

---

[1] This article was published in 1986. Since that time, the field of personality has become more settled and more

entific agenda may serve regenerative and guiding functions.

For this purpose, an historical perspective upon the development of personality research methods will be explored. This first broad-brush sketch will demarcate eras in personality research, identify a basic set of research methods, establish types of historical development, interpret our current situation, and offer lessons for future endeavor. * * *

* * *

Five historical periods in personality research will be demarcated: (1) the preidentity era, (2) the pre–World War II era, (3) the post–World War II era, (4) the contemporary era, and (5) the current situation. Consideration of trends in key research methods across these eras yields three types of historical development: (1) continued development, (2) interrupted development, and (3) halts and ar-

rested development. Two classes of influences upon the historical fate of methods are discussed: (1) conceptual formulations and (2) sociocultural factors. Finally, the implications of this historical perspective for the field of personality will be presented, along with a set of recommendations addressing them.

* * *

I. Types of Historical Development of Personality Research Methods

Perusal of trends across the entire five historical eras in personality research reveals three types of development and prominence for specific methods. A review of these courses, with illustrative cases, adds a component to our historical perspective upon personality research methods.

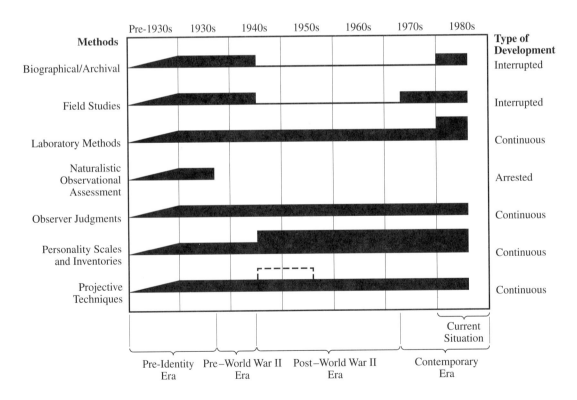

Figure 2.1   Historical trends in the prominence of personality methods

Figure 2.1 depicts in broad schematic form the trends for seven research methods in personality. This era-by-method analysis reveals three types of historical development. Four methods display continued development: (1) laboratory methods, (2) observer judgments, (3) personality scales and inventories, and (4) projective techniques. Two methods show interrupted development: (1) biographical and archival approaches and (2) field studies in personality. One method serves to illustrate halts or arrested development: naturalistic observational assessment.

A. CONTINUED DEVELOPMENT When the five historical eras of personality research are scanned, certain methods appear in prominent, continuing use. They are laboratory methods, observer judgments, personality scales and inventories, and projective techniques.

1. Laboratory methods.[2] Laboratory studies of "the dynamics of action" (Sears, 1950) can be traced at least as far back as Kurt Lewin's research program in Berlin in the 1920s and 1930s (Lewin, 1935, especially chapter VIII; MacKinnon & Dukes, 1962). Eysenck's (1967) research on extraversion has programmatically combined personality scale with laboratory methods (Wilson, 1978). The emergence of the state-trait distinction generated considerable research, especially on anxiety (Cattell & Scheier, 1961; Lamb, 1978; Spielberger, 1966, 1972). More recent topics have included psychological stress (e.g., Berglas, 1984; Lazarus, 1966), intrinsic motivation (e.g., Deci, 1975), learned helplessness (e.g., Polivy, 1982), and communication of affect (e.g., Buck, Barron, Goodman, & Shapiro, 1980). Calls for more systematic attention to aggregation and psychometric standards in laboratory studies of personality (Epstein,

1980, 1983) may strengthen this method and enhance the replicability of its findings.

2. Observer judgments.[3] Hollingworth (1922) and Roback (1927) document the considerable number of early empirical studies using ratings and other observer judgments. Such studies continue to appear, particularly within applied psychology (Kane & Lawler, 1978). Beginning with the work of Baumgarten (1933; John, Goldberg, & Angleitner, 1984) and especially with the impetus of the compilation of trait terms issued by G. W. Allport and Odbert (1936), a long series of studies has examined the descriptive language of personality (Cattell, 1943, 1946, 1947; Goldberg, 1982; Wiggins, 1979). The development of standard procedures (Block, 1978; Gough & Heilbrun, 1980) has facilitated the use of observer judgments in personality research.

3. Personality scales and inventories.[4] Goldberg (1971) provides thorough coverage of this continuing line of development in personality research methods, beginning with Heymans & Wiersma's (1906) symptom list. As previously noted, the post–World War II predominance of this methodological approach may be waning, but its impressive accomplishments and products will exert a sustained influence. Furthermore, inventories building upon the technical gains of that era continue to appear (e.g., Hogan, 1985; McKechnie, 1974; Tellegen, 1996).

4. Projective techniques.[5] The appearance of Jung's (1910) application of the word association technique and Rorschach's (1921) *Psychodiagnostics* in

---

[3]These are sometimes categorized as "I-data" (Funder, 1997), or "O-data" (Block, later in this section).

[4]Most personality tests belong to the category of "S-data" (Block, this section; Funder, 1997).

[5]"Projective tests" are those in which a person is shown an ambiguous stimulus and asked for her or his interpretation. The term comes from the idea that a person "projects" her or his personality into her or his response to an ambiguous stimulus. The most famous projective test is the Rorschach inkblot test.

---

[2]By "laboratory methods" Craik is referring to procedures in which subjects are brought into the lab, where their behavior is directly observed. An example would be the typical psychological experiment. The data yielded by such procedures are sometimes categorized as "T-data" (see the article by Block in this section and Funder, 1997).

the preidentity era establish the long-term use of projective techniques in personality research. L. K. Frank's (1939) influential explication of the projective hypothesis broadened the interpretational approach. The two-volume *Diagnostic Psychological Testing* by Rapaport, Gill, and Schafer (1946) and Schafer's (1948) related volume cast a strong psychodynamic influence upon the clinical application of psychological tests, including projective techniques, in the post–World War II era. During the contemporary era, projective techniques have markedly declined in prominence in scientific studies of personality (Lanyon, 1984), to the extent that the method might be considered for classification among those having experienced interrupted or arrested development. However, renewed advocacy (McClelland, 1980), continuing productive research programs using various forms of the method (e.g., Atkinson, 1958, 1983; Loevinger, 1979; Raynor & Entin, 1982), and new research approaches to the Rorschach (Blatt & Lerner, 1983; Exner, 1974, 1978; Exner & Weiner, 1982) illustrate continued attention to projective techniques within personality research.

B. INTERRUPTED DEVELOPMENT Across the five historical eras of personality research, certain methods appear to show interrupted development. Two illustrative methods were in use prior to World War II and then their application was attenuated during the post–World War II concentration upon personality scales and inventories.

1. Biographical/archival approaches. From its founding in 1934, *Character and Personality* (to become the *Journal of Personality* in 1943) regularly featured biographical studies in personality (Baumgarten, 1937; Cartwright & French, 1939; Frenkel, 1936; Polansky, 1941; Reitmann, 1939; Squires, 1938). The criteria for compiling life histories (Dollard, 1935) and the use of personal documents (G. W. Allport, 1942) were salient topics during this period. Allport's volume and Erickson's *Childhood and Society* (1950) were based primarily upon work done prior to the post–World

War II era. Despite certain exceptions (e.g., Allport, 1965; Erickson, 1958, 1969; White, 1952), the use of biographical and archival approaches in personality research was largely interrupted during the post–World War II era but has now reemerged in several forms (McAdams, 1985; Runyan, 1982; Tetlock, Crosby, & Crosby, 1981).

Longitudinal studies of personality (e.g., Bentz, 1967; Block, 1971; Bray, 1982; Conley, 1985; Costa, McCrae, & Arenberg, 1980; Eichorn, Clausen, Haan, Honzik, & Mussen, 1981) and life-span developmental psychology (Honzik, 1984) are providing a psychological framework for biographical studies, while psychological explanation in biography and life history analysis is receiving closer scrutiny (Runyan, 1981). Archival materials provide the basis for personality assessments of political leaders and historical figures at a temporal or societal distance (Hermann, 1977; Historical Figures Assessment Collaborative, 1977; Simonton, 1986). For example, the use of standard methods of content analysis has yielded useful personality measures from archival materials (Porter & Suedfeld, 1981; Tetlock, Bernzweig, & Gallant, 1985). Time series analysis is being productively applied to biographical and other archival materials (Simonton, 1981, 1984).

This pattern of interrupted development in the post–World War II era followed by a vigorous contemporary reemergence has been found for biographical approaches not only in personality research but also in anthropology and sociology (Runyan, 1982, pp. 9–13).

2. Field studies in personality. It is now generally recognized that the person-situation issue of the 1970s represented a rediscovery of a topic granted widespread attention in the pre–World War II era. The issue was often considered under the rubric of the specificity-generality issue (e.g., F. H. Allport, 1937; G. W. Allport, 1937, pp. 248–257; MacKinnon, 1944, pp. 25–28, 40–43), and it was treated with notable theoretical sophistication (Endler, 1984; Maddi, 1980).

The relevance of this methodological approach

to personality is evidenced by the frequent recourse in the post–World War II era and beyond to the citation of findings from Newcomb's (1929) observational study of extraversion-introversion (e.g., Block, Weiss, & Thorne, 1979; Buss & Craik, 1983b; Lamiell, Foss, & Cavenee, 1980; Shweder, 1975) and from the naturalistic experiments of the Character Education Inquiry (Hartshorne & May, 1928, 1929; Hartshorne, May, & Shuttleworth, 1930) (e.g., Block, 1977; Burton 1963; Jackson & Paunonen, 1980; Mischel, 1968, 1983; Nelson, Grinder, & Mutterer, 1969; Sherman & Fazio, 1983).

The reemergence of field studies reflects an interest in the flow of experience and behavior (Apter, 1984; Klinger, Barta, & Maxeiner, 1983; Pervin, 1983), attention to basic conceptual issues (Bem & Allen, 1974; Buss & Craik, 1983a; Mischel & Peake, 1982; Moskowitz, 1982) and new approaches to scale and rating validation (Buss & Craik, 1983c; Gormly, 1984; Gormly & Edelberg, 1974). The use of log books and accounts, beeper technology, and observer recordings can be adapted to research on personality (Csikszentmihalyi & Figurski, 1982; Eckenrode, 1984; Epstein, 1979, 1980; Hormuth, 1986; Kanner, Coyne, Shaefer, & Lazarus, 1981; Moskowitz & Schwarz, 1982; Pawlik, 1985; Peterson, 1979).

Methodological developments in behavioral assessment also deal with observation in natural settings and self-monitoring techniques (Goldfried & Kent, 1972; Haynes & Horn, 1982; Mash, 1979; Weinrot, Reid, Bauske, & Brummett, 1981). This research has clarified a number of important issues, such as the effects of observation upon conduct in naturalistic settings (i.e., the reactivity problem) (Goldfried, 1982; Haynes & Horn, 1982).

These trends collectively are expanding the domain of inquiry out of the assessment center, clinic, and laboratory into the everyday life and environments of persons. Psychological ecology can proceed productively without regard to person variables (Barker, 1968; Wicker, 1979) but in its fullest sense must encompass personality research (Craik, 1976; Little, in press).

C. Halts and Arrested Development Use of a personality research method can come to a halt before any sustained application or thorough exploration of it has occurred. The arrested development of a method may turn out to have been unwarranted.

A possible example is the naturalistic observational assessment of persons (Craik, 1985), which focuses upon public perceptions of personality held by members of an individual's own community of observers. Naturalistic observational assessment takes the technique of observer judgments of personality out of the assessment center and into the everyday social ecology of individuals. This analysis of reputation examines the structure of perceptions held by a stratified representative sample of each target person's idiographic community of observers.

Systematic approaches to reputational analysis in personality were strongly discouraged by G. W. Allport (1937). He dismissed Mark A. May's (1932) important call for an analysis of individuals' "social stimulus value" as merely a method dealing in rumor and gossip (G. W. Allport, 1937, pp. 42–43). Although attention to it can be found within the framework of sociometry, reputational analysis has not been pursued as a central method within personality research. Nevertheless, a theoretical case can be advanced for its revival and extension (Hogan, Jones, & Cheek, 1985).

Reputational analysis of personality can gauge the extent to which multiple vs. consensual perceptions of individuals prevail. It can facilitate examination of the social impact of reputation upon persons' conduct and their life course. However, over the years, use of observer judgments in personality research has been restricted to those of highly familiar informants and has required or assured consensual descriptions. Naturalistic observational assessment, in contrast to the typical use of peer ratings, analyzes the structure of perceptions of a target person throughout the individual's social network, and it treats reputation as a social resultant of personality as well as an influence upon personality (Craik, 1985).

2. Historical Perspective-Taking: Accuracy and Historical Analysis

The historical perspective schematically portrayed in Figure 2.1 conveys a story about personality research methods. This narrative has it that once upon a time, as our field achieved its initial scientific identity, at least seven more or less distinct methods were available for personality research. Over the past fifty years, the development of some methods was arrested or interrupted, while the development of other methods continued steadily. In the post–World War II era, the method of personality scales and inventories dominated mainstream research, with a secondary role played first by projective techniques and more recently by laboratory methods. Toward the end of the 1960s, the personality scale and inventory method matured in its scientific accomplishments and realization. Subsequently, a period of challenge and stocktaking saw the revival of pre–World War II issues and a reconsideration of alternative methods that had been arrested or interrupted in their development. We will turn soon to the implications of this perspective for our current situation. But first, our story line raises issues of descriptive accuracy and of historical analysis.

A. DESCRIPTIVE ACCURACY The schematic historical perspective conveyed by Figure 2.1 opens up a host of descriptive issues concerning the question: What *did* happen in the history of personality research methods? In moving from this impressionistic scheme to a more detailed and adequate historical perspective, criteria for gauging the state of development of a personality method at any given time would have to be specified. In the present context, the concept of state of development is being used to entail elements of attention, use, prestige, and intrinsic refinement. Thus, indices for estimating the state of development of personality research methods could include the number of publications reporting use of a method. However, the index must also incorporate information on the prestige of journals, the most widely cited

articles, treatment in reviews and textbooks, and inclusion in graduate research training programs. Expert judgment regarding the stage of intrinsic development of the method might also be employed (e.g., regarding realization of inherent potentials, establishment of self-critical standards).

No single criterion is likely to provide an adequate picture of the relative predominance or scientific vitality of a method. For example, Buros (1970, Table 4; 1975, Table 5) reports that among tests in print, published references to projective techniques predominated over nonprojective tests for nine continuous years, from 1948 through 1956, and enjoyed at least parity from 1942 through 1956. This index might suggest two subperiods during the post–World War II era, one characterized by projective techniques (1945–1956) and one dominated by personality scales and inventories (1957–1973). However, the restriction to published tests in print instead of all research instruments biases Buros' count against scales rather than against projective techniques. Nor do we have available comparable counts for laboratory and other methods.

By highlighting such questions, an historical perspective can serve to provoke and guide more detailed documentation of the development of specific research methods. Studies of this kind are needed in order to clarify the historical context of present-day personality research. These analyses should attend to the basic scientific refinement and realization of a method as well as to the consumer-oriented process of dissemination and adoption.

B. FACTORS INFLUENCING THE HISTORICAL FATE OF PERSONALITY RESEARCH METHODS An historical perspective loses credibility if its descriptive account of what has happened appears to be seriously inaccurate. However, it need not offer a full account of why events took the course they did nor provide a thorough analysis of what influences operated upon the fate of specific methods. Indeed, these concerns move us from historical perspective-taking to professional historical analysis. Nevertheless, two major classes of historical influencing factors can be noted briefly, to suggest the agenda that awaits the activities of historical scholars.

1. Reformulation of concepts. Personality research methods are implicitly or explicitly linked to theoretical concepts. Historical patterns in the use of methods cannot be considered independently of conceptual change. To illustrate these influences, two contemporary examples of the methodological implications of conceptual reformulations will be identified, dealing with the central concepts of motive and trait.

Motive. With the abandonment of drive theory, interest in the topic of human motivation declined steadily during the post–World War II era (Benjamin & Jones, 1978; Cofer, 1981). In more recent conceptual approaches to human motivation, purposive action is being analyzed in terms of goals (Pervin, 1983), life tasks (Cantor, Brower, & Korn, 1985) and personal projects (Little, 1983). These formulations appear to call for more detailed accounts of the flow of everyday human conduct than did drive theory. They are compatible with greater use of field studies and archival methods in examining the "serial hierarchical organization of goals over the course of a day and a lifetime" (Pervin, 1983). In this sense, they may advance beyond an earlier and similar formulation by F. H. Allport, whose promising concept of teleonomic trend (F. H. Allport, 1937; F. H. Allport & Frederiksen, 1941; Musgrave & F. H. Allport, 1941) never generated suitable methods and a sustained empirical research program.

Trait. The concept of trait or personal disposition is also being reexamined. The act frequency approach treats dispositional constructs as natural cognitive categories of topographically dissimilar acts (Buss & Craik, 1983a, 1984, 1985, in press). A dispositional assertion about an individual is viewed within this framework as a summary statement (Hampshire, 1953), referring to the frequency with which the individual has displayed acts counting as members of that dispositional category over a specified period of observation. The resulting multiple-act indices, or act trends, are treated as a basic form of personality data. This conceptual formulation of the concept of disposition demonstrates the relevance of dispositional constructs for analyzing the everyday flow of conduct. It points basic research in personality (Buss & Craik, 1983c, 1986) and the validation of personality scales (Buss & Craik, 1983b) toward field studies.

These contemporary reformulations of the concepts of motive and trait may embody fundamentally differing approaches to personality (Alston, 1975). However, they do share common ground with certain contemporary developments in the philosophical analysis of intention (Wright, 1976), disposition (Hampshire, 1953; O'Shaughnessy, 1970; Squires, 1970) and human agency (Brinkley, Bronaugh, & Marras, 1971; Davidson, 1980). They also share a methodological inclination toward the monitoring and analysis of everyday conduct and thus provide new impetus for field studies in personality.

2. Sociocultural influences. In addition to the pressures of the politics of science within psychology (Maddi, 1984), the broader sociocultural context of personality research without doubt exerts influences upon its direction and methods. In treating economic factors affecting personality, Stagner's (1937) text included a chapter in which the Great Depression of 1929 looms as a clear presence, while Elder (1974, 1981) has traced the Great Depression's role in the lives of two important samples in longitudinal personality research, those of the Oakland Growth Study and the Guidance Study.

The rise of totalitarian regimes and the impact of anti-Semitism occasioned a classic study of the authoritarian personality (Adorno, Frenkel-Brunswik, Levinson, & Sanford, 1950). The requirements of World War II transformed Murray's multimethod assessment program from the exploration of personality (Murray, 1938) to the more pragmatic aims of selection (OSS Assessment Staff, 1948). At the Harvard Psychological Clinic, Smith, Bruner, and White's (1956) postwar social-personality study of the functional role of attitudes appropriately took Russia as the focal attitude object.

The advent of Sputnik in 1957 appears to have been one source of the remarkable U.S. public interest in studies, already underway at the time, on the identification and encouragement of creative persons (Barron, 1969; Guilford, 1950; MacKinnon, 1978). One current societal challenge in 1986 is to link analyses of individual creativity to studies of organizational innovation, in light of the competitive technological and industrial pressures upon the United States (Botkin, Dimancescu, & Stata, 1984; Staw, 1984). A final illustration of sociocultural influences can be seen in the relationship between the increasing adoption of the assessment center method in industry and that method's compatibility with the requirements of the U.S. Equal Employment Opportunity Commission's affirmative action policies (Huck & Bray, 1976; Ritchie & Moses, 1983).

Further examination of sociocultural influences (e.g., feminism, health concerns) would eventually move us from the arena of psychological scholarship to the field of professional historical inquiry and analysis. A better understanding of the social, political, and cultural context of personality research over the past half century would enrich our historical perspective. However, these contributions will come not from scientists active in personality research but from scholars trained in the history of science.

3. Methodological Pluralism and the Current Situation[6]

The story generated by our historical perspective carries a major lesson for the current situation in personality research. The lesson is that methodo-

logical pluralism prevails and should be fostered in the field of personality research.

At the outset, our field of inquiry had available an array of research methods. The methods offer distinct and important information about individuals as persons living in society. In the most generic sense, our knowledge of persons derives from (1) their everyday conduct (field studies), (2) their imaginative productions (projective techniques), (3) the impressions they make upon others (observer judgments), (4) their life histories and fate in society (biographical/archival analysis), (5) their general reputations (naturalistic observational assessment), (6) their self-characterizations (personality scales and inventories), and (7) their behavior in standardized conditions (laboratory methods).

The inherent agenda of personality research encompasses each and every one of these sources of information about persons. Side by side with the devising of specific techniques for using these kinds of information has been an explicit advocacy of methodological pluralism and its importance. Cattell (1946, 1979) and others (Block, 1977; Buss & Craik, 1983a) have treated the need to identify and understand the basic types of personality data and their characteristics. Procedures recommended for the validation of construct measurement have called for examination of multiple method findings (Campbell & Fiske, 1959; Cronbach & Meehl, 1955; Gough, 1965). The institutional arrangements required to facilitate the gathering of findings derived from multiple methods and across data types have been delineated with some persistence across the eras (Bray, 1982; MacKinnon, 1975a, 1978; Murray, 1938; OSS Assessment Staff, 1948; Sanford, 1963; see also Pervin, 1985).

At any particular time, the relative success of our specific methods for accessing these forms of information about persons and employing them scientifically may be uneven, but each kind of information holds a fundamental place in our overall endeavor. Historical influences have unevenly distributed scientific attention and investment

---

[6]This article was published in 1986, and the "current situation" constantly changes. For an update, we recommend the chapter on personality psychology found in nearly any volume of the *Annual Review of Psychology*.

among the kinds of information and their associated methods. One method—personality scales and inventories—can for the present be recognized as having enjoyed a coherent, inventive, and sustained development to its current scientific maturity. Although scientific advances cannot be willed or prescribed, it is strategically sound now to devote special research attention to those methods that are less well developed (e.g., biographical/archival studies, field studies, naturalistic observational assessment). An even more basic goal is to move further toward a scientific integration of information about persons from all of these diverse sources.

Our historical perspective highlights the diversity of methods available to personality research in the current situation. In examining the ways in which the various methods and data types are now being deployed, three issues will be addressed. First, what is the present pattern of methodological usage, as indicated by representative journal publications in the field? Second, to what extent do institutional factors, such as societies, conferences, and journals, support an integrative application of personality research methods? And third, what are the prevailing conceptual orientations for marshaling and interpreting results from diverse methods and data types?

A. CURRENT PATTERNS OF METHODOLOGICAL USAGE A perusal of the personality section of the *Journal of Personality and Social Psychology* (*JPSP*) from its appearance in 1980 through 1983 and of the *Journal of Personality* (*JP*) for the same period provides an indication of trends in methodological practice. Over this period, the frequency of empirical studies enlisting only undergraduate samples remains comparable to that found by Carlson (1971) for the 1968 volume of these two journals: approximately 64%, with the incidence somewhat higher for this journal (*JP*) (77%) than for *JPSP* (61%). Carlson (1984) has reported a comparable figure for the 1982 personality section only of *JPSP* (65%).

The predominant methods used in the 1980–

1983 period for these two journals are self-report scales and laboratory tasks, separately or in conjunction (approximately 85%). The total use in *any* way of (1) observer judgments, (2) observer- or self-monitored field measures, (3) life history or other archival data, and (4) noncollege life outcome indices amounts to only about 15% or less of the studies reported during this period. It follows that research generating multimethod or cross data–type findings are rare, with the exception of the self-report/laboratory task linkage.

One noteworthy and salutary trend is the appearance of a new generation of personality measures during the contemporary era. These procedures assess, for example, sex role orientations (Bem, 1974; Spence, Helmreich, & Stapp, 1975), self-consciousness (Fenigstein, Scheier, & Buss, 1975), self-monitoring (Snyder, 1974), loneliness (Russell, Peplau, & Cutrona, 1980), and affect communication (Buck, Barron, Goodman, & Shapiro, 1980; Friedman, Prince, Riggio, & DiMatteo, 1980; Rosenthal, Hall, DiMatteo, Rogers, & Archer, 1979). Attention to these constructs and measures in part represents what has been termed the "social psychological invasion" of personality (Kenrick & Dantchik, 1983). The names of Allport, Crutchfield, Lewin, McDougall, Murphy, and Sarbin[7] among many others—evoke the more fitting term: the "welcome return" of social psychological collaboration within personality research (see also Blass, 1984; Rosenberg, 1983).

The newer measures are seldom used in conjunction with the multiscale personality inventories developed during the post–World War II era. Indeed, an impression from the current literature emerges of generational clustering in the joint usage of procedures from the post–World War II era vs. those from the contemporary era. This tendency, if it were to continue strongly, would constitute an unfortunate methodological generation gap. It would be ironic for a field whose theoret-

---

[7]The names just cited are important figures in the history of psychology who were equally important in the development of both personality and social psychology.

ical orientations include a recognition of the strength of generational continuity (Erikson, 1950, 1964) to fail to build upon its methodological accomplishments.[8]

B. THE GUILDING OF THE METHODS What research is conducted and becomes published has its origins in part in scientific programs and institutions. Certain institutional developments of the contemporary era serve as signs of methodological vigor but at the same time may function as obstacles to the integrative use of personality research methods. That is, special journals, societies, and regularly scheduled conferences and workshops— and their associated guilds—have formed around types of methods and specific instruments, procedures, and analyses.

Multivariate Behavioral Research, published through the Society of Multivariate Experimental Psychology, has purposes that reach beyond personality research (Cattell, Merrifield, Messick, Cartwright, & Sells, 1966; Royce, 1977) but remains a fitting and frequently used forum for studies using multiscale personality inventories. The *Rorschach Research Exchange* (Tallman, 1936) evolved into the *Journal of Projective Techniques* (Klopfer, 1947) and more recently emerged as the *Journal of Personality Assessment* (Farberow, 1970). The current *Journal* and the Society for Personality Assessment have expanded their focus from a single projective technique to the general class of those procedures and have now achieved a balance between reports on projective techniques and those on personality scales and inventories. The

Journal of Experimental Research in Personality, begun in 1965, changed its title to the *Journal of Research in Personality* in 1973, following explicit editorial policy to encompass other than strictly experimental (i.e., manipulative) studies (Wiggins, 1972). *Behavioral Assessment* (published through the Association for Advancement of Behavior Therapy) focuses upon naturalistic field studies as well as self-report procedures and has specific but broad conceptual commitments, while the *Journal of Behavioral Assessment* (Adams & Turner, 1979) is explicitly more eclectic.

The cross-cultural method, which includes but extends beyond topics in personality, is represented by the *Journal of Cross-Cultural Psychology* (published through the International Association for Cross-Cultural Psychology) (Lonner, 1980). *Biography* is becoming an outlet for biographical studies in personality (e.g., Conti & McCormack, 1984; Weissbourd & Sears, 1982) and is interdisciplinary in its coverage. The Assessment Center Research Group and the International Congress of Assessment Center Administrators are organized to promote research and to set ethical standards for assessment center operations (Cohen, 1982; Moses & Byham, 1977). Finally, a number of regularly scheduled conferences and workshops are devoted separately to *specific* inventories, projective techniques, and other methods in personality research.

The emergence of method guilds serves a variety of constructive scientific functions and offers evidence of the vitality of personality research in the contemporary era. However, without countervailing mechanisms, these institutional trends may inadvertently foster the isolated rather than integrated use of methods in personality research.

C. CONCEPTUAL ORIENTATIONS TO METHODOLOGICAL PLURALISM The most minimal adoption of a systems framework for the formulation of personality (Sanford, 1963; Smelser & Smelser, 1964) establishes the task of considering jointly the relations among data derived from biographical and other archival sources, from imaginative products, from time sampling of acts *in situ*, from observer

---

[8]Craik is referring here to the fact that a good deal of modern research fails to include older measures of personality along with the newer ones being developed. So it is unclear, for example, how a modern construct such as "self-consciousness" is related to the traits measured in a large amount of research over the years with the MMPI. Although not mentioned in Craik's article, a similar observation could be made about modern research in "cognitive-social" approaches to personality (Funder, 1997). This research, too, often includes measures of new constructs without including older measures to allow comparison and, as Craik notes, generational continuity.

judgments, from self-reports, from reputational analysis, and from laboratory task performance. For any given research analysis, the gauging of coherence among findings from various data types is guided by substantive theoretical assumptions and expectations (e.g., Block, 1977; Block & Block, 1979).

At the same time, interpretation of cross-method results is facilitated by general knowledge about each method and data type. Perturbation theory (Cattell, 1979; Cattell & Digman, 1964) represents one promising conceptual orientation to the constraints and distinctive modes of functioning of various data types. Within this framework, for example, trait-view theory (Cattell, 1968, 1979) seeks to organize the sources of perturbation due to the use of observer judgments (e.g., effects of observers' personality, role-relation effects, restrictions due to the range of observations and vantage points). The aim of perturbation theory is to locate knowledge of method effects (e.g., response set, halo effect) within a broad psychological framework and to apply it to the design and interpretation of cross-method studies involving multiple data types. Efforts of this kind possess useful implications for advancing the integrative deployment of multiple personality research methods.

4. Recommendations

Historical perspective-taking is a purposive activity, seeking to identify events and trends that hold implications for future endeavor. Viewing the current situation of personality research methods within an historical perspective suggests the following recommendations.

A. Promote Integrative Methodological Pluralism The infrequent and partial manifestations of cross-method analysis in current personality research are in part a function of institutional constraints. Major research projects of this kind place special demands upon facilities, staff training, and resources.

The influence of Murray's (1938) team at the

Harvard Psychological Clinic and the recommendations of the OSS Assessment Staff (1948) did not yield a widespread development of personality research centers organized around multimethod approaches. The Institute of Personality Assessment and Research (*IPAR*) established at Berkeley in 1949 and the longitudinal AT&T managerial studies initiated in 1956 represent continuing offsprings of this multimethod tradition (Bray, 1982; MacKinnon, 1975b, 1978). In addition to the managers being studied at AT&T (Bray, Campbell, & Grant, 1974; Bray & Howard, 1983), samples studied at IPAR have included architects (MacKinnon, 1962), managers (Barron & Egan, 1968), mathematicians (Helson & Crutchfield, 1970), and research scientists (Gough, 1976b).

More recently, the IPAR research program is being extended to include samples drawn from the general public such as married couples (e.g., Gough, 1976a); follow-up studies of persons intensively assessed at earlier points in their lives (e.g., Cartwright, 1977; Gough & Hall, 1975, 1977; Helson, Mitchell, & Moane, 1984); act frequency analyses of personality (Buss & Craik, 1983a, in press); biographical, life history and archival studies (e.g., Chodorow, in press; Helson, 1982; Mendelsohn, 1985; Runyan, 1982, 1983; Tetlock, 1984), and naturalistic observational assessment (Craik, 1985).

The goal of methodological pluralism is extending the scope of multimethod personality research institutes. The assessment program tradition has pioneered in the integration of observer judgments, self-report measures, simulation and laboratory tasks, and life outcome indices. The revival of biographical/archival methods presents new institutional requirements to create interdisciplinary ties (e.g., with the fields of history, literature, political science, journalism) and links to archival depositories (e.g., the presidential libraries). The logistical requirements of personality field studies of adult samples entail new kinds of staff and support facilities that have not yet been fully delineated.

The establishment of additional personality research centers of the expanded IPAR kind would contribute importantly to the advancement of knowledge in our field. They might be formed collaboratively on a regional basis by colleagues prepared to employ the full array of personality research methods. Centers of this breadth could conduct joint graduate programs as well, providing multimethod research training. For these and other purposes, the resurgence of personality research in the past decade warrants appropriate recognition and support by public and private funding agencies.

B. CONDUCT STUDIES FOSTERING THE INTEGRA-TIVE USE OF METHODS   Certain key studies would clarify issues in the use and interpretation of cross-method designs. First, an efficient and inexpensive means of gathering observer judgments of personality is to request each research participant to enlist the cooperation of two or more other persons (e.g., spouse and co-worker; roommate and parent) to describe the target person with an adjective checklist, rating scales, or a Q-sort deck. A series of sensitivity analyses showing, for example, that such informants provide descriptions comparable to those gathered when the investigator deals directly with them, would strengthen confidence in this procedure and warrant more general adoption of its use. The routine addition of observer judgments to data from self-reports and laboratory tasks would be a major methodological gain.

Second, studies interrelating the new generation of personality scales with the major multiscale inventories of the post–World War II era are needed. They would contribute to the psychological interpretation of both sets of measures and build methodological continuity.

Third, the steady high level of use of undergraduate research participants should be viewed with realistic acceptance. Less than 40% of the reports appearing in the personality section of *JPSP* and in *JP* for the 1980–1983 period acknowledge extramural funding support. Oversights aside, this low rate indicates that funding constraints as well as convenience must be recognized as factors in the use of undergraduate research participants. In-deed, the scientific productivity of the field is a tribute to researchers' commitment and resourcefulness. In this light, studies gauging the generality of findings from undergraduate samples would be useful. What is the impact of using psychology vs. nonpsychology students? What interactions with age/life stage factors are found when mail-out procedures are also obtained from various classes of alumni? What is the degree of generality of findings from academically select colleges to other colleges, and vice versa? Systematic sensitivity analyses of this kind would clarify the magnitude and type of consequences of this continuing methodological constraint in personality research.

C. ENCOURAGE COLLABORATION AMONG METHOD GUILDS   The notion of method guilds may exaggerate the current situation to some extent. Nevertheless, organizational initiatives to increase contacts and collaborative projects would be useful. These steps may be effectively taken by the guilds themselves, by broad-purpose units such as the Personality Section of the American Psychological Association and the European Association of Personality Psychology, or by personality research centers and programs.

*   *   *

D. FOSTER HISTORICAL PERSPECTIVE-TAKING IN GRADUATE TRAINING   How much emphasis should be placed in personality graduate training upon the historical development of our field? Certainly, enough to appreciate the magnitude of individual judgment that has entered into the historical perspective presented here and to appraise it critically.

The graduate proseminar in personality at UC Berkeley sometimes makes use of the "Decades Exercise." After devoting much of the term to current issues and directions, each seminar member randomly draws a decade assignment (e.g., the 1890s, the 1970s) and is then responsible for browsing through the personality literature for that decade and reporting on it at the final meetings of the course. The task is intentionally kept open-ended and playful. Experience has shown that the exercise itself can be counted upon to generate exceptional interest and engagement. The rediscovery of contemporary issues in earlier periods, the identification of significant continuities, the charm of prior styles of exposition, the novelty of subsequently abandoned ideas, projects, and instruments, the championing of an inappropriately halted development—all of these reactions are readily elicited by the materials themselves.

The cumulative impressions from all of the presentations in the Decades Exercise emphasize that historical perspective-taking entails the entire development of a field up to the present time. It is not simply the expression of antiquarian fondness for the ancient and temporally remote.

5. Conclusion

The history of personality research methods demonstrates recognition that the scientific understanding of personality must be grounded in a variety of distinct sources of information about persons. Compared to the recent past, our current situation more closely resembles the preidentity era in personality research, displaying a broader and more even distribution of scientific attention among the basic forms of research methods. The personality scale and inventory method has attained a relatively mature state of development, while renewed interest is being granted to methods (e.g., biographical/archival methods, field studies) whose development had been interrupted during the post–World War II era. This trend opens up the attractive opportunity to promote greater use of multimethod research programs and to move toward a more integrative methodological pluralism.

A focus upon methods alone yields only a partial historical perspective upon a field. A scientific program cannot be appraised or fully portrayed independently of its conceptual resources. Furthermore, self-critical methodological standards imply that a continuing tradition does not incorporate or retain everything from the past. And major redirections of the basic orientations of a scientific program can generate abrupt methodological discontinuities.

When Charles Spearman, as editor of this *Journal*, published F. W. Allport's (1937) "Teleonomic Description in the Study of Personality" almost fifty years ago, he appended the following footnote:

> To appreciate this article, we must remember the general verdict that the current methods of studying personality are in a very evil plight. Allport is presenting a remedy. So have several other writers, in this journal: G. W. Allport, Cantril, Lewin, McDougall, Mead, Meloun, Rand, Stephenson, Stern, Studman, and Vernon. Any further suggestions will be welcome.—The Editor (Spearman, 1937, p. 214)

The distressed cry of calamity has persisted over the eras in personality research, often as a gambit followed by advocacy of some new or specific methodological option. An historical perspective suggests that this favored strategic form of discourse does not in the aggregate convey a realistic account of the field's methodological condition and accomplishments. Instead, a half century of sustained endeavor reveals an intelligent, ingenious and self-critical response to a difficult scientific challenge by a vigorous, imaginative, dedicated and often contentious community of researchers.

Without doubt, the fiftieth anniversary in 1987–88 of the G. W. Allport, Murray, and Stagner volumes will properly be an occasion for hardheaded stocktaking. But it will also offer an opportunity to celebrate a worthy and inspiring heritage, to exercise the tolerance and civility required of an integrative methodological pluralism, to acknowledge the current reinvigorated condition of our field, and to plan and ensure an exciting future for personality research and its methods.

References

Adams, H. E., & Turner, S. M. (1979). Editorial. *Journal of Behavioral Assessment, 1*, 1–3.

Adorno, T. W., Frenkel-Brunswik, E., Levinson, D. J., & Sanford, R. N. (1950). *The authoritarian personality.* New York: Harper & Row.

Allport, F. H. (1937). Teleonomic description in the study of personality. *Character and Personality, 5*, 202–214.

Allport, F. H., & Frederiksen, N. (1941). Personality as a pattern of teleonomic trends. *Journal of Social Psychology, 13,* 141–182.

Allport, G. W. (1937). *Personality: A psychological interpretation.* New York: Holt.

Allport, G. W. (1942). *The use of personal documents in psychological science.* New York: Social Science Research Council.

Allport, G. W. (1965). *Letters from Jenny.* New York: Harcourt, Brace & World.

Allport, G. W., & Odbert, H. S. (1936). Trait-names: A psycho-lexical study. *Psychological Monographs, 47,* 1–171.

Alston, W. P. (1975). Traits, consistency, and conceptual alternatives for personality theory. *Journal for the Theory of Social Behavior, 5,* 17–48.

Apter, M. J. (1984). Reversal theory and personality: A review. *Journal of Research in Personality, 18,* 265–288.

Atkinson, J. W. (Ed.). (1958). *Motives in fantasy, action, and society.* Princeton, NJ: Van Nostrand.

Atkinson, J. W. (1983). *Personality, motivation, and action.* New York: Praeger.

Barker, R. G. (1968). *Ecological psychology: Concepts and methods for studying the environment of human behavior.* Stanford, CA: Stanford University Press.

Barron, F. (1969). *Creative person and creative process.* New York: Holt, Rinehart, & Winston.

Barron, F., & Egan, D. (1968). Leaders and innovators in Irish management. *Journal of Management Studies, 5,* 41–60.

Baumgarten, F. (1933). Die Charaktereigenschaften. *Beiträge zur Charakter—und Persönlichkeitsforschung: Monograph 1.* Bern: Verlag A. Francke.

Baumgarten, F. (1937). Character traits derived from biographies. *Character and Personality, 6,* 147–149.

Bem, D. J., & Allen, A. (1974). On predicting some of the people some of the time: The search for cross-situational consistencies in behavior. *Psychological Review, 81,* 506–520.

Bem, S. L. (1974). The measurement of psychological androgyny. *Journal of Consulting and Clinical Psychology, 42,* 155–162.

Benjamin, L. T., Jr., & Jones, M. R. (1978). From motivational theory to social cognitive development: Twenty-five years of the Nebraska Symposium. *Nebraska Symposium on Motivation, 26,* ix–xix.

Bentz, V. J. (1967). The Sears experience in the investigation, description, and prediction of executive behavior. In F. R. Wickert & D. E. McFarland (Eds.), *Measuring executive effectiveness* (pp. 147–205). New York: Appleton-Century-Crofts.

Berglas, S. (1984). Guest editor note—Special section: Stress and coping. *Journal of Personality and Social Psychology, 46,* 837–838.

Blass, T. (1984). Social psychology and personality: Toward a convergence. *Journal of Personality and Social Psychology, 47,* 1013–1027.

Blatt, S. J., & Lerner, H. (1983). The psychological assessment of object representation. *Journal of Personality Assessment, 47,* 7–28.

Block, J. (1971). *Lives through time.* Berkeley, CA: Bancroft.

Block, J. (1977). Advancing the psychology of personality: Paradigmatic shift or improving the quality of research? In D. Magnusson & N. S. Endler (Eds.), *Personality at the crossroads: Current issues in interactional psychology* (pp. 37–63). Hillsdale, NJ: Erlbaum.

Block, J. (1978). *The Q-sort method in personality assessment and psychiatric research.* Palo Alto, CA: Consulting Psychologists Press (orig. 1961).

Block, J. H., & Block, J. (1979). The role of ego control and ego resiliency in the organization of behavior. In W. A. Collins (Ed.), *Minnesota Symposia on Child Psychology,* (Vol. 13, pp. 39–101). Hillsdale, NJ: Erlbaum.

Block, J., Weiss, D. W., & Thorne, A. (1979). How relevant is a semantic similarity interpretation of personality ratings? *Journal of Personality and Social Psychology, 73,* 1055–1074.

Botkin, J., Dimancescu, D., & Stata, R. (1984). *The innovators: Re-discovering America's creative energy.* New York: Harper & Row.

Bray, D. W. (1982). The assessment center and the study of lives. *American Psychologist, 37,* 180–189.

Bray, D. W., Campbell, R. J., & Grant, D. L. (1974). *Formative years in business: A long-term AT&T study of managerial lives.* New York: Wiley.

Bray, D. W., & Howard, A. (1983). Personality and the assessment center method. In C. D. Spielberger & J. N. Butcher (Eds.), *Advances in personality assessment* (pp. 1–34). Hillsdale, NJ: Erlbaum.

Brinkley, R., Bronaugh, R., & Marras, A. (Eds.). (1971). *Agent, action, and reason.* Toronto: University of Toronto Press.

Buck, R., Barron, R., Goodman, N., & Shapiro, B. (1980). Unitization of spontaneous nonverbal behavior in the study of emotion communication. *Journal of Personality and Social Psychology, 39,* 522–529.

Buros, O. K. (Ed.). (1970). *Personality tests and reviews.* Highland Park, NJ: Gryphon Press.

Buros, O. K. (Ed.). (1975). *Personality tests and reviews II.* Highland Park, NJ: Gryphon Press.

Burton, R. V. (1963). Generality of honesty reconsidered. *Psychological Review, 70,* 481–499.

Buss, D. M., & Craik, K. H. (1983a). The act frequency approach to personality. *Psychological Review, 90,* 105–126.

Buss, D. M., & Craik, K. H. (1983b). The dispositional analysis of everyday conduct. *Journal of Personality, 51,* 393–412.

Buss, D. M., & Craik, K. H. (1983c). Act prediction and the conceptual analysis of personality scales: Indices of act density, bipolarity, and extensity. *Journal of Personality and Social Psychology, 45,* 1081–1095.

Buss, D. M., & Craik, K. H. (1984). Acts, dispositions, and personality. In B. A. Maher & W. B. Maher (Eds.), *Progress in experimental personality research: Normal personality processes* (pp. 241–301). New York: Academic Press.

Buss, D. M., & Craik, K. H. (1985). Why not measure that trait? Alternative criteria for identifying important dispositions. *Journal of Personality and Social Psychology, 48,* 934–946.

Buss, D. M., & Craik, K. H. (1986). Acts, dispositions, and clinical assessment: The psychopathology of everyday conduct. *Clinical Psychology Review.*

Buss, D. M., & Craik, K. H. (in press). The act frequency approach and the construction of personality. In A. Angleitner, A. Furnham, & G. Van Heck (Eds.), *Personality psychology in Europe.* Lisse, The Netherlands: Swets & Zeitlinger.

Campbell, D. T., & Fiske, D. W. (1959). Convergent and discriminant validity by the multitrait-multimethod matrix. *Psychological Bulletin, 56,* 81–105.

Cantor, N., Brower, A., & Korn, H. (1985). Cognitive bases of personality in a life transition. In E. E. Roskam (Ed.), *Measurement and personality assessment* (pp. 323–332) New York: Elsevier Science Publishers.

Carlson, R. (1971). Where is the person in personality research? *Psychological Bulletin, 75,* 203–219.

Carlson, R. (1984). What's social about social psychology? Where's the person in personality research? *Journal of Personality and Social Psychology, 47,* 1304–1309.

Cartwright, D., & French, J. R. P., Jr. (1939). The reliability of life-history studies. *Character and Personality, 8,* 110–119.

Cartwright, L. K. (1977). Personality changes in a sample of women physicians. *Journal of Medical Education, 52,* 467–474.

Cattell, R. B. (1943). The description of personality: Basic traits resolved into clusters. *Journal of Abnormal and Social Psychology, 38,* 476–506.

Cattell, R. B. (1946). The primary personality factors in women compared with those in men. *British Journal of Psychology, 1,* 114–130.

Cattell, R. B. (1947). Confirmation and clarification of primary personality factors. *Psychometrika, 12,* 197–220.

Cattell, R. B. (1968). Trait-view theory of perturbations in ratings and self-ratings (L(BR)- and Q-data): Its application to obtaining pure trait score estimates in questionnaires. *Psychological Review, 75,* 96–113.

Cattell, R. B. (1979). *Personality and learning theory: Volume 1, The structure of personality in its environment.* New York: Springer.

Cattell, R. B., & Digman, J. M. (1964). A theory of the structure of perturbations in observer ratings and questionnaire data in personality research. *Behavioral Science, 9,* 341–358.

Cattell, R. B., Merrifield, P. R., Messick, S. J., Cartwright, D. S., & Sells, S. B. (1966). Editorial statement. *Multivariate Behavioral Research, 1,* 2–3.

Cattell, R. B., & Scheier, I. H. (1961). *The meaning and measurement of neuroticism and anxiety.* New York: Ronald Press.

Chodorow, N. (in press). History and life histories of early women psychoanalysts. *Dialogue: Journal of the Friends of the San Francisco Psychoanalytic Institute.*

Cofer, C. N. (1981). The history of the concept of motivation. *Journal of the History of the Behavioral Sciences, 17,* 48–53.

Cohen, S. L. (1982). Journal readership survey. *Journal of Assessment Center Technology, 5,* 19–24.

Conley, J. J. (1985). The longitudinal stability of personality traits: A multitrait-multimethod-multioccasion analysis. *Journal of Personality and Social Psychology.*

Conti, I., & McCormack, W. A. (1984). Federico Fellini: Artist in search of self. *Biography, 7,* 292–308.

Costa, P. T., McCrae, R. R., & Arenberg, D. (1980). Enduring dispositions in adult males. *Journal of Personality and Social Psychology, 38,* 793–800.

Craik, K. H. (1976). The personality research paradigm in environmental psychology. In S. Wapner, S. Cohen, & B. Kaplan (Eds.), *Experiencing the Environment* (pp. 55–79). New York: Plenum.

Craik, K. H. (1985). Multiple perceived personalities: A neglected consistency issue. In E. E. Roskam (Ed.), *Measurement and personality assessment* (pp. 333–338). New York: Elsevier Science Publishers.

Cronbach, L. J., & Meehl, P. E. (1955). Construct validity in psychological tests. *Psychological Bulletin, 52,* 281–302.

Csikszentmihalyi, M., & Figurski, T. J. (1982). Self-awareness and aversive experience in everyday life. *Journal of Personality, 50,* 1–28.

Davidson, D. (1980). *Essays on actions and events.* New York: Oxford University Press.

Deci, E. L. (1975). *Intrinsic motivation.* New York: Plenum Press.

Dollard, J. (1935). *Criteria for the life history.* New Haven, CT: Yale University Press.

DuBois, P. H. (1970). *A history of psychological testing.* Boston, MA: Allyn and Bacon.

Eckenrode, J. (1984). Impact of chronic and acute stressors on daily reports of moods. *Journal of Personality and Social Psychology, 46,* 907–918.

Eichorn, D. H., Clausen, J. A., Haan, N., Honzik, M. P., & Mussen, P. H. (Eds.). (1981). *Present and past in middle life.* New York: Academic Press.

Elder, G. H., Jr. (1974). *Children of the Great Depression.* Chicago, IL: University of Chicago Press.

Elder, G. H., Jr. (1981). Social history and life experience. In D. H. Eichorn, J. A. Clausen, N. Haan, M. P. Honzik, & P. H. Mussen (Eds.). *Present and past in middle life* (pp. 1–32). New York: Academic Press.

Endler, N. S. (1984). Interactionism. In N. S. Endler & J. McV. Hunt (Eds.). *Personality and the behavioral disorders.* (Vol. 1, pp. 183–217) 2nd ed. New York: Wiley.

Epstein, S. (1979). The stability of behavior: I. On predicting most of the people much of the time. *Journal of Personality and Social Psychology, 37,* 1097–1126.

Epstein, S. (1980). The stability of behavior: II. Implications for psychological research. *American Psychologist, 35,* 790–806.

Epstein, S. (1983). Aggregation and beyond: Some basic issues on the prediction of behavior. *Journal of Personality, 51,* 360–392.

Erikson, E. H. (1950). *Childhood and society.* New York: Norton (2nd ed., 1963).

Erikson, E. H. (1958). *Young man Luther.* New York: Norton.

Erikson, E. H. (1964). *Insight and responsibility.* New York: Norton.

Erikson, E. H. (1969). *Gandhi's truth.* New York: Norton.

Exner, J. E., Jr. (1974). *The Rorschach: A comprehensive system* (Vol. 1). New York: Wiley.

Exner, J. E., Jr. (1978). *The Rorschach: A comprehensive system* (Vol. 2). New York: Wiley.

Exner, J. E., Jr., & Weiner, I. B. (1982). *The Rorschach: A comprehensive system. Volume 3: Assessment of children and adolescents.* New York: Wiley.

Eysenck, H. J. (1967). *The biological basis of personality.* Springfield, IL: Thomas.

Farberow, N. L. (1970). A society by any other name. *Journal of Projective Techniques and Personality Assessment, 34,* 3–5.

Fenigstein, A., Scheier, M. F., & Buss, A. H. (1975). Public and private self-consciousness: Assessment and theory. *Journal of Consulting and Clinical Psychology, 43,* 522–527.

Frank, L. K. (1939). Projective methods for the study of personality. *Journal of Psychology, 8,* 389–413.

Frenkel, E. (1936). Studies in biographical psychology. *Character and Personality, 5,* 1–34.

Friedman, H. S., Prince, L. M., Riggio, R. E., & DiMatteo, M. R. (1980). Understanding and assessing nonverbal expressiveness: The Affective Communication Test. *Journal of Personality and Social Psychology, 39,* 333–351.

Goldberg, L. R. (1971). A historical survey of personality scales and inventories. In P. McReynolds (Ed.), *Advances in psychological assessment* (Vol. 2, pp. 293–336). Palo Alto, CA: Science and Behavior Books.

Goldberg, L. R. (1982). From ace to zombie. Some explorations in the language of personality. In C. O. Spielberger & J. N. Butcher (Eds.), *Advances in personality assessment* (Vol. 1, pp. 203–234). Hillsdale, NJ: Erlbaum.

Goldfried, M. R. (1982). Behavioral assessment: An overview. In A. S. Bellack, M. Hersen, & A. E. Kazdin (Eds.), *International handbook of behavior modification and therapy* (pp. 81–107). New York: Plenum.

Goldfried, M. R., & Kent, R. N. (1972). Traditional versus behavioral personality assessment: A comparison of methodological and theoretical assumptions. *Psychological Bulletin, 77,* 409–420.

Gormly, J. (1984). Correspondence between personality trait ratings and behavioral events. *Journal of Personality, 52,* 220–232.

Gormly, J., & Edleberg, W. (1974). Validity in personality trait attributions. *American Psychologist, 29,* 189–193.

Gough, H. G. (1957). *Manual for the California Psychological Inventory.* Palo Alto, CA: Consulting Psychologists Press (revised, 1964, 1975).

Gough, H. G. (1965). Conceptual analysis of test scores and other diagnostic variables. *Journal of Abnormal Psychology, 70,* 294–302.

Gough, H. G. (1976a). Some methodological explorations in forecasting family-planning behavior. In S. H. Newman & V. D. Thompson (Eds.), *Population psychology: Research and educational issues* (pp. 59–85). (DHEW Publication No. [NIH] 76-574). Washington, DC: U.S. Government Printing Office.

Gough, H. G. (1976b). Studying creativity by means of word association tests. *Journal of Applied Psychology, 61,* 348–353.

Gough, H. G., & Hall, W. B. (1975). The prediction of academic and clinical performance in medical school. *Research in Higher Education, 3,* 301–314.

Gough, H. G., & Hall, W. B. (1977). Physicians' retrospective evaluation of their medical education. *Research in Higher Education, 7,* 29–42.

Gough, H. G., & Heilbrun, A. B., Jr. (1980). *The Adjective Check List manual: 1980 edition.* Palo Alto, CA: Consulting Psychologists Press (1st ed., 1965).

Guilford, J. P. (1950). Creativity. *American Psychologist, 5,* 444–454.

Hampshire, S. (1953). Dispositions. *Analysis, 14,* 5–11.

Hartshorne, H., & May, M. A. (1928). *Studies in the nature of character. Volume 1. Studies in deceit.* New York: Macmillan.

Hartshorne, H., & May, M. A. (1929). *Studies in the nature of character. Volume 2. Studies in service and self-control.* New York: Macmillan.

Hartshorne, H., May, M. A., & Shuttleworth, F. K. (1930). *Studies in the nature of character: Volume 3. Studies in the organization of character.* New York: Macmillan.

Haynes, S. N., & Horn, W. F. (1982). Reactivity in behavioral observation: A review. *Behavioral Assessment, 4,* 369–385.

Helson, R. (1982). Critics and their texts: An approach to Jung's theory of cognition and personality. *Journal of Personality and Social Psychology, 43,* 409–418.

Helson, R., & Crutchfield, R. S. (1970). Creative types in mathematics. *Journal of Personality, 38,* 177–197.

Helson, R., Mitchell, V., & Moane, G. (1984). Personality and patterns of adherence and nonadherence to the social clock. *Journal of Personality and Social Psychology, 46,* 1079–1096.

Hermann, M. G. (Ed.). (1977). *The psychological examination of political leaders.* New York: Free Press.

Heymans, G., & Weirsma, E. (1906). Beitrage zur Speziellen Psychologie auf Grund einer Massen-untersuchung. *Zeitschrift für Psychologie, 43,* 81–127.

Historical Figures Assessment Collaborative (1977). Assessing historical figures: The use of observer-based personality descriptions. *Historical Methods Newsletter, 10,* 66–76.

Hogan, R. (1985). *Hogan Personality Inventory: User's manual.* Minneapolis, MN: National Computer Systems.

Hogan, R., Jones, W., & Cheek, J. (1985). Socioanalytic theory: An alternative to armadillo psychology. In B. R. Schlenker (Ed.), *The Self and Social Life* (pp. 175–198). New York: Mc-Graw-Hill.

Hollingworth, H. L. (1922). *Judging human character.* New York: Appleton-Century.

Honzik, M. P. (1984). Life-span development. *Annual Review of Psychology, 35,* 309–332.

Hormuth, S. (1986). The sampling of experience *in situ. Journal of Personality, 54,* 262–293.

Huck, J. R., & Bray, D. W. (1976). Management assessment center evaluations and subsequent job performance of white and black females. *Personnel Psychology, 29,* 13–20.

Jackson, D. N., & Paunonen, S. V. (1980). Personality structure and assessment. *Annual Review of Psychology, 31,* 503–551.

John, O. P., Goldberg, L. R., & Angleitner, A. (1984). Better than the alphabet: Taxonomies of personality-descriptive terms in English, Dutch, and German. In H. Bonarius, G. Van Heck, & N. Smid (Eds.), *Personality psychology in Europe: Theoretical and empirical developments.* Lisse, The Netherlands: Swets & Zeitlinger.

Jung, C. G. (1910). The association method. *American Journal of Psychology, 21,* 219–269.

Kane, J. S., & Lawler, E. E. (1978). Methods of peer assessment. *Psychological Bulletin, 85,* 555–586.

Kanner, A. D., Coyne, J. C., Shaefer, C., & Lazarus, R. S. (1981). Comparison of two modes of stress measurement: Daily hassles and uplifts versus major life events. *Journal of Behavioral Medicine, 4,* 1–39.

Kenrick, D. T., & Dantchik, A. (1983). Interactionism, idiographics, and the social psychological invasion of personality. *Journal of Personality, 51,* 286–307.

Klinger, E., Barta, S. G., & Maxeiner, M. E. (1983). Motivational correlates of thought content frequency and commitment. *Journal of Personality and Social Psychology, 39,* 1222–1237.

Klopfer, B. (1947). Editorial comments. *Rorschach Research Exchange and Journal of Projective Techniques, 11,* 3–8.

Lamb, D. (1978). Anxiety. In H. London & J. E. Exner, Jr.

(Eds.), *Dimensions of personality* (pp. 37–83). New York: Wiley.

Lamiell, J. T., Foss, M. A., & Cavenee, P. (1980). On the relationship between conceptual schemes and behavior reports. *Journal of Personality, 48,* 54–73.

Lazarus, R. S. (1966). *Psychological stress and the coping process.* New York: McGraw-Hill.

Lewin, D. (1935). *A dynamic theory of personality.* New York: McGraw-Hill.

Little, B. R. (1983). Personal projects: A rationale and method for investigation. *Environment and Behavior, 15,* 273–309.

Little, B. R. (in press). Personality and environment. In D. Stokols & I. Altman (Eds.), *Handbook of environmental psychology.* New York: McGraw-Hill.

Littman, R. A. (1981). Psychology's histories: Some new ones and a bit about their predecessors—An essay review. *Journal of the History of the Behavioral Sciences, 17,* 516–532.

Loevinger, J. (1979). Construct validity of the sentence completion test of ego development. *Applied Psychological Measurement, 3,* 281–311.

Lonner, W. J. (1980). A decade of cross-cultural psychology: JCCP, 1970–1979. *Journal of Cross-Cultural Psychology, 11,* 7–34.

MacKinnon, D. W. (1944). The structure of personality. In J. McV. Hunt (Ed.), *Personality and the behavior disorders* (Vol. 1, pp. 3–48). New York: Ronald Press.

MacKinnon, D. W. (1962). The nature and nurture of creative talent. *American Psychologist, 17,* 484–495.

MacKinnon, D. W. (1975a). An overview of assessment centers. *CCL Technical Report No. 1.* Greensboro, NC: Center for Creative Leadership.

MacKinnon, D. W. (1975b). IPAR's contribution to the conceptualization and study of creativity (pp. 60–89). In I. A. Tayler & J. W. Getzels (Eds.), *Perspectives in creativity.* Chicago: Aldine.

MacKinnon, D. W. (1978). *In search of human effectiveness: Identifying and developing creativity.* Buffalo, NY: Creative Education Foundation.

MacKinnon, D. W., & Dukes, W. F. (1962). Repression. In L. Postman (Ed.), *Psychology in the making: Histories of selected research problems* (pp. 662–744). New York: A. A. Knopf.

Maddi, S. R. (1980). The uses of theorizing in personology. In E. Staub (Ed.), *Personality: Basic aspects and current research* (pp. 333–375). Englewood Cliffs, NJ: Prentice-Hall.

Maddi, S. R. (1984). Personology for the 1980s. In R. A. Zucker, J. Aronoff, & A. I. Rabin (Eds.), *Personality and the prediction of behavior* (pp. 7–41). New York: Academic Press.

Mash, E. J. (1979). What is behavioral assessment? *Behavioral Assessment, 1,* 23–29.

May, M. A. (1932). The foundations of personality. In P. S. Achilles (Ed.), *Psychology at work* (pp. 81–101). New York: McGraw-Hill.

McAdams, D. P. (1985). *Power, intimacy and the life story: Personological inquiries into identity.* Homewood, IL: Dorsey Press.

McClelland, D. C. (1951). *Personality.* New York: Sloane, Dryden, Holt.

McClelland, D. C. (1980). Motive dispositions: The merits of operant and respondent measures. In L. Wheeler (Ed.), *Review of personality and social psychology* (Vol. 1, pp. 10–41). Beverly Hills, CA: Sage.

McKechnie, G. E. (1974). *Manual for the Environmental Response Inventory.* Palo Alto, CA: Consulting Psychologists Press.

Mendelsohn, G. A. (1985). *La Dame aux Camélias* and *La Traviata*: A study of dramatic transformations in the light of biography. In R. Hogan & W. H. Jones (Eds.), *Perspectives in personality* (Vol. 1, pp. 271–303). Greenwich, CT: JAI Press.

Mischel, W. (1968). *Personality and assessment.* New York: Wiley.

Mischel, W. (1983). Alternatives in the pursuit of the predictability and consistency of persons: Stable data that yield unstable interpretations. *Journal of Personality, 51,* 578–604.

Mischel, W., & Peake, P. K. (1982). Beyond déjà vu in the search for cross-situational consistency. *Psychological Review, 89,* 730–755.

Moses, J. L., & Byham, W. (Eds.). (1977). *Applying the assessment center method.* New York: Pergamon Press.

Moskowitz, D. S. (1982). Coherence and cross-situational generality: A new analysis of old problems. *Journal of Personality and Social Psychology, 43,* 754–768.

Moskowitz, D. S., & Schwarz, J. C. (1982). Validity of behavior counts and ratings by knowledgeable informants. *Journal of Personality and Social Psychology, 42,* 518–528.

Murray, H. A. (1938). *Explorations in personality.* New York: Oxford University Press.

Musgrave, R. S., & Allport, F. H. (1941). Teleonomic description in the study of behavior. *Character and Personality, 9,* 326–343.

Nelson, E. A., Grinder, R. E., & Mutterer, M. L. (1969). Sources of variance in behavioral measures of honesty in temptation situations. *Developmental Psychology, 1,* 265–279.

O'Shaughnessy, B. (1970). The powerlessness of dispositions. *Analysis, 31,* 1–15.

Office of Strategic Services (OSS) Assessment Staff (1948). *Assessment of men.* New York: Rinehart.

Pawlik, K. (1985). Cross-situational consistency of behavior: Models, theories, and infield tests of the consistency issue. In E. E. Roskam (Ed.), *Measurement and personality assessment* (pp. 307–314). New York: Elsevier Science Publishers.

Pervin, L. A. (1983). The stasis and flow of behavior: Toward a theory of goals. In M. Page (Ed.), *Nebraska Symposium on Motivation* (Vol. 20, pp. 1–53). Lincoln, NB: University of Nebraska Press.

Pervin, L. A. (1985). Personality: Current controversies, issues, and directions. *Annual Review of Psychology, 36,* 83–114.

Peterson, D. R. (1979). Assessing interpersonal relationships in natural settings. In L. R. Kahle (Ed.), *Methods for studying person-situation interactions* (pp. 33–54). San Francisco, CA: Jossey-Bass.

Polansky, N. A. (1941). How shall a life history be written? *Character and Personality, 9,* 188–207.

Polivy, J. (1982). Introduction: Special issue on learned helplessness. *Journal of Personality, 50,* 385–386.

Porter, C. A., & Suedfeld, P. (1981). Integrative complexity in the correspondence of literary figures: Effects of personal and societal stress. *Journal of Personality and Social Psychology, 40,* 321–330.

Rapaport, D., Gill, M., & Schafer, R. (1946). *Diagnostic psychological testing* (Vols. 1 and 2). Chicago, IL: Year Book Publishers.

Raynor, J. O., & Entin, E. E. (1982). *Motivation, career striving, and aging.* Washington, DC: Hemisphere Publishing Company.

Reitmann, F. (1939). Goya: A medical study. *Character and Personality, 8,* 1–9.

Ritchie, R. J., & Moses, J. L. (1983). Assessment center correlates of women's advancement into middle management: A 7-year longitudinal study. *Journal of Applied Psychology, 68,* 227–231.

Roback, A. A. (1927). *A bibliography of character and personality.* Cambridge, MA: Sci-Art Publishers.

Rorschach, H. (1921). *Psychodiagnostics: A diagnostic test based on perception.* New York: Grune & Stratton.

Rosenberg, S. (1983). Contemporary perspectives and future directions of personality and social psychology. *Journal of Personality and Social Psychology, 45,* 57–73.

Rosenthal, R., Hall, J. A., DiMatteo, M. R., Rogers, P. L., & Archer, D. (1979). *Sensitivity to nonverbal communication: The PONS test.* Baltimore, MD: Johns Hopkins University Press.

Royce, J. R. (1977). Guest editorial: Have we lost sight of the original vision for SMEP and MBR? *Multivariate Behavioral Research, 12,* 135–141.

Runyan, W. M. (1981). Why did Van Gogh cut off his ear? The problem of alternative explanations in psychobiography. *Journal of Personality and Social Psychology, 40,* 1070–1077.

Runyan, W. M. (1982). *Life histories and psychobiography: Explorations in theory and method.* New York: Oxford University Press.

Runyan, W. M. (1983). Idiographic goals and methods in the study of lives. *Journal of Personality, 51,* 413–437.

Russell, D., Peplau, L. A., & Cutrona, E. C. (1980). The Revised UCLA Loneliness Scale: Concurrent and discriminant validity evidence. *Journal of Personality and Social Psychology, 39,* 472–480.

Sanford, N. (1963). Personality: Its place in psychology. In S. Koch (Ed.), *Psychology: A study of a science* (Vol. 5, pp. 488–592). New York: McGraw-Hill.

Sears, R. R. (1950). Personality. *Annual Review of Psychology, 1,* 105–118.

Sherman, S. J., & Fazio, R. H. (1983). Parallels between attitudes and traits as predictors of behavior. *Journal of Personality, 51,* 308–345.

Shweder, R. A. (1975). How relevant is an individual difference theory of personality? *Journal of Personality, 43,* 455–484.

Simonton, D. K. (1981). The library laboratory: Archival data in personality and social psychology. In L. Wheeler (Ed.), *Review of Personality and Social Psychology* (Vol. 2, pp. 217–243). Beverly Hills, CA: Sage.

Simonton, D. K. (1984). *Genius, creativity, and leadership.* Cambridge, MA: Harvard University Press.

Simonton, D. K. (1986). Presidential greatness: The historical consensus and its psychological significance. *Political Psychology, 7,* 259–283.

Smelser, N. J., & Smelser, W. T. (1964). Analyzing personality and social systems. In N. J. Smelser & W. T. Smelser (Eds.), *Personality and social systems* (pp. 1–18). New York: Wiley.

Smith, M. B., Bruner, J. S., & White, R. W. (1956). *Opinions and personality.* New York: Wiley.

Snyder, M. (1974). The self-monitoring of expressive behavior. *Journal of Personality and Social Psychology, 30,* 526–537.

Spearman, C. (1937). Editor's note. *Character and Personality, 5,* 214.

Spence, J. T., Helmreich, R., & Stapp, J. (1975). Ratings of self and peers on sex role attributes and their relations to self-esteem and conceptions of masculinity and femininity. *Journal of Personality and Social Psychology, 32,* 29–39.

Spielberger, C. D. (1966). Theory and research on anxiety. In C. D. Spielberger (Ed.), *Anxiety and behavior* (pp. 3–20). New York: Academic Press.

Spielberger, C. D. (1972). Anxiety as an emotional state. In C. D. Spielberger (Ed.), *Anxiety: Current trends in theory and research,* (Vol. 1, pp. 23–49). New York: Academic Press.

Squires, P. C. (1938). The creative psychology of Cesar Franck. *Character and Personality, 7,* 41–49.

Squires, R. (1970). Are dispositions lost causes? *Analysis, 31,* 15–18.

Stagner, R. (1937). *Psychology of personality.* New York: McGraw-Hill. (4th edition, 1974).

Staw, B. M. (1984). Organizational behavior: A review and reformulation of the field's outcome variables. *Annual Review of Psychology, 35,* 627–666.

Tallman, G. (1936). Foreword. *Rorschach Research Exchange, 1,* 2.

Tellegen, A. (1996). *Manual for the Multidimensional Personality Questionnaire.* Minneapolis: University of Minnesota Press.

Tetlock, P. E. (1984). Cognitive style and political belief systems in the British House of Commons. *Journal of Personality and Social Psychology, 46,* 365–375.

Tetlock, P. E., Bernzweig, J., & Gallant, J. L. (1985). Supreme Court decision making: Cognitive style as a predictor of ideological consistency of voting. *Journal of Personality and Social Psychology, 48,* 1227–1239.

Weinrot, M. R., Reid, J. B., Bauske, B. W., & Brummett, B. (1981). Supplementing naturalistic observation with observer impressions. *Behavioral Assessment, 3,* 141–159.

Weissbourd, R., & Sears, R. R. (1982). Mark Twain's exhibitionism. *Biography, 5,* 95–117.

White, R. W. (1952). *Lives in progress.* New York: Holt, Rinehart & Winston. (3rd ed., 1975).

Wicker, A. W. (1979). *An introduction to ecological psychology.* Monterey, CA: Brooks/Cole.

Wiggins, J. S. (1972). Editorial. *Journal of Experimental Research in Personality, 6,* iii–iv.

Wiggins, J. S. (1979). A psychological taxonomy of trait descriptive terms: 1. The interpersonal domain. *Journal of Personality and Social Psychology, 37,* 395–412.

Wilson, G. (1978). Introversion/extroversion. In H. London & J. E. Exner, Jr. (Eds.), *Dimensions of personality* (pp. 217–261). New York: Wiley.

Wright, L. (1976). *Teleological explanations.* Berkeley, CA: University of California Press.

Studying Personality the Long Way

Jack Block

This article by Jack Block, one of the most respected personality psychologists of his generation, introduces a research project he has conducted for more than two decades that has addressed a wide variety of topics. It has used many different methods to study people—he calls them L, O, T, and S data—but its most important methodological aspect is that the study is longitudinal. *That is, Block's research follows a group of the same people over a span of their lives when important psychological development takes place. At the time this article was written, the individuals he and his wife Jeanne Block began studying at age 3 were past college age. In this excerpt, Block presents his argument for the longitudinal method as a uniquely useful technique for tackling such topics, the guiding principles behind the design of the Block Project—which are those that should guide any major longitudinal investigation—and a sampling of the many, many methods this project has used to assess important aspects of personality.*

Block concluded this chapter with a summary of some of the project's most important empirical results at the time the chapter was written. We have omitted these summaries but direct your attention to the article by Shedler and Block in the second section of this reader. This article, on the personality antecedents of drug abuse, illustrates the kind of important information that can be gathered only through a major longitudinal investigation such as this one.

* * *

For various reasons, some of them overdetermined, it has seemed to me necessary to study people in the large, as they exist in their natural and real world, and the way and the why of their differences. And, to satisfyingly pursue this goal, the longitudinal study of personality development has seemed to me the compelled approach. By *longitudinal study*, I mean the close, comprehensive, systematic, objective, sustained study of individuals over significant portions of the life span. Such study permits unique and crucial scientific recognitions regarding human development and the factors influencing human development.

Longitudinal studies, once embarked on, perhaps inevitably become career investments of great personal significance and meaning to the investors. The commitment of self to so protracted a research enterprise runs the risk of distorting and subverting the subsequent scientific possibilities of the inquiry. It is also the case that such cathexis is required if the venture is to be carried through with care to a time of fruition and of harvest of what can be known in psychology no other way. No one longitudinal study will answer all the questions of developmental psychology, but also there is no alternative scientific approach that can begin to discern and disentangle the specific influential factors conjoining, interweaving, and reciprocating with each other as the individual reaches out to life, is enveloped by circumstance, and forges character. When we, as developmental or personality psychologists deign to observe a few conveniently accessible behaviors, here and there, now and then, for a moment or two, we are likely to be touching on or sampling rather little of the basis for comprehending a human life. It is the special merit of the longitudinal approach that by its scope, by its persistence, and by its analytical orientation toward the study of lives through time, it can perhaps permit a greater understanding of why it is people turn out as they do.

Aspirations for a Longitudinal Study of Personality Development

In 1968, my late wife, Jeanne, and I decided to initiate a longitudinal study of personality development. * * * We were moved to this commitment because we believed there was indeed an essential *coherence*, a deep structure to personality functioning and in personality development. Sure, it was crucial to recognize the ways in which the immediate environmental context influenced behavior, as personality psychologists Henry Murray (1938), Kurt Lewin (1946), Robert White (1959), and others earlier had observed. However, stimulus situations alone could not provide, we believed, a sufficient basis for understanding be-

havior. Human beings are not simply linear response systems effectively at the mercy of the situations they encounter. Besides making exquisite and unique discriminations, humans develop broad and adaptively functional, consistently applied generalizations. These constructed generalizations are shaped by a common evolutionary heritage, by modal perceptual and action patterns, and by commonly encountered environmental contingencies. Because of these constructed generalizations, individuals vary reliably and meaningfully and can be usefully dimensionalized or classified regarding the ways they perceive and react upon their world. We believed, 20 years ago, that the generally dismal state of empirical evidence for this proposition existed because, too often, the underlying coherence had not been sought well. In particular, we believed that consistency or continuity in behavior will not be found if one looks for expressions of personality consistency and continuity in ways that are conceptually obtuse or methodologically insufficient or empirically constrained. We thought we could do better and wanted to give it a try. We were by no means certain that, in our optimism, our faith would be fulfilled. We were certain, however, that those who would not try for coherence would not lead the way to understanding.

We sat down one evening to begin to list the desiderata for a longitudinal study of personality development. Gradually, as we thought about what had been done in the past and what we believed should be done in the future, we evolved a set of criterion dimensions in terms of which we planned our own effort.

Desiderata for a Longitudinal Study of Personality Development

1. *A longitudinal study should be an intentional rather than an accidental study, not a study begun for other reasons and only subsequently (and belatedly) declared to be a longitudinal study.* Some well-known longitudinal studies initially had not been conceived to be or to become long-term inquiries.

Because of this lack of anticipation, various simple, obvious, crucial kinds of research planning and data gathering had not been done at the outset, the one and only time when planning could have been effective or certain kinds of data could have been gathered. I am not referring to deficiencies of research design or research implementation easily and unfairly identified by cheap and virtuous retrospective wisdom. Instead, I have in mind omissions of data collection and failures of research design that could have been known at the time to be attenuating or vitiating of later analyses and hoped-for understandings. Our study, therefore, was to be deliberately longitudinal. Of course, intentionality did not prevent us from making our own mistakes, but it did permit us to avoid some important errors of the past.

2. *A longitudinal study should make public and communicable just what was done during the course of the study, how observations were made, how categories or numbers were generated, and how conclusions and interpretations were formulated.* We had observed that longitudinal investigators sometimes were carried away and infatuated by the aura of potential understanding that surrounds this well-regarded, if rarely used, approach. Too often, declamations and interpretations from longitudinal inquiries have been offered into the scientific literature on impressionistic and unspecifiable bases and, because of the positive aura surrounding longitudinal inquiry, have had unwarranted influence (see J. Block, 1981, for an account of one such unfortunate incident). Our longitudinal study, therefore, was to be one in which later psychologists could know what we had done, our rationales, the nature of our data and analyses, and the bases of our conclusions.

3. *A longitudinal study should be sufficiently extended in time so that developmental processes, continuities, and changes can be discerned.* Protracted, laborious, controlling of the researchers though a proper longitudinal study may be, there is not much point to a study so brief it cannot track development. Because of the cachet that now surrounds the term *longitudinal,* one sometimes encounters the oxymoron of "short-term longitudinal" studies. Our own plan and aspiration, therefore, was to conduct a long-term longitudinal study from early childhood (age 3 years) through the completion of high school (ages 17–18) and perhaps beyond. Although we viewed the then-incoming and increasingly popular emphasis on development throughout the life span to be salutary for those who had not earlier attained that important recognition, our own theoretical concerns were centered on the childhood and adolescent years, a time when personality development is relatively rapid and, as we believed, consequential.

4. *A longitudinal study should involve a sample of reasonable initial and continuing size, of reasonable relevance, and of both sexes seen a number of aptly selected times.* Given the diversity of personality development and the omnipresent noise in assessment measures, a sample size sufficient to permit discernment of relationships is crucial if this difficult game is to be worth the candle. Yet one cited longitudinal study involved a sample of 3 subjects that, when reassessed a final time 1 year later, showed a 33% attrition rate. Regarding sample relevance, in another longitudinal study the investigators apparently enlisted mothers from among their friends and friends of friends, with the consequence that 78% of their subjects came from Jewish, professional, urban, economically comfortable families. Certainly, one cannot aspire to a random or representative sample of subjects (representative of what, pray tell?) when close and continued study of development is being pursued, but certainly also, unusual, severely disproportionate subject selection that could well be relationship distorting is to be avoided. Other longitudinal researchers have considered subjects of only one sex, usually males; surely, this kind of exclusion is limiting of psychological understanding.

5. *A longitudinal study should have a conceptual or theoretically integrating rubric directing its doings and progression rather than be blandly or blindly eclectic.* In ranging widely in its coverage, a longitudinal study need not forsake theoretical pursuits. Indeed, the incisiveness and implicativeness of theoretical constructs are better seen when

a wide array of behaviors can be evaluated. Jeanne and I had developed some large, organizing personality constructs, ego-control and ego-resiliency, during our thesis days at Stanford University and demonstrated their behavioral implications in a variety of concurrent circumstances. Our constructs seemed to relate in intrinsic ways to other constructs formulated and studied by other investigators, encouraging us to think we were onto something of appreciable theoretical and behavioral importance. However, our constructs (and related ones) had never been studied developmentally. Obviously, to deepen understanding it was crucial to do so. We wished, therefore, to see how boys and girls over time evolved their personal systems for the modulation of motivations and the achievement of adaptive resourcefulness and perhaps to identify the environmental factors that differentially influenced these parameters of living. So we oriented our longitudinal study to examine developmentally our particular theoretical constructs.

6. *A longitudinal study should be comprehensive, intensive, systematic, and scientifically contemporary in coverage of its chosen conceptual domains.* Instead of being narrow and shallow, longitudinal inquiries should be broad and deep. They should involve *close psychological inquiry*, not just epidemiologically oriented surveys. Longitudinal studies are so rare that, although an already difficult research burden becomes even more difficult, a scientific responsibility is placed on the investigators to be catholic rather than parochial in designing and implementing their study. With broad and continuing assessments on the same set of subjects, there devolves the opportunity—which should not be missed—of relating within one sample research approaches customarily kept separate. Thereby, linkages among bodies of psychological research usually kept compartmentalized may possibly be established. The relationships, longitudinal or perhaps only concurrent, that subsequently may be discerned if there has been breadth of the research scan should have wide and cumulative import and speak to many psychological questions. Therefore, our longitudinal venture

was to range widely in the constructs to be covered and was to be alert to current thinking and procedures in the ongoing field of personality development. We expected to spend appreciable time with each of our subjects during each assessment for, as Robert White once informally remarked, one must look at personality in order to study it.

7. *A longitudinal study should be methodologically competent and display craftsmanship in its implementation.* Methodological competence should not be taken to mean simply and only knowledge of statistics; psychologists often incorrectly make this equivalence. Rather, methodological competence should mean competence of several kinds, invoked sequentially, with the recognition that later analytical possibilities depend crucially on earlier sensible decisions appropriately implemented. Competence with sophisticated or at least pertinent statistical methods is certainly required in the ultimate effort to discern relationships. However, prior to the invocation of such methods, a proper longitudinal research design must have been employed so that, from one time to another or from one context to another, data can be known to be absolutely independent and the subsequently obtained relationships indisputably can be recognized as inferentially clean. Prior to these considerations of research design, the measures being used must achieve sufficient psychometric status in terms of reliability and consequent discriminating power. Elaborate statistical analysis of logically independent measures will fail or will issue dismayingly null findings unless the measures employed are dependable. Finally, prior to concerns regarding measure dependability, it is essential to worry about the construct validity of the measures being used: Do they have the sweet reasonability and the supporting nomological network they must have if they are to represent the constructs the psychologist has in mind? Historically, longitudinal studies have been methodologically innocent and therefore interpreted sinfully. Measures have been awarded auspicious but unearned labels, with the consequence that subsequently observed relationships have been portrayed in misleading ways. Aware of these different

aspects of methodology and their logical sequence, we aspired, in our longitudinal effort, to a higher standard in this realm than previously had been achieved.

8. *A longitudinal study should seek to be innovative.* I mention this virtuous and grandiose aspiration, which modesty should perhaps cause me to conceal, to register my view that longitudinal studies often had been carried through in plodding, unthinking ways. Because head circumference was easy to measure, it was measured. In the home economics version of child psychology that prevailed prior to the 1950s, such parentally frowned-on behaviors as nail biting, eating problems, and enuresis were important topics and were longitudinally studied. Because the Rorschach Inkblot Test and the Thematic Apperception Test had become popular, they were administered. In short, a characteristic of previous longitudinal studies was that they brought together an agglomeration of readily available and unthought-about measures without much consideration being given to the concepts and issues to be studied and the necessary formulation of relevant assessment procedures bearing on these matters. A corollary of this passive, uncritical, atheoretical approach to longitudinal research is that when longitudinally studied subjects were followed up, it was too often the case that measures were reflexively, unthinkingly repeated *because they had been administered before* no matter how useless they had proved themselves to be or how age inappropriate they had become. We were determined to avoid such prosaicness in our longitudinal study. We therefore tried to seek out or create assessment procedures and concept-representing measures that were new, age appropriate, theoretically interesting, technically sound, and perhaps even elegant.

9. *A longitudinal study should be able to sustain the quality of the enterprise over the long period of time required.* An endemic disease of longitudinal studies seems to be that, after a time, they reach a point where they begin to falter, lose their vitality, and perhaps even their *raison d'être.* Staff demoralization occurs, and there is busyness without purpose. In part, this anomie may develop because the longitudinal idea takes so long before payoff. Also, some personnel replacements may be seeking a job rather than a purpose and so do not contribute to the necessary sense of meaning that must undergird the longitudinal enterprise. An especially troubling problem arises because longitudinal studies typically exist outside of academic departments and are supported by "soft" funds. In this insecure context, longitudinal researchers are hampered in their efforts to attract high-caliber research individuals for more than a few productive years. Understandably, such people must seize on ultimately more satisfying academic opportunities as they arise. Our longitudinal venture sought to forfend these problems by selecting and maintaining an intelligent, resourceful, dedicated cadre of professional staff, by encouraging an élan and group sense of meaning, by renewing and reinvigorating this small group over the years via carefully chosen replacements, and—perhaps primarily—by our very awareness that these problems could be expected to arise.

Taken altogether, these criteria for a longitudinal study represented a grandiose, quite adolescent ambition. I will not say that we achieved all of these worthy goals (indeed, I wish to be the first to criticize our enterprise), but these were the standards we set out for ourselves. I will leave to others and for another time the evaluation of how well we achieved our aspirations.

What, Indeed, Did We Do?

We began with 128 children from two nursery schools in Berkeley, a heterogeneous sample with regard to socioeconomic status, parental education, and ethnic background. Extensive individual assessments of these children were conducted at ages 3, 4, 5, 7, 11, 14, 18, and, most recently, at age 23. These time periods were selected for assessment because of our sense of when, developmentally, it would be most incisive to study our subjects. At age 23, we assessed 104 subjects. This small amount of subject attrition is due to the great attention we gave to motivating subjects and their parents, to repeated friendly contacts we initiated between assessment periods, to maintaining up-to-date records on subject locations, to paying the subjects a nominal sum for their participation once they entered adolescence, and to having the prescience to carry out such a study in the San Francisco Bay Area, from which there is a decided tendency not to move. Having interviewed just about all of our subjects during our most recent assessment, I have alerted them to our plans to see them again in their late 20s, after another eventful 5 years of life. ✶ ✶ ✶

During each of the eight assessment periods, every child (or adolescent or young adult) individually experienced an extensive battery of widely ranging procedures involving 10- or 11-hour-long sessions at ages 3 and 4, four or five longer sessions at ages 5 and 7, and six 2-hour (or longer) sessions at ages 11, 14, 18, and 23.

Various methodological or design principles guided our effort. We were oriented toward employing various kinds of data, not just life history, school, or demographic information (L-data); not just ratings of our subjects by teachers or parents or knowledgeable observers (O-data); not just formal experimental procedures or standardized tests (T-data); and not just questionnaires or other self-report techniques (S-data). Rather, we sought to include all (L-, O-, T-, and S-data) of these various approaches to generating useful data. Early on, we emphasized T-data in assessments because young children in their experimental and test behaviors rather directly express their motivations and characteristics. As our subjects moved into preadolescence and became "interiorized," we shifted to a greater use of S-data. Throughout our assessments, we collected various kinds of L-data information from the parents, school records, and the subjects themselves. And throughout the study we relied heavily on O-data, context-recognizing evaluations of our subjects at various ages, evaluations contributed by observers who had observed the subjects in diverse, often intimate situations, and often for appreciable periods of time.

We were also oriented toward the use of multiple measurements within each kind of data so as

to achieve dependability and generalizability of our measures. Instead of measuring the fidgetiness of a child by a single behavioral time sample, we measured fidgetiness on a number of occasions and developed an averaged index, which, of course, displayed much better reliability and subsequent relations with other variables. When measures were not sensibly repeatable, such as when we sought to study a broad construct such as style of categorizing, we sampled the conceptual domain using diverse measures of categorizing, which we then composited so as to rise above the problem of method variance. When we relied on observer evaluations of personality or interactions, we relied on a composite judgment of several independent observers—never just one—encoded by the Q-sort method so as to ensure observer comparability in the way they used numbers and to lessen the influence of response sets.

In successive assessments we used entirely different crews of assessors so that absolute independence was maintained between the data gathered at these different times. The T-procedures that were specifically repeated, such as the Witkin Rod-and-Frame Test, were not influenceable by prior testing or were separated by enough time so that memory could not play a vitiating role.

We used various data-reduction procedures with the thousands of variables that accumulated (e.g., factor analysis, hierarchical regression analysis, the compositing of standard scores derived from variables all conceptually or empirically linked, the generation of prototype scores to reflect how well a constellation of obtained scores fits a conceptual standard). In our analyses, we were sensitive to the problem of chance significance and applied an early version of the bootstrap method (J. Block, 1960) to our results and also catalyzed a method developed by truly mathematical statisticians (Alemayehu & Doksum, 1990) to further deal with the data analysis problems besetting us. Our most persuasive way of analyzing data, however, was to seek for and to find convergence of relationships from different kinds of data sets and from different times of assessment.

Routinely, we analyzed our data for the two

sexes separately. It is crucial to do so. When the same pattern of findings characterizes both boys and girls, both young men and young women, one has a cross-validated result. However, when, as happens surprisingly often, reliably different correlational patterns characterize the two sexes, a sex difference has been found that requires attention and thought. Over the years, I have been profoundly impressed by the differences between the sexes not so much in their respective mean levels on whatever is being measured as in the differences in the correlational *patterns* that characterize males as compared with females.

I now present an inundating listing (a sampling, really) of the measures and procedures and situations we imposed on our subjects over the years. The reader should not try to truly incorporate the meaning of the many measures so tersely mentioned; a sense of the scope and ambition of our effort is all that is needed.[1]

Thus, we used measures of activity level; delay of gratification; distractability; vigilance; exploratory behavior; motor inhibition (Simon Says!); susceptibility to priming; satiation and cosatiation; planfulness; curiosity; instrumental behavior when confronted by barriers or frustrations; dual focus (the ability to split attention); susceptibility to perceptual illusions; risk taking; level of aspiration; utilization of feedback; the Wechsler Intelligence Scale at ages 4, 11, and 18; the Raven Progressive Matrices; Piagetian measures of conservation; semantic retrieval; the Lowenfeld Mosaic Test; divergent thinking and other indexes of creativity; chained word association to index associative drift; various cognitive styles such as field dependence–independence, reflection–impulsivity, category breadth, and perceptual standards; sex role typing; egocentrism; physiognomic perception; incidental learning; the Stroop Color and Word Test; the Ko-

gan Metaphor Test for metaphor comprehension; metaphor generation; short-term memory via digit span; memory for sentences; and memory for narrative stories; moral development; Loevinger's Washington University Sentence Completion Test to measure ego development; Kelly's Role Construct Repertory Test; skin conductance while lying, when startled, and recovery rate from startle; the phenomenology of emotions; Spivack and Shure's interpersonal problem-solving measure; free play at age 3 and free play again at age 11 (patterned after Erik Erikson's approach); self-concept descriptions; descriptions of ideal self, of mother, of father, and of sought-for love object; decision time and decision confidence in situations varying in the intrinsic difficulty of decision; enacting a standard set of expressive situations (videotaped); experience sampling for a week via a beeper; blood pressure and heart rate in response to a set of stressors; depressive realism; false consensus; health indexes; activity and interest indexes; long and intensive clinical interviews (videotaped) relating to, among other topics, adult attachment, ways of knowing and ego development, and core conflict relationship themes; Diagnostic Interview Schedule screening so as to connect with the revised third edition of the *Diagnostic and Statistical Manual of Mental Disorders* (*DSM-III-R*) classification system; and hundreds of questionnaire and inventory items relating to dozens of personality scales.

Both the mothers and fathers of our subjects also participated in the study in various ways, contributing several kinds of data over the years. We have information at various times of their child-rearing orientations, their self-descriptions, their characterizations of the child, their responses to a personality inventory, home interviews and characterizations of the home environment, and videotapes of their interactions with their child during the preschool years and also during early adolescence.

In assembling and administering this array of procedures, there was continual concern for the age appropriateness of the procedures used. Some measures of conceptual interest sensibly could be

---

[1]The list of measures that follows is indeed inundating, as Block says. Even most psychologists would be unfamiliar with most of them. But this exhausting list does serve to illustrate how many different techniques exist for assessing different aspects of personality, and how many of them Block managed to include in his research project.

repeated in later years, such as the Rod-and-Frame Test, which we administered in six different assessments; others could not be, such as our procedure to measure delay of gratification by having nursery school children work for M&Ms. We were also attentive, as we went along, to the ongoing psychological literature, introducing into our assessments new topics and new measures that attracted our interest and to ensure continued contemporaneity of our broad-gauge inquiry. I offer as an observation and not as a boast that there is not another sample in psychology so extensively and intensively assessed for so long a period.[2]

* * *

---

[2]The rest of this chapter, omitted here, surveyed some recent empirical results. Block and his co-workers have published numerous articles over the years that present results concerning a wide array of topics, from drug use and depression to delay of gratification and moral development. One of the most important of these articles, on the personality antecedents of drug use and abuse, is excerpted in the next section of this reader.

References

Alemayehu, D., & Doksum, K. (1990). Using the bootstrap in correlation analysis, with applications to a longitudinal data set. *Journal of Applied Statistics, 17,* 357–368.

Block, J. (1960). On the number of significant findings to be expected by chance. *Psychometrika, 25,* 369–380.

Block, J. (1981). From infancy to adulthood: A clarification. *Child Development, 51,* 622–623.

Lewin, K. (1946). Behavior and development as a function of the total situation. In L. Carmichael (Ed.), *Manual of child psychology* (pp. 918–970). New York: Wiley.

Murray, H. A. (1938). *Explorations in personality.* New York: Oxford University Press.

White, R. W. (1959). Motivation reconsidered: The concept of competence. *Psychological Review, 66,* 297–333.

The Concept of Correlation

Leonard Horowitz

Most, but not all, empirical research in personality uses the correlational method. This means that rather than controlling variables experimentally, personality research usually measures two variables as they occur naturally, in real people, and assesses the degree to which they are related. Most commonly, the two variables that are correlated are two personality traits, or one personality trait and a behavior.

The degree to which the two variables are related is measured and reported using a statistic called the correlation coefficient. You cannot read personality research for very long without encountering this statistic repeatedly. The following selection, by the personality and clinical psychologist Leonard Horowitz, is one of the clearest expositions we could find of what this statistic means and how it is calculated.

The selection comes from an introductory statistics text, and does presuppose your knowledge of one thing, the meaning of a standard score. So, to bring you up to speed, the computation of a standard score—in the present case, called a z score—is a method for putting different variables onto a common scale. Each value of each variable is reexpressed in terms of the mean (average) and standard deviation (a measure of variability) of that variable.

For example, if a score of 20 on one variable, call it X, comes from a group of scores with a mean of 18 and standard deviation of 2, it would be expressed as a standard, z score of 1, because it is 1 standard deviation above the mean of X. Similarly, if a score of 40 on another variable, call it Y, came from a group of scores that had a mean of 36 and standard deviation of 4, it would also be expressed as a z of 1 because it is also 1 standard deviation above the mean of Y. In this way we could see that the two scores, 20 and 40, are equivalent in the sense that each score represents a value 1 standard deviation above the mean for X and Y, respectively.

The formula for the standard score is:

$$z = \frac{X - Mean\ of\ X}{Standard\ Deviation\ of\ X}$$

Now you are ready to follow Horowitz's explanation of the meaning and calculation of the correlation coefficient.

The concept of correlation is widely used in psychology. We hear claims that certain traits go together: Intelligence correlates with performance in school; learning time correlates with the subject's motivation; a word's frequency in English correlates with a speaker's ease of perceiving the word; a subject's personality correlates with his physique.

A correlation may be positive, negative, or zero. Height and weight are *positively* correlated. Tall people tend to be heavier, short people tend to be lighter. Of course, this relationship is not perfect since some short people weigh more than some tall people. The correlation is *negative* when the relationship is inverse: Individuals who are high on one trait tend to be low on the other. Word frequency, for example, correlates negatively with word length; frequent words are usually shorter.

The correlation is said to be a *zero correlation* when the traits are not related. An individual who is high on one trait might be high, medium, or low on the other trait. All combinations seem to occur. When the two traits are uncorrelated, they are said to be *distributed independently.*

First consider a simple, non-numerical example. Suppose four people are tested. Each person is asked to flip two pennies, Penny 1 and Penny 2. Then each person is assigned two scores, a score on Penny 1 and a score on Penny 2. The score can be H (for heads) or T (for tails). Here is one possible result:

Situation I illustrates a zero correlation: Subject 1 got an H both times, Subject 4 got a T both times, and Subjects 2 and 3 got one H and one T. All kinds of combinations occurred. There was no systematic relationship between the two events. Therefore, the Penny 1 score and the Penny 2

score are uncorrelated; they are independent of each other.

Situation I. A Zero Correlation

	Penny 1	Penny 2
Subject 1's result	H	H
Subject 2's result	H	T
Subject 3's result	T	H
Subject 4's result	T	T

To illustrate a *positive* correlation, suppose an invisible rod connects the two pennies. Then the score on Penny 1 *would* be related to the score on Penny 2. This relationship is shown in Situation II: An H on one accompanies an H on the other, and a T on one accompanies a T on the other. Finally, Situation III illustrates a *negative* correlation: In Situation III, an H on one penny accompanies a T on the other.

Situation II. A Positive Correlation

	Penny 1	Penny 2
Subject 1's result	H	H
Subject 2's result	H	H
Subject 3's result	T	T
Subject 4's result	T	T

Situation III. A Negative Correlation

	Penny 1	Penny 2
Subject 1's result	H	T
Subject 2's result	H	T
Subject 3's result	T	H
Subject 4's result	T	H

TABLE 4.1

COMPUTING r THROUGH z SCORES

Person	Trait X	Trait Y	z_X	z_Y	$z_X z_Y$
A	26	32	−0.8	−1.8	+1.44
B	24	40	−1.2	−1.0	+1.20
C	22	44	−1.6	−0.6	+0.96
D	33	44	+0.6	−0.6	−0.36
E	27	48	−0.6	−0.2	+0.12
F	36	52	+1.2	+0.2	+0.24
G	30	56	0.0	+0.6	0.00
H	38	56	+1.6	+0.6	+0.96
I	30	60	0.0	+1.0	0.00
J	34	68	+0.8	+1.8	+1.44

$$\bar{X} = 30 \qquad \bar{Y} = 50$$
$$S_X = 5 \qquad S_Y = 10$$

$$\sum z_X z_Y = +6.00$$

$$r_{XY} = \frac{\sum z_X z_Y}{N}$$

$$= \frac{+6.00}{10} = +0.60$$

Pearson's Correlation Coefficient

Frequently the scores are numerical and we need to describe the degree of correlation. The most common measure is Pearson's correlation coefficient, which is symbolized r. It originated with Sir Francis Galton, an English psychologist, and was extended by his student, Karl Pearson.

Consider the pairs of scores in Table 4.1. One score of each pair is denoted X, the other is denoted Y. (The r itself is denoted r_{XY}.) The mean of the X scores is 30, and the standard deviation is 5. The mean of the Y scores is 50, and the standard deviation is 10.

Table 4.1 shows one way to compute r_{XY}. First we convert each set of scores to z scores. (That makes the scores of one set comparable to those of the other set.) Thus, each X becomes a z_X, and each Y becomes a z_Y. For Subject A, $z_X = (26 − 30)/5 = −.80$; Subject A's score is therefore .8

standard deviation below the mean. The corresponding z_Y score is −1.8. Subject A's Y score therefore falls 1.8 standard deviations below the mean of the Y scores.

Then we multiply each z_X by the subject's z_Y and record the products in the last column. Then, to obtain r, we compute the mean of these $z_X \cdot z_Y$ products: We sum them and divide by N. The complete formula is written:

$$r_{XY} = \frac{\sum z_X z_Y}{N}$$

In Table 4.1, the mean of the $z_X \cdot z_Y$ column is positive. In general, negative z_X's accompany negative z_Y's, and positive z_X's accompany positive z_Y's. Most of the $z_X \cdot z_Y$ products are positive, so the mean is positive.

When r is negative, the mean $z_X \cdot z_Y$ is negative: Negative z_X's would generally accompany positive

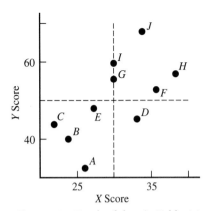

Figure 4.1   Graph of data in Table 4.1

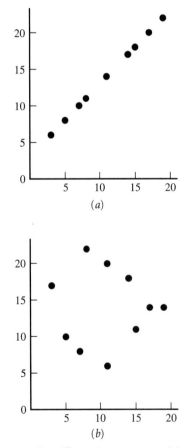

(a)

(b)

Figure 4.2   Data illustrating two cases: (a) $r = +1$ and (b) $r = 0$

z_Y's. Most of the products would be negative, so their mean would be negative.

The *sign* of r therefore describes the relationship as negative or positive. +.30 means a positive relationship; −0.60 means a negative relationship.

When r equals 0, the scores are not related. In that case, some negative z_X's accompany negative z_Y's, and other negative z_X's accompany positive z_Y's. Thus, some products are negative, while others are positive. If the negative products completely offset the positive ones, $\Sigma z_X \cdot z_Y = 0$, and r is 0.

If r differs from 0, the number tells how strong the relationship is. The farther it is from 0, the stronger the relationship. The relationship is strongest when r equals +1.00 or −1.00.[1] Thus, the possible values of r range from −1.00 through 0.00 to +1.00. In Table 4.1, $r = +0.60$—a moderately high, positive correlation.

To understand r, it is helpful to examine the data on a graph. Figure 4.1 presents the data of Table 4.1 graphically. Each subject's pair of scores appears as a dot on the graph. Notice that the points mainly fall in two quadrants—the lower left-hand quadrant and the upper right-hand quadrant. People with high X scores usually earned high Y scores; those with low X scores usually earned low Y scores.

Figure 4.2 shows other sets of data, too. When $r = +1.00$, the points fall along a perfectly straight line, and the relationship is perfect. The subject with the lowest X score has the lowest Y score; the one with the next highest X score has the next highest Y score, and so on. Each subject's z_X matches his z_Y, so a person's relative standing on X matches his relative standing on Y.

On the other hand, suppose $r = 0.00$. The z_X bears no relation to the z_Y. A positive z_X sometimes accompanies a negative z_Y and sometimes accompanies a positive z_Y. All combinations occur. Figure 4.2b illustrates a zero correlation. When $r = 0.00$, the points fall haphazardly on the graph.

---

[1]The absolute value of $\Sigma z_X z_Y$ is always less than or equal to N. Thus the maximum value of r is 1.00, and the minimum is −1.00.

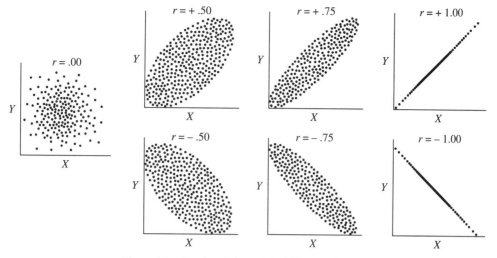

Figure 4.3 Graphs of data with different values of *r*

When *r* differs from 0, the points seem to fall within an ellipse. Some examples are shown in Figure 4.3. The ellipse grows thinner as *r* increases. Eventually, when *r* equals −1.00 or +1.00, the ellipse becomes a straight line.

*   *   *

Correlation Means Prediction

If someone is above average in height, we expect him to be above average in weight. If his IQ is low, we expect him to do poorly in school. Correlation means prediction: We can always use one variable to help predict the other. The main purpose of a psychological test is to make predictions about other variables.

For example, suppose the staff of a college admissions office were trying to predict ultimate grade-point averages. They might administer a one-hour test to every student just before the freshman year. Four years later, they might compute each student's grade-point average. The value of *r* would also be computed. Suppose the admissions office tested thousands of students and obtained the data of Figure 4.4. Thousands of datum points make a very thorough and accurate picture; future students would also fit into this picture.

Test scores can be gotten in one easy hour of mass testing. But grade-point averages cost four years of individual time, effort, and money. If grade-point averages could be *predicted* from test

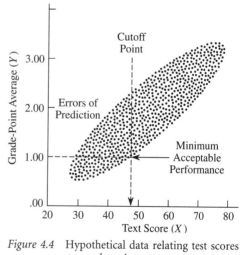

Figure 4.4 Hypothetical data relating test scores to grade-point averages

scores, some errors of admission and consequent heartache could be spared. The data of Figure 4.4 can help achieve this goal.

First, the admissions office must set the minimum acceptable grade-point average. Say this value is 1.00. They would like to screen out those people whose grade-point averages will ultimately fall below 1.00. Who are those people? In Figure 4.4 they all have test scores below 47. Therefore, in the future, the admissions office might require a score above 47 for admission. The college could thus eliminate potential failures.

This procedure does create one serious error. There are always some individuals whose test scores are low, but whose actual college performance is good. They might be people who become unusually anxious during a mass testing. Or they might be people who have not yet mastered the art of taking multiple-choice tests. It would be a mistake to reject those people from the college. Thus, as its next step, the admissions office would seek ways of identifying those people, perhaps through biographical data or personality tests.

A Simple, General-Purpose Display of Magnitude of Experimental Effect

Robert Rosenthal and Donald B. Rubin

As useful as it is, the correlation coefficient described in the preceding selection has been the source of considerable, needless confusion. As you have learned, an r of 1 (or −1) means that two variables are perfectly correlated, and an r of 0 means they are not correlated at all. But how should we interpret the r's in between, as most are?

Confusion has been engendered by a commonly taught practice of squaring correlations to yield the "percentage of variance explained" by the relationship. While this phrase sounds rather close to what one would want to know, it causes people to interpret correlations of .32, for example, as "explaining only 10% of the variance" (because .32 squared is about .10), which leaves 90% "unexplained." This does not make it sound like much has been accomplished.

In the next selection, psychologist Robert Rosenthal and statistician Donald Rubin team up to explain why this common calculation is misleading. In particular, they believe it causes strong effects, such as those indexed by a correlations between .30 and .40, to seem smaller than they are. They introduce a simple technique of their own invention for illustrating the real size and importance of correlations. The "binomial effect size display" (BESD) allows correlation coefficients to be interpreted in terms of the percentage of correct classification or effective treatment they represent.

The basic calculation is even simpler than this article may make it sound. Look at Table 5.1 and assume an r of 0. This would yield an entry of 50 in each of the four cells. To see what a correlation of .32 looks like, divide 32 by 2, which gives you 16. Add the 16 to 50 and put this 66 in the upper left-hand and lower right cells. Now subtract 16 from 50 and put 34 in the lower left and upper right cells. The rows and columns still each add up to 100, but now show what r = .32 looks like. It's easy! And it shows that a correlation between a treatment and an outcome, or between a predictor and a criterion, of a size of .32 would give you the right result almost twice as often as the wrong result.

The BESD is particularly important for personality psychology because most of the strongest relations between traits or between traits and behaviors are found to yield correlations between about .30 and .40. Rosenthal and Rubin show us that this means the prediction of one trait from another, or of a behavior on the basis of a trait, is usually more than twice as likely to be right as it is to be wrong.

---

* * *

Traditionally, behavioral researchers have concentrated on reporting significance levels of experimental effects. Recent years, however, have shown a welcome increase in emphasis on reporting the magnitude of experimental effects obtained (Cohen, 1977; Fleiss, 1969; Friedman, 1968; Glass, 1976; Hays, 1973; Rosenthal, 1978; Rosenthal & Rubin, 1978; Smith & Glass, 1977).

Despite the growing awareness of the importance of estimating sizes of effects along with estimating the more conventional levels of significance, there is a problem in interpreting various effect size estimators such as the Pearson r. For example, we found experienced behavioral researchers and experienced statisticians quite surprised when we showed them that the Pearson r of .32 associated with a coefficient of determination (r^2) of only .10 was the correlational equivalent of increasing a success rate from 34% to 66% by means of an experimental treatment procedure; for example, these values could mean that a death rate under the control condition is 66% but is only 34% under the experimental condition. We believe (Rosenthal & Rubin, 1979) that there may be a widespread tendency to underestimate the importance of the effects of behavioral (and biomedical) interventions (Mayo, 1978; Rimland, 1979) simply because they are often associated with what are thought to be low values of r^2.

The purpose of the present article is to introduce an intuitively appealing general purpose effect size display whose interpretation is perfectly transparent: the binomial effect size display (BESD). In no sense do we claim to have resolved the differences and controversies surrounding the use of various effect size estimators (e.g., Appelbaum & Cramer, 1974). Our display is useful because it is (a) easily understood by researchers,

TABLE 5.1

THE BINOMIAL EFFECT SIZE DISPLAY:
AN EXAMPLE
"ACCOUNTING FOR ONLY 10%
OF THE VARIANCE"

Condition	Alive	Dead	Σ
Treatment	66	34	100
Control	34	66	100
Σ	100	100	200

students, and lay persons; (b) applicable in a wide variety of contexts; and (c) conveniently computed.

The question addressed by BESD is: What is the effect on the success rate (e.g., survival rate, cure rate, improvement rate, selection rate, etc.) of the institution of a certain treatment procedure? It displays the change in success rate (e.g., survival rate, cure rate, improvement rate, selection rate, etc.) attributable to a certain treatment procedure. An example shows the appeal of our procedure.

In their meta-analysis of psychotherapy outcome studies, Smith and Glass (1977) summarized the results of some 400 studies. An eminent critic stated that the results of their analysis sounded the "death knell" for psychotherapy because of the modest size of the effect (Rimland, 1979). This modest effect size was calculated to be equivalent to an r of .32 accounting for "only 10% of the variance" (p. 192).

Table 5.1 is the BESD corresponding to an r of .32 or an r^2 of .10. The table shows clearly that it is absurd to label as "modest indeed" (Rimland, 1979, p. 192) an effect size equivalent to increasing the success rate from 34% to 66% (e.g., reducing a death rate from 66% to 34%).

TABLE 5.2

BINOMIAL EFFECT SIZE DISPLAYS CORRESPONDING TO VARIOUS VALUES OF r^2 AND r

r^2	r	Success rate increased From	Success rate increased To	Difference in success rates
.01	.10	.45	.55	.10
.04	.20	.40	.60	.20
.09	.30	.35	.65	.30
.16	.40	.30	.70	.40
.25	.50	.25	.75	.50
.36	.60	.20	.80	.60
.49	.70	.15	.85	.70
.64	.80	.10	.90	.80
.81	.90	.05	.95	90
1.00	1.00	.00	1.00	1.00

Table 5.2 shows systematically the increase in success rates associated with various values of r^2 and r. Even so small an r as .20, accounting for only 4% of the variance, is associated with an increase in success rate from 40% to 60%, such as a reduction in death rate from 60% to 40%. The last column of Table 5.2 shows that the difference in success rates is identical to r. Consequently the experimental success rate in the BESD is computed as $.50 + r/2$, whereas the control group success rate is computed as $.50 - r/2$. Cohen (1965) and Friedman (1968) have useful discussions of computing the r associated with a variety of test statistics, and Table 5.3 gives the three most frequently used equivalences.

We propose that the reporting of effect sizes can be made more intuitive and more informative by using the BESD. It is our belief that the use of the BESD to display the increase in success rate

---

TABLE 5.3

COMPUTATION OF r FROM COMMON TEST STATISTICS

Test statistic	r[a] given by
act	$\sqrt{\dfrac{t^2}{t^2 + df}}$
F[b]	$\sqrt{\dfrac{F}{F + df\,(error)}}$
$X^{2,c}$	$\sqrt{\dfrac{\chi^2}{N}}$

[a] The sign of r should be positive if the experimental group is superior to the control group and negative if the control group is superior to the experimental group.
[b] Used only when df for numerator = 1 as in the comparison of two group means or any other contrast.
[c] Used only when df for χ^2 = 1.

---

due to treatment will more clearly convey the real world importance of treatment effects than do the commonly used descriptions of effect size based on the proportion of variance accounted for. The BESD is most appropriate when the variances within the two conditions are similar, as they are assumed to be whenever we compute the usual t test.

It might appear that the BESD can be employed only when the outcome variable is dichotomous and the mean outcome in one group is the same amount above .5 as the mean outcome in the other group is below .5. Actually, the BESD is often a realistic representation of the size of treatment effect when the variances of the outcome variable are approximately the same in the two approximately equal sized groups, as is commonly the case in educational and psychological studies.

* * *

References

Appelbaum, M. I., & Cramer, E. M. (1974). The only game in town. *Contemporary Psychology, 19*, 406–407.

Cohen, J. (1965). Some statistical issues in psychological research. In B. B. Wolman (Ed.), *Handbook of clinical psychology*. New York: McGraw-Hill.

Cohen, J. (1977). *Statistical power analysis for the behavioral sciences* (Rev. ed.). New York: Academic Press.

Fleiss, J. L. (1969). Estimating the magnitude of experimental effects. *Psychological Bulletin, 72*, 273–276.

Friedman, H. (1968). Magnitude of experimental effect and a table for its rapid estimation. *Psychological Bulletin, 70*, 245–251.

Glass, G. V. (1976, April). *Primary, secondary, and meta-analysis of research.* Paper presented at the meeting of the American Educational Research Association, San Francisco.

Hays, W. L. (1973). *Statistics for the social sciences.* (2nd ed.). New York: Holt, Rinehart & Winston.

Mayo, R. J. (1978). Statistical considerations in analyzing the results of a collection of experiments. *The Behavioral and Brain Sciences, 3*, 400–401.

Rimland, B. (1979). Death knell for psychotherapy? *American Psychologist, 34*, 192.

Rosenthal, R. (1978). Combining results of independent studies. *Psychological Bulletin, 85*, 185–193.

Rosenthal, R., & Rubin, D. B. (1978). Interpersonal expectancy effects: The first 345 studies. *The Behavioral and Brain Sciences, 3*, 377–386.

Rosenthal, R., & Rubin, D. B. (1979). A note on percent variance explained as a measure of the importance of effects. *Journal of Applied Social Psychology, 9*, 395–396.

Smith, M. L., & Glass, G. V. (1977). Meta-analysis of psychotherapy outcome studies. *American Psychologist, 32*, 752–760.

Construct Validity in Psychological Tests

Lee J. Cronbach and Paul E. Meehl

Lee Cronbach and Paul Meehl are two of the most prominent methodologists in the history of psychology. In the following classic selection, they team up to address the knotty question of "construct validity," which is, how do you know whether a test—such as a personality test—really measures what it is supposed to measure? As is mentioned in the opening paragraphs, the article was occasioned by very real concerns in the mid-1950s over the proper way to establish the validity of a test. This issue generated political heat both within and outside the American Psychological Association, the professional organization of many psychologists, because the tests that people take often have real consequences. They are used for selection in education and employment, for example. Thus, the degree to which a test is valid is more than an academic issue. Its resolution has real consequences for real people.

This article is a fairly difficult piece, but worth some effort. Psychologists who have been doing research for years can reread this article and learn something important that escaped them on previous readings. The essential points to glean from this article are that no single study or one source of data will ever sufficiently explain any important aspect of personality, and that psychological theory plays an essential role in developing an understanding of what any measure of personality really means. Multiple methods must always be employed, and the validation of a test will emerge only gradually from an examination of how different methods produce results that are sometimes the same and sometimes different. The present excerpt concludes with the important observation that the aim of construct validation is not to conclude that a test "is valid," but rather to assess its degree of validity for various purposes.

From "Construct Validity in Psychological Tests," by L. J. Cronbach and P. E. Meehl (1955). In *Psychological Bulletin, 52,* 281–302. Adapted with permission.

Validation of psychological tests has not yet been adequately conceptualized, as the APA Committee on Psychological Tests learned when it undertook (1950–54) to specify what qualities should be investigated before a test is published. In order to make coherent recommendations the Committee found it necessary to distinguish four types of validity, established by different types of research and requiring different interpretation. The chief innovation in the Committee's report was the term *construct validity*. This idea was first formulated by a subcommittee (Meehl and R. C. Challman) studying how proposed recommendations would apply to projective techniques, and later modified and clarified by the entire Committee (Bordin, Challman, Conrad, Humphreys, Super, and the present writers). The statements agreed upon by the Committee (and by committees of two other associations) were published in American Psychological Association (APA) (1954). The present interpretation of construct validity is not "official" and deals with some areas where the Committee would probably not be unanimous. The present writers are solely responsible for this attempt to explain the concept and elaborate its implications.

Identification of construct validity was not an isolated development. Writers on validity during the preceding decade had shown a great deal of dissatisfaction with conventional notions of validity, and introduced new terms and ideas, but the resulting aggregation of types of validity seems only to have stirred the muddy waters. Portions of the distinctions we shall discuss are implicit in Jenkins's (1946) paper, Gulliksen (1950), Goodenough's (1950) distinction between tests as "signs" and "samples," Cronbach's (1949) separation of "logical" and "empirical" validity, Guilford's (1946) "factorial validity," and Mosier's (1947, 1951) papers on "face validity" and "validity generalization." Helen Peak (1953) comes close to an explicit statement of construct validity as we shall present it.

Four Types of Validation

The categories into which the *Recommendations* divide validity studies are: predictive validity, concurrent validity, content validity, and construct validity. The first two of these may be considered together as *criterion-oriented* validation procedures.

The pattern of a criterion-oriented study is familiar. The investigator is primarily interested in some criterion which he wishes to predict. He administers the test, obtains an independent criterion measure on the same subjects, and computes a correlation. If the criterion is obtained some time after the test is given, he is studying *predictive validity*. If the test score and criterion score are determined at essentially the same time, he is studying *concurrent validity*. Concurrent validity is studied when one test is proposed as a substitute for another (for example, when a multiple-choice form of spelling test is substituted for taking dictation), or a test is shown to correlate with some contemporary criterion (e.g., psychiatric diagnosis).

Content validity is established by showing that the test items are a sample of a universe in which the investigator is interested. Content validity is ordinarily to be established deductively, by defining a universe of items and sampling systematically within this universe to establish the test.

Construct validation is involved whenever a test is to be interpreted as a measure of some attribute or quality which is not "operationally defined." The problem faced by the investigator is, "What constructs account for variance in test performance?" Construct validity calls for no new scientific approach. Much current research on tests of personality (Child, 1954) is construct validation, usually without the benefit of a clear formulation of this process.

Construct validity is not to be identified solely by particular investigative procedures, but by the orientation of the investigator. Criterion-oriented validity, as Bechtoldt emphasizes (1951, p. 1245), "involves the *acceptance* of a set of operations as an adequate definition of whatever is to be measured." When an investigator believes that no criterion available in him is fully valid, he perforce becomes interested in construct validity because this is the only way to avoid the "infinite frustration" of relating every criterion to some more ultimate standard (Gaylord, unpublished manuscript). In content validation, *acceptance* of the universe of content as defining the variable to be measured is essential. Construct validity must be investigated whenever no criterion or universe of content is accepted as entirely adequate to define the quality to be measured. Determining what psychological constructs account for test performance is desirable for almost any test. Thus, although the MMPI was originally established on the basis of empirical discrimination between patient groups and so-called normals (concurrent validity), continuing research has tried to provide a basis for describing the personality associated with each score pattern. Such interpretations permit the clinician to predict performance with respect to criteria which have not yet been employed in empirical validation studies (cf. Meehl, 1954, pp. 49–50, 110–111).

We can distinguish among the four types of validity by noting that each involves a different emphasis on the criterion. In predictive or concurrent validity, the criterion behavior is of concern to the tester, and he may have no concern whatsoever with the type of behavior exhibited in the test. (An employer does not care if a worker can manipulate blocks, but the score on the block test may predict something he cares about.) Content validity is studied when the tester *is* concerned with the type of behavior involved in the test performance. Indeed, if the test is a work sample, the behavior represented in the test may be an end in itself. Construct validity is ordinarily studied when the tester has no definite criterion measure of the quality with which he is concerned, and must use indirect measures. Here the trait or quality underlying the test is of central importance, rather than either the test behavior or the scores on the criteria (APA, 1954, p. 14).

Construct validation is important at times for every sort of psychological test: aptitude, achievement, interests, and so on. Thurstone's statement is interesting in this connection:

In the field of intelligence tests, it used to be common to define validity as the correlation between a test score and some outside criterion. We have reached a stage of sophistication where the test-criterion correlation is too coarse. It is obsolete. If we attempted to ascertain the validity of a test for the second space-factor, for example, we would have to get judges [to] make reliable judgments about people as to this factor. Ordinarily their [the available judges'] ratings would be of no value as a criterion. Consequently, validity studies in the cognitive functions now depend on criteria of internal consistency . . . (Thurstone, 1952, p. 3).

Construct validity would be involved in answering such questions as: To what extent is this test of intelligence culture-free? Does this test of "interpretation of data" measure reading ability, quantitative reasoning, or response sets? How does a person with A in Strong Accountant, and B in Strong CPA, differ from a person who has these scores reversed?

Example of construct validation procedure. Suppose measure X correlates .50 with Y, the amount of palmar sweating induced when we tell a student that he has failed a Psychology I exam. Predictive validity of X for Y is adequately described by the coefficient, and a statement of the experimental and sampling conditions. If someone were to ask, "Isn't there perhaps another way to interpret this correlation?" or "What other kinds of evidence can you bring to support your interpretation?" we would hardly understand what he was asking because no interpretation has been made. These questions become relevant when the correlation is advanced as evidence that "test X measures anxiety proneness." Alternative interpretations are possible; e.g., perhaps the test measures "academic aspiration," in which case we will expect different results if we induce palmar sweating by economic threat. It is then reasonable to inquire about other *kinds* of evidence.

Add these facts from further studies: Test X correlates .45 with fraternity brothers' ratings on "tenseness." Test X correlates .55 with amount of intellectual inefficiency induced by painful electric shock, and .68 with the Taylor Anxiety scale. Mean X score decreases among four diagnosed groups in this order: anxiety state, reactive depression, "normal," and psychopathic personality. And palmar sweat under threat of failure in Psychology I correlates .60 with threat of failure in mathematics. Negative results eliminate competing explanations of the X score; thus, findings of negligible correlations between X and social class, vocational aim, and value-orientation make it fairly safe to reject the suggestion that X measures "academic aspiration." We can have substantial confidence that X does measure anxiety proneness if the current theory of anxiety can embrace the variates which yield positive correlations, and does not predict correlations where we found none.

* * *

The Relation of Constructs to "Criteria"

CRITICAL VIEW OF THE CRITERION IMPLIED An unquestionable criterion may be found in a practical operation, or may be established as a consequence of an operational definition. Typically, however, the psychologist is unwilling to use the directly operational approach because he is interested in building theory about a generalized construct. A theorist trying to relate behavior to "hunger" almost certainly invests that term with meanings other than the operation "elapsed-time-since-feeding." If he is concerned with hunger as a tissue need, he will not accept time lapse as *equivalent* to his construct because it fails to consider, among other things, energy expenditure of the animal.

In some situations the criterion is no more valid than the test. Suppose, for example, that we want to know if counting the dots on Bender-Gestalt figure five indicates "compulsive rigidity," and take psychiatric ratings on this trait as a criterion. Even a conventional report on the resulting correlation will say something about the extent and intensity of the psychiatrist's contacts and should describe his qualifications (e.g., diplomate status? analyzed?).

Why report these facts? Because data are needed to indicate whether the criterion is any good. "Compulsive rigidity" is not really intended to mean "social stimulus value to psychiatrists." The implied trait involves a range of behavior-dispositions which may be very imperfectly sampled by the psychiatrist. Suppose dot-counting does not occur in a particular patient and yet we find that the psychiatrist has rated him as "rigid." When questioned the psychiatrist tells us that the patient was a rather easy, free-wheeling sort: however, the patient *did* lean over to straighten out a skewed desk blotter, and this, viewed against certain other facts, tipped the scale in favor of a "rigid" rating. On the face of it, counting Bender dots may be just as good (or poor) a sample of the compulsive-rigidity domain as straightening desk blotters is.

Suppose, to extend our example, we have four tests on the "predictor" side, over against the psychiatrist's "criterion," and find generally positive correlations among the five variables. Surely it is artificial and arbitrary to impose the "test-should-predict-criterion" pattern on such data. The psychiatrist samples verbal content, expressive pattern, voice, posture, etc. The psychologist samples verbal content, perception, expressive pattern, etc. Our proper conclusion is that, from this evidence, the four tests and the psychiatrist all assess some common factor.

The asymmetry between the "test" and the so-designated "criterion" arises only because the terminology of predictive validity has become a commonplace in test analysis. In this study where a construct is the central concern, any distinction between the merit of the test and criterion variables would be justified only if it had already been shown that the psychiatrist's theory and operations were excellent measures of the attribute.

Inadequacy of Validation in Terms of Specific Criteria

The proposal to validate constructual interpretations of tests runs counter to suggestions of some others. Spiker and McCandless (1954) favor an operational approach. Validation is replaced by compiling statements as to how strongly the test predicts other observed variables of interest. To avoid requiring that each new variable be investigated completely by itself, they allow two variables to collapse into one whenever the properties of the operationally defined measures are the same: "If a new test is demonstrated to predict the scores on an older, well-established test, then an evaluation of the predictive power of the older test may be used for the new one." But accurate inferences are possible only if the two tests correlate so highly that there is negligible reliable variance in either test, independent of the other. Where the correspondence is less close, one must either retain all the separate variables operationally defined or embark on construct validation.

The practical user of tests must rely on constructs of some generality to make predictions about new situations. Test X could be used to predict palmar sweating in the face of failure without invoking any construct, but a counselor is more likely to be asked to forecast behavior in diverse or even unique situations for which the correlation of test X is unknown. Significant predictions rely on knowledge accumulated around the generalized construct of anxiety. The "Technical Recommendations" state:

> It is ordinarily necessary to evaluate construct validity by integrating evidence from many different sources. The problem of construct validation becomes especially acute in the clinical field since for many of the constructs dealt with it is not a question of finding an imperfect criterion but of finding any criterion at all. The psychologist interested in construct validity for clinical devices is concerned

with making an estimate of a hypothetical internal process, factor, system, structure, or state and cannot expect to find a clear unitary behavioral criterion. An attempt to identify any one criterion measure or any composite as *the* criterion aimed at is, however, usually unwarranted (APA, 1954, pp. 14–15).

This appears to conflict with arguments for specific criteria prominent at places in the testing literature. Thus Anastasi (1950) makes many statements of the latter character: "It is only as a measure of a specifically defined criterion that a test can be objectively validated at all . . . To claim that a test measures anything over and above its criterion is pure speculation" (p. 67). Yet elsewhere this article supports construct validation. Tests can be profitably interpreted if we "know the relationships between the tested behavior . . . and other behavior samples, none of these behavior samples necessarily occupying the preeminent position of a criterion" (p. 75). Factor analysis with several partial criteria might be used to study whether a test measures a postulated "general learning ability." If the data demonstrate specificity of ability instead, such specificity is "useful in its own right in advancing our knowledge of behavior; it should not be construed as a weakness of the tests" (p. 75).

We depart from Anastasi at two points. She writes, "The validity of a psychological test should not be confused with an analysis of the factors which determine the behavior under consideration." We, however, regard such analysis as a most important type of validation. Second, she refers to "the will-o'-the-wisp of psychological processes which are distinct from performance" (Anastasi, 1950, p. 77). While we agree that psychological processes are elusive, we are sympathetic to attempts to formulate and clarify constructs which are evidenced by performance but distinct from it. Surely an inductive inference based on a pattern of correlations cannot be dismissed as "pure speculation."

SPECIFIC CRITERIA USED TEMPORARILY: THE "BOOTSTRAPS" EFFECT Even when a test is constructed on the basis of a specific criterion, it may ultimately be judged to have greater construct validity than the criterion. We start with a vague concept which we associate with certain observations. We then discover empirically that these observations covary with some other observation which possesses greater reliability or is more intimately correlated with relevant experimental changes than is the original measure, or both. For example, the notion of temperature arises because some objects feel hotter to the touch than others. The expansion of a mercury column does not have face validity as an index of hotness. But it turns out that (a) there is a statistical relation between expansion and sensed temperature; (b) observers employ the mercury method with good interobserver agreement; (c) the regularity of observed relations is increased by using the thermometer (e.g., melting points of samples of the same material vary little on the thermometer; we obtain nearly linear relations between mercury measures and pressure of a gas). Finally, (d) a theoretical structure involving unobservable microevents—the kinetic theory—is worked out which explains the relation of mercury expansion to heat. This whole process of conceptual enrichment begins with what in retrospect we see as an extremely fallible "criterion"—the human temperature sense. That original criterion has now been relegated to a peripheral position. We have lifted ourselves by our bootstraps, but in a legitimate and fruitful way.

Similarly, the Binet scale was first valued because children's scores tended to agree with judgments by schoolteachers. If it had not shown this agreement, it would have been discarded along with reaction time and the other measures of ability previously tried. Teacher judgments once constituted the criterion against which the individual intelligence test was validated. But if today a child's IQ is 135 and three of his teachers complain about how stupid he is, we do not conclude that the test has failed. Quite to the contrary, if no error in test procedure can be argued, we treat the test score as a valid statement about an important quality, and define our task as that of finding out what other variables—personality, study skills, etc.—modify achievement or distort teacher judgment.

Experimentation to Investigate Construct Validity

VALIDATION PROCEDURES We can use many methods in construct validation. Attention should particularly be drawn to Macfarlane's survey of these methods as they apply to projective devices (Macfarlane, 1942).

Group differences. If our understanding of a construct leads us to expect two groups to differ on the test, this expectation may be tested directly. Thus Thurstone and Chave validated the Scale for Measuring Attitude Toward the Church by showing score differences between church members and nonchurchgoers. Churchgoing is not *the* criterion of attitude, for the purpose of the test is to measure something other than the crude sociological fact of church attendance; on the other hand, failure to find a difference would have seriously challenged the test.

Only coarse correspondence between test and group designation is expected. Too great a correspondence between the two would indicate that the test is to some degree invalid, because members of the groups are expected to overlap on the test. Intelligence test items are selected initially on the basis of a correspondence to age, but an item that correlates .95 with age in an elementary school sample would surely be suspect.

Correlation matrices and factor analysis. If two tests are presumed to measure the same construct, a correlation between them is predicted. (An exception is noted where some second attribute has positive loading in the first test and negative loading in the second test; then a low correlation is expected. This is a testable interpretation provided an external measure of either the first or the second variable exists.) If the obtained correlation departs from the expectation, however, there is no way to know whether the fault lies in test A, test B, or the formulation of the construct. A matrix of intercorrelations often points out profitable ways of dividing the construct into more meaningful parts, factor analysis being a useful computational method in such studies.

Guilford (1948) has discussed the place of factor analysis in construct validation. His statements may be extracted as follows:

"The personnel psychologist wishes to know 'why his tests are valid.' He can place tests and practical criteria in a matrix and factor it to identify 'real dimensions of human personality.' A factorial description is exact and stable; it is economical in explanation; it leads to the creation of pure tests which can be combined to predict complex behaviors." It is clear that factors here function as constructs. Eysenck (1950) in his "criterion analysis," goes further than Guilford and shows that factoring can be used explicitly to test hypotheses about constructs.

Factors may or may not be weighted with surplus meaning. Certainly when they are regarded as "real dimensions" a great deal of surplus meaning is implied, and the interpreter must shoulder a substantial burden of proof. The alternative view is to regard factors as defining a working reference frame, located in a convenient manner in the "space" defined by all behaviors of a given type. Which set of factors from a given matrix is "most useful" will depend partly on predilections, but in essence the best construct is the one around which we can build the greatest number of inferences, in the most direct fashion.

Studies of internal structure. For many constructs, evidence of homogeneity within the test is relevant in judging validity. If a trait such as *dominance* is hypothesized, and the items inquire about behaviors subsumed under this label, then the hypothesis appears to require that these items be generally intercorrelated. Even low correlations, if consistent, would support the argument that people may be fruitfully described in terms of a generalized tendency to dominate or not dominate. The general quality would have power to

predict behavior in a variety of situations represented by the specific items. Item-test correlations and certain reliability formulas describe internal consistency.

It is unwise to list uninterpreted data of this sort under the heading "validity" in test manuals, as some authors have done. High internal consistency may *lower* validity. Only if the underlying theory of the trait being measured calls for high item intercorrelations do the correlations support construct validity. Negative item-test correlations may support construct validity, provided that the items with negative correlations are believed irrelevant to the postulated construct and serve as suppressor variables (Horst, 1941, pp. 431–436; Meehl, 1945).

Study of distinctive subgroups of items within a test may set an upper limit to construct validity by showing that irrelevant elements influence scores. Thus a study of the PMA space tests shows that variance can be partially accounted for by a response set, tendency to mark many figures as similar (Cronbach, 1950). An internal factor analysis of the PEA Interpretation of Data Test shows that in addition to measuring reasoning skills, the test score is strongly influenced by a tendency to say "probably true" rather than "certainly true," regardless of item content (Damrin, 1952). On the other hand, a study of item groupings in the DAT Mechanical Comprehension Test permitted rejection of the hypothesis that knowledge about specific topics such as gears made a substantial contribution to scores (Cronbach, 1951).

Studies of change over occasions. The stability of test scores ("retest reliability," Cattell's "N-technique") may be relevant to construct validation. Whether a high degree of stability is encouraging or discouraging for the proposed interpretation depends upon the theory defining the construct.

More powerful than the retest after uncontrolled intervening experiences is the retest with experimental intervention. If a transient influence swings test scores over a wide range, there are definite limits on the extent to which a test result can be interpreted as reflecting the typical behavior of the individual. These are examples of experiments which have indicated upper limits to test validity: studies of differences associated with the examiner in projective testing, of change of score under alternative directions ("tell the truth" vs. "make yourself look good to an employer"), and of coachability of mental tests. We may recall Gulliksen's (1950) distinction: When the coaching is of a sort that improves the pupil's intellectual functioning in school, the test which is affected by the coaching has validity as a measure of intellectual functioning; if the coaching improves test taking but not school performance, the test which responds to the coaching has poor validity as a measure of this construct.

Sometimes, where differences between individuals are difficult to assess by any means other than the test, the experimenter validates by determining whether the test can detect induced intra individual differences. One might hypothesize that the Zeigarnik effect is a measure of ego involvement, i.e., that with ego involvement there is more recall of incomplete tasks. To support such an interpretation, the investigator will try to induce ego involvement on some task by appropriate directions and compare subjects' recall with their recall for tasks where there was a contrary induction. Sometimes the intervention is drastic. Porteus (1950) finds that brain-operated patients show disruption of performance on his maze, but do not show impaired performance on conventional verbal tests and argues therefrom that his test is a better measure of planfulness.

Studies of process. One of the best ways of determining informally what accounts for variability on a test is the observation of the person's process of performance. If it is supposed, for example, that a test measures mathematical competence, and yet observation of students' errors shows that erroneous reading of the question is common, the implications of a low score are altered. Lucas (1953) in this way showed that the Navy Relative Movement Test, an aptitude test, actually involved two different abilities: spatial visualization and mathematical reasoning.

Mathematical analysis of scoring procedures may provide important negative evidence on construct validity. A recent analysis of "empathy" tests is perhaps worth citing (Cronbach, 1955). "Empathy" has been operationally defined in many studies by the ability of a judge to predict what responses will be given on some questionnaire by a subject he has observed briefly. A mathematical argument has shown, however, that the scores depend on several attributes of the judge which enter into his perception of *any* individual, and that they therefore cannot be interpreted as evidence of his ability to interpret cues offered by particular others, or his intuition.

THE NUMERICAL ESTIMATE OF CONSTRUCT VALIDITY There is an understandable tendency to seek a "construct validity coefficient." A numerical statement of the degree of construct validity would be a statement of the proportion of the test score variance that is attributable to the construct variable. This numerical estimate can sometimes be arrived at by a factor analysis, but since present methods of factor analysis are based on linear relations, more general methods will ultimately be needed to deal with many quantitative problems of construct validation.

Rarely will it be possible to estimate definite "construct saturations," because no factor corresponding closely to the construct will be available. One can only hope to set upper and lower bounds to the "loading." If "creativity" is defined as something independent of knowledge, then a correlation of .40 between a presumed test of creativity and a test of arithmetic knowledge would indicate that at least 16 per cent of the reliable test variance is irrelevant to creativity as defined. Laboratory performance on problems such as Maier's "hatrack" would scarcely be an ideal measure of creativity, but it would be somewhat relevant. If its correlation with the test is .60, this permits a tentative estimate of 36 per cent as a lower bound. (The estimate is tentative because the test might overlap with the irrelevant portion of the laboratory measure.) The saturation seems to lie between

36 and 84 per cent; a cumulation of studies would provide better limits.

It should be particularly noted that rejecting the null hypothesis does not finish the job of construct validation (Kelly, 1954, p. 284). The problem is not to conclude that the test "is valid" for measuring the construct variable. The task is to state as definitely as possible the degree of validity the test is presumed to have.

* * *

References

American Psychological Association (1954). Technical recommendations for psychological tests and diagnostic techniques. *Psychological Bulletin Supplement, 51*, Part 2, 1–38.

Anastasi, A. (1950). The concept of validity in the interpretation of test scores. *Educational psychology Measurement, 10*, 67–78.

Bechtoldt, H. P. (1951). Selection. In S. S. Stevens (Ed.), *Handbook of experimental psychology*. (pp. 1237–1267). New York: Wiley.

Child, I. L. (1954). Personality. *Annual Review Psychology, 5*, 149–171.

Cronbach, L. J. (1949). *Essentials of psychological testing*. New York: Harper.

Cronbach, L. J. (1950). Further evidence on response sets and test design. *Educational psychology Measurement, 10*, 3–31.

Cronbach, L. J. (1951). Coefficient alpha and the internal structure of tests. *Psychometrika, 16*, 297–335.

Cronbach, L. J. (1955). Processes affecting scores on "understanding of others" and "assumed similarity." *Psychology Bulletin, 52*, 177–193.

Damrin, Dora E. (1952). A comparative study of information derived from a diagnostic problem-solving test by logical and factorial methods of scoring. Unpublished doctor's dissertation, University of Illinois.

Eysenck, H. J. (1950). Criterion analysis—an application of the hypothetico-deductive method in factor analysis. *Psychology Review, 57*, 38–53.

Gaylord, R. H. Conceptual consistency and criterion equivalence: a dual approach to criterion analysis. Unpublished manuscript (PRB Research Note No. 17). Copies obtainable from ASTIA-DSC, AD-21 440.

Goodenough, F. L. (1950). *Mental testing*. New York: Rinehart.

Guilford, J. P. (1946). New standards for test evaluation. *Educational psychology Measurement, 6*, 427–439.

Guilford, J. P. (1948). Factor analysis in a test-development program. *Psychology Review, 55*, 79–94.

Gulliksen, H. (1950). Intrinsic validity. *American Psychologist, 5*, 511–517.

Horst, P. (1941). The prediction of personal adjustment. *Social Science Research Council Bulletin*, No. 48.

Jenkins, J. G. (1946). Validity for what? *Journal consulting Psychology, 10*, 93–98.

Kelly, E. L. (1954). Theory and techniques of assessment. *Annual Review Psychology, 5*, 281–311.

Lucas, C. M. (1953). Analysis of the relative movement test by a method of individual interviews. *Bureau Naval Personnel Res. Rep.*, Contract Nonr-694 (00), NR 151-13, Educational Testing Service, March 1953.

Macfarlane, J. W. (1942). Problems of validation inherent in projective methods. *American Journal Orthopsychiatry, 12*, 405–410.

Meehl, P. E. (1945). A simple algebraic development of Horat's suppressor variables. *American Journal of Psychology, 58*, 550–554.

Meehl, P. E. (1954). *Clinical vs. statistical prediction*. Minneapolis: University of Minnesota Press.

Mosier, C. I. (1947). A critical examination of the concepts of face validity. *Educational psychology Measurement, 7*, 191–205.

Mosier, C. I. (1951). Problems and designs of cross-validation. *Educational psychology Measurement, 11*, 5–12.

Peak, H. (1953). Problems of objective observation. In L. Festinger and D. Katz (Eds.), *Research methods in the behavioral sciences* (pp. 243–300). New York: Dryden Press.

Porteus, S. D. (1950). *The Porteus maze test and intelligence*. Palo Alto: Pacific Books.

Spiker, C. C., & McCandless, B. R. (1954). The concept of intelligence and the philosophy of science. *Psychology Review, 61*, 255–267.

Thurstone, L. L. (1952). The criterion problem in personality research. *Psychometric Laboratory Report*, No. 78. Chicago: University of Chicago.

Convergent and Discriminant Validation by the Multitrait-Multimethod Matrix

Donald T. Campbell and Donald W. Fiske

If validity is not a simple property of a test, as Cronbach and Meehl argue, then what kinds of methods might be used to show that a particular measure has some degree of validity for a particular purpose? There are many possibilities, and Cronbach and Meehl briefly discussed a few of them. In the landmark paper that follows, the methodologists Donald Campbell and Donald Fiske propose that a "multitrait-multimethod matrix" of correlations provides especially useful information for examining construct validity. Their approach requires that one measure several different traits, each by several different methods. For example, sociability and impulsivity could each be assessed through self-descriptions and descriptions by peers. Once this kind of data is in hand, the correlations of each measure with all the others (the multitrait-multimethod matrix) can be examined. Measures of the same trait utilizing different methods (e.g., self- and peer-reports of sociability) should be positively correlated, demonstrating what Campbell and Fiske call "convergent" validity; and the self-reports of impulsivity and sociability should not be too strongly related to each other, despite their shared method of assessment ("discriminant validity"). Campbell and Fiske discuss the various kinds of information that might be gleaned from inspecting multitrait-multimethod matrices.

In the original version of this paper, Campbell and Fiske presented a number of previously published multitrait-multimethod matrices, and discussed the kinds of conclusions that each permitted. We have omitted this part of the article, because the data reported are now very old, and because the criteria used to evaluate multitrait-multimethod matrices have evolved considerably since the publication of this classic paper. More formal procedures using complex quantitative methods have replaced the informal rules described by Campbell and Fiske. These advanced methods (reviewed by Kenny & Kashy, 1992) remove some of the arbitrariness inherent to the informal judgment scheme of Campbell and Fiske, but require that one impose a formal model of a particular kind. While at least one of us has deep reservations (Ozer, 1989; Ozer & Reise, 1994) about using multitrait-multimethod matrices as the sine qua non (a favorite phrase from high school Latin, meaning "without that, nothing") of validity assessment, there is no question that contemporary practice of validity assessment begins (but too often ends) with the use of Campbell and Fiske's multitrait-multimethod matrices.

From "Convergent and Discriminant Validation by the Multitrait-Multimethod Matrix," by D. T. Campbell and D. W. Fiske (1959). In *Psychological Bulletin, 56*, 81–105. Adapted with permission.

In the cumulative experience with measures of individual differences over the past 50 years, tests have been accepted as valid or discarded as invalid by research experiences of many sorts. The criteria suggested in this paper are all to be found in such cumulative evaluations, as well as in the recent discussions of validity. These criteria are clarified and implemented when considered jointly in the context of a multitrait-multimethod matrix. Aspects of the validational process receiving particular emphasis are these:

1. Validation is typically *convergent*, a confirmation by independent measurement procedures. Independence of methods is a common denominator among the major types of validity (excepting content validity) insofar as they are to be distinguished from reliability.

2. For the justification of novel trait measures, for the validation of test interpretation, or for the establishment of construct validity, *discriminant* validation as well as convergent validation is required. Tests can be invalidated by too high correlations with other tests from which they were intended to differ.

3. Each test or task employed for measurement purposes is a *trait-method unit*, a union of a particular trait content with measurement procedures not specific to that content. The systematic variance among test scores can be due to responses to the measurement features as well as responses to the trait content.

4. In order to examine discriminant validity, and in order to estimate the relative contributions of trait and method variance, *more than one trait* as well as *more than one method* must be employed

in the validation process. In many instances it will be convenient to achieve this through a multitrait-multimethod matrix. Such a matrix presents all of the intercorrelations resulting when each of several traits is measured by each of several methods.

To illustrate the suggested validational process, a synthetic example is presented in Table 7.1. This illustration involves three different traits, each measured by three methods, generating nine separate variables. It will be convenient to have labels for various regions of the matrix, and such have been provided in Table 7.1. The reliabilities will be spoken of in terms of three *reliability diagonals*, one for each method. The reliabilities could also be designated as the monotrait-monomethod values. Adjacent to each reliability diagonal is the *heterotrait-monomethod* triangle. The reliability diagonal and the adjacent heterotrait-monomethod triangle make up a *monomethod block*. A *heteromethod block* is made up of a *validity* diagonal (which could also be designated as monotrait-heteromethod values) and the two *heterotrait-heteromethod* triangles lying on each side of it. Note that these two heterotrait-heteromethod triangles are not identical.

In terms of this diagram, four aspects bear upon the question of validity. In the first place, the entries in the validity diagonal should be significantly different from zero and sufficiently large to encourage further examination of validity. This requirement is evidence of convergent validity. Second, a validity diagonal value should be higher than the values lying in its column and row in the heterotrait-heteromethod triangles. That is, a validity value for a variable should be higher than

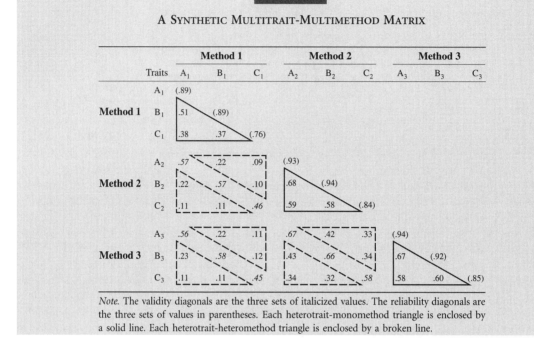

TABLE 7.1

A SYNTHETIC MULTITRAIT-MULTIMETHOD MATRIX

Note. The validity diagonals are the three sets of italicized values. The reliability diagonals are the three sets of values in parentheses. Each heterotrait-monomethod triangle is enclosed by a solid line. Each heterotrait-heteromethod triangle is enclosed by a broken line.

the correlations obtained between that variable and any other variable having neither trait nor method in common. This requirement may seem so minimal and so obvious as to not need stating, yet an inspection of the literature shows that it is frequently not met, and may not be met even when the validity coefficients are of substantial size. In Table 7.1, all of the validity values meet this requirement. A third common-sense desideratum is that a variable correlate higher with an independent effort to measure the same trait than with measures designed to get at different traits which happen to employ the same method. For a given variable, this involves comparing its values in the validity diagonals with its values in the heterotrait-monomethod triangles. For variables A_1, B_1, and C_1, this requirement is met to some degree. For the other variables, A_2, A_3 etc., it is not met and this is probably typical of the usual case in individual differences research, as will be discussed in what follows. A fourth desideratum is that the same pattern of trait interrelationship be

shown in all of the heterotrait triangles of both the monomethod and heteromethod blocks. The hypothetical data in Table 7.1 meet this requirement to a very marked degree, in spite of the different general levels of correlation involved in the several heterotrait triangles. The last three criteria provide evidence for discriminant validity.

* * *

CONVERGENCE OF INDEPENDENT METHODS: THE DISTINCTION BETWEEN RELIABILITY AND VALIDITY. Both reliability and validity concepts require that agreement between measures be demonstrated. A common denominator which most validity concepts share in contradistinction to reliability is that this agreement represent the convergence of independent approaches. The concept of independence is indicated by such phrases as "external variable," "criterion performance," "behavioral criterion" (American Psychological Association, 1954, pp. 13–15) used in connection with concurrent and predictive validity. For construct validity it has been stated thus: "Numerous successful predictions dealing with phenotypically diverse 'criteria' give greater weight to the claim of construct validity than do . . . predictions involving very similar behavior" (Cronbach & Meehl, 1955, p. 295). The importance of independence recurs in most discussions of proof. For example, Ayer, discussing a historian's belief about a past event, says "if these sources are numerous and independent, and if they agree with one another, he will be reasonably confident that their account of the matter is correct" (Ayer, 1956, p. 39). In discussing the manner in which abstract scientific concepts are tied to operations, Feigl speaks of their being "fixed" by "triangulation in logical space" (Feigl, 1958, p. 401).

Independence is, of course, a matter of degree, and in this sense, reliability and validity can be seen as regions on a continuum. (Cf. Thurstone, 1937, pp. 102–103.) Reliability is the agreement between two efforts to measure the same trait through maximally similar methods. Validity is represented in the agreement between two attempts to measure the same trait through maximally different methods. A split-half reliability is a little more like a validity coefficient than is an immediate test-retest reliability, for the items are not quite identical. A correlation between dissimilar subtests is probably a reliability measure, but is still closer to the region called validity.

Some evaluation of validity can take place even if the two methods are not entirely independent. In Table 7.1, for example, it is possible that Methods 1 and 2 are not entirely independent. If underlying Traits A and B are entirely independent, then the .10 minimum correlation in the heterotrait-heteromethod triangles may reflect method covariance. What if the overlap of method variance were higher? All correlations in the heteromethod block would then be elevated, including the validity diagonal. The heteromethod block involving Methods 2 and 3 in Table 7.1 illustrates this. The degree of elevation of the validity diagonal above the heterotrait-heteromethod triangles remains comparable and relative validity can still be evaluated. The interpretation of the validity di-

agonal in an absolute fashion requires the fortunate coincidence of both an independence of traits and an independence of methods, represented by zero values in the heterotrait-heteromethod triangles. But zero values could also occur through a combination of negative correlation between traits and positive correlation between methods, or the reverse. In practice, perhaps all that can be hoped for is evidence for relative validity, that is, for common variance specific to a trait, above and beyond shared method variance.

DISCRIMINANT VALIDATION While the usual reason for the judgment of invalidity is low correlations in the validity diagonal (e.g., the Downey Will-Temperament Test [Symonds, 1931, p. 337ff]) tests have also been invalidated because of too high correlations with other tests purporting to measure different things. The classic case of the social intelligence tests is a case in point. (See below and also Strang, 1930; R. Thorndike, 1936.) Such invalidation occurs when values in the heterotrait-heteromethod triangles are as high as those in the validity diagonal, or even where within a monomethod block, the heterotrait values are as high as the reliabilities. Loevinger, Gleser, and DuBois (1953) have emphasized this requirement in the development of maximally discriminating subtests.

When a dimension of personality is hypothesized, when a construct is proposed, the proponent invariably has in mind distinctions between the new dimension and other constructs already in use. One cannot define without implying distinctions, and the verification of these distinctions is an important part of the validational process. In discussions of construct validity, it has been expressed in such terms as "from this point of view, a low correlation with athletic ability may be just as important and encouraging as a high correlation with reading comprehension" (APA, 1954, p. 17).

THE TEST AS A TRAIT-METHOD UNIT In any given psychological measuring device, there are certain features or stimuli introduced specifically to represent the trait that it is intended to measure. There are other features which are characteristic of the method being employed, features which could also be present in efforts to measure other quite different traits. The test, or rating scale, or other device, almost inevitably elicits systematic variance in response due to both groups of features. To the extent that irrelevant method variance contributes to the scores obtained, these scores are invalid.

This source of invalidity was first noted in the "halo effects" found in ratings (E. Thorndike, 1920). Studies of individual differences among laboratory animals resulted in the recognition of "apparatus factors," usually more dominant than psychological process factors (Tryon, 1942). For paper-and-pencil tests, methods variance has been noted under such terms as "test-form factors" (Vernon, 1957, 1958) and "response sets" (Cronbach, 1946, 1950; Lorge, 1937). Cronbach has stated the point particularly clearly: "The assumption is generally made . . . that what the test measures is determined by the content of the items. Yet the final score . . . is a composite of effects resulting from the content of the item and effects resulting from the form of the item used" (Cronbach, 1946, p. 475). "Response sets always lower the logical validity of a test. . . . Response sets interfere with inferences from test data" (p. 484).

While E. L. Thorndike (1920) was willing to allege the presence of halo effects by comparing the high obtained correlations with common sense notions of what they ought to be (e.g., it was unreasonable that a teacher's intelligence and voice quality should correlate .63) and while much of the evidence of response set variance is of the same order, the clear-cut demonstration of the presence of method variance requires both several traits and several methods. Otherwise, high correlations between tests might be explained as due either to basic trait similarity or to shared method variance. In the multitrait-multimethod matrix, the presence of method variance is indicated by the difference in level of correlation between the parallel values of the monomethod block and the heteromethod blocks, assuming comparable reliabilities among all tests. Thus the contribution of method variance in Test A_1 of Table 7.1 is indicated by the elevation of r_{A1B1} above r_{A1B2}, i.e., the difference between .51 and .22, etc.

The distinction between trait and method is of course relative to the test constructor's intent. What is an unwanted response set for one tester may be a trait for another who wishes to measure acquiescence, willingness to take an extreme stand, or tendency to attribute socially desirable attributes to oneself (Cronbach, 1946, 1950; Edwards, 1957; Lorge, 1937).

* * *

Discussion

RELATION TO CONSTRUCT VALIDITY While the validational criteria presented are explicit or implicit in the discussions of construct validity (Cronbach & Meehl, 1955; APA, 1954), this paper is primarily concerned with the adequacy of tests as measures of a construct rather than with the adequacy of a construct as determined by the confirmation of theoretically predicted associations with measures of other constructs. We believe that before one can test the relationships between a specific trait and other traits, one must have some confidence in one's measures of that trait. Such confidence can be supported by evidence of convergent and discriminant validation. Stated in different words, any conceptual formulation of trait will usually include implicitly the proposition that this trait is a response tendency which can be observed under more than one experimental condition and that this trait can be meaningfully differentiated from other traits. The testing of these two propositions must be prior to the testing of other propositions to prevent the acceptance of erroneous conclusions. For example, a conceptual framework might postulate a large correlation between Traits A and B and no correlation between Traits A and C. If the experimenter then measures A and B by one method (e.g., questionnaire) and C by another method (such as the measurement of overt behavior in a situation test), his findings may be consistent with his hypotheses solely as a function of method variance common to his measures of A and B but not to C.

The requirements of this paper are intended to be as appropriate to the relatively atheoretical efforts typical of the tests and measurements field as to more theoretical efforts. This emphasis on validational criteria appropriate to our present atheoretical level of test construction is not at all incompatible with a recognition of the desirability of increasing the extent to which all aspects of a test and the testing situation are determined by explicit theoretical considerations, as Jessor and Hammond have advocated (Jessor & Hammond, 1957).

RELATION TO OPERATIONALISM Underwood (1957, p. 54) in his effective presentation of the operationalist point of view shows a realistic awareness of the amorphous type of theory with which most psychologists work. He contrasts a psychologist's "literary" conception with the latter's operational definition as represented by his test or other measuring instrument. He recognizes the importance of the literary definition in communicating and generating science. He cautions that the operational definition "may not at all measure the process he wishes to measure; it may measure something quite different" (1957, p. 55). He does not, however, indicate how one would know when one was thus mistaken.

The requirements of the present paper may be seen as an extension of the kind of operationalism Underwood has expressed. The test constructor is asked to generate from his literary conception or private construct not one operational embodiment, but two or more, each as different in research vehicle as possible. Furthermore, he is asked to make explicit the distinction between his new variable and other variables, distinctions which are almost certainly implied in his literary definition. In his very first validational efforts, before he ever rushes into print, he is asked to apply the several methods and several traits jointly. His literary definition, his conception, is now best represented in what his independent measures of the trait hold *distinctively* in common. The multitrait-multimethod matrix is, we believe, an important practical first step in avoiding "the danger . . . that the investigator will fall into the trap of thinking that because he went from an artistic or literary conception . . . to the construction of items for a scale to measure it, he has validated his artistic conception" (Underwood, 1957, p. 55). In contrast with the *single operationalism* now dominant in psychology, we are advocating a *multiple operationalism*, a *convergent operationalism* (Garner, 1954; Garner, Hake, & Eriksen, 1956), a *methodological triangulation* (Campbell, 1953, 1956), an *operational delineation* (Campbell, 1954), a *convergent validation.*

Underwood's presentation and that of this paper as a whole imply moving from concept to operation, a sequence that is frequent in science, and perhaps typical. The same point can be made, however, in inspecting a transition from operation to construct. For any body of data taken from a single operation, there is a subinfinity of interpretations possible; a subinfinity of concepts, or combinations of concepts, that it could represent. Any single operation, as representative of concepts, is equivocal. In an analogous fashion, when we view the Ames distorted room from a fixed point and through a single eye, the data of the retinal pattern are equivocal, in that a subinfinity of hexahedrons could generate the same pattern. The addition of a second viewpoint, as through binocular parallax, greatly reduces this equivocality, greatly limits the constructs that could jointly account for both sets of data. In Garner's (1954) study, the fractionation measures from a single method were equivocal—they could have been a function of the stimulus distance being fractionated, or they could have been a function of the comparison stimuli used in the judgment process. A multiple, convergent operationalism reduced this equivocality, showing the latter conceptualization to be the appropriate one, and revealing a preponderance of methods variance. Similarly for learning studies: in identifying constructs with the response data from animals in a specific operational setup there is equivocality which can operationally be reduced by introducing transposition tests, different operations so designed as to put to comparison the rival conceptualizations (Campbell, 1954).

Garner's convergent operationalism and our insistence on more than one method for measuring each concept depart from Bridgman's early position that "if we have more than one set of operations, we have more than one concept, and strictly there should be a separate name to correspond to each different set of operations" (Bridgman, 1927, p. 10). At the current stage of psychological progress, the crucial requirement is the demonstration of some convergence, not complete congruence, between two distinct sets of operations. With only one method, one has no way of distinguishing trait variance from unwanted method variance. When psychological measurement and conceptualization become better developed, it may well be appropriate to differentiate conceptually between Trait-Method Unit A_1 and Trait-Method Unit A_2, in which Trait A is measured by different methods. More likely, what we have called method variance will be specified theoretically in terms of a set of constructs. * * * It will then be recognized that measurement procedures usually involve several theoretical constructs in joint application. Using obtained measurements to estimate values for a single construct under this condition still requires comparison of complex measures varying in their trait composition, in something like a multitrait-multimethod matrix. Mill's joint method of similarities and differences still epitomizes much about the effective experimental clarification of concepts.

THE EVALUATION OF A MULTITRAIT-MULTI-METHOD MATRIX The evaluation of the correlation matrix formed by intercorrelating several trait-method units must take into consideration the many factors which are known to affect the magnitude of correlations. A value in the validity diagonal must be assessed in the light of the reliabilities of the two measures involved: e.g., a low reliability for Test A_2 might exaggerate the apparent method variance in Test A_1. Again, the whole approach assumes adequate sampling of individuals: The curtailment of the sample with respect

to one or more traits will depress the reliability coefficients and intercorrelations involving these traits. While restrictions of range over all traits produces serious difficulties in the interpretation of a multitrait-multimethod matrix and should be avoided whenever possible, the presence of different degrees of restriction on different traits is the more serious hazard to meaningful interpretation.

Various statistical treatments for multitrait-multimethod matrices might be developed. We have considered rough tests for the elevation of a value in the validity diagonal above the comparison values in its row and column. Correlations between the columns for variables measuring the same trait, variance analyses, and factor analyses have been proposed to us. However, the development of such statistical methods is beyond the scope of this paper. We believe that such summary statistics are neither necessary nor appropriate at this time. Psychologists today should be concerned not with evaluating tests as if the tests were fixed and definitive, but rather with developing better tests. We believe that a careful examination of a multitrait-multimethod matrix will indicate to the experimenter what his next steps should be: it will indicate which methods should be discarded or replaced, which concepts need sharper delineation, and which concepts are poorly measured because of excessive or confounding method variance. Validity judgments based on such a matrix must take into account the stage of development of the constructs, the postulated relationships among them, the level of technical refinement of the methods, the relative independence of the methods, and any pertinent characteristics of the sample of *Ss*. We are proposing that the validational process be viewed as an aspect of an ongoing program for improving measuring procedures and that the "validity coefficients" obtained at any one stage in the process be interpreted in terms of gains over preceding stages and as indicators of where further effort is needed.

THE DESIGN OF A MULTITRAIT-MULTIMETHOD MATRIX The several methods and traits included in a validational matrix should be selected with care. The several methods used to measure each trait should be appropriate to the trait as conceptualized. Although this view will reduce the range of suitable methods, it will rarely restrict the measurement to one operational procedure.

Wherever possible, the several methods in one matrix should be completely independent of each other: there should be no prior reason for believing that they share method variance. This requirement is necessary to permit the values in the heteromethod-heterotrait triangles to approach zero. If the nature of the traits rules out such independence of methods, efforts should be made to obtain as much diversity as possible in terms of data-sources and classification processes. Thus, the classes of stimuli *or* the background situations, the experimental contexts, should be different. Again, the persons providing the observations should have different roles *or* the procedures for scoring should be varied.

Plans for a validational matrix should take into account the difference between the interpretations regarding convergence and discrimination. It is sufficient to demonstrate convergence between two clearly distinct methods which show little overlap in the heterotrait-heteromethod triangles. While agreement between several methods is desirable, convergence between two is a satisfactory minimal requirement. Discriminative validation is not so easily achieved. Just as it is impossible to prove the null hypothesis, or that some object does not exist, so one can never establish that a trait, as measured, is differentiated from all other traits. One can only show that this measure of Trait A has little overlap with those measures of B and C, and no dependable generalization beyond B and C can be made. For example, social poise could probably be readily discriminated from aesthetic interests, but it should also be differentiated from leadership.

Insofar as the traits are related and are expected to correlate with each other, the monomethod correlations will be substantial and heteromethod correlations between traits will also be positive. For ease of interpretation, it may be best to include in the matrix at least two traits,

and preferably two sets of traits, which are postulated to be independent of each other.

In closing, a word of caution is needed. Many multitrait-multimethod matrices will show no convergent validation: no relationship may be found between two methods of measuring a trait. In this common situation, the experimenter should examine the evidence in favor of several alternative propositions: (a) Neither method is adequate for measuring the trait; (b) One of the two methods does not really measure the trait. (When the evidence indicates that a method does not measure the postulated trait, it may prove to measure some other trait. High correlations in the heterotrait-heteromethod triangles may provide hints to such possibilities.) (c) The trait is not a functional unity, the response tendencies involved being specific to the nontrait attributes of each test. The failure to demonstrate convergence may lead to conceptual developments rather than to the abandonment of a test.

*   *   *

References

American Psychological Association (1954). Technical recommendations for psychological tests and diagnostic techniques. *Psychological Bulletin Supplement, 51*, Part 2, 1–38.

Ayer, A. J. (1956). *The problem of knowledge.* New York: St Martin's Press.

Bridgman, P. W. (1927). *The logic of modern physics.* New York: Macmillan.

Campbell, D. T. (1953). *A study of leadership among submarine officers.* Columbus, OH: Ohio State University Research Foundation.

Campbell, D. T. (1954). Operational delineation of "what is learned" via the transposition experiment. *Psychological Review, 61*, 167–174.

Campbell, D. T. (1956). *Leadership and its effects upon the group.* Monograph No. 83. Columbus, OH: Ohio State University Bureau of Business Research.

Cronbach, L. J. (1946). Response sets and test validity. *Educational Psychology Measurement, 6*, 475–494.

Cronbach, L. J. (1950). Further evidence on response sets and test design. *Educational Psychology Measurement, 10*, 3–31.

Edwards, A. L. (1957). *The social desirability variable in personality assessment and research.* New York: Dryden.

Feigl, H. (1958). The mental and the physical. In H. Feigl, M. Scriven, & G. Maxwell (Eds.), *Minnesota studies in the philosophy of science.* Vol. II. *Concepts, theories and the mind-body problem.* Minneapolis: University of Minnesota Press.

Garner, W. R. (1954). Context effects and the validity of loudness scales. *Journal of Experimental Psychology, 48*, 218–224.

Garner, W. R., Hake, H. W., & Eriksen, C. W. (1956). Operationism and the concept of perception. *Psychological Review*, *63*, 149–159.

Jessor, R., & Hammond, K. R. (1957). Construct validity and the Taylor Anxiety Scale. *Psychological Bulletin, 54*, 161–170.

Loevinger, J., Gleser, G. C., & DuBois, P. H. (1953). Maximizing the discriminating power of a multiple-score test. *Psychometrika, 18*, 309–317.

Lorge, I. (1937). Gen-like: Halo or reality? *Psychological Bulletin, 34*, 545–546.

Mayo, G. D. (1956). Peer ratings and halo. *Educational Psychology Measurement, 16*, 317–323.

Strang, R. (1930). Relation of social intelligence to certain other factors. *Schools & Sociology, 32*, 268–272.

Symonds, P. M. (1931). *Diagnosing personality and conduct.* New York: Appleton-Century.

Thorndike, E. L. (1920). A constant error in psychological ratings. *Journal of Applied Psychology, 4*, 25–29.

Thorndike, R. L. (1936). Factor analysis of social and abstract intelligence. *Journal of Educational Psychology, 27*, 231–233.

Thurstone, L. L. (1937). *The reliability and validity of tests.* Ann Arbor: Edwards.

Tryon, R. C. (1942). Individual differences. In F. A. Moss (Ed.), *Comparative Psychology.* (2nd ed., pp. 330–365) New York: Prentice-Hall.

Underwood, B. J. (1957). *Psychological research.* New York: Appleton-Century-Crofts.

Vernon, P. E. (1957). Educational ability and psychological factors. Address given to the Joint Education-Psychology Colloquium, University of Illinois, March 29, 1957.

Vernon, P. E. (1958). *Educational testing and test-form factors.* (Res. Bull. RB-58-3.) Princeton: Educational Testing Service.

MAKING CLAIMS WITH STATISTICS

Robert Abelson

In this final methodological selection, the cognitive and social psychologist Robert Abelson offers an unusual and refreshing view of what statistical data analysis is all about. He argues that a statistical analysis is not a formal proof of a proposition but simply a particularly persuasive kind of reasoned argument. Contrary to what some of us were originally taught, statistical analysis is not a judge to which you submit your data for a verdict as to whether the data are worthwhile. Instead, it is a tool for understanding and communicating results. The better a researcher becomes at using this tool, the better she or he becomes at reaching psychological understanding and at helping others to understand.

Abelson's lesson is important. If you have already taken a course or two in statistics, you will find that he tells you more in this chapter about (1) why you learned it and (2) what you can do with it, than do most courses. If you have not yet taken a statistics course, we cannot imagine a better invitation than Abelson offers for learning more about quantitative methods in psychology.

From *Statistics as Principled Argument*, by R. P. Abelson (1995), pp. 1–16. Hillsdale, NJ: Lawrence Erlbaum Associates. Adapted with permission.

Misunderstandings of Statistics

The field of statistics is misunderstood by students and nonstudents alike. The general public distrusts statistics because media manipulators often attempt to gull them with misleading statistical claims. Incumbent politicians, for example, quote upbeat economic statistics, whereas their challengers cite evidence of wrack and ruin. Advertisers promote pills by citing the proportion of doctors who supposedly recommend them, or the average time they take to enter the bloodstream. The public suspects that in the interest of making particular points, propagandists can use any numbers they like in any fashion they please.

Suspicion of false advertising is fair enough, but to blame the problem on statistics is unreasonable. When people lie with words (which they do quite often), we do not take it out on the English language. Yes, you may say, but the public can more readily detect false words than deceitful statistics. Maybe true, maybe not, I reply, but when statistical analysis is carried out responsibly, blanket public skepticism undermines its potentially useful application. Rather than mindlessly trashing any and all statements with numbers in them, a more mature response is to learn enough about statistics to distinguish honest, useful conclusions from skullduggery or foolishness.

It is a hopeful sign that a considerable number of college and university students take courses in statistics. Unfortunately, the typical statistics course does not deal very well, if at all, with the argumentative, give-and-take nature of statistical claims. As a consequence, students tend to develop their own characteristic misperceptions of statistics. They seek certainty and exactitude, and emphasize calculations rather than points to be drawn from statistical analysis. They tend to state statistical conclusions mechanically, avoiding imaginative rhetoric (lest they be accused of manipulativeness).

My central theme is that good statistics involves principled argument that conveys an interesting and credible point. Some subjectivity in statistical presentations is unavoidable, as acknowledged even by the rather stuffy developers of statistical hypothesis testing. Egon Pearson (1962), for example, wrote retrospectively of his work with Jerzy Neyman, "We left in our mathematical model a gap for the exercise of a more intuitive process of personal judgment" (p. 395). Meanwhile, Sir Ronald Fisher (1955) accused Neyman and Pearson of making overmechanical recommendations, himself emphasizing experimentation as a continuing process requiring a community of free minds making their own decisions on the basis of shared information.

Somewhere along the line in the teaching of statistics in the social sciences, the importance of good judgment got lost amidst the minutiae of null hypothesis testing. It is all right, indeed essential, to argue flexibly and in detail for a particular case when you use statistics. Data analysis should not be pointlessly formal. It should make an interesting claim; it should tell a story that an informed audience will care about, and it should do so by intelligent interpretation of appropriate evidence from empirical measurements or observations.

Claims Made with Statistics: Comparison and Explanation

* * *

STAND-ALONE STATISTICS Many statistics are isolated, stand-alone figures such as: "The average life expectancy of famous orchestral conductors is 73.4 years" (Atlas, 1978), or "adults who watched television 3–4 hours a day had nearly *double* the prevalence of high cholesterol as those who watched less than one hour a day" (Tucker & Bagwell, 1992), or ". . . college-educated women who are still single at the age of thirty-five have only a 5 percent chance of ever getting married" ("Too Late," 1986; discussed by Cherlin, 1990, and Maier, 1991). The point of the life-expectancy statistic was supposedly that conducting an orchestra is so fulfilling that it lengthens life. The cholesterol story was somewhat puzzling, but the implication was that increased junk food consumption accompanied heavy TV watching. The marriage statistic was based on shaky projections of future trends, and could be variously explained or dismissed, depending on who was doing the explaining or dismissing.

A problem in making a claim with an isolated number is that the audience may have no context within which to assess the meaning of the figure and the assertion containing it. How unusual is it to live until age 73.4? Does "nearly double" mean I shouldn't watch TV? If one can't answer such questions, then a natural reaction to this type of numerical pronouncement would be, "So what?"

THE IMPORTANCE OF COMPARISON In the example about women and percentage marrying, a background context is readily available, and most people would regard 5% as a startlingly low marriage rate compared to the general average (or compared to what was true 50 years ago). The idea of *comparison* is crucial. To make a point that is at all meaningful, statistical presentations must refer to differences between observation and expectation, or differences among observations. Observed differences lead to why questions, which in turn trigger a search for explanatory factors. Thus, the big difference between the 5% future marriage rate for 35-year-old, college-educated single women and one's impression that some 80% or 90% of women in general will marry, evokes the question, "I wonder why that is? Is it career patterns, the lack of appeal of marriage, or a shortage of eligible men? . . . Or maybe the 5% figure is based on a faulty statistical procedure." Such candidate explanations motivate the investigators (or their critics) to a reanalysis of existing evidence and assumptions, or the collection of new data, in order to choose a preferred explanation.

Apart from the standard statistical questions of why there is a difference between one summary statistic and another, or between the statistic and a baseline comparison figure, there occasionally arises a need to explain a lack of difference. When we expect a difference and don't find any, we may ask, "Why is there *not* a difference?" Galileo's fabled demonstration that heavy and light objects take the same time to fall a given distance is a case in point. The observed constancy stands in contrast with a strong intuition that a heavy object should fall faster, thus posing a puzzle requiring explanation.

STANDARDS OF COMPARISON At the outset of the explanation process, there is a complication. Given a single statistic, many different observations or expectations may be used as standards of comparison; what is compared with what may have a substantial influence on the question asked and the answer given. Why questions are said to have a *focus*. The longevity datum on famous orchestral conductors (Atlas, 1978) provides a good example. With what should the mean age at their deaths, 73.4 years, be compared? With orchestral *players*?

With *nonfamous* conductors? With the general public?

All of the conductors studied were men, and almost all of them lived in the United States (though born in Europe). The author used the mean life expectancy of males in the U.S. population as the standard of comparison. This was 68.5 years at the time the study was done, so it appears that the conductors enjoyed about a 5-year extension of life—and indeed, the author of the study jumped to the conclusion that involvement in the activity of conducting *causes* longer life. Since the study appeared, others have seized upon it and even elaborated reasons for a causal connection (e.g., as health columnist Brody, 1991, wrote, "it is believed that arm exercise plays a role in the longevity of conductors" [p. B8]).

However, as Carroll (1979) pointed out in a critique of the study, there is a subtle flaw in life-expectancy comparisons: The calculation of average life expectancy includes infant deaths along with those of adults who survive for many years. Because no infant has ever conducted an orchestra, the data from infant mortalities should be excluded from the comparison standard. Well, then, what about teenagers? They also are much too young to take over a major orchestra, so their deaths should also be excluded from the general average. Carroll argued that an appropriate cutoff age for the comparison group is at least 32 years old, an estimate of the average age of appointment to a first orchestral conducting post. The mean life expectancy among U.S. males who have already reached the age of 32 is 72.0 years, so the relative advantage, if any, of being in the famous conductor category is much smaller than suggested by the previous, flawed comparison. One could continue to devise ever and ever more finely tuned comparison groups of nonconductors who are otherwise similar to conductors. Thoughtful attention to comparison standards (usually "control groups") can substantially reduce the occurrence of misleading statistical interpretations.

CHOOSING AMONG CANDIDATE EXPLANATIONS
For any observed comparative difference, several possible candidate explanations may occur to the investigator (and to critics). In a given case, this set of explanations may include accounts varying widely in their substance and generality, ranging from a dismissal of the observed difference as a fluke or an artifactual triviality to claims that the observations support or undermine some broad theoretical position. In our orchestra conductors example, the set of candidate explanations includes at least the following: (a) The result arose fortuitously from the particular sample of conductors included; (b) the comparison standard is still flawed, as it does not account for subpopulations with shorter life spans who are also ineligible to become conductors (e.g., the chronically ill); and (c) conductors *do* live longer, because of some common genetic basis for longevity and extraordinary musical talent, health benefits from the activity of conducting (or from a larger class of activities that includes conducting), or health benefits from something associated with conducting, such as receiving adulation from others, or having a great deal of control over others.

It is the task of data analysis and statistical inference to help guide the choice among the candidate explanations. The chosen explanation becomes a *claim*. (If this term implies more force than appropriate, we may use the blander word *point*.) In the conductor example, it is risky to make a claim, because of a lack of relevant data that would help winnow the set of explanations. It would be helpful to have information on such matters as the life expectancy of well-known pianists, actors, professors, lawyers, and so forth; the life expectancy of eminent conductors who retire early (for reasons other than health); the life expectancy of siblings of famous conductors (ideally, twin siblings—but there would not be enough cases); and the comparative life expectancies of elderly people who stay active and those who are inactive (for reasons other than poor health).

Experimentalists would despair at the vagueness of specification of the needed evidence (how should one define "poor health," "active," "retire"), and the sinking feeling that there are just too many variables (some of them unknown) that might be associated with longevity. The experimental investigator would be in a much more comfortable position if he or she could isolate and *manipulate* the factors assumed to be relevant in one or more of the proposed causal accounts. An experimenter, as distinct from an observer, tries to *create* (or re-create) comparative differences rather than just to observe them passively.

Consider the possible explanation that orchestral conducting is so personally satisfying or otherwise beneficial that it extends life beyond the age at which the individual would have died in the absence of this activity. The standard experimental way to try to recreate such an effect would be to assemble a group of potentially outstanding conductors, arrange for a random half of them to have prestigious orchestra posts whereas the other half have less involving career activities, and then collect longevity data on all of them. Of course this test would be absurdly impractical. I mention it because it suggests the possibility of conceptually similar experiments that might be feasible. For example, one could recruit a group of elderly people, provide a random half of them with social or physical activities, or social control, and monitor their subsequent feelings of well-being and state of health relative to that of the other half, who had received no intervention. The bottom line for the conductors example, though, is that casual, one-shot tabulations of statistical observations will almost certainly be difficult to interpret. Therefore it is rhetorically weak to make claims based on them, and such claims deserve to be regarded with great skepticism. Well-justified explanations of comparative differences typically depend on well-controlled comparisons such as can be provided by careful experiments. (Sometimes, one can also do well by the sophisticated collection of converging lines of evidence in field observations.) The quality of explanation improves dramatically when there are many interrelated data sets, some of them repeated demonstrations of the core result(s) or of closely related results, some of them ruling out alternative explanations, and yet others showing that when the explanatory factor is absent, the result(s) fail to appear.

SYSTEMATIC VERSUS CHANCE EXPLANATIONS To understand the nature of statistical argument, we must consider what *types* of explanation qualify as answers to why questions. One characteristic type, the *chance* explanation, is expressed in statements such as, "These results could easily be due to chance," or "A random model adequately fits the data." Indeed, statistical inference is rare among scientific logics in being forced to deal with chance explanations as alternatives or additions to systematic explanations.

In the discussion to follow, we presume that data are generated by a single measurement procedure applied to a set of objects or events in a given domain. We suppose that the observations comprising the data set differ, some from others, and we ask why. A *systematic factor* is an influence that contributes an orderly relative advantage to particular subgroups of observations, for example, a longevity gain of a certain number of years by elderly people who stay active. A *chance factor* is an influence that contributes haphazardly to each observation, with the amount of influence on any given observation being unspecifiable.

THE TENDENCY TO EXAGGERATE SYSTEMATIC FACTORS Inexperienced researchers and laypeople alike usually overestimate the influence of systematic factors relative to chance factors. As amateur everyday psychologists and would-be controllers of the world around us, we exaggerate our ability to predict the behavior of other people. We have difficulty thinking statistically about human beings.

Kunda and Nisbett (1986) showed that in matters of human *ability*, especially athletic ability, there is some degree of appreciation of inexplicable variations in performance from one occasion to the next. We understand, for example, that a tennis player might be on his game one day but flat the next, so that a sample of performances is necessary to make a reliable judgment of ability. Even so, the relative importance of chance influ-

ences is seriously underestimated in many athletic contexts. Abelson (1985) asked baseball-wise psychologists to consider whether or not a major league batter would get a hit in a given turn at bat, and to estimate the proportion of variance in this event explained by differences in the skill of different batters, as opposed to chance factors affecting the success of a given batter. The median estimate was around 25%, but the true answer is less than one half of 1%! In part this is due to the highly stingy properties of "explained variance" as a measure of relationship between two variables (Rosenthal & Rubin, 1979), but more interestingly, it is because we as baseball fans are prone to regard a .330 hitter as a hero who will almost always come through in the clutch, and the .260 hitter as a practically certain out when the game is on the line.

The underappreciation of chance variability extends to other domains. For events such as lottery drawings in which skill plays no objective role whatever, subjects under many conditions act as though some control can be exerted over the outcome (Langer, 1975). Kunda and Nisbett (1986) concluded that in matters of *personality*, inferences based on a single encounter are made with undue confidence, ignoring the possibility of situational influences that vary over time and place. We tend to feel, for example, that the person who is talkative on one occasion is a generally talkative person (the "fundamental attribution error," Ross, 1977).[1]

The upshot of all this is a natural tendency to jump to systematic conclusions in preference to chance as an explanation. As researchers, we need

---

[1] In this passage Abelson demonstrates a common bias among cognitive-social psychologists against the existence and importance of personality traits. In relation to the specific example just cited, ample empirical evidence indicates that a person who is talkative on one occasion generally *is* talkative on another—talkativeness is a reasonably consistent trait of personality (Funder & Colvin, 1991). However, people may still be too quick to infer general attributes of personality from brief observations of behavior, which is Abelson's larger point.

principled data-handling procedures to protect us from inventing elaborate overinterpretations for data that could have been dominated by chance processes. We need to understand that even though statistical calculations carry an aura of numerical exactitude, debate necessarily surrounds statistical conclusions, made as they are against a background of uncertainty. A major step in the winnowing of explanations for data is to make a judgment about the relative roles played by systematic and chance factors.

*   *   *

Language and Limitations of Null Hypothesis Tests

A staple procedure used in psychological research to differentiate systematic from chance explanations is the significance test of a null hypothesis. Elementary statistics texts describe many varieties of them, but students often regard null hypothesis testing as counterintuitive, and many critics (e.g., Cohen, 1995; Falk & Greenbaum, 1995; Tukey, 1991) find much to fault in null hypothesis tests. It is worthwhile to set forth here the quirky logic of these tests. * * *

Consider the simplest type of laboratory experiment, in which subjects are assigned at random to either an experimental group or a control group. Members of the two groups perform the identical experimental task, except for the additional manipulation of a single factor of interest in the experimental group—say, the receipt of prior information or training, or the administration of a drug. The experimenter wishes to test whether the experimental factor makes a systematic difference on some appropriate measure of task performance.

Presumably, performance measures on the task differ from individual to individual, and we ask a rhetorical why question. The systematic explanatory factor is the manipulation introduced by the experimenter. To say that this factor is systematic is to assume that on average it improves (or damages) task performances in the experimental group by some unknown amount over and above performances in the control group. We can try to estimate the magnitude of this systematic effect simply by calculating the difference between the mean performance scores of the two groups.

But there are also chance factors in this situation—things that add noise to individual measurements in an unknown way. We mention two categories here: sampling errors and measurement errors. Sampling errors arise from the "luck of the draw" in randomly assigning subjects to the two groups; the experimental group may contain a predominance of people with somewhat higher (or lower) task ability than members of the control group, thus introducing a mean difference that could be mistaken for a systematic effect. Measurement errors refer to unknown and unrepeatable causes of variability in task performance over time, place, and circumstance. The laboratory room may be too warm when Subject 17 performs the task; Subject 42 may have a headache that day; and so on.

In qualitative terms, there are three possible accounts for the data arising from this experimental design: (a) The variability of task scores can be entirely explained by the systematic factor, (b) the variability of task scores can be entirely explained by chance factors (sampling and measurement errors), or (c) the variability requires explanation by both chance factors and the systematic factor.

The first and the second accounts are simpler, and parsimony would suggest that they be tested before falling back on the third account. Why tell a complicated story if a simpler story will do? The third account can be held in reserve if both of the first two accounts are inadequate. The first possibility, completely systematic data with no chance variability, would be immediately apparent in the data set: All the scores in the experimental group would be equal, and different from all the equal scores in the control group. This outcome may be approximated in the physical and biological sciences, where chance variability is typically very small. With psychological data, however, this outcome is quite rare—but if and when it occurs, statistical inference is not used (Skinner, 1963).

Setting aside these rare, errorless cases, we are left with the choice between the all-chance explanation and the systematic-plus-chance explanation. We can tell if we need to invoke a systematic factor by first testing the all-chance explanation; if chance factors do not adequately account for the data, then the systematic factor is needed. This is in essence the justification for significance tests of the null hypothesis.

THE LANGUAGE OF NULL HYPOTHESIS TESTING   A null hypothesis test is a ritualized exercise of devil's advocacy. One assumes as a basis for argument that there is no systematic difference between the experimental and control scores—that except for errors of sampling and measurement the two groups' performances are indistinguishable. If (according to a formal procedure such as a *t* test) the data are not sharply inconsistent with this conception, then an all-chance explanation is tenable, so far as this one data set is concerned. This is often described as "accepting the null hypothesis." If, on the other hand, the data are inconsistent with the all-chance model, the null hypothesis is rejected, and the systematic-plus-chance model is preferred.

An important caveat here is that the standard terms, "accept" or "reject" the null hypothesis, are semantically too strong. Statistical tests are aids to (hopefully wise) judgment, not two-valued logical declarations of truth or falsity. Besides, common sense tells us that the null hypothesis is virtually never (Cohen, 1990; Loftus, 1991) literally true to the last decimal place. It is thus odd to speak of accepting it. We often use other terms for this outcome, such as "retaining the null hypothesis" or "treating the null hypothesis as viable."[2] Similarly, rejection can be softened with alternative phrases like "discrediting the null hypothesis."

In any case, the investigator wanting to show the influence of some experimental factor proceeds by discrediting the assumption that it

doesn't matter. The backhandedness of this procedure reflects the fact that null hypothesis tests are motivated by rhetorical considerations. Suppose an experimental investigator announces that the data demonstrate—despite considerable variability from case to case—the systematic efficacy of a particular educational or medical intervention or the operation of a particular theoretical principle, but a critic counters that the data could easily have arisen from fortuitous sampling or measurement errors. Who wins this scientific debate? The critic does, unless the investigator can come up with a *counter*-counter, to the effect that the data are in fact quite unlikely to be explained entirely by chance factors. With such a rebuttal, the investigator discredits the null hypothesis (and therefore the critic will in practice usually be deterred from raising this argument in the first place).

SIGNIFICANCE TESTS PROVIDE VERY LIMITED INFORMATION   The answer to the simple question, "Is there some systematic difference between the experimental group and the control group?" is not usually electrifying. As mentioned earlier, there is virtually always some difference caused by sensible experimental manipulations. Indeed, the only examples where the exact satisfaction of the null hypothesis is worth considering occur when there is widespread disbelief that some strange phenomenon exists at all. For example, the null hypothesis is interesting when discrediting it implies that mental telepathy is possible, or that stimuli below the level of conscious awareness can have reliable effects on attitudes and behavior. The complementary case is also interesting, in which everybody believes beforehand that an effect must exist. For instance, virtually everyone who follows sports believes that there is such a thing as "streak shooting" in basketball, and it caused a considerable furor when Gilovich, Vallone, and Tversky (1985) argued from a set of sensitive statistical tests on sequences of shots that the null hypothesis of no streak shooting is tenable.

---

[2]A good way to think about what it means to retain a null hypothesis of no mean difference is that the analyst is insufficiently confident to assert which mean is larger (Tukey, 1991).—Author

SINGLE STUDIES ARE NOT DEFINITIVE Even in these rare cases, though, where the outcome of a simple significance test may have scientific (and possibly popular) news value, a single study never is so influential that it eliminates all argument. Replication of research findings is crucial. After all, if a result of a study is contrary to prior beliefs, the strongest holders of those prior beliefs will tend to marshal various criticisms of the study's methodology, come up with alternative interpretations of the results, and spark a possibly long-lasting debate.

Sometimes critics prove right in the long run, and sometimes they prove wrong. To take an example from the physical sciences, skepticism about the existence of "cold fusion" prevailed after a year or two of debate (Pool, 1988) over a claim of success. The opposite outcome of debate is illustrated by the reality of "subliminal perception"— meaningful stimulus registration without awareness—that after a period of skepticism has been widely accepted (Kihlstrom, 1987).

Debate about the existence of extrasensory perception (ESP) went on for years in an inconclusive, rather sterile fashion (Hyman, 1991; Utts, 1991). Argument had not progressed much beyond the "mere existence," null-hypothesis-testing stage to a more interesting, focused examination of the strength and generality (if any) of ESP, the conditions that encourage it, and the process by which it may operate. (Recently, the debate has become more usefully focused on the properties of a particular type of demonstration, the *Ganzfeld* procedure [Bem & Honorton, 1994; Hyman, 1994].)

Thus even in the rare cases where the literal truth of the null hypothesis is at issue, and especially in the preponderance of cases where the null hypothesis is a straw man, the investigator wants to formulate a position going beyond a primitive test of a single null hypothesis. Scientific arguments are much more rich than that. Before working up to the issues in some typical debates, however, we stay at an elementary level and discuss in detail what makes statistical arguments rhetorically forceful and narratively compelling.

Persuasive Arguments: The Magic Criteria

There are several properties of data, and its analysis and presentation, that govern its persuasive force. We label these by the acronym MAGIC, which stands for *magnitude, articulation, generality, interestingness*, and *credibility*.[3]

MAGNITUDE The strength of a statistical argument is enhanced in accord with the quantitative magnitude of support for its qualitative claim. There are different ways to index magnitude, the most popular of which is the so-called "effect size" (Cohen, 1988; Glass, 1978; Hedges & Olkin, 1985; Mullen, 1989; Rosenthal, 1991). In the basic case of the comparison between two means, effect size can be simply given as the difference between the means; often, however, this difference is divided by the standard deviation of observations within groups. * * *

ARTICULATION By articulation, we refer to the degree of comprehensible detail in which conclusions are phrased. Suppose, for example, that the investigator is comparing the mean outcomes of five groups: A, B, C, D, E. The conclusion "there exist some systematic differences among these means" has a very minimum of articulation. A statement such as, "means C, D, and E are each

---

[3]There are other schemes for classifying the quality of statistical evidence and its presentation. The enumeration of various forms of *validity* (internal, external, construct, trait, discriminant, ecological, predictive, etc.) is a well-known alternative (Campbell, 1960; Cook & Campbell, 1979). The analysis of validity has been very useful, but it has never caught on as a coherent whole. It strikes the student as rather formal and esoteric. Another system has been given in an exquisitely sensible little book on the importance of statistical analysis in medical research (Hill, 1977). This author named but did not elaborate on criteria similar to mine. If my approach has any claim to novelty, it is that I have chosen and developed my criteria within the unifying premise of statistics as argument, and I know of no previous source that has systematically pursued such an approach.—Author

systematically higher than means A and B, although they are not reliably different from each other" contains more articulation. Still more would attach to a quantitative or near-quantitative specification of a pattern among the means, for example, "in moving from Group A to B to C to D to E, there is a steady increase in the respective means." ∗ ∗ ∗

GENERALITY Generality denotes the breadth of applicability of the conclusions. The circumstances associated with any given study are usually quite narrow, even though investigators typically intend their arguments to apply more broadly. To support broad conclusions, it is necessary to include a wide range of contextual variations in a comprehensive research plan, or to cumulate outcome data from many interrelated but somewhat different studies, as can be done within the context of meta-analysis (Mullen, 1989; Rosenthal, 1991).

High-quality evidence, embodying sizable, well-articulated, and general effects, is necessary for a statistical argument to have maximal persuasive impact, but it is not sufficient. Also vital are the attributes of the research story embodying the argument. We discuss two criteria for an effective research narrative: interestingness, and credibility.

INTERESTINGNESS Philosophers, psychologists, and others have pondered variously what it means for a story to be interesting (e.g., Davis, 1971; Hidi & Baird, 1986; Schank, 1979; Tesser, 1990), or to have a point (Wilensky, 1983). Our view is that for a statistical story to be *theoretically* interesting, it must have the potential, through empirical analysis, to change what people believe about an important issue. This conceptual interpretation of statistical interestingness has several features requiring further explanation. The key ideas are *change of belief*—which typically entails surprising results—and the *importance* of the issue, which is a function of the number of theoretical and applied propositions needing modification in light of the new results.

CREDIBILITY Credibility refers to the believability of a research claim. It requires both *methodological* soundness, and *theoretical* coherence. Claims based on sloppy experimental procedures or mistaken statistical analyses will fall victim to criticism by those with an interest in the results. Clues suggested by funny-looking data or wrongly framed procedures provide skeptics with information that something is amiss in the statistical analysis or research methodology. (Of course, you might yourself be in the role of critic, whereby you can track these clues in other people's research reports.)

∗ ∗ ∗

The credibility of a research claim can sustain damage from another source—the claim may violate prevailing theory, or even common sense. The research audience cannot bring itself to believe a discrepant claim, such as a purported demonstration of extrasensory perception, which would require vast revision of existing views. In such cases, debate tends to occur on two fronts simultaneously. The critic will typically pick on suspected methodological errors, thus accounting for the claim as a methodological artifact. The investigator must be prepared to try to rule out such accounts. Also, a theoretical battle will develop, in which the investigator is challenged to show that her alternative theory is *coherent*, tht is, capable of explaining a range of interconnected findings. If result A requires explanation X, result B calls forth explanation Y, and result C explanation Z, where explanations X, Y, and Z have little relation to each other, the narrative of results A, B, and C is incoherent (Thagard, 1989). On the other hand, if a single explanatory principle accounts for several different results, the story is coherent. When the results would be unrelated were it not for sharing the same explanation, the story is not only coherent, it is *elegant*.

The outcome of a theoretical debate depends on the comparative adequacy of the respective accounts of existing data. But the contest may also hinge on who has the *burden of proof* in the exchange of criticisms and rebuttals. Usually, this burden rests with the investigator, especially at the outset. Critics are often freewheeling in their invention of counterexplanations: It could be this, it may be that, it's merely such-and-so. Some types of counterexplanations are so vague as to be untestable—which gives the critic a substantial debating advantage. Nevertheless, despite occasional abuse of the ability to criticize, science is better off being tolerant of kibitzers and second-guessers. The critic is often right. Anyway, science should have both a conservative bias—which prevents rapid and bewildering shifts of views—and ultimate openness, such that persistent innovators can ultimately triumph if their claims are indeed meritorious.

The requisite skills for producing credible statistical narratives are not unlike those of a good detective (Tukey, 1969). The investigator must solve an interesting case, similar to the "whodunit" of a traditional murder mystery, except that it is a "howcummit"—how come the data fall in a particular pattern. She must be able to rule out alternatives, and be prepared to match wits with supercilious competitive colleagues who stubbornly cling to presumably false alternative accounts, based on somewhat different clues. (This is analogous to the problems faced by heroic fictional detectives who must put up with interference from cloddish police chiefs.)

* * *

The Bottom Line

A research story can be interesting and theoretically coherent, but still not be persuasive—if the data provide only weak support for the rhetoric of the case. On the other hand, a lot of high-quality rhetoric can be squandered by a poor narrative— for example, if the research is so dull that no one cares which way the results come out. Thus rhetoric and narrative combine multiplicatively, as it were, in the service of persuasive arguments based on data analysis. If either component is weak, the product is weak. The argument is strong only when it has the MAGIC properties of forceful rhetoric and effective narrative. In making his or her best case, the investigator must combine the skills of an honest lawyer, a good detective, and a good storyteller.

References

Abelson, R. P. (1985). A variance explanation paradox: When a little is a lot. *Psychological Bulletin, 97,* 128–132.

Atlas, D. H. (1978). Longevity of orchestra conductors. *Forum on Medicine, 1*(9), 50–51.

Bem, D. J., & Honorton, C. (1994). Does psi exist? Replicable evidence for an anomolous process of information transfer. *Psychological Bulletin, 115,* 4–18.

Brody, J. E. (1991, March 14). Personal health. *The New York Times,* p. B8.

Campbell, D. T. (1960). Recommendations for APA test standards regarding construct, trait, or discriminant validity. *American Psychologist, 15,* 546–553.

Carroll, J. D. (1979, January 23). Music and age. *The New York Times,* p. C2.

Cherlin, A. (1990). The strange career of the "Harvard-Yale study". *Public Opinion Quarterly, 54,* 117–124.

Cohen, J. (1988). *Statistical power analysis for the behavioral sciences* (2nd ed.). Hillsdale, NJ: Lawrence Erlbaum Associates.

Cohen, J. (1990). Things I have learned (so far). *American Psychologist, 45,* 1304–1312.

Cohen, J. (1995). The earth is round (*p* < .05). *American Psychologist.*

Cook, T. D., & Campbell, D. T. (1979). *Quasi-experimentation: Design and analysis issues for field settings.* Chicago: Rand McNally.

Davis, M. S. (1971). That's interesting! *Philosophy of the Social Sciences, 1,* 309–344.

Falk, R., & Greenbaum, C. W. (1995). Significance tests die hard: The amazing persistence of a probabilistic misconception. *Theory and Psychology.*

Fisher, R. A. (1955). Statistical methods and scientific induction. *Journal of the Royal Statistical Society* (Series B), *17,* 69–77.

Gilovich, T., Vallone, R., & Tversky, A. (1985). The "hot hand" in basketball: On the misperception of random sequences. *Cognitive Psychology, 17,* 295–314.

Glass, G. V. (1978). Integrating findings: The meta-analysis of research. *Review of Research in Education, 5,* 351–379.

Hedges, L. V., & Olkin, I. (1985). *Statistical methods for meta-analysis.* New York: Academic Press.

Hidi, S., & Baird, W. (1986). Interestingness—A neglected variable in discourse processing. *Cognitive Science, 10,* 179–194.

Hill, B. (1977). *A short textbook of medical statistics* (10th ed.). Philadelphia: Lippincott. (Original work published 1937)

Hyman, R. (1991). Comment. *Statistical Science, 6,* 389–392.

Hyman, R. (1994). Anomaly or artifact? Comments on Bem and Honorton. *Psychological Bulletin, 115,* 19–24.

Kihlstrom, J. (1987). The cognitive unconscious. *Science, 237,* 1445–1452.

Kunda, Z., & Nisbett, R. E. (1986). The psychometrics of everyday life. *Cognitive Psychology, 18,* 195–224.

Langer, E. J. (1975). The illusion of control. *Journal of Personality and Social Psychology, 32,* 311–328.

Loftus, G. R. (1991). On the tyranny of hypothesis testing in the social sciences. *Contemporary Psychology, 36,* 102–105.

Maier, M. H. (1991). *The data game: Controversies in social science statistics.* Armonk, NY: M. E. Sharpe.

Pearson, E. S. (1962). Some thoughts on statistical inference. *Annals of Mathematical Statistics, 33*, 394–403.

Pool, R. (1988). Similar experiments, dissimilar results. *Science, 242*, 192–193.

Rosenthal, R., & Rubin, D. B. (1979). A note on percent variance explained as a measure of the importance of effects. *Journal of Applied Social Psychology, 9*, 395–396.

Ross, L. (1977). The intuitive psychologist and his shortcomings: Distortions in the attribution process. In L. Berkowitz (Ed.), *Advances in experimental social psychology* (Vol. 10, pp. 173–220). New York: Academic Press.

Schank, R. C. (1979). Interestingness: Controlling inferences. *Artificial Intelligence, 12*, 273–297.

Skinner, B. F. (1963). Operant behavior. *American Psychologist, 18*, 503–515.

Tesser, A. (1990, August). *Interesting models in social psychology: A personal view.* Invited address presented at the meeting of the American Psychological Association, Boston.

Thagard, P. (1989). Explanatory coherence. *Behavioral and Brain Sciences, 12*, 435–462.

Tucker, L. A., & Bagwell, M. (1992). Relationship between serum cholesterol levels and television viewing in 11,947 adults. *American Journal of Health Promotion, 6*(6), 437–442.

Tukey, J. W. (1969). Analyzing data: Sanctification or detective work? *American Psychologist, 24*, 83–91.

Tukey, J. W. (1991). The philosophy of multiple comparisons. *Statistical Science, 6*, 100–116.

Utts, J. (1991). Replication and meta-analysis in parapsychology. *Statistical Science, 6*, 363–378.

Wilensky, R. (1983). Story grammars versus story points. *Behavioral and Brain Sciences, 6*, 579–623.

PART II

The Trait Approach to Personality

People are not all the same. They think differently, feel differently, and act differently. This fact raises an important question: What is the best way to describe enduring psychological differences among persons? The purpose of the trait approach to personality psychology is to attempt to answer this question. The ordinary language of personality—found in any dictionary—consists of terms like "sociable" and "anxious" and "dominant." The goal of many researchers who follow the trait approach is to transform this everyday language into a scientifically valid technology for describing individual differences in personality that can be used for predicting people's behavior and, more importantly, for understanding what they do and how they feel.

This section begins with a brief excerpt from a novel that illustrates how a person (in this case, a fictional one) can be vividly described in trait terms. In the second selection, the person widely recognized as the founder of modern personality psychology, Gordon Allport, describes what he thinks a personality trait is and why it is important. The third selection is one of the classics from the golden age of traits—the introduction of the term "authoritarian personality" and use of the F scale (F standing for fascism) to identify people with antidemocratic and racist tendencies.

The fourth selection marks the end of the golden age. It is an excerpt from a book by Walter Mischel that was widely read as a frontal assault on the very existence of personality. Although Allport anticipated many of Mischel's criticisms, the book had a widespread impact and inspired numerous rebuttals. One of the shortest of these rebuttals is the fifth selection, by Jack Block. This article briefly and elegantly describes the uncertain connection between behavior and personality and the reasons why variability in the first does not necessarily imply inconsistency in the second. The sixth selection, by Douglas Kenrick and David Funder, sums up the lessons learned from the controversy over the existence of personality, which include not just the conclusion that "traits exist," but concern the circumstances under which personality is most likely to be clearly seen.

The seventh and eighth selections return to the Allportian theme of using traits to understand behavior. Mark Snyder introduces the concept of "self-monitoring" to examine the differences between people who do and do not adjust their expressive behavior to match the situation they find themselves in. Jonathan Shedler and Jack Block show how drug abuse can be predicted from personality traits measured in childhood, years before abusers encounter their first drug. The ninth and final selection, by Paul Costa and Robert McCrae, asks which of the 17,953 traits of personality in the unabridged dictionary are truly basic and important. Their number they offer is 5. This does not mean the other 17,948 can be safely ignored. But Costa and McCrae argue that a wide swath of the personality domain is encompassed by broad traits they call extraversion, neuroticism, openness, agreeableness, and conscientiousness.

FROM *THE LAST HURRAH*

Edwin O'Connor

The first selection in this section is an excerpt from Edwin O'Connor's famous political novel, The Last Hurrah. *The passage describes the mayor's impression of the personality of his disappointing son. It provides a vivid demonstration of how trait terms are used in daily life—there is certainly nothing unusual about a person thinking about another in this way. It also shows how useful such terms can be. A few well-chosen words link the son's personality traits to his typical behaviors, and these are sufficient to convey a clear impression of what he is like. It seems likely that if you were actually to meet the mayor's son, you would recognize him, and you might even be able to predict what he would do under a wide range of circumstances.*

In the terminology used by Block in his article in Part I, the father's impressions of his son constitute O-data (judgments by an observer). And as O-data often do, these impressions have their own consequences. The father may not be right about his son's personality, but his beliefs no doubt have a profound effect on their relationship. Finally, notice that even though this selection describes the son from the father's viewpoint, it tells you nearly as much about the father as it does about the son.

From *The Last Hurrah*, by E. O'Connor, pp. 17–19. Copyright © 1956 by Edwin O'Connor. By permission of Little, Brown and Company.

On the way out he thought suddenly of his son; he stopped and said to the maid, "Has Francis come downstairs yet?"

"No sir. I think he's still asleep."

A growing boy needs his rest, Skeffington thought sardonically; the only question was whether or not Francis Jr., at the age of thirty-seven, might properly qualify as a growing boy. For years Skeffington had been baffled and badly disappointed by his only son. Francis Jr. was virtually a physical duplicate of his father—the resemblance was so astonishing that Skeffington, looking at his son in recent years, could only groan at the unkind mockery of the mnemonic shell, smiling emptily at him across the dinner table. For some important if not quite definable ingredient had been omitted from the boy's makeup; he had been a pleasant, well-mannered, lazy youngster who had grown placidly into manhood without betraying a sign of ambition or, indeed, of intelligence. He had skinned through high school, preparatory school, college, and law school, gaining in this educational passage but a single distinction: in his junior year at college he had been voted Best Dancer in his class. It was an honor that Skeffington had failed to appreciate.

"I've sired a featherhead," he had said to his wife. "A waltzing featherhead. Or am I doing the boy an injustice? Perhaps he fox-trots as well."

"Ah, Frank, you expect too much," she had replied. A gentle woman, she knew and in part shared his disappointment in the boy, yet she had kept herself the buffer between the uncomprehending father and the smiling phantom son. "You want him to be like you and the simple fact of it is he can't be. It's not fair to expect it of him."

He had shrugged. "I don't expect it. I merely expect him to be like some recognizable adult. He's not like me, he's not like you, he's not like anybody. Possibly he's a throwback: a throwback to some dancing ancestor. He claims he wants to be a lawyer; do you suppose he plans to dance his way into court?"

She had persisted. "He's very young yet, after all. It's much too early to pass judgment. And he *is* a good boy; that's no small thing, surely?"

"He's good, he's moral, he's likable," he had agreed, "but he's also a puffball. No weight at all. Twenty-one years old, and everybody still calls him Junior; they'll call him Junior when he's ninety. I don't find that particularly encouraging, Kate."

She had returned to a long-cherished ambition. "I don't know, I always thought that one day he might surprise us all by going to the seminary.

He still might, I suppose. I wish he would; I think he'd be happy there."

"Well, he's made a grand start," Skeffington had said dryly. "I understand the seminaries want only the best dancers. No, Kate, the boy will go through law school. He'll go through without too much trouble, I think I can promise you that; the good Dean Gillis is a fine old-fashioned scholar with a healthy respect for his own skin. Then when he gets through he'll get a place in a decent firm; it's barely possible I may have something to do with that, too. But what's to happen to him after I'm gone I haven't the least idea. Maybe he'll be all right as long as his legs hold out."

Now, sixteen years later, Skeffington's bleak prediction for the most part had been fulfilled. At thirty-seven, his son, unmarried, still danced: he could be seen nightly at any one of the city's numerous nightclubs in the company of any one of a number of young women who danced well, laughed immoderately, and were remarkably similar in appearance. He was a thoroughly agreeable, well-tailored man, with a face as unlined as that of a child, who perhaps drank a bit more with the passing of each year, but whose behavior had remained untouched by scandal or disgrace. He was by occupation a practicing attorney, although the practice was largely limited to routine and undemanding labors in the offices of the city's Corporation Counsel, a department of government which had been for some years under Skeffington's control. And, by friend and foe alike, he was still called Junior.

Now that you have finished reading about Junior, you can see how this passage exemplifies not only what the trait approach includes, but what it leaves out. Traits provide a view from the outside only. We have a vivid impression of how the son appears to others, but we have learned nothing about his opinions of his father, his goals in life, his emotional experience, his values, his fears, or anything else that is part of what could be considered his "inner life." It can be useful to keep in mind what a trait approach to personality—and O-data in particular—can and cannot do.

WHAT IS A TRAIT OF PERSONALITY?

Gordon W. Allport

The trait section of this reader now really begins, with a classic statement by the original and still perhaps most important trait theorist. What Sigmund Freud is to psychoanalysis, Gordon Allport is—almost—to trait psychology.

In this selection, Allport offers one of the earliest—and still one of the best—psychological definitions of a personality trait. This article was written for a conference held in 1929, when the modern field of personality psychology was just beginning to be formed. Allport's fundamental contribution, in efforts like this paper, was to take the study of normal variations in personality out of the exclusive hands of novelists, dramatists, theologians, and philosophers and to begin to transform it into a scientific discipline.

Especially considering how old this article is, it is remarkable to observe how many modern issues it anticipates, and how cogently it addresses them. These issues include the person-situation debate (see the upcoming selection by Mischel), the issue of whether a trait is a cause or just a summary of behavior (Allport says it is a cause), and the distinction between focusing on how traits are structured within a single individual (now called the idiographic approach) and focusing on how traits distinguish between people (now called the nomothetic approach). Almost 70 years after it was written, this article still has much to say to the modern field of personality psychology.

From "What Is a Trait of Personality?" by G. W. Allport (1931). *Journal of Abnormal and Social Psychology, 25,* 368–372. Adapted with permission.

At the heart of all investigation of personality lies the puzzling problem of the nature of the unit or element which is the carrier of the distinctive behavior of a man. *Reflexes* and *habits* are too specific in reference, and connote constancy rather than consistency in behavior; *attitudes* are ill defined, and as employed by various writers refer to determining tendencies that range in inclusiveness from the *Aufgabe* to the *Weltan-* schanung;[1] *dispositions* and *tendencies* are even less definitive. But *traits*, although appropriated by all manner of writers for all manner of purposes, may still be salvaged, I think, and limited in their refer-

[1]With these German words, Allport is describing the range from the specific tasks an individual must perform (*Aufgabe*) to his or her entire view of the world (*Weltanschanung*).

ence to a certain definite conception of a generalized response-unit in which resides the distinctive quality of behavior that reflects personality. Foes as well as friends of the doctrine of traits will gain from a more consistent use of the term.

The doctrine itself has never been explicitly stated. It is my purpose with the aid of eight criteria to define *trait*, and to state the logic and some of the evidence for the admission of this concept to good standing in psychology.

1. A trait has more than nominal existence. A trait may be said to have the same kind of existence that a habit of a complex order has. Habits of a complex, or higher, order have long been accepted as household facts in psychology. There is no reason to believe that the mechanism which produces such habits (integration, *Gestaltung*, or whatever it may be) stops short of producing the more generalized habits which are here called traits of personality.

2. A trait is more generalized than a habit. Within a personality there are, of course, many independent habits; but there is also so much integration, organization, and coherence among habits that we have no choice but to recognize great systems of interdependent habits. If the habit of brushing one's teeth can be shown, statistically or genetically, to be unrelated to the habit of dominating a tradesman, there can be no question of a common trait involving both these habits; but if the habit of dominating a tradesman can be shown, statistically or genetically, to be related to the habit of bluffing one's way past guards, there is the presumption that a common trait of personality exists which includes these two habits. Traits may conceivably embrace anywhere from two habits to a legion of habits. In this way, there may be said to be major, widely extensified traits and minor, less generalized traits in a given personality.

3. A trait is dynamic, or at least determinative. It is not the stimulus that is the crucial determinant in behavior that expresses personality; it is the trait itself that is decisive. Once formed a trait seems to have the capacity of directing responses to stimuli into characteristic channels. This emphasis upon the dynamic nature of traits, ascribing to them a capacity for guiding the specific response, is variously recognized by many writers. The principle is nothing more than that which has been subscribed to in various connections by Woodworth, Prince, Sherrington, Coghill, Kurt Lewin, Troland, Lloyd Morgan, Thurstone, Bentley, Stern, and others.[2] From this general point of view traits might be called "derived drives" or "derived motives." Whatever they are called they may be regarded as playing a motivating role in each act, thus endowing the separate adjustments of the individual to specific stimuli with that *adverbial* quality that is the very essence of personality.

* * *

4. The existence of a trait may be established empirically or statistically. In order to know that a person has a *habit* it is necessary to have evidence of repeated reactions of a constant type. Similarly in order to know that an individual has a trait it is necessary to have evidence of repeated reactions which, though not necessarily constant in type, seem none the less to be consistently a function of the same underlying determinant. If this evidence is gathered casually by mere observation of the subject or through the reading of a case-history or biography, it may be called empirical evidence.

More exactly, of course, the existence of a trait may be established with the aid of statistical techniques that determine the degree of coherence among the separate responses. Although this employment of statistical aid is highly desirable, it is not necessary to wait for such evidence before speaking of traits, any more than it would be necessary to refrain from speaking of the habit of bit-

---

[2]This is an all-star list of important psychologists and scientists at the time this article was written. Of these, Kurt Lewin and Allport himself had the most lasting influence on personality psychology.

ing fingernails until the exact frequency of the occurrence is known. Statistical methods are at present better suited to intellective than to conative functions, and it is with the latter that we are chiefly concerned in our studies of personality.[3]

5. *Traits are only relatively independent of each other.* The investigator desires, of course, to discover what the fundamental traits of personality are, that is to say, what broad trends in behavior do exist independently of one another. Actually with the test methods and correlational procedures in use, completely independent variation is seldom found. In one study expansion correlated with extroversion to the extent of +.39, ascendance with conservatism, +.22, and humor with insight, +.83, and so on. This overlap may be due to several factors, the most obvious being the tendency of the organism to react in an integrated fashion, so that when concrete acts are observed or tested they reflect not only the trait under examination, but also simultaneously other traits; several traits may thus converge into a final common path. It seems safe, therefore, to predict that traits can never be completely isolated for study, since they never show more than a relative independence of one another.

In the instance just cited, it it doubtful whether humor and insight (provided their close relationship is verified in subsequent studies) represent distinct traits. In the future perhaps it may be possible to agree upon a certain magnitude of correlation below which it will be acceptable to speak of *separate* traits, and above which *one* trait only will be recognized. If one trait only is indicated it will presumably represent a broadly generalized disposition. For example, if humor and insight cannot be established as independent traits,

it will be necessary to recognize a more inclusive trait, and name it perhaps "sense of proportion."

6. *A trait of personality, psychologically considered, is not the same as moral quality.* A trait of personality may or may not coincide with some well-defined, conventional, social concept. Extroversion, ascendance, social participation, and insight are free from preconceived moral significance, large because each is a word newly coined or adapted to fit a psychological discovery. It would be ideal if we could in this way find our traits first and then name them. But honesty, loyalty, neatness, and tact, though encrusted with social significance, *may* likewise represent true traits of personality. The danger is that in devising scales for their measurement we may be bound by the conventional meanings, and thus be led away from the precise integration as it exists in a given individual. Where possible it would be well for us to find our traits first, and then seek devaluated terms with which to characterize our discoveries.

7. *Acts, and even habits, that are inconsistent with a trait are not proof of the non-existence of the trait.* The objection most often considered fatal to the doctrine of traits has been illustrated as follows: "An individual may be habitually neat with respect to his person, and characteristically slovenly in his handwriting or the care of his desk."[4]

In the first place this observation fails to state that there are cases frequently met where a constant level of neatness is maintained in all of a person's acts, giving unmistakable empirical evidence that the trait of neatness is, in some people at least, thoroughly and permanently integrated. All people must not be expected to show the same

---

[3]"Conative functions" here refer to motivation; at the time this was written statistical methods of psychological measurement (psychometrics) had been used exclusively for the measurement of intellectual skills, not motivation or personality. Over the following decades, this situation changed and psychometrics became a foundation of modern personality psychology.

[4]This comment anticipates the "person-situation" debate that flared up in 1968, almost 40 years later, with the publication of a book by Walter Mischel (excerpted in a following selection). Interestingly, the inconsistency of neatness, almost exactly as Allport here describes it, *was* used as an argument against the doctrine of traits in an even later article by Mischel and Peake (1982).

degree of integration in respect to a given trait. *What is a major trait in one personality may be a minor trait, or even nonexistent in another personality.*[5]

In the second place, we must concede that there may be opposed integrations, i.e., contradictory traits, in a single personality. The same individual may have a trait *both* of neatness *and* of carelessness, of ascendance *and* submission, although frequently of unequal strength.

In the third place there are in every personality instances of acts that are unrelated to existent traits, the product of the stimulus and of the attitude of the moment. Even the characteristically neat person may become careless in his haste to catch a train.

But to say that not all of a person's acts reflect some higher integration is not to say that no such higher integrations exist.

---

[5]This comment—that not all traits apply to all people—was developed into an important article many years later by the psychologists Daryl Bem and Andrea Allen (1974).

8. *A trait may be viewed either in the light of the personality which contains it, or in the light of its distribution in the population at large.* Each trait has both its unique and its universal aspect. In its unique aspect, the trait takes its significance entirely from the role it plays in the personality as a whole. In its universal aspect, the trait is arbitrarily isolated for study, and a comparison is made between individuals in respect to it. From this second point of view traits merely extend the familiar field of the psychology of individual differences.

There may be relatively few traits, a few hundred perhaps, that are universal enough to be scaled in the population at large; whereas there may be in a single personality a thousand traits distinguishable to a discerning observer. For this reason, after a scientific schedule of universal traits is compiled, there will still be the field of *artistic* endeavor for psychologists in apprehending correctly the subtle and unique traits peculiar to one personality alone, and in discovering the *pattern* which obtains *between* these traits in the same personality.

The Measurement of Implicit Antidemocratic Trends

R. Nevitt Sanford, T. W. Adorno, Else Frenkel-Brunswik, and Daniel J. Levinson

Trait psychology flourished over the decades that followed Allport's pioneering efforts. Many different researchers formulated a huge number of personality trait constructs and an equally large number of tests to measure them. Some of these tests were used to assist in the diagnosis of psychopathology, some predicted important aspects of behavior, and some described what people do in their daily lives. But as you have seen, Allport's goal for traits went beyond these worthy purposes. Allport thought that traits cause *behavior, and therefore can be used not just to predict but to* explain *what people do.*

The premier example of the use of a trait to explain the underpinnings of behavior came from the famous research project on the "authoritarian personality." This project was begun during the waning days of World War II as an attempt to understand the psychological roots of anti-Semitism and the other attitudes and behaviors that produced the Holocaust in Europe. It provides an early and classic example of a major psychological research project initiated specifically to understand a serious social problem. It also featured an unusual melding of trait and psychoanalytic (Freudian) viewpoints. As you will see, the authoritarian personality is not just a collection of overt behaviors, but is seen as the product of a complex interplay of underlying psychodynamic forces that extend back to early childhood.

The book on the authoritarian personality is several hundred pages long. The selection that follows focuses on the main personality measurement instrument—the "F scale" (F standing for fascism)—that this project produced. Earlier work in this project had produced several scales to measure ethnic prejudice, but these all asked questions that explicitly mentioned the names of various minority groups. Researchers became concerned that some subjects might deny holding prejudiced attitudes in order to look good, but might be racists nonetheless. So they began to work on a measure of a "subtle" measure of ethnic prejudice that did not mention any minority by name.

Not only did they succeed in developing a subtle measure of prejudice, but they also discovered a constellation of attitudes and motivations that went deeper than racism even as it formed part of its foundation. These attitudes and motivations produced "antidemocratic trends" in a person's character, and the syndrome ended up being called the authoritarian personality.

The authoritarian personality is inconsistent in an interesting way. He or she is completely obedient to superiors in the hierarchy, and completely dominating of and contemptuous of those lower in the hierarchy. In the selection that follows, the researchers describe how these attitudes both stem from the same source, and outline nine dynamic underpinnings of authoritarianism that they believe are captured by the F scale.

A. Introduction

There gradually evolved a plan for constructing a scale that would measure prejudice without appearing to have this aim and without mentioning the name of any minority group. * * * It might be used to survey opinion in groups where "racial questions" were too "ticklish" a matter, e.g., a group which included many members of one or another ethnic minority. It might be used for measuring prejudice among minority group members themselves. Most important, by circumventing some of the defenses which people employ when asked to express themselves with respect to "race issues," it might provide a valid measure of prejudice.

* * * What was needed was a collection of items each of which was correlated with [racial prejudice] but which did not come from an area ordinarily covered in discussions of political, economic, and social matters. The natural place to turn was to the clinical material already collected, where, particularly in the subjects' discussions of such topics as the self, family, sex, interpersonal relations, moral and personal values, there had appeared numerous trends which, it appeared, might be connected with prejudice.

At this point the second—and major—purpose of the new scale began to take shape. Might not such a scale yield a valid estimate of antidemocratic tendencies at the personality level? It was clear, at the time the new scale was being planned, that anti-Semitism and ethnocentrism were not merely matters of surface opinion, but general tendencies with sources, in part at least, deep within the structure of the person. Would it not be possible to construct a scale that would approach more directly these deeper, often unconscious forces? If so, and if the scale could be validated by means of later clinical studies, would we not have a better estimate of antidemocratic *potential* than could be obtained from the scales that were more openly ideological? The prospect was intriguing. And experience with clinical techniques and with the other scales gave considerable promise of success. * * * The task then was to formulate scale items which, though they were statements of opinions and attitudes and had the same form as those appearing in ordinary opinion-attitude questionnaires, would actually serve as "giveaways" of underlying antidemocratic trends in the personality. This would make it possible to carry over into group studies the insights and hypotheses derived from clinical investigation; it would test whether we could study on a mass scale features ordinarily regarded as individualistic and qualitative.

＊ ＊ ＊ The new instrument was termed the F scale, to signify its concern with implicit prefascist tendencies.

＊   ＊   ＊

B. Construction of the Fascism (F) Scale

1. THE UNDERLYING THEORY The 38 items of the original F scale are shown in [the following pages]. It will be apparent that in devising the scale we did not proceed in a strictly empirical fashion. We did not consider starting with hundreds of items chosen more or less at random and then seeing by trial and error which ones might be associated with [racial prejudice]. For every item there was a hypothesis, sometimes several hypotheses, stating what might be the nature of its connection with prejudice.[1]

＊   ＊   ＊

It will have been recognized that the interpretation of the material of the present study was guided by a theoretical orientation that was present at the start. The same orientation played the most crucial role in the preparation of the F scale. Once a hypothesis had been formulated concerning the way in which some deep-lying trend in the personality might express itself in some opinion or attitude that was dynamically, though not logically, related to prejudice against outgroups, a preliminary sketch for an item was usually not far to seek: a phrase from the daily newspaper, an

utterance by an interviewee, a fragment of ordinary conversation was usually ready at hand. (The actual formulation of an item was a technical proceeding to which considerable care had to be devoted.)

＊ ＊ ＊ For example, when it was discovered that the anti-Semitic individual objects to Jews on the ground that they violate conventional moral values, one interpretation was that this individual had a particularly strong and rigid adherence to conventional values, and that this general disposition in his personality provided some of the motivational basis for anti-Semitism, and at the same time expressed itself in other ways, e.g., in a general tendency to look down on and to punish those who were believed to be violating conventional values. ＊ ＊ ＊ Accordingly, therefore, *adherence to conventional values* came to be thought of as a *variable* in the person—something which could be approached by means of scale items of the F type and shown to be related functionally to various manifestations of prejudice. Similarly, underlying several of the prejudiced responses was a general disposition to glorify, to be subservient to and remain uncritical toward authoritative figures of the ingroup and to take an attitude of punishing outgroup figures in the name of some moral authority. Hence, *authoritarianism* assumed the proportions of a variable worthy to be investigated in its own right.

In the same way, a number of such variables were derived and defined, and they, taken together, made up the basic content of the F scale. Each was regarded as a more or less central trend in the person which, in accordance with some dynamic process, expressed itself on the surface in ethnocentrism as well as in diverse psychologically related opinions and attitudes. These variables are listed below, together with a brief definition of each.

a. *Conventionalism.* Rigid adherence to conventional, middle-class values.
b. *Authoritarian submission.* Submissive, uncritical attitude toward idealized moral authorities of the ingroup.

---

[1]Thus, items from the F scale were assembled using the "rational method" of test construction. This is as opposed to the "empirical method," a technique that was widely used in the 1940s and 1950s to assemble personality tests based on the association between item scores and criteria without regard for the content of the items. The developers of the F scale, by contrast, wrote items they thought had theoretical reasons for being associated with the construct they hoped to measure.

c. *Authoritarian aggression.* Tendency to be on the lookout for, and to condemn, reject, and punish people who violate conventional values.

d. *Anti-intraception.* Opposition to the subjective, the imaginative, the tender-minded.

e. *Superstition and stereotypy.* The belief in mystical determinants of the individual's fate; the disposition to think in rigid categories.

f. *Power and "toughness."* Preoccupation with the dominance-submission, strong-weak, leader-follower dimension; identification with power figures; overemphasis upon the conventionalized attributes of the ego; exaggerated assertion of strength and toughness.

g. *Destructiveness and cynicism.* Generalized hostility, vilification of the human.

h. *Projectivity.* The disposition to believe that wild and dangerous things go on in the world; the projection outward of unconscious emotional impulses.

i. *Sex.* Exaggerated concern with sexual "goings-on."

These variables were thought of as going together to form a single syndrome, a more or less enduring structure in the person that renders him receptive to antidemocratic propaganda. One might say, therefore, that the F scale attempts to measure the potentially antidemocratic personality. This does not imply that *all* the features of this personality pattern are touched upon in the scale, but only that the scale embraces a fair sample of the ways in which this pattern characteristically expresses itself. Indeed, as the study went on, numerous additional features of the pattern, as well as variations within the overall pattern, suggested themselves—and it was regretted that a second F scale could not have been constructed in order to carry these explorations further. It is to be emphasized that one can speak of personality here only to the extent that the coherence of the scale items can be better explained on the ground of an inner structure than on the ground of external association.

The variables of the scale may be discussed in more detail, with emphasis on their organization and the nature of their relations to ethnocentrism. As each variable is introduced, the scale items deemed to be expressive of it are presented. It will be noted, as the variables are taken up in turn, that the same item sometimes appears under more than one heading. This follows from our approach to scale construction. In order to cover efficiently a wide area it was necessary to formulate items that were maximally rich, that is, pertinent to as much as possible of the underlying theory—hence a single item was sometimes used to represent two, and sometimes more, different ideas. It will be noted also that different variables are represented by different numbers of items. This is for the reason that the scale was designed with first attention to the whole pattern into which the variables fitted, some with more important roles than others.

a. *Conventionalism*

- The modern church, with its many rules and hypocrisies, does not appeal to the deeply religious person; it appeals mainly to the childish, the insecure, and the uncritical.
- One should avoid doing things in public which appear wrong to others, even though one knows that these things are really all right.
- There is too much emphasis in colleges on intellectual and theoretical topics, not enough emphasis on practical matters and on the homely virtues of living.
- Although leisure is a fine thing, it is good hard work that makes life interesting and worthwhile.
- *What* a man does is not so important so long as he does it well.
- Which of the following are the most important for a person to have or to be? *Mark X the three most important.*

artistic and sensuous
popular, good personality
drive, determination, will power
broad, humanitarian social outlook
neatness and good manners
sensitivity and understanding
efficiency, practicality, thrift
intellectual and serious
emotional expressiveness, warmth,
    intimacy
kindness and charity

It is a well-known hypothesis that susceptibility to fascism is most characteristically a middle-class phenomenon, that it is "in the culture" and, hence, that those who conform the most to this culture will be the most prejudiced. Items referring to the holding of conventional values were included in order to gather data bearing on this hypothesis. Many of the early findings of the present study, however, gave evidence that the matter was not quite so simple. The correlation between conventional values and prejudice seemed to be positive but not very high; whereas unconventional people tended to be free of prejudice, it was clear that some conventional people were prejudiced while others were not. It seemed that, among the conventional group, what might make the difference was the deeper source of the conventionality, or rather the type of broader personality structure within which it had a functional role. If the adherence to conventional values was an expression of a fully established individual conscience, then we should expect no necessary connection between these values and antidemocratic potential. The same standards which render the individual easily offended by what he conceives to be the morally loose behavior of unassimilated minority group members or of "lower-class" people, would—if they are well internalized—cause him to resist the violence and delinquency which characterize the advanced stages of fascism. If, on the other hand, adherence to conventional values is determined by contemporary external social pressure, if it is based upon the individual's adherence to the standards of the collective powers with which he, for the time being, is identified, then we should expect a close association with antidemocratic receptivity. It is this latter state of affairs that we wish to call conventionalism—and to distinguish from mere acceptance of conventional values. The conventionalistic individual could in good conscience follow the dictates of the external agency wherever they might lead him and, moreover, he would be capable of totally exchanging one set of standards for another quite different one—as in a conversion from official Communism to Catholicism.

*   *   *

* * * Extreme conventionalism going with a strong inclination to punish those who violate conventional values is a different thing from conventional values associated with a philosophy of live and let live. In other words, the meaning of a high score on this variable, as on any of the others, is to be known from the broader context within which it occurs.

b. *Authoritarian Submission*

- One of the main values of progressive education is that it gives the child great freedom in expressing those natural impulses and desires so often frowned upon by conventional middle-class society.
- He is indeed contemptible who does not feel an undying love, gratitude, and respect for his parents.
- It is essential for learning or effective work that our teachers or bosses outline in detail what is to be done and exactly how to go about it.
- Every person should have a deep faith in some supernatural force higher than himself to which he gives total allegiance and whose decisions he does not question.
- Sciences like chemistry, physics, and medicine have carried men very far, but there are many important things that can never possibly be understood by the human mind.

- Obedience and respect for authority are the most important virtues children should learn.
- What this country needs is fewer laws and agencies, and more courageous, tireless, devoted leaders whom the people can put their faith in.
- No sane, normal, decent person could ever think of hurting a close friend or relative.

Submission to authority, desire for a strong leader, subservience of the individual to the state, and so forth, have so frequently and, as it seems to us, correctly, been set forth as important aspects of the Nazi creed that a search for correlates of prejudice had naturally to take these attitudes into account.[2] These attitudes have indeed been so regularly mentioned in association with anti-Semitism that it was particularly difficult to formulate items that would express the underlying trend and still be sufficiently free of logical or direct relations to prejudice—and we cannot claim to have been entirely successful. Direct references to dictatorship and political figures were avoided for the most part, and the main emphasis was on obedience, respect, rebellion, and relations to authority in general. Authoritarian submission was conceived of as a very general attitude that would be evoked in relation to a variety of authority figures—parents, older people, leaders, supernatural power, and so forth.

The attempt was made to formulate the items in such a way that agreement with them would indicate not merely a realistic, balanced respect for valid authority but an exaggerated, all-out, emotional need to submit. This would be indicated, it seemed, by agreement that obedience and respect for authority were the *most important* virtues that children should learn, that a person should *obey without question* the decisions of a supernatural power, and so forth. It was considered that here, as in the case of conventionalism, the subservience

to external agencies was probably due to some failure in the development of an inner authority, i.e., conscience. Another hypothesis was that authoritarian submission was commonly a way of handling ambivalent feelings toward authority figures: underlying hostile and rebellious impulses, held in check by fear, lead the subject to overdo in the direction of respect, obedience, gratitude, and the like.

It seems clear that authoritarian submission by itself contributes largely to the antidemocratic potential by rendering the individual particularly receptive to manipulation by the strongest external powers. The immediate connection of this attitude with ethnocentrism has been suggested in earlier chapters: Hostility against ingroup authorities, originally the parents, has had to be repressed; the "bad" aspects of these figures—that they are unfair, self-seeking, dominating—are then seen as existing in outgroups, who are charged with dictatorship, plutocracy, desire to control, and so forth. And this displacement of negative imagery is not the only way in which the repressed hostility is handled; it seems often to find expression in authoritarian aggression.

c. *Authoritarian Aggression*

- It is only natural and right that women be restricted in certain ways in which men have more freedom.
- He is indeed contemptible who does not feel an undying love, gratitude, and respect for his parents.
- Homosexuality is a particularly rotten form of delinquency and ought to be severely punished.
- No insult to our honor should ever go unpunished.
- Sex crimes, such as rape and attacks on children, deserve more than mere imprisonment; such criminals ought to be publicly whipped.

The individual who has been forced to give up basic pleasures and to live under a system of rigid

---

[2]E. Fromm, E. H. Erikson, A. Maslow, M. B. Chisholm, and W. Reich are among the writers whose thinking about authoritarianism has influenced our own.—Author

restraints, and who therefore feels put upon, is likely not only to seek an object upon which he can "take it out" but also to be particularly annoyed at the idea that another person is "getting away with something." Thus, it may be said that the present variable represents the sadistic component of authoritarianism just as the immediately foregoing one represents its masochistic component. It is to be expected, therefore, that the conventionalist who cannot bring himself to utter any real criticism of accepted authority will have a desire to condemn, reject, and punish those who violate these values. As the emotional life which this person regards as proper and a part of himself is likely to be very limited, so the impulses, especially sexual and aggressive ones, which remain unconscious and ego-alien are likely to be strong and turbulent. Since in this circumstance a wide variety of stimuli can tempt the individual and so arouse his anxiety (fear of punishment), the list of traits, behavior patterns, individuals, and groups that he must condemn grows very long indeed. * * * It is here hypothesized that this feature of ethnocentrism is but a part of a more general tendency to punish violators of conventional values: homosexuals, sex offenders, people with bad manners, etc. Once the individual has convinced himself that there are people who ought to be punished, he is provided with a channel through which his deepest aggressive impulses may be expressed, even while he thinks of himself as thoroughly moral. If his external authorities, or the crowd, lend their approval to this form of aggression, then it may take the most violent forms, and it may persist after the conventional values, in the name of which it was undertaken, have been lost from sight.

One might say that in authoritarian aggression, hostility that was originally aroused by and directed toward ingroup authorities is *displaced*[3] onto outgroups. This mechanism is superficially

similar to but essentially different from a process that has often been referred to as "scapegoating." According to the latter conception, the individual's aggression is aroused by frustration, usually of his economic needs; and then, being unable due to intellectual confusion to tell the real causes of his difficulty, he lashes out about him, as it were, venting his fury upon whatever object is available and not too likely to strike back. While it is granted that this process has a role in hostility against minority groups, it must be emphasized that according to the present theory of displacement, the authoritarian *must*, out of an inner necessity, turn his aggression against outgroups. He must do so because he is psychologically unable to attack ingroup authorities, rather than because of intellectual confusion regarding the source of his frustration. If this theory is correct, then authoritarian aggression and authoritarian submission should turn out to be highly correlated. Furthermore, this theory helps to explain why the aggression is so regularly justified in moralistic terms, why it can become so violent and lose all connection with the stimulus which originally set it off.

Readiness to condemn other people on moral grounds may have still another source: it is not only that the authoritarian must condemn the moral laxness that he sees in others, but he is actually driven to see immoral attributes in them whether this has a basis in fact or not. This is a further device for countering his own inhibited tendencies; he says to himself, as it were: "I am not bad and deserving of punishment, he is." In other words the individual's own unacceptable impulses are *projected* onto other individuals and groups who are then rejected.

* * *

Although conventionalism and authoritarianism might thus be regarded as signs of ego weakness, it seemed worthwhile to seek other, more direct, means for estimating this trend in personality, and to correlate this trend with the others. Ego weakness would, it seemed, be expressed fairly directly in such phenomena as opposition to in-

---

[3]Displacement is the psychoanalytic mechanism by which feelings for one object are moved onto another object.

trospection, in superstition and stereotypy, and in overemphasis upon the ego and its supposed strength. The following three variables deal with these phenomena.

d. *Anti-intraception*

- Novels or stories that tell about what people think and feel are more interesting than those which contain mainly action, romance, and adventure.
- There is too much emphasis in colleges on intellectual and theoretical topics, not enough emphasis on practical matters and on the homely virtues of living.
- There are some things too intimate or personal to talk about even with one's closest friends.
- Although leisure is a fine thing, it is good hard work that makes life interesting and worthwhile.
- *What* a man does is not so important so long as he does it well.
- Books and movies ought not to deal so much with the sordid and seamy side of life; they ought to concentrate on themes that are entertaining or uplifting.

Intraception is a term introduced by Murray[4] to stand for "the dominance of feelings, fantasies, speculations, aspirations—an imaginative, subjective human outlook." The opposite of intraception is extraception, "a term that describes the tendency to be determined by concrete, clearly observable, physical conditions (tangible, objective facts)." The relations of intraception/extraception to ego weakness and to prejudice are probably highly complex, and this is not the place to consider them in detail. It seems fairly clear, however, that *anti*-intraception, an attitude of impatience with and opposition to the subjective and tenderminded, might well be a mark of the weak ego. The extremely anti-intraceptive individual is afraid

of thinking about human phenomena because he might, as it were, think the wrong thoughts; he is afraid of genuine feeling because his emotions might get out of control. Out of touch with large areas of his own inner life, he is afraid of what might be revealed if he, or others, should look closely at himself. He is therefore against "prying," against concern with what people think and feel, against unnecessary "talk"; instead he would keep busy, devote himself to practical pursuits, and instead of examining an inner conflict, turn his thoughts to something cheerful. An important feature of the Nazi program, it will be recalled, was the defamation of everything that tended to make the individual aware of himself and his problems; not only was "Jewish" psychoanalysis quickly eliminated but every kind of psychology except aptitude testing came under attack. This general attitude easily leads to a devaluation of the human and an overevaluation of the physical object; when it is most extreme, human beings are looked upon as if they were physical objects to be coldly manipulated—even while physical objects, now vested with emotional appeal, are treated with loving care.

e. *Superstition and Stereotypy*

- Although many people may scoff, it may yet be shown that astrology can explain a lot of things.
- It is more than a remarkable coincidence that Japan had an earthquake on Pearl Harbor Day, December 7, 1944.
- Every person should have a deep faith in some supernatural force higher than himself to which he gives total allegiance and whose decisions he does not question.
- Sciences like chemistry, physics, and medicine have carried men very far, but there are many important things that can never possibly be understood by the human mind.
- It is entirely possible that this series of wars and conflicts will be ended once and for all by a world-destroying earthquake, flood, or other catastrophe.

---

[4]Henry Murray (1938) was a personality psychologist and contemporary of Gordon Allport. Murray's theorizing was notable for its use of psychoanalytic ideas.

Superstitiousness, the belief in mystical or fantastic external determinants of the individual's fate, and stereotypy the disposition to think in rigid categories are so obviously related to ethnocentrism that they need little discussion here. A question that must be raised concerns the relations of these trends to general intelligence—and the relations of intelligence to ethnocentrism. Probably superstition and stereotypy tend to go with low intelligence, but low intelligence appears to be correlated with ethnocentrism to only a slight degree. It appears likely that superstition and stereotypy embrace, over and above the mere lack of intelligence in the ordinary sense, certain dispositions in thinking which are closely akin to prejudice, even though they might not hamper intelligent performance in the extraceptive sphere. These dispositions can be understood, in part at least, as expressions of ego weakness. Stereotypy is a form of obtuseness particularly in psychological and social matters. It might be hypothesized that one reason why people in modern society—even those who are otherwise "intelligent" or "informed"—resort to primitive, oversimplified explanations of human events is that so many of the ideas and observations needed for an adequate account are not allowed to enter into the calculations: because they are affect-laden and potentially anxiety-producing, the weak ego cannot include them within its scheme of things. More than this, those deeper forces within the personality which the ego cannot integrate with itself are likely to be projected onto the outer world; this is a source of bizarre ideas concerning other peoples' behavior and concerning the causation of events in nature.

Superstitiousness indicates a tendency to shift responsibility from within the individual onto outside forces beyond one's control; it indicates that the ego might already have "given up," that is to say, renounced the idea that it might determine the individual's fate by overcoming external forces. It must, of course, be recognized that in modern industrial society the capacity of the individual to determine what happens to himself has *actually* decreased, so that items referring to external causation might easily be realistic and hence of no significance for personality. It seemed necessary, therefore, to select items that would express ego weakness in a nonrealistic way by making the individual's fate dependent on more or less fantastic factors.

f. *Power and "Toughness"*

- Too many people today are living in an unnatural, soft way; we should return to the fundamentals, to a more red-blooded, active way of life.
- There are some activities so flagrantly un-American that, when responsible officials won't take the proper steps, the wide-awake citizen should take the law into his own hands.
- No insult to our honor should ever go unpunished.
- To a greater extent than most people realize, our lives are governed by plots hatched in secret by politicians.
- What this country needs is fewer laws and agencies, and more courageous, tireless, devoted leaders whom the people can put their faith in.

* * *

Closely related to the phenomenon of exaggerated toughness is something which might be described as a "power complex." Most apparent in its manifestations is overemphasis on the power motif in human relationships; there is a disposition to view all relations among people in terms of such categories as strong-weak, dominant-submissive, leader-follower, "hammer-anvil." And it is difficult to say with which of these roles the subject is the more fully identified. It appears that he wants to get power, to have it and not to lose it, and at the same time is afraid to seize and wield it. It appears that he also admires power in others and is inclined to submit to it—and at the same time is afraid of the weakness thus implied. The individual whom we expected to score high on this cluster readily identifies himself with the "little people," or "the average," but he does so, it seems, with little or no humility, and he seems actually to think of himself as strong or to believe that he can somehow become so. In short, the power complex contains elements that are essentially contradictory, and we should expect that sometimes one feature and sometimes another will predominate at the surface level. We should expect that both leaders and followers will score high on this variable, for the reason that the actual role of the individual seems to be less important than his concern that leader-follower relations shall obtain. One solution which such an individual often achieves is that of alignment with power figures, an arrangement by which he is able to gratify both his need for power and his need to submit. He hopes that by submitting to power he can participate in it. For example, a man who reports that the most awe-inspiring experience for him would be "to shake hands with the President" probably finds his gratification not in submission alone but in the idea that some of the big man's power has, as it were, rubbed off onto him, so that he is a more important person for having "shaken his hand" or "known him" or "been there." The same pattern of gratification can be obtained by acting in the role of "the lieutenant" or by functioning in a middle position in some clearly structured hierarchy where there is always somebody above and somebody below.

The power complex has immediate relations with certain aspects of ethnocentrism. An individual who thinks of most human relations in such terms as strong versus weak is likely to apply these categories in his thinking about ingroups and outgroups e.g., to conceive of "superior" and "inferior races." And one of the psychologically least costly devices for attaining a sense of superiority is to claim it on the basis of membership in a particular "race."

g. *Destructiveness and Cynicism*

- America is getting so far from the true American way of life that force may be necessary to restore it.
- Too many people today are living in an unnatural, soft way; we should return to the fundamentals, to a more red-blooded, active way of life.
- After we finish off the Germans and Japs, we ought to concentrate on other enemies of the human race such as rats, snakes, and germs.
- Familiarity breeds contempt.
- Today everything is unstable; we should be prepared for a period of constant change, conflict, and upheaval.
- Reports of atrocities in Europe have been greatly exaggerated for propaganda purposes.
- There are some activities so flagrantly un-American that, when responsible officials won't take the proper steps, the wide-awake citizen should take the law into his own hands.
- No matter how they act on the surface, men are interested in women for only one reason.
- After the war, we may expect a crime wave; the control of gangsters and ruffians will become a major social problem.
- Human nature being what it is, there will always be war and conflict.
- When you come right down to it, it's human nature never to do anything without an eye to one's own profit.

According to the present theory, the antidemocratic individual, because he has had to accept numerous externally imposed restrictions upon the satisfaction of his needs, harbors strong underlying aggressive impulses. As we have seen, one outlet for this aggression is through displacement onto outgroups leading to moral indignation and authoritarian aggression. Undoubtedly this is a very serviceable device for the individual; yet the strong underlying aggression seems at the same time to express itself in some other way—in a nonmoralized way. It was assumed, of course, that primitive aggressive impulses are rarely expressed with complete directness by adults, but must instead be sufficiently modified, or at least justified, so that they are acceptable to the ego.

The present variable, then, refers to rationalized, ego-accepted, nonmoralized aggression. The supposition was that a subject could express this tendency by agreeing with statements which though thoroughly aggressive were couched in such terms as to avoid his moral censorship. Thus, some items offered justifications for aggression, and were formulated in such a way that strong agreement would indicate that the subject needed only slight justification in order to be ready for all-out aggression. Other items dealt with contempt for mankind, the theory being that here the hostility is so generalized, so free of direction against any particular object, that the individual need not feel accountable for it. Still another guiding conception was that a person can most freely express aggression when he believes that everybody is doing it and, hence, if he wants to be aggressive, he is disposed to believe that everybody *is* doing it, e.g., that it is "human nature" to exploit and to make war upon one's neighbors. It goes without saying that such undifferentiated aggressiveness could easily, by means of propaganda, be directed against minority groups, or against any group the persecution of which was politically profitable.

h. *Projectivity*

- The sexual orgies of the old Greeks and Romans are nursery school stuff compared to some of the goings-on in this country today, even in circles where people might least expect it.
- After the war, we may expect a crime wave; the control of gangsters and ruffians will become a major social problem.
- It is entirely possible that this series of wars and conflicts will be ended once and for all by a world-destroying earthquake, flood, or other catastrophe.
- To a greater extent than most people realize, our lives are governed by plots hatched in secret by politicians.
- Nowadays when so many different kinds of people move around so much and mix together so freely, a person has to be especially careful to protect himself against infection and disease.

The mechanism of projection was mentioned in connection with authoritarian aggression: The suppressed impulses of the authoritarian character tend to be projected onto other people who are then blamed out of hand. Projection is thus a device for keeping id drives ego-alien, and it may be taken as a sign of the ego's inadequacy in carrying out its function. Indeed, in one sense most of the items of the F scale are projective: they involve the assumption that judgments and interpretations of fact are distorted by psychological urges. The subject's tendency to project is utilized, in the present group of items, in an attempt to gain access to some of the deeper trends in his personality. If the antidemocratic individual is disposed to see in the outer world impulses which are suppressed in himself, and we wish to know what these impulses are, then something may be learned by noting what attributes he most readily, but unrealistically, ascribes to the world around him. If an individual insists that someone has hostile designs on him, and we can find no evidence that this is true, we have good reason to suspect that our subject himself has aggressive intentions and is seeking by means of projection to justify them. ✳ ✳ ✳ Similarly, it seemed that the greater a subject's preoccupation with "evil forces" in the world, as shown by his readiness to think about and to believe in the existence of such phenomena as wild erotic excesses, plots and conspiracies, and danger from natural catastrophes, the stronger would be his own unconscious urges of both sexuality and destructiveness.

i. *Sex*

- Homosexuality is a particularly rotten form of delinquency and ought to be severely punished.
- No matter how they act on the surface, men are interested in women for only one reason.
- The sexual orgies of the old Greeks and Romans are nursery school stuff compared to some of the goings-on in this country today, even in circles where people might least expect it.

- Sex crimes, such as rape and attacks on children, deserve more than mere imprisonment; such criminals ought to be publicly whipped.

Concern with overt sexuality is represented in the F scale by four items, two of which have appeared in connection with authoritarian aggression and one other as an expression of projectivity. This is an example of the close interaction of all the present variables; since taken together they constitute a totality, it follows that a single question may pertain to two or more aspects of the whole. * * *

The present variable is conceived of as ego-alien sexuality.[5] A strong inclination to punish vi-olators of sex mores (homosexuals, sex offenders) may be an expression of a general punitive attitude based on identification with ingroup authorities, but it also suggests that the subject's own sexual desires are suppressed and in danger of getting out of hand. A readiness to believe in "sex orgies" may be an indication of a general tendency to distort reality through projection, but sexual content would hardly be projected unless the subject had impulses of this same kind that were unconscious and strongly active. The three items pertaining to the punishment of homosexuals and of sex criminals and to the existence of sex orgies may, therefore, give some indication of the strength of the subject's unconscious sexual drives.

* * *

---

[5]Ego-alien sexuality consists of sexual feelings that one has difficulty accepting as part of the self. It can lead to feeling that one's own impulses are mysterious or disgusting and—by projection—that the behavior of others is as well.

Consistency and Specificity in Behavior

Walter Mischel

The "book that launched a thousand rebuttals" is Walter Mischel's (1968) Personality and Assessment. This book, widely perceived as an all-out frontal assault on the existence of personality traits and the viability of personality psychology, touched off the "person-situation debate," which lasted 20 years. Put briefly, the debate was over this issue: For determining what an individual does, which is more important, stable aspects of his or her personality, or the situation he or she happens to be in at the time? You have already seen that Allport's view, which is the traditional view of the trait approach, is that personality is an important determinant of behavior. And you saw in the previous selection how this assumption can lead to explaining behavior in terms of important traits like authoritarianism. Mischel's view is that people act very differently in different situations, to the point that characterizing them in terms of broad personality traits may be neither meaningful nor useful.

The next selection is drawn from one of the key chapters of Mischel's book. In it, Mischel argues that inconsistency in behavior is the rule rather than the exception. He surveys, very briefly, a large number of studies that attempted to find strong relationships between what individuals did in one situation and what they did in another. In Mischel's view, such studies generally have failed. Specifically, Mischel assumes that if the relationship between behaviors in two different situations yields a correlation coefficient (see the Horowitz selection in Part I) of less than about .30, not enough of the variance in behavior has been explained to make it useful to assume that both behaviors are affected by the same underlying personality trait. Of course, the selection by Rosenthal and Rubin in Part I provides a different—and more optimistic—interpretation of a correlation of about .30.

Although the field of personality and what Allport called the "doctrine of traits" ultimately survived the Mischelian onslaught, the book and this chapter remain important landmarks in the recent history of personality psychology. First, the ideas presented in this chapter had a powerful effect on the viewpoint of many psychologists within and outside the field of personality, an effect that more than 25 years later has still not dissipated. To this day, a surprising number of psychologists "don't believe in personality." Second and even more impor-

tant, with the words you are about to read Mischel forced the field of personality into an agonizing reappraisal of some of its most basic and cherished assumptions. Although these assumptions can be said to have survived, their close reexamination was on the whole potentially beneficial for our understanding of personality (see the selection by Kenrick and Funder later in this section).

From *Personality and Assessment*, by W. Mischel (1968), pp. 13–39. New York: Wiley. Adapted with permission of the author and Lawrence Erlbaum Associates.

For more than 50 years personality psychologists have tried to measure traits and states in order to discover personality structure and dynamics. There has been an enormous effort to investigate the reliability and, more recently, the validity of the results. This chapter examines some of the evidence for the assumption of generalized personality traits and states. Empirically, the generality of a trait is established by the associations found among trait indicators. The evidence consists of obtained correlations between behaviors measured across similar situations. Data that demonstrate strong generality in the behavior of the same person across many situations are critical for trait and state personality theories; the construct of personality itself rests on the belief that individual behavioral consistencies exist widely and account for much of the variance in behavior. Most definitions of personality hinge on the assumption that an individual's behavior is consistent across many stimulus conditions (e.g., Sanford, 1963).

Data on the generality-specificity of behavior usually fall under the rubric of "reliability" and are separated from "validity" evidence. This distinction between reliability and validity is not very sharp. Both reliability and validity are established by demonstrating relations between responses to various stimulus conditions. The stimulus conditions are the particular measures and settings used to sample responses. *Reliability* concerns the congruence among responses measured under maximally *similar* stimulus conditions (Campbell, 1960; Campbell & Fiske, 1959). *Validity*, in contradistinction to reliability, requires convergence between responses to maximally *different*, independent stimulus conditions or measures.[1] The distinction between reliability and validity research depends chiefly on judgments about the degree of similarity among the stimuli used to evoke responses with the particular eliciting techniques or tests employed. For example, correlations among two similar tests, or of two forms of one test, or of the same test administered to the same person on different occasions, all are taken as reliability evidence; correlations among more dissimilar tests, on the other hand, are interpreted as validity data. This chapter is concerned mainly with reliability evidence and evaluates the behavioral consistencies obtained under relatively similar stimulus conditions. We shall look at several kinds of data, first examining the consistency of intellectual variables and then turning to measures of personality. Throughout this chapter some of the empirical evidence for the cross-situational generality of behavior will be reviewed in order to assess more concretely the appropriateness of the

---

[1] Our reading of Cronbach and Meehl and of Campbell and Fiske (see Part I) suggests that validity implies something much more, and sometimes much different than this simple characterization. Validity concerns the convergence between patterns of data that are theoretically predicted and those that are empirically obtained. The patterns are not necessarily simple consistency of the sort Mischel describes. For example, recall that the authoritarian is subservient to authority and domineering with subordinates, which is at a surface level inconsistent. Yet this very inconsistency is an important part of the authoritarian syndrome.

trait assumptions which have had such a marked impact on the field.

* * *

Personality Variables

* * *

Personality variables have been examined thoroughly to determine individual consistencies with respect to particular dimensions or dispositions. The following personality dimensions are representative of those attracting most theoretical and research interest during the last decade, and some of the evidence for their consistency is examined. It will become apparent rapidly that the generality of these dispositions usually is far less than that found for cognitive and intellectual variables.[2]

ATTITUDES TOWARD AUTHORITY AND PEERS. The belief that an individual has generalized attitudes toward classes of persons pervades clinical, diagnostic, and research practice. This belief is reflected in the common assumption that problems of sibling rivalry repeat themselves in peer relations, and that attitudes toward parental figures are mirrored in reactions to diverse authority figures throughout life and toward the psychotherapist in particular. Psychologists of many theoretical orientations often agree that persons develop highly generalized attitudes toward authority. Freud, Piaget, and Rogers, among others, all posit that reactions toward authority originate in the family situation and manifest themselves as broadly generalized attitudes expressed in many contexts toward superiors in later social situations. As Piaget puts it:

> Day to day observation and psycho-analytic experience show that the first personal schemas are afterward generalised and applied to many people. According as the first inter-individual experiences of the child who is just learning to speak are con-

nected with a father who is understanding or dominating, loving or cruel, etc., the child will tend (even throughout life if these relationships have influenced his whole youth) to assimilate all other individuals to this father schema. (Piaget, 1951, p. 207)

These assumptions have been subjected to a rare and extensive test by Burwen and Campbell (1957). Burwen and Campbell studied a large sample of Air Force personnel by means of interviews, TAT,[3] description of self and others, judgments of photos, and autobiographical inventories, as well as an attitude survey and sociometric questionnaire.[4] Through each of these techniques, where possible, attitudes were scored toward own father, symbolic authority (e.g., in responses to pictures of older persons on the TAT), immediate boss, immediate peers, and symbolic peers. The topics or attitude objects and the measures for scoring attitudes toward authority on each are summarized below:

Topic	Measures
Father	Interview; description of self and others; autobiographical inventory
Symbolic authority	Interview; TAT (scored globally); TAT (scored objectively); judgments of photos (of older persons); attitude survey
Boss	Interview; description of self and others; autobiographical inventory; sociometric questionnaire

---

[2]In a section of this chapter that has been omitted, Mischel acknowledged that cognitive and intellectual variables, such as IQ and cognitive style, are relatively consistent over time and across situations.

[3]The TAT is the Thematic Apperception Test, in which a person looks at a picture (e.g., of a person working at a desk) and makes up a story about what is going on. This story can then be scored in various ways, most commonly as to the motivations that it reveals.

[4]A sociometric questionnaire is one in which members of a group are asked about their impressions of or feelings about one another.

TABLE 12.1

MEAN CORRELATIONS AMONG ATTITUDES MEASURED
BY DIFFERENT METHODS

Attitude toward		F	SA	B	P	SP
Father	F	.35	.12	.03	.06	.08
Symbolic authority	SA		.15	.08	.10	.06
Boss	B			.09	.13	.03
Peer	P				.22	.07
Symbolic peer	SP					.01

(Adapted from Burwen & Campbell, 1957, p. 26.)

Similar measures were used to score attitudes toward real and symbolic peers.

The interjudge reliability of all ratings on each instrument was adequately high, and scores were available on twenty variables. Their intercorrelations revealed, first of all, the major impact of stimulus similarity or "method variance": for three quarters of all the variables the highest correlations occurred between measures of different attitudes based on the *same* instrument. When these method-produced correlations were disregarded, there was little evidence for generality of attitudes either toward authority or toward peers. Attitudes toward father, symbolic authority, and boss were no more highly correlated with each other than they were with attitudes toward real or symbolic peers, and all correlations tended to be low.

Table 12.1 shows the average of transformed correlations between attitude topics, eliminating those based on the same instrument. Of the correlations between different measures of attitude toward a *single* type of authority figure, only among attitudes toward father and among attitudes toward peers are there any indications that independent methods tap a specific attitude focus at least to some extent. Even these associations among different measures of attitudes toward the same type of authority were very modest, being .35 for father and .22 for peers. Attitude toward *different* types of authority figures showed no consistency at all. For example, attitude toward one's

father correlated .03 with attitude toward one's boss. The authors appropriately concluded that:

> Evidence for a generalized attitude toward authority which encompasses attitudes toward father, symbolic authority, and boss is totally negative, suggesting the need for reconsideration of the applicability of commonly held theory in this area. (Burwen & Campbell, 1957, p. 31)

MORAL BEHAVIOR Psychodynamic theory has emphasized the role of the "superego" as an internalized moral agency that has a critical role in the regulation of all forms of conduct and in the control of impulses. Theorizing regarding the superego has focused on the way in which authority figures and their values become "incorporated" during the course of socialization. It has been assumed that as a result of this process the child adopts parental standards and controls as his own. There is no doubt that in the course of development most children acquire the capacity to regulate, judge, and monitor their own behavior even in the absence of external constraints and authorities. An important theoretical issue, however, is the consistency of these self-regulated patterns of conduct and self-control.

In the extraordinarily extensive and sophisticated Character Education Inquiry, more than thirty years ago,[5] thousands of children were ex-

---

[5]That is, more than 30 years before this book was published in 1968.

posed to various situations in which they could cheat, lie, and steal in diverse settings, including the home, party games, and athletic contexts (Hartshorne & May, 1928; Hartshorne, May, & Shuttleworth, 1930).

Although moral conduct was relatively inconsistent, the children showed substantial consistency in their self-reported opinions and thoughts about moral issues elicited on paper-and-pencil tests administered in the classroom. High correlations also were found between various forms of these paper-and-pencil tests. However, if children took alternate equivalent forms of the same tests in diverse social settings—such as at home, in Sunday school, at club meetings, as well as in the classroom—the correlations of their scores among situations were reduced to about .40. The investigators concluded that children vary their opinions to "suit the situation" (Hartshorne, May, & Shuttleworth, 1930, p. 108) and do not have a generalized code of morals.

The specificity of responses, and their dependence on the exact particulars of the evoking situation, was keenly noted by Hartshorne and May (1928). For example:

> . . . even such slight changes in the situation as between crossing out A's and putting dots in squares are sufficient to alter the amount of deception both in individuals and in groups. (p. 382)

To illustrate further from their data, copying from an answer key on one test correlated .696 with copying from a key on another test, and cheating by adding on scores from a speed test correlated .440 with adding on scores on another speed test. However, copying from a key on one test correlated only .292 with adding on scores. Moreover, the average intercorrelations among four classroom tests was only .256 (Hartshorne & May, 1928, p. 383). The more the situation changed the lower the correlations became. The average correlation between four classroom tests and two out-of-classroom tests (contests and stealing) was .167. The lying test given in the classroom averaged .234 with the other classroom tests but

only .061 with the two out-of-classroom deception tests (p. 384).

* * *

The observations that Hartshorne and May reported for the relative specificity of moral behavior accurately foreshadowed the findings that emerged from later research on other behavioral consistencies. Response specificity of the kind emphasized by Hartshorne and May is also reflected, for example, in the finding that questionnaires dealing with attitudes and hypothetical matters may correlate with other questionnaires but are less likely to relate to non-self-report behavior (Mischel, 1962). In one study, children were asked questions about whether or not they would postpone immediate smaller rewards for the sake of larger but delayed outcomes in hypothetical situations. Their answers in these hypothetical delay of reward situations were found to relate to other questionnaires dealing with trust and a variety of verbally expressed attitudes. What they said, however, was unrelated to their actual delay of reward choices in real situations (Mischel, 1962). Likewise, measures eliciting direct nonverbal behavior may relate to other behavioral indices in the same domain but not to questionnaires. Thus real behavioral choices between smaller but immediately available gratifications, as opposed to larger but delayed rewards, correlated significantly with such behavioral indices as resistance to temptation, but not with self reports on questionnaires (Mischel, 1962).

Moral guilt also has been studied utilizing projective test[6] responses. For example, in a study with teenage boys (Allinsmith, 1960) moral feelings were inferred from the subjects' projective story completions in response to descriptions of various kinds of immoral actions. The findings led Allinsmith to the view that a person with a truly generalized conscience is a statistical rarity. Johnson (1962) also found that moral judgments across situations

---

[6]A projective test is one in which a subject is shown an ambiguous stimulus (e.g., an inkblot, a TAT picture) and asked for his or her interpretation. The subject's answer is assumed to be a "projection" of some aspect of his or her underlying psychology.

tend to be highly specific and even discrepant.

Recent research on moral behavior has concentrated on three areas: moral judgment and verbal standards of right and wrong (e.g., Kohlberg, 1963); resistance to temptation in the absence of external constraint (e.g., Aronfreed & Reber, 1965; Grinder, 1962; MacKinnon, 1938; Mischel & Gilligan, 1964); and post-transgression indices of remorse and guilt (e.g., Allinsmith, 1960; Aronfreed, 1961; Sears, Maccoby, & Levin, 1957; Whiting, 1959). These three areas of moral behavior turn out to be either completely independent or at best only minimally interrelated (Becker, 1964; Hoffman, 1963; Kohlberg, 1963). Within each area specificity also tends to be the rule. For example, an extensive survey of all types of reactions to transgression yielded no predictable relationships among specific types of reaction (Aronfreed, 1961). Similarly, Sears and his coworkers (1965, chapter 6) did not find consistent associations among various reactions to transgression. Thus the data on moral behavior provide no support for the widespread psychodynamic belief in a unitary intrapsychic moral agency like the superego, or for a unitary trait entity of conscience or honesty. Rather than acquiring a homogeneous conscience that determines uniformly all aspects of their self-control, people seem to develop subtler discriminations that depend on many considerations.

SEXUAL IDENTIFICATION, DEPENDENCY, AND AGGRESSION It is widely assumed in most dynamic and trait theories that people develop firm masculine or feminine identifications early in life. These stable identifications, in turn, are believed to exert pervasive effects on what the person does in many diverse situations (e.g., Kohlberg, 1966). There is, of course, no doubt that boys and girls rapidly learn about sex differences and soon recognize their own gender permanently. A much less obvious issue is the extent to which children develop highly consistent patterns of masculine or feminine "sex-typed" behavior. This question has received considerable research attention. The chief strategy has involved studying the associations among different indicators of masculine and feminine sex-typed behavior.

Dependency and aggression often serve conceptually as behavioral referents for sex typing, with boys expected to be more aggressive and girls more dependent. In dependency research, although Beller's (1955) correlations ranged from .48 to .83 for teacher ratings of five dependency components in nursery school children, it is likely that a "halo" effect spuriously inflated the teachers' ratings.[7] Mann (1959) obtained ratings of 55 two-minute observations of 41 nursery school children in free play on six kinds of dependency behavior. He found only 1 of 15 intercorrelations among components of dependency significant. Likewise, observations of nursery school children revealed that the frequencies of "affection seeking" and "approval seeking" were unrelated (Heathers, 1953).

Sears (1963) extensively studied the intercorrelations between five categories of dependency behavior in preschool girls and boys. The five categories were: *negative attention seeking*, e.g., attention getting by disruption or aggressive activity; *positive attention seeking*, as in seeking praise; nonaggressive *touching or holding; being near*, e.g., following a child or teacher; and *seeking reassurance*. The frequency of these behaviors was carefully and reliably scored by observing the children at nursery school with an extensive time-sampling procedure. Each child was observed in free play for a total of 7 to 10 hours. The intercorrelations among the five dependency categories for 21 boys and 19 girls are shown in Table 12.2. Note that only 1 of the 20 correlations reached statistical significance since for 20 degrees of freedom correlations of .423 and .537 would have been needed to reach significance at the .05 and .01 levels respectively.[8]

---

[7]A "halo effect" occurs when a rater's global positive or negative evaluation of a target person affects all of her or his ratings.

[8]The .05 and .01 significance levels are conventional criteria by which findings are judged not to have occurred merely by chance.

TABLE 12.2

INTERCORRELATIONS AMONG DEPENDENCY MEASURES[a]

Measures		I	II	III	IV	V
Negative attention	I		.06	.10	.15	.37
Reassurance	II	.24		.25	.19	.26
Positive attention	III	.23	.11		.11	.03
Touching and holding	IV	.01	.11	.16		.71
Being near	V	.03	.12	.14	.13	

(Adapted from Sears, 1963, p. 35.)
[a]Girls above diagonal, boys below.

* * *

Some support for sex differences in the generality of particular patterns of sex-typed behaviors comes in the form of more (and stronger) intercorrelations for girls than boys on five observation measures of dependency (Sears, 1963), whereas the reverse holds for aggression, with more intercorrelations among aggression variables for boys than for girls (Lansky, Crandall, Kagan, & Baker, 1961; Sears, 1961). However, individuals discriminate sharply between situations. The specificity of aggressive behavior, for example, is documented in a study of highly aggressive boys by Bandura (1960). Parents who punished aggression in the home, but who simultaneously modeled aggressive behavior and encouraged it in their sons' peer relationships, produced boys who were nonaggressive at home but markedly aggressive at school.

RIGIDITY AND TOLERANCE FOR AMBIGUITY If individuals did develop strongly consistent character structures that channelized them in stable ways, it would be important to identify these syndromes. One of the most thoroughly studied personality patterns is the "authoritarian personality." Intolerance for ambiguity attracted considerable interest as a characteristic of the authoritarian personality (Adorno Frenkel-Brunswik, Levinson, & Sanford, 1950), and a voluminous literature was devoted to elaborating its correlates.

Several behavioral signs have been used as the referents for intolerance for ambiguity. These signs include resistance to reversal of apparent fluctuating stimuli, early selection and adherence to one solution in perceptually ambiguous situations, seeking for certainty, rigid dichotomizing into fixed categories, premature closure, and the like. In one study, an extensive battery of tests to measure intolerance of ambiguity was designed and administered (Kenny & Ginsberg, 1958). Only 7 of the 66 correlations among intolerance of ambiguity measures reached significance and the relationship for 2 of these was opposite to the predicted direction. Moreover, the measures in the main failed to correlate with the usual questionnaire indices of authoritarianism submissiveness as elicited by a form of the California F scale.

Closely related to authoritarianism, "rigidity" is another personality dimension that has received much attention as a generalized trait (Chown, 1959; Cronbach, 1956). In one study (Applezweig, 1954), among 45 correlations between behaviors on six measures of rigidity (including arithmetic problems, Rorschach,[9] and F scale), 22 were negative, 21 were positive, and 2 were zero; only 3 of the 45 correlations were significant and 2 of these were negative. Likewise, Pervin's (1960) data on five noninventory performance measures of rigidity, including the water-jars problems, provide generally low associations and suggest that "individuals may be rigid in one area of personality functioning and not in another" and that "rigidity

---

[9]The Rorschach is the famous projective test in which subjects are asked what they see in blots of ink.

is not a general personality characteristic" (p. 394). The conclusion that rigidity is not a unitary trait is also supported by the modest intercorrelations between measures obtained by Wrightsman and Baumeister (1961) and by the specificity found earlier by Maher (1957).

* * *

Thus investigators frequently measure and describe a purportedly general dimension of behavior only to discover later that it has dubious consistency. As a result the popular dimensions of personality research often wax and wane almost like fashions. Research on the generality of the behavioral indices of personality dimensions has generated its own truisms. Over and over again the conclusions of these investigations, regardless of the specific content area, are virtually identical and predictable. The following paragraph, from Applezweig's (1954) own summary, is essentially interchangeable with those from a plethora of later researches on the generality of many different traits:

> The following conclusions appear to be justified: (a) There is no general factor of rigidity among a number of so-called measures of rigidity; the interrelationships of these measures appear to vary with the nature of the tests employed and the conditions of test administration as well as behavioral determinants within S's. (b) Scores obtained by an individual on any so-called measure of rigidity appear to be a function not only of the individual, but also of the nature of the test and the conditions of test administration. (Applezweig, 1954, p. 228)

* * *

CONDITIONABILITY Classical learning formulations place great emphasis on conditioning as a basic process in learning. Consequently psychologists with an interest in both learning and individual differences have been especially interested in studying conditionability as a personality dimension. In spite of a great deal of research, however, there is no evidence for the existence of a general factor or trait of "conditionability" in either classical or operant conditioning paradigms.

Correlations among different measures and types of conditioning tend to be low or zero (e.g., Bunt & Barendregt, 1961; Campbell, 1938; Davidson, Payne, & Sloane, 1964; Eysenck, 1965; Franks, 1956; Lovibond, 1964; Moore & Marcuse, 1945; Patterson & Hinsey, 1964). Moore and Marcuse (1945) noted many years ago that "the concept of good or poor conditioners must always be with reference to a specific response." Reviewing the literature two decades later, Eysenck (1965) points out that correlations between conditionability measures depend on specific peripheral factors (sweat glands in the hand, pain sensitivity of the cornea). He also notes that even if these sources were eliminated correlations would still be affected by situational circumstances such as the sequence and massing of stimuli, the scheduling of reinforcement, the strength of CS and UCS, temporal intervals, and so on.

The evidence that learning variables like conditionability are unitary traitlike entities is no more convincing than the data for the consistency of personality traits couched in any other theoretical language. Whenever individual differences are elicited, however, the failure to demonstrate impressive reliability does not preclude the existence of extensive correlations with other response measures (e.g., Franks, 1961).

MODERATOR VARIABLES Wallach (1962) and Kogan and Wallach (1964) have called attention to the fact that "moderator variables" may influence the correlations found in research on behavioral consistency. By moderator variables Wallach and Kogan mean interactions among several variables that influence the correlations obtained between any one of the variables and other data. For example, correlations between two response patterns may be found for males, but not for females, or may even be positive for one sex but negative for the other. Thus, if the correlations between two response patterns are examined for both sexes combined, the different relations that might be obtained if each sex were taken into account separately could become obscured. Similarly, relations between two measures might be positive for children with high IQ but negative for those with low IQ. In other words, there are complex interactions so that the relations between any two variables depend on several other variables.

By analyzing their data to illuminate higher-order interactions of this kind, these investigators have been able to demonstrate significant associations among various measures of risk taking, and between risk taking and other variables. The resulting associations of course apply only to some subjects under a few conditions. This strategy of searching for interactions holds some promise. Since the interactions are obtained post hoc rather than predicted, however, considerable interpretative caution must be observed. Otherwise the analysis of the same data for many interactions provides many additional chances to obtain seemingly statistically significant results that actually monopolize on chance. That is, more "significant" associations occur by chance when more correlations are computed.

TEMPORAL STABILITY So far, our discussion of consistency has focused on relationships among a person's behaviors across situations sampled more or less at the same time. Equally important, however, are data that examine how stable the individual's behavior remains in any one particular domain when he is reassessed at later times.

Results from the Fels Longitudinal Study give some typical examples of the stability of a person's behavior patterns over time (Kagan & Moss, 1962). The overall findings suggest some significant consistency between childhood and early adulthood ratings of achievement behavior, sex-typed activity, and spontaneity for both sexes. For certain other variables, like dependency, some consistency was found for one sex but not the other. Thus the rated dependency of girls at age six years to ten years correlated .30 with their adult dependence on family; the comparable correlation for boys was near zero. In the same longitudinal study of middle class subjects the most highly significant positive associations were found between ratings of achievement and recognition strivings obtained at various periods of childhood and in

early adulthood (Kagan & Moss, 1962; Moss & Kagan, 1961). Children who were rated as showing strong desires for recognition also tended to be rated as more concerned with excellence and with the attainment of high self-imposed standards when they were interviewed as young adults. Some of the many correlations between achievement strivings in childhood and comparable adult preoccupation with attaining excellence were exceptionally high, in several instances reaching the .60 to .70 range.

Apart from ratings the motive or need to achieve ("n Ach") has also been studied most extensively by scoring the subject's achievement imagery in the stories he tells to selected TAT cards. For example, if the person creates stories in which the hero is studying hard for a profession and aspires and strives to improve himself and to advance in his career, the story receives high n Ach scores. This technique, developed thoroughly by McClelland and his associates (1953), has become the main index of the motive to achieve and to compete against standards of excellence. As a result considerable attention has been devoted to studying the stability of this need by comparing n Ach scores obtained from the same individuals at different times. Moss and Kagan (1961) reported a stability coefficient of .31 for their sample over a 10-year period from adolescence to adulthood. They also reported a 3-year stability coefficient of .32 for TAT achievement themes obtained at ages 8 and 11 (Kagan & Moss, 1959). However, the correlation between n Ach at age 8 and at age 14 was only .22; the correlation between n Ach at age 11 and at 14 years was a nonsignificant .16.

The stability of achievement motivation was also studied closely for shorter time intervals with other samples of people. Birney (1959) reported a coefficient of only .29 for n Ach on equivalent picture forms administered to college students within six months. He concluded that ". . . the n Ach measure is highly situational in character . . ." (p. 267). Similarly, a significant but modest coefficient of .26 was reported for a 9-week test-retest study with college students (Krumboltz & Farquhar, 1957). Higher correlations ranging from .36 to .61

have been found for shorter time intervals of 3 weeks to 5 weeks (Haber & Alpert, 1958; Morgan, 1953). Reviewing a great deal of information from many studies, Skolnick (1966a, b) reported extensive correlations between diverse adolescent and adult measures. Many correlations reached significance, especially for achievement and power imagery indices, although the associations tended to be extremely complicated and most often of modest magnitude.

Just as with consistency across situations, stability over time tends to be greatest for behaviors associated with intelligence and cognitive processes (e.g., Bloom, 1964; Gardner & Long, 1960; Kagan & Moss, 1962; Moss & Kagan, 1961). Most notably, extremely impressive stability over long time periods has been found for certain cognitive styles. Retest correlations on Witkin's rod-and-frame test (RFT), for example, were as high as .92 for time intervals of a few years (Witkin, Goodenough, & Karp, 1967). A time lapse of 14 years was the lengthiest interval sampled in their longitudinal study. Even after such a long period, the stability correlation for boys tested with the RFT at age 10 and retested at age 24 was .66. Data of this kind demonstrate genuine durability in aspects of cognitive and perceptual functioning.

A representative illustration of temporal stability comes from studies of behavior during interviews. Reasonable stability has been demonstrated for certain interaction patterns during interviews. These patterns were measured by an interaction chronograph devised to record selected temporal aspects of verbal and gestural behavior (e.g., Matarazzo, 1965; Saslow, Matarazzo, Phillips, & Matarazzo, 1957). In these studies the interviewer followed a standardized pattern of behavior, including systematic periods of "not responding," "interrupting," and other variations in style. The subject's corresponding behavior was scored on formal dimensions such as the frequency of his actions, their average duration, and the length of his silences. The results indicated that these interactions are highly stable across short time periods (such as 1-week retests) when the interviewer's behavior remains fixed. The same

interactions, however, were readily and predictably modifiable by planned changes in the interviewer's behavior.

The trait-descriptive categories and personality labels with which individuals describe themselves on questionnaires and trait-rating scales seem to be especially long lasting. E. L. Kelly (1955) compared questionnaire trait self-descriptions obtained almost 20 years apart. During the years 1935–1938 several personality questionnaires were administered to 300 engaged couples, and most of them were retested with the same measures in 1954. The questionnaires included the Strong Vocational Interest Blank, the Allport-Vernon values test, and the Bernreuter personality questionnaire, among others. Self-reports of attitudes about marriage were highly unstable ($r < .10$), but the stability coefficients for self-descriptions of interests, of economic and political values, of self-confidence and sociability were high. The coefficients for these areas of self-reported traits ranged from about .45 to slightly over .60, indicating impressive stability, considering the long temporal delay between assessments.

As another example, the test retest correlations on the California Psychological Inventory scales for high school students retested after 1 year, and for a sample of prisoners retested after a lapse of 7 to 21 days, were also high (Gough, 1957). In general, trait self-descriptions on many personality questionnaires show considerable stability (Byrne, 1966). Studies of the semantic differential also suggest that the meanings associated with semantic concepts may be fairly stable (Osgood, Suci, & Tannenbaum, 1957).

Research on the temporal stability of personal constructs evoked by Kelly's Role Construct Repertory Test (Reptest) also indicates considerable consistency in constructs over time (Bonarius, 1965). For example, a retest correlation of .79 was found for constructs after a 2-week interval (Landfield, Stern, & Fjeld, 1961). * * * Thus the trait categories people attribute to themselves and others may be relatively permanent, and may be more enduring than the behaviors to which they refer.

Implications

The data on cross-situational consistency and stability over time reviewed in this chapter merely provide representative examples from an enormous domain. The results indicate that correlations across situations tend to be highest for cognitive and intellectual functions. Moreover, behaviors sampled in closely similar situations generally yield the best correlations. Considerable stability over time has been demonstrated for some domains, and again particularly for ability and cognitive measures. Self-descriptions on trait dimensions also seem to be especially consistent even over very long periods of time.

As early as 1928 Hartshorne and May surprised psychologists by showing that the honesty or moral behavior of children is not strongly consistent across situations and measures. The Hartshorne and May data were cited extensively but did not influence psychological theorizing about the generality of traits. Similar evidence for behavioral specificity across situations has been reported over and over again for personality measures since the earliest correlational studies at the turn of the century. Considerable specificity has been found regularly even for syndromes like attitudes toward authority, or aggression and dependency, whose assumed generality has reached the status of a cliché in psychological writings.

The interpretation of all data on behavioral consistency is affected of course by the criteria selected. Consistency coefficients averaging between .30 and .40, of the kind obtained by Hartshorne and May, can be taken either as evidence for the relative specificity of the particular behaviors or as support for the presence of underlying generality. Indeed, the Hartshorne and May data have been reinterpreted as evidence for generality in children's moral behavior, at least across related situations (Burton, 1963). Similarly, McGuire (1968) reviewed data on the consistency of suggestibility, persuasibility, and conformity and concluded that each has the status of a generalized, although "weak," trait. McGuire noted the tenuousness of the evidence, since the data consisted mostly of low but positive correlations which often reached the .05 statistical confidence level, sometimes did not, and which never accounted for more than a trivial proportion of the variance.[10]

There is nothing magical about a correlation coefficient, and its interpretation depends on many considerations. The accuracy or reliability of measurement increases with the length of the test. Since no single item is a perfect measure, adding items increases the chance that the test will elicit a more accurate sample and yield a better estimate of the person's behavior. Second, a test may be reliable at one score level but unreliable at another. That is, the accuracy of the test is not necessarily uniform for different groups of people; a test that yields reliable achievement scores for 10-year-old children may be so difficult for 7-year-olds that they are reduced to guessing on almost all items. Moreover, different items within the same test do not necessarily yield uniformly reliable information (Cronbach, 1960). The interpretation of reliability coefficients is influenced by the relative homogeneity or heterogeneity in the tested behavior range of the sample of subjects. For example, if an ability test is given to a more or less uniformly bright group of college students, very slight errors in measurement could obscure actual individual differences. Any one set of observations provides merely a sample of behavior whose meaning may be confounded by numerous errors of measurement.

These and similar statistical considerations (Cronbach, 1960) caution us to interpret the meaning of particular coefficients with care. In spite of methodological reservations, however, it is

---

[10]Mischel is here following the common practice of squaring a correlation to yield the percent of variance "explained" (see the selection by Rosenthal and Rubin in Part I). Thus a correlation of .30 is said to explain 9% of the variance (.30 squared being .09) and a correlation of .40 is said to explain 16% of the variance (.40 squared being .16). Mischel regards these percentages as "trivial." But recall that Rosenthal and Rubin (Part I) demonstrated that a correlation of .32 yields correct classification twice as often as incorrect classification.

evident that the behaviors which are often construed as stable personality trait indicators actually are highly specific and depend on the details of the evoking situations and the response mode employed to measure them.

* * *

It is important to distinguish clearly between "statistically significant" associations and equivalence. A correlation of .30 easily reaches statistical significance when the sample of subjects is sufficiently large, and suggests an association that is highly unlikely on the basis of chance. However, the same coefficient accounts for less than 10 percent of the relevant variance. Statistically significant relationships of this magnitude are sufficient to justify personality research on individual and group differences. It is equally plain that their value for making statements about an individual is severely limited. Even when statistically significant behavioral consistencies are found, and even when they replicate reliably, the relationships usually are not large enough to warrant individual assessment and treatment decisions except for certain screening and selection purposes.

It is very easy to misunderstand the meaning of the findings on behavioral consistency and specificity surveyed in this chapter. It would be a complete misinterpretation, for instance, to conclude that individual differences are unimportant.[11] To remind oneself of their pervasive role one need merely observe the differences among people's responses to almost any complex social stimulus under most supposedly uniform laboratory conditions. The real questions are not the existence of differences among individuals but rather their nature, their causes and consequences, and the utility of inferring them for particular purposes and by particular techniques.

Consistency coefficients of the kind reviewed in this chapter are only one of several types of data pertinent to an appropriate evaluation of the em-

pirical status of the main trait and state approaches to personality. It would be premature therefore to attempt to draw conclusions at this point. Sophisticated dispositional personality theories increasingly have come to recognize that behavior tends to change with alterations in the situations in which it occurs. They note, however, that the same basic underlying disposition (or "genotype") may manifest itself behaviorally in diverse ways in different situations so that heterogeneous behaviors can be signs of the same underlying trait or state. According to this argument, the dependent person, for example, need not behave dependently in all situations; indeed his basic dependency may show itself in diverse and seemingly contradictory overt forms. Although fundamentally dependent, he may, for instance, try to appear aggressively dependent, he may, for instance, try to appear aggressively independent under some circumstances, and even may become belligerent and hostile in other settings in efforts to deny his dependency. Similarly, and in accord with psychodynamic theorizing, seemingly diverse acts may be in the service of the same underlying motivational force. For example, a person's overtly liberal political behavior and his overt social conservativism, although apparently inconsistent, may actually both be understandable as expressions of a more fundamental motive, such as his desire to please and win approval and recognition. These arguments for basic consistencies that underlie surface diversity are theoretically defensible, but they ultimately depend, of course, on supporting empirical evidence.

* * *

References

Adorno, I. W., Frenkel-Brunswik, Else, Levinson, D. J., & Sanford, R. N. *The authoritarian personality.* New York: Harper, 1950.

Allinsmith, W. (1960). The learning of moral standards. In D. R. Miller & G. E. Swanson (Eds.), *Inner conflict and defense* (pp. 141–176). New York: Holt.

Applezweig, Dee G. (1954). Some determinants of behavioral rigidity. *Journal of Abnormal and Social Psychology, 49,* 224–228.

Aronfreed, J. (1961). The nature, variety, and social patterning of moral responses to transgression. *Journal of Abnormal and Social Psychology, 63,* 223–240.

---

[11]Despite this disclaimer, the book from which this excerpt is drawn *was* widely interpreted as arguing—even proving—that stable individual differences in personality are unimportant.

Aronfreed, J. (1964). The origin of self-criticism. *Psychological Review, 71,* 193–218.

Aronfreed, J., & Reber, A. (1965). Internalized behavioral suppression and the timing of social punishment. *Journal of Personality and Social Psychology, 1,* 3–16.

Bandura, A. (1960). Relationship of family patterns to child behavior disorders. Progress Report, U.S.P.H. Research Grant M-1734, Stanford University.

Becker, W. C. (1964). Consequences of different kinds of parental discipline. In M. L. Hoffman & Lois W. Hoffman (Eds.), *Review of child development research,* (Vol. 1, pp. 169–208) New York: Russell Sage Foundation.

Belter, E. K. (1955). Dependency and independence in young children. *Journal of Genetic Psychology, 87,* 25–35.

Birney, R. C. (1959). The reliability of the achievement motive. *Journal of Abnormal and Social Psychology, 58,* 266–267.

Bloom, R. S. (1964). *Stability and change in human characteristics.* New York: Wiley.

Bonarius, J. C. J. (1965). Research in the personal construct theory of George A. Kelly: Role Construct Repertory Test and basic theory. In B. A. Maher (Ed.), *Progress in experimental personality research.* (Vol. 2, pp. 1–46) New York: Academic Press.

Bunt, A. van de, & Barendregt, J. T. (1961). Inter-correlations of three measures of conditioning. In J. T. Barendregt (Ed.), *Research in psychodiagnostics.* The Hague: Mouton.

Burton, R. V. (1963). Generality of honesty reconsidered. *Psychological Review, 70,* 481–499.

Burwen, L. S., & Campbell, D. T. (1957). The generality of attitudes toward authority and nonauthority figures. *Journal of Abnormal and Social Psychology, 54,* 24–31.

Byrne, D. (1966). *An introduction to personality.* Englewood Cliffs, N. J.: Prentice-Hall.

Campbell, A. A. (1938). The interrelations of two measures of conditioning in man. *Journal of Experimental Psychology, 22,* 225–243.

Campbell, D. T. (1960). Recommendations for APA test standards regarding construct, trait, or discriminant validity. *American Psychologist, 15,* 546–553.

Campbell, D., & Fiske, D. (1959). Convergent and discriminant validation by the multitrait-multimethod matrix. *Psychological Bulletin, 56,* 81–105.

Chown, Sheila M. (1959). Rigidity—A flexible concept. *Psychological Bulletin, 56,* 195–223.

Cronbach, L. J. (1956). Assessment of individual differences. *Annual Review of Psychology, 7,* 173–196.

Cronbach, L. J. *Essentials of psychological testing.* (2nd ed.) New York: Harper, 1960.

Davidson, P. O., Payne, R. W., & Sloane, R. B. (1964). Introversion, neuroticism, and conditioning. *Journal of Abnormal and Social Psychology, 68,* 136–148.

Eysenck, II. J. (1965). Extraversion and the acquisition of eyeblink and GSR conditioned responses. *Psychological Bulletin, 63,* 258–270.

Franks, C. M. (1956). Conditioning and personality: A study of normal and neurotic subjects. *Journal of Abnormal and Social Psychology, 52,* 143–150.

Franks, C. M. (1961). Conditioning and abnormal behaviour. In H. J. Eysenck (Ed.), *Handbook of abnormal psychology,* (pp. 457–487). New York: Basic Books.

Gardner, R. W., & Long, R. I. (1960). The stability of cognitive controls. *Journal of Abnormal Social Psychology, 61,* 485–487.

Gough, H. G. (1957). *Manual for the California Psychological Inventory,* Palo Alto, Calif: Consulting Psychologists Press.

Grinder, R. E. (1962). Parental childrearing practices, conscience, and resistance to temptation of sixth-grade children. *Child Development, 33,* 803–820.

Haber, R. N., & Alpert, R. (1958). The role of situation and picture cues in projective measurement of the achievement motive. In J. W. Atkinson (Ed.), *Motives in fantasy, action, and society,* (pp. 644–663). Princeton: Van Nostrand.

Hartshorne, H., & May, M. A. (1928). *Studies in the nature of character.* Vol. I., *Studies in deceit.* New York: Macmillan.

Hartshorne, H., May, M. A., & Shuttleworth, F. K. (1930). *Studies in the nature of character.* Vol. 3, *Studies in the organization of character.* New York: Macmillan.

Heathers, G. (1953). Emotional dependence and independence in a physical threat situation. *Child Development, 24,* 169–179.

Hoffman, M. L. (1963). Child rearing practices and moral development: Generalizations from empirical research. *Child Development, 34,* 295–318.

Johnson, R. C. (1962). A study of children's moral judgments. *Child Development, 33,* 327–354.

Kagan, J., & Moss, H. A. (1959). Stability and validity of achievement fantasy. *Journal of Abnormal and Social Psychology, 58,* 357–364.

Kagan, J., & Moss, H. A. (1962). *Birth to maturity: A study in psychological development.* New York: Wiley.

Kelly, E. L. (1955). Consistency of the adult personality. *American Psychologist, 10,* 659–681.

Kenny, D. T., & Ginsberg, Rose. (1958). The specificity of intolerance of ambiguity measures. *Journal of Abnormal and Social Psychology, 56,* 300–304.

Kogan, N., & Wallach, M. A. (1964). *Risk taking: A study in cognition and personality.* New York: Holt, Rinehart & Winston.

Kohlberg, L. (1963). The development of children's orientations toward a moral order: I. Sequence in the development of moral thought. *Vita Humana, 6,* 11–33.

Kohlberg, L. (1966). A cognitive-developmental analysis of children's sex-role concepts and attitudes. In Eleanor E. Maccoby (Ed.), *The development of sex differences* (pp. 25–55). Stanford: Stanford University Press.

Krumboltz, J. D., & Farquhar, W. W. (1957). Reliability and validity of the *n*-Achievement test. *Journal of Consulting Psychology, 21,* 226–228.

Landfield, A. W., Stern, M., & Fjeld, S. (1961). Social conceptual processes and change in students undergoing psychotherapy. *Psychological Reports, 8,* 63–68.

Lansky, L. M., Crandall, V. J., Kagan, J., & Baker, C. T. (1961). Sex differences in aggression and its correlates in middle-class adolescents. *Child Development, 32,* 45–58.

Lovibond, S. H. (1964). Personality and conditioning. In B. A. Maher (Ed.), *Progress in experimental personality research* (pp. 115–168). Vol. 1. New York: Academic Press.

MacKinnon, D. W. (1938). Violation of prohibitions. In H. A. Murray, *Explorations in personality* (pp. 491–501). New York: Oxford University Press.

Maher, B. A. (1957). Personality, problem solving, and the Einstellung effect. *Journal of Abnormal and Social Psychology, 54,* 70–74.

Mann, R. D. (1959). A review of the relationships between personality and performance in small groups. *Psychological Bulletin, 56*, 241–270.

Matarazzo, J. D. (1965). The interview. In B. B. Wolman (Ed.), *Handbook of clinical psychology* (pp. 403–450). New York: McGraw-Hill.

McClelland, D. C., Atkinson, J. W., Clark, R. A., & Lowell, E. I. (1953). *The achievement motive.* New York: Appleton-Century-Crofts.

McGuire, W. J. (1968). Personality and susceptibility to social influence. In E. F. Borgatta & W. W. Lambert (Eds.), *Handbook of personality theory and research* (pp. 1130–1187). Chicago: Rand McNally.

Mischel, W. (1962). Delay of gratification in choice situations. NIMH Progress Report, Stanford University.

Moore, A. U., & Marcuse, F. I. (1945). Salivary, cardiac and motor indices of conditioning in two sows. *Journal of Comparative Psychology, 38*, 1–16.

Morgan, H. H. (1953). Measuring achievement motivation with "picture interpretations." *Journal of Consulting Psychology, 17*, 289–292.

Moss, H. A., & Kagan, J. (1961). Stability of achievement and recognition seeking behaviors from early childhood through adulthood. *Journal of Abnormal and Social Psychology, 62*, 504–518.

Osgood, C. E., Suci, G. J., & Tannenbaum, P. H. (1957). *The measurement of meaning.* Urbana: University of Illinois Press.

Patterson, G. R., & Hinsey, W. C. (1964). Investigations of some assumptions and characteristics of a procedure for instrumental conditioning in children. *Journal of Experimental Child Psychology, 1*, 111–122.

Pervin, L. A. (1960). Rigidity in neurosis and general personality functioning. *Journal of Abnormal and Social Psychology, 61*, 389–395.

Piaget, J. (1951). *Play, dreams, and imitation in childhood.* New York: Norton.

Sanford, N. (1963). Personality: Its place in psychology. In S.

Koch (Ed.), *Psychology: A study of a science.* Vol. 5 (pp. 488–592). New York: McGraw-Hill.

Saslow, G., Matarazzo, J. D., Phillips, Jeanne S., & Matarazzo, Ruth C. (1957). Test-retest stability of interaction patterns during interviews conducted one week apart. *Journal of Abnormal and Social Psychology, 54*, 295–802.

Sears, R. R. (1961). Relation of early socialization experiences to aggression in middle childhood. *Journal of Abnormal and Social Psychology, 63*, 466–492.

Sears, R. R. (1963). Dependency motivation. In M. R. Jones (Ed.), *Nebraska symposium on motivation* (pp. 25–64). Lincoln: University of Nebraska Press.

Sears, R. R., Maccoby, Eleanor E., & Levin, H. (1957). *Patterns of child rearing.* Evanston, IL: Row, Peterson.

Sears, R. R., Rau, Lucy, & Alpert, R. (1965). *Identification and child rearing.* Stanford, CA: Stanford University Press.

Skolnick, Arlene. (1966a). Motivational imagery and behavior over twenty years. *Journal of Consulting Psychology, 30*, 463–478.

Skolnick, Arlene. (1966b). Stability and interrelations of thematic test imagery over 20 years. *Child Development, 37*, 389–396.

Wallach, M. A. (1962). Commentary: Active-analytical vs. passive-global cognitive functioning. In S. Messick & J. Ross (Eds.), *Measurement in personality and cognition* (pp. 199–215). New York: Wiley.

Whiting, J. W. M. (1959). Sorcery, sin, and the superego. A cross-cultural study of some mechanisms of social control. In M. R. Jones (Ed.), *Nebraska symposium on motivation* (pp. 174–195). Lincoln: University of Nebraska Press.

Witkin, H. A., Goodenough, D. R., & Karp, S. A. (1967). Stability of cognitive style from childhood to young adulthood. *Journal of Personality and Social Psychology, 7*, 291–300.

Wrightsman, L. S., Jr., & Baumeister, A. A. (1961). A comparison of actual and paper-and-pencil versions of the Water Jar Test of Rigidity. *Journal of Abnormal and Social Psychology, 63*, 191–198.

SOME REASONS FOR THE APPARENT INCONSISTENCY OF PERSONALITY

Jack Block

The next selection may have been the first and was ultimately one of the most important of the rebuttals to Mischel's argument in the previous selection. This brief article, by the same Jack Block who wrote the essay on longitudinal research in Part I, sets forth several reasons why actions that seem inconsistent might in fact all be produced by a stable personality structure. If trivial behaviors are correlated with important ones, or if the context of behavior is not taken into account, or if the underlying dynamics of behavior are ignored, then behavior *will appear inconsistent even though* personality *is not. This article appeared at about the same time as Mischel's book and does not mention it by name, but the several possible misunderstandings Block lists are ones that some observers believe to have been present in many of the demonstrations, reviewed by Mischel, that "behavior is inconsistent."*

    However, the most important aspect of this article is not the way in which it rebuts Mischel but in its clear illustration of the complex and far-from-obvious processes by which personality affects what a person does.

From "Some Reasons for the Apparent Inconsistency of Personality," by J. Block. In *Psychological Bulletin, 70*, 210–212. Copyright © 1968 by the American Psychological Association. Adapted with permission.

The study of personality seeks regularities in behavior and this search is usually made operational by evaluations of the correlations among different, theoretically related behaviors. To date, the empirical evidence for personality consistency has not been inspiring. As a principle or aspiration of a science aimed at human understanding, the idea of continuity and coherence in personality functioning must be affirmed. Whereupon the question becomes: Why have psychologists, in their many research efforts, been unable to display the presumed harmonies in individual behavior?

The present note collects and lists some of the reasons for this state of affairs. The problem is viewed as arising both from deficiencies in the way psychologists operationalize their concepts and from deficiencies in the way they conceptualize their operations; and it is in these terms that our discussion will proceed. There are some psychometric reasons, as well, for the apparent inconsistency observed in behaviors, having to do with such matters as attenuation effects and the vexing influence of "method variance," but these statistical concerns have been dealt with elsewhere (Block, 1963, 1964; Humphreys, 1960); so the present argument can be entirely psychological.

To exemplify the several points to be made, the personality dimension of ego control will be used, although, of course, other personality constructs instead might have been employed. By ego control is meant something akin to excessive behavioral constraint or rigidity ("the over-controller") at one end of the dimension and something like excessive behavioral reactivity or spontaneity ("the undercontroller") at the other end of the continuum. For further articulation of the ego-control concept, the reader may wish to consult other sources (e.g., Block, 1965; Block & Turula, 1963).

There is evidence for a common thread through a large variety of behaviors that can be accounted for by the concept of ego control. Undercontrollers in one situation are often undercontrollers in another context as well and the same is true of overcontrollers. But also, and often, an individual who is impulsive in one situation will appear constrained in another circumstance; such behavior apparently denies the usefulness of a generalizing personality variable. This last kind of datum, of apparent inconsistency, cannot be questioned or explained away by psychometric manipulation;[1] it is there and further instances can be multiplied at will. What can be questioned, however, is the implication immediately, frequently, and strongly drawn from such observations to the effect that a personality dimension—in the present instance, ego control—necessarily loses its cogency as a basis for conceptualizing behavior because of the inconsistencies observed. We can question this implication if, and only if, a higher form of lawfulness can be found in the behaviors pointed to as evidence for temperamental inconsistency. The apparent discordancies must be resolved within a framework provided by a theory,

or, at least, a theory must have the promise of integrating these otherwise upsetting data.

There are at least four ways in which these superficially embarrassing behavioral inconsistencies may come about:

1. *The behaviors being contrasted and correlated may not all be significant or salient for the individual.* Thus, it is psychologically uneconomical and as a rule not necessary to deliberate excessively before deciding whether to walk down the right aisle or the left aisle of a theater. The decision problem confronting the individual in this particular situation is essentially unimportant. Consequently, an individual may make his theater-lobby decision in a rather cavalier or "impulsive" way. Or he may give reign to a slight position preference which, because it is consistent, may suggest a "rigidity" or highly controlled patterning in his behavior. It is specious to contrast such peripheral behaviors of an individual with the way in which he copes with centrally involving situations such as friendship formation or aggression imposition, and yet, unwittingly, the comparison is often made. When correlation is sought between behaviors formulated in salient situations on the one hand and behaviors formulated in uninvolving situations on the other, then behavior will appear more whimsical than congruent. If we are to seek consistency, it must be sought among behaviors that are at comparable levels in the hierarchy of behaviors.

2. *Formulations of personality which are context blind or do not attempt to take environmental factors into account will encounter many behaviors that will appear inconsistent.* Thus, a generally spontaneous child may in certain circumstances behave in a highly constricted way. This vacillation and apparent inconsistency readily becomes understandable when it is realized that these certain circumstances are always *unfamiliar* ones for the child. Behavior often appears capricious because the nature of the stimulus situation in which the individual finds himself is not comprehended or attended to by the observer and his theory. Explicit theoretical conceptualization of environmental factors is a fruitful way of integrating and

---

[1] In other words, these inconsistencies are not just a matter of statistical imprecision or error.

assimilating behaviors which from a context-blind viewpoint appear inconsistent. It is still a way that is almost untried.[2]

3. *The behaviors being related may not be mediated by the same underlying variables.* Thus, in a basketball game two players may each demonstrate a wide variety of shots and sequencing of shots at the basket. The one player may have spent solitary, obsessive years before a hoop, planfully developing precisely the repertoire and combinations he is now manifesting. The second player, in the heat of athletic endeavor, may in spontaneous and impromptu fashion manifest a fully equivalent variety of basket-making attempts (and with no less accuracy if he is a good athlete). These phenotypically equivalent behaviors are in the first player mediated by controlled, deliberate development of a differentiated behavioral repertoire; in the second player, behavioral variety is mediated by his kinesthetic spontaneity. In a rather different situation, where prior cultivation of ability is not available as a resource, the first player may now appear rigid and behaviorally impoverished; the second player can continue to be spontaneous. These two individuals, behaviorally equivalent in the first situation, are quite different in the second situation; and this difference suggests an inconsistency of behavior. If the mediating variables underlying a given action are not analyzed or considered, behavior can appear paradoxical when closer assessment will reveal a lawful basis for the discrepancy.

4. *When an individual has reached certain personal limits, previous behavioral consistencies may break down.* Thus, an acutely paranoid individual will manifest both extremely overcontrolled behaviors and extremely undercontrolled behaviors more or less conjointly. Etiologically, this contrary

behavioral state appears to come about when the preparanoid individual finds his former ability to consistently contain his excessive impulses is becoming exceeded in certain directions of expression, with a resultant absence of control in these special areas. The former, often quite striking coherence the preparanoid personality manifests has been disrupted because the *bounds* or *limits* within which the coherence can be maintained have been transcended. Such extremist behaviors are especially likely to be judged psychopathological. Indeed, one of the explanations why psychiatrists and clinical psychologists often argue against the existence of an internally consistent ego apparatus is that they in their practice so often encounter those relatively few individuals in whom personal limits have been reached and therefore personal consonance shattered. More generally, psychologists have not given the notion of bounds or limits sufficient attention and application. Relationships tend to be posited unequivocally, without recognizing the bounds within which the relationship can be expected to hold and beyond which the relationship fails and is replaced by other relationships.

The foregoing remarks and recognitions are not new but their implications are often neglected by the busy psychologist concerned more with the action of research than with contemplative conceptualization. But both are required. If we are to respond to our empirical disappointments in the pursuit of personality consistency, that response should comprehend the reasons for former failure rather than perpetuate and proliferate a fundamentally unpsychological approach to the understanding of personality.

[2]More than 2 decades later, the integration of situational context into our understanding of how personality affects behavior is still seldom even attempted. Part of the problem seems to be that we lack a vocabulary and technology for assessing the psychologically important aspects of situations that is comparable to our vocabulary and technology for assessing persons (see Bem & Funder, 1978).

References

Block, J. (1963). The equivalence of measures and the correction for attenuation. *Psychological Bulletin, 60,* 152–156.

Block, J. (1964). Recognizing attenuation effects in the strategy of research. *Psychological Bulletin, 62,* 214–216.

Block, J. (1965). *The challenge of response sets.* New York: Appleton-Century-Crofts.

Block, J., & Turula, E. (1963). Identification, ego control, and adjustment. *Child Development, 34,* 945–953.

Humphreys, L. G. (1960). Note on the multitrait-multimethod matrix. *Psychological Bulletin, 57,* 86–88.

PROFITING FROM CONTROVERSY: LESSONS FROM THE PERSON-SITUATION DEBATE

Douglas T. Kenrick and David C. Funder

When Mischel proposed that personality traits are not important, this proposal immediately ran into the fact that nearly everybody thinks that they are. Personality traits are not only an important topic of psychological research, but obviously a major part of the way we think and talk about people in daily life. Mischel's response to this paradox was a further proposal, that our perceptions of personality traits in ourselves and each other are cognitive illusions. This position was bolstered by the development of research in social psychology describing many errors that people make in their judgments of each other. Indeed, the tendency to see personality traits as affecting behaviors that are really due to the situation became dubbed the "fundamental attribution error" (Ross, 1977).

The following article, by the social-personality psychologist Douglas Kenrick and one of the editors of this reader, was intended to sum up the person-situation debate by directly addressing this question: Are personality traits merely illusions? The article is structured by considering seven hypotheses that range from the most to the least pessimistic about the existence and importance of personality traits. Traits are not just illusions in the eye of the beholder, Kenrick and Funder conclude, nor is their appearance the mere by-product of processes—such as discussion among peers about what somebody is like—that may have nothing to do with the personality of the person who is being described. Rather, the accumulated evidence supports the conclusion that traits are real and have a major influence on what people do.

Kenrick and Funder conclude—contrary to the opinion of some—that the person-situation controversy was good for personality psychology. It forced the reconsideration of some of the basic premises of the field in the light of new evidence and illuminated a number of ways in which the influence of personality can and cannot be validly demonstrated. For example, personality judgments of traits that are visible (such as "talkative") are more likely to be accurate than judgments of traits that are hard to see (such as "tends to fantasize"), and judgments by people who know well the people they are judging are more likely to be valid than judgments by relative strangers. These points might seem obvi-

ous in retrospect but, Kenrick and Funder point out, it took the field of personality a surprisingly long time to realize how important they are.

Notice that this article originally appeared in 1988, exactly 20 years after the publication of Mischel's influential book. The article attempted not just to sum up the lessons learned from the person-situation controversy, but to declare the war over. In the years since 1988, the field of personality largely has turned its attention to other issues.

From "Profiting from Controversy: Lessons from the Person-Situation Debate," by D. T. Kenrick and D. C. Funder. In *American Psychologist*, 43, 23–34. Copyright © 1988 by the American Psychological Association. Adapted with permission.

* * *

Whether we are acting as professional psychologists, as academic psychologists, or simply as lay psychologists engaging in everyday gossip, the assumption that people have "traits" (or enduring cross-situational consistencies in their behavior) provides a basis for many of our decisions. When a clinical or counseling psychologist uses a standard assessment battery, he or she assumes that there is some degree of trait-like consistency in pathological behavior to be measured. When an organizational psychologist designs a personnel selection procedure, he or she assumes that consistent individual differences between the applicants are there to be found. When an academic psychologist teaches a course in personality, he or she must either assume some consistency in behavior or else face a bit of existential absurdity for at least 3 hours a week. Likewise, a good portion of our courses on clinical and developmental psychology would be unimaginable unless we assumed some cross-situational consistency. Even in everyday lay psychology, our attempts to analyze the behaviors of our friends, relatives, and co-workers are riddled with assumptions about personality traits.

Despite the wide appeal of the trait assumption, personality psychologists have been entangled for some time in a debate about whether it might be based more on illusion than reality (e.g., Alker, 1972; Allport, 1966; Argyle & Little, 1972; Bem, 1972; Block, 1968, 1977; Bowers, 1973; Epstein, 1977, 1979, 1980; Fiske, 1974; Gormly & Edelberg, 1974; Hogan, DeSoto, & Solano, 1977; Hunt, 1965; Magnusson & Endler, 1977; Mischel, 1968, 1983; West, 1983). Murmurs of the current debate could be heard more than 40 years ago (Ichheisser, 1943), but the volume increased markedly after Mischel's (1968) critique, and things have not quieted down yet (Bem, 1983; Epstein, 1983; Funder, 1983; Kenrick, 1986; Mischel, 1983; Mischel & Peake, 1982, 1983). Of late, discussants have begun to express yearning to end what some see as an endless cycle of repeating the same arguments. Mischel and Peake (1982) and Bem (1983), for instance, both use the term *déjà vu* in the titles of recent contributions, suggesting that they feel as if they have been here before. Other commentators maintain that the debate has been a "pseudo-controversy" (Carlson, 1984; Endler, 1973) that never should have occurred in the first place.

However fatiguing it may now seem to some of its erstwhile protagonists, the debate over the alleged inconsistency of personality has been more than an exercise in sophistry. In the course of the nearly two decades since Mischel's (1968) critique, a number of provocative hypotheses have been put forward, along with a host of studies to evaluate them. Platt (1964) and Popper (1959), among others, maintained that science typically progresses through the accumulation of negative information—that is, by eliminating hypotheses that data suggest are no longer tenable. From this perspective, it may be worth taking a look back at the hypotheses suggested during the consistency controversy, this time in the improved light shed by two decades of research. In this light, the debate can be seen as an intellectually stimulating chapter in the history of the discipline, replete with useful lessons for professionals who include assessment in their repertoire.

The "Pure Trait" Model and Its Alternatives

Discussions of the "person versus situation" debate traditionally begin with the "pure trait" model (Alston, 1975; Argyle & Little, 1972; Mischel, 1968): that people show powerful, unmodulated consistencies in their behavior across time and diverse situations. This position has been attacked frequently over the years. However, it is really just a "straw man," and even traditional personality researchers find it unacceptable (see, e.g., Allport, 1931, 1966; Block, 1977; Hogan et al., 1977; Jackson, 1983; Wiggins, 1973; Zuroff, 1986). Complete invariance in behavior is associated more with severe psychopathology than with "normal" behavior.

If the consensus rejects the "pure trait" position, then what can replace it? Several alternative hypotheses have been advanced over the years. These hypotheses differ with regard to four issues, which can be arranged into a logical hierarchy:

1. *Consensus versus solipsism.* Are traits merely idiosyncratic constructs that reside solely inside the heads of individual observers, or can observers reach agreement in applying trait terms?

2. *Discriminativeness versus generality.* If observers can agree with one another in ascribing traits to targets, is it simply because they apply a nondiscriminative "one size fits all" approach?

3. *Behavior versus labeling.* If observers can agree with one another, and can also differentiate be-

tween who is low or high on a given trait, does this occur because they really observe behavior? Or do they merely provide their judgments based on superficial stereotypes, targets' self-presentations, or other socially assigned labels?

4. *Internal versus external locus of causal explanation.* If observers can agree with one another and can distinguish individual differences on the basis of *actual behavior* of the people they are observing, are the causes of these consistencies located within each person or within his or her situation and role?

Each of these issues depends on the resolution of those earlier in the list. For instance, if observers cannot agree with one another about who has which traits, there is no point in going on to debate whether traits have a behavioral basis. Ultimately, assumptions about traits must pass the tests of consensus, discriminativeness, behavioral foundation, and internality. We will discuss seven hypotheses that assume that traits fail one or more of these tests. In Table 14.1, we list the hypotheses in terms of the four hierarchical issues just discussed. As can be seen, the hypotheses can be arranged more or less in order of their pessimism regarding the existence of (consensually verifiable, discriminative, internal) traitlike consistencies.

We will consider each hypothesis in its purest form and, for the moment, disregard the various qualifications that have sometimes been attached to each. Placing each hypothesis in bold relief allows us to assess it most clearly, and philosophers of science tell us that we learn most when hypotheses are stated in such a way as to allow disproof (e.g., Platt, 1964; Popper, 1959). Moreover, each of these hypotheses has, at some time, actually been stated in its bold form. In 1968, for instance, one social psychologist argued that

> the prevalent view that the normal behavior of individuals tends toward consistency is misconceived [and the research evidence] . . . strongly suggests that consistency, either in thought or action, does not constitute the normal state of affairs. (Gergen, 1968, pp. 305–306)

TABLE 14.1

HIERARCHY OF HYPOTHESES FROM THE PERSON-SITUATION
CONTROVERSY, ARRANGED FROM MOST TO LEAST PESSIMISTIC

Critical assumptions	Hypotheses
Solipsism over consensus	1. Personality is in the eye of the beholder.
Consensus without discrimination	2. Agreement between raters is an artifact of the semantic structure of the language used to describe personality.
	3. Agreement is an artifact of base-rate accuracy (rater's tendency to make similar guesses about what people in general are like).
Discriminative consensus without behavioral referents	4. Differential agreement is an artifact of the shared use of invalid stereotypes.
	5. Observers are in cahoots with one another; that is, their agreement results from discussion rather than accurate observation.
Differential agreement about behavior without internal traits	6. Raters see targets only within a limited range of settings and mistake situational effects for traits.
	7. Compared with situational pressures, cross-situational consistencies in behavior are too weak to be important.

In the same year, a behavioral psychologist stated that "I, for one, look forward to the day when personality theories are regarded as historical curiosities" (Farber, 1964, p. 37).

Such extreme pessimism was clearly unwarranted. The data available now, more than two decades later, argue strongly against all seven of the hypotheses in Table 14.1. However, it would be a mistake to presume, as some personologists seem to do, that the issues raised by the "situationists" were merely diversions from the true path that can now be safely disregarded. We have learned, in the course of the debate, about a number of sources of distortion in trait judgments. These not only are of interest in their own right but are useful to personality assessment professionals, whose main goal may be to eliminate as much clutter from their path as possible.

HYPOTHESIS 1: PERSONALITY IS IN THE EYE OF THE BEHOLDER The first and most pessimistic hypothesis that must be considered is that our perceptions of personality traits in our friends, acquaintances, and selves might be largely or exclusively by-products of the limitations and flaws of human information processing. Although no personality researcher has ever advocated that personality exists solely in the head and not in the external world, social psychologists such as Gergen (1968) and behavioral analysts such as Farber (1964) have done so. Moreover, the issue lies in the logical path of any further inquiries into the origin of trait attributions.

Social psychologists have often emphasized how personality impressions can arise in the absence of supporting evidence in the real world:

> Unwitting evidence provided by countless personality psychologists shows how objectively low or nonexistent covariations (between personality and behavior) can be parlayed into massive perceived covariations through a priori theories and assumptions. (Nisbett & Ross, 1980, p. 109)

> The personality theorists' (and the layperson's) conviction that there are strong cross-situational consistencies in behavior may be seen as merely another instance of theory-driven covariation assessments operating in the face of contrary evidence. (Nisbett & Ross, 1980, p. 112)

Research relevant to the "eye of the beholder" hypothesis has mainly consisted of (a) demonstrations of various "errors" in the way that people process social information, or (b) claims that different judges rating the same personality rarely agree with each other or with the person being rated.

The demonstrations of error (for reviews, see Nisbett & Ross, 1980; Ross, 1977) establish that information given to subjects in laboratory settings is frequently distorted. People tend to jump to conclusions, biasing their judgments and their memories on the basis of their "implicit personality theories" (Schneider, 1973) or "scripts" (Abelson, 1976; Schank & Abelson, 1977). Studies of these attributional errors clearly demonstrate that people have biased expectations and that they routinely go beyond the information they are given.

However, for two reasons such studies do not establish that personality resides solely in the eye of the beholder. First, some of the errors are more a product of the unusual experimental situation than of a fundamentally biased cognitive process (cf. Block, Weiss, & Thorne, 1979; Trope, Bassok, & Alon, 1984). More important, the existence of judgmental biases does not necessarily imply the existence of mistakes. The expectations and biases

demonstrated in laboratory tasks are, in principle, liable to lead to correct judgments in the real world (Funder, 1987). Many demonstrations of this principle can be found in the field of visual perception, where a useful rule of thumb underlies every "optical illusion" (Gregory, 1971). The "Ponzo" or "railroad lines" illusion, for example, produces errors in the lab but correct judgments when applied to three-dimensional reality. In the field of social perception, even the "fundamental attribution error" will lead to correct judgments to the extent that real people actually are somewhat consistent in their behavior. In short, demonstrations of laboratory errors are not informative, one way or the other, as to whether the associated judgmental biases lead mostly to mistakes or correct judgments in real life (see also McArthur & Baron, 1983).

A different line of support for the "eye of the beholder" hypothesis has been the belief that people generally do not agree with each other in their judgments of the same personality. For example, Dornbusch, Hastorf, Richardson, Muzzy, and Vreeland (1965) found that the constructs children in a summer camp used to describe personality were more a function of the person doing the ratings than they were of the person being rated. Such studies do show that people have individually preferred constructs for thinking about others. But these judgmental idiosyncrasies must be interpreted in the light of frequent findings that (a) when raters and ratees get a chance to know one another, their ratings come to agree with each other more (Funder & Colvin, 1987; Norman & Goldberg, 1966), and (b) when common rating categories are imposed on raters, their judgments will show substantial agreement in orderings of individual targets (e.g., Amelang & Borkenau, 1986; Bem & Allen, 1974; Cheek, 1982; Funder, 1987, Funder & Dobroth, 1987; Kenrick & Braver, 1982; Koretzky, Kohn, & Jeger, 1978; McCrae, 1982; Mischel & Peake, 1982).

Table 14.2 demonstrates some fairly typical findings in the area. In each of these studies, adult targets rated their own personalities and were also rated by more than one person who knew them

TABLE 14.2

INTERRATER CORRELATIONS FROM RECENT TRAIT STUDIES

Trait	Kenrick & Stringfield (1980) (n = 71)	Obs[a] (n = 34)	Funder & Dobroth (1987) (n = 69)	Danchik (1985) (n = 92)	Obs[a] (n = 36)	Cheek (1982) 1/2/3[b] (n = 81)	Obs[a] (n = 40)	McCrae (1982) (n = 139)	Paunonen & Jackson (1985) (n = 90)	Mischel & Peake (1982) (n = 63)
Intellectance	.17	.04	.36	.40	.52		.36	.50	.53	
Likability	.35	.52	.41	.14	.14	.22/.33/.39	.49	.47	.57	
Self-control	.26	.26	.25	.19	.47	.27/.40/.47	.64	.48	.67	.52
Sociability	.40	.55	.34	.46	.53	.43/.53/.59	.46	.53	.74	
Adjustment	.23	.43	.23	.38	.40	.22/.25/.27		.58	.48	
Dominance	.35	.41	.40	.58	.61			.52	.60	
M	.29	.37	.34	.37	.45	.29/.38/.44	.50	.51	.59	.52
	(.53)[c]	(.67)		(.51)	(.64)					

Note. The trait labels used here are based on Hogan's (1982) terminology, and we have used roughly equivalent scales from studies that did not use those exact terms (denoting the major "factors" usually found in trait rating studies).

[a] Data from subjects who rated their behaviors on a given dimension as publicly observable (Obs).

[b] Data based on 1, 2, and 3 judges, respectively.

[c] Figures in parentheses are corrected for attenuation.

well (parents, spouses, housemates, or friends). Correlations represent agreement about the same person by different raters who filled out the scales independently. Studies on the left side of the table used single-item scales (Funder & Dobroth, 1987; Kenrick & Stringfield, 1980); Dantchik (1985) and Cheek (1982) used 5-item and 3-item scales, respectively; and the studies to the right used lengthier scales with better established psychometric properties. It is clear that the use of reliable rating scales leads to high agreement regarding a target's personality, but even single-item scales can produce consistently positive (and statistically significant) levels of agreement.[1] * * *

A consideration of this first hypothesis has taught us something about when the eyes of different beholders will behold different characteristics in the persons at whom they are looking. For instance, when rating strangers, observers will be quite happy to make attributions about what the strangers are like but will show little consensus (Funder & Colvin, 1987; Monson, Keel, Stephens, & Genung, 1982; Passini & Norman, 1966). So, although strangers' ratings provide an excellent domain for the study of bias (Fiske & Taylor, 1984), it is probably futile to expect them to manifest much validity. However, when observers are well acquainted with the person they are judging, they nevertheless do manage to see something on which they can agree. The findings of consensus (such as those in Table 14.2) are sufficient to rule out the radical hypothesis that personality resides solely in the eye of the beholder.

* * *

[1]Most rating scales consist of a total score computed across the ratings of several or more individual items. The more the ratings of these different items within a scale tend to agree with each other, the more reliable the total scale is. More reliable scales tend to yield larger correlations with other variables. Single-item scales, by contrast, usually produce lower correlations.

HYPOTHESIS 2: AGREEMENT IS DUE TO SEMANTIC GENERALIZATION

The first hypothesis, in its radical form, considered traits to be idiosyncratic constructions of the individual perceiver. The second hypothesis concedes that there is consensus in the use of trait terms but views that agreement as due simply to shared delusions based on common linguistic usage. According to the semantic generalization hypothesis, as soon as one judgment about another person is made, many other judgments follow based on nothing more than implicit expectations about which words "go together." Anyone judged as "friendly" may also be judged as "empathic," "altruistic," and "sincere" because the concepts are semantically linked, even though the component behaviors themselves may not be so linked. For instance, "helping others in distress" and "contributing to charities" (behavioral components of "altruism") may not be correlated with "smiling a lot" and "talking to strangers" (behavioral components of "friendliness"), but judges who see evidence of "smiling a lot" might still infer "altruism," at least sometimes incorrectly. Shweder (1975) argued that shared preconceptions about "what goes with what" affected judgments so pervasively as to raise the question "How relevant is an individual differences theory of personality?" (See also D'Andrade, 1974.) Bourne (1977) went even further, suggesting that trait ratings might not reflect "anything more than raters' conceptual expectancies about which traits go together" (p. 863).

* * *

It is crucial to realize, as Block, Weiss, and Thorne (1979) pointed out, that semantic generalization cannot explain how different judges agree on attributing a *single* trait to a target person (as research such as that in Table 14.2 shows they do). To take a well-known example, the Passini and Norman (1966) study has been cited as evidence that trait ratings are based on "nothing more" than semantic similarity judgments. Indeed, Passini and Norman's data yielded a similar factor structure for ratings of friends and for ratings of strangers (who had been observed only briefly).[2]

Because the strangers had very little time to observe one another, it is clear that an implicit personality theory guided their judgments. However, this issue of the relationships between trait words is completely orthogonal to the question of accuracy in application of any one of those words. Passini and Norman's subjects not only reached significant agreement about which trait applied to which person but they also agreed more about friends' ratings than about strangers' (see also Funder & Colvin, 1987; Norman & Goldberg, 1966).

In light of such arguments, Shweder and D'Andrade (1979) seem to have reversed their earlier claim that semantic generalization negates the importance of judgments of individual differences. Although semantic structure might tell us to expect "friendly" to go with "altruistic" and not with "aggressive," it does not tell us whether we should apply the term more strongly to Walter or Seymour or Daryl. We must seek further for an adequate explanation of findings like those in Table 14.2.

HYPOTHESIS 3: AGREEMENT IS DUE TO BASE-RATE ACCURACY According to this hypothesis, interrater agreement is an artifact of the highly stable base rates that many traits have in the population at large. For example, the trait "needs to be with other people" characterizes most of us, whereas "has murderous tendencies" characterizes few. If one is trying to describe someone one does not know, therefore, one can achieve a certain degree of "accuracy" just by rating the first trait higher than the second. The base-rate hypothesis, like the semantic structure hypothesis, allows for consensus between observers but regards their judgments as indiscriminate. "Accuracy" of this sort might reflect knowledge about what people in general are like, what Cronbach (1955) called "stereotype accuracy," but does not necessarily reflect any knowledge specific to the person being described.

The base-rate accuracy problem helps us understand phenomena such as the "Barnum effect" (Ulrich, Stachnik, & Stainton, 1963), reflected in widespread acceptance of generalized descriptions

---

[2]This reference to "factor structure" means that the different traits on which raters judged others tended to be correlated with each other in a similar manner whether the targets of judgment were close acquaintances or strangers. For example, people rated high on "talkativeness" also tend to be rated high on "friendliness," whether these people are well known to the rater or not.

such as, "You have a strong need for other people to like you and for them to admire you."[3] Questions of when and for whom base-rate accuracy becomes an issue are interesting ones. For example, a recent study by Miller, McFarland, and Turnbull (1985) found that Barnum statements are more likely to be accepted by subjects when the statements refer to attributes that are publicly observable and flattering. However, to argue that base-rate accuracy is a basis for doubting whether we "can . . . describe an individual's personality" (Bourne, 1977) takes things too far. The base-rate accuracy hypothesis, like the semantic similarity hypothesis, can explain how judges reach consensus but not how they distinguish *between* the targets they judge. To take a simple case, imagine that a group of sorority sisters rates one another on a dichotomous item (as either "friendly" or "unfriendly"). If "friendly" is chosen over "unfriendly" 9 out of 10 times, there could be a very high percentage of "agreement," in terms of overlapping judgments, even if there were absolutely no agreement about who the 10th, unfriendly person is. But if there is truly no agreement about individual targets, correlations calculated between judges will show no relationship at all. So base-rate accuracy cannot explain the results of interrater studies such as those in Table 14.2 either (cf. Funder, 1980a; Funder & Colvin, 1987; Funder & Dobroth, 1987).

Summarizing thus far, we may say that whatever role solipsism and glittering generality play as noise in personality assessment, a signal of consensus and discrimination comes through. Can that signal be explained without acceding to the existence of trait-like consistencies in behavior? The answer is still yes, and in at least three ways.

HYPOTHESIS 4: AGREEMENT IS DUE TO STEREOTYPES BASED ON OBVIOUS (BUT ERRONEOUS) CUES None of the arguments considered so far can account for interjudge agreement about the differences between people. One hypothesis that does is this: Perhaps agreement about peers is due to shared (but incorrect) stereotypes based on one or another readily accessible (e.g., physical) cues. Many such stereotypes come to mind: physical types (athlete, fat person, dumb blonde), racial and ethnic stereotypes, and so forth. Judges might share cultural stereotypes and so "agree" about burly, obese, or blond targets regardless of whether there were any corresponding consistencies in the targets' behavior.

Note that this hypothesis is very different from the sort of "stereotype accuracy" discussed under Hypothesis 3. That hypothesis referred to the possibility of indiscriminate responding based on raters' common preconceptions about what *everybody* is like. Hypothesis 4 refers to consensual agreement about traits that are *differentially* assigned to others. None of the first three hypotheses requires the observer to really "observe" anything distinctive about the person he or she is describing. This hypothesis, however, does require that the observer at least take a look at the target person—but assumes that the observer hardly looks much further than the end of his or her nose, just enough to assign the target person to a general category.

Such categorical stereotypes undoubtedly exist, but this does not mean we cannot become more accurate after getting to know someone beyond their "surface" categorization. Raters will try to make "reasonable" (i.e., stereotypic) guesses in the absence of real behavioral information. But as we mentioned earlier, their ratings increasingly converge as they actually observe the person's behavior (e.g., Funder & Colvin, 1987; Monson, Tanke, & Lund, 1980; Moskowitz & Schwarz, 1982; Norman & Goldberg, 1966; Passini & Norman, 1966).

The data that are most difficult for the stereotype hypothesis to explain are relationships between judgments and independent, objective behavioral measurements. For example, parents

---

[3]The "Barnum effect" was named for the circus promoter P. T. Barnum, who is said to have claimed "there's a sucker born every minute." In demonstrations of this effect a group of people are all given descriptions of their personalities that include phrases such as "you have a strong need for other people to like you." People often report that the descriptions are remarkably accurate, but in reality they were all given the same description!

and teachers can provide general personality descriptions of children that not only agree with each other but also predict the children's "delay of gratification" behavior, measured in minutes and seconds, in a lab situation that none of the raters have ever seen (Bem & Funder, 1978; Funder, Block, & Block, 1983; Mischel, 1984). Other examples include Funder's studies of personality correlates of attributional style (1980b), attitude change (1982), and social acuity (Funder & Harris, 1986b); Gormly and Edelberg's (1974) work on aggression; Moskowitz and Schwarz's (1982) work on dominance; and Alker and Owen's (1977) research on reactions to stressful events. This sort of predictive capability must arise from something beyond the use of invalid stereotypes.

Although the existence of stereotypes does not negate the existence of traits, it is useful to consider how stereotypes and personality traits interact. For example, physical attractiveness may actually lead one to become more friendly, via self-fulfilling prophecies (Goldman & Lewis, 1977; Snyder, Tanke, & Berscheid, 1977). Likewise, burly males really are more aggressive (Glueck & Glueck, 1956), probably because aggressiveness has a higher payoff for a muscular youth than it does for a skinny or flabby one.

In sum, although stereotypes may be informative about the genesis of some traits, and may account for judgments of strangers, the findings that observers agree more with one another after they have gotten to know the target and the correlations between ratings and independent assessments of behavior rule out the possibility that interrater agreement is due solely to the use of shared stereotypes based on superficial cues.

HYPOTHESIS 5: AGREEMENT IS DUE TO DISCUSSION BETWEEN OBSERVERS We just considered evidence that observers agree with each other better when they know the target person well. Is this because acquaintances have had more time to observe the relevant behaviors and hence are more truly accurate than strangers? Perhaps not. It could be argued that observers ignore the truly

relevant nonverbal behaviors of a target person but are attentive to the target's verbalizations about himself or herself and come to regard the target as the target does for that reason (cf. Funder, 1980a; Funder & Colvin, 1987). Alternatively, observers might get together and discuss the target (McClelland, 1972), agree on his or her reputation, and then inform the target about how to regard himself or herself (as in the classical "looking glass self" formulations of C. H. Cooley, 1902).

The research cited earlier, showing how ratings of personality traits can predict behavior in unique settings, strongly suggests that such explicit "negotiation" is not all that underlies interjudge agreement. Moreover, several researchers have found that agreement between parents "back home" and peers at college is about as good as that among peers or among parents (Bem & Allen, 1974; Kenrick & Stringfield, 1980). Likewise, Koretzky et al. (1978) found respectable agreement between judges from different settings. In that study, the various settings were all within the same (mental) institution, but the Kenrick and Stringfield (1980) study was conducted in an isolated college town in Montana and used parents who often lived several hundred miles away from campus and were unlikely to have met the peers (whose home towns may have been hundreds of miles in the opposite direction), much less to have had intimate discussions with them about their children's traits.

Findings of higher agreement on traits that relate to observable behaviors (such as "friendliness" as opposed to "emotionality") are also relevant here. Kenrick and Stringfield (1980) found that "observable" traits are reported with better agreement than "unobservable" ones. * * * Related findings are reported by Amelang and Borkenau (1986), Cheek (1982), Funder and Colvin (1987), Funder and Dobroth (1987), and McCrae (1982) and in two unpublished studies, one by Dantchik (1985) and one by McCall, Linder, West, and Kenrick (1985). If judges simply manufacture a reputation for a subject, it seems that it would be just as easy to agree about terms relating to emotionality as it would be to agree about terms relating to extraversion. Higher agreement about publicly observable traits thus suggests that behavior is in fact being observed and accurately reported.

A tenacious adherent could still rescue this hypothesis by adding one more assumption. Perhaps we talk more about the so-called observable traits like extraversion than about "unobservable" traits. However, other findings further undermine the "discussion" hypothesis. Several studies have shown that when subjects' self-reports contradict their nonverbal behaviors, observers pay more attention to what is done than to what is said (Amabile & Kabat, 1982; Bryan & Walbek, 1970). In the Amabile and Kabat study, subjects viewed a target who described herself as either "introverted" or "extraverted," and they also watched her behave in a way that was either consistent with, or inconsistent with, her self-description. Observers' subsequent judgments were much more strongly influenced by her actual behaviors than by the way she had described herself. It seems, then, that observers give more credence to trait-relevant behaviors than to self-descriptions.

Summarizing our arguments thus far, there is good evidence that trait ratings are more than solipsistic fantasies. Observers can agree in their trait ratings and can use them differently for different people. For those we know well, at least, trait ratings involve more than just stereotypes based on easily observable categories, and they are based more on behavioral observation than on unfounded gossip. Are we therefore now compelled to allow some veracity to the trait construct? Alas, the answer is still no, not necessarily.

HYPOTHESIS 6: AGREEMENT IS DUE TO SEEING OTHERS IN THE SAME SETTING It is possible to allow for consensus and discrimination in the use of trait terms, and even to allow that observers are really and truly observing behavioral consistencies, without allowing that those behavioral consistencies stem from factors that are "internal" to the target person. As William James (1890), noted,

Many a youth who is demure enough before his parents and teachers, swears and swaggers like a pirate among his "tough" young friends. We do not show ourselves to our children as to our club-companions, to our customers as to the laborers we employ, to our masters and employers as to our intimate friends. (p. 294)

Fellow club-companions may all agree that a particular merchant is consistently rather "wild," whereas his customers agree that he is quite "conventional." Because club-companions and customers live in "separate worlds," their different mutual delusions about the merchant's traits can be maintained. If behavior is mostly due to the situation, then the people who inhabit a given situation with a target will agree about that person's behavioral attributes, even if they are not actually general attributes of the individual's personality.

A good deal of the evidence we have already discussed poses difficulties for this hypothesis as a final explanation of rater agreement. Much of the research that uses trait ratings is based on studies of students who are rated by fellow fraternity members or college roommates (e.g., Bem & Allen, 1974; Cheek, 1982; Funder, 1980a; Funder & Dobroth, 1987; Kenrick & Stringfield, 1980). These individuals see each other across many settings, yet agree well. Recall also that studies such as those done by Bem and Allen (1974) and Kenrick and Stringfield (1980) found agreement across peer and parent groups—who see the targets in very different situations. In the Kenrick and Stringfield (1980) study, for instance, peers knew the target as a college student (and perhaps fellow beer drinker), whereas parents knew the target as a child (and perhaps a ranch hand). Restriction of range of environmental experience could even constrain correlations. For example, perhaps the college dorm is a setting that constrains one to be "friendly." If so, it will be a difficult and subtle task for raters who know two targets only in that setting to agree about which one is the more "dispositionally" friendly.

Finally, a good deal of the research just discussed shows how personality ratings made by parents, teachers, and friends often correlate well with behavior measured in settings that are very different from the contexts from which their judgments were derived. From observing their children at home, for example, parents can provide personality descriptions that predict behavior measured in a unique experimental setting (Bem & Funder, 1978)—even when a dozen or more years separate the personality judgments from the behavior (Mischel, 1984). Such predictability has to be based on the parents' detection of true "cross-situational consistency."

Although the "situational" hypothesis is often viewed as an alternative to the trait position, they need not be at odds with one another. Researchers have begun to uncover useful information about how persons and situations "interact" (e.g., Bem & Funder, 1978; Kenrick & Dantchik, 1983; Magnusson & Endler, 1977; Snyder & Ickes, 1985):

1. Traits influence behavior only in relevant situations (Allport, 1966; Bem & Funder, 1978). Anxiety, for example, shows up only in situations that the person finds threatening.

2. A person's traits can change a situation (Rausch, 1977). For instance, an aggressive child can bring out the hostility in a previously peaceful playground.

3. People with different traits will choose different settings (Snyder & Ickes, 1985). Highly sex-typed males, for example, seek out sexually stimulating situations; highly sex-typed females avoid them (Kenrick, Stringfield, Wagenhals, Dahl, & Ransdell, 1980).

4. Traits can change with chronic exposure to certain situations. For instance, Newcomb's students became less conservative during their Bennington college experience and stayed that way for decades (Newcomb, Koenig, Flacks, & Warwick, 1967).

5. Traits are more easily expressed in some situations than others. They have more influence when situations are low in constraint—for example, a picnic as opposed to a funeral (Monson et al., 1982; Price & Bouffard, 1974; Schutte, Kenrick, & Sadalla, 1985). Traits are also more likely

to be influential in settings that are highly prototypical or exemplary (Schutte et al., 1985). For instance, the postinterview cocktail party for an academic job applicant is more difficult to categorize than the in-office interview or the office Christmas party and would probably allow for the operation of greater individual differences. Note that laboratory situations, where psychologists often look for evidence of individual differences, will constrain the operation of traits precisely because they are rigidly controlled, are imposed arbitrarily on subjects, and are usually not reactive to anything the subject does (Monson & Snyder, 1977; Wachtel, 1973).

The data we have discussed thus far require us to concede that some degree of consensus, discrimination, and internality exist in the trait domain. Is it time, therefore, to give the store back to the "trait" position? Even with the distance we have come, the answer is still no. It is possible to argue that although some true cross-situational consistencies in behavior may exist, they are too small to worry about.

HYPOTHESIS 7: THE RELATIONSHIPS BETWEEN TRAITS AND BEHAVIOR ARE "TOO SMALL" TO BE IMPORTANT Just how small is "too small"? Mischel's (1968) review concluded that correlations between trait scores and behaviors and between different behaviors are seldom larger than about .30. This conclusion hit the field of personality with devastating force because of two separable assumptions: (a) The coefficient .30 is not simply an artifact of poorly developed research tools but is the true upper limit for the predictability of behavior from personality, and (b) this upper limit is a small upper limit. Acceptance of both of these assumptions was necessary for Mischel's critique to have had a major impact, and many initially did accept them.

Several personologists (e.g., Block, 1977; Hogan, DeSoto, & Solano, 1977) have challenged the first assumption, arguing that Mischel's review did not give a fair hearing to the better studies in the personality literature. More than the several studies cited in earlier sections of this article have used direct behavioral observations and found larger correlations with behavior (see also Block, Buss, Block, & Gjerde, 1981; Block, von der Lippe, & Block, 1973; McGowen & Gormly, 1976; Moskowitz, 1982). Epstein (1979, 1983) reported that such correlations can be especially high when aggregates of behavior[4] rather than single instances are used.

Indeed, in everyday life, what we usually wish to predict on the basis of our personality judgments are not single acts, but aggregate trends: Will this person make an agreeable friend, a reliable employee, an affectionate spouse? Given such broad criteria, the Spearman-Brown formula shows how even "small" single-act correlations compound into extremely high predictive validities. For example, Mischel and Peake (1982) found that interitem correlations between behavior measures are relatively low (.14 to .21) for single, unaggregated observations but that coefficient alpha for their total behavioral aggregate is .74. That is, a similar aggregate of behaviors would correlate .74 with that one. Along the same lines, Epstein and O'Brien (1985) reanalyzed several classical studies in the field of personality. In all of these studies behavior was situation specific at the single-item level (in line with Mischel's point) but cross-situationally general at the level of behavioral aggregates. Protagonists on both sides of the controversy now seem ready to allow that the ".30 ceiling" applies only to behavior in unaggregated form (Epstein, 1983; Mischel, 1983).

Even if one were to allow that it is difficult to surpass correlations of .30 to .40 (e.g., in the case of unaggregated measures), it may be a mistake to assume that such correlations are "small." In fact, correlations in this range characterize the strength of some of the most interesting and important situational effects found by experimental social psychology (Funder & Ozer, 1983; Sarason, Smith, & Diener, 1975) and even some of Mischel's own work on situational determinants of delay of gratification behavior (Funder & Harris, 1986a). These observations echo Hogan et al.'s (1977) warning that a correlation of .30 does not necessarily mean that the "remaining 91% of the variance" can be assigned, by subtraction, to the situation.

Moreover, a correlation of .30 may not be as small as many psychologists seem to believe. Common practice, as exemplified in the above warning, is to square such a correlation and report that it "accounts for 9% of the variance." However, Ozer (1985) claimed that, contrary to common belief and practice, the unsquared correlation coefficient is directly interpretable as the percentage of the variance accounted for. For example, $r = .30$ accounts for 30%, not 9%, of the relevant variance. Another way of clarifying the size of an effect in this range is Rosenthal and Rubin's (1979, 1982) binomial effect size display, which reveals that a predictor that correlates .30 with a dichotomous criterion will yield correct discriminations 65% of the time.[5] Abelson (1985) made the point in a vivid way with an application of the "percentage of variance" approach to batting performances in major league baseball players. Noting that most are in the .200s to .300s, he calculates that the percentage of variance explained in a single batting performance is less than 1%. Yet, with aggregation over seasons, these minuscule differences compound to result in discriminations important enough to determine hundreds of thousands of dollars in salary differentials. Thus, the .30 statistic that had such a devastating effect on the enterprise of personality assessment may have been badly misunderstood.

The hypothesis that personality coefficients are "too small" has been quite useful in elucidating some important limitations on what can be measured and how it should be measured. Minute and unaggregated behavioral indexes, no matter what

---

[4]An "aggregate" is an average of several variables or observations. Aggregates tend to be more reliable and therefore more predictable than single observations. For example, the average of your friendliness on 10 different occasions over the next 3 weeks would be easier to predict than how friendly you will be tomorrow at 3 p.m.

---

[5]See the selection by Rosenthal and Rubin in Part I, which is what is being referred to here.

their face validity, are not necessarily good criterion measures (Golding, 1978; West, 1983). They may be full of various sorts of error, lack temporal stability, or measure something other than what they seem to measure (Bem & Funder, 1978; Moskowitz & Schwarz, 1982; Romer & Revelle, 1984). Even if it is true, as Fiske (1979) pointed out, that judges can agree quite well about the occurrence of a given facial twitch, the twitch may be meaningless unless its context is understood (Block et al., 1979; Dahlstrom, 1972; Hogan, DeSoto & Solano, 1977). These problems may account for the repeated finding that when objective behavioral measures are compared with observers' ratings, the results do not support the superiority of behavioral measures (e.g., Eaton & Enns, 1986; Moskowitz & Schwarz, 1982).

What Have We Learned?

As with most controversies, the truth finally appears to lie not in the vivid black or white of either extreme, but somewhere in the less striking gray area. It would be a mistake, however, to claim that the interchange served only to bring out a number of "straw man" positions that no one ever took seriously anyway, that the repetitive cycle of argument and reply produced no more than fatigue and déjà vu, or that we are no closer to understanding personality traits than we were two decades ago. Radical versions of each of these hypotheses were suggested, not just for rhetorical purposes, and were passed uncritically onward to a generation of students in psychology courses. We were trained as experimental social psychologists during the heat of the debate, and the shade of gray we see now seemed much closer to a gloomy black back then. Indeed, for a time, and in some places, it was not unusual for the very idea of personality traits to be dismissed out of hand and even ridiculed.

On the other hand, one of us also underwent clinical training during that era and came across a viewpoint much closer to the "pure trait" position than is remotely tenable on the basis of the data available now. Ten years ago, there were, and

probably still are (Mischel, 1983; Wade & Baker, 1977), clinical professionals overconfidently making grand predictions from minute samples of behavior of highly questionable reliability and validity. We can eliminate the radical forms of each of the seven critical hypotheses, but that does not imply that the so-called "pure trait" position has regained the day. Systematic sources of judgmental bias, systematic effects of situations, and systematic interactions between persons and situations must be explicitly dealt with before we can predict from trait measures.

So although there may be enough signal amidst the noise in this research area to make it worthwhile to turn on the radio, the device must still be carefully tuned. Instead of simply viewing each of the seven critical hypotheses as being resolved in favor of the trait position, it is better to view each as a clue about one ever-present source of noise to be tuned out. Kenny and La Voie (1984) showed how factors such as idiosyncratic rater bias (the problem of Hypothesis 1) can even, under the proper circumstances, be turned to statistical advantage in estimating a person's "true" trait score.

Other practical lessons have emerged from this controversy. The research now indicates quite clearly that anyone who seeks predictive validity from trait ratings will do better to use (a) raters who are thoroughly familiar with the person being rated; (b) multiple behavioral observations; (c) multiple observers; (d) dimensions that are publicly observable; and (e) behaviors that are relevant to the dimension in question.

On the other hand, one should *not* expect great accuracy when predicting (a) behavior in "powerful" and clearly normatively scripted situations from trait ratings and (b) a single behavioral instance from another single behavioral instance.

Those who would respond to this list by claiming that they "knew it all along" may or may not be guilty of hindsight bias (Fischoff, 1975). But they should at least acknowledge that many of us did not know these principles all along and needed the light generated by controversy to open our eyes. For instance, the apparently "obvious" in-sight that we should not rely on ratings made by strangers can help us understand why some of the data on clinical assessment (e.g., Goldberg & Werts, 1966; Golden, 1964; Soskin, 1959) have been so disappointing, and the awareness that traits will not show up in overpowering situations has led to a dramatic reassessment of failures to find "consistency" in brief laboratory observa-tions. Likewise, if these issues and that of the un-reliability of single behavioral instances were so obvious, one is left to wonder why the field re-sponded so strongly to Mischel's (1968) critique. "Déjà vu" may be an accurate description of our current situation after all, because the term actu-ally refers to the *illusion* that one has previously experienced something that is really new.

One side effect of the person-situation debate has been an intensification of the antagonism be-tween personality and social psychology. Social psychologists have historically focused on situa-tional determinants of behavior and were there-fore quite willing to join with behavioral clinicians in the situationist attack on personality (Hogan & Emler, 1978; Kenrick & Dantchik, 1983). Person-ologists share a very different set of assumptions, and the two subdisciplines have sometimes seemed intent on defining each other out of ex-istence (Kenrick, 1986). To continue such sepa-ration between the two fields would be a mistake. Many exciting developments are beginning to emerge at the interface of social and personality psychology. For instance, research that combines personality with biology suggests a vast array of questions about the connection between person-ality traits and social interaction (Kenrick, 1987; Kenrick & Trost, 1987; Sadalla, Kenrick, & Ver-shure, 1987). And research on the accuracy of interpersonal judgment draws equally on both personality and social psychology (Funder, 1987; Funder & Colvin, 1987; Funder & Dobroth, 1987).

Houts, Cook, and Shadish (1986) made a strong case that science best progresses through multiple and mutually critical attempts to under-stand the same problem. When camps with strongly opposing sets of biases manage to come

to some level of agreement, we may be more con-fident of the validity of the conclusions that are agreed upon. Viewed in this light, the controversy stimulated by the situationist attack on personality may be seen more as a life-giving transfusion than as a needless bloodletting.

References

Abelson, R. P. (1976). A script theory of understanding, atti-tude, and behavior. In J. Carroll & J. Payne (Eds.), *Cognition and social behavior* (pp. 33–45). Hillsdale, NJ: Erlbaum.

Abelson, R. P. (1985). A variance explanation paradox: When a little is a lot. *Psychological Bulletin, 97,* 129–133.

Alker, H. A. (1972). Is personality situationally specific or in-trapsychically consistent? *Journal of Personality, 40,* 1–16.

Alker, H. A., & Owen, D. W. (1977). Biographical, trait, and behavioral-sampling predictions of performance in a stress-ful life setting. *Journal of Personality and Social Psychology, 35,* 717–723.

Allport, G. W. (1931). What is a trait of personality? *Journal of Abnormal and Social Psychology, 25,* 368–372.

Allport, G. W. (1966). Traits revisited. *American Psychologist, 21,* 1–10.

Alston, W. P. (1975). Traits, consistency, and conceptual alter-natives for personality theory. *Journal for the Theory of Social Behavior, 5,* 17–48.

Amabile, T. M., & Kabat, L. G. (1982). When self-description contradicts behavior: Actions do speak louder than words. *Social Cognition, 1,* 311–335.

Amelang, M., & Borkenau, P. (1986). The trait concept: Cur-rent theoretical considerations, empirical facts, and im-plications for personality inventory construction. In A. Angleitner & J. S. Wiggins (Eds.), *Personality assessment via questionnaire* (pp. 7–24). Berlin: Springer-Verlag.

Argyle, M., & Little, B. R. (1972). Do personality traits apply to social behavior? *Journal for the Theory of Social Behavior, 2,* 1–35.

Bem, D. J. (1972). Constructing cross-situational consistencies in behavior: Some thoughts on Alker's critique of Mischel. *Journal of Personality, 40,* 17–26.

Bem, D. J. (1983). Further *déjà vu* in the search for cross sit-uational consistency: A reply to Mischel and Peake. *Psycho-logical Review, 90,* 390–393.

Bem, D. J., & Allen, A. (1974). On predicting some of the people some of the time: The search for cross-situational consistencies in behavior. *Psychological Review, 81,* 506–520.

Bem, D. J., & Funder, D. C. (1978). Predicting more of the people more of the time: Assessing the personality of situa-tions. *Psychological Review, 85,* 485–501.

Block, J. (1968). Some reasons for the apparent inconsistency of personality. *Psychological Bulletin, 70,* 210–212.

Block, J. (1977). Advancing the science of personality: Paradig-matic shift or improving the quality of research? In D. Mag-nusson & N. S. Endler (Eds.), *Personality at the crossroads: Current issues in interactional psychology* (pp. 37–63). Hills-dale, NJ: Erlbaum.

Block, J., Buss, D. M., Block, J. M., & Gjerde, P. F. (1981). The cognitive style of breadth of categorization: The longitudinal consistency of personality correlates. *Journal of Personality and Social Psychology, 40*, 770–779.

Block, J., von der Lippe, A., & Block, J. H. (1973). Sex-role and socialization patterns: Some personality concomitants and environmental antecedents. *Journal of Consulting and Clinical Psychology, 41*, 321–341.

Block, J., Weiss, D. S., & Thorne, A. (1979). How relevant is a semantic similarity interpretation of personality ratings? *Journal of Personality and Social Psychology, 37*, 1055–1074.

Bourne, E. (1977). Can we describe an individual's personality? Agreement on stereotype versus individual attributes. *Journal of Personality and Social Psychology, 35*, 863–872.

Bowers, K. S. (1973). Situationism in psychology: An analysis and critique. *Psychological Review, 80*, 307–336.

Bryan, J., & Walbek, N. (1970). Impact of words and deeds concerning altruism upon children. *Child Development, 41*, 747–757.

Carlson, R. (1984). What's social about social psychology? Where's the person in personality research? *Journal of Personality and Social Psychology, 35*, 1055–1074.

Cheek, J. M. (1982). Aggregation, moderator variables, and the validity of personality tests: A peer-rating study. *Journal of Personality and Social Psychology, 43*, 1254–1269.

Cooley, C. H. (1902). *Human nature and the social order.* New York: Scribner's.

Cronbach, L. J. (1955). Processes affecting scores on "understanding of others" and "assumed similarity." *Psychological Bulletin, 52*, 177–193.

Dahlstrom, W. G. (1972). *Personality systematics and the problem of types.* Morristown, NJ: General Learning Press.

D'Andrade, R. G. (1974). Memory and the assessment of behavior. In H. M. Blalock (Ed.), *Measurement in the social sciences* (pp. 159–186). Chicago: Aldine-Atherton.

Dantchik, A. (1985). *Idiographic approaches to personality assessment.* Unpublished master's thesis, Arizona State University, Tempe.

Dornbusch, S. M., Hastorf, A. H., Richardson, S. A., Muzzy, R. E., & Vreeland, R. S. (1965). The perceiver and perceived: Their relative influence on categories of interpersonal perception. *Journal of Personality and Social Psychology, 1*, 434–440.

Eaton, W. D., & Enns, L. R. (1986). Sex differences in human activity level. *Psychological Bulletin, 100*, 19–28.

Endler, N. S. (1973). The person vs. situation: A pseudo issue? *Journal of Personality, 41*, 287–303.

Epstein, S. (1977). Traits are alive and well. In D. Magnusson & N. S. Endler (Eds.), *Personality at the crossroads: Current issues in interactional psychology* (pp. 83–98). Hillsdale, NJ: Erlbaum.

Epstein, S. (1979). The stability of behavior: I. On predicting most of the people much of the time. *Journal of Personality and Social Psychology, 37*, 1097–1126.

Epstein, S. (1980). The stability of behavior: II. Implications for psychological research. *American Psychologist, 35*, 790–806.

Epstein, S. (1983). The stability of confusion: A reply to Mischel and Peake. *Psychological Review, 90*, 390–393.

Epstein, S., & O'Brien, E. J. (1985). The person-situation debate in historical and current perspective. *Psychological Bulletin, 98*, 513–537.

Farber, I. E. (1964). A framework for the study of personality

as a behavioral science. In P. Worchel & D. Bryne (Eds.), *Personality change* (pp. 3–37). New York: Wiley.

Fischoff, B. (1975). Hindsight does not equal foresight: The effect of outcome knowledge on judgment under uncertainty. *Journal of Experimental Psychology: Human Perception and Performance, 1*, 288–299.

Fiske, D. W. (1974). The limits for the conventional science of personality. *Journal of Personality, 42*, 1–11.

Fiske, D. W. (1979). Two worlds of psychological phenomena. *American Psychologist, 34*, 733–739.

Fiske, S., & Taylor, S. (1984). *Social cognition.* New York: Random House.

Funder, D. C. (1980a). On seeing ourselves as others see us: Self-other agreement and discrepancy in personality ratings. *Journal of Personality, 48*, 473–493.

Funder, D. C. (1980b). The "trait" of ascribing traits: Individual differences in the tendency to trait ascription. *Journal of Research in Personality, 14*, 376–385.

Funder, D. C. (1982). On assessing social psychological theories through the study of individual differences: Template matching and forced compliance. *Journal of Personality and Social Psychology, 43*, 100–110.

Funder, D. C. (1983). Three issues in predicting more of the people: A reply to Mischel and Peake. *Psychological Review, 90*, 283–289.

Funder, D. C. (1987). Errors and mistakes: Evaluating the accuracy of social judgment. *Psychological Bulletin, 101*, 75–90.

Funder, D. C., Block, J., & Block, J. H. (1983). Delay of gratification: Some longitudinal personality correlates. *Journal of Personality and Social Psychology, 44*, 1198–1213.

Funder, D. C., & Colvin, C. R. (1987). *Friends and strangers: Acquaintanceship, agreement, and the accuracy of personality judgment.* Manuscript submitted for publication.

Funder, D. C., & Dobroth, J. M. (1987). Differences between traits: Properties associated with interjudge agreement. *Journal of Personality and Social Psychology, 52*, 409–418.

Funder, D. C., & Harris, M. J. (1986a). Experimental effects and person effects in delay of gratification. *American Psychologist, 41*, 476–477.

Funder, D. C., & Harris, M. J. (1986b). On the several facets of personality assessment: The case of social acuity. *Journal of Personality, 54*, 528–550.

Funder, D. C., & Ozer, D. J. (1983). Behavior as a function of the situation. *Journal of Personality and Social Psychology, 44*, 107–112.

Gergen, K. J. (1968). Personal consistency and the presentation of self. In C. Gordon & K. J. Gergen (Eds.), *The self in social interaction* (pp. 299–308). New York: Wiley.

Glueck, S., & Glueck, E. (1956). *Physique and delinquency.* New York: Harper & Row.

Goldberg, L. R., & Werts, C. E. (1966). The reliability of clinician's judgments: A multitrait-multimethod approach. *Journal of Consulting Psychology, 30*, 199–206.

Golden, M. (1964). Some effects of combining psychological tests on clinical inferences. *Journal of Consulting Psychology, 28*, 440–446.

Golding, S. L. (1978). Toward a more adequate theory of personality: Psychological organizing principles. In H. London (Ed.), *Personality: A new look at metatheories* (pp. 69–96). New York: Wiley.

Goldman, W., & Lewis, P. (1977). Beautiful is good: Evidence that the physically attractive are more socially skilled. *Journal of Experimental Social Psychology, 13,* 125–130.

Gormly, J., & Edelberg, W. (1974). Validity in personality trait attributions. *American Psychologist, 29,* 189–193.

Gregory, R. L. (1971). Visual illusions. In R. C. Atkinson (Ed.), *Contemporary psychology* (pp. 167–177). San Francisco: W. H. Freeman.

Hogan, R., DeSoto, C. B., and Solano, C. (1977). Traits, tests, and personality research. *American Psychologist, 32,* 255–264.

Hogan, R. T., & Emler, N. P. (1978). The biases in contemporary social psychology. *Social Research, 45,* 478–534.

Houts, A. C., Cook, T. D., & Shadish, W. R. (1986). The person-situation debate: A critical multiplist perspective. *Journal of Personality, 54,* 52–105.

Hunt, J. McV. (1965). Traditional personality theory in the light of recent evidence. *American Scientist, 53,* 80–96.

Ichheisser, G. (1943). Misinterpretations of personality in everyday life and the psychologist's frame of reference. *Character and Personality, 12,* 145–160.

Jackson, D. N. (1983). Some preconditions for valid person perception. In M. P. Zanna, E. T. Higgins, & C. P. Herman (Eds.), *Consistency in social behavior: The Ontario Symposium* (pp. 251–279). Hillsdale, NJ: Erlbaum.

James, W. (1890). *Principles of psychology* (Vol. 1). London: Macmillan.

Kenny, D. A., & La Voie, L. (1984). The social relations model. In L. Berkowitz (Ed.), *Advances in experimental social psychology* (Vol. 18, pp. 141–182). Orlando, FL: Academic Press.

Kenrick, D. T. (1986). How strong is the case against contemporary social and personality psychology? A response to Carlson. *Journal of Personality and Social Psychology, 50,* 839–844.

Kenrick, D. T. (1987). Gender, genes, and the social environment. In P. C. Shaver & C. Hendrick (Eds.), *Review of personality and social psychology: Vol. 7. Sex and gender* (pp. 14–43). Beverly Hills, CA: Sage.

Kenrick, D. T., & Braver, S. L. (1982). Personality: Idiographic and nomothetic! A rejoinder. *Psychological Review, 89,* 182–186.

Kenrick, D. T., & Dantchik, A. (1983). Interactionism, idiographics, and the social psychological invasion of personality. *Journal of Personality, 51,* 286–307.

Kenrick, D. T., & Stringfield, D. O. (1980). Personality traits and the eye of the beholder: Crossing some traditional philosophical boundaries in the search for consistency in all of the people. *Psychological Review, 87,* 88–104.

Kenrick, D. T., Stringfield, D. O., Wagenhals, W. L., Dahl, R. H., & Ransdell, H. J. (1980). Sex differences, androgyny, and approach responses to erotica: A new variation on the old volunteer problem. *Journal of Personality and Social Psychology, 40,* 1039–1056.

Kenrick, D. T., & Trost, M. R. (1987). A biosocial theory of heterosexual relationships. In K. Kelley (Ed.), *Males, females, and sexuality: Theory and research* (pp. 59–100). Albany: State University of New York Press.

Koretzky, M. B., Kohn, M., & Jeger, A. M. (1978). Cross-situational consistency among problem adolescents: An application of the two-factor model. *Journal of Personality and Social Psychology, 36,* 1054–1059.

Magnusson, D., & Endler, N. S. (Eds.). (1977). *Personality at the crossroads: Current issues in interactional psychology.* Hillsdale, NJ: Erlbaum.

McArthur, L. Z., & Baron, R. M. (1983). Toward an ecological theory of social perception. *Psychological Review, 90,* 215–235.

McCall, M., Linder, D. E., West, S. G., & Kenrick, D. T. (1985). *Some cautions on the template-matching approach to assessing person/environment interactions.* Unpublished manuscript, Arizona State University, Tempe.

McClelland, D. C. (1972). Opinions reflect opinions: So what else is new? *Journal of Consulting and Clinical Psychology, 38,* 325–326.

McCrae, R. R. (1982). Consensual validation of personality traits: Evidence from self-reports and ratings. *Journal of Personality and Social Psychology, 43,* 293–303.

McGowen, J., & Gormly, J. (1976). Validation of personality traits: A multicriteria approach. *Journal of Personality and Social Psychology, 34,* 791–795.

Miller, D. T., McFarland, C., & Turnbull, W. (1985). *Pluralistic ignorance: Its causes and consequences.* Paper presented at the annual meeting of the Eastern Psychological Association, Boston.

Mischel, W. (1968). *Personality and assessment.* New York: Wiley.

Mischel, W. (1983). Alternatives in the pursuit of the predictability and consistency of persons: Stable data that yield unstable interpretations. *Journal of Personality, 51,* 578–604.

Mischel, W. (1984). Convergences and challenges in the search for consistency. *American Psychologist, 39,* 351–364.

Mischel, W. (1985, October). *Diagnosticity of situations.* Paper presented at the meeting of the Society for Experimental Social Psychology, Evanston, IL.

Mischel, W., & Peake, P. K. (1982). Beyond *déjà vu* in the search for cross-situational consistency. *Psychological Review, 89,* 730–755.

Mischel, W., & Peake, P. K. (1983). Some facets of consistency: Replies to Epstein, Funder, and Bem. *Psychological Review, 90,* 394–402.

Monson, T. C., Keel, R., Stephens, D., & Genung, V. (1982). Trait attributions: Relative validity, covariation with behavior, and prospect of future interaction. *Journal of Personality and Social Psychology, 42,* 1014–1024.

Monson, T. C., Tanke, E. D., & Lund, J. (1980). Determinants of social perception in a naturalistic setting. *Journal of Research in Personality, 14,* 104–120.

Monson, T. C., & Snyder, M. (1977). Actors, observers, and the attribution process: Toward a reconceptualization. *Journal of Experimental Social Psychology, 13,* 89–111.

Moskowitz, D. S. (1982). Coherence and cross-situational generality in personality: A new analysis of old problems. *Journal of Personality and Social Psychology, 43,* 754–768.

Moskowitz, D. S., & Schwarz, J. C. (1982). Validity comparison of behavior counts and ratings by knowledgeable informants. *Journal of Personality and Social Psychology, 42,* 518–528.

Newcomb, T. M., Koenig, K. E., Flacks, R., & Warwick, D. P. (1967). *Persistence and change: Bennington College and its students after twenty-five years.* New York: Wiley.

Nisbett, R. E., & Ross, L. D. (1980). *Human inference: Strategies and shortcomings of social judgment.* New York: Prentice-Hall.

Norman, W. T., & Goldberg, L. R. (1966). Raters, ratees, and randomness in personality structure. *Journal of Personality and Social Psychology, 4,* 681–691.

Ozer, D. J. (1985). Correlation and the coefficient of determination. *Psychological Bulletin, 97,* 307–315.

Passini, F. T., & Norman, W. T. (1966). A universal conception of personality structure? *Journal of Personality and Social Psychology, 4,* 44–49.

Platt, J. R. (1964). Strong inference. *Science, 146,* 347–353.

Popper, K. (1959). *The logic of scientific discovery.* New York: Basic Books.

Price, R. H., & Bouffard, D. L. (1974). Behavioral appropriateness and situational constraint as dimensions of social behavior. *Journal of Personality and Social Psychology, 30,* 579–586.

Rausch, M. L. (1977). Paradox, levels, and junctures in person-situation systems. In D. Magnusson & N. S. Endler (Eds.), *Personality at the crossroads* (pp. 287–304). Hillsdale, NJ: Erlbaum.

Romer, D., & Revelle, W. (1984). Personality traits: Fact or fiction? A critique of the Shweder and D'Andrade systematic distortion hypothesis. *Journal of Personality and Social Psychology, 47,* 1028–1042.

Rosenthal, R., & Rubin, D. B. (1979). A note on percent variance explained as a measure of the importance of effects. *Journal of Applied Social Psychology, 9,* 385–396.

Rosenthal, R., & Rubin, D. B. (1982). A simple, general purpose display of magnitude of experimental effect. *Journal of Educational Psychology, 74,* 166–169.

Ross, L. (1977). The intuitive psychologist and his shortcomings: Distortions in the attribution process. In L. Berkowitz (Ed.), *Advances in experimental social psychology* (Vol. 10, pp. 174–221). New York: Academic Press.

Sadalla, E. K., Kenrick, D. T., & Vershure, B. (1987). Dominance and heterosexual attraction. *Journal of Personality and Social Psychology, 52,* 730–738.

Sarason, I. G., Smith, R. E., & Diener, E. (1975). Personality research: Components of variance attributable to the person and the situation. *Journal of Personality and Social Psychology, 32,* 199–204.

Schank, R. C., & Abelson, R. P. (1977). *Scripts, plans, goals, and understanding.* Hillsdale, NJ: Erlbaum.

Schneider, D. (1973). Implicit personality theory: A review. *Psychological Bulletin, 79,* 294–309.

Schutte, N. A., Kenrick, D. T., & Sadalla, E. K. (1985). The search for predictable settings: Situational prototypes, constraint, and behavioral variation. *Journal of Personality and Social Psychology, 49,* 121–128.

Shweder, R. A. (1975). How relevant is an individual-difference theory of personality? *Journal of Personality, 43,* 455–485.

Shweder, R. A., & D'Andrade, R. G. (1979). Accurate reflection or systematic distortion: A reply to Block, Weiss, and Thorne. *Journal of Personality and Social Psychology, 37,* 1075–1084.

Snyder, M., & Ickes, W. (1985). Personality and social behavior. In G. Lindzey & E. Aronson (Eds.), *Handbook of social psychology* (3rd ed., Vol. 2, pp. 883–948). Reading, MA: Addison-Wesley.

Snyder, M., Tanke, E. D., & Berscheid, E. (1977). Social perception and interpersonal behavior: On the self-fulfilling nature of social stereotypes. *Journal of Personality and Social Psychology, 35,* 656–666.

Soskin, W. F. (1959). Influence of four types of data on diagnostic conceptualization in psychological testing. *Journal of Abnormal and Social Psychology, 58,* 69–78.

Trope, Y., Bassok, M., & Alon, E. (1984). The questions lay interviewers ask. *Journal of Personality, 52,* 90–106.

Ulrich, R. E., Stachnik, T. J., & Stainton, N. R. (1963). Student acceptance of generalized personality interpretations. *Psychological Reports, 13,* 831–834.

Wachtel, P. (1973). Psychodynamics, behavior therapy, and the implacable experimenter: An inquiry into the consistency of personality. *Journal of Abnormal Psychology, 82,* 324–334.

Wade, T. C., & Baker, T. B. (1977). Opinions and use of psychological tests: A survey of clinical psychologists. *American Psychologist, 32,* 874–882.

West, S. G. (1983). Personality and prediction: An introduction. *Journal of Personality, 51,* 275–285.

Wiggins, J. S. (1973). *Personality and prediction: Principles of personality assessment.* Reading, MA: Addison-Wesley.

Zuroff, D. C. (1986). Was Gordon Allport a trait theorist? *Journal of Personality and Social Psychology, 51,* 993–1000.

SELF-MONITORING OF EXPRESSIVE BEHAVIOR

Mark Snyder

As the person-situation debate began to be resolved, researchers again turned their attention to interesting and consequential psychological processes that could be addressed through personality assessment. The following selection, by the influential social-personality psychologist Mark Snyder, concerns expressive behavior.

An important part of social interaction is the way we express our feelings and attitudes to one another. Snyder points out that such expressive behavior could have two sources. First, one could simply act the way one feels in a "what you see is what you get" manner. Or, second, one could adjust what one expresses with great sensitivity to the current social context. In other words, expressive behavior can be affected by both the person and the situation.

Snyder hypothesized that these two possible influences on expressive behavior vary in their relative important to different individuals. Some people, high on the trait Snyder calls "self-monitoring," sensitively adjust their expressive behavior to match what is appropriate and socially useful in the particular situational context. Others, low on self-monitoring, do not adjust their behavior so much and instead are relatively likely to express their feelings, attitudes, and personality through their behavior regardless of the situation they find themselves in.

Snyder's self-monitoring scale is short and clearly written (see Table 15.1). Take a moment, before you read the article, and answer its questions yourself. Then you will be able to compute your own score and compare your own style of social and expressive behavior with those of the people discussed in this article.

We would not be responsible editors if we did not mention that in the ensuing years the SM scale produced a small controversy of its own. In a sense it became a victim of its own success. As dozens and perhaps hundreds of studies were done using this scale, it gradually became less clear what it really measured. For example, some researchers concluded that it measured not one trait but three—extraversion, acting ability, and "other-directedness" (concern with the opinions of others, Briggs & Cheek, 1986, 1988). Snyder responded that the construct was still valid and its key findings held despite these concerns (Snyder & Gangestad, 1986). The controversy was never completely settled, and many personality psychologists remain somewhat wary of this scale and its psychometric properties.

The bottom line, though, is that the construct and scale of self-monitoring reintroduced an important topic—the study of expressive behavior—into personality psychology. Moreover, as illustrated in this article, scores on SM have been shown to be relevant to interesting behaviors and relevant group memberships (e.g., being an actor or mental patient). Despite some technical complications, the SM scale remains an interesting and useful way to identify one way in which people differ.

From "Self-Monitoring of Expressive Behavior," by M. Snyder. In *Journal of Personality and Social Psychology, 30,* 526–537. Copyright © 1974 by the American Psychological Association. Adapted with permission.

A common observation in literature and cultural folklore has been that certain nonlanguage behaviors, such as voice quality, body motion, touch, and the use of personal space appear to play a prominent role in communication. Furthermore, laboratory and field research clearly indicates that much information about a person's affective states, status and attitude, cooperative and competitive nature of social interaction, and interpersonal intimacy is expressed and accurately communicated to others in nonverbal expressive behavior (e.g., Ekman, 1971; Hall, 1966; Mehrabian, 1969; Sommer, 1969).

Much interest in nonverbal expressive behavior stems from a belief that it may not be under voluntary control and might function as a pipeline or radarscope to one's true inner "self" (e.g., Freud, 1905/1959). Although nonverbal behavior may often escape voluntary attempts at censorship (Ekman & Friesen, 1969), there have been numerous demonstrations that individuals can voluntarily express various emotions with their vocal and/or facial expressive behavior in such a way that their expressive behavior can be accurately interpreted by observers (e.g., Davitz, 1964). In fact, some social observers have proposed that the ability to manage and control expressive presentation is a prerequisite to effective social and interpersonal functioning. Thus Goffman (1955) has likened social interaction to a theatrical performance or "line" of verbal and nonverbal self-expressive acts which are managed to keep one's line appropriate to the current situation. Such self-management requires a repertoire of face-saving devices, an awareness of the interpretations which others place on one's acts, a desire to maintain social approval, and the willingness to use this repertoire of impression management tactics. Within the more restricted domain of facial expressions of emotional affect, Ekman (1971) has suggested that individuals typically exercise control over their facial expressions to intensify, deintensify, neutralize, or mask the expression of a felt affect, according to various norms of social performance.

There are, however, striking and important individual differences in the extent to which individuals can and do monitor their self-presentation, expressive behavior, and nonverbal affective display. Clearly, professional stage actors can do what I cannot. Politicians have long known how important it is to wear the right face for the right constituency. LaGuardia learned the expressive repertoires of several different cultures in New York and became, "chameleon-like," the son of whatever people he was facing. Yet little research has directly concerned such individual differences in the self-control of expressive behavior. At best, some dispositional correlates[1] of spontaneous and natural expression of emotion have been reported (e.g., Buck, Savin, Miller, & Caul, 1972; Davitz, 1964).

A CONCEPT OF SELF-MONITORING OF EXPRESSIVE BEHAVIOR How might individual differences in the self-control of expressive behavior arise? What might be the developmental, historical, and current motivational origins of self-control ability and performance? Perhaps some individuals have learned that their affective experience and expression are either socially inappropriate or lacking. Such people may *monitor* (observe and control) their self-presentation and expressive behavior. The goals of self-monitoring may be (a) to communicate accurately one's true emotional state by means of an intensified expressive presentation; (b) to communicate accurately an arbitrary emotional state which need not be congruent with actual emotional experience; (c) to conceal adaptively an inappropriate emotional state and appear unresponsive and unexpressive; (d) to conceal adaptively an inappropriate emotional state and appear to be experiencing an appropriate one; (e) to appear to be experiencing some emotion when one experiences nothing and a nonresponse is inappropriate.

An acute sensitivity to the cues in a situation which indicate what expression or self-presentation is appropriate and what is not is a corollary ability to self-monitoring. One such set of cues for guiding self-monitoring is the emotional expressive behavior of other similar comparison persons in the same situation.

There is some evidence of an acute version of this process. When persons are made uncertain of their emotional reactions, they look to the behavior of others for cues to define their emotional states and model the emotional expressive behavior of others in the same situation who appear to be behaving appropriately (Schachter & Singer, 1962).

On the other hand, persons who have not learned a concern for appropriateness of their self-presentation would not have such well-developed self-monitoring skills and would not be so vigilant to social comparison information about appropriate patterns of expression and experience. This is not to say that they are not emotionally expressive or even that they are less so than those who monitor their presentation. Rather, their self-presentation and expressive behavior seem, in a functional sense, to be controlled from within by their affective states (they express it as they feel it) rather than monitored, controlled, and molded to fit the situation.

SELF-MONITORING AND CONSISTENCY IN EXPRESSION: BETWEEN MODALITIES AND ACROSS SITUATIONS Do people, as Freud (1905/1959) believed, say one thing with their lips and another with their fingertips? More specifically, what governs the consistency between expression in different channels of expression, such as vocal and facial, and the consistency between nonverbal and verbal expression? The self-monitoring approach provides one perspective on differences and consistencies across channels of expression, including verbal self-presentation.

It is likely that when one is monitoring, various channels are monitored differentially, and perhaps some forgotten. Thus, what may be communicated by one channel may differ from what is communicated by another. For example, I may cover my sadness by putting on a happy face but forget to use a happy voice.

Ekman and Friesen (1969, 1972) have demonstrated with psychiatric patients and student nurses that in deception situations people are more likely to monitor their facial than body presentation, with the result that the deception is more likely to be detected from an examination of body cues than facial cues. Thus, the information encoded in monitored channels should differ from that encoded in nonmonitored channels. However, it is likely that great consistency characterizes that set of channels of expressive (verbal or nonverbal) behaviors which are simultaneously

_____

[1]A "dispositional correlate" is a trait found to be related to a particular behavior.

monitored according to the same criteria. Furthermore, self-monitored expressive behavior should vary more from situation to situation than nonmonitored expressive behavior. Self-monitoring individuals should be most likely to monitor and control their expression in situations which contain reliable cues to social appropriateness. Thus, such a person would be more likely to laugh at a comedy when watching it with amused peers than when watching it alone. The laughing behavior of the non-self-monitoring person should be more invariant across those two situations and more related to how affectively amused he himself actually is. The expressive behavior of self-monitoring individuals should be more reflective of an internal affect state when it is generated in a situation with minimal incentives for, and cues to, self-monitoring.

The cross-situational variability of the self-monitoring versus the consistency of the non-self-monitoring individuals is similar to the "traits versus situations" issue: Is behavior controlled by situational factors and hence predictable from characteristics of the surrounding situation, or is it controlled by internal states and dispositions which produce cross-situational consistency and facilitate prediction from characteristics of the person, measures of internal states, or dispositions (Mischel, 1968; Moos, 1968, 1969)? Bem (1972) has proposed that the issue be redirected from an "either traits or situations for all behavior of all people" debate to a search for moderating variables which would allow the specification for an individual of equivalence classes of situations and responses across which he monitors his behavior with respect to a particularly central self-concept. In these areas he would show traitlike cross-situational and interresponse mode consistency; in others he would not. In the domain of expressive behavior, individual differences in self-monitoring are a moderating variable which identifies individuals who demonstrate or fail to demonstrate consistency across channels of expression and between situations differing in monitoring properties.

IN SEARCH OF A MEASURE OF INDIVIDUAL DIFFERENCES IN SELF-MONITORING

* * *

Self-monitoring would probably best be measured by an instrument specifically designed to discriminate individual differences in concern for social appropriateness, sensitivity to the expression and self-presentation of others in social situations as cues to social appropriateness of self-expression, and use of these cues as guidelines for monitoring and managing self-presentation and expressive behavior. Accordingly, an attempt was made to transpose the self-monitoring concept into a self-report scale which reliably and validly measures it.

The convergence between diverse methods of measuring self-monitoring was examined according to the strategy of construct validation (Cronbach & Meehl, 1955). To demonstrate discriminant validity (Campbell & Fiske, 1959), comparisons were made between self-monitoring and need for approval in the prediction of each external criterion in the validation strategy.[2] Need for approval was chosen for these critical comparisons. * * *

Construction of the Self-Monitoring Scale

Forty-one true–false self-descriptive statements were administered to 192 Stanford University undergraduates. The set included items which describe (a) concern with the social appropriateness of one's self-presentation (e.g., "At parties and social gatherings, I do not attempt to do or say things that others will like"); (b) attention to social comparison information as cues to appropriate self-expression (e.g., "When I am uncertain how to act in social situations, I look to the behavior of others for cues"); (c) the ability to control and modify one's self-presentation and

---

[2]The two basic methodological articles referred to in this sentence are excerpted in Part I. It is nearly impossible to introduce a new personality scale without making reference to Cronbach-Meehl and Campbell-Fiske.

expressive behavior (e.g., "I can look anyone in the eye and tell a lie with a straight face [if for a right end]"); (d) the use of this ability in particular situations (e.g., "I may deceive people by being friendly when I really dislike them"); and (e) the extent to which the respondent's expressive behavior and self-presentation are cross-situationally consistent or variable (e.g., "In different situations and with different people, I often act like very different persons").

The individual items were scored in the direction of high self-monitoring. For approximately half the items, agreement was keyed as high SM; for the remainder, disagreement was keyed as high SM.

An item analysis was performed to select items to maximize internal consistency.

* * *

The 25 items of the SM are presented in Table 15.1.

CORRELATIONS WITH OTHER SCALES Correlations between the SM and related but conceptually distinct individual differences measures provide some evidence for its discriminant validity.[3] There is a slight negative relationship ($r = -.1874$, $df = 190$, $p < .01$) between the SM and the Marlowe-Crowne Social Desirability Scale (M-C SDS, Crowne & Marlowe, 1964). Individuals who report that they observe, monitor, and manage their self-presentation are unlikely to report that they engage in rare but socially desirable behaviors.

There is a similarly low negative relationship ($r = -.2002$, $df = 190$, $p < .01$) between the SM and the Minnesota Multiphasic Personality Inventory Psychopathic Deviate scale. High-SM subjects are unlikely to report deviant psychopathological behaviors or histories of maladjustment.

_____

[3]Discriminant validity, discussed by Campbell and Fiske in Part I, means that a scale is not redundant with other, preexisting measures. Here Snyder has decided to contrast SM with a widely used measure of "social desirability," to ensure that the SM construct is different and new.

There is a small and nonsignificant negative relationship ($r = -.25$, $df = 24$, ns) between the SM and the c scale of the Performance Style Test, (e.g., Ring & Wallston, 1968). The c scale was designed to identify a person who is knowledgeable about the kind of social performance required in a wide range of situations and who seeks social approval by becoming whatever kind of person the situation requires. He is literally a chameleon. Clearly the SM and c do not identify the same individuals.

The SM was also found to be unrelated to Christie and Geis's (1970) Machiavellianism ($r = -.0931$, $df = 51$, ns), Alpert-Haber (1960) Achievement Anxiety Test ($r = +.1437$, $df = 51$, ns), and Kassarjian's (1962) inner-other directedness ($r = -.1944$, $df = 54$, ns).

It thus appears that SM is relatively independent of the other variables measured.

* * *

Validation: Self-Monitoring, Stage Actors, and Psychiatric Ward Patients

[One] means of establishing the validity of an instrument is by predicting how predetermined groups of individuals would score when the instrument is administered to them. According to this strategy, SM scores of criterion groups chosen to represent extremes in self-monitoring were compared with the unselected sample of Stanford University undergraduates.

PROFESSIONAL STAGE ACTORS Groups of individuals known to be particularly skilled at controlling their expressive behavior (e.g., actors, mime artists, and politicians) should score higher on the SM than an unselected sample. The SM was administered to a group of 24 male and female dramatic actors who were appearing in professional productions at Stanford and in San Francisco.

Their average score on the SM was 18.41 with a standard deviation of 3.38. This is significantly

TABLE 15.1

INSTRUCTIONS. ITEMS, AND SCORING KEY, INDEXES FOR THE SELF-MONITORING SCALE[a]

Item and scoring key[a]

1. I find it hard to imitate the behavior of other people. (F)
2. My behavior is usually an expression of my true inner feelings, attitudes, and beliefs. (F)
3. At parties and social gatherings, I do not attempt to do or say things that others will like. (F)
4. I can only argue for ideas which I already believe. (F)
5. I can make impromptu speeches even on topics about which I have almost no information.(T)
6. I guess I put on a show to impress or entertain people. (T)
7. When I am uncertain how to act in a social situation, I look to the behavior of others for cues. (T)
8. I would probably make a good actor. (T)
9. I rarely need the advice of my friends to choose movies, books, or music. (F)
10. I sometimes appear to others to experiencing deeper emotions than I actually am. (T)
11. I laugh more when I watch a comedy with others than when alone. (T)
12. In a group of people I am rarely the center of attention. (F)
13. In different situations and with different people, I often act like very different persons. (T)
14. I am not particularly good at making other people like me. (F)
15. Even if I am not enjoying myself, I often pretend to be having a good time. (T)
16. I'm not always the person I appear to be. (T)
17. I would not change my opinions (or the way I do things) in order to please someone else or win their favor. (F)
18. I have considered being an entertainer.(T)
19. In order to get along and be liked, I tend to be what people expect me to be rather than anything else. (T)
20. I have never been good at games like charades or improvisational acting. (F)
21. I have trouble changing my behavior to suit different people and different situations. (F)
22. At a party I let others keep the jokes and stories going. (F)
23. I feel a bit awkward in company and do not show up quite so well as I should.(F)
24. I can look anyone in the eye and tell a lie with a straight face (if for a right end). (T)
25. I may deceive people by being friendly when I really dislike them.(T)

Note. T = true; F = false; SM = Self-monitoring scale.

[a] Directions for Personal Reaction Inventory were: The statements on the following pages concern your personal reactions to a number of different situations. No two statements are exactly alike, so consider each statement carefully before answering. If a statement is *TRUE* or *MOSTLY TRUE* as applied to you, blacken the space marked *T* on the answer sheet. If a statement is *FALSE* or *NOT USUALLY TRUE* as applied to you, blacken the space marked *F*. Do not put your answers on this test booklet itself.

It is important that you answer as frankly and as honestly as you can. Your answers will be kept in the strictest confidence.

[b] Items keyed in the direction of high SM.

higher than the mean SM score for the Stanford sample ($t = 8.27$, $df = 555$, $p < .001$).[4]

Thus, stage actors do score higher than non-actors on the SM. Actors probably do have particularly good self-control of their expressive behavior and self-presentation while on stage. It is not clear that actors are any more concerned about monitoring their expressive presentation in other situations.

HOSPITALIZED PSYCHIATRIC WARD PATIENTS
The behavior of hospitalized psychiatric patients is less variable across situations than that of "normals." Moos (1968) investigated the reactions of patients and staff in a representative sample of daily settings in a psychiatric inpatient ward in order to assess the relative amount of variance accounted for by settings and individual differences. The results indicated that for patients, individual differences accounted for more variance than setting differences; whereas for staff, individual differences generally accounted for less variance than setting differences. One interpretation of this finding is that psychiatric ward patients are unable or unwilling to monitor their social behavior and self-presentation to conform to variations in contingencies of social appropriateness between situations. In fact, diagnoses of "normal" and "psychopathological" may be closely related to cross-situational plasticity or rigidity (Cameron, 1950). Moos (1969) has reported that situational factors play an increasingly potent role in the behavior of institutionalized individuals as therapy progresses.

Accordingly, it was expected that a sample of hospitalized psychiatric ward patients should score lower on the SM than nonhospitalized normals.

The SM was administered to 31 male hospitalized psychiatric patients at the Menlo Park Veterans Administration Hospital. Their psychiatric diagnoses varied, and most had been previously institutionalized. Each patient's cumulative length of hospitalization varied from several months to several years.

The average SM score for this group was 10.19 with a standard deviation of 3.63. This is significantly lower than the mean SM score for the Stanford sample ($t = 3.44$, $df = 562$, $p < .001$).

Validation: Self-Monitoring and the Expression of Emotion

If the SM discriminates individual differences in the self-control of expressive behavior, this should be reflected behaviorally. In a situation in which individuals are given the opportunity to communicate an arbitrary affective state by means of nonverbal expressive behavior, a high-SM individual should be able to perform this task more accurately, easily, and fluently than a low SM.

METHOD

Subjects: Expression of Emotion. Male and female students whose SM scores were above the 75th percentile ($SM > 15$) or below the 25th percentile ($SM < 9$) were recruited by telephone from the pool of pretested introductory psychology students. In all, 30 high-SM and 23 low-SM subjects participated in the study and received either course credit or $1.50.

Procedure: Expression of Emotion. Each subject was instructed to read aloud an emotionally neutral three-sentence paragraph (e.g., "I am going out now. I won't be back all afternoon. If anyone calls, just tell him I'm not here.") in such a way as to express each of the seven emotions anger, happiness, sadness, surprise, disgust, fear, and guilt or remorse using their vocal and facial expressive behavior. The order of expression was determined randomly for each subject. The subject's facial and upper-body expressive behavior was filmed and his voice tape-recorded. It was suggested that he

---

[4]The t statistic reported here is a standard method for evaluating the difference between two means; *df* stands for "degrees of freedom" and is related to (but is not exactly the same as) the number of subjects.

TABLE 15.2

SM AND ACCURACY OF EXPRESSION OF
EMOTION: NAIVE JUDGES

Stimulus	High-SM judge		Low-SM judge	
	Face	Voice	Face	Voice
High SM				
(n = 30)				
Mᵃ	3.353	4.047	3.196	3.564
Variance	.718	.636	1.117	1.769
Low SM				
(n = 23)				
M	2.518	2.957	2.493	3.094
Variance	1.348	.982	1.479	2.102

Note. SM = Self-monitoring scale.

[a] Average accuracy computed for each stimulus across all judges who rated him and then averaged across n stimulus persons; range = 0–7.

imagine he was trying out for a part in a play and wanted to give an accurate, convincing, natural, and sincere expression of each emotion—one that someone listening to the tape or watching the film would be able to understand as the emotion the subject had been instructed to express. The procedure is similar to one used by Levitt (1964).

These filmed and taped samples of expressive behavior were scored by judges who indicated which of the seven emotions the stimulus person was expressing. Accuracy of the judges was used as a measure of the expressive self-control ability of the stimulus subjects.

Judgments of Expressive Behavior: Subjects. The films and tapes of expressive behavior were scored by a group of 20 high-SM (SM > 15, or top 25%) and 13 low-SM (SM < 9, or bottom 25%) naive judges who were paid $2.00 an hour.

Judgments of Emotional Expressive Behavior: Procedure. Judges participated in small groups of both high- and low-SM judges who watched films for approximately one fourth of the subjects in the expression experiment and listened to the tapes of

approximately another one fourth of the subjects. For each stimulus segment, judges indicated which of the seven emotions had been expressed.

RESULTS AND DISCUSSION

Accuracy of Expression and SM Scores. Accuracy of the judges in decoding the filmed and taped expressive behavior for each stimulus person was used as a measure of his self-control of expressive behavior ability. For each of the 53 subjects in the expression task, the average accuracy of his judges was computed separately for films and tapes and high- and low-SM judges. Table 15.2 represents these accuracy scores as a function of stimulus (expresser) SM scores, facial or vocal channel of expression, and judge SM score for naive judges. Each stimulus person expressed seven emotions. Therefore, mean accuracy scores can range from 0 to 7.

* * *

The following pattern of results emerges. Individuals who scored high on the SM were better able to communicate accurately an arbitrarily chosen emotion to naive judges than were individuals who scored low on the SM. That is, judges were more often accurate in judging both the facial and vocal expressive behavior generated in this emotion communication task by high-SM stimuli than by low-SM stimuli ($F = 11.72$, $df = 1/51$, $p < .01$).[5] For both high- and low-SM stimuli, accuracy was greater in the vocal than the facial channel ($F = 19.12$, $df = 1/153$, $p < .001$). Finally, there was a tendency for high-SM judges to be better judges of emotion than low-SM judges ($F = 1.69$, $df = 1/153$, $p < .25$). In addition, high-SM judges may have been more differentially sensitive to the expressive behavior of high- and low-SM stimuli. That is, the difference in accuracy for judging

[5]The analysis of variance and F statistics reported here are another way of evaluating mean differences. If you are not familiar with this statistic, don't worry; Snyder is just showing that the means of the high and low SM groups are different from each other on a variety of measures of nonverbal accuracy.

high-SM and low-SM stimuli for high-SM judges was greater than the corresponding difference for low-SM judges. However, once again the differences are not significant ($F = 2.41$, $df = 1/153$, $p < .25$).

* * *

Conclusions

Individuals differ in the extent to which they monitor (observe and control) their expressive behavior and self-presentation. Out of a concern for social appropriateness, the self-monitoring individual is particularly sensitive to the expression and self-presentation of others in social situations and uses these cues as guidelines for monitoring and managing his own self-presentation and expressive behavior. In contrast, the non-self-monitoring person has little concern for the appropriateness of his presentation and expression, pays less attention to the expression of others, and monitors and controls his presentation to a lesser extent. His presentation and expression appear to be controlled from within by his experience rather than by situational and interpersonal specifications of appropriateness.

* * *

References

Bem, D. J. (1972). Constructing cross-situational consistencies in behavior: Some thoughts on Alker's critique of Mischel. *Journal of Personality, 40,* 17–26.

Buck, R., Savin, V. J., Miller, R., & Caul, W. F. (1972). Nonverbal communication of affect in humans. *Journal of Personality and Social Psychology, 23,* 362–371.

Cameron, N. W. (1950). Role concepts in behavior pathology. *American Journal of Sociology, 55,* 464–467.

Campbell, D. J., & Fiske, D. W. (1959). Convergent and discriminant validation by the multitrait-multimethod matrix. *Psychological Bulletin, 56,* 81–105.

Christie, R., & Geis, F. L. (1970). *Studies in Machiavellianism.* New York: Academic Press.

Cronbach, L. J., & Meehl, P. E. (1955). Construct validity in psychological tests. *Psychological Bulletin, 52,* 281–302.

Crowne, D. P., & Marlowe, D. (1964). *The approval motive.* New York: Wiley.

Davitz, J. R. (Ed.) (1964). *The communication of emotional meaning.* New York: McGraw-Hill.

Ekman, P. (1971). Universals and cultural differences in facial expressions of emotion. In J. Cole (Ed.), *Nebraska Symposium on Motivation: 1971.* Lincoln, NE: University of Nebraska Press.

Ekman, P., & Friesen, W. V. (1969). Nonverbal leakage and clues to deception. *Psychiatry, 32,* 88–105.

Ekman, P., & Friesen, W. V. (1972). Judging deception from the face or body. Paper presented at the meeting of the Western Psychological Association, Portland, OR.

Freud, S. (1959). Fragment of an analysis of a case of hysteria. In *Collected Papers* (Vol. 3). New York: Basic Books, 1959. (Original work published 1905)

Goffman, E. (1955). On face work: An analysis of ritual elements in social interaction. *Psychiatry, 18,* 213–221.

Hall, E. T. (1966). *The hidden dimension.* Garden City, NY: Doubleday.

Kassarjian, W. M. (1962). A study of Riesman's theory of social character. *Sociometry, 25,* 213–230.

Levitt, E. A. (1964). The relationship between abilities to express emotional meanings vocally and facially. In J. R. Davitz (Ed.), *The communication of emotional meaning.* New York: McGraw-Hill.

Mehrabian, A. (1969). Significance of posture and position in the communication of attitude and status relationship. *Psychological Bulletin, 71,* 359–372.

Mischel, W. (1968). *Personality and assessment.* New York: Wiley.

Moos, R. H. (1968). Situational analysis of a therapeutic community milieu. *Journal of Abnormal Psychology, 73,* 49–61.

Moos, R. H. (1969). Sources of variance in responses to questionnaires and in behavior. *Journal of Abnormal Psychology, 74,* 403–412.

Ring, K., & Wallston, K. (1968). A test to measure performance styles in interpersonal relations. *Psychological Reports, 22,* 147–154.

Schachter, S., & Singer, J. (1962). Cognitive, social, and physiological determinants of emotional state. *Psychological Review, 69,* 379–399.

Sommer, R. (1969). *Personal space.* Englewood Cliffs, NJ: Prentice-Hall.

Adolescent Drug Use and Psychological Health: A Longitudinal Inquiry

Jonathan Shedler and Jack Block

Whether one will become a drug abuser, an experimental user, or a complete abstainer is to an important degree dependent upon one's personality. That is the important message of the following article, by Jack Block and his former research associate Jonathan Shedler. This study uses Block's longitudinal study, described in his chapter in Part I, to examine the personality correlates and antecedents of drug use and abuse. The data show that a large number of personality traits are associated with patterns of drug use, and perhaps even more importantly show that these associations can be found in childhood, years before subjects encountered drugs for the first time.

The latter finding implies that many of the psychological problems associated with drug abuse precede rather than follow the behavior, and therefore interventions designed around "just saying no" largely miss the point. They miss the point because the situation is not so much that drug use causes problems, but that psychological problems cause drug abuse. The most effective interventions, therefore, would attempt to prevent potential drug abusers from developing psychological difficulties in the first place.

Another finding from this study became more widely publicized, and generated quite a bit of controversy for a time. This was the finding that "experimenters," the vast majority of adolescents in this sample who had briefly tried various drugs (typically marijuana), were in psychologically better shape than either drug abusers or complete abstainers. This finding implies that some of the experimentation with drugs by American youth during the time of this sample's adolescence was not a pathology but a normal pattern of trying out a variety of different behaviors, some forbidden. But as Shedler and Block anticipated in the last section of their article, this is a finding seemingly born to be misinterpreted. As they feared, a surprising number of media reports of their research said they had claimed that moderate drug use is good for you!

It is difficult, as Shedler and Block found, to do research on an emotionally charged topic like drug abuse and not have one's results distorted and misunderstood. Still, this study has been importantly beneficial, and is one of the mostly frequently cited investigations in personality in recent years. It demonstrates how personality research can be important for understanding the roots of important behaviors and even for the intelligent design of social policy.

From "Adolescent Drug Use and Psychological Health: A Longitudinal Inquiry," by J. Shedler and J. Block. In *American Psychologist*, 45, 612–630. Based on the findings of "The Longitudinal Study of Personality and Cognitive Development" originated by Jack and Jeanne Block in 1969. Funding for the study provided by the National Institute of Mental Health. Copyright © 1990 by the American Psychological Association. Adapted with permission.

* * *

Drug abuse among young people is one of the greatest challenges of our time. Almost daily, we are besieged by media reports of drug-related tragedy, of shootings in our schools, gang warfare, and overdose-related deaths. Many see the drug problem as epidemic (Robins, 1984). As an increasing share of society's resources is diverted toward coping with the drug problem and its consequences, the need for sound, scientific information on the factors contributing to drug use is urgent.

Considerable research has already been directed toward studying the causes and correlates of drug use, and important recognitions have developed (for reviews, see Bush & Iannotti, 1985; Cox, 1985; Hawkins, Lishner, & Catalano, 1985; Jessor, 1979; Jones & Battjes, 1985; Kandel, 1980). Nevertheless, many studies to date have been interpretively constrained by various research-design or empirical limitations.

Large-scale epidemiological studies (e.g., Jessor, Chase, & Donovan, 1980; Johnston, O'Malley, & Bachman, 1984, 1986; National Institute on Drug Abuse [NIDA], 1986) have provided much-needed information about the prevalence and patterns of drug use, about the demographics of drug users, and about certain psychosocial characteristics of drug users. In general, however, these studies have been unable to provide the kind of in-depth, psychologically rich, clinically oriented information needed to inform intervention efforts. And by their very nature, cross-sectional studies and panel studies of relatively brief duration can offer only limited or confounded understandings of the antecedents of drug use.

* * *

The present study reports on the Block and Block sample, studied in late adolescence when the subjects had reached age 18. * * * The findings we report span 13 years, from preschool through age 18. By virtue of their prospective nature, these data allow inferences about the antecedents of drug use that cannot be made from retrospective, cross-sectional, or short-term panel studies.

Beyond the length of time spanned by the present investigation, the study differs from previous studies in two important ways. In most empirical studies, psychological descriptions are limited to a small number of variables that are selected by researchers on a priori grounds. In the present study, psychological descriptions are, for all practical purposes, comprehensive and open-ended. They are based on extensive evaluations of participants by panels of psychologists, and they encompass the full range of constructs subsumed by the California Adult Q-sort (CAQ; Block, 1961/1978) and the California Child Q-sort (CCQ; J. Block & J. H. Block, 1980)—personality assessment instruments specifically designed to allow clinicians to provide in-depth, comprehensive psychological descriptions. The intention was to gather information psychologically rich enough to speak to clinical concerns and to inform intervention efforts.

The study also differs from previous studies in its approach to data analysis. Previous investigators have tended to assume (and test for) linear relations between level of drug use and measures of psychosocial disturbance. In effect, such an approach assumes that occasional experimentation with drugs is psychologically problematic, if not quite as problematic as regular use, and that complete avoidance of drugs is psychologically optimal.

However, the majority of young adults in the United States, nearly two thirds, have experimented with marijuana at one time or another (Johnston et al., 1986; Johnston, Bachman, & O'Malley, 1981a, 1981b; Miller et al., 1983; NIDA, 1986), and the vast majority of these young people do not subsequently become drug *abusers*. Little is known about the relative psychosocial adjustment of adolescents who have experimented with drugs on an occasional basis and of adolescents who have avoided drugs entirely. Indeed, a number of researchers have suggested that occasional drug use among adolescents may be best understood as a manifestation of *developmentally appropriate* experimentation. Newcomb and Bentler (1988), for example, have observed that

> one defining feature of adolescence is a quest for or establishment of independence and autonomous identity and functioning. This may involve experimentation with a wide range of behaviors, attitudes, and activities before choosing a direction and way of life to call one's own. This process of testing attitudes and behavior may include drug use. In fact, experimental use of various drugs, both licit and illicit, *may be considered a normative behavior among United States teenagers in terms of prevalence, and from a developmental task perspective.* (p. 214, emphasis added)

These empirical and developmental considerations suggest that the relations between psychological variables and level of drug use may not be linear at all. To the extent that drug experimentation may represent normative behavior during the prolonged adolescent period, as individuals seek a sense of self and possibility, it may be wrong to pathologize adolescents who experiment with drugs by assuming that they fall between nonusers and drug abusers on a continuum of psychosocial adjustment. To evaluate this conceptual possibility in the present study, we identify and contrast discrete groups of nonusers, experimenters, and frequent drug users. * * *

Method

SUBJECTS Subjects were 101 18-year-olds, 49 boys and 52 girls, from an initial sample of 130 participating in a longitudinal study of ego and cognitive development. The subjects were initially recruited into the study at age 3, while attending either a university-run nursery school or a parent-cooperative nursery school in the San Francisco Bay area. They were assessed on wide-ranging batteries of psychological measures at ages 3, 4, 5, 7, 11, 14, and 18 (see J. H. Block & J. Block, 1980, for an extended description of the study). Because so few subjects were lost over the years, there can be little influence of differential attrition.

The subjects live primarily in urban settings and are heterogeneous with respect to social class and parent education. About two thirds are white, one fourth are black, and one twelfth are Asian. Not all subjects are used in all analyses to be reported, as will be discussed.

MEASURING DRUG USE Information about drug use was collected at age 18 during individual interviews with the subjects. Skilled clinicians conducted these interviews, which ranged over a variety of topics including schoolwork, peer relations, family dynamics, personal interests, dating experiences, and so on. Total interview time was typically four hours per subject, and all interviews were videotaped.

The subjects were asked whether they "smoked pot or used it in another form." Their responses were coded from the interview videotapes as follows: (0) never used marijuana; (1) used once or twice; (2) used a few times; (3) used once a month; (4) used once a week; (5) used two or three times a week; and (6) used daily. The subjects were also given a list of other substances and were asked to check which (if any) they had used at least once on a "recreational" basis. The list included inhalants (e.g., glue, nitrous oxide), cocaine, hallucinogens, barbiturates, amphetamines, tranquilizers, heroin, and an open-ended category for "other" drugs not specifically listed.

Although self-report data on drug use are always subject to underreporting, the findings of a number of investigations indicate that such data have high validity (e.g., Block, Block, & Keyes, 1988; Haberman, Josephson, Zanes, & Elinson, 1972; Jessor & Jessor, 1977; Perry, Killen, & Slinkard, 1980; Single, Kandel, & Johnston, 1975). Additionally, there is every reason to believe that the subjects in this investigation answered our questions honestly. The interviewers were skilled in gaining rapport and in eliciting information without inducing discomfort. Moreover, the subjects had been involved in the longitudinal study from earliest childhood; they not only had been assured that their individual responses would be held in confidence, but they knew from years of prior experience that this promise had been honored.

MEASURING PERSONALITY *Age 18 assessment.* At age 18, the personality characteristics of each subject were described by four psychologists, using the standard vocabulary of the California Adult Q-sort (Block, 1961/1978). The CAQ is a personality assessment instrument that allows psychologists to provide comprehensive personality descriptions in a conceptually systematic, quantifiable, and readily comparable form. The CAQ consists of 100 personality-descriptive statements, each printed on a separate index card. The psychologist sorts these statements into a fixed nine-step distribution, according to their evaluated salience vis-à-vis the person being described. Thus, the CAQ yields a score of 1 through 9 for each of 100 personality-descriptive statements; higher scores indicate that a statement is relatively characteristic of a person, and lower scores indicate that it is relatively uncharacteristic. The validity and usefulness of Q-sort personality

descriptions have been demonstrated frequently (see, e.g., Bem & Funder, 1978; Block, 1961/1978; Block, 1971; Gjerde, Block, & Block, 1988; Mischel, Shoda, & Peake, 1988).

The psychologists based their CAQ descriptions of each subject on observations made while administering a variety of experimental procedures designed to tap various aspects of psychological functioning. These psychologists were *not* the interviewers who gathered information about drug use; they had no knowledge of subjects' drug use or of any other information elicited during the interviews. Each of the four psychologists who provided CAQ-based personality descriptions saw the subjects in a different assessment context, so that four entirely independent Q-sort descriptions were available per subject. The scores assigned to each Q-sort item were then averaged across the four psychologists, to yield a final, composite Q-sort for each subject. These composite Q-sorts thus represent the consensual judgment of four independent assessors. The reliabilities of the composite Q-sorts differed somewhat from subject to subject, and were of the order of .70 to .90.[1]

Childhood assessments. At ages 7 and 11, the personality characteristics of the subjects were described in a similar manner, each time by entirely different sets of psychologists, using the standard vocabulary of the California Child Q-sort (CCQ). The CCQ is an age-appropriate modification of the California Adult Q-sort, and consists of statements describing the personality, cognitive, and social characteristics of children (see J. Block & J. H. Block, 1980; J. H. Block & J. Block, 1980). At age 7, the standard 100-item CCQ was used; at age 11, an abridged 63-item version was used. Three psychologists observed the children at age 7, and five psychologists observed the children at age 11, while administering a variety of age-

---

[1] Reliability refers to the consistency of measurement across occasions or judges. In this context, the averaged ratings of four *new* assessors of the same subjects would be expected to correlate with these averages with an *r* of .70 to .90.

appropriate experimental procedures. The scores assigned to the CCQ items were averaged across the psychologists to produce a composite Q-sort for age 7 and a composite Q-sort for age 11. Again, the reliabilities of the composite Q-sorts were of the order of .70 to .90.

* * *

Results

RATES OF DRUG USE   The primary purpose of this study was to investigate the relations between drug use and psychological characteristics. However, it is first useful to consider the rate of drug use in the sample in absolute terms.

Of the 101 subjects for whom information about drug use was available, 68% had tried marijuana (four years earlier, 51% of the subjects had used marijuana; see Keyes & Block, 1984). Thirty-nine percent of the subjects reported using marijuana once a month or more, and 21% reported using it weekly or more than weekly. These figures are comparable to figures obtained in nationwide probability samples of adolescents and young adults (Johnston et al., 1986; Johnston, Bachman & O'Malley, 1981a, 1981b; Miller et al., 1983; NIDA, 1986).

Approximately 37% of the subjects reported trying cocaine, and 25% reported trying hallucinogens. Approximately 10% of the subjects reported trying amphetamines, barbiturates, tranquilizers, or inhalants. Only one subject reported that she had used heroin.

CREATION OF COMPARISON GROUPS   Based on the drug use information collected at age 18, the subjects were divided into three nonoverlapping groups, as follows.

Abstainers were defined as subjects who had never tried marijuana or any other drug. This group contained 29 subjects, 14 boys and 15 girls.

Experimenters were defined as subjects who had used marijuana "once or twice," "a few times," or "once a month," and who had tried *no more* than one drug other than marijuana. This group contained 36 subjects, 16 boys and 20 girls.

The mean number of other drugs tried by the subjects in this group was 0.31 (i.e., 11 of the 36 subjects had tried one drug other than marijuana).

Frequent users were defined as subjects who reported using marijuana frequently; that is, once a week or more, and who had tried *at least* one drug other than marijuana. This group contained 20 subjects, 11 boys and 9 girls. The mean number of other drugs tried by the subjects in this group was 2.70.

Sixteen subjects "fell between the cracks" of the classification scheme, and did not meet the definitional criteria for any of the groups. In general, these were subjects who were excluded from the abstainer and experimenter groups because of their use of drugs other than marijuana.

The basis for the groupings derives from conceptual considerations, as well as from some recognitions derived from prior evaluation of the subjects in early adolescence (Block et al., 1988). Obviously, a degree of arbitrariness is unavoidable in any such classification scheme; however, the results to be reported are robust with respect to the various group definitions. That is, we considered both broader and narrower definitions for the various groups (e.g., excluding from the group of experimenters subjects who had tried any drug other than marijuana, or including subjects who had tried as many as two other drugs). As long as the sample was divided into three groups that could be broadly construed in terms of nonusers, experimenters, and regular users, the pattern of results we report emerged reliably.

* * *

Personality Concomitants of Drug Use

The major findings from the age 18 personality assessment are presented in Table 16.1, which lists mean scores for the CAQ items differentiating between frequent drug users, experimenters, and abstainers.

Findings are presented using the experimenters as a reference group, and the personality characteristics associated with the other groups are elucidated through comparison with them. The experimenters are used as a frame of reference for two reasons: (a) they constitute the largest group and reflect the pattern of drug use most typical for this sample and most typical for adolescents in the nation as a whole; (b) the group of experimenters lies between the other groups on the continuum of frequency of drug use; therefore, its use as a reference group facilitates the discernment of possible curvilinear relations between drug use and personality measures. As will be seen, this second consideration takes on considerable importance.

PERSONALITY CHARACTERISTICS OF FREQUENT USERS The frequent users were compared with the experimenters on each of the 100 Q-sort items, by means of separate t-tests. The number of statistically significant differences between the groups is striking and far exceeds the number to be expected by chance. Fully 51 of the 100 Q-sort items revealed differences at the .05 significance level.[2]

The following set of Q-sort items, all of which discriminate beyond the .05 level, serve to characterize the frequent users. The items are grouped according to general conceptual similarity. Inspection of Table 16.1 will reveal additional items that supplement this summary characterization.

Relative to experimenters, frequent users are described as not dependable or responsible, not productive or able to get things done, guileful and deceitful, opportunistic, unpredictable and changeable in attitudes and behavior, unable to delay gratification, rebellious and nonconforming, prone to push and stretch limits, self-indulgent, not ethically consistent, not having high aspirations, and prone to express hostile feelings directly.

Relative to experimenters, frequent users are also described as critical, ungiving, not sympathetic or considerate, not liked and accepted by others, not having warmth or the capacity for

close relationships, having hostility toward others, prone to avoid close relationships, distrustful of people, not gregarious, not personally charming, and not socially at ease.

Finally, frequent users are described as relatively overreactive to minor frustrations, likely to think and associate to ideas in unusual ways, having brittle ego-defense systems, self-defeating, concerned about the adequacy of their bodily functioning, concerned about their adequacy as persons, prone to project their feelings and motives onto others, feeling cheated and victimized by life, and having fluctuating moods.

Consistent with the CAQ descriptions suggesting alienation and poor impulse control, the frequent users attain significantly lower high school grade-point averages than the experimenters, 2.3 versus 3.0 ($p < .01$).[3]

When the Q-sort descriptions are considered as a set, the picture of the frequent user that emerges is one of a troubled adolescent, an adolescent who is interpersonally alienated, emotionally withdrawn, and manifestly unhappy, and who expresses his or her maladjustment through undercontrolled, overtly antisocial behavior.

PERSONALITY CHARACTERISTICS OF ABSTAINERS The abstainers were compared with the experimenters on each of the 100 Q-sort items, by means of separate t-tests. Once again, the number of statistically significant CAQ items well exceeds chance, with 19 of the 100 CAQ items showing differences between the groups at the .05 level.

The following Q-sort items, all significant beyond the .05 level, serve to characterize the abstainers.

Relative to experimenters, abstainers are described as fastidious, conservative, proud of being "objective" and rational, overcontrolled and prone to delay gratification unnecessarily, not liked or accepted by people, moralistic, unexpressive,

---

[2]The .05 significance level is conventionally taken to mean that these correlations have an only 5% probability of appearing if the true correlation is zero.

[3]This notation refers to a .01 significance level, which in this case means that if there truly were no difference between the groups, the differences reported would be obtained less than 1% of the time.

TABLE 16.1

MEAN SCORES FOR AGE 18 CALIFORNIA ADULT Q-SORT (CAQ) ITEMS

CAQ item	Group		
	Abstainers	Experimenters	Frequent users
1. Is critical, skeptical, not easily impressed.	4.9	4.6	5.6***
2. Is genuinely dependable and responsible person.	7.7	7.5	5.9***
5. Behaves in a giving way with others.	6.4	6.5	5.5***
6. Is fastidious.	5.3**	4.9	4.2**
7. Favors conservative values in a variety of areas.	5.6**	5.0	3.6***
13. Thin-skinned; sensitive to anything that can be construed as criticism.	4.2	4.0	4.7**
17. Behaves in a sympathetic or considerate manner.	7.2	7.3	6.2***
18. Initiates humor.	5.3*	5.7	5.3
19. Seeks reassurance from others.	5.0	4.9	4.3*
21. Arouses nurturant feelings in others.	5.1*	5.4	4.7***
22. Feels a lack of personal meaning in life.	2.6	2.7	3.8***
23. Extrapunitive; tends to transfer or project blame.	3.7*	3.4	4.0**
24. Prides self on being "objective," rational.	6.2***	5.5	5.1
25. Overcontrols needs and impulses; delays gratification unnecessarily.	4.8***	3.9	3.3**
26. Is productive; gets things done.	7.1*	6.7	5.6***
27. Shows condescending behavior to others.	2.5	2.2	3.0***
28. Tends to arouse liking and acceptance in people.	7.0***	7.6	6.2***
29. Is turned to for advice and reassurance	5.0	5.0	4.3***
30. Gives up and withdraws in face of frustration, adversity.	3.6	4.0	4.7*
31. Regards self as physically attractive.	5.4**	5.8	5.4
34. Overreactive to minor frustrations; irritable.	3.5	3.4	4.4***
35. Has warmth, capacity for close relationships.	7.2	7.5	6.7***
36. Is subtly negativistic; tends to undermine, sabotage.	2.9	2.5	4.0***
37. Is guileful and deceitful, manipulative, opportunistic.	1.7	1.6	2.4***
38. Has hostility toward others.	3.5	3.3	4.4***
39. Thinks and associates to ideas in unusual ways.	4.2	4.3	5.0**
41. Is moralistic.	4.6***	4.2	3.9
42. Delays or avoids action.	3.4*	3.8	4.1
43. Is facially and/or gesturally expressive.	5.2***	5.9	5.5
45. Has a brittle ego-defense system; maladaptive under stress.	3.0	2.9	3.6**
48. Keeps people at a distance; avoids close interpersonal relationships.	3.7**	3.0	3.9**
49. Is basically distrustful of people in general.	3.4	3.1	4.2***

50. Is unpredictable and changeable in behavior, attitudes.	3.7**	4.0	4.9***
51. Genuinely values intellectual and cognitive matters.	7.0*	6.5	6.0
53. Undercontrols needs and impulses; unable to delay gratification.	2.9***	3.7	4.4***
54. Emphasizes being with others; gregarious.	5.6**	6.2	5.3***
55. Is self-defeating.	3.2	3.0	4.1***
56. Responds to humor.	6.8*	7.2	6.8
58. Enjoys sensuous experiences (touch, taste, smell, physical contact).	5.3***	5.7	6.0**
62. Tends to be rebellious and nonconforming.	3.5	3.8	5.8***
63. Judges self and others in conventional terms (e.g., "popularity").	5.4	5.2	4.4***
65. Characteristically pushes and tries to stretch limits.	3.6	3.7	5.2***
67. Is self-indulgent.	4.1	4.2	4.9***
68. Is basically anxious.	4.3**	3.8	4.3
69. Is sensitive to anything that can be construed as a demand.	4.7	4.4	5.1**
70. Behaves in an ethically consistent manner.	6.8	6.5	6.0**
71. Has high aspiration level for self.	7.0	6.4	5.4***
72. Concerned with own adequacy as a person.	5.4	5.0	6.0***
73. Tends to perceive many different contexts in sexual terms.	3.9***	4.3	4.7*
74. Subjectively unaware of self-concern, satisfied with self.	5.1	5.5	4.9*
75. Has clear-cut, internally consistent personality.	6.7	6.6	5.9***
76. Tends to project own feelings and motivations onto others.	4.5	4.5	4.9**
77. Appears straightforward, forthright, candid with others.	7.1***	7.6	6.0***
78. Feels cheated and victimized by life; self-pitying.	2.2	2.1	3.0***
80. Interested in members of the opposite sex.	6.1***	6.6	6.6
81. Is physically attractive; good-looking.	5.9***	6.6	6.1*
82. Has fluctuating moods.	4.8	4.9	5.5***
84. Is cheerful.	6.9*	7.6	5.7***
86. Handles anxiety and conflict by denial, repression.	4.5	4.2	4.7*
88. Is personally charming.	5.9**	6.5	5.5***
92. Has social poise and presence; is socially at-ease.	6.3**	6.9	5.6***
93. Is sex-typed (masculine/feminine).	6.8	7.0	6.4**
94. Expresses hostile feelings directly.	3.8	3.9	4.3**
96. Values own independence and autonomy.	7.0	7.1	7.8***

* Differs from experimenters, $p < .10$. ** Differs from experimenters, $p < .05$. *** Differs from experimenters, $p < .01$.

prone to avoid close interpersonal relationships, predictable in attitudes and behavior, not gregarious, not able to enjoy sensuous experiences, basically anxious, not straightforward and forthright with others, not physically attractive, not personally charming, and not socially at ease.

The abstainers and the experimenters achieve identical high school grade point averages, 3.0 in both cases.

When the Q-sort items are considered as a set, the picture of the abstainer that emerges is of a relatively tense, overcontrolled, emotionally constricted individual who is somewhat socially isolated and lacking in interpersonal skills.

Personality Antecedents of Drug Use

An unusual feature of the present study is that psychological descriptions of subjects are available from early childhood on. Moreover, the psychological descriptions obtained at different ages are wholly independent of one another. We wish to emphasize this independence: The psychologists who saw the subjects at different ages were different people, they saw the subjects under different conditions, they saw the subjects only at the age at which they served as assessors, and they had no contact with one another. Because of the safeguards taken to ensure the independence of the data, relations between psychological characteristics observed at age 18 and psychological characteristics observed in early childhood must be attributed to continuities in psychological development over time (and not to artifacts of the research design).

On the basis of the CAQ descriptions obtained at age 18, a priori directional hypotheses were generated for virtually all of the age 11 and age 7 California Child Q-Sort items. Specifically, it was hypothesized that abstainers would show signs of impulse overcontrol, and frequent users would show signs of impulse undercontrol, relative to experimenters; and that abstainers and frequent users would both show signs of interpersonal

alienation and psychological distress, relative to experimenters. In view of the existence of directional hypotheses and the independence of the data collected at different ages, one-tailed statistical tests were employed in evaluating the childhood CCQ data. Table 16.2 lists the mean scores for the age 11 CCQ items discriminating between the groups (recall that an abridged 63-item Q-sort was used at the age 11 assessment, so fewer significant relationships can be expected), and Table 16.3 lists the mean scores for the age 7 CCQ items discriminating between groups.

THE CHILDHOOD PERSONALITY OF FREQUENT USERS The frequent users were compared with the experimenters on each of the CCQ items by means of separate *t*-tests. At age 11, frequent users were described (in comparison to experimenters) as visibly deviant from their peers, emotionally labile, inattentive and unable to concentrate, not involved in what they do, stubborn (preceding items significant at the .05 level), unhelpful and uncooperative, pushing and stretching limits, not eager to please, immobilized under stress, not curious and open to new experience, likely to give up easily, likely to withdraw under stress, not having high performance standards, suspicious and distrustful, and overreactive to minor frustrations (preceding items significant at the .10 level).

At age 7, the frequent users were described as not getting along well with other children, not showing concern for moral issues (e.g., reciprocity, fairness), having bodily symptoms from stress, tending to be indecisive and vacillating, not planful or likely to think ahead, not trustworthy or dependable, not able to admit to negative feelings, not self-reliant or confident (preceding items significant at the .05 level), preferring nonverbal methods of communication, not developing genuine and close relationships, not proud of their accomplishments, not vital or energetic or lively, not curious and open to new experience, not able to recoup after stress, afraid of being deprived, appearing to feel unworthy and "bad," not likely to identify with admired adults, inappropriate in emotive behavior, and easily victimized and scapegoated by other children (preceding items significant at the .10 level).

In short, the frequent users appear to be relatively maladjusted as children. As early as age 7, the picture that emerges is of a child unable to form good relationships, who is insecure, and who shows numerous signs of emotional distress. These data indicate that the relative social and psychological maladjustment of the frequent users predates adolescence, and predates initiation of drug use.

THE CHILDHOOD PERSONALITY OF ABSTAINERS The abstainers were compared with the experimenters on each of the CCQ items. At age 11, the abstainers were described as relatively fearful and anxious, using and responding to reason, not physically active, not vital or energetic or lively, inhibited and constricted, not liking to compete, not curious and open to new experiences, not interesting or arresting, physically cautious, neat and orderly (implies fussiness), anxious in unpredictable environments, not having a rapid personal tempo, looking to adults for help and direction, not responsive to humor, not self-assertive, not self-reliant or confident, shy and reserved (preceding items significant at the .05 level), cold and unresponsive, immobilized under stress, obedient and compliant, not calm or relaxed, planful and likely to think ahead, not cheerful, not talkative, and not aggressive (preceding items significant at the .10 level).

At age 7, the abstainers were described as relatively eager to please, inhibited and constricted, conventional in thought, neat and orderly, planful and likely to think ahead, not verbally expressive, not seeking to be independent and autonomous (preceding items significant at the .05 level), not proud of their accomplishments, not physically active, immobilized under stress, obedient and compliant, not self-assertive, not competent and skillful, and not creative (preceding items significant at the .10 level).

These descriptions present a picture of a child who is relatively overcontrolled, timid, fearful, and morose. While the characterizations of these children as "anxious," "inhibited," and "immobilized under stress" are telling, more telling, perhaps, may be the descriptions of what these children are not; relative to the reference group of experimenters, they are not warm and responsive, not curious and open to new experience, not active, not vital, and not cheerful.

* * *

General Discussion

SUMMARY OF MAJOR FINDINGS On the basis of the drug use information collected at age 18, subjects were divided into nonoverlapping groups made up of frequent drug users, experimenters, and abstainers. At age 18, frequent users were observed to be alienated, deficient in impulse control, and manifestly distressed, compared with experimenters. At age 18, abstainers were observed to be anxious, emotionally constricted, and lacking in social skills, compared with experimenters.

Differences between the groups were evident during childhood as well, at the age 7 and age 11 assessments. Consistent with the age 18 findings, frequent users were judged to be relatively insecure, unable to form healthy relationships, and emotionally distressed as children, compared with experimenters. Also consistent with the age 18 findings, abstainers were judged to be relatively anxious, inhibited, and morose as children, compared with experimenters.

* * *

ON THE RELATION BETWEEN DRUG USE AND PSYCHOLOGICAL HEALTH When the psychological findings are considered as a set, it is difficult to escape the inference that experimenters are the psychologically healthiest subjects, healthier than either abstainers or frequent users. Psychological health is meant here in a global and nonspecific sense, consistent with ordinary conversational usage, and consistent also with empirical recognitions by mental health researchers that a general psychological health/psychological distress factor underlies diverse clinical syndromes (e.g., Dohrenwend, Shrout, Egri, & Mendelsohn, 1980; Tanaka & Huba, 1984; Watson & Clark, 1984). * * *

The finding that frequent users are relatively

TABLE 16.2

MEAN SCORES FOR AGE 11 CALIFORNIA CHILD Q-SORT (CCQ) ITEMS

CCQ item	Group		
	Abstainers	Experimenters	Frequent users
1. Prefers nonverbal methods of communication.	4.6	4.5	5.1*
3. Is warm and responsive.	5.3**	6.2	5.2**
6. Is helpful and cooperative.	7.0	7.2	6.5**
8. Tends to keep thoughts, feelings, or products to self.	5.6*	4.7	5.3
13. Characteristically pushes and tries to stretch limits.	3.0*	3.6	4.2
14. Is eager to please.	6.0	6.1	5.3**
21. Tries to be the center of attention.	3.1**	3.8	3.9
23. Is fearful and anxious.	4.5***	3.3	4.0
25. Uses and responds to reason.	7.3**	6.6	6.5
26. Is physically active.	5.2**	5.9	5.7
27. Is visibly deviant from peers in physical appearance.	3.3	3.0	3.7**
28. Is vital, energetic, lively.	4.9**	5.9	5.2
30. Tends to arouse liking and acceptance in adults.	6.1	6.5	5.9*
34. Is restless and fidgety.	3.7***	4.6	5.1
35. Is inhibited and constricted.	5.1**	3.9	4.4
37. Likes to compete; tests and compares self with others.	4.1**	4.5	4.6
39. Becomes rigidly repetitive or immobilized under stress.	4.2*	3.5	4.2*
40. Is curious, eager to learn, open to new experiences.	5.4***	6.4	5.7*
41. Is persistent in activities; does not give up easily.	5.9	5.6	5.1*
42. Is an interesting, arresting child.	5.1**	5.8	5.1*
45. Tends to withdraw and disengage when under stress.	5.0*	4.2	5.2**
47. Has high standards of performance for self.	6.1	5.9	5.1**

maladjusted has been obtained by many other investigators. The finding that abstainers also show some signs of relative maladjustment (albeit of a very different kind) is, perhaps, unusual. In order to understand this latter finding, we suggest it is important to consider both the *meaning* of drug use within adolescent peer culture, as well as the psychology of adolescent development.

First, it is necessary to recognize that in contemporary American culture, there is wide prevalence and apparent acceptability of marijuana use in late adolescence. The majority of the 18-year-olds in our sample—approximately two thirds—had tried marijuana at one time or another. Such a high usage rate is consistent with the findings from national probability samples (Johnston et al., 1986; Johnston, Bachman, & O'Malley, 1981a, 1981b, Miller et al., 1983; NIDA, 1986). Thus, some experimentation with marijuana cannot be considered *deviant* behavior for high school seniors in this culture at this time. In a statistical sense it is *not* trying marijuana that has become deviant.

52. Is physically cautious.	5.1***	4.0	4.5
54. Has rapid shifts in mood; is emotionally labile.	3.5	3.4	4.2**
59. Is neat and orderly in dress and behavior.	6.5***	5.5	5.2
60. Becomes anxious in unpredictable environment.	4.9**	4.0	4.8*
62. Is obedient and compliant.	6.5*	58	5.6
63. Has a rapid personal tempo; reacts and moves quickly.	4.2**	5.0	4.6
64. Is calm and relaxed, easygoing.	5.0*	5.6	5.2
66. Is attentive and able to concentrate.	7.0	6.6	5.9*
67. Is planful; thinks ahead.	6.9**	6.1	5.9
71. Looks to adults for help and direction.	5.6*	5.0	4.6
73. Responds to humor.	4.9**	5.7	5.7
74. Becomes strongly involved in what she or he does.	5.8	6.2	5.2**
75. Is cheerful (low placement implies unhappiness).	5.4**	6.3	5.6
79. Tends to be suspicious and distrustful of others.	3.8**	2.9	3.8*
82. Is self-assertive.	4.4**	5.3	5.2
84. Is a talkative child.	4.6*	5.4	4.6*
85. Is aggressive (physically or verbally).	2.9*	3.4	3.8
88. Is self-reliant, confident; trusts own judgment.	5.4*	5.9	5.8
90. Is stubborn.	4.3	4.0	4.8**
94. Tends to be sulky or whiny.	3.7	3.1	4.0**
95. Overreacts to minor frustrations; is easily irritated.	3.5	3.1	3.9**
98. Is shy and reserved; makes social contacts slowly.	5.6**	4.3	5.0
99. Is reflective; deliberates before speaking or acting.	6.7*	6.0	6.1

* Differs from experimenters, $p < .10$. ** Differs from experimeenters, $p < .05$. *** Differs from experimenters, $p < .01$.

Second, the extended period of adolescence is a time of transition, a time when young people face the developmental task of differentiating themselves from parents and family and forging independent identities. Experimenting with values and beliefs, exploring new roles and identities, and testing limits and personal boundaries are normative behaviors during adolescence, and they serve important developmental ends (cf. Erikson, 1968; Havinghurst, 1972).

Given these factors—the ubiquity and apparent acceptability of marijuana in the peer culture and the developmental appropriateness of experimentation and limit-testing during adolescence—

it is not surprising that by age 18, psychologically healthy, sociable, and reasonably inquisitive individuals would have been tempted to try marijuana. We would not expect these essentially normal and certainly normative adolescents to *abuse* the drug (and it is crucial to distinguish between experimentation and abuse) because they would have little need for drugs as an outlet for emotional distress or as a means of compensating for lack of meaningful human relationships—but we should not be surprised if they try it. Indeed, not to do so may reflect a degree of inhibition and social isolation in an 18-year-old.

Although no prior study has focused explicitly

TABLE 16.3

MEAN SCORES FOR AGE 7 CALIFORNIA CHILD Q-SORT (CCQ) ITEMS

CCQ item	Group		
	Abstainers	Experimenters	Frequent users
1. Prefers nonverbal methods of communication.	4.6*	4.4	4.7**
3. Is warm and responsive.	5.6	5.7	5.5*
4. Gets along well with other children.	6.1	5.8	5.3**
5. Is admired and sought out by other children.	5.1	5.2	4.8*
7. Seeks physical contact with others (touching, hugging, etc.).	4.9	4.9	4.6*
8. Tends to keep thoughts, feelings, or products to self.	5.0*	4.7	5.1*
14. Is eager to please.	5.6*	5.4	5.3
15. Shows concern for moral issues (fairness, reciprocity).	5.4	5.5	5.1*
16. Tends to be pleased with his/her accomplishments.	5.6*	5.8	5.6*
20. Tries to take advantage of others.	4.1**	3.8	4.0
23 Is fearful and anxious.	4.5	4.3	4.5*
26. Is physically active.	5,4*	5.6	5.5
28. Is vital, energetic, lively.	5.6	5.7	5.3**
32. Tends to give, lend, and share.	5.7*	5.4	5.2
34. Is restless and fidgety.	4.5*	4.8	4.8
35. Is inhibited and constricted.	4.6**	4.3	4.6
38. Has unusual thoughts processes.	4.6***	5.2	5.2
39. Becomes rigidly repetitive or immobilized under stress.	4.2*	4.0	4.3*
40. Is curious, eager to learn, open to new experiences.	5.5	5.6	5.4*
43. Can recoup or recover after stressful experience.	5.3	5.2	5.0*
44. When in conflict with others, yields and gives in.	4.7	4.5	4.9**

on the psychology of adolescent abstainers, there is some empirical precedent for the present finding that abstainers are not the most well-adjusted of adolescents. Hogan, Mankin, Conway, and Fox (1970), using a self-report personality inventory, compared marijuana users with nonusers in a college population and found that users "are more socially skilled, have a broader range of interests, are more adventuresome, and more concerned with the feelings of others" (p. 63). Nonusers were characterized as "too deferential to external authority, narrow in their interests, and overcon- trolled" (p. 61). These findings, based on entirely different methodology, are strikingly similar to our own. In a similar vein, Bentler (1987) reported a small but reliable association between marijuana use and the development of a *positive* self-concept.

We do not suggest that the inverted U-shaped relation between level of drug use and psychological health expresses a fundamental psychological "principle" or "law." Rather, we view this finding as a function of historical and social circumstances—specifically, of the current prevalence of drug use in this culture, conjoined with the de-

45. Tends to withdraw and disengage when under stress.	4.6	4.5	4.8*
50. Has bodily symptoms as a function of stress.	4.2	4.2	4.9***
53. Tends to be indecisive and vacillating.	4.3	4.3	4.6**
55. Is afraid of being deprived.	4.4	4.2	4.5*
59. Is neat and orderly in dress and behavior.	5.7***	5.2	5.2
62. Is obedient and compliant.	5.6*	5.3	5.4
67. Is planful; thinks ahead.	5.1**	5.4	5.1**
69. Is verbally fluent; can express ideas well.	5.2***	5.7	5.5*
72. Has a readiness to feel guilty; puts blame on self.	4.1**	4.5	4.4
76. Can be trusted; is dependable.	6.1	6.1	5.7*
77. Appears to feel unworthy; thinks of self as "bad."	4.0	4.0	4.5**
81. Can admit to own negative feelings.	5.1	5.0	4.5***
83. Seeks to be independent and autonomous.	5.1**	5.4	5.2
84. Is a talkative child.	5.1	5.3	5.0*
86. Likes to be by him/herself, enjoys solitary activities.	4.8	4.6	5.1**
87. Tends to imitate characteristics of those admired.	4.8	4.9	4.5**
88. Is self-reliant, confident; trusts own judgment.	5.4	5.5	5.3*
89. Is competent, skillful.	5.6*	5.9	5.7
91. Is inappropriate in emotive behavior.	4.1	4.4	4.8**
92. Is physically attractive, good-looking.	5.9***	5.5	5.7
96. Is creative in perception, work, thought, or play.	5.3*	5.5	5.3
97. Has an active fantasy life.	4.9	4.9	5.3*
100. Is easily victimized or scapegoated by other children.	4.1	4.1	4.6**

* Differs from experimenters, $p < .10$. ** Differs from experimenters, $p < .05$. *** Differs from experimenters, $p < .01$.

velopmentally appropriate propensity of adolescents to explore and experiment. Gergen's (1973) arguments regarding "social psychology as history" may be applicable here.[4]

The U-shaped relations between psychological health and drug use are reminiscent of U-shaped relations between psychological health and alcohol use noted in an earlier generation of subjects.[5] Thus, Jones (1968, 1971) found that moderate drinkers were psychologically healthier than either problem drinkers or abstainers. Moreover, the undercontrolled, alienated personality attributes of problem drinkers and the overcontrolled, diffident personality attributes of alcohol abstainers were quite similar to the personality attributes that

[4]In an influential article, the social psychologist Kenneth Gergen has argued that "social psychology is history," meaning that research results pertain only to a particular group of people at the time they happened to have been studied. Shedler and Block are acknowledging that this may be true about their results, which are drawn from individuals who were adolescents in the San Francisco Bay area during the 1970's. The same results might not be obtained today or in a different area of the country.

[5]A U-shaped relationship is one where the extreme groups score higher than the middle. In this case, the extremely low drug use group and the extremely high drug use group had the most psychological difficulties.

characterize frequent drug users and drug abstainers in the present study. Given the prevalence and apparent acceptability of marijuana use among adolescents today, it would seem that marijuana use has taken on psychological and sociological meanings for young people that, in earlier generations, were associated with alcohol use.

TOWARD AN UNDERSTANDING OF FREQUENT DRUG USERS If drug use among experimenters reflects normative adolescent exploration and inquisitiveness, it reflects something quite different in the group we have labeled frequent users. Frequent users differ profoundly from the comparison group of experimenters, and indications of their social and psychological maladjustment are pervasive.

At age 18, the frequent users appear unable to invest in, or derive pleasure from, meaningful personal relationships. Indeed, they seem fortified against the possibility of such relationships through their hostility, distrust, and emotional withdrawal. Neither do they appear to be capable of investing in school and work, or of channeling their energies toward meaningful future goals. They are, then, alienated from the "love and work" that lend a sense of satisfaction and meaning to life.[6] Consistent with this, they appear to *feel* troubled and inadequate. It is easy to see how these characteristics could create a vicious cycle: Feeling troubled and inadequate, these adolescents withdraw from work and relationships, and alienated from work and relationships, they feel all the more troubled and inadequate.

Such a pattern of alienation can be expected to go hand in hand with an impaired ability to control and regulate impulses. When there is little investment in either work or relationships, that is, when there is little connection with those things that give life a sense of stability and purpose, then the impulses of the moment become paramount. The impulses are not adequately transformed or

mediated by a broader system of values and goals because such a system is lacking.

Shapiro (1965) has written eloquently on this point:

> The normal person "tolerates" frustration or postpones the satisfaction of his whim at least in part because he is also interested in other things; his heart is set on goals and interests that are independent of the immediate frustration or extend beyond the whim and supersede it in subjective significance. This is not simply a matter of intellectual choice. Rather, the existence of these general goals and interests automatically provides a perspective, a set of dimensions in which a passing whim or an immediate frustration is experienced. In the absence of such goals and interests, the immediately present frustration or the promised satisfaction must, accordingly, gain in subjective significance, and under these conditions forbearance or tolerance is unthinkable. (pp. 145–146)

Drugs would have a special appeal to the alienated and impulsive individuals we are discussing. The temporary effects of various drugs "numb out" feelings of isolation and inadequacy; they offer transient gratification to individuals who lack deeper and more meaningful gratifications (i.e., through relationships and work); and given the poor ability of these individuals to regulate impulse, the urge toward drug use would meet with little inner resistance and would be little modified by a broader value system.

The traits that characterize the frequent users can be seen, then, to form a theoretically coherent syndrome, characterized by the psychological triad of *alienation*, *impulsivity*, and *subjective distress*. The data indicate that the roots of this syndrome predate adolescence and predate initiation of drug use.

As early as age 7, the frequent users show signs of the alienation, undercontrol, and emotional distress that will characterize them at age 18. Relative to experimenters, they are described as not getting along well with other children, as not developing genuine and close relationships, as not showing concern for moral issues, as not trustworthy or dependable, as having bodily symptoms

---

[6]Freud's definition of mental health—still widely acknowledged as one of the best—was the ability to love and to work.

from stress, as afraid of being deprived, as appearing to feel unworthy, as inappropriate in emotive behavior, and so on (see Table 16.2). The data clearly indicate, then, that *the relative maladjustment of the frequent users precedes the initiation of drug use.*

*　*　*

TOWARD AN UNDERSTANDING OF ABSTAINERS
Adolescents who have never experimented with marijuana or any other drug have not been the subject of research attention, if only because their behavior does not pose an obvious, confronting societal problem and because it has been presumed categorically that *not* using drugs goes hand in hand with psychological health. However, our data suggest that, relative to experimenters, abstainers in late adolescence are somewhat maladjusted. Unlike the patent, blatant maladjustment of frequent drug users, however, the psychological inadequacies of abstainers are largely a private matter, limiting of life as it is led, and do not attract societal attention. The constriction, uneasiness with affect, and interpersonal deficiencies of abstainers are recognizable more by way of *omission* than commission.

By omission, we refer to personal potentialities that seem to remain unfulfilled, specifically, potentialities for emotional gratifications, friendship, and human warmth and closeness. It is the relative capacity (or rather, *incapacity*) to experience these positive qualities of life that distinguishes abstainers from experimenters. Relative to experimenters, the abstainers are described at age 18 as overcontrolled and prone to delay gratification unnecessarily, not able to enjoy sensuous experiences, prone to avoid close interpersonal relationships, not gregarious, not liked and accepted by people, and so on. Thus, their avoidance of drugs seems less the result of "moral fiber" or successful drug education than the result of relative alienation from their peers and a characterological overcontrol of needs and impulses.

It seems likely that the relative overcontrol and emotional constriction of the abstainers serve the psychological purpose of containing or masking feelings of vulnerability. There is some evidence for this hypothesis in the age 18 personality descriptions of our subjects, for the abstainers are described at this age as relatively anxious. However, the strongest support for this hypothesis comes from the childhood data, when the relative maladjustment of these subjects is most manifest. At age 11, for example, prior to initiation of drug use, the abstainers are described (relative to experimenters) as fearful and anxious, inhibited and constricted, immobilized under stress, anxious in unpredictable environments, not curious and open to new experience, not vital or energetic or lively, not confident, not responsive to humor, and not cheerful. These traits would appear to reflect a susceptibility to anxiety and, perhaps, a consequent avoidance of circumstances or behaviors perceived as risky.

*　*　*

IMPLICATIONS FOR THEORY AND SOCIAL POLICY
Taken as a whole, the present data indicate that drug use and drug abstinence have theoretically coherent antecedents and must be understood within the context of an individual's total psychology. Because experimenters and frequent users are, psychologically, very different kinds of people, the meaning of drug use in these two groups is very different. In the case of experimenters, drug use appears to reflect age-appropriate and developmentally understandable experimentation. In the case of frequent users, drug use appears to be a manifestation of a more general pattern of maladjustment, a pattern that appears to predate adolescence and predate initiation of drug use. Undoubtedly, drug use exacerbates this earlier established pattern but, of course, the logic of a longitudinal research design precludes invocation of drug use as causing this personality syndrome.

Current theories (e.g., Akers, Krohn, Lanze-Kaduce, & Radosevich, 1979; Jessor & Jessor, 1977, 1978; Kaplan, Martin, & Robbins, 1982) tend to emphasize the role of peers in influencing drug use. The importance of peers in providing an encouraging surround for *experimentation* cannot be denied, but "peer-centered" or "environmental" explanations of *problem* drug use seem inadequate, given the present longitudinal findings (cf. Margulies, Kessler, & Kandel, 1977).

The discovery of psychological antecedents predating drug use (see also Block et al., 1988, Kellam, Branch, Agrawal, & Ensminger, 1975, Kellam, Brown, Rubin, & Ensminger, 1983; Kellam, Ensminger, & Simon, 1980) can to some extent be integrated with explanations of drug use that emphasize environmental factors, once it is recognized that individuals, from early childhood, actively construct and seek out environments that, given their essential personality, motivational, and intellectual characteristics, they find particularly harmonious and vivifying (see, e.g., Scarr & McCartney, 1983). Rather than being passive recipients of "environmental" influences, by the time of adolescence, individuals are already appreciably formed psychologically and are actively evoking, actively seeking, and actively forging the circumstances that will suit them and that will then, in an adventitious way, "impinge" on them.

The recognition that *problem* drug use (and, for that matter, abstinence) has developmental antecedents, that it is a part of a broad and theoretically coherent psychological syndrome, and that it is not adequately explained in terms of peer influence has important implications for social policy.

Current social policy seems to follow from the assumption that peer influence leads to experimentation, which in turn leads to abuse. Thus, efforts at drug education are aimed at discouraging experimentation by emphasizing the need to "just say no" to peer influence. But adolescent experimentation in and of itself does not appear to be personally or societally destructive (see also Kandel, Davies, Karus, & Yamaguchi, 1986, and Newcomb & Bentler, 1988), and peer influence does not appear to be an adequate explanation for *problem* drug use. Moreover, given the developmental tasks of the prolonged adolescent period, efforts aimed at eliminating adolescent experimentation are likely to be costly and to meet with limited success.

Current efforts at drug "education" seem flawed on two counts. First, they are alarmist, pathologizing normative adolescent experimentation and limit-testing, and perhaps frightening parents and educators unnecessarily. Second, and of far greater concern, they *trivialize* the factors underlying drug *abuse*, implicitly denying their depth and pervasiveness. For so long as problem drug use is construed primarily in terms of "lack of education," so long is attention diverted from its disturbing psychological underpinnings: the psychological triad of alienation, impulsivity, and distress. Paradoxically, then, the "just say no" approach may be concerned with a "problem" that, from a developmental viewpoint, need not be seen as alarming (adolescent experimentation), and it may be dismayingly oblivious to a serious problem that is extremely alarming (the ubiquity of the psychological syndrome that appears to underlie *problem* drug use).

The concept of drug "education" may have its current popular appeal in part because the link between the problem (drugs) and the attempted solution (drug education) is self-evident and thus reassures concerned parents, educators, and policymakers that "something is being done." But educational approaches to drug prevention have had limited success (Tobler, 1986), and society's limited resources might better be invested in interventions focusing on the personality syndrome underlying problem drug use.

Given current understandings of personality development, it would seem that the psychological triad of alienation, impulsivity, and distress would be better addressed through efforts aimed at encouraging sensitive and empathic parenting, at building childhood self-esteem, at fostering sound interpersonal relationships, and at promoting involvement and commitment to meaningful goals. Such interventions may not have the popular appeal of programs that appear to tackle the drug problem "directly," but may have greater individual and societal payoff in the end.

FORFENDING MISINTERPRETATION The finding that experimenters are the psychologically healthiest adolescents, and the observation that some drug experimentation, in and of itself, does not seem to be psychologically destructive, may sit badly with some. In particular, it may sit badly with drug counselors who "know" from clinical experience that there is no level of drug use that is safe, that it is dangerous to suggest otherwise, and that the most effective intervention is one aiming at total abstinence. To avoid any misunderstanding, we wish to make clear that there is no contradiction between this therapeutic perspective and the findings we have reported. On the contrary, we are in agreement with the therapeutic perspective.

The present data indicate that in a nonselected late-adolescent sample, occasional experimentation with marijuana is not personally or societally destructive. This view is supported by longitudinal studies of the consequences of drug use (as well as by the present study of the antecedents and concomitants of drug use; see, e.g., Kandel et al., 1986; Newcomb & Bentler, 1988), and by the fact that the majority of adolescents in the United States have experimented with marijuana but have not subsequently become drug abusers. The apparent contradiction between clinical wisdom, on the one hand, and the present findings, on the other, is resolved when it is recognized that individuals who present themselves for drug treatment are *not* representative of the general population of adolescents, but instead constitute a special, highly selected subpopulation. The psychological meaning of drug use is very different for this fractional group existing within the larger population of adolescents. For them, experimentation with drugs is highly destructive because drugs easily become part of a broader pathological syndrome. For adolescents more generally, some drug experimentation apparently does not have psychologically catastrophic implications.

In closing, one final clarification is in order. In presenting research on a topic as emotionally charged as drug use, there is always the danger that findings may be misinterpreted or misrepresented. Specifically, we are concerned that some segments of the popular media may misrepresent our findings as indicating that drug use might somehow improve an adolescent's psychological health. Although the incorrectness of such an interpretation should be obvious to anyone who has actually read this article, our concern about media misrepresentation requires us to state categorically that our findings do *not* support such a view, nor should anything we have said remotely encourage such an interpretation.

References

Akers, R. L., Krohn, M. D., Lanze-Kaduce, L., & Radosevich, M. (1979). Social learning and deviant behavior: A specific test of a general theory. *American Sociological Review, 44,* 636–655.

Bem, D. J., & Funder, D. C. (1978). Predicting more of the people more of the time: Assessing the personality of situations. *Psychological Review, 85,* 485–501.

Bentler, P. M. (1987). Drug use and personality in adolescence and young adulthood: Structural models with nonnormal variables. *Child Development, 58,* 65–79.

Block, J. (1971). *Lives through time.* Berkeley, CA: Bancroft.

Block, J. (1978). *The Q-sort method in personality assessment and psychiatric research.* Palo Alto, CA: Consulting Psychologists Press. (Original work published 1961)

Block, J., & Block, J. H. (1980). *The California Child Q-set.* Palo Alto, CA: Consulting Psychologists Press.

Block, J., Block, J. H., & Keyes, S. (1988). Longitudinally foretelling drug usage in adolescence: Early childhood personality and environmental precursors. *Child Development, 59,* 336–355.

Block, J. H., & Block, J. (1980). The role of ego-control and ego-resiliency in the organization of behavior. In W. A. Collins (Ed.), *Minnesota symposia on child psychology* (Vol. 13, pp. 39–101). Hillsdale, NJ: Erlbaum.

Bush, P. J., & Iannotti, R. (1985). The development of children's health orientations and behaviors. Lessons for substance use prevention. In C. L. Jones & R. J. Battjes (Eds.), *Etiology of drug abuse: Implications for prevention* (Research Monograph No. 56, pp. 45–74). Rockville, MD: National Institute on Drug Abuse.

Cox, W. M. (1985). Personality correlates of substance abuse. In M. Galizio & S. A. Maisto (Eds.), *Determinants of substance abuse: Biological, psychological, and environmental factors* (pp. 209–246). New York: Plenum.

Dohrenwend, B. S., Shrout, P. E., Egri, G., & Mendelsohn, F. S. (1980). Nonspecific psychological distress and other dimensions of psychopathology. *Archives of General Psychiatry, 37,* 1229–1236.

Erikson, E. H. (1968). *Identity: Youth and crisis.* New York: Norton.

Gergen, K. J. (1973). Social psychology as history. *Journal of Personality and Social Psychology, 36,* 309–320.

Gjerde, P. F., Block, J., & Block, J. H. (1988). Depressive symptomatology and personality during late adolescence: Gender differences in the externalization-internalization of symptom expression. *Journal of Abnormal Psychology, 97,* 475–486.

Haberman, P. W., Josephson, E., Zanes, A., & Elinson, J. (1972). High school drug behavior: A methodological report on pilot studies. In S. Einstein & S. Allen (Eds.), *Proceedings of the First International Conference on Student Drug Surveys* (pp. 103–121). Farmingdale, NY: Baywood.

Havinghurst, R. J. (1972). *Developmental tasks and education* (3rd ed.). New York: McKay.

Hawkins, J. D., Lishner, D. M., & Catalano, R. F. (1985). Childhood predictors and the prevention of adolescent substance abuse. In C. L. Jones & R. J. Battjes (Eds.), *Etiology of drug abuse: Implications for prevention* (Research Monograph No. 56, pp. 75–125). Rockville, MD: National Institute on Drug Abuse.

Hogan, R., Mankin, D., Conway, J., & Fox, S. (1970). Personality correlates of undergraduate marijuana use. *Journal of Consulting and Clinical Psychology, 35,* 58–63.

Jessor, R. (1979). Marijuana: A review of recent psychosocial research. In R. L. Dupont, A. Goldstein, & J. O'Donnell (Eds.), *Handbook on drug abuse* (pp. 337–355). Washington, DC: Government Printing Office.

Jessor, R., Chase, J. A., & Donovan, J. E. (1980). Psychosocial correlates of marijuana use and problem drinking in a national sample of adolescents. *American Journal of Public Health, 70,* 604–613.

Jessor, R., & Jessor, S. L. (1977). *Problem behavior and psychological development: A longitudinal study of youth.* New York: Academic Press.

Jessor, R., & Jessor, S. L. (1978). Theory testing in longitudinal research on marijuana use. In D. B. Kandel (Ed.), *Longitudinal research on drug use: Empirical findings and methodological issues* (pp. 41–71). Washington, DC: Hemisphere.

Johnston, L. D., Bachman, J. G., & O'Malley, P. M. (1981a). *Highlights from student drug use in America 1975–1981.* Rockville, MD: National Institute on Drug Abuse.

Johnston, L. D., Bachman, J. G., & O'Malley, P. M. (1981b). *Student drug use in America 1975–1981.* Rockville, MD: National Institute on Drug Abuse.

Johnston, L. D., O'Malley, P. M., & Bachman, J. G. (1984). *Drugs and American high school students, 1975–1983* (National Institute of Drug Abuse, DHHS Publication No. ADM 84-1317). Washington, DC: Government Printing Office.

Johnston, L. D., O'Malley, P. M., & Bachman, J. G. (1986). *Drug use among American high school students, college students, and other young adults: National trends through 1985.* Rockville, MD: National Institute on Drug Abuse.

Jones, C. L., & Battjes, R. J. (Eds.). (1985). *Etiology of drug abuse: Implications for prevention.* (Research Monograph No. 56; DHHS Publication No. ADM 85-1335). Rockville, MD: National Institute of Drug Abuse.

Jones, M. C. (1968). Personality correlates and antecedents of drinking patterns in adult males. *Journal of Consulting and Clinical Psychology, 31,* 1–12.

Jones, M. C. (1971). Personality antecedents and correlates of drinking patterns in women. *Journal of Consulting and Clinical Psychology, 36,* 61–69.

Kandel, D. B. (1980). Drug and drinking behavior among youth. *Annual Review of Sociology, 6,* 235–285.

Kandel, D. B., Davies, M., Karus, D., & Yamaguchi, K. (1986).

The consequences in young adulthood of adolescent drug involvement. *Archives of General Psychiatry, 43,* 746–754.

Kaplan, H. B., Martin, S. S., & Robbins, C. (1982). Application of a general theory of deviant behavior: Self-derogation and adolescent drug use. *Journal of Health and Social Behavior, 23,* 274–294.

Kellam, S. G., Branch, J. D., Agrawal, K. C., & Ensminger, M. E. (1975). *Mental health and going to school: The Woodlawn program of assessment, early intervention, and evaluation.* Chicago: University of Chicago Press.

Kellam, S. G., Brown, C. H., Rubin, B. R., & Ensminger, M. E. (1983). Paths leading to teenage psychiatric symptoms and substance use: Developmental epidemiological studies in Woodlawn. In S. B. Guze, F. J. Earls, & J. E. Barrett (Eds.), *Childhood psychopathology and development* (pp. 17–47). New York: Raven.

Kellam, S. G., Ensminger, M. E., & Simon, M. B. (1980). Mental health in first grade and teenage drug, alcohol, and cigarette use. *Drug and Alcohol Dependence, 5,* 273–304.

Keyes, S., & Block, J. (1984). Prevalence and patterns of substance abuse among early adolescents. *Journal of Youth and Adolescence, 13,* 1–14.

Margulies, R. Z., Kessler, R. C., & Kandel, D. B. (1977). A longitudinal study of onset of drinking among high school students. *Journal of Studies of Alcohol, 38,* 897–912.

Miller, J. D., Cisin, I. H., Gardner-Keaton, H., Harrel, A. V., Wirtz, P. W., Abelson, H. I., & Fishburne, P. M. (1983). *National survey on drug abuse: Main findings 1982.* Rockville, MD: National Institute on Drug Abuse.

Mischel, W., Shoda, Y., & Peake, P. K. (1988). The nature of adolescent competencies predicted by preschool delay of gratification. *Journal of Personality and Social Psychology, 54,* 687–696.

National Institute on Drug Abuse. (1986). *Capsules: Overview of the 1985 household survey on drug abuse.* Rockville, MD: Author.

Newcomb, M., & Bentler, P. (1988). *Consequences of adolescent drug use: Impact on the lives of young adults.* Newbury Park, CA: Sage.

Perry, C. L., Killen, J., & Slinkard, L. A. (1980). Peer teaching and smoking prevention among junior high students. *Adolescence, 15,* 277–281.

Scarr, S., & McCartney, K. (1983). How people make their own environments: A theory of genotype (arrow) environmental effects. *Child Development, 54,* 424–435.

Shapiro, D. (1965). *Neurotic styles.* New York: Basic Books.

Single, E., Kandel, D., & Johnson, B. D. (1975). The reliability and validity of drug use responses in a large scale longitudinal survey. *Journal of Drug Issues, 5,* 426–443.

Tanaka, J. S., & Huba, G. J. (1984). Confirmatory hierarchical factor analysis of psychological distress measures. *Journal of Personality and Social Psychology, 46,* 621–635.

Tobler, N. S. (1986). Meta-analysis of 143 adolescent drug prevention programs: Quantitative outcome results of program participants compared to a control or comparison group. *Journal of Drug Issues, 16,* 537–568.

Watson, D. W., & Clark, L. A. (1984). Negative affectivity: The disposition to experience aversive emotional states. *Psychological Bulletin, 96,* 465–490.

Four Ways Five Factors Are Basic

Paul T. Costa, Jr., and Robert R. McCrae

More than 60 years ago, Gordon Allport and one of his students did a count of trait words in an unabridged dictionary and reported finding a total of 17,953 (Allport & Odbert, 1936)! Personality psychologists have not made up tests to measure all of these, but it is safe to estimate that at least a couple of thousand different personality traits have been investigated by one researcher or another. It is reasonable to wonder whether all these different traits are strictly necessary. Can we reduce the vast number of trait terms in the language and the research literature down to an essential few? If so, this would be an important accomplishment, for it would vastly simply the task of personality assessment and go a long way toward making it possible to compare the research of different psychologists with each other.

In recent years, the personality psychologists Paul Costa and Robert McCrae have argued that the "Big Five" traits of personality are the truly essential ones. They call these traits extraversion, neuroticism, openness to experience, agreeableness, and conscientiousness. Not everybody believes these traits are important (see Block, 1995 for one vigorous dissent), but many psychologists find the Big Five to be a useful—if not all-encompassing—common framework for the conceptualization of individual differences in personality.

In the last article in this section Costa and McCrae present "four reasons five factors are basic." Their four reasons are: (1) research demonstrates that these traits can be rated consistently by different observers of the same person, and can be used to predict behavior, (2) the Big Five show up repeatedly in different systems and lists of traits, (3) the Big Five are found in both sexes as well as in many different languages and cultures, and (4) they appear to have a biological basis because they are to some degree "heritable," or influenced by genetics.

Research on the Big Five—pro and con—continues to be lively, and the final chapter on this topic has not yet been written. In the meantime, it is worth pondering two questions. First, how much of human personality can be encompassed by five basic traits? And second, what is left out?

From "Four Ways Five Factors Are Basic," by P. T. Costa, Jr., and R. R. McCrae (1992). Reprinted with permission from *Personality and Individual Differences, 13*, pp. 653–665. Oxford, England: Elsevier Science Ltd.

* * *

What are the criteria by which we determine that a personality dimension is *basic*, and which dimensions of personality meet these criteria? There is perhaps more agreement on the former than on the latter question. In this article we will argue that basic dimensions must demonstrate their psychological reality through evidence of temporal stability and cross-observer validity;[1] must pervade the trait systems of both laypersons and personality theorists; must recur in many different cultures; and must have some biological basis, although they need not be tied to any particular neuro- or psychophysiological theory. We will also summarize data showing that the dimensions of the five-factor model meet these criteria.

* * *

Critics of the model sometimes object that five factors cannot adequately account for the full range of personality traits (Mershon & Gorsuch, 1988), and of course they are correct. The term "Big Five"[2] is perhaps misleading here, because it suggests that the model posits only five important traits. The alternative label, "the five-factor model," may be more descriptive, because a factor matrix contains both rows and columns, both variables and factors. The variables in this model are specific personality traits. The instrument we have developed to measure the model, the Revised NEO Personality Inventory (NEO-PI-R: Costa & Mc-Crae, 1992), assesses 30 separate traits organized by the model into five domains: Neuroticism (N), Extraversion (E), Openness (O), Agreeableness (A), and Conscientiousness (C). The model helps us specify the range of traits that a comprehensive personality instrument should measure, and the factors that emerge from an analysis of these traits are what we consider the basic dimensions of personality.

As an illustration of the traits and their structure, Table 17.1 presents a factor analysis of NEO-PI-R facets in a sample of 411 men and women, aged 19 to 96, who completed the NEO-PI-R between 1989 and 1991.[3] These subjects were participants in the Baltimore Longitudinal Study of Aging (BLSA: Shock, et al., 1984), but their data were not used in any of the item selection studies for the NEO-PI-R. In Table 17.1, most facets have their largest loading on the intended factor, and the secondary loadings are similar to those seen in other analyses. * * *

Another frequent criticism of the five-factor model is based on a more general skepticism about factor analysis itself as a way to understanding personality (Block, 1991).[4] Certainly it is true that there is nothing magical about factor analysis; if it were an infallible approach, the questions addressed by this article would long since have been answered. But factor analysis is a useful tool for processing the quantities of data that are needed to understand something as complicated as individual differences in personality. It identifies clusters of variables that are related to each other and unrelated to other clusters of variables, and in this

---

[1] *Temporal stability* refers to the degree that measuring the same trait of a person at two different times will yield the same result; *cross-observer validity* refers to the degree that two different raters of the same person will yield the same personality judgment.

[2] The "Big Five" is a widely used term among psychologists for the five basic traits that Costa and McCrae favor.

---

[3] Factor analysis is a statistical method that summarizes the degree to which different traits (or behaviors) are related to one another. The results in Table 17.1 can be considered correlations between each of the lower-level traits listed and each of the Big Five, the factors or higher-order traits. Thus, anxiety correlates .80 with neuroticism but no larger than −.09 with any other of the five.

[4] Factor analysis has a long history of use in personality research, but there has never been full agreement about how the statistical results that so readily spew from the computer should be interpreted to yield psychological meaning. Part of the problem is that factor analysis is so quantitatively complex that only a few specialists are really qualified to have an opinion worth listening to. Block's reservations are noteworthy because he has, in other contexts (e.g., Block, 1965), adroitly used factor analysis himself as an aid to solving difficult and long-standing problems.

TABLE 17.1

FACTOR ANALYSIS OF COMPUTER-ADMINISTERED REVISED NEO PERSONALITY INVENTORY FACET SCALES

NEO-PI-R facet scale	Varimax-rotated principal component				
	N	E	O	A	C
Neuroticism facets					
N1: Anxiety	**.80**	−.09	.05	−.01	−.03
N2: Angry hostility	**.64**	.02	−.04	**−.49**	−.02
N3: Depression	**.77**	−.15	.00	−.04	−.20
N4: Self-consciousness	**.75**	−.22	−.08	.04	−.07
N5: Impulsiveness	**.48**	**.47**	.11	−.25	−.15
N6: Vulnerability	**.67**	−.14	−.16	.11	−.40
Extraversion facets					
E1: Warmth	−.21	**.57**	.26	**.46**	.09
E2: Gregariousness	−.22	**.69**	−.01	.19	.01
E3: Assertiveness	−.27	**.52**	.17	−.31	**.43**
E4: Activity	.00	**.49**	.18	−.20	**.58**
E5: Excitement seeking	−.12	**.63**	.10	−.22	−.05
E6: Positive emorions	−.22	**.58**	.37	.23	.17
Openness facets					
O1: Fantasy	.02	.13	**.66**	−.24	−.12
O2: Aesthetics	.08	−.08	**.68**	.23	.02
O3: Feelings	.21	.18	**.68**	.01	.26
O4: Actions	−.13	.28	**.57**	.17	−.07
O5: Ideas	−.17	.01	**.69**	−.13	.08
O6: Values	−.06	.08	**.63**	−.03	−.10
Agreeableness facets					
A1: Trust	−.27	.25	.10	**.57**	.14
A2: Straightforwardness	−.03	−.11	−.15	**.68**	.02
A3: Altruism	−.14	.26	.06	**.63**	.34
A4: Compliance	−.13	−.20	−.02	**.77**	.00
A5: Modesty	.15	−.23	−.12	**.56**	−.13
A6: Tender-mindedness	.17	.11	.18	**.66**	.08
Conscientiousness facets					
C1: Competence	−.41	.01	.17	.03	**.67**
C2: Order	.11	−.09	−.16	.11	**.66**
C3: Dutifulness	−.17	−.06	−.14	.32	**.67**
C4: Achievement striving	−.05	.14	.07	−.09	**.77**
C5: Self-discipline	−.33	−.07	−.02	.11	**.75**
C6: Deliberation	−.19	**−.48**	−.01	.21	.40

$N=411$ adult men and women. Loadings greater than ±0.40 are shown in boldface.

respect it systematizes the quest for those basic requirements of scientific constructs, convergent and discriminant validity. Used intelligently, it can yield valuable insights.

In any case, the test of whether factor analysis is useful does not lie in an analysis of the technique, but in an evaluation of the constructs it yields. Do the dimensions of the five-factor model make conceptual sense? Do they show convergence across different instruments and observers? Are they useful in predicting important social and psychological outcomes? We think so.

Four Criteria for Basic Dimensions of Personality

THE REALITY OF THE FACTORS Surely no one would dispute that the basic dimensions of personality must refer to some objective psychological reality. But the belief that personality traits were nothing more than cognitive fictions was widespread only a few years ago. And ironically, although it was Mischel's (1968) influential critique that popularized this idea, earlier research on the five-factor model provided the most powerful argument for it.

As shown by D'Andrade (1965) and by Passini and Norman (1966), the five-factor structure of personality could be recovered from ratings made on complete strangers. Because nothing was known about the actual traits of these ratees, and thus about the covariation of those traits, the clear implication of this finding was that the structure itself must somehow be built into our cognitive system of person perception, constituting an implicit personality theory. But this fact itself was subject to radically different interpretations. At one extreme, it was seen as evidence that traits were nothing but fictions, projections of our cognitive structure onto the interpersonal world. At the other, it was taken as an indication that individuals learned the true structure of personality from their observations of the real world and simply applied it to unknown cases. Borkenau (1992) has recently reviewed the evidence on these hypotheses and a number of more sophisticated variants, and concluded that "traits are real and accurately perceived, provided that the judges have the necessary information."

This conclusion is based in large part on evidence of the stability and cross-observer validity of the five factors. Traits are defined as enduring dispositions that can be inferred from patterns of behavior; they should therefore be stable across long periods of time and be similarly assessed by different observers. By these criteria, N, E, O, A, and C are all indisputably real traits.

Because most questionnaires include scales measuring aspects of N and E, there are many longitudinal studies of personality in adulthood that demonstrate the stability of these two dimensions. For example, Finn (1986) reported uncorrected stability coefficients of .56 for MMPI measures of both N and Social E in a sample of 78 middle-aged men retested after 30 years. Using the NEO-PI, we found 6-yr retest correlations of .83, .82, and .83 for N, E, and O, respectively, in self-reports from 398 men and women; similarly, we found 6-yr stability coefficients of .83, .77, and .80 for spouse ratings of N, E, and O on 167 of these individuals (Costa & McCrae, 1988b). A 7-yr longitudinal peer rating study of all five factors found stability coefficients of .67 for N, .81 for E, .84 for O, .63 for A, and .78 for C (Costa & McCrae, 1992). Corrected for unreliability, these values would approach unity.[5]

All five factors have also been consensually validated in studies examining agreement across observers—a fact demonstrated as long ago as 1966 by Norman and Goldberg, and subsequently replicated by Funder and Colvin (1988) and others. Table 17.2 presents correlations across observers for factor scores from the NEO-PI-R. The first column gives intraclass correlations between peer raters; the second and third columns give correlations of self-reports with single peer and spouse ratings. All these correlations are statistically significant, and the median value of .50 shows that they are substantial in magnitude. Indeed, all of them meet or exceed the so-called .30 barrier for validity coefficients.[6] Self-reports and various kinds of ratings are not interchangeable, and discrepancies between them may sometimes be of clinical interest (Muten, 1991), but the consistent convergences attest to the reality of these five factors.

The reality of the factors is also seen in their practical utility. O is an important predictor of

---

[5]"Unity" refers to a perfect correlation of 1.0. These correlations just summarized are about as high as they could possibly get, given the degree of measurement instability or "unreliability" they manifest.

[6]This is a not-so-veiled reference to Walter Mischel's claim that correlation coefficients pertaining to personality traits rarely if ever exceed .30.

vocational interests (Costa, McCrae, & Holland, 1984), and C has recently emerged as the best overall predictor of job performance (Barrick & Mount, 1991). A and C are related to life satisfaction even after accounting for the major effects of E and N (McCrae & Costa, 1991). A is essential in understanding the literature in coronary-prone behavior (Costa, McCrae, & Dembroski, 1989), C is a predictor of academic achievement (Digman & Takemoto-Chock, 1981), and knowledge of all five factors has proven to be useful in clinical psychology (Miller, 1991). The five-factor model has much to offer applied psychology.

THE PERVASIVENESS OF THE FACTORS If someone were to suggest that the only basic dimensions of personality were E and A, the two axes of the interpersonal circumplex (McCrae & Costa, 1989b), the proposal would be greeted with astonishment: How could one possibly omit N, so crucial to measures of both normal personality and psychopathology, to perceived stress and ways of coping, to psychological well-being, to somatic concerns,

TABLE 17.2

CROSS-OBSERVER CORRELATIONS FOR NEO-PI-R FACTORS

NEO-PI-R Factor	Peer/ peer	Peer/ self	Spouse/ self
Neuroticism	.35	.33	.61
Extraversion	.41	.43	.58
Openness	.50	.55	.67
Agreeableness	.52	.51	.57
Conscientiousness	.30	.46	.37

For intraclass correlations between peer raters. N=193 pairs; for peer/self correlations. N=250; for spouse/self correlations, N=68. All correlations are significant at P <.001.

to low self-esteem? Surely we need N in our model as a basic dimension. Just as surely, we would argue, we need C and O. The basic dimensions of personality are those which together summarize with maximal efficiency the covariation among all

the traits in the personality sphere; they must account for all the major variables that have been studied by psychologists as well as those traits that are used by laypersons to characterize themselves and their acquaintances. All five factors are needed to do that.

There is relatively little dispute about the dimensions of E and N, which have long been recognized as the Big Two (Wiggins, 1968). We will therefore focus attention on O, A, and C, pointing out the range of traits that would be lost if these three dimensions were omitted. In particular, we wish to correct the impression that A and C are narrow, first-order traits (Eysenck, 1991). As the facet scales in Table 17.1 show, A and C are broad, second-order factors defined by many specific traits.

The first source of evidence on the pervasiveness of the five factors comes from studies of trait terms in natural languages (John, Angleitner, & Ostendorf, 1988). The tradition of research that stretches from Allport and Odbert (1936) to Ostendorf (1990) through Cattell (1946), Tupes and Christal (1961), and Goldberg (1981) was, of course, the origin of the five-factor model. The English language includes thousands of terms to describe aspects of personality, and analysis after analysis has found five similar factors (Goldberg, 1990).

It is true that the five factors are not equally well represented among trait adjectives. At one extreme, there are hundreds of terms relevant to the A factor, including at the low pole *abrasive, abusive, acrimonious, aggressive, altercative, antagonistic, argumentative, arrogant, autocratic,* and *avaricious,* and at the high pole *acceding, accommodating, acquiescent, affable, affectionate, altruistic, amiable, approachable, assistful,* and, of course, *agreeable* (cf. Norman, 1967). At the other extreme, there are relatively few adjectives that describe O (McCrae, 1990), and most of them, like *curious, creative, inquisitive,* and *intellectual* refer only to the more cognitive forms of O, leading many lexical researchers to call this factor "Intellect."

Some psychologists might object that lay vocabularies are not the best source for scientific descriptions of personality. More psychologically informed descriptions are provided by the items in Block's (1961) California Q-Set. Table 17.3 lists items that define the O, A, and C factors found in this instrument (McCrae, Costa & Busch, 1986).

Scales related to these three factors can also be found in instruments designed to operationalize many of the classic theories of personality. Henry Murray's (1938) catalog of needs includes Understanding, Change, Sentience, and Autonomy, all related to O; Abasement, Nurturance, and low Aggression, all related to A; and Achievement, Order, Endurance, and Cognitive Structure, all related to C (Costa & McCrae, 1988a). C. G. Jung's (1923/1971) psychological functions are the basis of the Myers-Briggs Type Indicator; correlations of its scales with measures of the five-factor model show that Sensing vs Intuition, Thinking vs Feeling, and Perceiving vs Judging are related to O, A, and C, respectively (McCrae & Costa, 1989a). Angleitner and Ostendorf (1991) recently recovered the five factors in an analysis of temperament scales. There the O factor was defined in part by Zuckerman's (1979) Experience Seeking scale, the A factor included Strelau, Angleitner, Bantelmann and Ruch's (1990) Inhibition scale, and the C factor was marked by Windel and Lerner's (1986) Persistence scale.

Aspects of O are seen in Tellegen's (1982) absorption; Gough's (1987) flexibility, Rokeach's (1960) dogmatism, Fenigstein, Scheier, and Buss's (1975) private self-consciousness, Holland's (1985) artistic interests, Guilford, Zimmerman and Guilford's (1976) thoughtfulness, Kris's (1952) regression in the service of the ego. Aspects of A are seen in Erikson's (1950) trust vs mistrust, Snyder's (1974) self-monitoring, James' (1907) tough vs tender-mindedness, Horney's (1945) "moving against" tendency, Freud's (1914/1957) narcissism, Adler's (1938/1964) social interest. Aspects of C are seen in White's (1959) competence, Cattell, Eber and Tatsuoka's (1970) superego strength, Rotter's (1966) locus of control, Hartshorn, May, and Maller's (1929) character, Lorr's (1986) persistence, and McClelland, Atkinson,

TABLE 17.3

SOME ITEM DEFINERS OF O, A, AND C FACTORS IN THE CALIFORNIA Q-SET

Openness
  Aesthetically reactive
  Values intellectual matters
  Wide range of interests
  Rebellious, nonconforming
    —vs—
  Sex-role stereotyped behavior
  Favors conservative values
  Uncomfortable with complexities
  Judges in conventional terms

Agreeableness
  Sympathetic, considerate
  Arouses liking
  Warm, compassionate
  Behaves in giving way
    —vs—
  Expresses hostility directly
  Basically distrustful
  Shows condescending behavior
  Critical, skeptical

Conscientiousness
  Productive
  Behaves ethically
  Has high aspiration level
  Dependable, responsible
    —vs—
  Self-indulgent
  Interested in opposite sex
  Enjoys sensuous experiences
  Unable to delay gratification

Adapted from McCrae et al. (1986).

Clark, and Lowell's (1953) achievement motive. O, A, and C—like N and E—are basic themes that have recurred in innumerable forms throughout the history of personality psychology. Each of them is indispensable.

THE UNIVERSALITY OF THE FACTORS Truly basic dimensions of personality ought to be universal—found in both sexes, in all races, in various age groups, in different cultures. Whether such dimensions exist is an empirical question. There is no guarantee that thoughts, feelings, and actions must covary in the same way in all different groups. For example, it is unlikely that the same personality factors found in adults would also be found in infants, and it would surprise few social psychologists if the factors found in modern industrial societies differed from those found in hunting and gathering cultures.

However, if any personality factors can be found that do cross all these boundaries, they would surely have more claim to being basic than would factors that are only found in specialized populations. Each of the dimensions of the five-factor model has evidence of universality.

The factors have been found in teachers' ratings of children (Digman & Inouye, 1986), in college students (Goldberg, 1990), in adults (see for example Table 17.1). In a sample of 1,539 individuals tested as part of a study of job performance (Costa, McCrae, & Holland, 1991), we examined factors of the NEO-PI-R in men and women, in older and younger adults, and in white and nonwhite subjects. In each case, five very similar factors were found, with coefficients of congruence for the 15 comparisons ranging from .91 to .99.

Beginning with Bond's work in the 1970s, a number of cross-cultural studies on the five-factor model have been conducted, many using translations of Norman's (1963) instrument (Bond, 1979; Bond, Nakazato, & Shiraishi, 1975; Borkenau & Ostendorf, 1990; Yang & Bond, 1990). Most of these studies have recovered factors very similar to those reported by Norman. For example, Yang and Bond factored 718 ratings of father made by Chinese college students. Of the 20 Norman scales, they found 19 with their highest loading on the intended factor.

Borkenau and Ostendorf (1990) provided a more formal analysis of the five-factor model, using both the Norman rating scales and their German translation of the NEO-PI. When separate results for men and women were compared using Everett's (1983) procedure, five and only five factors were replicable in both instruments, and confirmatory factor analyses showed that these were the factors hypothesized.

Currently there is considerable interest in the question of whether a different factor structure might be found if more culture-specific variables were included. Ostendorf (1990) reported analyses of the German language lexicon that provide an almost perfect replication of the structure in English. Yang and Bond (1990) sought to examine the structure of personality using representative Chinese trait adjectives; they found five factors, but they were not identical to the standard five. Church and Katigbak (1989) used items generated by Filipino students in both English and Tagalog, and found factors they interpreted in terms of the Big Five. Yang and Bond chose to emphasize the cultural differences; Church and Katigbak seemed more impressed by the similarities. Clearly, this is an issue that will require more research.

Some of that research is currently being conducted by Michael Bond, who, with Wai-kwan Li, has translated the NEO-PI-R into Chinese. Fung Yi Liu (1991) administered this Chinese NEO-PI-R to a sample of 100 college students; she also administered a set of items intended to measure distinctively Chinese characteristics organized into three scales. When the 30 NEO-PI-R scales were factored, the five factors were recovered, with 26 facets having their highest loading on the intended factor. Of more interest is the fact that a joint analysis showed that the three indigenous Chinese scales also fit within the five-factor solution. For example, one of the Chinese scales was Filial Piety, a variable measuring deference to parents. It loaded on the A factor.

Perhaps what these cross-cultural studies really show is that the ways in which the basic factors of personality are manifested differ somewhat from culture to culture. Among American college students, disregard for one's parents' wishes is more or less the norm, and says relatively little about personality. Among Chinese students, however, it seems that only highly antagonistic individuals lack filial piety.

THE BIOLOGICAL BASIS OF THE FACTORS The fact that the five factors are found in many different cultures suggests that they are basic features of human nature itself. This does not necessarily mean that they are biologically based, because human beings share more than a common biology. They are, for example, all social beings with the capacity for abstract thought through symbolization: the five factors may represent alternative ways in which people in a social environment can respond to their life experience.

But as it happens there are good reasons to suspect that all five factors have some biological foundation, because measures of all five have shown evidence of heritability. This should be reassuring to those who prefer to "select personality variables that are genotypically rooted in our biology as much as possible" (Caspi & Bem, 1990, p. 556). There is a large body of research on genetic influences on N and E (Eaves, Eysenck, & Martin, 1989), and the few studies that have examined the heritability of O have also shown consistent genetic influences. Using a short Swedish version of the NEO-PI, Plomin and McClearn (1990) reported that 41% of the variance in the O scale was attributable to additive genetic influences. Tellegen and Waller (in press) reported substantial heritabilities for two Multidimensional Personality Questionnaire (MPQ) scales related to O, Absorption and (low) Harmavoidance. Loehlin's (1987) cross-pair analysis of California Psychological Inventory items recovered a genetic factor that included "the pursuit of culture— lectures, discussion, opera—and a willingness to tackle uncertain and ambiguous problems" (p. 142) that Loehlin identified with Norman's fifth factor, Culture, and that we would call O.

* * *

It seems likely that there are neurobiological structures that underlie such heritable personality traits, and Tooby and Cosmides (1990) argued that shared neurophysiological systems may account for the covariation of specific traits into broad factors. Cloninger (1988) presented a theory of personality structure based on such a principle, and some, like Claridge (1986), have argued that no personality dimension can be taken seriously unless it is supported by theory linking it to a biological mechanism.

We believe that this latter view is profoundly mistaken. The fact is that we know much more about personality structure than we do about the functioning of the brain, and it is poor science to try to explain the known on the basis of the unknown. Consider for a moment the far-reaching developments in our understanding of neurophysiology that have occurred since 1961. In retrospect, it would have been folly for Tupes and Christal to attempt to explain their five factors in terms of the comparatively primitive neuroscience of the day. Their factors have survived the past 30 years very well; any biological explanation they might have proposed would surely be hopelessly outdated. Will today's neurobiological explanations fare any better?

We do not mean to suggest that studies of personality and psychophysiology are unimportant; they may teach us much about both individual differences and neuroscience. But it seems to us that such studies should begin with our current understanding of the organization of personality into five factors. Every psychophysiological study should include measures of all five; empirical links between these factors and neurophysiological variables, even if they are not anticipated by theory, may give valuable clues to the biological basis of personality.

* * *

References

Adler, A. (1964). *Social interest: A challenge to mankind.* New York: Capricorn Books. (Original work published 1938)

Allport, G. W., & Odbert, H. S. (1936). Trait names: A psycholexical study. *Psychological Monographs, 47* (211).

Angleitner, A., & Ostendorf, F. (1991). Temperament and the Big Five factors of personality. Paper presented at the *Conference on the Development of the Structure of Temperament and Personality from Infancy to Adulthood.* Wassenaar. The Netherlands, June.

Barrick, M. R., & Mount, M. K. (1991). The Big Five personality dimensions and job performance: A meta-analysis. *Personnel Psychology, 44,* 1–26.

Block, J. (1961). *The Q-sort method in personality assessment and psychiatric research.* Springfield, IL: Charles C Thomas.

Block, J. (1991). My uneasiness with the five-factor model of personality. Paper presented at the *Conference on the Development of the Structure of Temperament and Personality from Infancy to Adulthood,* Wassenaar, The Netherlands, June.

Bond, M. H. (1979). Dimensions of personality used in perceiving peers: Cross-cultural comparisons of Hong Kong,

Japanese, American, and Filipino university students. *International Journal of Psychology, 14*, 47–56.

Bond, M. H., Nakazato, H., & Shiraishi, D. (1975). Universality and distinctiveness in dimensions of Japanese person perception. *Journal of Cross-Cultural Psychology, 6*, 346–357.

Borkenau, P. (1992). Implicit personality theory and the five-factor model. *Journal of Personality, 60*, 295–327.

Borkenau, P., & Ostendorf, F. (1990). Comparing exploratory and confirmatory factor analysis: A study on the 5-factor model of personality. *Personality and Individual Differences, 11*, 515–524.

Caspi, A., & Bem, D. J. (1990). Personality continuity and change across the life course. In Pervin, L. A. (Ed.), *Handbook of personality: theory and research* (pp. 549–575). New York: Guilford.

Cattell, R. B. (1946). *The description and measurement of personality.* Yonkers, NY: World Book.

Cattell, R. B., Eber, H. W., & Tatsuoka, M. M. (1970). *The handbook for the Sixteen Personality Factor Questionnaire.* Champaign, IL: Institute for Personality and Ability Testing.

Church, T. A., & Katigbak, M. S. (1989). Internal, external, and self-report structure of personality in a non-Western culture: An investigation of cross-language and cross-cultural generalizability. *Journal of Personality and Social Psychology, 57*, 857–872.

Claridge, G. (1986). Eysenck's contribution to the psychology of personality. In Modgil, S. & Modgil, C. (Eds), *Hans Eysenck: consensus and controversy* (pp. 73–85). London: Falmer Press.

Cloninger, C. R. (1988). A unified biosocial theory of personality and its role in the development of anxiety states: A reply to commentaries. *Psychiatric Development, 2*, 83–120.

Costa, P. T., Jr., & McCrae, R. R. (1988a). From catalog to classification: Murray's needs and the five-factor model. *Journal of Personality and Social Psychology, 55*, 258–265.

Costa, P. T., Jr., & McCrae, R. R. (1988b). Personality in adulthood: A six-year longitudinal study of self-reports and spouse ratings on the NEO Personality Inventory. *Journal of Personality and Social Psychology, 54*, 853–863.

Costa, P. T., Jr., & McCrae, R. R. (1992). *Revised NEO Personality Inventory (NEO-PI-R) and NEO Five-Factor Inventory (NEO-FFI) professional manual.* Odessa, FL: Psychological Assessment Resources.

Costa, P. T., Jr., & McCrae, R. R. (1992). Trait psychology comes of age. In Sonderegger, T. B. (Ed.), *Nebraska Symposium on motivation: Psychology and aging.* Lincoln, NE: University of Nebraska Press.

Costa, P. T., Jr., McCrae, R. R., & Dembroski, T. M. (1989). Agreeableness vs. antagonism: Explication of a potential risk factor for CHD. In Siegman, A. & Dembroski, T. M. (Eds.), *In search of coronary-prone behavior: Beyond Type A* (pp. 41–63). Hillsdale, NJ: Lawrence Erlbaum Associates.

Costa, P. T., Jr., McCrae, R. R., & Dye, D. A. (1991). Facet scales for Agreeableness and Conscientiousness: A revision of the NEO Personality Inventory. *Personality and Individual Differences, 12*, 887–898.

Costa, P. T., Jr., McCrae, R. R., & Holland, J. L. (1984). Personality and vocational interests in an adult sample. *Journal of Applied Psychology, 69*, 390–400.

D'Andrade, R. B. (1965). Trait psychology and componential analysis. *American Anthropologist, 67*, 215–228.

Digman, J. M., & Inouye, J. (1986). Further specification of the five robust factors of personality. *Journal of Personality and Social Psychology, 50*, 116–123.

Digman, J. M., & Takemoto-Chock, N. K. (1981). Factors in the natural language of personality: Re-analysis, comparison, and interpretation of six major studies. *Multivariate Behavioral Research, 16*, 149–170.

Eaves, L. J., Eysenck, H. J., & Martin, N. G. (1989). *Genes, culture, and personality: An empirical approach.* New York: Academic Press.

Erikson, E. H. (1950). *Childhood and society.* New York: Norton.

Everett, J. E. (1983). Factor comparability as a means of determining the number of factors and their rotation. *Multivariate Behavioral Research, 18*, 197–218.

Eysenck, H. J. (1991). Dimensions of personality: 16, 5, or 3? —Criteria for a taxonomic paradigm. *Personality and Individual Differences, 12*, 773–790.

Fenigstein, A., Scheier, M. F., & Buss, A. H. (1975). Public and private self-consciousness: Assessment and theory. *Journal of Consulting and Clinical Psychology, 43*, 522–528.

Finn, S. E. (1986). Stability of personality self-ratings over 30 years: Evidence for an age/cohort interaction. *Journal of Personality and Social Psychology, 50*, 813–818.

Freud, S. (1957). On narcissism: An introduction. In Strachey, J. (Ed.), *The standard edition of the complete psychological works of Sigmund Freud* (Vol. 19, pp. 73–102). London: Hogarth Press. (Original work published 1914)

Funder, D. C., & Colvin, C. R. (1988). Friends and strangers: Acquaintanceship, agreement, and the accuracy of personality judgment. *Journal of Personality and Social Psychology, 55*, 149–158.

Fung Yi Liu. (1991). The generalizability of the NEO Personality Inventory to an university sample in Hong Kong. Unpublished manuscript, Chinese University of Hong Kong.

Goldberg, L. R. (1981). Language and individual differences: The search for universals in personality lexicons. In Wheeler, L. (Ed.), *Review of personality and social psychology* (Vol. 2, pp. 141–165). Beverly Hills, CA: Sage.

Goldberg, L. R. (1990). An alternative "description of personality": The Big-Five factor structure. *Journal of Personality and Social Psychology, 59*, 1216–1229.

Gough, H. G. (1987). *California Psychological Inventory administrator's guide.* Palo Alto, CA: Consulting Psychologists Press.

Guilford, J. S., Zimmerman, W. S., & Guilford, J. P. (1976). *The Guilford-Zimmerman Temperament Survey Handbook: twenty-five years of research and application.* San Diego, CA: EdITS Publishers.

Hartshorn, H., May, M. A., & Maller, J. B. (1929). *Studies in the nature of character, Vol. 2: studies in service and self-control.* New York: Macmillan.

Holland, J. L. (1985). *Self-Directed Search—1985 edition.* Odessa, FL: Psychological Assessment Resources.

Horney, K. (1945). *Our inner conflicts.* New York: W. W. Norton.

James, W. (1907). *Pragmatism: a new name for some old ways of thinking.* London: Longmans Green.

John, O. P., Angleitner, A., & Ostendorf, F. (1988). The lexical approach to personality: A historical review of trait taxonomic research. *European Journal of Personality, 2,* 171–203.

Jung, C. G. (1971). *Psychological types* (Baynes, H. G. Trans., revised by Hull, R. F. C.). Princeton, NJ: Princeton University Press. (Original work published 1923)

Kris, E. (1952). *Psychoanalytic explorations in art.* New York: International Universities.

Loehlin, J. C. (1987). Heredity, environment, and the structure of the California Psychological Inventory. *Multivariate Behavioral Research, 22,* 137–148.

Lorr, M. (1986). *Interpersonal Style Inventory (ISI) manual.* Los Angeles: Western Psychological Services.

McClelland, D. C., Atkinson, J. W., Clark, R. A., & Lowell, E. L. (1953). *The achievement motive.* New York: Appleton-Century-Crofts.

McCrae, R. R. (1990). Controlling neuroticism in the measurement of stress. *Stress Medicine, 6,* 237–241.

McCrae, R. R., & Costa, P. T., Jr (1989a). Reinterpreting the Myers-Briggs Type Indicator from the perspective of the five-factor model of personality. *Journal of Personality, 57,* 17–40.

McCrae, R. R., & Costa, P. T., Jr (1989b). The structure of interpersonal traits: Wiggins's circumplex and the five-factor model. *Journal of Personality and Social Psychology, 56,* 586–595.

McCrae, R. R., & Costa, P. T., Jr (1991). Adding *Liebe und Arbeit*: The full five-factor model and well-being. *Personality and Social Psychology Bulletin, 17,* 227–232.

McCrae, R. R., Costa, P. T., Jr., & Busch, C. M. (1986). Evaluating comprehensiveness in personality systems: The California Q-Set and the five-factor model. *Journal of Personality, 54,* 430–446.

Mershon, B., & Gorsuch, R. L. (1988). Number of factors in the personality sphere: Does increase in factors increase predictability of real-life criteria? *Journal of Personality and Social Psychology, 55,* 675–680.

Miller, T. (1991). The psychotherapeutic utility of the five-factor model of personality: A clinician's experience. *Journal of Personality Assessment, 57,* 415–433.

Mischel, W. (1968). *Personality and assessment.* New York: Wiley.

Murray, H. A. (1938). *Explorations in personality.* New York: Oxford University Press.

Muten, E. (1991). Self-reports, spouse ratings, and psychophysiological assessment in a behavioral medicine program: An application of the five-factor model. *Journal of Personality Assessment, 57,* 449–464.

Norman, W. T. (1963). Toward an adequate taxonomy of personality attributes: Replicated factor structure in peer nomination personality ratings. *Journal of Abnormal and Social Psychology, 66,* 574–583.

Norman, W. T. (1967). *2800 Personality trait descriptors: normative operating characteristics for a university population.* Ann Arbor: University of Michigan.

Norman, W. T., & Goldberg, L. R. (1966). Raters, ratees, and randomness in personality structure. *Journal of Personality and Social Psychology, 4,* 681–691.

Ostendorf, F. (1990). *Sprache und Persönlichkeitsstruktur: Zur Validität des Fünf-Faktoren-Modells der Persönlichkeit* [Language and personality structure: Toward the validation of the five-factor model of personality]. Regensburg: S. Roderer Verlag.

Passini, F. T., & Norman, W. T. (1966). A universal conception of personality structure? *Journal of Personality and Social Psychology, 4,* 44–49.

Plomin, R., & McClearn, G. E. (1990). Human behavioral genetics of aging. In Birren, J. E. & Schaie, K. W. (Eds), *Handbook of the psychology of aging* (3rd Ed., pp. 67–78). New York: Academic Press.

Rokeach, M. (1960). *The open and closed mind.* New York: Basic Books.

Rotter, J. B. (1966). Generalized expectancies for internal versus external control of reinforcement. *Psychological Monographs, 80*(1).

Shock, N. W., Greulich, R. C., Andres, R., Arenberg, D., Costa, P. T., Jr, Lakatta, E. G., & Tobin, J. D. (1984). *Normal human aging: The Baltimore Longitudinal Study of Aging* (NIH Publication No. 84–2450). Bethesda, MD: National Institutes of Health.

Synder, M. (1974). Self-monitoring of expressive behavior. *Journal of Personality and Social Psychology, 30,* 526–537.

Strelau, J., Angleitner, A., Bantelmann, J., & Ruch, W. (1990). The Strelau Temperament Inventory—Revised (STI-R): Theoretical considerations and scale development. *European Journal of Personality, 4,* 209–235.

Tellegen, A. (1982). Brief manual for the Differential Personality Questionnaire. Unpublished manuscript, University of Minnesota.

Tellegen, A., & Waller, N. G. (in press). Exploring personality through test construction: Development of the Multidimensional Personality Questionnaire. In Briggs, S. R. & Cheek, J. M. (Eds), *Personality measures: Development and evaluation* (Vol. 1). Greenwich, CT: JAI Press.

Tooby, J. & Cosmides, L. (1990). On the universality of human nature and the uniqueness of the individual: The role of genetics and adaptation. *Journal of Personality, 58,* 17–68.

Tupes, E. C., & Christal, R. E. (1961). Recurrent personality factors based on trait ratings (USAF ASD Technical Report No. 61–97). Lackland Air Force Base, TX: U.S. Air Force.

White, R. W. (1959). Motivation reconsidered: The concept of competence. *Psychological Review, 66,* 297–333.

Wiggins, J. S. (1968). Personality structure. In Farnsworth, P. R., Rosenzweig, M. R. & Polefka, J. T. (Eds), *Annual review of psychology* (Vol. 19, pp. 293–350). Palo Alto, CA: Annual Reviews.

Windel, M., & Lerner, R. M. (1986). Reassessing the dimensions of temperament individuality across the life span: The Revised Dimensions of Temperament Survey (DOTS-R). *Journal of Adolescent Research, 1,* 213–230.

Yang, K., & Bond, M. H. (1990). Exploring implicit personality theories with indigenous or imported constructs: The Chinese case. *Journal of Personality and Social Psychology, 58,* 1087–1095.

Zuckerman, M. (1979). *Sensation seeking: Beyond the optimal level of arousal.* Hillsdale, NJ: Lawrence Erlbaum Associates.

PART III

Biological Approaches to Personality

The field of biology has made remarkable progress over the past century, and particularly in the past few decades. It was only natural, therefore, for personality psychologists to begin to use biology to help them understand the roots of important human behaviors. A biological psychology of personality has developed that is based upon four different areas of biology and that therefore comprises four rather different approaches.

One approach relates the anatomy of the brain to personality. Perhaps the oldest field of biological psychology, work in this area began by cataloging the ways in which accidental brain damage affected behavior. A second approach, very active today, relates the physiology of the nervous system to personality. This approach can to traced back to the ancient Greeks, who proposed that "humors," or bodily fluids, influenced personality. Modern research addresses the complex interactions still being discovered between neurotransmitters, hormones, and behavior. A third approach, called behavioral genetics, studies the way individual differences in personality are inherited from one's parents and shared among family members. Finally, a fourth approach applies Darwin's theory of evolution—a foundation of all of modern biology—to understand the behavioral propensities of the human species.

The readings in this section sample all of these approaches. Be forewarned: Some of these articles contain a fair amount of technical detail that is not really part of psychology at all. You will read about neurohormonal assays and even the kind of paste used to attach an electrode to a subject's hand. These details are included to provide a flavor of this enterprise and for your reference. But the general principles concerning the relationships between biological markers and psychological characteristics are what matter. Even among psychologists, only a few researchers develop—or need to develop—a real expertise in all of these details.

The section begins with a chapter, more than a century old, that describes the ancient humoral theory of personality and proposes a "modern"—as of the mid-19th century—modification. The next selection, by James Dabbs and his colleagues, describes research on the association between a "humor" of modern interest—testosterone—and violent behavior. Then a selection by Marvin Zuckerman reviews the state of the art in research on the biological bases of personality, including the influence of both brain structures and biochemicals.

Behavioral genetics is introduced in the next selection, by Thomas Bouchard, Jr. Bouchard reviews the current evidence that many personality traits have a substantial heritable component. Next, a selection by Robert Plomin describes a particularly important conclusion from research in behavioral genetics, that the aspects of family environment shared by siblings have a surprisingly small influence on the way their personality ultimately develops.

The evolutionary biology of personality is illustrated in the sixth and seventh selections. David Buss and his co-workers describe research that measures gender differences in jealousy through self-report and physiological indicators, and provide an evolutionarily based account of their results. Then Margo Wilson and Martin Daly describe what they see as the evolutionary basis of "uxoricide," the propensity to kill one's spouse in a jealous rage.

The final section, by Daryl Bem, illustrates what may be the wave of the future for biological approaches to personality. Bem introduces a theory of sexual orientation that explains this important personality characteristic as a result of a complex interplay between predisposing biological factors, basic biological mechanisms, and a child's and adolescent's social interactions in a sexually polarized society. Other theories of sexual development are likely to appear in the future to compete with Bem's. Even more importantly, we may begin to see other complete theories of complex phenomena such as violence, extraversion, jealousy, and even wife-beating, that move step by step from genes to temperament to early experience to interaction with society.

The Temperaments

Samuel R. Wells

*Modern biological psychology attempts to connect physical form and function
with psychological outcomes by studying the anatomy of the brain and nervous
system, and substances in the body such as neurotransmitters and hormones, to
determine their effect upon behavior and personality.*

*The attempt to connect the physical with the mental has a very long history.
The ancient physicians Hippocrates and Galen believed that the balance of four
"humors," or fluids, in the body produced four distinct personality types. As recently as 100 years ago, it was widely believed that the structure of the brain
could be determined by feeling bumps in the head, and in this way "phrenology" could be used to assess an individual's personality.*

*The first selection in the biological section is an excerpt from a book pub-
lished more than a century ago by Samuel R. Wells. Not much is known about
Wells today except that he was the editor of something called* The Phrenological
Journal and Life Illustrated. *In this book, Wells summarized the ancient humoral theory of personality and then replaced it with one of his own. Wells
seems to have been what would today be called a biological reductionist; he believed that all aspects of human character and personality reside and can be
seen in the physical form. The book provides detailed guidance on how to assess
personality from appearance.*

*The excerpted chapter begins with a brief summary of the theory he attrib-
utes to Hippocrates, then quickly moves on to his own modification. It is interesting to see that more than 2,000 years after Hippocrates, and just over 100
years ago, this ancient theory was still taken seriously enough to be the jumping-
off place for what was portrayed as state-of-the-art knowledge.*

*Perhaps this book marks the last gasp of the ancient humoral and phreno-
logical approach. The research of the 20th century, based upon dramatic
breakthroughs in the study of physiology, genetics, and evolution, quickly began
to look very different.*

*And maybe it doesn't. Recent research in health psychology relates some of
the ancient types to disease-proneness. The "choleric" person, described not
much differently today than by the ancient Greeks, seems at exceptional risk for
heart attack (Booth-Kewley & Friedman, 1987)!*

Still, and perhaps needless to say, the specific biological factors and psychological characteristics do not *in fact relate to each other in the manner described by Wells. Please do not read this selection to learn how to do personality assessment by looking at the individual's face. Instead, read it for historical background, its style of argument, and the richness of its description of psychological types. Wells may have been wrong in his biology, but he provides a description of some types of people that seem recognizable.*

From *New Physiognomy, or, Signs of Character, as Manifested Through Temperament and External Forms, and Especially in 'the Human Face Divine,'* by S. R. Wells (1873), pp. 94–109. New York: Samuel R. Wells, Publisher.

Made him of well-attempered clay,
As such high destiny befitted,
And bade him rule.

—MARVEL

The first condition to be noted in the study of character through its physical manifestations, is temperament; which may be defined as "a particular state of the constitution, depending upon the relative proportion of its different masses, and the relative energy of its different functions."

In their last analysis, the temperaments are as numerous as the individuals of the human race, no two persons being found with precisely the same physical constitution. Tracing them back, however, we find them all to result from the almost infinite combinations of a few simple elements.

The Ancient Doctrine

Hippocrates, "the father of medicine," describes four temperamental conditions depending, according to his theory, upon what he called the four primary components of the human body—the blood, the phlegm, the yellow bile, and the black bile. The preponderance of one or the other of these components in a person produces his peculiar constitution or temperament. Bodies in which blood superabounds have, he says, the sanguine temperament; if phlegm be in excess, the phlegmatic temperament; if yellow bile be most

fully developed, the choleric temperament is produced; and if the black bile (*atrabilis*) be most abundant, the melancholic or atrabilious temperament. These four temperaments are thus described by Paulus Ægineta, an ancient physician, who adopts the theory and follows the classification of Hippocrates:

1. The sanguine or hot and moist temperament is more fleshy than is proper, hairy, and hot to the touch. Persons having this temperament in excess are liable to putrid disorders.

2. The phlegmatic or cold and moist temperament is gross, fat, and lax. The skin is soft and white; the hair tawny and not abundant; the limbs and muscles weak; the veins invisible, and the character timid, spiritless, and inactive.

3. The choleric or warm and dry temperament is known by abundant dark hair; large and prominent veins and arteries, dark skin, and a firm, well-articulated, and muscular body.

4. The melancholic or cold and dry temperament is known by hard, slender, and white bodies; fine muscles, small joints, and little hair. As to disposition, persons of this temperament are spiritless, timid, and desponding.

*   *   *

The New Classification

The human body is composed of three grand classes or systems of organs, each of which has its

Figure 18.1   Hon. Wm. Maule Panmure, M.P.

Figure 18.2   Thomas Moore

Figure 18.3   D. C. McCallum

Figure 18.4   McDonald Clarke

special function in the general economy. We denominate them—

1. The Motive or Mechanical System;
2. The Vital or Nutritive System; and
3. The Mental or Nervous System.

On this natural anatomical basis rests the most simple and satisfactory doctrine of the temperaments, of which there are primarily three, corresponding with the three systems of organs just named. We call them—

1. The Motive Temperament;
2. The Vital Temperament; and,
3. The Mental Temperament.

Each of these temperaments is determined by the predominance of the class of organs from which it takes its name. The first is marked by a superior development of the osseous and muscular systems, forming the locomotive apparatus; in the second the vital organs, the principal seat of which is in the trunk, give the tone to the organization; while in the third the brain and nervous system exert the controlling power.

I. THE MOTIVE TEMPERAMENT The bony framework of the human body determines its general configuration, which is modified in its details by the muscular fibers and cellular tissues which overlay it. In the motive temperament, the bones are proportionally large and generally long rather than broad, and the outlines of the form manifest a tendency to angularity. The figure is commonly tall and striking if not elegant; the face oblong, the cheekbones rather high; the front teeth large; the neck rather long; the shoulders broad and definite; the chest moderate in size and fullness; the abdomen proportional; and the limbs long and tapering. The muscles are well developed and correspond in form with the bones. The complexion and eyes are generally but not always dark, and the hair dark, strong, and abundant. The features are strongly marked, and their expression striking. Firmness of texture characterizes all the organs, imparting great strength and endurance.

This temperament gives great bodily strength,

MOTIVE.

Figure 18.5   James Monroe

ease of action, love of physical exercise, energy, and capacity for work. Those in whom it predominates generally possess strongly marked characters, and are in a high degree capable of receiving and combining rapidly many and varied impressions. They are the acknowledged leaders and rulers in the sphere in which they move; and are often carried away, bearing others with them, by the torrent of their own imagination and passions. This is the temperament for rare talents—especially of the executive kind—great works, great errors, great faults, and great crimes. It is sometimes, though not necessarily, characterized by an objectionable degree of coarseness and harshness of feelings, manifested by a corresponding coarseness of fiber in the bodily organs, bushy hair and beard, and a harsh expression of countenance.

The motive temperament is emphatically the American temperament, as it was that of the ancient Romans, though with us it is modified by a larger proportion of the mental temperament than with them. An aquiline or a Roman nose, great ambition, and an insatiable love of power and conquest go with it.

Figure 18.6 Silas Wright

ligaments and the articulations which they form are proportionally small, which corrects the tendency to angularity which is characteristic of this temperament, and tends to round the contour of the joints. This will be particularly observable in the wrists and ankles.

The third modification of this temperament is that which presents proportionally shorter bones, and, except around the pelvis, smaller and more rounded muscles, affording less strongly marked reliefs and more of that rounded plumpness essential to the highest style of female beauty. In this characteristic, it approaches the vital temperament, to which this modification is allied.

In accordance with the law of homogeneousness, we find, on examining this temperament more closely, that it is characterized in details, as well as in general form, by length. The face is oblong, the head high, the nose long and prominent, and all the features correspond. This structure indicates great power and activity in some particular direction, but lack of breadth or comprehensiveness.

* * *

II. The Vital Temperament As this temperament depends upon the preponderance of the vital or nutritive organs, which occupy the great cavities of the trunk, it is necessarily marked by a breadth and thickness of body proportionally greater, and a stature and size of limbs proportionally less than the motive temperament. Its most striking physical characteristic is *rotundity*. The face inclines to roundness; the nostrils are wide; the neck rather short; the shoulders broad and rounded; the chest full; the abdomen well developed; the arms and legs plump but tapering, and terminating in hands and feet relatively small. The complexion is generally florid; the countenance smiling; the eyes light; the nose broad, and the hair soft, light, and silky.

In a woman of this temperament (which seems to be peculiarly the temperament of woman), the shoulders are softly rounded, and owe any breadth they may possess rather to the expanded chest, with which they are connected, than to the bony

Men of this temperament often pursue their ends with a stern and reckless disregard of their own and others' physical welfare. Nothing can turn them aside from their purpose; and they attain success by means of energy and perseverance rather than by forethought or deep scheming. They are men of the field rather than of the closet—men with whom to think and to feel is to act. As speakers, they make use of strong expressions, emphasize many words, and generally hit the nail with a heavy blow.

In its typical form, the motive temperament is less proper to woman than to man, but there are several modifications of it which give much elegance and beauty to the female figure.

The first is that in which the bones, except those of the pelvis, are proportionally small, which gives the figure additional delicacy and grace. This conformation, while it adds to the beauty of the female figure, detracts from the strength and consequently the beauty of the masculine form. The Diana of Grecian sculpture furnishes a fine example of the motive temperament thus modified.

The second modification is that in which the

or muscular size of the shoulders themselves; the bust is full and rounded; the waist, though sufficiently marked, is, as it were, encroached upon by the plumpness of the contiguous parts; the haunches are greatly expanded; the limbs tapering; the feet and hands small, but plump; the complexion, depending on nutrition, has the rose and the lily so exquisitely blended that we are surprised that it should defy the usual operations of the elements; and there is a profusion of soft, and fine flaxen or auburn hair. The whole figure is plump, soft and voluptuous. This temperament is not so common among American women as could be desired.

Persons of this temperament have greater vigor, but less density and toughness of fiber than those in whom the motive predominates. They love fresh air and exercise, and must be always doing something to work off their constantly accumulating stock of vitality; but they generally love play better than hard work.

Mentally, they are characterized by activity, ardor, impulsiveness, enthusiasm, versatility, and sometimes by fickleness. They are distinguished by elasticity rather than firmness, and possess more diligence than persistence, and more brilliancy than depth. They are frequently violent and passionate, but are as easily calmed as excited; are generally cheerful, amiable, and genial; always fond of good living, and more apt than others to become addicted to the excessive use of stimulants. Their motto is *dum vivimus, vivamus*—let us live while we live. There is great enjoyment to them in the mere sense of being alive—in the consciousness of animal existence. The English furnish some of the best examples of the vital temperament. Our illustration gives a good idea of it so far as its outlines are concerned.

* * *

III. THE MENTAL TEMPERAMENT The mental temperament, depending upon the brain and nervous system, is characterized by a slight frame; a head relatively large, an oval or a pyriform face; a high, pale forehead; delicate and finely chiseled

Figure 18.7 Prof. Tholuck

features; bright and expressive eyes; slender neck; and only a moderate development of the chest. The whole figure is delicate and graceful, rather than striking or elegant. The hair is soft, fine, and not abundant or very dark; the skin soft and delicate in texture; the voice somewhat high-keyed, but flexible and varied in its intonations; and the expression animated and full of intelligence.

Women in whom this temperament predominates, though often very beautiful, lack the rounded outlines, the full bosom, and the expanded pelvis, which betoken the highest degree of adaptation to the distinctive offices of the sex.

The mental temperament indicates great sensitiveness, refined feelings; excellent taste; great love of the beautiful in nature and art; vividness of conception; and intensity of emotion. The thoughts are quick, the senses acute, the imagination lively and brilliant, and the moral sentiments active and influential.

This is the literary, the artistic, and especially the poetic temperament.

There is at the present day, in this country

especially, an excessive and morbid development of this temperament which is most inimical to health, happiness, and longevity. It prevails particularly among women (to whom even in its normal predominance it is less proper than the preceding), and answers to the nervous temperament of the old classification. It is characterized by the smallness and emaciation of the muscles, the quickness and intensity of the sensations, the suddenness and fickleness of the determinations, and a morbid impressibility. It is caused by sedentary habits, lack of bodily exercise, a premature or disproportionate development of the brain, the immoderate use of tea and coffee, late hours, and other hurtful indulgences.

The three primary temperaments, combining with each other in different proportions and being modified by various causes, form sub-temperaments innumerable, presenting differences and resemblances depending upon the relative proportion of the primitive elements. The simplest combination of which the three temperaments already described are susceptible, gives us six sub-temperaments, which we designate as—

1. The Motive-Vital Temperament;
2. The Motive-Mental Temperament;
3. The Vital-Motive Temperament;
4. The Vital-Mental Temperament;
5. The Mental-Motive Temperament; and,
6. The Mental-Vital Temperament.

The names of these compound temperaments sufficiently indicate their character. The motive-vital and the vital-motive differ but slightly, the name placed first in either case indicating the element which exists in the larger proportion. The same remark applies to the motive-mental and the mental-motive, and to the vital-mental and mental-vital.

Perfection of constitution, it is evident, must consist in a proper balance of temperaments. Where any one of them exists in great excess, the result must necessarily be a departure from symmetry and harmony, both of form and character. Whatever, therefore, has a tendency to promote this disproportionate development should be carefully avoided.

Each person is born with a particular temperament in which there is an inherent tendency to maintain and increase itself, since it gives rise to habits which exercise and develop it; but this tendency may be greatly modified, if not counteracted entirely, by external circumstances—by education, occupation, superinduced habits, climate, and so forth; and more especially by direct and special training instituted for that purpose.

It will be seen by the foregoing statements, which we have aimed to make as clear and explicit as the nature of the subject will admit, that a thorough practical knowledge of the temperaments alone will enable one to form a very correct general estimate of individual character. The character, as a whole, which we have attributed to the motive temperament, is never found in connection with either of the others; and the same remark applies equally to the vital and the mental. The difficulty (which is not insurmountable, however) lies in estimating correctly the relative proportion of the different elements in each individual temperament so as to give to each its due degree of influence on the character. Study, observation, and practice will enable the persevering student to do this, in time, with great exactness.

Testosterone, Crime, and Misbehavior Among 692 Male Prison Inmates

James M. Dabbs, Jr., Timothy S. Carr, Robert L. Frady, and Jasmin K. Riad

Of all the substances in the body that might affect behavior, the male sex hormone testosterone probably has received the most attention. Although both males and females have testosterone in their bodies, males have much more and, it is commonly observed, are more aggressive. These observations have led directly to the hypothesis that testosterone might be a cause of aggressive behavior.

This hypothesis is tested in the next selection by the personality psychologist James Dabbs and several of his collaborators. Dabbs has spent much of his career in pursuit of the relationship between testosterone, behavior, and personality. His usual technique is to have subjects spit in a cup and measure testosterone level from the saliva. He then gathers some measure of his subjects' personality or behavior, and correlates the two measurements.

For the research reported in the next selection, Dabbs was looking for subjects who might be unusually aggressive. So he went to a maximum security prison, induced prisoners to donate some of their saliva, and obtained records of the crimes for which they had been incarcerated as well as of their rule infractions in prison. He found both related to testosterone. High-testosterone inmates were more likely to have committed violent crimes outside of prison and to have violated prison rules inside of prison.

Of course, as Dabbs points out at the end of this article, these are correlational data. That means the direction of causality is not certain. Perhaps testosterone causes violent behavior, but perhaps, too, violent behavior raises one's testosterone level. In the end, the relationship is likely to turn out to be complex. Dabbs points out that it is too simple to say "testosterone causes violence." But the evidence is strong that this hormone has something to do with it.

A final note before you begin reading this selection. Dabbs provides quite a bit of technical material and describes a complex set of statistical analyses. These are included here for reference, but do not be troubled if you cannot follow the technical material in detail. The basic finding of a relationship between testoster-

one and behavior should shine through clearly, particularly in the article's tables and its graph.

From "Testosterone, Crime, and Misbehavior Among 692 Male Prison Inmates," by J. M. Dabbs, Jr., T. S. Carr, R. L. Frady, and J. K. Riad (1995). Reprinted with permission from *Personality and Individual Differences*, Vol. 18, pp. 627–633. Oxford, England: Elsevier Science Ltd.

The link between testosterone and criminal behavior has been studied for more than 20 years, with mixed results. Testosterone has been related to toughness, status, dominance, and violence in the criminal history and prison behavior of inmates (Dabbs, Frady, Carr, & Besch, 1987; Dabbs, Jurkovic, & Frady, 1991; Ehrenkranz, Bliss, & Sheard, 1974; Kreuz & Rose, 1972), although not all researchers have found these relationships (Bain, Langevin, Dickey, Hucker, & Wright, 1988; Bain, Langevin, Dickey, & Ben-Aron, 1987). There have been no reports of overall differences in testosterone between criminal and noncriminal populations.

Uncertainty about the role of testosterone has arisen in part from the use of small samples, ranging from fewer than 30 to about 100 prison inmates. Small samples lack the statistical power to detect relationships that may be weak. Small samples also make it difficult to study differences in testosterone levels across different kinds of crime, because the subjects committing a particular crime, such as murder, will be few indeed. If testosterone is to be useful in criminology, we need more confidence regarding its overall relationship to crime, along with more knowledge about the crimes to which it is mostly related.

The present study employed a relatively large sample, containing 692 Ss.[1] The sample comprises two sets, one with 202 Ss about whom some findings have been reported before (Dabbs et al, 1987, 1991), and one with 490 new Ss. In examining overall relationships of testosterone to criminal violence and prison behavior, the second set was used to cross-validate findings from the first set.

In examining detailed relationships between testosterone and different crimes and behaviors in prison, the two sets were combined into a single sample.

Method

SUBJECTS Ss were adult male inmates in a maximum security state prison. Their mean age was 19.8 years (SD = 2.6).[2] Two thirds were black and one third white. Thirty-four percent had prior juvenile or adult convictions, 37% had prior incarcerations since age 17, and only 5% had been fully employed during the 6 months prior to committing the crime for which they were currently incarcerated. Their mean Wide Range Aptitude Test reading score was at seventh grade level. Their median sentence length was 6.1 year (range 0.5–89.0). In prison they lived in prison dormitories (15%), cells (21%), and a diagnostic unit where all incoming inmates spend 1–2 months (64%). A comparison of Ss in the two sets is presented in the results section.

TESTOSTERONE SCORES Testosterone was measured from saliva samples. Each S voluntarily consented to participate and collected 3 ml saliva in a 20-ml vial for testosterone assay. Salivary and serum testosterone levels are highly correlated (Navarro, Jaun, & Bonnin, 1986). Day-to-day reliability of salivary testosterone measurements is

---

[1] S is a standard abbreviation for "subject."

[2] SD stands for standard deviation, a commonly used measure of variation (it is the square root of the average squared deviations from the mean within a sample). If you are not familiar with this statistic, don't worry.

about $r = .64$ (Dabbs, 1990),[3] about the same as the reliability of serum testosterone measurements (Gutai, Dai, LaPorte, & Kuller, 1988). The reliability of measurements among 15 Ss who appeared in our present prison sample on two occasions a mean of 15 months apart was $r = .76$. Saliva was collected unstimulated for the first 202 Ss and stimulated by sugar-free chewing gum for the last 490; using gum makes it easier to collect saliva and does not affect assay scores (Dabbs, 1991). Ss had been in prison a median of 47 days (range 0–2,546) when samples were collected. Samples were collected between 8:30 and 10:00 a.m. and stored frozen until assayed.

Saliva samples from the first 202 Ss were collected in 1985 and 1987 and assayed in one clinical laboratory (Dabbs et al., 1987, 1991). Samples from the remaining Ss were collected during the years 1990–1992 and assayed in a second laboratory. Each laboratory assayed samples in duplicate, using in-house[125] I-Testosterone radioimmunoassays with ether extraction and charcoal separation. The mean within-assay coefficient of variation was less than 10%.

Combining data from different assays requires considerable care, because changes in reagents, personnel, and other factors in routine laboratory operation can affect results. Samples from the first 202 Ss were assayed in two groups, of 89 and 113 samples each. Samples from the remaining 490 Ss were assayed in batches of 15–50 samples each. Scores from different assays were adjusted as follows and then combined into a single data set. Samples from a control pool that remained constant across the study period were included in each assay among the 490 Ss, and interassay variation was statistically controlled by multiplying each testosterone score by the ratio of the mean control value for all assays, divided by the control value for its own assay. Among the first 202 Ss, comprising the two groups of 89 and 113 each, control values were not available, and constants were added to the scores to make the mean of each group equal to the mean of the last 490 Ss.[4]

PRISON RECORDS Information on Ss' behavior was obtained from prison system computer records, which are updated continuously. This information was extracted at the end of the study and merged with Ss' testosterone scores.

Each S had a crime of record, it being either the crime, or the most serious of several crimes, for which he was currently serving time. The crime of record was designated by the Department of Corrections as violent or nonviolent, following a Federal Bureau of Investigation (1984) distinction between personal crimes and property crimes. The most frequent violent crimes were robbery (25%) and assault (11%), and the most frequent nonviolent crimes were burglary (21%) and drug offenses (10%). No information was available on what crimes Ss committed prior to the crime for which they were currently incarcerated.

While in prison, Ss receive disciplinary reports (DR's) for violations of prison rules. Our Ss received a total of 7,416 DR's for 85 different violations, ranging from fighting to wearing unauthorized clothing. The frequency of DR's per S was skewed, with a mean of 11 and a range from 0 to 151. We assigned an overall 0–1 score to indicate whether each S had any DR's at all. We also assigned 85 separate 0–1 scores to indicate whether the S had DR's for each of the 85 different kinds of violation.

Results

CROSS-VALIDATION: TESTOSTERONE, CRIME, AND PRISON BEHAVIOR IN TWO SAMPLES Table 19.1 describes the two sets of Ss. Ss in Set 2 were older, more often black, and more often incarcerated for violent crimes, but the differences were not sta-

---

[3]This finding means that testosterone measures taken from an individual on one day could be expected correlate with measures from the same individual on another day with an $r = .64$.

[4]Because the two samples of subjects were studied at different times, Dabbs and his co-workers took pains to make sure the testosterone assays were comparable. These efforts are described in the preceding paragraph.

tistically significant ($P > .10$). Ss in Set 2 did have significantly higher WRAT reading levels, $t(690) = 5.80$, $P < .001$, and longer sentences, $t(690) = 2.81$, $P < .01$, than Ss in Set 1, and more of them had received DR's, χ^2 ($df = 1$, $N = 692$), $P < 0.05$.[5]

The standard deviation among testosterone scores was 2.6 ng/dl in Set 1 and 3.4 ng/dl in Set 2. Mean testosterone scores were 8.3 ng/dl for the first 87 Ss in Set 1 (Dabbs et al., 1987), 6.6 ng/dl for the second 113 Ss in Set 1 (Dabbs et al., 1991), and 9.0 ng/dl for the 490 Ss in Set 2. These means are within the normal range and similar to means reported for men in various occupations (Dabbs, de La Rue, & Williams, 1990). Differences among the means were due in part to having the assays conducted in different laboratories. We added constants to make the means in Set 1 equal to the mean of Set 2, as described above. This adjustment to a common mean level did not introduce bias into the relationships reported below, and it eliminated a between-groups source of error.[6]

Testosterone in both sets was related to crime of record and behavior in prison. Testosterone was correlated with violence of crime marginally in Set 1 (biserial $r = .12$, $df = 201$, $P < .10$) and significantly in Set 2 (biserial $r = .19$, $df = 489$, $P < .01$). The marginal relationship in Set 1 reflected a combination of a significant relationship in the first 87 cases (Dabbs et al., 1987) and a nonsignificant relationship in the next 113 cases (Dabbs et al., 1991). Testosterone was correlated with having at least one DR in Set 1 (biserial $r = .20$, $df = 201$, $P < .001$) and in Set 2 (biserial $r = .23$, $df = 489$, $P < .001$). For the combined sets, more higher testosterone Ss committed violent crimes (biserial $r = .18$, $df = 691$, $P < .001$) and received at least one DR in prison (biserial $r = .22$, $df = 691$, $P < .001$). Mean testosterone levels for Ss who committed violent or nonviolent crimes

TABLE 19.1

CHARACTERISTICS OF Ss IN SET 1 AND SET 2

	Set 1	Set 2
Mean age	19.7 yr	19.9 yr
Mean WRAT reading level	6.0	7.6
Mean sentence length	10.6 yr	8.6 yr
% of inmates white	34	28
% of inmates black	66	72
% of crimes violent	52	57
% of inmates with DR's	82	73

were 9.5 (SD = 3.3) and 8.4 (SD = 3.0) ng/dl, respectively. Mean testosterone levels for Ss who had no DR's or one or more DR's were 7.7 (SD = 2.4) and 9.4 (SD = 3.3) ng/dl, respectively.[7]

COMBINED SAMPLE

Crimes. In addition to treating testosterone as a continuous variable in the combined sample of 692 Ss, we classified each S as being in the lower, middle, or upper third of the testosterone distribution. This loses some information available in the continuous distribution, but it has the advantage of focusing on extreme groups.[8] We then followed an epidemiological approach, treating high testosterone as a factor increasing the risk (or likelihood) of criminal violence and misbehavior in prison. We computed Cochran-Mantel-Haenszel statistics (SAS Institute, 1985) to contrast the risk of a behavior occurring among Ss in the upper third of testosterone with the risk of the same behavior occurring in the lower third. A risk ratio

---

[5]The χ^2 or "chi-square" statistic is a measure of the degree to which the distribution of observations across categories is nonrandom.

[6]The preceding paragraph describes technical adjustments to testosterone measurements to make them comparable across all the subjects in the sample.

[7]The biserial correlation is a correlation coefficient calculated in a case where one of the two variables is dichotomous, in this case, whether a crime was violent or not. The df is related to the number of subjects, the p level refers to the probability of the results given a correlation of zero.

[8]Treating a variable as "continuous" means that the actual value of the variable is entered into all calculations; the alternative used here is to break all subjects into three groups, such as high, medium, and low. The latter practice loses information, but Dabbs argues it is useful for comparing individuals who score near the extremes.

PERCENTAGE OF LOW, MEDIUM, AND HIGH TESTOSTERONE INMATES COMMITTING VIOLENT CRIMES AND VIOLATING PRISON RULES

Activity	Testosterone group[a]			Upper/lower risk ratio[b]
	Lower third	Mid third	Upper third	
Committed violent crimes ($n = 395$)	46	54	66	1.4*
Violated prison rules ($n = 524$)	67	71	88	1.3*

[a]Cell entries are rounded to the nearest per cent.
[b]Risk ratios represent the likelihood of an activity among Ss in the upper third of the testosterone distribution, relative to its likelihood among Ss in the lower third. If the likelihoods in the upper and lower thirds are equal, the risk ratio will be 1.0.
*Confidence intervals of the risk ratio do not overlap 1.0 ($P<.05$).

of 2.0, for example, would characterize a behavior twice as likely in the upper third as in the lower third. A risk ratio is statistically significant when its confidence interval excludes 1.0. Table 19.2 shows the risk of having committed violent crime was 1.4 times greater for a S in the upper third than the lower third of the testosterone distribution. The risk of receiving a DR was 1.3 times greater in the upper third than the lower third.[9]

In the combined sample, we also examined the relationship of testosterone to different crimes. We examined nine specific types of crime, all committed by more than 25 inmates, and a combined type made up of the remaining less frequent crimes. We used χ^2 as an overall test to determine whether different crimes were committed by Ss in the lower, middle, and upper thirds of testosterone. We computed risk ratios to reflect the difference in likelihood of committing specific crimes in the upper and lower thirds of the testosterone distribution. Table 19.3 summarizes this information.

The crimes in Table 19.3 are ordered by their risk ratios from those committed most by high testosterone Ss to those committed most by low testosterone Ss. Testosterone level was significantly related to type of crime, χ^2 ($df = 18$, $N = 692$) = 43.73, $P < .001$ (although the χ^2 test does not speak to the particular ordering of crimes in Table 19.3). Risk ratios indicated 4 of the 10 crimes were significantly associated with testosterone. High testosterone was associated with crimes of sex and violence, and low testosterone was associated with burglary, theft, and drug offenses. Figure 19.1 displays this information differently, showing the percentage of each kind of crime committed by high, medium, and low testosterone Ss.[10]

Disciplinary reports. We used analysis of variance to determine whether the pattern of DR's received was different for Ss in the lower, middle, and upper thirds of testosterone. χ^2 was not appropriate for this analysis, because a S could have several different kinds of DR's and the responses were thus not independent. We computed risk ratios of the difference in likelihood of receiving specific DR's in the upper and lower thirds of the testosterone distribution.

The DR's in Table 19.4 are ordered by their risk ratios from those received most by high tes-

[9]The "epidemiological" analyses reported in this paragraph are techniques commonly used in medical research to examine risk for disease; they are relatively unusual in a psychological report such as this one.

[10]If you are unfamiliar with these statistics, the important numbers to focus on are the percentages in Table 19.3.

TABLE 19.3

PERCENTAGE OF LOW, MEDIUM, AND HIGH TESTOSTERONE INMATES
COMMITTING VIOLENT CRIMES

Type of crime	Testosterone group[a]			Upper/lower risk ratio[b]
	Lower third	Mid third	Upper third	
Rape ($n = 35$)[c]	2	5	8	3.6*
Child molestation ($n = 25$)[d]	2	3	6	2.6
Homicide ($n = 45$)[e]	4	6	9	2.1*
Robbery ($n = 72$)	8	12	12	1.5
Armed robbery ($n = 100$)	13	15	16	1.2
Assault ($n = 77$)	11	9	13	1.2
Misc. other ($n = 56$)[f]	8	10	6	0.8
Burglary ($n = 147$)	25	21	18	0.7
Theft ($n = 65$)	11	12	6	0.5*
Drugs ($n = 70$)	16	7	7	0.4*

[a]Cell entries are rounded to the nearest per cent.
[b]Risk ratios represent the likelihood of an activity among Ss in the upper third of the testosterone distribution, relative to its likelihood among Ss in the lower third. If the likelihoods in the upper and lower thirds are equal, the risk will be 1.0.
[c]Does not include statutory rape.
[d]Includes 16 cases of child molestation and 9 cases of aggravated child molestation. Mean testosterone levels for molestation and aggravated molestation were 9.8 and 11.4 ng/dl, respectively, $t<1.0$.
[e]Includes murder and voluntary homicide; does not include involuntary homicide.
[f]Includes 31 violent and 25 nonviolent crimes.
*Confidence intervals of the risk ratio do not overlap 1.0 ($P<.05$).

tosterone Ss to those received most by low testosterone Ss. In the analysis of variance, the 0–1 DR scores were treated as dichotomous measures of continuous variables. The three testosterone levels constituted three levels of a between-subjects factor, and the 10 DR categories constituted 10 levels of a within-subjects factor. A significant group effect indicated more DR's among higher testosterone Ss, $F(2,689) = 6.55$, $P < 0.01$. A significant DR effect indicated some DR's more likely than others, $F(2,6201) = 169.62$, $P < 0.001$. And a significant group by DR interaction indicated that Ss with different testosterone levels had different DR's, $F(18,6201) = 3.97$, $P < 0.001$. Risk ratios indicated five of the 10 DR categories significantly associated with testosterone. High testosterone was associated especially with violations involving overt confrontation. As with the crimes, Figure

19.1 displays this information differently, showing the percent of each kind of DR received by high, medium, and low testosterone Ss.

*   *   *

Discussion

The present study supports earlier findings relating testosterone to criminal violence, and it provides details not available from earlier studies. Similar testosterone effects were found in two different subsets of data, even though there were significant differences between Ss in the two sets. Pooling the subsets to produce a large overall sample allowed us to draw conclusions about different kinds of crime. We found testosterone related to crimes of sex and violence. We clarified Rada, Laws, Kellner, Stivastava, and Peake's (1983)

TABLE 19.4

PERCENTAGE OF LOW, MEDIUM, AND HIGH TESTOSTERONE INMATES WITH AT LEAST ONE
DISCIPLINARY REPORT FOR VIOLATION OF PRISON RULES

Type of violation	Testosterone group[a]			Upper/lower risk ratio[b]
	Lower third	Mid third	Upper third	
Unauthorized presence ($n = 113$)	11	19	19	1.7*
Assault with injury to inmate ($n = 189$)	21	29	32	1.6*
Assault on inmate ($n = 200$)	23	29	35	1.5*
Failure to follow instructions ($n = 452$)	56	59	81	1.5*
Participation in disturbance ($n = 131$)	15	21	21	1.4
Verbal threat ($n = 108$)	14	13	20	1.4
Insubordination ($n = 328$)	43	45	54	1.3*
Lying ($n = 134$)	17	20	21	1.2
Property damage ($n = 87$)	13	12	13	0.9
Unauthorized absence ($n = 89$)	15	12	12	0.8

The ten most common violations are included in the table.
[a]Cell entries are rounded to the nearest per cent.
[b]Risk ratios represent the likelihood of an activity among Ss in the upper third of the testosterone distribution, relative to its likelihood among Ss in the lower third. If the likelihoods in the upper and lower thirds are equal, the risk ratio will be 1.0.
*Confidence intervals of the risk ratio do not overlap 1.0 ($P < .05$).

mixed evidence linking testosterone to rape and child molestation. And we related testosterone to prison behavior as well as to type of prior criminal behavior outside of prison.

The findings provide information about criminal behavior among low as well as high testosterone individuals. While certain crimes and misbehaviors are characteristic of high testosterone, others are characteristic of low testosterone. The rule violations shown at the top and bottom of Figure 19.1 may be emblematic of high and low testosterone individuals. High testosterone individuals are dominant and confrontational, and they showed up where they did not belong (often to engage in illicit activity, according to prison staff). Those low in testosterone hold back, and they are notable more by their absence than their presence.

The relationship of testosterone to specific rule violations should not obscure the fact that higher testosterone inmates overall had more rule violations. The variety of rule violations suggests the behavior of high testosterone individuals reflects

intractability, unmanageability, and lack of docility as well as aggression and violence. This fits with findings about occupations (Dabbs, 1992) and college fraternities (Dabbs, Hargrove, & Heusel, 1993), as well as with Albert, Walsh, and Jonik's (1993) conclusion that testosterone is related to something other than simple aggression.

A question may arise as to whether Ss who committed drug offenses were low in testosterone because activity with drugs lowered testosterone, or because lower testosterone led to their drug crimes. Prison system records contained information on prior drug use for 476 of the 692 Ss and among these Ss drug use was reported more for those who committed drug crimes, χ^2 ($df = 1$, $N = 476$) = 32.53, $P < .001$. Both marijuana and heroin have a temporary effect of lowering testosterone levels (Kolodny, Lessin, Toro, Masters, & Cohen, 1976; Mendelson & Mello, 1975). But even if Ss' testosterone levels had been lower when they committed drug crimes, because they were using drugs at that time, it seems likely their levels would have recovered by the time we collected their saliva samples in prison. We doubt that those who committed drug offenses were using more drugs in prison than other Ss were. Correctional officers told us the primary drug found in prison was marijuana, and they did not associate its use more with one kind of inmate than with another.

The true relationships between testosterone and behavior are probably higher than indicated in the present study. The day-to-day reliability of testosterone measurements from Ss assayed in the same laboratory is about $r = .64$ (Dabbs, 1990). The Spearman-Brown formula indicates this much unrealibility in measurements will reduce an observed testosterone-behavior relationship to about .8 of its true value. For example, an observed relationship of $r = .20$ would reflect an underlying true relationship of about $r = .25$. The observed testosterone-behavior relationships will be further attenuated by the unreliability of assays performed in different laboratories (Dabbs et al., 1994) and unreliability in the measurement of Ss' characteristic behavior.[11]

The present study documents relationships between testosterone and behavior in a sizable sample of prison inmates. We need now to examine the casual role of testosterone, and to explore the pathways through which testosterone might operate and conditions that might modify its effects. These mediating and moderating variables (Baron & Kenny, 1986) can lead to different effects in different settings and populations. For example, social control forces in education and family background can attenuate the negative effects of testosterone (Dabbs & Morris, 1990; Udry, 1990). And although there are significant mean differences in testosterone between inmates who commit different kinds of crimes, inmates who commit a given crime vary greatly among themselves in testosterone. We plan now to examine

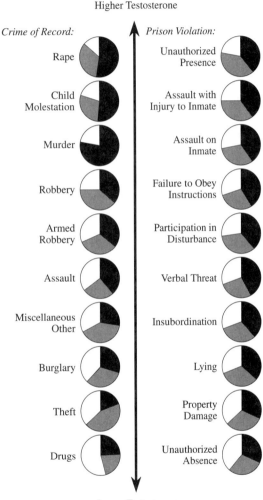

Testosterone and Misbehavior

Higher Testosterone

Crime of Record:
Rape
Child Molestation
Murder
Robbery
Armed Robbery
Assault
Miscellaneous Other
Burglary
Theft
Drugs

Prison Violation:
Unauthorized Presence
Assault with Injury to Inmate
Assault on Inmate
Failure to Obey Instructions
Participation in Disturbance
Verbal Threat
Insubordination
Lying
Property Damage
Unauthorized Absence

Lower Testosterone

Figure 19.1 Percentage of different crime sand prison violations attributable to Ss in lower (white), middle (gray), and upper (black) thirds of the testosterone distribution. Crimes and prison violations are ordered such that high testosterone Ss more often do those near the top of the figure, and low testosterone Ss more often do those near the bottom.

---

[11]Dabbs is saying that because testosterone level varies from day to day within a given individual, it is difficult to detect relationships between this level and proneness to violence. Moreover, it is likely the "true" relationship between testosterone and violence is larger than reported in this paper.

within-crime variation, looking for example at differences in the activities of high and low testosterone murderers, or of high and low testosterone burglars. Research involving such detailed questions is aided by having large samples of Ss and using salivary measures makes it easier to get Ss.

References

Albert, D. J., Walsh, M. L., & Jonik, R. H. (1993). Aggression in humans: What is its biological foundation? *Neuroscience and Biobehavioral Reviews, 17*, 405–425.

Bain, J., Langevin, R., Dickey, R., & Ben-Aron, M. (1987). Sex hormones in murderers and assaulters. *Behavioral Science & The Law, 5*, 95–101.

Bain, J., Langevin, R., Dickey, R., Hucker, S., & Wright, P. (1988). Hormones in sexually aggressive men. I. Baseline values for eight sex hormones. II. The ACTH test. *Annals of Sex Research, 1*, 63–78.

Baron, R. M., & Kenny, D. A. (1986). The moderator-mediator variable distinction in social psychological research: Conceptual, strategic, and statistical considerations. *Journal of Personality and Social Psychology, 51*, 1173–1182.

Dabbs, J. M. Jr. (1990). Salivary testosterone measurements: Reliability across hours, days, and weeks. *Physiology and Behavior, 48*, 83–86.

Dabbs, J. M. Jr. (1991). Salivary testosterone measurements: Collecting, storing, and mailing saliva samples. *Physiology and Behavior, 49*, 815–817.

Dabbs, J. M. Jr. (1992). Testosterone and occupational achievement. *Social Forces, 70*, 813–824.

Dabbs, J. M. Jr., Campbell, B. C., Gladue, B. A., Midgley, A. R., Navarro, M. A., Read, G. F., Susman, E., Swinkels, L. M. J. W., & Worthman, C. M. (1994). Reliability of salivary testosterone measurements: A multicenter evaluation. Unpublished manuscript, Georgia State University.

Dabbs, J. M. Jr., Frady, R. L., Carr, T. S., & Besch, N. F. (1987). Saliva testosterone and criminal violence in young adult prison inmates. *Psychosomatic Medicine, 49*, 174–182.

Dabbs, J. M. Jr., Hargrove, M. F., & Heusel, C. (1993). Testosterone differences among college fraternities: Well-behaved vs. rambunctious. Unpublished manuscript, Georgia State University.

Dabbs, J. M. Jr., Jurkovic, G. L., & Frady, R. L. (1991). Saliva testosterone and cortisol among late adolescent juvenile offenders. *Journal of Abnormal Child Psychology, 19*, 469–478.

Dabbs, J. M. Jr., de La Rue, D., & Williams, P. M. (1990). Testosterone and occupational choice: Actors, ministers, and other men. *Journal of Personality and Social Psychology, 59*, 1261–1265.

Dabbs, J. M. Jr., & Morris, R. (1990). Testosterone, social class, and antisocial behavior in a sample of 4,462 men. *Psychological Science, 1*, 209–211.

Ehrenkranz, J., Bliss, E., & Sheard. M. H. (1974). Plasma testosterone: Correlation with aggressive behavior and social dominance in man. *Psychosomatic Medicine, 36*, 469–475.

Federal Bureau of Investigation (1984). *Uniform crime reports: Crime in the United States.* Washington, DC: U.S. Government Printing Office.

Gutai, J. P., Dai, W. S., LaPorte, R. E., & Kuller, L. H. (1988). The reliability of sex hormone measurements in men for epidemiologic research. Unpublished manuscript, University of Pittsburgh.

Kolodny, R., Lessin, P., Toro, G., Masters, W. H., & Cohen. S. (1976). Depression of plasma testosterone with acute marihuana administration. In Braude, M. C. & Szara, S. (Eds.). *The pharmacology of marihuana.* New York: Raven.

Kreuz, L. E., & Rose, R. M. (1972). Assessment of aggressive behavior and plasma testosterone in a young criminal population. *Psychosomatic Medicine, 34*, 321–332.

Mendelson, J. H., & Mello, N. K. (1975). Plasma testosterone levels during chronic heroin use and protracted abstinence. *Clinical Pharmacology and Therapeutics, 17*, 529–533.

Navarro, M. A., Juan, L., & Bonnin, M. R. (1986). Salivary testosterone: Relationship to total and free testosterone in serum. *Clinical Chemistry, 32*, 231–232.

Rada, R. T., Laws, D. R., Kellner, R., Stivastava, L., & Peake, G. (1983). Plasma androgens in violent and nonviolent sex offenders. *American Academy of Psychiatry and the Law Bulletin, 11*, 149–158.

SAS Institute (1985). *SAS user's guide: Statistics, version 5 edition.* Carey, NC: SAS Institute.

Thompson, W. M., Dabbs, J. M. Jr., & Frady, R. L. (1990). Changes in saliva testosterone levels during a 90-day shock incarceration program. *Criminal Justice and Behavior, 17*, 246–252.

Udry, J. R. (1990). Biosocial models of adolescent behavior problems. *Social Biology, 37*, 1–10.

Good and Bad Humors: Biochemical Bases of Personality and Its Disorders

Marvin Zuckerman

Over the past couple of decades, rapid and simultaneous advances have been made in the study of the anatomy and physiology of the nervous system. While most of the new knowledge is not directly relevant to personality, a few brave researchers have made a serious attempt to integrate what we have learned about neurobiology with what we know about personality. One of the most successful and sophisticated of these researchers is the personality psychologist Marvin Zuckerman. In the next selection, written for a general audience of psychologists, Zuckerman reviews the state of the art in research on the neurobiological basis of personality. He mentions some of the complex relations between brain anatomy and behavior, but focuses more closely on the biochemical bases of personality. He draws an explicit connect between the ancient theory of temperaments and recent discoveries concerning "good and bad humors."

Unlike some of his neurobiological colleagues, and to his credit, Zuckerman is not a biological reductionist. That is, he does not think that states of the brain can be mapped one to one onto states of the mind, nor that in the end personality is "nothing but" the anatomy and physiology of the nervous system. Instead, Zuckerman has been unusually sensitive to the interactive relationships among various determinants of behavior and personality. Look at his Figure 1 not to memorize it, but to understand how complex the interactions are among the various biochemicals that influence what people do. In his conclusion, Zuckerman goes even further, pointing out that the functions of the nervous system interact with an equally complex social world outside the organism, and it is from that interaction—not the nervous system nor the outer environment alone —that personality emerges.

It might be particularly illuminating, after you have read this article, to compare Zuckerman's approach to that of Wells in the first selection. Zuckerman provides detailed and highly technical biological explanations, but describes the psychological correlates in only the broadest and most abstract of terms. Wells, by contrast, is quite vague (and largely wrong) in what he says about biology, but provides descriptions of personality much richer than anything included by Zuckerman. Yet the two investigators reach the same basic conclusion:

No "humor" or other biological substance is good or bad in itself. It is the balance of humors that matters.

From "Good and Bad Humors: Biochemical Bases of Personality and Its Disorders," by M. Zuckerman (1995). In *Psychological Science*, 6, 325–332. Copyright © 1991 by the American Psychological Society. Reprinted with the permission of Cambridge University Press.

Greek physicians in the fifth century B.C. proposed biochemical bases (humors) for normal and disordered personalities. For many centuries, this model for temperament and mental illness struggled against demon possession, satanic collaboration, divine punishment, and other supernatural or moralistic theories.

In the first part of the 20th century, the psychodynamic perspective emerged from the work of Freud and his disciples. Freud, the neurologist and "biologist of the mind" (Sulloway, 1979), regarded his psychological theories as an expedient strategy pending the development of a mature neuroscience (Freud, 1920/1955). In the second half of the century, the discovery of effective drugs for treatment of anxiety, mood, and schizophrenic disorders resulted in a new science: psychopharmacology. Research on the neurochemical basis of brain functions and the delineation of neurochemical pathways mediated by specific neurotransmitters enlarged our understanding of the chemistry of brain function and its relation to cognition, emotion, and behavior. The Greek physicians had the right idea, but the wrong humors. Given the advances in the brain sciences in the last quarter of the century, Freud would probably have agreed that it is time to have another look at the psychobiology of personality and its disorders (Zuckerman, 1991).

Levels of Personality Analysis

Personality can be studied at many levels from the top down, starting with the abstractions of basic traits from social behaviors and emotional expressions, and descending to the behavioral mechanisms and cognitions mediating the learning of social behavior, and the psychophysiological, biochemical, neurological, and genetic determinants of the mechanisms (Zuckerman, 1993). This is not a reductionistic paradigm because each level is worthy of study in itself.[1] But this method of analysis encourages seeking connections between levels and establishing biological "cause" and effect derived from experimental, comparative work with other species. Because we cannot ethically experiment with human brains, insights about the role of biological mechanisms in human behavior are largely derived from neuropsychological and psychopharmacological studies of psychopathology and the effects of drugs used to treat behavioral-cognitive disorders (Bloom & Kupfer, 1995). Until we get down to the genetic level, causation may be bidirectional between levels. For instance, characteristic levels of hormone and neurotransmitter activity may predispose behavior in certain directions, but prolonged stress and emotional experiences may affect the biochemical states. Chronic states may evolve into biological traits, which may in turn affect future reactions.

This article is concerned primarily with trait and biochemical levels of analysis. A more extended treatment of all levels may be found in other sources (Gray, 1982, 1987b; Zuckerman, 1991, 1993). The fact that the focus of this article is on the biological does not minimize the importance of the social environment in personality traits, but the latter topic is amply covered in another literature, in which the genetic and biolog-

---

[1]Reductionism in this context would imply that each layer of determination could be completely explained by the next layer down. Zuckerman explicitly disavows this belief; each kind of determinant is important in its own right.

ical makeup of the individual are less adequately considered, if not completely ignored.

Traits

Recent years have witnessed a narrowing of the range of what are considered basic dimensions of personality from 16 or so to five or three. Furthermore, there is substantial agreement on two of these basic traits (extraversion or sociability, and neuroticism or anxiety) in nearly all taxonomic systems. Eysenck (1967, 1991) has proposed three basic personality factors: extraversion (E), neuroticism (N), and psychoticism (P). Tellegen's (1985) three-factor model includes positive affectivity (PA), negative affectivity (NA), and constraint (C) as the basic factors. Tellegen has found consistent correlations between his "big three" and Eysenck's three (E correlates with PA, N with NA, and P with C). The "Big Five" model emerged from rating scales based on lexical analyses and was translated into a questionnaire form by Costa and McCrae (1992). The Big Five factors are extraversion, neuroticism, conscientiousness, agreeableness, and openness to experience (or intellect).

Based on factor analyses of personality scales (Zuckerman, Kuhlman, Thornquist, & Kiers, 1991) and questionnaire items (Zuckerman, Kuhlman, Joireman, Teta, & Kraft, 1993), I (Zuckerman, 1994a) have proposed an "Alternative Five": sociability, neuroticism-anxiety, impulsive sensation seeking, aggression-hostility, and activity. * * *

* * *

Brain Structures

Nineteenth-century phrenology suggested that each trait has a specific locus in the brain. The modern conception of brain structure sees neural structures like the amygdala, hypothalamus, or hippocampus as way stations for complex neural systems serving a variety of behavioral functions. Within any one distinguishable structure, such as the amygdala, different nuclei may be involved in different functions. A thorough discussion of the

neuropsychology of personality is impossible here, but a few observations are in order.

Systems involved in emotional responses have been suggested as the basis of some of the basic personality traits. Tellegen (1985), for instance, postulated that extraversion is based on positive affectivity and neuroticism on negative affectivity (anxiety and depression).[2] Do the structure-function relationships within the brain support this distinction? Studies of the effects of cortical lesions[3] on emotional behavior, the effects of arousal of particular emotions on brain activity, and individual differences in emotional response and their cortical correlates[4] suggest that the right-hemisphere frontal lobes are primarily involved in negative affects and inhibition in children (Davidson, 1992). Damage to the right orbito-frontal brain area in humans produces anger and aggression, perhaps through disinhibition (Grafman, Vance, Weingarten, Salazar, & Amin, 1986). At the subcortical level, Davis (1986) suggested that the central nucleus of the amygdala is an organizing center for the various aspects of fear response through its efferent connections to other nuclei mediating behavioral inhibition, cardiovascular and respiratory responses, startle response, facial expressions of fear, and vigilance and hyperalertness.

Positive affect, as expressed by smiling, is associated with activation of left-frontal and anterior brain activity (Davidson, 1992). Positive emotions

---

[2]Positive and negative "affectivity" refer to the tendency to experience positive and negative emotions. Some psychologists hypothesize that positive and negative emotions—e.g., joy and anxiety—stem from independent systems.

[3]A "cortical lesion" is a bit of physical damage to the cortex, or outer layer of the brain, usually seen as the location of higher mental functions. The damage can be experimentally induced (as in animal studies) or the result of accidents (in people).

[4]Techniques have been developed to measure the biochemical and electrical activity of the cortex in living organisms using electrodes or sophisticated scanning devices. The research referred to here has shown that different parts of the cortex become active as different emotions are experienced.

are probably related to the limbic reward systems first identified by Olds and Milner (1954). The lateral hypothalamus and medial forebrain bundle are sites where self-stimulation of the brain is powerfully supported, and their destruction reduces approach behavior.

The distinctions between positive and negative affect and between negative affects of anxiety and hostility (associated with aggression) seem to have possible bases in brain systems from the higher frontal lobe centers to limbic structures involved in particular circuits. But it is difficult to separate particular structures uniquely related to particular behavioral mechanisms or traits. When one nucleus is lesioned, the effects may ramify along a number of other pathways. Analyses of pathways mediated by specific neurotransmitters allow a more specific examination of biobehavioral mechanisms, and chemical lesioning of these pathways is more informative than surgical lesioning of structures or their nuclei. I agree with Kagan's (1995) conclusion that "it appears likely at the present time that much of the temperamentally based variation . . . will rest on differences in neurochemistry and associated physiology rather than anatomy" (p. 51).

Humors (Neurotransmitters and Hormones)

The biochemical makeup of the organism determines the physiological characteristics of the nervous systems, which in turn predispose toward the relatively consistent patterns of behavior (in certain ranges of situations) that we call traits. Neurotransmitters govern the transmission of nerve impulses through specific neuronal pathways. The production, release, catabolic breakdown, reuptake, and storage of neurotransmitters are regulated by particular enzymes. The activity in specific neurotransmitter systems in humans is often estimated from inactive metabolites of the neurotransmitters found in cerebrospinal fluid (CSF), blood, or urine after breakdown of the transmitter and prior to disposal. These estimates are impre-

cise and confounded with the results of activity in the peripheral nervous systems rather than in the brain itself. New neurotransmitter-specific brain-imaging methods may eventually yield more direct measures.

*   *   *

Information about the behavioral functions of particular neurotransmitter systems or hormones is obtained largely from comparative studies of nonhuman species because direct experimentation on the brain is possible in these species. Neurotransmitter systems may be stimulated directly or lesioned and the behavioral results observed. Inferences to human brain-behavior relationships depend on the adequacy of the animal models of behavior and psychopathology. The data from comparative studies may be compared with results from biological psychiatry studies in which drugs are used to ameliorate human mood and behavior disorders.

MONOAMINE OXIDASE (MAO) MAO is an enzyme that is found in the neurons of the monoamine systems, where it regulates the levels of the monoamines by breaking down certain neurotransmitters after reuptake or in the synaptic cleft. The primary monoamines in the brain include the catecholamines, norepinephrine and dopamine, and the indoleamine, serotonin. The type B MAO, assayed from blood platelets, is particularly important in dopamine breakdown and regulation in brains of humans and nonhuman primates. No correlation has been obtained between platelet MAO and MAO from the cortex in humans, but the possibility remains that platelet MAO is related to brain MAO in particular limbic brain areas. The effects of MAO inhibitors on both behavior and platelet MAO, and the broad range of behavioral, personality trait, and psychopathological correlates of platelet MAO, to be presented next, also argue for the relevance of MAO to brain-behavior relations. Platelet MAO is highly heritable and is related to behavioral activity and emotionality of infants in the first 3 days of postnatal life (Sostek, Sostek, Murphy, Martin, & Born, 1981).

The most consistent correlate of MAO is the

trait of sensation seeking. MAO was significantly and negatively correlated with sensation seeking in 9 of 13 male-only, female-only, and mixed groups (Zuckerman, 1994b) and with extraversion in several other studies. Although most of these correlations are low and do not account for a large amount of variance in the psychological trait, the consistency of the findings implies a significant role for some of the monoamine systems in personality. Furthermore, low MAO is related to behavioral correlates of sensation seeking and extraversion, including criminality; alcohol, tobacco, and illegal drug use; sexual experience; and sociability in humans. Low MAO is also correlated with social dominance, sociability, aggression, and sexual and play activity in monkeys. The cross-species similarities in behavioral traits associated with MAO are impressive. Low levels of MAO are associated with three of the five major traits in the alternative five-factor model: impulsive sensation seeking, sociability, and aggression-hostility.

* * *

MONOAMINE SYSTEMS Simple correlational studies relating neurotransmitters or their metabolites to personality traits in normal subjects and patients have not yielded many consistent findings. Sensation seeking is correlated negatively with norepinephrine in the CSF (Ballenger et al., 1983). Five hydroxyindoleacetic acid (5-HIAA), the metabolite of serotonin, is negatively correlated with Eysenck's P scale in normal and patient groups (Schalling, Asberg, & Edman, 1984). However, the dopamine metabolite, homovanyllic acid (HVA), has not shown consistent correlation with personality traits.

Experimental studies on the monoamine systems in the brain are difficult in humans; lesioning studies are out of the question, and stimulation studies are done only during brain operations in special populations, like epileptics.[5] Animal behav-

ioral models for human personality traits provide an opportunity to study the effects of brain lesions on personality-relevant behavior. Exploration of novel situations has been proposed as a model for extraversion (Garcia-Sevilla, 1984) and sensation seeking (Dellu, Mayo, Piazza, Le Moal, & Simon, 1993; Zuckerman, 1984). The behavioral trait defined by responsiveness to signals of reward and the tendency to approach and investigate novel situations and stimuli has been called *behavioral approach* (Gray, 1971, 1987b; Schneirla, 1959; Zuckerman, 1984), *activation* (Fowles, 1980), or *facilitation* (Depue & Iacono, 1989). Theories and comparative research have linked this behavioral system to dopaminergic systems (Cloninger, 1987; Dellu et al., 1993; Depue & Iacono, 1989; Gray, 1987b; Panksepp, 1982; Zuckerman, 1984, 1991). At the human level, the approach system would probably subsume several basic traits, including extraversion, impulsivity, and sensation seeking. In nonhuman species, "personality," defined by behavioral traits, is probably organized in broader factors, like approach-dominance-impulsivity and inhibition-fearfulness-asociability.

Experimental research linking dopaminergic activity directly to personality in humans is rare. Indirect studies using catecholamine agonists such as amphetamine and cocaine are more common, but cannot separate the dopaminergic effects from the noradrenergic ones. These studies often reveal curvilinear relations between dosage and behavior: Stimulant drugs often produce euphoria, activity, sociability, and disinhibition at low doses but anxiety, withdrawal, and even brief psychosis at high doses. There is probably an optimal level of catecholamine system activity (CSA) for mood, performance, and social behavior; too little activity and too much activity of catecholamine systems are not optimal (Zuckerman, 1984).

High sensation seekers may have a higher optimal level of CSA than low sensation seekers. The low levels of CSF norepinephrine in high sensation seekers (Ballenger et al., 1983) might indicate that they are chronically underaroused and seek stimulation to activate the system. * * *

* * *

---

[5]In a lesioning study, part of the brain is purposely damaged or removed. In a stimulation study, part of the brain is electrically stimulated.

Depue, Luciana, Arbisi, Collins, and Leon (1994) selected subjects on the basis of both positive emotionality (extraversion) and constraint (impulsivity), using subjects who were high on extraversion and low on constraint (impulsive extraverts) at one extreme and low on extraversion and high on constraint at the other. They gave subjects a dopamine receptor agonist[6] and found a positive relationship between the effects of the agonist and extraversion (but not impulsivity or neuroticism), suggesting enhanced dopaminergic activity in extraverts.

The dorsal ascending noradrenergic system originating in the locus coeruleus has been characterized as an alarm system at moderate levels of activity and a panic-producing system at higher levels (Gray, 1982; Redmond, 1987). Stimulation of the locus coeruleus produces behavioral signs of anxiety in monkeys (Redmond, 1987). However, other researchers have characterized this noradrenergic system as a simple arousal system, involved in focused attention. Of course, a threatening stimulus or one associated with punishment does focus the attention, but other kinds of significant stimuli, such as cues associated with sexual arousal and reward, may do the same. Novel stimuli are not necessarily fear provokers, and in sensation seekers they are attractants for attention and interest. Some neurotransmitter other than noradrenalin may mediate the "sensitivity to signals of punishment" of anxious neurotics (Gray, 1982). The recently discovered benzodiazepine receptors may provide some explanation for the trait of neuroticism or anxiety. Benzodiazepines are produced by drug companies, not by the brain, but the finding of specific receptors for these drugs suggests that some chemically similar endogenous tranquilizer must exist in the brain. The benzodiazepine receptors are parts of a larger receptor complex for the neuroregulator gamma-aminobutyric acid (GABA). GABA is generally inhibitory in its actions on neurons in other systems, including the noradrenergic. There are inverse agonists that act on GABA receptors and produce anxiety

in humans. Either an excess of endogenous agents resembling these inverse agonists or a lack of endogenous benzodiazepine-like transmitters may underlie the trait of anxiety. Another possibility is that trait anxiety is a function of a low concentration of benzodiazepine receptors (Weizman et al., 1987). A final possibility is that endogenous opiates, or endorphins, may be involved in anxiety as a natural extension of their primary function in pain reduction. It would be a deficit of endorphins that would make one vulnerable to anxiety.

Whereas the mesolimbic dopaminergic system seems to mediate many kinds of approach motivations in rats, including aggression, sex, and exploration, the serotonergic system that originates in the raphe nuclei and extends to many of the same limbic and frontal cortical structures seems to serve a general behavioral inhibition function (Soubrié, 1986). Both Cloninger (1987) and Gray (1987b) identified this serotonergic system with harm-avoidance or anxiety traits, but Gray stipulated that serotonin mediates primarily the inhibition effects of anxiety and not the arousal effects. Serotonergic lesions produce disinhibition in animals. Low levels of serotonin in humans are associated with psychopathy and impulsive aggression, murder, and suicide. An underreactive serotonergic system may be related to impulsive sensation seeking, a trait characterized by disinhibition of behavior and lack of planning or caution. Netter and Rammsayer (1989) found that a serotonin-receptor blocker improved reaction time performance in low sensation seekers but slowed performance in high sensation seekers. Their results suggest that the low sensation seekers are inhibited in speed of reaction by an overactive serotonergic system, whereas an underreactive serotonergic system might account for the fast, impulsive reactions of high sensation seekers.

HORMONES The gonadal hormone testosterone is produced in the male by the testes, but is also produced in the female, primarily by the adrenal cortex. Estrogen is produced in the female by the ovaries and largely by conversion from testosterone in the male. Aggression in humans has been

---

[6]An agonist is a chemical that combines with a drug or another chemical to produce an effect.

attributed to excess testosterone, partly because of direct evidence of its involvement in aggressive-competitive behavior in other species and because of the sex differences in aggressiveness in our own species. But this association has not been as clear in humans as in other animals, possibly because of the different forms that aggression can take in humans and the high socialization of the trait. Although men may compete for the favors of women, they rarely engage in direct combat to resolve the issue. In the normal range of aggression-hostility, the results relating the trait to testosterone are mixed, but in groups of male delinquents and male and female prisoners, testosterone levels are high in prisoners with histories of very violent and unprovoked crimes of aggression, and in those high in social dominance over other prisoners (Dabbs, Carr, Frady, & Riad, 1995; Dabbs, Ruback, Frady, Hopper, & Sgoritas, 1988; Ehrenkranz, Bliss, & Sheard, 1974).[7] Anabolic-androgenic steroids self-administered by male athletes frequently produce manic episodes, often accompanied by aggressive or violent behavior (Pope & Katz, 1994).

Testosterone in normal young males is strongly related to sensation seeking, particularly of the disinhibitory type (Daitzman & Zuckerman, 1980), as well as to extraversion, dominance, and heterosexual experience. Testosterone is the hormone related to sexual arousal in women as well as men. Testosterone in married women is correlated with their reported sexual gratification and responsivity and with frequency of intercourse. Of course, sex is one of the major modes of sensation seeking of the disinhibitory type.

Testosterone has a reputation as a "bad humor," probably because of its reputed association with male aggression. However, this hormone seems to be related to many positively adaptive traits, including sexual arousability, assertiveness, and sociability.

Cortisol is a hormone that is secreted by the adrenal cortex during physical and psychological stress, as well as during normal metabolic functioning. Its release is the end result of a neurochemical chain beginning with secretion of corticotrophin-releasing factor (CRF) from the hypothalamus. CRF flows to the anterior pituitary gland, which releases adrenocorticotropic hormone (ACTH). ACTH travels via the bloodstream to the adrenal cortex, where it results in the release of a number of cortico-steroid hormones, including cortisol. Cortisol is involved in the release of glycogen from storage in the liver into the bloodstream, where it can be utilized in stress-responding tissues like those in brain and muscle.

Cortisol release is a prominent effect of stress in humans, but high tonic levels of the hormone are more characteristic of depressive mood disorders than anxiety disorders. Cortisol varies with depression in many persons on a day-to-day basis (Rubinow, Post, Gold, Ballenger, & Wolff, 1984), but it is not clear what is cause and what is effect in the relationship between depression and cortisol. Injection of cortisol into normal volunteers did not affect depression, anxiety, anger, or sociable feelings (Born, Hitzler, Pietrowsky, Pauschinger, & Fehm, 1988), suggesting that cortisol is not the direct cause of emotional changes, but may be an effect of other factors, such as the reduction of levels of norepinephrine in the brain.

However, cortisol, norepinephrine, and the enzyme dopamine-β-hydroxylase (DBH, which is involved in the production of norepinephrine) in the CSF of normal volunteers are negatively related to more stable traits like sensation seeking, hypomania (Minnesota Multiphasic Personality Inventory scale), and the Eysenck P scale (Zuckerman, 1994b), suggesting that cortisol may play a role in the inhibition of behavior associated with overcontrol and constraint at high levels of cortisol activity and disinhibition and unsocialized sensation seeking at low levels of cortisol activity. High levels of cortisol were found in timid infants and children who showed fear rather than interest in response to novel stimuli and strangers (Kagan, Reznik, & Snidman, 1988). Cortisol is neither a good nor a bad humor at moderate levels of activity, but at extremes of activity it may be

---

[7]See the preceding selection on the relationship between testosterone and violence.

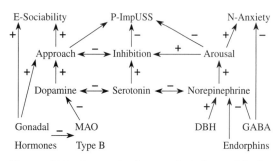

Figure 20.1 A psychopharmacological model for extraversion-sociability (E-Sociability), impulsive unsocialized sensation seeking (P-ImpUSS), and neuroticism-anxiety (N-Anxiety) showing underlying behavioral mechanisms (approach, inhibition, and arousal) and neurotransmitters, enzymes, and hormones involved. Agonistic interactions between factors are indicated by a plus sign, and antagonistic interactions are indicated by a minus sign. MAO = monoamine oxidase; DBH = dopamine-β-hydroxylase; GABA = gamma-aminobutyric acid. Modified from Figure 14.2 in Zuckerman (1994b). Copyright © 1994 by Cambridge University Press. Reprinted by permission.

associated with personality disorders of either undercontrol (antisocial and borderline personalities) or overcontrol (avoidant, depressive, and obsessive-compulsive personalities).

INTERACTIONS OF HORMONES, MONOAMINE SYSTEMS, AND BEHAVIORAL MECHANISMS Phrenological thinking suggests simple one-to-one isomorphic relationships between personality traits, neurotransmitters, hormones, and neural structures. Such isomorphism would simplify models for psychobiologists. But biology is not simple, and evolution has produced many redundancies and interactions in the neural mechanisms mediating behavioral mechanisms. Figure 20.1 shows a model summarizing the hypothesized neurochemical and behavioral mechanisms underlying three of the basic traits identifiable in all three- and five-factor models.

The approach mechanism is mediated by dopaminergic activity in the medial forebrain bundle and lateral hypothalamus and is involved in the traits of sociability and impulsive sensation seeking. It is potentiated by gonadal hormones, par-

ticularly testosterone, and enzyme MAO through its regulating influence in dopamine neurons. Behavioral inhibition is a function of serotonergic activity and is weak in the trait of impulsive sensation seeking. Cortical arousal is in part a function of the ascending noradrenergic system from the locus coeruleus. Descending tracts arouse the sympathetic part of the autonomic nervous system. The noradrenergic system is regulated by the enzyme DBH, GABA, and the endorphins. Low arousability of this system is found in impulsive sensation seekers, and high arousability is a component of neuroticism-anxiety. Low levels of GABA play a specific role in anxiety as the mediator of endogenous agonists and inverse agonists acting on benzodiazepine receptors. Not shown in the diagram are the influences of noradrenergic arousal on activity and aggression-hostility traits, and serotonergic inhibition on aggression. Also not shown in the diagram are possible influences of cortisol in both inhibition and arousal.

The interactions at the level of behavioral mechanisms are obvious. Inhibition and approach are incompatible. Very high noradrenergic arousal is associated with behavioral inhibition and very low arousal with disinhibition. But interactions also occur at the neurotransmitter level, where serotonin may inhibit both dopamine and norepinephrine.

One consequence of these interactions is that there is no simple one-to-one relationship between a personality trait and a single neurotransmitter, enzyme, or hormone. Gray (1987a) criticized Cloninger's theory for assigning a single neurotransmitter system to each dimension of personality. My model also rejects this kind of simplistic isomorphism. Impulsive sensation seeking, for instance, is a function of strong approach, weak inhibition, and low arousal, and therefore a high level of the personality trait could be due to various combinations of the three monoamines involved in these mechanisms, as well as the enzymes and hormones influencing the activity of the neurotransmitters.

As the ancient Greek "psychopharmacologists" surmised, there are no good or bad humors; disordered personalities are a result of imbalances in humors. Even if the indirect indicators of neurochemical activity in the human were perfectly reliable and valid indicators of brain activity (which they are not), and even if other neurotransmitters and enzymes were not involved (and they probably are), one could not expect to find a very strong correlation between any one personality trait and a single measure of monoamine activity. The fact that some reliable and generalizable findings have emerged, even if they are not powerful relationships, suggests that there is a biochemical basis for personality, although it is a multivariate, complex one.

Conclusions

We do not inherit personality traits or even behavior mechanisms as such. What is inherited are chemical templates that produce and regulate proteins involved in building the structure of nervous systems and the neurotransmitters, enzymes, and hormones that regulate them. We are not born as extraverts, neurotics, impulsive sensation seekers, or antisocial personalities, but we are born with differences in reactivities of brain structures and levels of regulators like MAO. How do these differences in biological traits shape our choices in life from the manifold possibilities provided by environments? The answers cannot be found in the unproven theories of parental influence contained in most textbooks of personality.[8] Nor can they be found solely in those life experiences outside of the family over which people have no control. Only cross-disciplinary, developmental, and comparative psychobiological research can provide the answers.

References

Ballenger, J. C., Post, R. M., Jimerson, D. C., Lake, C. R., Murphy, D. L., Zuckerman, M., & Cronin, C. (1983). Bio-

---

chemical correlates of personality traits in normals: An exploratory study. *Personality and Individual Differences*, 4, 615–625.

Bloom, F. E., & Kupfer, D. J. (Eds.). (1995). *Psychopharmacology: The fourth generation of progress*. New York: Raven Press.

Born, J., Hitzler, V., Pietrowsky, R., Pauschinger, P., & Fehm, H. L. (1988). Influences of cortisol on auditory evoked potentials and mood in humans. *Neuropsychobiology*, 20, 145–151.

Cloninger, C. R. (1987). A systematic method for clinical description and classification of personality. *Archives of General Psychiatry*, 44, 573–588.

Costa, P. T., Jr., & McCrae, R. R. (1992). *NEO-PI-R: Revised personality inventory*. Odessa, FL: Psychological Assessment Resources.

Dabbs, J. M., Jr., Carr, T. S., Frady, R. L., & Riad, J. K. (1995). Testosterone, crime, and misbehavior among 692 male prison inmates. *Personality and Individual Differences*, 19, 627–633.

Dabbs, J. M., Jr., Ruback, R. B., Frady, R. L., Hopper, C. H., & Sgoritas, D. S. (1988). Saliva testosterone and criminal violence among women. *Personality and Individual Differences*, 9, 269–275.

Daltzman, R. J., & Zuckerman, M. (1980). Disinhibitory sensation seeking, personality, and gonadal hormones. *Personality and Individual Differences*, 1, 103–110.

Davidson, R. J. (1992). Emotion and affective style: Hemispheric substrates. *Psychological Science*, 3, 39–43.

Davis, M. (1986). Pharmacological and anatomical analysis of fear conditioning using the fear-potentiated startle paradigm. *Behavioral Neuroscience*, 100, 814–824.

Dellu, F., Mayo, W., Piazza, P. V., Le Moal, M., & Simon, H. (1993). Individual differences in behavioral responses to novelty in rats: Possible relationship with the sensation-seeking trait in man. *Personality and Individual Differences*, 14, 411–418.

Depue, R. A., & Iacono, W. G. (1989). Neurobehavioral aspects of affective disorders. *Annual Review of Psychology*, 40, 457–492.

Depue, R. A., Luciana, M., Arbisi, P., Collins, P., & Leon, A. (1994). Dopamine and the structure of personality: Relationship of agonist-induced dopamine activity to positive emotionality. *Journal of Personality and Social Psychology*, 67, 485–498.

Ehrenkranz, J., Bliss, E., & Sheard, M. H. (1974). Plasma testosterone: Correlation with aggressive behavior and social dominance in man. *Psychosomatic Medicine*, 36, 469–475.

Eysenck, H. J. (1967). *The biological basis of personality*. Springfield, IL: Charles C. Thomas.

Eysenck, H. J. (1991). Dimensions of personality: The biosocial approach to personality. In J. Strelau & A. Angleitner (Eds.), *Explorations in temperament* (pp. 87–103). London: Plenum Press.

Fowles, D. C. (1980). The three arousal model: Implications for Gray's two-factor learning theory for heart rate, electrodermal activity, and psychopathy. *Psychophysiology*, 17, 87–104.

Freud, S. (1955). Beyond the pleasure principle. In J. Strachey (Ed.), *The standard edition of the complete psychological works* (Vol. 18). London: Hogarth Press. (Original work published 1920)

---

[8]This observation foreshadows Plomin's conclusion, presented in a later selection, that the shared family environment has only a small influence on personality development.

Garcia-Sevilla, L. (1984). Extraversion and neuroticism in rats. *Personality and Individual Differences*, 5, 511–532.

Grafman, J., Vance, S. C., Weingarten, H., Salazar, A. M., & Amin, D. (1986). The effects of lateralized frontal lesions on mood regulation. *Brain*, 109, 1127–1148.

Gray, J. A. (1971). *The psychology of fear and stress*. New York: McGraw Hill.

Gray, J. A. (1982). *The neuropsychology of anxiety: An enquiry into the functions of the septo-hippocampal system*. New York: Oxford University Press.

Gray, J. A. (1987a). Discussions arising from: Cloninger, C. R. A unified biosocial theory of personality and its role in the development of anxiety states. 1. Gray, J. A. *Psychiatric Developments*, 4, 377–394.

Gray, J. A. (1987b). The neuropsychology of emotion and personality. In S. M. Stahl, S. D. Iverson, & E. C. Goodman (Eds.), *Cognitive neurochemistry* (pp. 171–190). Oxford, England: Oxford University Press.

Kagan, J. (1995). *Galen's prophecy: Temperament in human nature*. New York: Basic Books.

Kagan, J., Reznik, J. S., & Snidman, N. (1988). Biological bases of childhood shyness. *Science*, 240, 167–171.

Loehlin, J. C. (1992). *Genes and environment in personality development*. Newbury Park, CA: Sage.

Netter, P., & Rammsayer, T. (1989). Serotonergic effects on sensory and motor responses in extraverts and introverts. *International Clinical Psychopharmacology*, 4(Suppl. 1), 21–26.

Olds, J., & Milner, P. (1954). Positive reinforcement produced by electrical stimulation of septal area and other regions of rat brain. *Journal of Comparative and Physiological Psychology*, 47, 419–427.

Panksepp, J. (1982). Toward a general psychobiological theory of emotions. *The Behavioral and Brain Sciences*, 5, 407–422.

Pope, H. G., & Katz, D. L. (1994). Psychiatric and medical effects of anabolic-androgenic steroid use: A controlled study of 160 athletes. *Archives of General Psychiatry*, 51, 375–382.

Redmond, D. E., Jr. (1987). Studies of locus coeruleus in monkeys and hypotheses for neuropsychopharmacology. In H. Y. Meltzer (Ed.), *Psychopharmacology: The third generation of progress* (pp. 967–975). New York: Raven Press.

Rubinow, D. R., Post, R. M., Gold, P. W., Ballenger, J. C., & Wolff, E. A. (1984). The relationship between cortisol and clinical phenomenology of affective illness. In R. M. Post & J. C. Ballenger (Eds.), *Neurobiology of mood disorders* (pp. 271–289). Baltimore, MD: Williams & Wilkins.

Schalling, D., Asberg, M., & Edman, G. (1984). *Personality and CSF monoamine metabolites*. Unpublished manuscript, Department of Psychiatry and Psychology, Karolinska Hospital and Department of Psychology, University of Stockholm. Stockholm, Sweden.

Schneirla, T. C. (1959). An evolutionary and development theory of biphasic processes underlying approach and withdrawal. In M. R. Jones (Ed.), *Nebraska Symposium on Motivation* (Vol. 7, pp. 1–42). Lincoln: University of Nebraska Press.

Sostek, A. J., Sostek, A. M., Murphy, D. L., Martin, E. B., & Born, W. S. (1981). Cord blood amine oxidase activities relate to arousal and motor functioning in human newborns. *Life Sciences*, 28, 2561–2568.

Soubrié, P. (1986). Reconciling the role of central serotonin neurons in human and animal behavior. *Behavioral and Brain Sciences*, 9, 319–364.

Sulloway, F. J. (1979). *Freud: Biologist of the mind*. New York: Basic Books.

Tellegen, A. (1985). Structures of mood and personality and their relevance to assessing anxiety with an emphasis on self-report. In A. H. Tuma & J. D. Maser (Eds.), *Anxiety and the anxiety disorders* (pp. 681–706). Hillsdale, NJ: Erlbaum.

Weizman, R., Tanne, Z., Granek, M., Karp, L., Golomb, M., Tyano, S., & Gavish, M. (1987). Peripheral benzodiazepine binding sites on platelet membranes are increased during diazepam treatment of anxious patients. *European Journal of Pharmacology*, 138, 289–292.

Zuckerman, M. (1984). Sensation seeking: A comparative approach to a human trait. *Behavioral and Brain Sciences*, 7, 413–471.

Zuckerman, M. (1991). *Psychobiology of personality*. Cambridge, England: Cambridge University Press.

Zuckerman, M. (1993). Personality from top (traits) to bottom (genetics) with stops at each level between. In J. Hettema & I. J. Deary (Eds.), *Foundations of personality* (pp. 73–100). Dordrecht, Netherlands: Kluwer Academic.

Zuckerman, M. (1994a). An alternative five factor model for personality. In C. F. Halverson, G. A. Kohnstamm, & R. P. Martin (Eds.), *The developing structure of temperament and personality from infancy to adulthood* (pp. 53–68). Hillsdale, NJ: Erlbaum.

Zuckerman, M. (1994b). *Behavioral expressions and biosocial bases of sensation seeking*. New York: Cambridge University Press.

Zuckerman, M., Kuhlman, D. M., Joireman, J., Teta, P., & Kraft, M. (1993). A comparison of three structural models for personality: The big three, the big five, and the alternative five. *Journal of Personality and Social Psychology*, 65, 757–768.

Zuckerman, M., Kuhlman, D. M., Thornquist, M., & Kiers, H. (1991). Five (or three) robust questionnaire scale factors of personality without culture. *Journal of Personality and Individual Differences*, 12, 929–941.

Genes, Environment, and Personality

Thomas J. Bouchard, Jr.

We have seen that modern research on the anatomy and physiology of personality can be traced back to the ancient Greek physicians. The other important area of research on the biology of personality has a different and more recent foundation, the late-19th-century writings of Charles Darwin. Darwin's theory of evolution has a strong influence on modern research on the genetic inheritance of personality. This research itself has two threads. One pursues quantitative studies of the extent to which individual differences in personality are affected by genetic as opposed to environmental factors; and the other tries to bring Darwinian evolutionary theorizing to bear in explaining behavioral propensities in the modern human race.

The next selection, by one of the most prominent practitioners of research in "behavioral genetics," Thomas Bouchard, provides a brief and up-to-date review of the evidence concerning the inheritance of personality. (Selections later in this section will address the evolutionary angle.) Drawing on the five-factor model of personality we saw espoused in the selection by Costa and McCrae in Part II, Bouchard reviews evidence that all five of these basic traits have substantial "heritabilities." That is, monozygotic twins are more similar on these traits than are dizygotic twins, which implies that part of the basis of these traits is genetic.

As Bouchard notes, the news that personality is influenced by one's genes has not always been welcomed by other psychologists. But research of the sort summarized in this article establishes convincingly that genes are important for personality, and this finding will not be wished away. On the other hand, it is important to remember that a high heritability does not mean a trait is determined by genetics alone; all organisms must grow up in an environment; and even if this environment is simply a stage for "genetic actors," it is hard to imagine how Julius Caesar would play on the set of "Gilligan's Island." The role that a gene plays in development could have completely different effects in two different environments. Bouchard notes correctly that much remains to be learned about the complex interplay of our genes in our environments.

Notice also that although genetic analysis has come in for some unfair criticism, Bouchard himself takes an extreme position on the other side. When he says that the effect of variation of environments on personality "may even turn out to be the equivalent of noise," he is saying the environment in which a child grows up may not matter at all. This conclusion runs at variance with decades of research in developmental psychology, and many psychologists remain unwilling to accept it.

From "Genes, Environment, and Personality," by T. J. Bouchard, Jr. (1994). Excerpted with permission from *Science*, 264, 1700–1701. Copyright © 1994, American Association for the Advancement of Science.

The idea that genetic factors influence behavior, including personality, is very old. The most compelling evidence has always been, as Darwin (1871–1967) noted, the successful domestication of animals:

> So in regard to mental qualities, their transmission is manifest in our dogs, horses and other domestic animals. Besides special tastes and habits, general intelligence, courage, bad and good tempers, etc., are certainly transmitted.

Unlike genetic influences on the intelligence quotient, which have been studied continuously since the time of Galton a century ago, the study of genetic influences on personality has had a much briefer history. Although Galton discussed genetic influence on personality, the lack of reliable and valid measures of personality qualities hampered progress. In addition, until recently, psychologists could not agree on which were the important traits of personality. Currently there is a modest consensus that five broad traits or "super factors" are necessary to describe personality—extraversion, neuroticism, conscientiousness, agreeableness, and openness (Goldberg, 1993) (see Table 21.1).

Until the early 1980s, the evidence for genetic influence on personality derived almost exclusively from twin studies that utilized very modest sample sizes and measured different variables. Heritability was estimated as twice the difference between the correlation for identical or monozygotic (MZ) twins and that for fraternal or dizygotic (DZ) twins. The typical conclusion was that about 50% of the observed variance in personality is due to genetic factors (Nichols, 1978). The influence on

personality of the shared home environment (estimated as twice the DZ correlation minus the MZ value) was concluded to be small or even negligible. These simple equations make a number of assumptions, including (1) on average DZ twins share half as many genes in common by descent as MZ twins, (2) the genes act additively, and (3) MZ and DZ twins experience the same shared environmental influences. If the assumptions are correct, the difference between the two types of twins reflects one half the genetic influence on the trait being studied.

The conclusion that 50% of the variation in personality is genetic was not universally embraced. Many psychologists questioned that MZ and DZ twins experience the same home environment and ascribed much of the greater similarity of MZ twins over DZ twins to more similar environmental treatment of the MZ than the DZ twins. It also seemed implausible to psychologists that being reared in the same home would have so little influence on sibling similarity. Consequently these findings were not generally accepted outside of behavioral genetics.

In recent years, three trends have converged to transform our understanding of genetic and environmental influences on personality traits. First, studies of twins reared together with very large sample sizes, in some instances over 2,000 pairs of each sex and zygosity, have been carried out. Second, data have been gathered from monozygotic and dizygotic twins reared apart (MZA and DZA), as well as from both biological and adoptive families. Third, powerful methods of model fitting have been introduced that allow full utilization of the available information and statistical testing of

TABLE 21.1

FIVE MAIN DETERMINANTS OF PERSONALITY

Extraversion: Surgency, Introversion-Extraversion (−), Dominance, *Positive Emotionality*

| Is outgoing, decisive, persuasive, and enjoys leadership roles | Is retiring, reserved, withdrawn, and does not enjoy being the center of attention |

Neuroticism: Anxiety, Emotional Stability (−), Stress Reactivity, *Negative Emotionality*

| Is emotionally unstable, nervous, irritable, and prone to worry | Quickly gets over upsetting experiences, stable, and not prone to worries and fears |

Conscientiousness: Conformity, Dependability, Authoritarianism (−), *Constraint*

| Is planful, organized, responsible, practical, and dependable | Is impulsive, careless, irresponsible, and cannot be depended upon |

Agreeableness: Likability, Friendliness, Pleasant, *Aggression* (−)

| Is sympathetic, warm, kind, good-natured, and will not take advantage of others | Is quarrelsome, aggressive, unfriendly, cold, and vindictive |

Openness: Culture, Intellect, Sophistication, Imagination, *Absorption*

| Is insightful, curious, original, imaginative, and open to novel experiences and stimuli | Has narrow interests, is unintelligent, unreflective, and shallow |

Negative signs indicate trait names that characterized to opposite end of the dimension. The italic trait terms indicate the Multidimensional Personality Questionnaire factors or scales used to measure these five characteristics in the Minnesota study of twins reared apart.

competing hypotheses (Eaves, Eysenck, & Martin, 1989; Neale & Cardon, 1992).

Figure 21.1 compares the results of the early twin studies, an analysis of an extremely large data set assembled by Loehlin (1992), and our own analysis of MZA (n = 59) and DZA (n = 47)[1] data from the Minnesota study of twins reared apart (MISTRA) and MZT (n = 522) and DZT (n = 408) twins from the Minnesota Twin Registry (Bouchard, Lykken, McGue, Segal, & Tellegen, 1990). The Loehlin analysis yields an estimated genetic influence of 42% (with a sizable contribution from nonadditive genetic factors—influences that are configural and not inherited in a simple additive manner) and a very modest contribution of the shared environment. The most parsimonious fit to the Minnesota data is a simple additive ge-

netic model for all five traits with an estimate of genetic influence of 46%. Addition of nonadditive genetic and shared environmental parameters do not, however, significantly change the fit of the model, and those data are shown in the figure for comparison with the Loehlin analysis. Both approaches yield estimates of genetic influence of just over 40% and modest estimates of shared environmental influence (7%). Of the remaining variance, about half is due to nonshared environmental influences and half to error of measurement. Thus, about two thirds of the reliable variance in measured personality traits is due to genetic influence.

The early studies of twins appear to have only slightly overestimated the degree of genetic influence on personality variation, and the main contribution of the more sophisticated recent analyses is that some of the genetic influence seems to be due to nonadditive genetic variance for all five

---

[1]n refers to the number of subjects or, in this case, the number of twin-pairs.

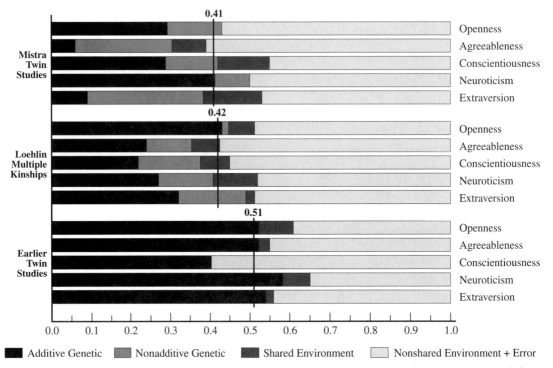

Figure 21.1 Sources of variation in personality in three sets of data. Percentages of variance accounted for by various genetic and environmental influences in personality traits. The solid lines indicate the mean Falconer heritability for the twin data from earlier studies and the mean broad heritability from model fitting for the other data sets.

traits. All three analyses yield quite small estimates of shared environmental influence. This is now a well-replicated finding in behavior genetics, and its implications are straightforward. The similarity we see in personality between biological relatives is almost entirely genetic in origin. If we wish to study environmental influences on personality development in families, we must look for influences that operate differentially among children in the same family (Rowe, 1994).

However, simply demonstrating that systematic differences in treatment within the family exist does not suffice to prove that such treatments explain personality differences. First, the treatment may have no effect. For example, differences in socialization due to birth order exist, but contrary to widespread belief (Hoffman, 1991), they do not influence personality. Second, as Lytton (1990)

has demonstrated, the differential behavior of children is often the cause of differential parental behavior rather than a consequence. Third, arguments as to the purported importance of environmental factors in shaping personality, though superficially plausible, often fail to stand up to scrutiny when subjected to quantitative analysis. Consider physical attractiveness. It is often argued that because twins reared apart are similar in physical attractiveness they must be treated alike, and therefore this is an important source of their similarity in personality (Hoffman, 1991; Ford, 1993). The problem with this argument is that physical attractiveness is so poorly correlated with personality traits that, when numbers are fit to the model implied by the argument, it can explain only a trivial portion of the similarity between MZA twins (Rowe, 1994). In truth, how nontraumatic environmental determinants influence the normal range of variance in adult personality remains largely a mystery. This variation may even turn out to be the equivalent of noise (Molenar, Boomsma, & Dolan, 1993).

Current thinking holds that each individual picks and chooses from a range of stimuli and events largely on the basis of his or her genotype and creates a unique set of experiences—that is, people help to create their own environments (Scarr, 1992). This view of human development does not deny the existence of inadequate and debilitating environments nor does it minimize the role of learning. Rather, it views humans as dynamic creative organisms for whom the opportunity to learn and to experience new environments amplifies the effects of the genotype on the phenotype. It also reminds us of our links to the biological world and our evolutionary history. This brings us to the core problem of the genetics of personality—the function of the variation in personality traits. The purpose of this variation is undoubtedly rooted in the fact that humans have adapted to life in face-to-face groups (sociality). Unraveling the role human individual differences play in evolution is the next big hurdle (Buss, 1993), and its solution will turn the behavior genetics of human personality from a descriptive discipline to an explanatory one.

References

Bouchard, T. J., Jr., Lykken, Dt. T., McGue, M., Segal, N. L., & Tellegen, A. (1990). Sources of human psychological differences: the Minnesota study of twins reared apart. *Science*, 250, 223–228.

Buss, D. M. (1993). Strategic individual differences: The evolutionary psychology of selection, evocation, and manipulation. In T. J. Bouchard, Jr., & P. Propping (Eds.), *Twins as a tool of behavioral genetics* (pp. 121–137). Chichester, England: Wiley.

Darwin, C. (1967). *The descent of man and selection in relation to sex.* New York: Modern Library. (Original work published 1871)

Eaves, L. J., Eysenck, H. J., & Martin, N. G. (1989). *Culture and personality: An empircal approach.* New York: Academic Press.

Ford, B. D. (1993). Emergenesis: An alternative and a confound. *American Psychologist, 48*, 1294.

Goldberg, L. R. (1993). The structure of phenotype personality traits. *American Psychologist, 48*, 26–34.

Hoffman, L. W. (1991). The influence of the family environment on personality: Accounting for sibling differences. *Psychological Bulletin, 110*, 187–203.

Loehlin, J. C. (1992). *Genes and environment in personality development.* Newbury Park, CA: Sage.

Lytton, H. (1990). Child effects: Still unwelcome? *Developmental Psychology, 26*, 705–709.

Molenar, P. C. M., Boomsma, D. I., & Dolan, C. V. (1993). A 3rd source of developmental differences. *Behavior Genetics, 23*, 519–524.

Neale, M. C., & Cardon, L. R. (Eds.). (1992). *Methodology for genetic studies of twins and families.* Boston: Kluwer Academic.

Nichols, R. C. (1978). Twin studies of ability, personality, and interests. *Homo, 29*, 158–173.

Rowe, D. (1994). *The limits of family influence: Genes, experience, and behavior.* New York: Guilford.

Scarr, S. (1992). Developmental theories for the 1990s: Development and individual differences. *Child Development, 63*, 1–19.

ENVIRONMENT AND GENES: DETERMINANTS OF BEHAVIOR

Robert Plomin

According to many behavioral geneticists, a major finding of their research concerns not genetics so much as the environment: Their results seem to indicate that the part of the family environment that is shared by siblings growing up together does not make them similar to each other. In the following selection, the prominent behavioral genetics researcher Robert Plomin describes this finding, its basis, and some of its implications.

As Plomin notes, the proposal that the shared family environment is unimportant remains controversial. There are several reasons why. First, many psychologists were trained to be environmental determinists, believing that how you turn out depends critically on how you were raised—and that children in the same family tend to be raised in the same way. Second, at least some findings from developmental psychology seem to contradict the conclusion from behavioral genetics research. For example, the number of siblings in a child's family has been shown by the developmentalist Arnold Sameroff to be a risk factor in development—a child growing up in a family with more than four children is more likely to develop problems in intellectual and social development (Barocas, Seifer, & Sameroff, 1985; Sameroff & Seifer, 1995). Yet the number of siblings is a "shared environment" variable that is equivalent for all the children in a family! The large literature on child development and the more recent and smaller literature on the developmental psychology of behavioral genetics have still not successfully integrated seemingly contradictory findings like these.

A third reason for controversy is the fact that, as Plomin himself has noted, nearly all behavioral genetics studies rely on self-report questionnaires as their measures of behavioral outcome. Perhaps the seemingly contradictory findings in the literature will be reconciled when behavioral genetics research begins to be conducted using a wider range of measures, including direct observations of behavior, life outcomes, and peers' reports of personality. Until that happens, many findings from behavioral genetics are likely to remain both intriguing and perplexing.

* * *

Environmental Influences Do Not Make Children in the Same Family Similar

Children growing up in the same family are not very similar. Sibling correlations are about .40 for cognitive abilities and about .20 for personality, and sibling concordances for psychopathology are typically less than 10%.[1] In other words, siblings show greater differences than similarities for the major domains of psychology. What is more, behavioral genetic research has shown that nearly all of the sibling resemblance found in these domains is due to heredity shared by siblings rather than to shared family environment. By no means do these findings imply that environmental influences—or more specifically, family environmental influences—are unimportant. Rather, the data imply that environmental influences important to behavioral development operate in such a way as to make children in the same family different from one another. That is, environmental influences do not operate on a family-by-family basis but rather on an individual-by-individual basis. They are specific to each child rather than general for an entire family.

IMPORTANCE OF NONSHARED ENVIRONMENT The case for the importance of so-called nonshared environmental influences was presented in a target article in *Behavioral and Brain Sciences,* which was published with 32 commentaries (Plomin & Daniels, 1987). One of several results that converge on

the conclusion that shared family environment is unimportant is the correlation for adoptive "siblings," genetically unrelated children adopted early in life into the same adoptive families. Their resemblance cannot be due to shared heredity, and thus their resemblance directly assesses the importance of environmental influence shared by children growing up in the same family. Results are clear in showing little influence of shared environment. For personality, adoptive sibling correlations are about .05 on average. Genetically unrelated individuals adopted together show no-greater-than-chance resemblance for psychopathology. For cognitive abilities, although adoptive siblings are similar in childhood (correlations of about .25), by adolescence, their correlations are near zero, suggesting that the long-term impact of shared family environment is slight (Plomin, 1988).

The importance of nonshared environmental factors suggests the need for a reconceptualization of environmental influences that focuses on experiential differences between children in the same family. That is, many environmental factors differ across families; these include socioeconomic status, parental education, and child-rearing practices. However, to the extent that these environmental factors do not differ between children growing up in the same family, they do not influence behavioral development. The critical question becomes, Why are children in the same family so different from one another? The key to unlock this riddle is to study more than one child per family. This permits the study of experiential differences within a family and their association with differences in outcome. Because heredity contributes to differences between siblings, sibling differences in experiences might reflect as well as affect differences in their behavior. Behavioral genetic methods are useful in addressing this issue. For

---

[1]These correlational statistics are described in the selection by Horowitz in Part I. A "concordance" is a statistic that reflects the probability of one sibling developing a disorder if the other one does.

example, because members of identical twin pairs do not differ genetically, one approach is to relate behavioral differences within pairs of identical twins to their experiential differences.

SOURCES OF NONSHARED ENVIRONMENTAL INFLU- ENCES What are these nonshared environmental influences that are so important in development? They need not be mysterious: Any environmental factor that has been studied in the traditional fam- ily-by-family manner can be reconsidered in terms of experiential differences within a family, as long as environmental measures are specific to each child in the family. For example, differential pa- rental behavior toward their two children could create or magnify differences between the chil- dren. Even small differences in relative parental affection within the family might have large effects on differences in siblings' outcomes. Siblings' per- ceptions of differences in treatment may be im- portant even if their perceptions are not veridical. In addition to differential treatment within the family, family composition variables such as birth order and gender differences might contribute to sibling differences. Experiences outside the family could also play a role; for example, siblings in the same family often have nonoverlapping friends. These are systematic sources of nonshared envi- ronment. It is also possible that nonsystematic fac- tors such as accidents and illnesses and other idiosyncratic experiences initiate differences be- tween siblings that, when compounded over time, make children in the same family different, per- haps in unpredictable ways.

So far, research on this new topic indicates that siblings in the same family experience consid- erably different environments in terms of parental treatment and their interaction with one another and with their peers. Evidence is beginning to ac- cumulate that these differential experiences are systematically related to sibling differences in de- velopmental outcomes. Although the first few steps have been taken toward identifying specific sources of nonshared environment, much remains to be learned. Answers to the question, Why are children in the same family so different from one another? are not only answers to the question about sibling differences. Their importance is far more general: understanding the environmental origins of individual differences in development.

Nature and Nurture

Behavioral genetics is likely to make other contri- butions to understanding environmental processes in development. For example, the special 1979 is- sue of *American Psychologist* on children included a behavioral genetic article that discussed an im- portant implication of the fact that family mem- bers share heredity as well as family environment: Measured environmental influences in families "are not solely environmental but confound he- redity with environment and are causally ambig- uous with respect to the direction of effects" (Willerman, 1979, p. 925). Recent research has shown that heredity can affect measures of the family environment (Plomin, Pedersen, McClearn, Nesselroade, & Bergeman, 1988; Rowe, 1981, 1983a) and that heredity can also mediate associ- ations between measures of the family environ- ment and developmental outcomes of children (Plomin, Loehlin, & DeFries, 1985). Other exam- ples of the usefulness of behavioral genetic strat- egies for understanding environmental influences include the analysis of genotype-environment in- teraction (differential effects of environments on children with different genetic propensities) and genotype-environment correlation (the extent to which children receive or create environments correlated with their genetic propensities; Plomin, 1986; Scarr & McCartney, 1983).

The move away from a rigid adherence to en- vironmental explanations of behavioral devel- opment to a more balanced perspective that recognizes genetic as well as environmental sources of individual differences must be viewed as healthy for the social and behavioral sciences. The danger now, however, is that the swing from environmentalism will go too far. During the 1970s, I found I had to speak gingerly about ge- netic influence, gently suggesting heredity might be important in behavior. Now, however, I more often have to say, "Yes, genetic influences are significant and substantial, but environmental influences are just as important." This seems to be happening most clearly in the field of psychopathology, where evidence of significant genetic influence has led to a search for single genes and simple neurochemical triggers at the expense of research on its psychosocial origins. It would be wonderful if some simple, and presumably inexpensive, biochemical cure could be found for schizophrenia. However, this happy outcome seems highly unlikely given that schizophrenia is as much influenced by environmental factors as it is by heredity.

Furthermore, genetic effects on behavior are polygenic and probabilistic, not single-gene and deterministic. The characteristics in the pea plant that Mendel studied and a few diseases such as Huntington's disease and sickle-cell anemia are due to single genes that have their effects regardless of the environment or the genetic background of the individual. The complexity of behaviors studied by psychologists makes it unlikely that such a deterministic model and the reductionistic approach that it suggests will pay off. There is as yet no firm evidence for a single-gene effect that accounts for a detectable amount of variation for any complex behavior. For example, earlier reports of a major gene effect for spatial ability have not been replicated, a recent suggestion of a major gene effect for spelling disability has been questioned, and the widely publicized major gene effects for schizophrenia and manic-depressive psychosis may be limited to particular families.

The complex interplay between environment and genes is most apparent in the case of development. For example, the lowly roundworm has become distinguished by being the first multicelled organism to have the developmental fate of each of its 959 adult cells mapped from the initial fer-

tilized egg, by having the complete wiring diagram of the nervous system worked out, and by having many of its 2,000 genes mapped. Despite these tremendous advances, we have learned little about the genetics of development except to appreciate its complexity. Clearly, development is not coded in DNA in the same way that the triplet code determines the amino acid sequence of proteins. The point is that a reductionistic, deterministic view is not likely to be a profitable way to think about genetic effects on behavioral development in the roundworm, and certainly not in children.

As the pendulum swings from environmentalism, it is important that the pendulum be caught midswing before its momentum carries it to biological determinism. Behavioral genetic research clearly demonstrates that both nature and nurture are important in human development.

References

Plomin, R. (1986). *Development, genetics, and psychology.* Hillsdale, NJ: Erlbaum.

Plomin, R. (1988). The nature and nurture of cognitive abilities. In R. J. Sternberg (Ed.), *Advances in the psychology of human intelligence* (Vol. 4, pp. 1–33). Hillsdale, NJ: Erlbaum.

Plomin, R., & Daniels, D. (1987). Why are children in the same family so different from each other? *Behavioral and Brain Sciences, 10,* 1–16.

Plomin, R., Loehlin, J. C., & DeFries, J. C. (1985). Genetic and environmental components of "environmental" influences. *Developmental Psychology, 21,* 391–402.

Plomin, R., Pedersen, N. L., McClearn, G. E., Nesselroade, J. R., & Bergeman, C. S. (1988). EAS temperaments during the last half of the life span: Twins reared apart and twins reared together. *Psychology and Aging, 3,* 43–50.

Rowe, D. C. (1981). Environmental and genetic influences on dimensions of perceived parenting: A twin study. *Developmental Psychology, 17,* 203–208.

Rowe, D. C. (1983a). A biometrical analysis of perceptions of family environment: A study of twin and singleton sibling kinships. *Child Development, 54,* 416–423.

Scarr, S., & McCartney, K. (1983). How people make their own environments: A theory of genotype ∩ environment effects. *Child Development, 54,* 424–435.

Wilerman, L. (1979). Effects of families on intellectual development. *American Psychologist, 34,* 923–929.

Sex Differences in Jealousy: Evolution, Physiology, and Psychology

David M. Buss, Randy J. Larsen, Drew Westen, and Jennifer Semmelroth

The essence of Darwin's theory of evolution is that those traits that are associated with successful reproduction will be increasingly represented in succeeding generations. For this reason, the obvious place to look for an evolutionarily based influence on behavior is in the area of sex. It is unsurprising, therefore, that as the evolutionary biology of personality has grown into an active research area in its own right, sex has come in for special attention.

The following article is a collaboration of several personality psychologists led by David Buss, one of the leaders in the application of evolutionary theory to personality. It derives hypotheses about the different approaches to mating that evolutionary theory would expect to be manifest by women and by men. In a nutshell, evolutionary considerations would lead one to expect men to be particularly worried that "their" children might have been fathered by other men, and therefore to be prone to sexual jealousy. Women, however, are not doubtful about their maternity but rather about the possibility that their mates might not continue to provide resources and protection for their children. They would therefore be more prone to emotional jealousy.

The next step taken by Buss and his co-workers is to test this hypothesis in a sample of undergraduates, presenting each with scenarios designed to trigger emotional and sexual jealousy. Not only are the expected sex differences found, but physiological indices of emotional arousal, such as heart rate, yield results that are consistent with the feelings that the subjects report.

The final paragraphs of this article acknowledge that these results might all be the result of cultural conditioning, not a process biologically built in through evolution. Nonetheless, Buss et al. point out that their results were predicted *by their evolutionary theorizing, not merely explained after they were obtained. This fact does not prove their theory, but does give it added plausibility.*

*   *   *

In species with internal female fertilization and gestation, features of reproductive biology characteristic of all 4,000 species of mammals, including humans, males face an adaptive problem not confronted by females—uncertainty in their paternity of offspring. Maternity probability in mammals rarely or never deviates from 100%. Compromises in paternity probability come at substantial reproductive cost to the male—the loss of mating effort expended, including time, energy, risk, nuptial gifts, and mating opportunity costs. A cuckolded male also loses the female's parental effort, which becomes channeled to a competitor's gametes. The adaptive problem of paternity uncertainty is exacerbated in species in which males engage in some postzygotic parental investment (Trivers, 1972). Males risk investing resources in putative offspring that are genetically unrelated.

These multiple and severe reproductive costs should have imposed strong selection pressure on males to defend against cuckoldry. Indeed, the literature is replete with examples of evolved anti-cuckoldry mechanisms in lions (Bertram, 1975), bluebirds (Power, 1975), doves (Erickson & Zenone, 1976), numerous insect species (Thornhill & Alcock, 1983), and nonhuman primates (Hrdy, 1979). Since humans arguably show more paternal investment than any other of the 200 species of primates (Alexander & Noonan, 1979), this selection pressure should have operated especially intensely on human males. Symons (1979); Daly, Wilson, and Weghorst (1982); and Wilson and Daly (1992) have hypothesized that male sexual jealousy evolved as a solution to this adaptive problem (but see Hupka, 1991, for an alternative view). Men who were indifferent to sexual contact between their mates and other men presumably experienced lower paternity certainty, greater investment in competitors' gametes, and lower reproductive success than did men who were motivated to attend to cues of infidelity and to act on those cues to increase paternity probability.

Although females do not risk maternity uncertainty, in species with biparental care they do risk the potential loss of time, resources, and commitment from a male if he deserts or channels investment to alternative mates (Buss, 1988; Thornhill & Alcock, 1983; Trivers, 1972). The redirection of a mate's investment to another female and her offspring is reproductively costly for a female, especially in environments where offspring suffer in survival and reproductive currencies without investment from both parents.

In human evolutionary history, there were likely to have been at least two situations in which a woman risked losing a man's investment. First, in a monogamous marriage, a woman risked having her mate invest in an alternative woman with whom he was having an affair (partial loss of investment) or risked his departure for an alternative woman (large or total loss of investment). Second, in polygynous marriages, a woman was at risk of having her mate invest to a larger degree in other wives and their offspring at the expense of his investment in her and her offspring. Following Buss (1988) and Mellon (1981), we hypothesize that cues to the development of a deep emotional attachment have been reliable leading indicators to women of potential reduction or loss of their mate's investment.

Jealousy is defined as an emotional "state that is aroused by a perceived threat to a valued relationship or position and motivates behavior aimed at countering the threat. Jealousy is 'sexual' if the valued relationship is sexual" (Daly et al., 1982, p. 11; see also Salovey, 1991; White & Mullen, 1989). It is reasonable to hypothesize that jealousy involves physiological reactions (autonomic arousal) to perceived threat and motivated action to reduce the threat, although this hypothesis has not been examined. Following Symons (1979) and Daly et al. (1982), our central hypothesis is that the events that activate jealousy physiologically and psychologically differ for men and women because of the different adaptive problems they have faced over human evolutionary history in mating contexts. Both sexes are hypothesized to be distressed over both sexual and emotional infidelity, and previous findings bear this out (Buss, 1989). However, these two kinds of infidelity should be weighted differently by men and women. Despite the importance of these hypothesized sex differences, no systematic scientific work has been directed toward verifying or falsifying their existence (but for suggestive data, see Francis, 1977; Teismann & Mosher, 1978; White & Mullen, 1989).

Study 1: Subjective Distress Over a Partner's External Involvement

This study was designed to test the hypothesis that men and women differ in which form of infidelity—sexual versus emotional—triggers more upset and subjective distress, following the adaptive logic just described.

METHOD After reporting age and sex, subjects ($N = 202$ undergraduate students) were presented with the following dilemma:

> Please think of a serious committed romantic relationship that you have had in the past, that you currently have, or that you would like to have. Imagine that you discover that the person with whom you've been seriously involved became interested in someone else. What would distress or upset you more (*please circle only one*):
> (A) Imagining your partner forming a deep emotional attachment to that person.
> (B) Imagining your partner enjoying passionate sexual intercourse with that other person.

> Subjects completed additional questions, and then encountered the next dilemma, with the same instructional set, but followed by a different, but parallel, choice:
> (A) Imagining your partner trying different sexual positions with that other person.

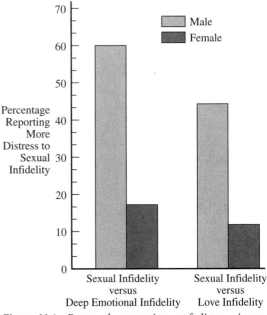

Figure 23.1 Reported comparisons of distress in response to imagining a partner's sexual or emotional infidelity. The panel shows the percentage of subjects reporting more distress to the sexual infidelity scenario than to the emotional infidelity (left) and the love infidelity (right) scenarios.

> (B) Imagining your partner falling in love with that other person.

RESULTS Shown in Figure 23.1 are the percentages of men and women reporting more distress in response to sexual infidelity than emotional infidelity. The first empirical probe, contrasting distress over a partner's sexual involvement with distress over a partner's deep emotional attachment, yielded a large and highly significant sex difference ($\chi^2 = 47.56$, $df = 3$, $p < .001$).[1] Fully 60% of the male sample reported greater distress over their partner's potential sexual infidelity; in contrast, only 17% of the female sample chose that option, with 83% reporting that they would ex-

---

[1]This "chi-square" statistic is a test for the randomness of arrangement of outcomes into categories; here, if there were no sex difference, the results obtained would be found less than one time in a thousand.

perience greater distress over a partner's emotional attachment to a rival.

This pattern was replicated with the contrast between sex and love. The magnitude of the sex difference was large, with 32% more men than women reporting greater distress over a partner's sexual involvement with someone else, and the majority of women reporting greater distress over a partner's falling in love with a rival ($\chi^2 = 59.20$, $df = 3$, $p < .001$).

Study 2: Physiological Responses to a Partner's External Involvement

Given the strong confirmation of jealousy sex linkage from Study 1, we sought next to test the hypotheses using physiological measures. Our central measures of autonomic arousal were electrodermal activity (EDA), assessed via skin conductance, and pulse rate (PR). Electrodermal activity and pulse rate are indicators of autonomic nervous system activation (Levenson, 1988). Because distress is an unpleasant subjective state, we also included a measure of muscle activity in the brow region of the face—electromyographic (EMG) activity of the *corrugator supercilii* muscle. This muscle is responsible for the furrowing of the brow often seen in facial displays of unpleasant emotion or affect (Fridlund, Ekman, & Oster, 1987). Subjects were asked to image two scenarios in which a partner became involved with someone else—one sexual intercourse scenario and one emotional attachment scenario. Physiological responses were recorded during the imagery trials.

SUBJECTS Subjects were 55 undergraduate students, 32 males and 23 females, each completing a 2-hr laboratory session.

PHYSIOLOGICAL MEASURES Physiological activity was monitored on the running strip chart of a Grass Model 7D polygraph and digitized on a laboratory computer at a 10-Hz rate, following principles recommended in Cacioppo and Tassinary (1990).

Electrodermal activity. Standard Beckman Ag/AgCl surface electrodes, filled with a .05 molar NaCl solution in a Unibase paste, were placed over the middle segments of the first and third fingers of the right hand. A Wheatstone bridge applied a 0.5-V voltage to one electrode.

Pulse rate. A photoplethysmograph was attached to the subject's right thumb to monitor the pulse wave. The signal from this pulse transducer was fed into a Grass Model 7P4 cardiotachometer to detect the rising slope of each pulse wave, with the internal circuitry of the Schmitt trigger individually adjusted for each subject to output PR in beats per minute.

Electromyographic activity. Bipolar EMG recordings were obtained over the *corrugator supercilii* muscle. The EMG signal was relayed to a wideband AC-preamplifier (Grass Model 7P3), where it was band-pass filtered, full-wave rectified, and integrated with a time constant of 0.2 s.[2]

PROCEDURE After electrode attachment, the subject was made comfortable in a reclining chair and asked to relax. After a 5-min waiting period, the experiment began. The subject was alone in the room during the imagery session, with an intercom on for verbal communication. The instructions for the imagery task were written on a form which the subject was requested to read and follow.

Each subject was instructed to engage in three separate images. The first image was designed to be emotionally neutral: "Imagine a time when you were walking to class, feeling neither good nor bad, just neutral." The subject was instructed to press a button when he or she had the image clearly in mind, and to sustain the image until the experimenter said to stop. The button triggered the computer to begin collecting physiological

---

[2]The preceding paragraphs are a detailed technical description of state-of-the-art techniques for measuring autonomic arousal, for the use of researchers who might want to replicate these results.

data for 20 s, after which the experimenter instructed the subject to "stop and relax."

The next two images were infidelity images, one sexual and one emotional. The order of presentation of these two images was counterbalanced. The instructions for sexual jealousy imagery were as follows: "Please think of a serious romantic relationship that you have had in the past, that you currently have, or that you would like to have. Now imagine that the person with whom you're seriously involved becomes interested in someone else. *Imagine you find out that your partner is having sexual intercourse with this other person.* Try to feel the feelings you would have if this happened to you."

The instructions for emotional infidelity imagery were identical to the above, except the italicized sentence was replaced with "*Imagine that your partner is falling in love and forming an emo-*

tional attachment to that person." Physiological data were collected for 20 s following the subject's button press indicating that he or she had achieved the image. Subjects were told to "stop and relax" for 30 s between imagery trials.

RESULTS

Physiological scores. The following scores were obtained: (a) the amplitude of the largest EDA response occurring during each 20-s trial; (b) PR in beats per minute averaged over each 20-s trial; and (c) amplitude of EMG activity over the *corrugator supercilii* averaged over each 20-s trial. Difference scores were computed between the neutral imagery trial and the jealousy induction trials. Within-sex *t* tests revealed no effects for order of presentation of the sexual jealousy image, so data were collapsed over this factor.

Jealousy induction effects. Table 23.1 shows the mean scores for the physiological measures for men and women in each of the two imagery conditions. Differences in physiological responses to the two jealousy images were examined using paired-comparison *t* tests for each sex separately for EDA, PR, and EMG. The men showed significant increases in EDA during the sexual imagery compared with the emotional imagery ($t = 2.00$, $df = 29$, $p < .05$).[3] Women showed significantly greater EDA to the emotional infidelity image than to the sexual infidelity image ($t = 2.42$, $df = 19$, $p < .05$). A similar pattern was observed with PR. Men showed a substantial increase in PR to both images, but significantly more so in response to the sexual infidelity image ($t = 2.29$, $df = 31$, $p < .05$). Women showed elevated PR to both images, but not differentially so. The results of the *corrugator* EMG were similar, although less strong. Men showed greater brow contraction to the sex-

---

TABLE 23.1

MEANS AND STANDARD DEVIATIONS ON PHYSIOLOGICAL MEASURES DURING TWO IMAGERY CONDITIONS

Measure	Imagery type	Mean	SD
Males			
EDA	Sexual	1.30	3.64
	Emotional	−0.11	0.76
Pulse rate	Sexual	4.76	7.80
	Emotional	3.00	5.24
Brow EMG	Sexual	6.75	32.96
	Emotional	1.16	6.60
Females			
EDA	Sexual	−0.07	0.49
	Emotional	0.21	0.78
Pulse rate	Sexual	2.25	4.68
	Emotional	2.57	4.37
Brow EMG	Sexual	3.03	8.38
	Emotional	8.12	25.60

Note. Measures are expressed as changes from the neutral image condition. EDA is in microsiemen units, pulse rate is in beats per minute, and EMG is in microvolt units.

---

[3]The *t* statistic here indicates that given the number of subjects (related to *df*) in this sample, the data obtained would have occurred less than 5% of the time if there were no sex differences.

ual infidelity image, and women showed the opposite pattern, although results with this nonautonomic measure did not reach significance ($t = 1.12$, $df = 30$, $p < .14$, for males; $t = -1.24$, $df = 22$, $p < .12$, for females). The elevated EMG contractions for both jealousy induction trials in both sexes support the hypothesis that the affect experienced is negative.

* * *

Discussion

The results of the empirical studies support the hypothesized sex linkages in the activators of jealousy. Study 1 found large sex differences in reports of the subjective distress individuals would experience upon exposure to a partner's sexual infidelity versus emotional infidelity. Study 2 found a sex linkage in autonomic arousal to imagined sexual infidelity versus emotional infidelity; the results were particularly strong for the EDA and PR. * * *

These studies are limited in ways that call for additional research. First, they pertain to a single age group and culture. Future studies could explore the degree to which these sex differences transcend different cultures and age groups. Two clear evolutionary psychological predictions are (a) that male sexual jealousy and female commitment jealousy will be greater in cultures where males invest heavily in children, and (b) that male sexual jealousy will diminish as the age of the male's mate increases because her reproductive value decreases. Second, future studies could test the alternative hypotheses that the current findings reflect (a) domain-specific psychological adaptations to cuckoldry versus potential investment loss or (b) a more domain-general mechanism such that any thoughts of sex are more interesting, arousing, and perhaps disturbing to men whereas any thoughts of love are more interesting, arousing, and perhaps disturbing to women, and hence that such responses are not specific to jealousy or infidelity. Third, emotional and sexual infidelity are clearly correlated, albeit imperfectly, and a sizable percentage of men in Study 1 reported greater distress to a partner's emotional infidelity. Emotional infidelity may signal sexual infidelity and vice versa, and hence both sexes should become distressed at both forms (see Buss, 1989). Future research could profitably explore in greater detail the correlation of these forms of infidelity as well as the sources of within-sex variation.

Within the constraints of the current studies, we can conclude that the sex differences found here generalize across both psychological and physiological methods—demonstrating an empirical robustness in the observed effect. The degree to which these sex-linked elicitors correspond to the hypothesized sex-linked adaptive problems lends support to the evolutionary psychological framework from which they were derived. Alternative theoretical frameworks, including those that invoke culture, social construction, deconstruction, arbitrary parental socialization, and structural powerlessness, undoubtedly could be molded post hoc to fit the findings—something perhaps true of any set of findings. None but the Symons (1979) and Daly et al. (1982) evolutionary psychological frameworks, however, generated the sex-differentiated predictions in advance and on the basis of sound evolutionary reasoning. The recent finding that male sexual jealousy is the leading cause of spouse battering and homicide across cultures worldwide (Daly & Wilson, 1988a, 1988b) offers suggestive evidence that these sex differences have large social import and may be species-wide.

References

Alexander, R. D., & Noonan, K. M. (1979). Concealment of ovulation, parental care, and human social evolution. In N. Chagnon & W. Irons (Eds.), *Evolutionary biology and human social behavior* (pp. 436–453). North Scituate, MA: Duxbury.

Bertram, B. C. R. (1975). Social factors influencing reproduction in wild lions. *Journal of Zoology, 177,* 463–482.

Buss, D. M. (1988). From vigilance to violence: Tactics of mate retention. *Ethology and Sociobiology, 9,* 291–317.

Buss, D. M. (1989). Conflict between the sexes: Strategic interference and the evocation of anger and upset. *Journal of Personality and Social Psychology, 56,* 735–747.

Cacioppo, J. T., & Tassinary, L. G. (Eds.). (1990). *Principles of psychophysiology: Physical, social, and inferential elements.* Cambridge, England: Cambridge University Press.

Daly, M., & Wilson, M. (1988a). Evolutionary social psychology and family violence. *Science, 242,* 519–524.

Daly, M., & Wilson, M. (1988b). *Homicide.* Hawthorne, NY: Aldine.

Daly, M., Wilson, M., & Weghorst, S. J. (1982). Male sexual jealousy. *Ethology and Sociobiology, 3,* 11–27.

Erickson, C. J., & Zenone, P. G. (1976). Courtship differences in male ring doves: Avoidance of cuckoldry? *Science, 192,* 1353–1354.

Francis, J. L. (1977). Toward the management of heterosexual jealousy. *Journal of Marriage and Family Counseling, 10,* 61–69.

Fridlund, A., Ekman, P., & Oster, J. (1987). Facial expressions of emotion. In A. Siegman & S. Feldstein (Eds.), *Nonverbal behavior and communication* (pp. 143–224). Hillsdale, NJ: Erlbaum.

Hrdy, S. B. G. (1979). Infanticide among animals: A review, classification, and examination of the implications for the reproductive strategies of females. *Ethology and Sociobiology, 1,* 14–40.

Hupka, R. B. (1991). The motive for the arousal of romantic jealousy: Its cultural origin. In P. Salovey (Ed.), *The psychology of jealousy and envy* (pp. 252–270). New York: Guilford Press.

Levenson, R. W. (1988). Emotion and the autonomic nervous system: A prospectus for research on autonomic specificity. In H. Wagner (Ed.), *Social psychophysiology: Theory and clinical applications* (pp. 17–42). London: Wiley.

Mellon, L. W. (1981). *The evolution of love.* San Francisco: W. H. Freeman.

Power, H. W. (1975). Mountain bluebirds: Experimental evidence against altruism. *Science, 189,* 142–143.

Salovey, P. (Ed.). (1991). *The psychology of jealousy and envy.* New York: Guilford Press.

Symons, D. (1979). *The evolution of human sexuality.* New York: Oxford University Press.

Teismann, M. W., & Mosher, D. L. (1978). Jealous conflict in dating couples. *Psychological Reports, 42,* 1211–1216.

Thornhill, R., & Alcock, J. (1983). *The evolution of insect mating systems.* Cambridge, MA: Harvard University Press.

Trivers, R. (1972). Parental investment and sexual selection. In B. Campbell (Ed.), *Sexual selection and the descent of man, 1871–1971* (pp. 136–179). Chicago: Aldine.

White, G. L., & Mullen, P. E. (1989). *Jealousy: Theory, research, and clinical strategies.* New York: Guilford Press.

Wilson, M., & Daly, M. (1992). The man who mistook his wife for a chattel. In J. Barkow, L. Cosmides, & J. Tooby (Eds.), *The adapted mind: Evolutionary psychology and the generation of culture.* New York: Oxford University Press.

Male Sexual Proprietariness and Violence Against Wives

Margo I. Wilson and Martin Daly

The preceding selection provided an evolutionary explanation of the causes of jealousy; the following selection provides an evolutionary explanation of one of its effects. Margo Wilson and Martin Daly, two Canadian researchers on interpersonal conflict and violence, propose that thousands of years of evolutionary processes have produced modern men so concerned about the sexual ownership of their mates that they may physically harm and even kill their wives to prevent other men from taking possession of them. (In an interesting twist of evolutionary logic, they suggest that the seemingly self-defeating behavior—from a reproductive point of view—of killing one's own wife is the result of the necessity of maintaining a credible threat that one's wife will be killed if she strays.)

This article presents a set of ideas that are provocative to say the least. It takes a phenomenon, here called "uxoricide," that is usually considered due to a variety of poor social conditions and criminal psychopathology and describes it as a built-in element of the male behavioral repertoire. This account may disturb some readers.

If you find yourself disturbed, inspired, offended, or just intrigued by this and the previous selection, you might want to do further reading in evolutionary biology. In fact, the editors of your reader have misgivings about several aspects of this paper, particularly its explanation of why spouses are sometimes killed. The crucial missing piece in Wilson and Daly's explanation is any description of a psychological mechanism by which ancient evolutionary history could influence contemporary behavior. Rather than focusing exclusively on the behavioral outcome of uxoricide, they might have done better to concentrate on the rage of a jealous husband, much as Buss and his co-workers (in the previous selection) concentrated on the experience of jealousy.

The issues raised by this article are stimulating, thought-provoking, and illustrate the ambitious reach of evolutionary personality psychology. A good place to begin further reading would be the references at the end of this and the preceding selection. The issues raised by an evolutionary approach are not simple, wide differences of opinion exist, and it takes some study to be in a position to be able to make up one's own mind intelligently for oneself.

There is a cross-culturally ubiquitous connection between men's sexual possessiveness and men's violence (Wilson & Daly, 1992, 1993). We have studied accounts of uxoricides (wife killings) from a broad range of societies, and find that male sexual proprietariness—broadly construed to encompass resentment both of infidelity and of women's efforts to leave marriages—is everywhere implicated as the dominant precipitating factor in a large majority of cases (Daly & Wilson, 1988). The discovery of wifely infidelity is viewed as an exceptional provocation, likely to elicit a violent rage, both in societies where such a reaction is considered a reprehensi-

ble loss of control and in those where it is considered a praiseworthy redemption of honor. Indeed, such a rage is widely presumed to be so compelling as to mitigate the responsibility of even homicidal cuckolds.

Battered women nominate "jealousy" as the most frequent motive for their husbands' assaults, and their assailants commonly make the same attribution (Wilson & Daly, 1992, 1993; Daly & Wilson, 1988). Moreover, assaulted wives often maintain that their husbands are not only violently jealous about their interactions with other men, but are so controlling as to curtail contacts with female friends and family. In a 1993 national

---

TABLE 24.1

ASSOCIATION BETWEEN VIOLENCE AGAINST WIVES AND HUSBANDS' AUTONOMY-LIMITING BEHAVIORS, ACCORDING TO A NATIONAL PROBABILITY SAMPLE OF CANADIAN WIVES (WILSON ET AL., 1995)

Statement	History of violence against wife		
	Serious violence N = 286	Relativity minor only N = 1,039	None N = 6,990
"He is jealous and doesn't want you to talk to other men"	39	13	4
"He tries to limit your contact with family or friends"	35	11	2
"He insists on knowing who you are with and where you are at all times"	40	24	7
"He calls you names to put you down or make you feel bad"	48	22	3
"He prevents you from knowing about or having access to the family income, even if you ask"	15	5	1

Note. Table entries are the percentages of respondents affirming that each item applied to their husbands. Violence was categorized as "serious" or "relatively minor" on the basis of the alleged assaultive acts; the validity of this distinction is supported by sample interviews indicating that an injury required medical attention occurred in 72% of the incidents that met the "serious" criterion versus 18% of the "relatively minor" violent incidents.

survey, Statistics Canada interviewed more than 8,000 women currently residing with male partners. In addition to answering questions about their experiences of violence, the women indicated whether five statements about autonomy-limiting aspects of some men's behavior applied to their husbands. Autonomy-limiting behavior was especially likely to be attributed to those husbands who were also reported to have behaved violently, and women who had experienced relatively serious or frequent assaults were much more likely to affirm each of the five statements than were women who had experienced only lesser violence (Table 24.1) (Wilson, Johnson, & Daly, 1995). These and other data suggest that unusually controlling husbands are also unusually violent husbands. Rather than being one of a set of alternative controlling tactics used by proprietary men, wife assault appears to go hand in hand with other tactics of control.

Evolutionary Psychology, Intrasexual Competition, and Marital Alliance

Why should sexually proprietary feelings be linked with violence in this way? Although it is often supposed that wives are assaulted mainly because they are accessible, legitimate targets when men are frustrated or angry, mere opportunity cannot account for the differential risk of violent victimization within households. Wives are far more likely than other relatives to be murdered by an adult in their household (Figure 24.1) (Daly & Wilson, 1988). Wife assault has distinct motives. We propose that a satisfactory account of the psychological links between male sexual proprietariness and violence will depend on an understanding of the adaptive problems that men have faced in the course of human evolutionary history and the ways in which the psyche is organized to solve them. Those adaptive problems include both the risk of losing the wife, a valued reproductive resource, to a rival and the risk of directing paternal investments to another man's child (Wilson & Daly, 1992, 1993).

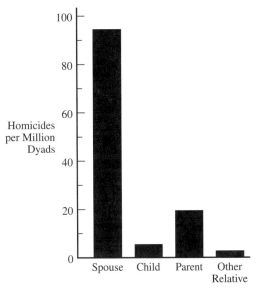

Figure 24.1 Homicide victimization rates characteristic of different categories of co-residing relatives (considering only adults as potential perpetrators) in the city of Detroit, 1972 (Daly & Wilson, 1988)

Adaptations are organismic attributes that are well "designed," as a result of a history of natural selection, to achieve functions that promoted reproductive success in ancestral environments (Williams, 1966). Because organisms can usefully be analyzed into numerous distinct parts with complementary functions, investigation in the life sciences is almost invariably conducted in the shadow of (often inexplicit) adaptationist ideas. Sound hypotheses about what the heart or lungs or liver are "for" were essential first steps for investigating their physiology, for example. Psychological research is similarly (and equally appropriately) infused with adaptationist premises.

The goal of psychological science is and always has been the discovery and elucidation of psychological adaptations. Evolutionary thinking can help. By paying explicit attention to adaptive significance and selective forces, evolutionists are better able to generate hypotheses about which developmental experiences and proximate causal cues are likely to affect which aspects of behavior, and what sorts of contingencies, priorities, and combinatorial information-processing algorithms are likely to be instantiated in the architecture of the mind (Toby & Cosmides, 1992; Buss, 1995; Daly & Wilson, 1995, in press). Psychological constructs from self-esteem to color vision to sexual jealousy are formulated at a level of abstraction intended to be of panhuman (cross-cultural) generality. If these things exist and are complexly structured and organized, they almost certainly evolved to play some fitness-promoting role in our ancestors' lives. But although psychologists usually recognize that the phenomena they study have utility, jealousy in particular has often been dismissed as a functionless epiphenomenon or pathology. In light of what is known about evolution by selection, this is scarcely plausible.

In a sexual population, all the males are engaged in a *zero-sum game* in which the paternal share of the ancestry of all future generations is divided among them, while the females are engaged in a parallel contest over the maternal share of that ancestry. In a fundamental sense, then, one's principal competitors are same-sex members of one's own species. But although it is true for both females and males that selection entails a zero-sum competitive contest for genetic posterity, the evolutionary consequences are not necessarily similar in the two sexes. In particular, *sexual selection* (the component of selection that is attributable to differential access to mates) is generally of differential intensity, leading to a variety of sexually differentiated adaptations for intrasexual competition (Andersson, 1994).

In most mammals, the variance in male fitness is greater than the variance in female fitness, with the result that male mammals are generally subject to more intense sexual selection than females, and that the psychological and morphological attributes that have evolved for use in intrasexual competition are usually costlier and more dangerous in males than in females. The human animal is no exception to these generalizations, and rivalry among men is a ubiquitous and sometimes deadly source of conflict. Where homicide rates are high, most victims are men, and their killers are mainly unrelated male acquaintances; the predominant

motive is not robbery, but some sort of interpersonal conflict, especially a status or "face" dispute, with an overt element of sexual rivalry apparent in a substantial minority of the cases (Daly & Wilson, 1988). Of course, killing often oversteps the bounds of utility, but the circumstances under which dangerous violence is used in these cases bespeak its more typical functionality in its much more numerous nonlethal manifestations. And although the principal victims of men's lethal assaults are other men, violence is a coercive social tool that can be used on women, too, including wives.

From a selectionist perspective, the marital relationship has special properties. The fitnesses of genetic relatives overlap in proportion to genealogical proximity, a situation that engenders selection for altruistic and cooperative inclinations toward kin. Mates share genetic interests, too, but their solidarity is more fragile. By reproducing together, a monogamous couple may attain a state in which all exigencies affect their fitnesses identically, a situation conducive to consensus and harmony. However, the correlation between their expected fitnesses can be abolished or even rendered negative if one or both betray the relationship (Daly & Wilson, 1995, in press).

Is it reasonable to propose the existence of an evolved social psychology specific to the marital relationship? Certainly, marital alliance is neither a sporadically distributed cultural option nor a modern discovery or invention, like agriculture or writing. Women and men everywhere enter into socially recognized unions, with a set of complementary sex-specific entitlements and obligations predicated on the complementarity of female and male sexual and reproductive roles, and they have done so for many millennia. We therefore expect that there are certain fundamental, universal sources of marital conflict, reflecting situations in which one marriage partner could have gained fitness in ancestral human environments at the other partner's expense. These situations would include conflicts over equity of contributions to the couple's joint endeavors (work sharing), over each partner's nepotistic interest in the welfare of his or her distinct kindred (in-law disputes), over asymmetrical temptations to abandon the union, and over sexual infidelity. In a pair-forming, bi-parental species, most of these conflicts can apply both ways, but the potential effects of infidelity are an exception: Males, unlike females, can be cuck-olded and unwittingly invest their parental efforts in the service of rivals' fitness.

* * *

Undetected cuckoldry poses a major threat to a man's fitness, but for women the threat is slightly different: that a husband's efforts and re-sources will be diverted to the benefit of other women and their children. It follows that the arousal of men's and women's proprietary feelings toward their mates is likely to have evolved to be differentially attuned to distinct cues indicative of the sex-specific threats to fitness in past environ-ments. Diverse evidence on feelings, reactions, and cultural practices supports the hypothesis that men are more intensely concerned with sexual infidelity per se and women more intensely con-cerned with the allocation of their mates' re-sources, affection, and attentions (Wilson & Daly, 1992, 1993; Buss, Larsen, Western, & Semmelroth, 1992).

Contingent Cuing of Male Sexual Proprietariness and the Epidemi-ology of Violence Against Wives

If sexual proprietariness is aroused by cues of threats to sexual monopoly, and if use of violence is contingent on cues of its utility (including tol-erable costs), then variations within and between societies in the frequency and severity of violence against wives may be largely attributable to vari-ations in such cues (Wilson & Daly, 1992, 1993). Those relevant to the arousal of sexual proprie-tariness are likely to include cues of pressure from potential rivals and cues of one's partner's fertility and attractiveness to those rivals. Regarding the former issue, we would expect a husband to be sensitive to indicators of the local intensity of male competition and sexual poaching, and to indica-

tors of the status, attractiveness, and resources of potential rivals relative to himself. Being part of a relatively large age cohort may also be expected to intensify male-male competition, especially if same-age women are unavailable; thus, cohort-size effects on intrasexual rivalry and hence on the coercive constraint of women may be especially evident where age disparities at marriage are large. Parameters like relative cohort size, local marital instability, and local prevalence of adultery clearly cannot be cued simply by stimuli immediately present, but must be induced from experience ac-cumulated over large portions of the life span.

If men's violence and threats function to limit female autonomy, husbands may be motivated to act in these ways in response to probabilistic cues that their wives may desert them. Women who actually leave their husbands are often pursued, threatened, and assaulted; separated wives are even killed by their husbands at substantially higher rates than wives who live with their husbands (Figure 24.2) (Wilson, Daly, & Scheib, in press). The elevation of uxoricide risk at separation is even more severe than the contrasts in Figure 2 suggest because the rate denominators include all separated wives regardless of the duration of sep-aration, whereas when separated wives are killed, it is usually soon after separation. Of course, the temporal association between separation and vio-lence does not necessarily mean that the former caused the latter; however, many husbands who have killed their wives had explicitly threatened to do so should their wives ever leave, and explain their behavior as a response to the intolerable stimulus of their wives' departure.

Why are men ever motivated to pursue and kill women who have left them? Such behavior is spiteful in that it is likely to impose a net cost on its perpetrator as well as its victim, and therefore challenges the evolutionary psychological hypoth-esis that motives and emotions are organized in such a way as to promote the actors' interests. Moreover, if the adaptive function of the moti-vational processes underlying violence against wives resides in retaining and controlling one's mate, as we have suggested, killing is all the more

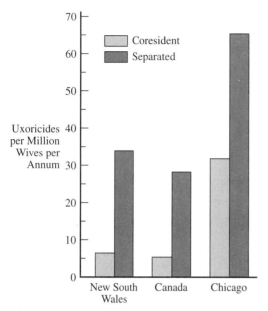

Figure 24.2 Rates of uxoricides perpetrated by registered-marriage husbands, for coresiding versus estranged couples in New South Wales (NSW), Australia (1968–1986); Canada (1974–1990); and Chicago (1965–1989) (Wilson et al., in press)

paradoxical. The problem is akin to that of understanding vengeance (Daly & Wilson, 1988). A threat is an effective social tool, and usually an inexpensive one, but it loses its effectiveness if the threatening party is seen to be bluffing, that is, to be unwilling to pay the occasional cost of following through when the threat is ignored or defied. Such vengeful follow-through may appear counter-productive—a risky or expensive act too late to be useful—but effective threats cannot "leak" signs of bluff and may therefore have to be sincere. Although killing an estranged wife appears futile, threatening one who might otherwise leave can be self-interested, and so can pursuing her with further threats, as can advertisements of anger and ostensible obliviousness to costs.

Evolutionary psychologists have predicted and confirmed that men are maximally attracted to young women as sexual and marital partners (Symons, 1995). This fact suggests that sexual proprietariness will be relatively intensely aroused in

men married to younger women, and young wives indeed incur the highest rates of both lethal (Daly & Wilson, 1988; Wilson et al., 1995, in press) (Figure 24.3) and nonlethal[4] violence by husbands. (It might be suggested that male sexual jealousy cannot be an evolved adaptation because men remain sexually jealous of postmenopausal or otherwise infertile women, but adaptations can have evolved only to track ancestrally informative cues of fertility and not fertility itself. In a modern society with contraception, improved health, and diverse cosmetic manipulations, postmenopausal women are likely to exhibit fewer cues of age-related declining reproductive value than still-fertile women in ancestral societies; Symons, 1995.)

There are several reasons to suppose that husbands may be relatively insecure in their proprietary claims in de facto marriages, which have higher rates of dissolution and a weaker or more ambiguous legal status than registered unions. And, indeed, wives in de facto marital unions in Canada incur an eight times greater risk of uxoricide and a four times greater risk of nonlethal assault by husbands (Wilson et al., 1995). However, registered and de facto unions differ in many ways, and the higher risk of uxoricide and assault in the latter may be due to a complex combination of factors, including youth, poverty, parity, and the presence of stepchildren (Daly & Wilson, 1988, 1995, in press; Wilson et al., 1995); whether adultery and desertion are greater sources of conflict in de facto unions than in registered unions is unknown. Demographic risk markers such as type of marital union and age are undoubtedly correlated with several variables that may be more directly causal to the risk of violence; elucidation of their relative roles awaits further research. However, it was the logic of evolution by selection which suggested to us that these demographic variables are likely correlates of breaches of sexual exclusivity and hence of violence.

Evolution by selection offers a framework for the development of hypotheses about the functional design of motivational-emotional-cognitive subsystems of the mind such as male sexual proprietariness, providing hints about proximate

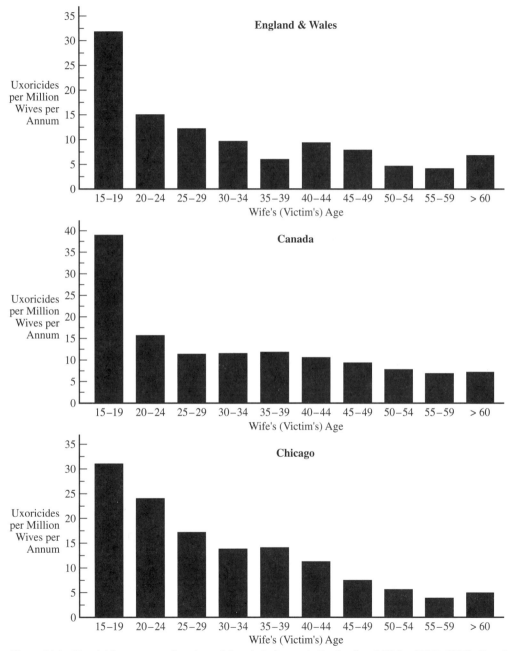

Figure 24.3 Uxoricide rates as a function of the victim's age, in England and Wales (1977–1990), Canada (1974–1990), and Chicago (1965–1989) (Wilson et al., in press)

causal cues, modulated expression, attentional priorities, and perceptual and informational processing. We have argued that the development and modulation of male sexual proprietariness is contingent on ecologically valid cues of threats to a sexually exclusive relationship. The link between male sexual proprietariness and violent inclinations has presumably been selected for because violence and threat work to deter sexual rivals and limit female autonomy. (This is not to say that violent capacities and inclinations were not also subject to selection pressures in other contexts, including intergroup warfare and hunting.) The expression of male sexual proprietariness, including violent manifestations, will depend not only on the presence and incidence of ecologically valid cues, but also on community, family, and person-specific factors that are likely to affect the thresholds and other parameter settings of the psychological mechanisms involved.

References

Andersson, M. (1994). *Sexual Selection*. Princeton, NJ: Princeton University Press.

Buss, D. M. (1995). Evolutionary psychology: A new paradigm for psychological science. *Psychological Inquiry, 6*, 1–30.

Buss, D. M., Larsen, R. J., Westen, D., & Semmelroth, J. (1992). Sex differences in jealousy: Evolution, physiology, and psychology. *Psychological Science, 3*, 251–255.

Daly, M., & Wilson, M. I. (1988). *Homicide*. Hawthorne, NY: Aldine de Gruyter.

Daly, M., & Wilson, M. I. (1995). Discriminative parental solicitude and the relevance of evolutionary models to the analysis of motivational systems. In M. Gazzaniga (Ed.), *The Cognitive Neurosciences* (pp. 1269–1286). Cambridge, MA: MIT Press.

Daly, M., & Wilson, M. I. (in press). Evolutionary psychology and marital conflict: The relevance of stepchildren. In D. M. Buss & N. Malamuth (Eds.), *Sex, Power, Conflict: Feminist and Evolutionary Perspectives*. New York: Oxford University Press.

Symons, D. S. (1995). Beauty is in the adaptations of the beholder: The evolutionary psychology of human female sexual attractiveness. In P. R. Abramson & S. D. Pinkerton (Eds.), *Sexual Nature/Sexual Culture* (pp. 80–119). Chicago: University of Chicago Press.

Tooby, J., & Cosmides, L. (1992). The psychological foundations of culture. In J. H. Barkow, L. Cosmides, & J. Tooby (Eds.), *The Adapted Mind* (pp. 19–136). New York: Oxford University Press.

Williams, G. C. (1996). *Adaptation and Natural Selection*. Princeton, NJ: Princeton University Press.

Wilson, M. I., & Daly, M. (1992). The man who mistook his wife for a chattel. In J. H. Barkow, L. Cosmides, & J. Tooby (Eds.), *The Adapted Mind* (pp. 289–322). New York: Oxford University Press.

Wilson, M. I., & Daly, M. (1993). An evolutionary psychological perspective on male sexual proprietariness and violence against wives. *Violence & Victims, 8*, 271–294.

Wilson, M. I., Daly, M., & Scheib, J. (in press). Femicide: An evolutionary psychological perspective. In P. A. Gowaty (Ed.), *Evolutionary Biology and Feminism*. New York: Chapman and Hall.

Wilson, M. I., Johnson, H., & Daly, M. (1995). Lethal and nonlethal violence against wives. *Canadian Journal of Criminology, 37*, 331–361.

Exotic Becomes Erotic: A Developmental Theory of Sexual Orientation

Daryl J. Bem

Despite the rapid and impressive gains made by biological approaches to personality in recent years, some observers have found the results disappointing, for a couple of reasons. First, biological approaches to psychological issues too often have become reductionistic—treating the identification of a gene associated with a behavior as a complete explanation, for example, or even concluding that behavior and personality are "nothing but" by-products of a bioneurological system best explained in terms of anatomy and physiology. A second and related criticism of biological approaches is that they generally limit themselves to positing a biological cause on one hand, a psychological result on the other hand, and then showing that the two are connected. As we have seen, the biological cause might be testosterone, cortisol, one's DNA, or the evolutionary history of the species. And the behavioral result might be violence, overreaction to stress, one's degree of extraversion, or the murder of one's wife!

Although such demonstrations of connections between biology and behavior are interesting and useful, they typically leap over all the processes in between—the traditional domain of psychology. For example, what does it feel like to be a high-testosterone prison inmate, and how does that feeling affect your motivations? What is it, exactly, that develops in the DNA of two extraverted twins, and how does that interact with their early experiences to produce the people they eventually become? And what really goes on the mind of a wife murderer? These are the kinds of questions many people—including psychologists—expect psychology to address. But, as we have seen, biological approaches to personality typically neither answer nor ask questions like these.

The real potential for a biological approach to psychology, therefore, is for it to be integrated with psychological and social factors in a way that leads all the way and step by step from genetically based predeterminants, on the one hand, to important behavioral outcomes on the other. Such integration is yet rare, but a superb example is provided by the final selection in this section. The well-known social and personality psychologist Daryl Bem tackles the issue of sexual orientation—what makes a person turn out to be heterosexual or homosexual.

Although this article contains a wide range of interesting commentary on many issues, the heart of the theory is portrayed in a simple fashion in Figure 25.1. Notice how the development of sexual orientation begins with genes, prenatal hormones, and other purely biological variables. These variables produce the basic personality styles, evident in early childhood, called temperaments. These temperaments in turn lead to preferences and aversions to different kinds of activities. Since our gender-polarized society sees rough-and-tumble play as appropriate for boys but more sedate activities as appropriate for girls, the activity preferences of a given child quickly become identified as either appropriate or inappropriate to his or her gender. Depending on which kind of activities one prefers, one associates with either same-sex or opposite-sex peers, leading in turn to a viewing of the nonassociated sex as mysterious or, in Bem's term, "exotic." A basic biological mechanism then engages, which leads stimuli seen as exotic to become endowed with erotic appeal. Finally, one has eroticized either the opposite or same sex, and thus become either heterosexual or homosexual.

Bem's theory may be right or it may be wrong. Although he arrays an impressive amount of evidence in its favor, new theories as complex as this one have a small chance of being correct in their entirety. But the most important aspect of the theory is how it points the way for biological personality psychology in general. Unlike so many other biologically based explanations, Bem's is complete. Rather than leaping over the gap between biology and behavior, it explains how each link in a complex chain leads to an important attribute of the person.

From "Exotic Becomes Erotic: A Developmental Theory of Sexual Orientation," by D. J. Bem (1996). In *Psychological Review, 103*, 320–335. Copyright © 1996 by the American Psychological Association. Adapted with permission.

* * *

The question "What causes homosexuality?" is both politically suspect and scientifically misconceived. Politically suspect because it is so frequently motivated by an agenda of prevention and cure. Scientifically misconceived because it presumes that heterosexuality is so well understood, so obviously the "natural" evolutionary consequence of reproductive advantage, that only deviations from it are theoretically problematic. Freud himself did not so presume: "[Heterosexuality] is also a problem that needs elucidation and is not a self-evident fact based upon an attraction that is ultimately of a chemical nature" (1905/1962, pp. 11–12).

Accordingly, this article proposes a developmental theory of erotic/romantic attraction that provides the same basic account for both opposite-sex and same-sex desire—and for both men and women. In addition to finding such parsimony politically, scientifically, and aesthetically satisfying, I believe that it can also be sustained by the evidence.

The academic discourse on sexual orientation is currently dominated by the biological essentialists—who can point to a corpus of evidence linking sexual orientation to genes, prenatal hormones, and brain neuroanatomy—and the social constructionists—who can point to a corpus of historical and anthropological evidence showing that the very concept of sexual orientation is a culture-bound notion (De Cecco & Elia, 1993). The personality, clinical, and developmental theorists who once dominated the discourse on this topic have fallen conspicuously silent. Some have probably become closet converts to biology because they cannot point to a coherent corpus of evidence that supports an experience-based account of sexual orientation. This would be understandable; experience-based theories have not fared well empirically in recent years.

The most telling data come from an intensive, large-scale interview study conducted in the San Francisco Bay Area by the Kinsey Institute for Sex Research (Bell, Weinberg, & Hammersmith, 1981a). Using path analysis to test several developmental hypotheses,[1] the investigators compared approximately 1,000 gay men and lesbians with 500 heterosexual men and women. The study (hereinafter, the San Francisco study) yielded virtually no support for current experience-based accounts of sexual orientation. With respect to the classical psychoanalytic account, for example,

> our findings indicate that boys who grow up with dominant mothers and weak fathers have nearly the same chances of becoming homosexual as they would if they grew up in "ideal" family settings. Similarly, the idea that homosexuality reflects a failure to resolve boys' "Oedipal" feelings during childhood receives no support from our study. Our data indicate that the connection between boys' relationships with their mothers and whether they become homosexual or heterosexual is hardly worth mentioning. . . . [Similarly,] we found no evidence that prehomosexual girls are "Oedipal victors"—having apparently usurped their mothers' place in the fathers' affections. . . . [Finally,] respondents' identification with their opposite-sex parents while they were growing up appears to have had no significant impact on whether they turned out to be homosexual or heterosexual. (pp. 184, 189)

More generally, no family variables were strongly implicated in the development of sexual orientation for either men or women.[2]

The data also failed to support any of several possible accounts based on mechanisms of learning or conditioning, including the popular layperson's "seduction" theory of homosexuality. In particular, the kinds of sexual encounters that would presumably serve as the basis for such learning or conditioning typically occurred after, rather than before, the individual experienced the relevant sexual feelings. Gay men and lesbians, for example, had typically not participated in any "advanced" sexual activities with persons of the same sex until about 3 years after they had become aware of same-sex attractions. Moreover, they neither lacked opposite-sex sexual experiences during their childhood and adolescent years nor found them unpleasant.

And finally, there was no support for "labeling" theory, which suggests that individuals might adopt a homosexual orientation as a consequence of being labeled homosexual or sexually different by others as they were growing up. Although gay men and lesbians were, in fact, more likely to report that they had been so labeled, the path analysis revealed the differential labeling to be the result of an emerging homosexual orientation rather than a cause of or even a secondary contributor to it.

But before we all become geneticists, biopsychologists, or neuroanatomists, I believe it's worth another try. In particular, I believe that the theoretical and empirical building blocks for a coherent, experience-based developmental theory of sexual orientation are already scattered about in the literature. What follows, then, is an exercise in synthesis and construction—followed, in turn, by analysis and deconstruction.

---

[1] Path analysis is a statistical technique that evaluates numerous correlations in complex data sets to try to disentangle cause and effect.

[2] This is reminiscent of Plomin's conclusion, in the earlier selection, that shared family experience has a small impact on development.

Overview of the Theory

The theory proposed here claims to specify the causal antecedents of an individual's erotic or romantic attractions to opposite-sex and same-sex persons. In particular, Figure 25.1 displays the proposed temporal sequence of events that leads to sexual orientation for most men and women in a gender-polarizing culture like ours—a culture that emphasizes the differences between the sexes by pervasively organizing both the perceptions and realities of communal life around the male-female dichotomy (S. Bem, 1993). The sequence begins at the top of the figure with biological variables (labeled **A**) and ends at the bottom with erotic/romantic attraction (**F**).

A → B. Biological variables such as genes or prenatal hormones do not code for sexual orientation per se but for childhood temperaments, such as aggression or activity level.

B → C. A child's temperaments predispose him or her to enjoy some activities more than others. One child will enjoy rough-and-tumble play and competitive team sports (male-typical activities); another will prefer to socialize quietly or play jacks or hopscotch (female-typical activities). Children will also prefer to play with peers who share their activity preferences; for example, the child who enjoys baseball or football will selectively seek out boys as playmates. Children who prefer sex-typical activities and same-sex playmates are referred to as gender conforming; children who prefer sex-atypical activities and opposite-sex playmates are referred to as gender nonconforming.

C → D. Gender-conforming children will feel different from opposite-sex peers, perceiving them as dissimilar, unfamiliar, and exotic. Similarly, gender-nonconforming children will feel different—even alienated—from same-sex peers, perceiving them as dissimilar, unfamiliar, and exotic.

D → E. These feelings of dissimilarity and unfamiliarity produce heightened autonomic arousal. For the male-typical child, it may be felt as antipathy or contempt in the presence of girls ("girls are yucky"); for the female-typical child, it may be felt as timidity or apprehension in the presence of

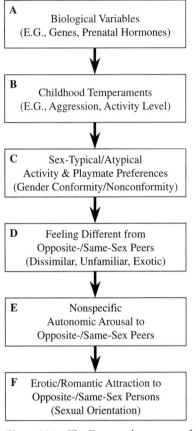

Figure 25.1 The Temporal sequence of events leading to sexual orientation for most men and women in a gender-polarizing culture

boys. A particularly clear example is provided by the "sissy" boy who is taunted by male peers for his gender nonconformity and, as a result, is likely to experience the strong autonomic arousal of fear and anger in their presence. Although girls are punished less than boys for gender nonconformity, a "tomboy" girl who is ostracized by her female peers may feel similar, affectively toned arousal in their presence. The theory claims, however, that every child, conforming or nonconforming, experiences heightened, nonspecific autonomic arousal in the presence of peers from whom he or she feels different. In this modal case,

TABLE 25.1

PERCENTAGE OF RESPONDENTS REPORTING GENDER-NONCONFORMING PREFERENCES AND
BEHAVIORS DURING CHILDHOOD

| | Men | | Women | |
| | Gay ($n = 686$) | Heterosexual ($n = 337$) | Lesbian ($n = 293$) | Heterosexual ($n = 140$) |
Response				
Had not enjoyed sex-typical activities	63	10	63	15
Had enjoyed sex-atypical activities	48	11	81	61
Atypical sex-typed (masculinity/femininity)	56	8	80	24
At least half of childhood friends were of the opposite sex	42	13	60	40

Note. Percentages have been calculated from the data given in Bell, Weinberg, and Hammersmith (1981b, pp. 74–75, 77). All chi-square comparisons between gay and heterosexual subgroups are significant at $p < .0001$.

the arousal will not necessarily be affectively toned or consciously felt.

E → F. Regardless of the specific source or affective tone of the childhood autonomic arousal, it is transformed in later years into erotic/romantic attraction. Steps **D → E** and **E → F** thus encompass specific psychological mechanisms that transform exotic into erotic (**D → F**). For brevity, the entire sequence outlined in Figure 25.1 will be referred to as the EBE (Exotic Becomes Erotic) theory of sexual orientation.

As noted above, Figure 25.1 does not describe an inevitable, universal path to sexual orientation but the modal path followed by most men and women in a gender-polarizing culture like ours. Individual variations, alternative paths, and cultural influences on sexual orientation are discussed in the final sections of the article.

Evidence for the Theory

Evidence for EBE theory is organized into the following narrative sequence: Gender conformity or nonconformity in childhood is a causal antecedent of sexual orientation in adulthood (**C → F**). This is so because gender conformity or nonconformity causes a child to perceive opposite or same sex

peers as exotic (**C → D**), and the exotic class of peers subsequently becomes erotically or romantically attractive to him or her (**D → F**). This occurs because exotic peers produce heightened autonomic arousal (**D → E**) which is subsequently transformed into erotic/romantic attraction (**E → F**). This entire sequence of events can be initiated, among other ways, by biological factors that influence a child's temperaments (**A → B**), which, in turn, influence his or her preferences for gender-conforming or gender-nonconforming activities and peers (**B → C**).

GENDER CONFORMITY OR NONCONFORMITY IN CHILDHOOD IS A CAUSAL ANTECEDENT OF SEXUAL ORIENTATION (**C → F**) In a review of sex-role socialization in 1980, Serbin asserted that "there is no evidence that highly sex-typed children are less likely to become homosexual than children showing less extreme sex-role conformity" (p. 85).

Well, there is now. In the San Francisco study, childhood gender conformity or nonconformity was not only the strongest but the only significant childhood predictor of later sexual orientation for both men and women (Bell et al., 1981a). As Table 25.1 shows, the effects were large and significant. For example, gay men were significantly more likely than heterosexual men to report that as children they had not enjoyed boys' activities (e.g., baseball and football), had enjoyed girls' activities (e.g., hopscotch, playing house, and jacks), and had been nonmasculine. These were the three variables that defined gender nonconformity in the study. Additionally, gay men were more likely than heterosexual men to have had girls as childhood friends. The corresponding comparisons between lesbian and heterosexual women were also large and significant. Moreover, the path analyses implied that gender conformity or nonconformity in childhood was a causal antecedent of later sexual orientation for both men and women—with the usual caveat that even path analysis cannot "prove" causality.

It is also clear from the table that relatively more women than men had enjoyed sex-atypical activities and had opposite-sex friends during childhood. (In fact, more heterosexual women than gay men had enjoyed boys' activities as children—61% versus 37%, respectively.) As I suggest later, this might account, in part, for differences between men and women in how their sexual orientations are distributed in our society.

The San Francisco study does not stand alone. A meta-analysis of 48 studies with sample sizes ranging from 34 to 8,751 confirmed that gay men and lesbians were more likely to recall gender-nonconforming behaviors and interests in childhood than were heterosexual men and women (Bailey & Zucker, 1995). The differences were large and significant for both men and women, ranging (in units of standard deviation) from 0.5 to 2.1 across studies, with means of 1.31 and 0.96 for men and women, respectively. As the authors noted, "these are among the largest effect sizes ever reported in the realm of sex-dimorphic behaviors" (p. 49).[3]

Prospective studies have come to the same conclusion. The largest of these involved a sample of 66 gender-nonconforming and 56 gender-conforming boys with a mean age of 7.1 years

(Green, 1987). The researchers were able to assess about two thirds of each group in late adolescence or early adulthood, finding that about 75% of the previously gender-nonconforming boys were either bisexual or homosexual compared with only one (4%) of the gender-conforming boys. In six other prospective studies, 63% of gender-nonconforming boys whose sexual orientations could be ascertained in late adolescence or adulthood had homosexual orientations (Zucker, 1990). Unfortunately, there are no prospective studies of gender-nonconforming girls.

This body of data has led one researcher in the field to assert that the link between childhood gender nonconformity and an adult homosexual orientation "may be the most consistent, well-documented, and significant finding in the entire field of sexual-orientation research and perhaps in all of human psychology" (Hamer & Copeland, 1994, p. 166). That may be a bit hyperbolic —Hamer is a molecular geneticist, not a psychologist—but it is difficult to think of other individual differences (besides IQ or sex itself) that so reliably and so strongly predict socially significant outcomes across the life span, and for both sexes, too. Surely it must be true.

GENDER CONFORMITY AND NONCONFORMITY PRODUCE FEELINGS OF BEING DIFFERENT FROM OPPOSITE AND SAME-SEX PEERS, RESPECTIVELY (C → D) EBE theory proposes that gender-conforming children will come to feel different from their opposite-sex peers and gender-nonconforming children will come to feel different from their same-sex peers. To my knowledge, no researcher has ever asked children or adults whether they feel different from opposite-sex peers, probably because they expect the universal answer to be yes. The San Francisco researchers, however, did ask respondents whether they felt different from same-sex peers in childhood. They found that 71% of gay men and 70% of lesbian women recalled having felt different from same-sex children during the grade-school years, compared with 38% and 51% of heterosexual men and

---

[3]In other words, these differences are as large or larger than sex differences in general usually are.

women, respectively ($p < .0005$ for both gay/heterosexual comparisons).

When asked in what way they felt different, gay men were most likely to say that they did not like sports; lesbians were most likely to say that they were more interested in sports or were more masculine than other girls. In contrast, the heterosexual men and women who had felt different from their same-sex peers in childhood typically cited differences unrelated to gender. Heterosexual men tended to cite such reasons as being poorer, more intelligent, or more introverted. Heterosexual women frequently cited differences in physical appearance.

Finally, the data showed that the gender-nonconforming child's sense of being different from same-sex peers is not a fleeting early experience but a protracted and sustained feeling throughout childhood and adolescence. For example, in the path model for men, gender nonconformity in childhood was also a significant predictor of feeling different for gender reasons during adolescence (which was, in turn, a significant predictor of a homosexual orientation). Similarly, the statistically significant difference between the lesbians and heterosexual women in feeling different from same-sex peers during childhood remained significant during adolescence. This is, I believe, why sexual orientation displays such strong temporal stability across the life course for most individuals.

EXOTIC BECOMES EROTIC (D ➞ F) The heart of EBE theory is the proposition that individuals become erotically or romantically attracted to those who were dissimilar or unfamiliar to them in childhood. We have already seen some evidence for this in Table 25.1: Those who played more with girls in childhood, gay men and heterosexual women, preferred men as sexual/romantic partners in later years; those who played more with boys in childhood, lesbian women and heterosexual men, preferred women as sexual/romantic partners in later years. As we shall now see, however, the links between similarity and erotic/romantic attraction are complex.

Similarity and complementarity. One of the most widely accepted conclusions in social psychology, cited in virtually every textbook, is that similarity promotes interpersonal attraction and that complementarity ("opposites attract") does not.

For example, the vast majority of married couples in the United States are of the same race and religion, and most are significantly similar in age, socioeconomic class, educational level, intelligence, height, eye color, and even physical attractiveness (Feingold, 1988; Murstein, 1972; Rubin, 1973; Silverman, 1971). In one study, dating couples who were the most similar were the most likely to be together a year later (Hill, Rubin, & Peplau, 1976). In a longitudinal study of 135 married couples, spouses with similar personalities reported more closeness, friendliness, shared enjoyment in daily activities, marital satisfaction, and less marital conflict than less similar couples (Caspi & Herbener, 1990). In contrast, attempts to identify complementarities that promote or sustain intimate relationships have not been very successful (Levinger, Senn, & Jorgensen, 1970; Strong et al., 1988). Marital adjustment among couples married for up to 5 years was found to depend more on similarity than on complementarity (Meyer & Pepper, 1977).

But there is an obvious exception: sex. Most people choose members of the opposite sex to be their romantic and sexual partners. It is an indication of how unthinkingly heterosexuality is taken for granted that authors of articles and textbooks never seem to notice this quintessential complementarity and its challenge to the conclusion that similarity produces attraction. They certainly don't pause to ponder why we are not all gay or lesbian.

The key to resolving this apparent paradox is also a staple of textbooks: the distinction between liking and loving or between companionate and passionate love (Berscheid & Walster, 1974; Brehm, 1992). The correlation among dating or engaged couples between liking their partners and loving them is only .56 for men and .36 for women (Rubin, 1973). Both fiction and real life provide numerous examples of erotic attraction between two incompatible people who may not even like each other. Collectively, these observations suggest that similarity may promote friendship, compatibility, and companionate love, but it is dissimilarity that sparks erotic/romantic attraction and passionate love.

This is the resolution proposed by both Tripp (1975) and Bell (1982), the senior author of the San Francisco study:

> a necessary ingredient for romantic attachment is one's perception of the loved one as essentially different from oneself in terms of gender-related attributes. According to this view it would be argued that, among homosexuals and heterosexuals alike, persons perceived as essentially *different* from ourselves become the chief candidates for our early romantic and, later, erotic investments. Only a superficial view of the matter would maintain that *heterogamy*, as it has been called, operates only among heterosexuals where anatomical differences make the principle, "opposites attract," most obvious. Among both groups we find romantic and sexual feelings aroused by others perceived to be different from ourselves, unfamiliar in manner, attitude, and interests, and whose differences offer the possibility of a relationship based upon psychological (not necessarily genital) complementarity. On the other side of the coin is the principle of *homogamy* in which perceived similarity and mutual identification and familiarity makes for friendship as opposed to the romantic . . . state. (Bell, 1982, p. 2)

But this account fails to resolve the paradox because it errs in the opposite direction, failing to account for the previously cited evidence that, except for sex itself, it is similarity and not complementarity that sustains the majority of successful heterosexual relationships. Similarly, for every gay or lesbian relationship that conforms to the "butch-femme" stereotype of the popular imagination, there appear to be many more in which the partners are strikingly similar to each other in both psychological and physical attributes—including sex. Bell's account resolves the paradox only if one is willing to accept the implausible im-

plication that all those happy, similar partners must be devoid of erotic enthusiasm for each other.

Like the accounts of Tripp and Bell, EBE theory also proposes that dissimilarity promotes erotic/romantic attraction, but it locates the animating dissimilarity in childhood. Consider, for example, a gender-nonconforming boy whose emerging homoeroticism happens to crystallize around the muscular athlete or leather-jacketed motorcyclist. As he moves into adolescence and adulthood, he may deliberately begin to acquire the attributes and trappings of his eroticized hypermasculine ideal—working out at the gym, buying a leather jacket, getting a body tattoo, and so forth. This acquired "macho" image is not only self-satisfying but is also attractive to other gay men who have eroticized this same idealized image. Two such men will thus be erotically attracted to each other, and their striking similarities, including their shared eroticism, will have been produced by their shared childhood dissimilarities from highly masculine boys.

EBE theory thus proposes that once the dissimilarities of childhood have laid the groundwork for a sustained sexual orientation, the noncriterial attributes of one's preferred partners within the eroticized class can range from extremely similar to extremely dissimilar. More generally, the theory proposes that the protracted period of feeling different from same- or opposite-sex peers during childhood and adolescence produces a stable sexual orientation for most individuals but that within that orientation there can be wide ranging—and changing—idiosyncratic preferences for particular partners or kinds of partners.

Familiarity and unfamiliarity. Like similarity, familiarity is a major antecedent of liking. In fact, similarity probably promotes liking precisely because it increases familiarity: Social norms, situational circumstances, and mutual interests conspire to bring people together who are similar to one another, thereby increasing their mutual familiarity. When college roommates were systematically paired for similarity or dissimilarity in Newcomb's (1961) ambitious 2-year study of the acquaintance process, familiarity turned out to be a stronger facilitator of liking than similarity.

The "familiarity-breeds-liking" effect has been confirmed in so many contexts that it is now considered to be a general psychological principle. For example, rats repeatedly exposed to compositions by Mozart or Schönberg have shown an enhanced preference for the composer they heard, and humans repeatedly exposed to nonsense syllables, Chinese characters, or real people have come to prefer those they saw most often (Harrison, 1977).

But like childhood similarity, childhood familiarity does not produce erotic or romantic attraction; on the contrary, it appears to be antithetical to it. This was observed over a century ago by Westermarck (1891), who noted that two individuals who spent their childhood years together did not find each other sexually attractive even when there were strong social pressures favoring a bond between them. For example, he reported problematic sexual relations in arranged marriages in which the couple was betrothed in childhood and the girl was taken in by the future husband's family and treated like one of the siblings; similar findings have emerged from more recent studies of arranged marriages in Taiwan (cited in Bateson, 1978a).

A contemporary example is provided by children on Israeli kibbutzim, who are raised communally with age-mates in mixed-sex groups and exposed to one another constantly during their entire childhood. Sex play is not discouraged and is quite intensive during early childhood. After childhood, there is no formal or informal pressure or sanction against heterosexual activity within the peer group from educators, parents, or members of the peer group itself. Yet despite all this, there is a virtual absence of erotic attraction between peer group members in adolescence or adulthood (Bettelheim, 1969; Rabin, 1965; Shepher, 1971; Spiro, 1958; Talmon, 1964). A review of nearly 3,000 marriages contracted by second-generation adults in all Israeli kibbutzim revealed that there was not a single case of an intrapeer group marriage (Shepher, 1971).

* * *

The Sambian culture in New Guinea illustrates the phenomenon in a homosexual context. As described by Herdt in several publications (1981, 1984, 1987, 1990), Sambian males believe that boys cannot attain manhood without ingesting semen from older males. At age 7 years, Sambian boys are removed from the family household and initiated into secret male rituals, including ritualized homosexuality. For the next several years, they live in the men's clubhouse and regularly fellate older male adolescents. When they reach sexual maturity, they reverse roles and are fellated by younger initiates. During this entire time, they have no sexual contact with girls or women. And yet, when it comes time to marry and father children in their late teens or early twenties, all but a tiny minority of Sambian males become preferentially and exclusively heterosexual. Although Sambian boys enjoy their homosexual activities, the context of close familiarity in which it occurs either extinguishes or prevents the development of strongly charged homoerotic feelings.

During the years that a Sambian boy is participating in homosexual activities with his male peers, he is taught a misogynist ideology that portrays women as dangerous and exotic creatures—almost a different species. According to EBE theory, this should enhance their erotic attractiveness for him. More generally, EBE theory proposes that heterosexuality is the modal outcome across time and culture because virtually all human societies polarize the sexes to some extent, setting up a sex-based division of labor and power, emphasizing or exaggerating sex differences, and, in general, superimposing the male-female dichotomy on virtually every aspect of communal life. These gender-polarizing practices ensure that most boys and girls will grow up seeing the other sex as dissimilar, unfamiliar, and exotic—and, hence, erotic. Thus, the theory provides a culturally based alternative to the assumption that heterosexuality must necessarily be coded in the genes. I return to this point later.

Finally, the assertion that exotic becomes erotic should be amended to exotic—but not too exotic—becomes erotic (cf. Tripp, 1987). Thus, an erotic or romantic preference for partners of a different sex, race, or ethnicity is relatively common, but a preference for lying with the beasts in the field is not. This phenomenon appears to be a special case of the well-established motivational principle that there is an optimal, nonzero level of stimulus novelty and a correspondingly optimal nonzero level of internal arousal that an organism will seek to attain or maintain (Mook, 1987).

HOW DOES EXOTIC BECOME EROTIC? (D → E → F) In Plato's *Symposium*, Aristophanes explains sexual attraction by recounting the early history of human beings. Originally, we were all eight-limbed creatures with two faces and two sets of genitals. Males had two sets of male genitals, females had two sets of female genitals, and androgynes had one set of each kind. As punishment for being overly ambitious, Zeus had all humans cut in half. But because the two halves of each former individual clung to each other in such a desperate attempt to reunite, Zeus took pity on them and invented sexual intercourse so that they might at least reunite temporarily. Sexual attraction thus reflects an attempt to complete one's original self, and heterosexual attraction is what characterizes the descendents of the androgynes.

It is a durable myth. Both Bell (1982) and Tripp (1987) propose that we are erotically attracted to people who are different from us because we are embarked on a "quest for androgyny" (Bell); we seek to complete ourselves by "importing" gender-related attributes that we perceive ourselves as lacking (Tripp). As noted earlier, I do not believe this accurately characterizes the data; but even if it did, it would constitute only a description of them, not an explanation. There may not be much evidence for Aristophanes' historical account, but epistemologically at least, it is an explanation.

Because I prefer mechanism to metaphor, EBE theory is unabashedly reductionistic. As already discussed, it proposes that exotic becomes erotic because feelings of dissimilarity and unfamiliarity in childhood produce heightened nonspecific

autonomic arousal (D → E) which is subsequently transformed into erotic/romantic attraction (E → F). To my knowledge, there is no direct evidence for the first step in this sequence beyond the well-documented observation that novelty and unfamiliarity produce heightened arousal (Mook, 1987); filling in this empirical gap in EBE theory must await future research. In contrast, there are at least three mechanisms that can potentially effect the second step, transforming generalized arousal into erotic/romantic attraction: the extrinsic arousal effect, the opponent process, and imprinting.[4]

The extrinsic arousal effect. In his 1st-century Roman handbook, *The Art of Love*, Ovid advised any man who was interested in sexual seduction to take the woman in whom he was interested to a gladiatorial tournament, where she would more easily be aroused to passion. He did not say why this should be so, however, and it was not until 1887 that an elaboration appeared in the literature:

> Love can only be excited by strong and vivid emotion, and it is almost immaterial whether these emotions are agreeable or disagreeable. The Cid wooed the proud heart of Donna Ximene, whose father he had slain, by shooting one after another of her pet pigeons. (Horwicz, quoted in Finck, 1887, p. 240)

A contemporary explanation of this effect was introduced by Walster (1971; Berscheid & Walster, 1974), who suggested that it constituted a special case of Schachter and Singer's (1962) two-factor theory of emotion. That theory states that the physiological arousal of our autonomic nervous system provides the cues that we are feeling emotional but that the more subtle judgment of which emotion we are feeling often depends on our cognitive appraisal of the surrounding circumstances. According to Walster, then, the experience of passionate love or erotic/romantic attraction results from the conjunction of physiological arousal and

---

[4]Bem's discussion of "imprinting" and the "opponent process" are not included in this excerpt.

the cognitive causal attribution (or misattribution) that the arousal has been elicited by the potential lover.

There is now extensive experimental evidence that an individual who has been physiologically aroused will show heightened sexual responsiveness to an appropriate target stimulus. In one set of studies, male participants were physiologically aroused by running in place, by hearing an audiotape of a comedy routine, or by hearing an audiotape of a grisly killing (White, Fishbein, & Rutstein, 1981). They then viewed a taped interview with a woman who was either physically attractive or physically unattractive. Finally, they rated the woman on several dimensions, including her attractiveness, her sexiness, and the degree to which they would be interested in dating her and kissing her. The results showed that no matter how the arousal had been elicited, participants were more erotically responsive to the attractive woman and less erotically responsive to the unattractive women than were control participants who had not been aroused. In other words, the arousal intensified both positive or negative reactions to the woman, depending on which was cognitively appropriate.

This extrinsic arousal effect (my term) is not limited to the individual's cognitive appraisal of his or her emotional state. In two studies, men or women watched a sequence of two videotapes. The first portrayed either an anxiety-inducing or non-anxiety-inducing scene; the second videotape portrayed a nude heterosexual couple engaging in sexual foreplay. Preexposure to the anxiety-inducing scene produced greater penile tumescence in men and greater vaginal blood volume increases in women in response to the erotic scene than did preexposure to the non-anxiety-inducing scene (Hoon, Wincze, & Hoon, 1977; Wolchik et al., 1980).

In addition to the misattribution explanation, several other explanations for the extrinsic arousal effect have been proposed, but experimental attempts to determine which explanation is the most valid have produced mixed results and the dispute is not yet settled (Allen, Kenrick, Linder, &

McCall, 1989; Kenrick & Cialdini, 1977; McClanahan, Gold, Lenney, Ryckman, & Kulberg, 1990; White & Kight, 1984; Zillmann, 1983). For present purposes, however, it doesn't matter. It is sufficient to know that autonomic arousal, regardless of its source or affective tone, can subsequently be experienced cognitively, emotionally, and physiologically as erotic/romantic attraction. At that point, it *is* erotic/romantic attraction.

The pertinent question, then, is whether this effect can account for the link between autonomic arousal in childhood and erotic/romantic attraction later in life. In one respect, the experiments may actually underestimate the strength and reliability of the effect in real life. In the experiments, the arousal is deliberately elicited by a source extrinsic to the intended target, and there is disagreement over whether the effect even occurs when participants are aware of that fact (Allen et al., 1989; Cantor, Zillmann, & Bryant, 1975; McClanahan et al., 1990; White & Kight, 1984). But in the real-life scenario envisioned by EBE theory, the autonomic arousal is genuinely elicited by the class of individuals to which the erotic/romantic attraction develops. The exotic arousal and the erotic arousal are thus likely to be phenomenologically indistinguishable.

*   *   *

THE BIOLOGICAL CONNECTION: (A → F) VERSUS (A → B) In recent years, researchers, the mass media, and segments of the lesbian/gay/bisexual community have rushed to embrace the thesis that a homosexual orientation is coded in the genes or determined by prenatal hormones and brain neuroanatomy. Even the authors of the San Francisco study, whose findings disconfirm most experience-based theories of sexual orientation, seem ready to concede the ball game to biology. In contrast, EBE theory proposes that biological factors influence sexual orientation only indirectly, by intervening earlier in the chain of events to determine a child's temperaments and subsequent activity preferences. Accordingly, my persuasive task in this section is to argue that any nonartifactual correlation between a biological factor and sexual orientation is more plausibly attributed to its influence in early childhood than to a direct link with sexual orientation.

Genes. Recent studies have provided some evidence for a correlation between an individual's genotype and his or her sexual orientation. For example, in a sample of 115 gay men who had male twins, 52% of monozygotic twin brothers were also gay compared with only 22% of dizygotic twin brothers and 11% of gay men's adoptive brothers (Bailey & Pillard, 1991). In a comparable sample of 115 lesbians, 48% of monozygotic twin sisters were also lesbian compared with only 16% of dizygotic twin sisters and 6% of lesbian women's adoptive sisters (Bailey, Pillard, Neale, & Agyei, 1993). A subsequent study of nearly 5,000 twins who had been systematically drawn from a twin registry confirmed the significant heritability of sexual orientation for men but not for women (Bailey & Martin, 1995). And finally, a pedigree and linkage analysis of 114 families of gay men and a DNA linkage analysis of 40 families in which there were two gay brothers suggested a correlation between a homosexual orientation and the inheritance of genetic markers on the X chromosome (Hamer & Copeland, 1994; Hamer, Hu, Magnuson, Hu, & Pattatucci, 1993).[5]

But these same studies have also provided evidence for the link proposed by EBE theory between an individual's genotype and his or her childhood gender nonconformity, even when sexual orientation is held constant. For example, in the 1991 twin study of gay men, childhood gender nonconformity was assessed by a composite of three scales that have been shown to discriminate between gay and heterosexual men: childhood aggressiveness, interest in sports, and effeminacy. Across twin pairs in which both brothers were gay ("concordant" pairs), the correlation on gender nonconformity for monozygotic twins was as high as the reliability of the scale would permit,

.76 ($p < .0001$), compared with a correlation of only .43 for concordant dizygotic twins, implying significant heritability (Bailey & Pillard, 1991). In the family pedigree study of gay men, pairs of gay brothers who were concordant for the genetic markers on the X chromosome were also more similar on gender nonconformity than were genetically discordant pairs of gay brothers (Hamer & Copeland, 1994). Finally, childhood gender nonconformity was significantly heritable for both men and women in the large twin registry study, even though sexual orientation itself was not heritable for the women (Bailey & Martin, 1995).

These studies are thus consistent with the link specified by EBE theory between the genotype and gender nonconformity ($\mathbf{A \rightarrow C}$). The theory further specifies that this link is composed of two parts, a link between the genotype and childhood temperaments ($\mathbf{A \rightarrow B}$) and a link between those temperaments and gender nonconformity ($\mathbf{B \rightarrow C}$). This implies that the mediating temperaments should possess three characteristics: First, they should be plausibly related to those play activities that define gender conformity and nonconformity. Second, because they manifest themselves in sex-typed preferences, they should show sex differences. And third, because they are hypothesized to derive from the genotype, they should have significant heritabilities.

One likely candidate is aggression and its benign cousin, rough-and-tumble play. As noted above, gay men score lower than heterosexual men on a measure of childhood aggression (Blanchard, McConkey, Roper, & Steiner, 1983), and parents of gender-nonconforming boys specifically rate them as having less interest in rough-and-tumble play than do parents of gender-conforming boys (Green, 1976). Second, the sex difference in aggression during childhood is about half a standard deviation, one of the largest psychological sex differences known (Hyde, 1984). Rough-and-tumble play in particular is more common in boys than in girls (DiPietro, 1981; Fry, 1990; Moller, Hymel, & Rubin, 1992). And third, individual differences in aggression have a large heritable component (Rushton, Fulker, Neale, Nias, & Eysenck, 1986).

---

[5]This last finding is currently in dispute, and an independent attempt to replicate it has failed (Rice, Anderson, Risch, & Ebers, 1995).—Author

Another likely candidate is activity level, considered to be one of the basic childhood temperaments (Buss & Plomin, 1975, 1984). Like aggression, differences in activity level would also seem to characterize the differences between male-typical and female-typical play activities in childhood, and gender-nonconforming boys and girls are lower and higher on activity level, respectively, than are control children of the same sex (Bates, Bentler, & Thompson, 1973, 1979; Zucker & Green, 1993). Second, the sex difference in activity level is as large as it is for aggression. A meta-analysis of 127 studies found boys to be about half a standard deviation more active than girls. Even before birth, boys in utero are about one-third of a standard deviation more active than girls (Eaton & Enns, 1986). And third, individual differences in activity level have a large heritable component (Plomin, 1986).

In sum, existing data are consistent with both a direct path between the genotype and sexual orientation and the EBE path which channels genetic influence through the child's temperaments and subsequent activity preferences. So why should one prefer the EBE account?

The missing theory for the direct path. The EBE account may be wrong, but I submit that a competing theoretical rationale for a direct path between the genotype and sexual orientation has not even been clearly articulated, let alone established. At first glance, the theoretical rationale would appear to be nothing less than the powerful and elegant theory of evolution. The belief that sexual orientation is coded in the genes would appear to be just the general case of the implicit assumption, mentioned in the introduction, that heterosexuality is the obvious, "natural" evolutionary consequence of reproductive advantage.

But if that is true, then a homosexual orientation is an evolutionary anomaly that requires further theoretical explication. How do lesbians and gay men manage to pass on their gene pool to successive generations? Several hypothetical scenarios have been offered (for a review, see Savin-Williams, 1987). One is that social institu-

tions such as universal marriage can ensure that lesbians and gay men will have enough children to sustain a "homosexual" gene pool (Weinrich, 1987). Another is that the genes for homosexuality are linked to, or piggyback on, other genes that themselves carry reproductive advantage, such as genes for intelligence or dominance (Kirsch & Rodman, 1982; Weinrich, 1978). A third, based on kin selection, speculates that homosexual individuals may help nurture a sufficient number of their kin (e.g., nieces and nephews) to reproductive maturity to ensure that their genes get passed along to successive generations (Weinrich, 1978; Wilson, 1975, 1978).

Although these speculations have been faulted on theoretical, metatheoretical, and empirical grounds (Futuyma & Risch, 1983/84), a more basic problem with such arguments is their circularity. As Bleier has noted about similar accounts,

> this logic makes a *premise* of the genetic basis of behaviors, then cites a certain animal or human behavior, constructs a speculative story to explain how the behavior (*if* it were genetically based) could have served or could serve to maximize the reproductive success of the individual, and this *conjecture* then becomes evidence for the *premise* that the behavior was genetically determined. (1984, p. 17)

When one does attempt to deconstruct the evolutionary explanation for sexual orientation, homosexual *or* heterosexual, some problematic assumptions become explicit. For example, the belief that sexual orientation is coded in the genes embodies the unacknowledged assumption that knowledge of the distinction between male and female must also be hardwired into the human species, that sex is a natural category of human perception. After all, we cannot be erotically attracted to a class of persons unless and until we can discriminate exemplars from nonexemplars of that class.

Given what psychology has learned about human language and cognition in recent decades, the notion that humans have innate knowledge of the male-female distinction is not quite so inconceivable as it once was. An explicit version of this notion is embodied in the Jungian belief that an animus-anima archetype is part of our collective unconscious. It could also be argued that functional, if not cognitive, knowledge of the male-female distinction is embodied in innate responses to pheromones or other sensory cues, as it is for several other species.

As it happens, I find all these possibilities implausible, but that is not the point. Rather, it is that those who argue for the direct heritability of sexual orientation should be made cognizant of such assumptions and required to shoulder the burden of proof for them. More generally, any genetic argument, including a sociobiological one, must spell out the developmental pathway by which genotypes are transformed into phenotypes (Bronfenbrenner & Ceci, 1994). This is precisely what EBE theory attempts to do and what the competing claim for a direct path between genes and sexual orientation fails to do. It is not that an argument for a direct path has been made and found wanting, but that it has not yet been made.

I am certainly willing to concede that heterosexual behavior is reproductively advantageous, but it does not follow that it must therefore be sustained through genetic transmission. As noted earlier, EBE theory implies that heterosexuality is the modal outcome across time and culture because virtually every human society ensures that most boys and girls will grow up seeing the other sex as exotic and, hence, erotic.

The more general point is that as long as the environment supports or promotes a reproductively successful behavior sufficiently often, it will not necessarily get programmed into the genes. For example, it is presumably reproductively advantageous for ducks to mate with other ducks, but as long as most baby ducklings encounter other ducks before they encounter an ethologist, evolution can simply implant the imprinting process itself into the species rather than the specific content of what, reproductively speaking, needs to be imprinted. Analogously, because most cultures ensure that the two sexes will see each other as exotic, it would be sufficient for evolution to implant exotic-becomes-erotic processes into our

species rather than heterosexuality per se. In fact, as noted earlier, an exotic-becomes-erotic mechanism is actually a component of sexual imprinting. If ducks, who are genetically free to mate with any moving object, have not perished from the earth, then neither shall we.

Prenatal hormones. One of the oldest hypotheses about sexual orientation is that gay men have too little testosterone and lesbians have too much. When the data failed to support this hypothesis (for reviews, see Gartrell, 1982, and Meyer-Bahlburg, 1984), attention turned from adult hormonal status to prenatal hormonal status. Reasoning from research on rats in which the experimental manipulation of prenatal androgen levels can "masculinize" or "feminize" the brain and produce sex-atypical mating postures and mounting responses, some researchers hypothesized that human males who are exposed prenatally to substantially lower than average amounts of testosterone and human females who are exposed to substantially higher than average amounts of testosterone will be predisposed toward a homosexual orientation in adult life (Ellis & Ames, 1987).

One body of data advanced in support of this hypothesis comes from interviews with women who have congenital adrenal hyperplasia (CAH), a chronic endocrine disorder that exposes them to abnormally high levels of androgen during the prenatal period, levels comparable to those received by normal male fetuses during gestation. Most of these women were born with virilized genitalia, which were surgically corrected soon after birth, and placed on cortisol medication to prevent further anatomical virilization. In three studies, CAH women have now reported more bisexual or homosexual responsiveness than control women (Dittmann et al., 1990a; Money, Schwartz, & Lewis, 1984; Zucker et al., 1992).

But a number of factors suggest that this link from prenatal hormones to sexual orientation is better explained by their effects on childhood temperaments and activity preferences. For example, both boys and girls who were exposed to high levels of androgenizing progestins during gestation show have shown increased aggression later in childhood (Reinisch, 1981), and girls with CAH have shown stronger preferences for male-typical activities and male playmates in childhood than control girls (Berenbaum & Hines, 1992; Berenbaum & Snyder, 1995; Dittmann et al., 1990b; Money & Ehrhardt, 1972).

It is also possible that the correlation itself is artifactual, having nothing to do with prenatal hormonal exposure—let alone ''masculinization'' of the brain. The contemporaneous hormonal status of CAH girls could be producing some of these childhood effects. It is even conceivable that the cortisol medication could be increasing their activity level, thereby promoting their preference for male-typical activities (Quadagno, Briscoe, & Quadagno, 1977).

But from the perspective of EBE theory, the major reason for expecting CAH girls to be disproportionately homoerotic in adulthood is that they are overwhelmingly likely to feel different from other girls. Not only are they gender nonconforming in their play activities and peer preferences, as most lesbians are during the childhood years, but the salience of their CAH status itself aids and abets their perception of being different from other girls on gender-relevant dimensions. For example, they know about their virilized genitalia and they may be concerned that they will not be able to conceive and bear children when they grow up, one of the frequent complications of the CAH disorder. According to EBE theory, these are not girls who need masculinized brains to make them homoerotic.

A more critical test of the direct link between prenatal hormones and sexual orientation would seem to require a prenatal hormonal condition that is correlated with an adult homosexual orientation but uncorrelated with any of these childhood effects. Meyer-Bahlburg et al. (1995) have hypothesized that abnormally high levels of prenatal estrogens might produce such an outcome in women by masculinizing their brains.

Although the theoretical reasoning behind this hypothesis has been questioned (Byne & Parsons, 1993), Meyer-Bahlburg et al. (1995) cited some supporting evidence from women whose mothers had taken diethylstilbestrol (DES), a synthetic estrogen that was used to maintain high-risk pregnancies until it was banned in 1971. Three samples of such women have now been interviewed and rated on several Kinsey-like scales for heterosexual and homosexual responsiveness. According to the investigators, ''more DES-exposed women than controls were rated as bisexual or homosexual . . .'' (p. 12). Because DES does not produce any visible anomalies during childhood and evidence for childhood gender nonconformity among DES-exposed women was weak, this outcome would seem to favor the argument for a direct link between prenatal hormones and sexual orientation over the EBE account.

But the evidence for a bisexual or homosexual orientation among the DES-exposed women was also very weak. As Meyer-Bahlburg et al. (1995) themselves noted, ''the majority of DES-exposed women in our study were exclusively or nearly exclusively heterosexual, in spite of their prenatal DES exposure'' (p. 20). In fact, of 97 DES-exposed women interviewed, only 4 were rated as having a predominantly homosexual orientation, and not a single woman was rated as having an exclusively homosexual orientation. I think the jury is still out on the link between prenatal estrogens and sexual orientation.

* * *

Neuroanatomical correlates of sexual orientation. Even the general public now knows that there are neuroanatomical differences between the brains of gay men and those of heterosexual men and that some of these correspond to differences between the brains of women and men (Allen & Gorski, 1992; LeVay, 1991, 1993; Swaab & Hofman, 1990). Gay men also perform less well than heterosexual men on some cognitive, motor, and spatial tasks on which women perform less well than men (e.g., Gladue, Beatty, Larson, & Staton, 1990; McCormick & Witelson, 1991). (There are no comparable studies of lesbian women.)

But such differences are also consistent with the EBE account. Any biological factor that correlates with one or more of the intervening processes proposed by EBE theory could also emerge as a correlate of sexual orientation. For example, any neuroanatomical feature of the brain that correlates with childhood aggression or activity level could also emerge as a difference between gay men and heterosexual men, between women and men, and between heterosexual women and lesbians. Even if EBE theory turns out to be wrong, the more general point, that a mediating personality variable could account for observed correlations between biological variables and sexual orientation, still holds.

Like all well-bred scientists, biologically oriented researchers in the field of sexual orientation dutifully murmur the mandatory mantra that correlation is not cause. But the reductive temptation of biological causation is so seductive that the caveat cannot possibly compete with the excitement of discovering yet another link between the anatomy of our brains and the anatomy of our lovers' genitalia. Unfortunately, the caveat vanishes completely as word of the latest discovery moves from *Science* to *Newsweek*. The public can be forgiven for believing that research is but one government grant away from pinpointing the penis preference gene.

INDIVIDUAL VARIATIONS AND ALTERNATIVE PATHS As noted earlier, Figure 25.1 is not intended to describe an inevitable, universal path to sexual orientation but only the modal path followed by most men and women in a gender-polarizing culture like ours. Individual variations can arise in several ways. First, different individuals might enter the EBE path at different points in the sequence. For example, a child might come to feel different from same-sex peers not because of a temperamentally induced preference for gender-nonconforming activities but because of an atypical lack of contact with same-sex peers, a physical disability, or an illness (e.g., the CAH girls). Similarly, I noted earlier that the nonmasculine lesbians in the San Francisco study were not significantly gender nonconforming in childhood. But they were more likely than heterosexual

women to have mostly male friends in grade school, and, consistent with the subsequent steps in the EBE path, this was the strongest predictor for these women of homosexual involvements in adolescence and a homosexual orientation in adulthood.

In general, EBE theory predicts that the effect of any childhood variable on an individual's sexual orientation depends on whether it prompts him or her to feel more similar to or more different from same-sex or opposite-sex peers. For example, it has recently been reported that a gay man is likely to have more older brothers than a heterosexual man (Blanchard & Bogaert, 1996). This could come about, in part, if having gender-conforming older brothers especially enhances a gender-nonconforming boy's sense of being different from other boys.

Individual variations can also arise from differences in how individuals interpret the "exotic" arousal emerging from the childhood years, an interpretation that is inevitably guided by social norms and expectations. For example, girls might be more socially primed to interpret the arousal as romantic attraction whereas boys might be more primed to interpret it as sexual arousal. Certainly most individuals in our culture are primed to anticipate, recognize, and interpret opposite-sex arousal as erotic or romantic attraction and to ignore, repress, or differently interpret comparable same-sex arousal. In fact, the heightened visibility of gay men and lesbians in our society is now prompting individuals who experience same-sex arousal to recognize it, label it, and act on it at earlier ages than in previous years (Fox, 1995).

In some instances, the EBE process itself may be supplemented or even superseded by processes of conditioning or social learning, both positive and negative. Such processes could also produce shifts in an individual's sexual orientation over the life course. For example, the small number of bisexual respondents in the San Francisco study appeared to have added same-sex erotic attraction to an already established heterosexual orientation after adolescence. Similar findings were reported in a more extensive study of bisexual individuals

(Weinberg, Williams, & Pryor, 1994), with some respondents adding heterosexual attraction to a previously established homosexual orientation. This same study also showed that different components of an individual's sexual orientation need not coincide; for example, some of the bisexual respondents were more erotically attracted to one sex but more romantically attracted to the other.

Negative conditioning also appears to be an operative mechanism in some cases of childhood sexual abuse or other upsetting childhood sexual experiences. For example, a reanalysis of the original Kinsey data revealed that a woman was more likely to engage in sexual activity with other women as an adult if she had been pressured or coerced into preadolescent sexual activity with an older male (Van Wyk & Geist, 1984).

Finally, some women who would otherwise be predicted by the EBE model to have a heterosexual orientation might choose for social or political reasons to center their lives around other women. This could lead them to avoid seeking out men for sexual or romantic relationships, to develop affectional and erotic ties to other women, and to self-identify as lesbians or bisexuals. In general, issues of sexual orientation *identity* are beyond the formal scope of EBE theory.

Deconstructing the Concept of Sexual Orientation

As noted in the introduction, the academic discourse on sexual orientation is currently dominated by the debate between the biological essentialists, who can point to the empirical links between biology and sexual orientation, and the social constructionists, who can point to the historical and anthropological evidence that the concept of sexual orientation is itself a culture-bound notion (De Cecco & Elia, 1993). I suggest that EBE theory can accommodate both kinds of evidence. I have already shown how the theory incorporates the biological evidence. To demonstrate how EBE theory also accommodates the cultural relativism of the social constructionists, it is necessary to de-

construct the theory itself, to explicitly identify its essentialist and culture-specific elements and to see what remains when the latter are stripped away.

There are three essentialist assumptions underlying the scenario outlined in Figure 25.1. First, it is assumed that childhood temperaments are partially coded in the genes and, second, that those temperaments can influence a child's preferences for male-typical or female-typical activities. Third, and most fundamentally, it is assumed that the psychological processes that transform exotic into erotic are universal properties of the human species. That's it. Everything else is cultural overlay, including the concept of sexual orientation itself.

* * *

References

Allen, J. B., Kenrick, D. T., Linder, D. E., & McCall, M. A. (1989). Arousal and attraction: A response-facilitation alternative to misattribution and negative-reinforcement models. *Journal of Personality and Social Psychology, 57,* 261–270.

Allen, L. S., & Gorski, R. A. (1992). Sexual orientation and the size of the anterior commissure in the human brain. *Proceedings of the National Academy of Sciences, 89,* 7199–7202.

Bailey, J. M., & Martin, N. G. (1995, September). *A twin registry study of sexual orientation.* Paper presented at the annual meeting of the International Academy of Sex Research, Provincetown, MA.

Bailey, J. M., & Pillard, R. C. (1991). A genetic study of male sexual orientation. *Archives of General Psychiatry, 48,* 1089–1096.

Bailey, J. M., Pillard, R. C., Neale, M. C., & Agyei, Y. (1993). Heritable factors influence sexual orientation in women. *Archives of General Psychiatry, 50,* 217–223.

Bailey, J. M., & Zucker, K. J. (1995). Childhood sex-typed behavior and sexual orientation: A conceptual analysis and quantitative review. *Developmental Psychology, 31,* 43–55.

Bates, J. E., Bentler, P. M., & Thompson, S. K. (1973). Measurement of deviant gender development in boys. *Child Development, 44,* 591–598.

Bates, J. E., Bentler, P. M., & Thompson, S. K. (1979). Gender-deviant boys compared with normal and clinical controls boys. *Journal of Abnormal Child Psychology, 7,* 243–259.

Bateson, P. P. G. (1978a). Early experience and sexual preferences. In J. B. Hutchison (Ed.), *Biological determinants of sexual behavior* (pp. 29–53). New York: Wiley.

Bell, A. P. (1982, November). Sexual preference: A postscript. *Siecus Report, 11,* 1–3.

Bell, A. P., Weinberg, M. S., & Hammersmith, S. K. (1981a). *Sexual preference: Its development in men and women.* Bloomington: Indiana University Press.

Bell, A. P., Weinberg, M. S., & Hammersmith, S. K. (1981b).

Sexual preference: Its development in men and women. Statistical appendix. Bloomington: Indiana University Press.

Bem, S. L. (1993). *The lenses of gender: Transforming the debate on sexual inequality.* New Haven, CT: Yale University Press.

Berenbaum, S. A., & Hines, M. (1992). Early androgens are related to childhood sex-typed toy preferences. *Psychological Science, 3*, 203–206.

Berenbaum, S. A., & Snyder, E. (1995). Early hormonal influences on childhood sex-typed activity and playmate preferences: Implications for the development of sexual orientation. *Developmental Psychology, 31*, 31–42.

Berscheid, E., & Walster, E. (1974). A little bit about love. In T. Huston (Ed.), *Foundations of interpersonal attraction* (pp. 355–381). New York: Academic Press.

Bettelheim, B. (1969). *The children of the dream.* New York: Macmillan.

Blanchard, R., & Bogaert, A. F. (1996). Homosexuality in men and number of older brothers. *American Journal of Psychiatry, 153*, 27–31.

Blanchard, R., McConkey, J. G., Roper, V., & Steiner, B. W. (1983). Measuring physical aggressiveness in heterosexual, homosexual, and transsexual males. *Archives of Sexual Behavior, 12*, 511–524.

Bleier, R. (1984). *Science and gender: A critique of biology and its theories on women.* New York: Pergamon Press.

Brehm, S. S. (1992). *Intimate relationships* (2nd ed.). New York: McGraw-Hill.

Bronfenbrenner, U., & Ceci, S. J. (1994). Nature-nurture reconceptualized in developmental perspective: A bioecological model. *Psychological Review, 101*, 568–586.

Buss, A. H., & Plomin, R. (1975). *A temperament theory of personality development.* New York: Wiley.

Buss, A. H., & Plomin, R. (1984). *Temperament: Early developing personality traits.* Hillsdale, NJ: Erlbaum.

Byne, W., & Parsons, B. (1993). Human sexual orientation: The biologic theories reappraised. *Archives of General Psychiatry, 50*, 228–239.

Cantor, J. R., Zillmann, D., & Bryant, J. (1975). Enhancement of experienced sexual arousal in response to erotic stimuli through misattribution of unrelated residual excitation. *Journal of Personality and Social Psychology, 32*, 69–75.

Caspi, A., & Herbener, E. S. (1990). Continuity and change: Assortative marriage and the consistency of personality in adulthood. *Journal of Personality and Social Psychology, 58*, 250–258.

De Cecco, J. P., & Elia, J. P. (Eds.). (1993). *If you seduce a straight person, can you make them gay? Issues in biological essentialism versus social constructionism in gay and lesbian identities.* New York: Harrington Park Press.

DiPietro, J. A. (1981). Rough and tumble play: A function of gender. *Developmental Psychology, 17*, 50–58.

Dittmann, R. W., Kappes, M. H., Kappes, M. E., Borger, D., Meyer-Bahlburg, H. F. L., Stegner, H., Willig, R. H., & Wallis, H. (1990a). Congenital adrenal hyperplasia: II. Gender-related behavior and attitudes in female salt-wasting and simple-virilizing patients. *Psychoneuroendocrinology, 15*, 421–434.

Dittmann, R. W., Kappes, M. H., Kappes, M. E., Borger, D., Stegner, H., Willig, R. H., & Wallis, H. (1990b). Congenital adrenal hyperplasia: I. Gender-related behavior and attitudes

in female patients and sisters. *Psychoneuroendocrinology, 15*, 410–420.

Eaton, W. O., & Enns, L. R. (1986). Sex differences in human motor activity level. *Psychological Bulletin, 100*, 19–28.

Ellis, L., & Ames, M. A. (1987). Neurohormonal functioning and sexual orientation: A theory of homosexuality-heterosexuality. *Psychological Bulletin, 101*, 233–258.

Feingold, A. (1988). Matching for attractiveness in romantic partners and same-sex friends: A meta-analysis and theoretical critique. *Psychological Bulletin, 104*, 226–235.

Finck, H. T. (1887). *Romantic love and personal beauty: Their development, causal relations, historic and national peculiarities.* London: Macmillan.

Fox, R. C. (1995). Bisexual identities. In A. R. D'Augelli & C. J. Patterson (Eds.), *Lesbian, gay and bisexual identities over the lifespan* (pp. 48–86). New York: Oxford University Press.

Freud, S. (1962). *Three essays on the theory of sexuality.* New York: Basic Books. (Original work published 1905)

Fry, D. P. (1990). Play aggression among Zapotec children: Implications for the practice hypothesis. *Aggressive Behavior, 17*, 321–340.

Futuyma, D. J., & Risch, S. J. (1983/84). Sexual orientation, sociobiology, and evolution. *Journal of Homosexuality, 9*, 157–168.

Gartrell, N. K. (1982). Hormones and homosexuality. In W. Paul, J. D. Weinrich, J. C. Gonsiorek, & M. E. Hotvedt (Eds.), *Homosexuality: Social psychological and biological issues* (pp. 169–182). Beverly Hills, CA: Sage.

Gladue, B. A., Beatty, W. W., Larson, J., & Staton, R. D. (1990). Sexual orientation and spatial ability in men and women. *Psychobiology, 28*, 101–108.

Green, R. (1976). One-hundred ten feminine and masculine boys: Behavioral contrasts and demographic similarities. *Archives of Sexual Behavior, 5*, 425–426.

Green, R. (1987). *The "sissy boy syndrome" and the development of homosexuality.* New Haven, CT: Yale University Press.

Hamer, D., & Copeland, P. (1994). *The science of desire: The search for the gay gene and the biology of behavior.* New York: Simon & Schuster.

Hamer, D. H., Hu, S., Magnuson, V. L., Hu, N., & Patatucci, A. M. L. (1993). A linkage between DNA markers on the X chromosome and male sexual orientation. *Science, 261*, 321–327.

Harrison, A. A. (1977). Mere exposure. In L. Berkowitz (Ed.), *Advances in Experimental Social Psychology* (Vol. 10, pp. 39–83). New York: Academic Press.

Herdt, G. (1981). *Guardians of the flutes: Idioms of masculinity.* New York: McGraw-Hill.

Herdt, G. (1987). *Sambia: Ritual and gender in New Guinea.* New York: Holt, Rinehart & Winston.

Herdt, G. (1990). Developmental discontinuities and sexual orientation across cultures. In D. P. McWhirter, S. A. Sanders, & J. M. Reinisch (Eds.), *Homosexuality/heterosexuality: Concepts of sexual orientation* (pp. 208–236). New York: Oxford University Press.

Herdt, G. (Ed.). (1984). *Ritualized homosexuality in Melanesia.* Berkeley: University of California Press.

Hill, C., Rubin, Z., & Peplau, L. A. (1976). Breakups before marriage: The end of 103 affairs. *Journal of Social Issues, 32*, 147–168.

Hoon, P. W., Wincze, J. P., & Hoon, E. F. (1977). A test of

reciprocal inhibition: Are anxiety and sexual arousal in women mutually inhibitory? *Journal of Abnormal Psychology, 86,* 65–74.

Hyde, J. S. (1984). How large are gender differences in aggression? A developmental meta-analysis. *Developmental Psychology, 20,* 722–736.

Kenrick, D. T., & Cialdini, R. B. (1977). Romantic attraction: Misattribution versus reinforcement explanations. *Journal of Personality and Social Psychology, 35,* 381–391.

Kirsch, J. A. W., & Rodman, J. E. (1982). Selection and sexuality: The Darwinian view of homosexuality. In W. Paul, J. D. Weinrich, J. C. Gonsiorek, & M. E. Hotvedt (Eds.), *Homosexuality: Social psychological and biological issues* (pp. 183–195). Beverly Hills, CA: Sage.

LeVay, S. (1991). A difference in hypothalamic structure between heterosexual and homosexual men. *Science, 253,* 1034–1037.

LeVay, S. (1993). *The sexual brain.* Cambridge, MA: MIT Press.

Levinger, G., Senn, D. J., & Jorgensen, B. W. (1970). Progress toward permanence in courtship: A test of the Kerckhoff-Davis hypotheses. *Sociometry, 33,* 427–443.

McClanahan, K. K., Gold, J. A., Lenney, E., Ryckman, R. M., & Kulberg, G. E. (1990). Infatuation and attraction to a dissimilar other: Why is love blind? *Journal of Social Psychology, 130,* 433–445.

McCormick, C. M., & Witelson, S. F. (1991). A cognitive profile of homosexual men compared to heterosexual men and women. *Psychoneuroendocrinology, 16,* 459–473.

Meyer, J. P., & Pepper, S. (1977). Need compatibility and marital adjustment in young married couples. *Journal of Personality and Social Psychology, 35,* 331–342.

Meyer-Bahlburg, H. F. L. (1984). Psychoendocrine research on sexual orientation: Current status and future options. *Progress in Brain Research, 61,* 375–398.

Meyer-Bahlburg, H. F. L., Erhhardt, A. A., Rosen, L. R., Gruen, R. S., Veridiano, N. P., Vann, F. H., & Neuwalder, H. F. (1995). Prenatal estrogens and the development of homosexual orientation. *Developmental Psychology, 31,* 12–21.

Moller, L. C., Hymel, S., & Rubin, K. H. (1992). Sex typing in play and popularity in middle childhood. *Sex Roles, 26,* 331–353.

Money, J., & Ehrhardt, A. A. (1972). *Man and woman, boy and girl: The differentiation and dimorphism of gender identity from conception to maturity.* Baltimore: Johns Hopkins Press.

Money, J., Schwartz, M., & Lewis, V. G. (1984). Adult erotosexual status and fetal hormonal masculinization and demasculinization: 46, XX congenital virilizing adrenal hyperplasia and 46, XY androgen-insensitivity syndrome compared. *Psychoneuroendocrinology, 9,* 405–414.

Mook, D. B. (1987). *Motivation: The organization of action.* New York: Norton.

Murstein, B. I. (1972). Physical attractiveness and marital choice. *Journal of Personality and Social Psychology, 22,* 8–12.

Newcomb, T. M. (1961). *The acquaintance process.* New York: Holt, Rinehart & Winston.

Pitz, G. F., & Ross, R. B. (1961). Imprinting as a function of arousal. *Journal of Comparative and Physiological Psychology, 54,* 602–604.

Plomin, R. (1986). *Development, genetics, and psychology.* Hillsdale, NJ: Erlbaum.

Quadagno, D. M., Briscoe, R., & Quadagno, J. S. (1977). Effect of perinatal gonadal hormones on selected nonsexual behavior patterns: A critical assessment of the nonhuman and human literature. *Psychological Bulletin, 84,* 62–80.

Rabin, I. A. (1965). *Growing up in a kibbutz.* New York: Springer.

Reinisch, J. M. (1981). Prenatal exposure to synthetic progestins increases potential for aggression in humans. *Science, 211,* 1171–1173.

Rice, G., Anderson, C., Risch, N., & Ebers, G. (1995, September). *Male homosexuality: Absence of linkage to micro satellite markers on the X-chromosome in a Canadian study.* Paper presented at the annual meeting of the International Academy of Sex Research, Provincetown, MA.

Rubin, Z. (1973). *Liking and loving.* New York: Holt, Rinehart & Winston.

Rushton, J. P., Fulker, D. W., Neale, M. C., Nias, D. K. B., & Eysenck, H. J. (1986). Altruism and aggression: The heritability of individual differences. *Journal of Personality and Social Psychology, 50,* 1192–1198.

Savin-Williams, R. C. (1987). An ethological perspective on homosexuality during adolescence. *Journal of Adolescent Research, 2,* 283–302.

Schachter, S., & Singer, J. E. (1962). Cognitive, social, and physiological determinants of emotional state. *Psychological Review, 69,* 379–399.

Serbin, L. A. (1980). Sex-role socialization: A field in transition. In B. B. Lahey & A. E. Kazdin (Eds.), *Advances in clinical child psychology* (Vol. 3, pp. 41–96). New York: Plenum.

Shepher, J. (1971). Mate selection among second generation kibbutz adolescents and adults: Incest avoidance and negative imprinting. *Archives of Sexual Behavior, 1,* 293–307.

Silverman, I. (1971). Physical attractiveness and courtship. *Archives of Sexual Behavior, 1,* 22–25.

Spiro, M. E. (1958). *Children of the kibbutz.* Cambridge, MA: Harvard University Press.

Strong, S. R., Hills, H. I., Kilmartin, C. T., DeVries, H., Lanier, K., Nelson, B. N., Strickland, D., & Meyer, C. W., III. (1988). The dynamic relations among interpersonal behaviors: A test of complementarity and anticomplementarity. *Journal of Personality and Social Psychology, 54,* 798–810.

Swaab, D. F., & Hofman, M. A. (1990). An enlarged suprachiasmatic nucleus in homosexual men. *Brain Research, 537,* 141–148.

Talmon, Y. (1964). Mate selection in collective settlements. *American Sociological Review, 29,* 481–508.

Tripp, C. A. (1975). *The homosexual matrix.* New York: McGraw-Hill.

Tripp, C. A. (1987). *The homosexual matrix* (2nd ed.). New York: New American Library.

Van Wyk, P. H., & Geist, C. S. (1984). Psychological development of heterosexual, bisexual, and homosexual behavior. *Archives of Sexual Behavior, 13,* 505–544.

Walster, E. (1971). Passionate love. In B. I. Murstein (Ed.), *Theories of attraction and love* (pp. 85–99). New York: Springer.

Weinberg, M. S., Williams, C. J., & Pryor, D. W. (1994). *Dual attraction: Understanding bisexuality.* New York: Oxford University Press.

Weinrich, J. D. (1978). Nonreproduction, homosexuality, transsexualism, and intelligence: I. A systematic literature search. *Journal of Homosexuality, 2,* 275–289.

Weinrich, J. D. (1987). A new sociobiological theory of homosexuality applicable to societies with universal marriage. *Ethology and Sociobiology, 8,* 37–47.

Westermarck, E. (1891). *The history of human marriage.* London: Macmillan.

White, G. L., Fishbein, S., & Rutstein, J. (1981). Passionate love and the misattribution of arousal. *Journal of Personality and Social Psychology, 41,* 56–62.

White, G. L., & Kight, T. D. (1984). Misattribution of arousal and attraction: Effects of salience of explanations for arousal. *Journal of Experimental Social Psychology, 20,* 55–64.

Wilson, E. O. (1975). *Sociobiology: The new synthesis.* Cambridge, MA: Harvard University Press.

Wilson, E. O. (1978). *On human nature.* Cambridge, MA: Harvard University Press.

Wolchik, S. A., Beggs, V. E., Wincze, J. P., Sakheim, D. K., Barlow, D. H., & Mavissakalian, M. (1980). The effect of emotional arousal on subsequent sexual arousal in men. *Journal of Abnormal Psychology, 89,* 595–598.

Zillmann, D. (1983). Transfer of excitation in emotional behavior. In J. T. Cacioppo & R. E. Petty (Eds.), *Social psychophysiology: A sourcebook.* New York: Guilford Press.

Zucker, K. J. (1990). Gender identity disorders in children: Clinical descriptions and natural history. In R. Blanchard & B. W. Steiner (Eds.), *Clinical management of gender identity disorders in children and adults* (pp. 1–23). Washington, DC: American Psychiatric Press.

Zucker, K. J., Bradley, S. J., Oliver, G., Hood, J. E., Blake, J., & Fleming, S. (1992, July). *Psychosexual assessment of women with congenital adrenal hyperplasia: Preliminary analyses.* Paper presented at the 18th Annual meeting of the International Academy of Sex Research, Prague, Czechoslovakia.

Zucker, K. J., & Green, R. (1993). Psychological and familial aspects of gender identity disorder. *Child and Adolescent Psychiatric Clinics of North America, 2,* 513–542.

PART IV

Psychoanalytic Approaches to Personality

About a century ago, the brilliant Viennese psychiatrist Sigmund Freud began to present his psychoanalytic theory of personality to the world. Freud continued to publish prolifically and to develop his theory right up to the time of his death, in 1939. The result of all this labor was not only a long-lasting and pervasive influence on the field of psychology, but a fundamental influence on the way members of Western culture think about people. The "Freudian slip" is the commonplace idea most obviously identified with Freud, but his writings also continue to affect the way we talk about child-rearing, psychological conflict, sexuality, and emotion.

Freud's own contributions were impressive enough, but he also attracted a remarkable group of followers, several of whom eventually broke away from his influence. These include some of the major intellectual figures of the early twentieth century, including Carl Jung, Alfred Adler, Karen Horney, and Erik Erikson. And Freud's theory continues to influence modern psychological research both directly and indirectly.

The readings in this section sample from the writings of Freud himself and several other important figures in psychoanalysis. The two lectures by Freud that begin this section concern the basic structure of the mind and the widely observed phenomenon of Freudian slips, or "parapraxes." The next four selections are articles by Jung, Adler, Horney, and Erikson that describe key parts of the theoretical approaches of each psychologist and also address topics of interest in their own right. Jung describes the nature of extraversion and introversion; Adler speaks of love and marriage; Horney explains the "distrust" between the sexes; and Erikson outlines the eight stages of psychological development that occur over an individual's entire lifetime.

Two modern articles end this section. One, by the psychologists Lloyd Silverman and Joel Weinberger, describes a controversial program of research concerning a "dynamic proposition" of psychoanalytic theory. They propose that people have strong unconscious wishes for a state of oneness with the good mother of early childhood and that the operation of this wish can be demonstrated by showing subjects sentences such as "Mommy and I are one" too quickly to be consciously perceived.

The last selection is a scathing but also humorous critique of psychoanalytic theory, written by the feminist Gloria Steinem. Vehemently attacking psychoanalysis at perhaps its weakest point—its obvious sexism—Steinem describes how the theory might have looked if Freud were a woman, living in a matriarchy.

Perhaps no theory in psychology has been as admired, and as reviled, as psychoanalysis. As you will see in the following articles, there are good reasons for both kinds of reaction.

Lecture XXXI: The Dissection of the Psychical Personality

Sigmund Freud

In this first selection the founder of psychoanalysis, Sigmund Freud himself, describes the core of the theory. Freud describes how the mind is divided into three parts, the now-famous id, ego, and super-ego. These roughly map onto the animalistic part, the logical part, and the moral part of the mind.

One of your editors remembers years ago having seen a Donald Duck cartoon in which the unfortunate duck was tormented by an angel who rode on one shoulder and a devil who rode on the other. The angel was always scolding him, and the devil was always egging him on to do things he knew he shouldn't do. Donald himself, in the middle, was confused and prone to obey first one of his tormentors, then the other.

Disney's animators seem to have known their Freud. The situation described near the end of this selection is nearly identical. When Freud has the poor ego cry, "Life is not easy!" he is describing the torment of having to resolve the three-way conflict between what one believes one should do, what one wants to do, and what is really possible.

This selection was written late in Freud's career and published six years before his death. Freud had 15 years earlier delivered a famous set of introductory lectures on psychoanalysis, and he hit upon the idea of writing a new set of lectures to update and expand upon the earlier ones. But by this time Freud, an old man, had undergone repeated surgeries for cancer of the palate and could not speak in public. So although this and several other articles were written in the form of lectures, they were never meant to be delivered. In Freud's own words (from his preface),

> If, therefore, I once more take my place in the lecture room during the remarks that follow, it is only by an artifice of the imagination; it may help me not to forget to bear the reader in mind as I enter more deeply into my subject. . . . [this lecture is] addressed to the multitude of educated people to whom we may perhaps attribute a benevolent, even though cautious, interest in the characteristics and discoveries of the young science. (Freud, 1965/1933, p, 5).

From *New Introductory Lectures on Psycho-analysis*, by Sigmund Freud, in *The Standard Edition of the Complete Psychological Works of Sigmund Freud*, edited and translated by James Strachey, pp. 51–71. Translation copyright © 1965, 1964 by James Strachey. Reprinted by permission of W. W. Norton & Company, Inc., Sigmund Freud Copyrights, the Institute of Psycho-Analysis, and the Hogarth Press.

* * *

The situation in which we find ourselves at the beginning of our enquiry may be expected itself to point the way for us. We wish to make the ego the matter of our enquiry, our very own ego.[1] But is that possible? After all, the ego is in its very essence a subject; how can it be made into an object? Well, there is no doubt that it can be. The ego can take itself as an object, can treat itself like other objects, can observe itself, criticize itself, and do Heaven knows what with itself. In this, one part of the ego is setting itself over against the rest. So the ego can be split; it splits itself during a number of its functions—temporarily at least. Its parts can come together again afterwards. That is not exactly a novelty, though it may perhaps be putting an unusual emphasis on what is generally known. On the other hand, we are familiar with the notion that pathology, by making things larger and coarser, can draw our attention to normal conditions which would otherwise have escaped us. Where it points to a breach or a rent, there may normally be an articulation present. If we throw a crystal to the floor, it breaks; but not into haphazard pieces. It comes apart along its lines of cleavage into fragments whose boundaries, though they were invisible, were predetermined by the crystal's structure. Mental patients are split and broken structures of this same kind. Even we cannot withhold from them something of the reverential awe which peoples of the past felt for the insane. They have

turned away from external reality, but for that very reason they know more about internal, psychical reality and can reveal a number of things to us that would otherwise be inaccessible to us.

We describe one group of these patients as suffering from delusions of being observed. They complain to us that perpetually, and down to their most intimate actions, they are being molested by the observation of unknown powers—presumably persons—and that in hallucinations they hear these persons reporting the outcome of their observation: "now he's going to say this, now he's dressing to go out," and so on. Observation of this sort is not yet the same thing as persecution, but it is not far from it; it presupposes that people distrust them, and expect to catch them carrying out forbidden actions for which they would be punished. How would it be if these insane people were right, if in each of us there is present in his ego an agency like this which observes and threatens to punish, and which in them has merely become sharply divided from their ego and mistakenly displaced into external reality?

I cannot tell whether the same thing will happen to you as to me. Ever since, under the powerful impression of this clinical picture, I formed the idea that the separation of the observing agency from the rest of the ego might be a regular feature of the ego's structure, that idea has never left me, and I was driven to investigate the further characteristics and connections of the agency which was thus separated off. The next step is quickly taken. The content of the delusions of being observed already suggests that the observing is only a preparation for judging and punishing, and we accordingly guess that another function of this

---

[1] "Ego" has also been translated as "the I." Here Freud is referring to the self as it experiences itself—a paradoxical but common situation that leads Freud to conclude that dividing up the self is not so odd as it might first seem.

agency must be what we call our conscience. There is scarcely anything else in us that we so regularly separate from our ego and so easily set over against it as precisely our conscience. I feel an inclination to do something that I think will give me pleasure, but I abandon it on the ground that my conscience does not allow it. Or I have let myself be persuaded by too great an expectation of pleasure into doing something to which the voice of conscience has objected and after the deed my conscience punishes me with distressing reproaches and causes me to feel remorse for the deed. I might simply say that the special agency which I am beginning to distinguish in the ego is conscience. But it is more prudent to keep the agency as something independent and to suppose that conscience is one of its functions and that self-observation, which is an essential preliminary to the judging activity of conscience, is another of them. And since when we recognize that something has a separate existence we give it a name of its own, from this time forward I will describe this agency in the ego as the '*super-ego*'.

* * *

Hardly have we familiarized ourselves with the idea of a super-ego like this which enjoys a certain degree of autonomy, follows its own intentions and is independent of the ego for its supply of energy, than a clinical picture forces itself on our notice which throws a striking light on the severity of this agency and indeed its cruelty, and on its changing relations to the ego. I am thinking of the condition of melancholia,[2] or, more precisely, of melancholic attacks, which you too will have heard plenty about, even if you are not psychiatrists. The most striking feature of this illness, of whose causation and mechanism we know much too little, is the way in which the super-ego—"conscience," you may call it, quietly—treats the ego. While a melancholic can, like other people, show a greater or lesser degree of severity to himself in his healthy periods, during a melancholic attack his super-ego

becomes over-severe, abuses the poor ego, humiliates it and ill-treats it, threatens it with the direst punishments, reproaches it for actions in the remotest past which had been taken lightly at the time—as though it had spent the whole interval in collecting accusations and had only been waiting for its present access of strength in order to bring them up and make a condemnatory judgement on their basis. The super-ego applies the strictest moral standard to the helpless ego which is at its mercy; in general it represents the claims of morality, and we realize all at once that our moral sense of guilt is the expression of the tension between the ego and the super-ego. It is a most remarkable experience to see morality, which is supposed to have been given us by God and thus deeply implanted in us, functioning [in these patients] as a periodic phenomenon. For after a certain number of months the whole moral fuss is over, the criticism of the super-ego is silent, the ego is rehabilitated and again enjoys all the rights of man till the next attack. In some forms of the disease, indeed, something of a contrary sort occurs in the intervals; the ego finds itself in a blissful state of intoxication, it celebrates a triumph, as though the super-ego had lost all its strength or had melted into the ego; and this liberated, manic ego permits itself a truly uninhibited satisfaction of all its appetites. Here are happenings rich in unsolved riddles!

No doubt you will expect me to give you more than a mere illustration when I inform you that we have found out all kinds of things about the formation of the super-ego—that is to say, about the origin of conscience. Following a well-known pronouncement of Kant's which couples the conscience within us with the starry Heavens, a pious man might well be tempted to honor these two things as the masterpieces of creation. The stars are indeed magnificent, but as regards conscience God has done an uneven and careless piece of work, for a large majority of men have brought along with them only a modest amount of it or scarcely enough to be worth mentioning. We are far from overlooking the portion of psychological

---

[2] "Modern terminology would probably speak of 'depression.'"—Translator

truth that is contained in the assertion that conscience is of divine origin; but the thesis needs interpretation. Even if conscience is something "within us," yet it is not so from the first. In this it is a real contrast to sexual life, which is in fact there from the beginning of life and not only a later addition. But, as is well known, young children are amoral and possess no internal inhibitions against their impulses striving for pleasure. The part which is later taken on by the super-ego is played to begin with by an external power, by parental authority. Parental influence governs the child by offering proofs of love and by threatening punishments which are signs to the child of loss of love and are bound to be feared on their own account. This realistic anxiety is the precursor of the later moral anxiety. So long as it is dominant there is no need to talk of a super-ego and of a conscience. It is only subsequently that the secondary situation develops (which we are all too ready to regard as the normal one), where the external restraint is internalized and the super-ego takes the place of the parental agency and observes, directs and threatens the ego in exactly the same way as earlier the parents did with the child.

The super-ego, which thus takes over the power, function and even the methods of the parental agency, is however not merely its successor but actually the legitimate heir of its body. It proceeds directly out of it, we shall learn presently by what process. First, however, we must dwell upon a discrepancy between the two. The super-ego seems to have made a one-sided choice and to have picked out only the parents' strictness and severity, their prohibiting and punitive function, whereas their loving care seems not to have been taken over and maintained. If the parents have really enforced their authority with severity we can easily understand the child's in turn developing a severe super-ego. But, contrary to our expectation, experience shows that the super-ego can acquire the same characteristic of relentless severity even if the upbringing had been mild and kindly and had so far as possible avoided threats and punishments. * * *

* * *

The basis of the process is what is called an 'identification'—that is to say, the assimilation of one ego to another one,[3] as a result of which the first ego behaves like the second in certain respects, imitates it and in a sense takes it up into itself. Identification has been not unsuitably compared with the oral, cannibalistic incorporation of the other person. It is a very important form of attachment to someone else, probably the very first, and not the same thing as the choice of an object. The difference between the two can be expressed in some such way as this. If a boy identifies himself with his father, he wants to *be like* his father; if he makes him the object of his choice, he wants to *have* him, to possess him. In the first case his ego is altered on the model of his father; in the second case that is not necessary. Identification and object-choice are to a large extent independent of each other; it is however possible to identify oneself with someone whom, for instance, one has taken as a sexual object, and to alter one's ego on his model. It is said that the influencing of the ego by the sexual object occurs particularly often with women and is characteristic of femininity. I must already have spoken to you in my earlier lectures of what is by far the most instructive relation between identification and object-choice. It can be observed equally easily in children and adults, in normal as in sick people. If one has lost an object or has been obliged to give it up, one often compensates oneself by identifying oneself with it and by setting it up once more in one's ego, so that here object-choice regresses, as it were, to identification.

I myself am far from satisfied with these remarks on identification; but it will be enough if you can grant me that the installation of the super-ego can be described as a successful instance of identification with the parental agency. The fact that speaks decisively for this view is that this new creation of a superior agency within the ego is most intimately linked with the destiny of the

---

[3]"I.e., one ego coming to resemble another one."—Translator.

Oedipus complex[4] so that the super-ego appears as the heir of that emotional attachment which is of such importance for childhood. With his abandonment of the Oedipus complex a child must, as we can see, renounce the intense object-cathexes[5] which he has deposited with his parents, and it is as a compensation for this loss of objects that there is such a strong intensification of the identifications with his parents which have probably long been present in his ego. Identifications of this kind as precipitates of object-cathexes that have been given up will be repeated often enough later in the child's life; but it is entirely in accordance with the emotional importance of this first instance of such a transformation that a special place in the ego should be found for its outcome. Close investigation has shown us, too, that the super-ego is stunted in its strength and growth if the surmounting of the Oedipus complex is only incompletely successful. In the course of development the super-ego also takes on the influences of those who have stepped into the place of parents —educators, teachers, people chosen as ideal models. Normally it departs more and more from the original parental figures; it becomes, so to say, more impersonal. Nor must it be forgotten that a child has a different estimate of its parents at different periods of its life. At the time at which the Oedipus complex gives place to the super-ego they are something quite magnificent; but later they lose much of this. Identifications then come about with these later parents as well, and indeed they regularly make important contributions to the formation of character; but in that case they only affect the ego, they no longer influence the super-ego, which has been determined by the earliest parental imagos.

*   *   *

---

[4]The Oedipus complex is the result of a complex process in which, according to Freud, a young boy falls in love with his mother, fears his father's jealous retaliation, and as a defense against that fear comes to identify with his father.

[5]An object-cathexis is an investment of emotional energy in an important "object," usually a person.

*   *   * In face of the doubt whether the ego and super-ego are themselves unconscious or merely produce unconscious effects, we have, for good reasons, decided in favour of the former possibility. And it is indeed the case that large portions of the ego and super-ego can remain unconscious and are normally unconscious. That is to say, the individual knows nothing of their contents and it requires an expenditure of effort to make them conscious. It is a fact that ego and conscious, repressed and unconscious do not coincide. We feel a need to make a fundamental revision of our attitude to the problem of conscious-unconscious. At first we are inclined greatly to reduce the value of the criterion of being conscious since it has shown itself so untrustworthy. But we should be doing it an injustice. As may be said of our life, it is not worth much, but it is all we have. Without the illumination thrown by the quality of consciousness, we should be lost in the obscurity of depth-psychology; but we must attempt to find our bearings afresh.

There is no need to discuss what is to be called conscious: it is removed from all doubt. The oldest and best meaning of the word "unconscious" is the descriptive one; we call a psychical process unconscious whose existence we are obliged to assume—for some such reason as that we infer it from its effects—but of which we know nothing. In that case we have the same relation to it as we have to a psychical process in another person, except that it is in fact one of our own. If we want to be still more correct, we shall modify our assertion by saying that we call a process unconscious if we are obliged to assume that it is being activated *at the moment*, though *at the moment* we know nothing about it. This qualification makes us reflect that the majority of conscious processes are conscious only for a short time; very soon they become *latent*, but can easily become conscious again. We might also say that they had become unconscious, if it were at all certain that in the condition of latency they are still something psychical. So far we should have learnt nothing new; nor should we have acquired the right to introduce the concept of an unconscious into psychology. [But] in order to explain a slip of the tongue, for instance, we find ourselves obliged to assume that the intention to make a particular remark was present in the subject. We infer it with certainty from the interference with his remark which has occurred; but the intention did not put itself through and was thus unconscious. If, when we subsequently put it before the speaker, he recognizes it as one familiar to him, then it was only temporarily unconscious to him; but if he repudiates it as something foreign to him, then it was permanently unconscious. From this experience we retrospectively obtain the right also to pronounce as something unconscious what had been described as latent. A consideration of these dynamic relations permits us now to distinguish two kinds of unconscious—one which is easily, under frequently occurring circumstances, transformed into something conscious, and another with which this transformation is difficult and takes place only subject to a considerable expenditure of effort or possibly never at all. In order to escape the ambiguity as to whether we mean the one or the other unconscious, whether we are using the word in the descriptive or in the dynamic sense, we make use of a permissible and simple way out. We call the unconscious which is only latent, and thus easily becomes conscious, the "preconscious" and retain the term "unconscious" for the other. We now have three terms, "conscious," "preconscious," and "unconscious," with which we can get along in our description of mental phenomena. Once again: the preconscious is also unconscious in the purely descriptive sense, but we do not give it that name, except in talking loosely or when we have to make a defence of the existence in mental life of unconscious processes in general.

You will admit, I hope, that so far that is not too bad and allows of convenient handling. Yes, but unluckily the work of psychoanalysis has found itself compelled to use the word "unconscious" in yet another, third, sense, and this may, to be sure, have led to confusion. Under the new and powerful impression of there being an extensive and important field of mental life which is normally withdrawn from the ego's knowledge so

that the processes occurring in it have to be regarded as unconscious in the truly dynamic sense, we have come to understand the term "unconscious" in a topographical or systematic sense as well; we have come to speak of a "system" of the preconscious and a "system" of the unconscious, of a conflict between the ego and the system Ucs. [unconscious], and have used the word more and more to denote a mental province rather than a quality of what is mental. The discovery, actually an inconvenient one, that portions of the ego and super-ego as well are unconscious in the dynamic sense, operates at this point as a relief—it makes possible the removal of a complication. We perceive that we have no right to name the mental region that is foreign to the ego "the system Ucs.," since the characteristic of being unconscious is not restricted to it. Very well; we will no longer use the term "unconscious" in the systematic sense and we will give what we have hitherto so described a better name and one no longer open to misunderstanding. Following a verbal usage of Nietzsche's and taking up a suggestion by Georg Groddeck [1923],[6] we will in future call it the 'id'.[7] This impersonal pronoun seems particularly well suited for expressing the main characteristic of this province of the mind—the fact of its being alien to the ego. The super-ego, the ego and the id— these, then, are the three realms, regions, provinces, into which we divide an individual's mental apparatus, and with the mutual relations of which we shall be concerned in what follows.

* * *

You will not expect me to have much to tell you that is new about the id apart from its new name. It is the dark, inaccessible part of our personality; what little we know of it we have learnt from our study of the dream-work and of the construction of neurotic symptoms, and most of that is of a negative character and can be described only as a contrast to the ego. We approach the id

---

[6]"A German physician by whose unconventional ideas Freud was much attracted."—Translator

[7]"In German, Es, the ordinary word for 'it.' "—Translator

with analogies: we call it a chaos, a cauldron full of seething excitations. We picture it as being open at its end to somatic influences, and as there taking up into itself instinctual needs which find their psychical expression in it, but we cannot say in what substratum. It is filled with energy reaching it from the instincts, but it has no organization, produces no collective will, but only a striving to bring about the satisfaction of the instinctual needs subject to the observance of the pleasure principle. The logical laws of thought do not apply in the id, and this is true above all of the law of contradiction. Contrary impulses exist side by side, without cancelling each other out or diminishing each other: at the most they may converge to form compromises under the dominating economic pressure towards the discharge of energy. There is nothing in the id that could be compared with negation; and we perceive with surprise an exception to the philosophical theorem that space and time are necessary forms of our mental acts. There is nothing in the id that corresponds to the idea of time; there is no recognition of the passage of time, and—a thing that is most remarkable and awaits consideration in philosophical thought—no alteration in its mental processes is produced by the passage of time. Wishful impulses which have never passed beyond the id, but impressions, too, which have been sunk into the id by repression, are virtually immortal; after the passage of decades they behave as though they had just occurred. They can only be recognized as belonging to the past, can only lose their importance and be deprived of their cathexis of energy, when they have been made conscious by the work of analysis, and it is on this that the therapeutic effect of analytic treatment rests to no small extent.

Again and again I have had the impression that we have made too little theoretical use of this fact, established beyond any doubt, of the unalterability by time of the repressed. This seems to offer an approach to the most profound discoveries. Nor, unfortunately, have I myself made any progress here.

The id of course knows no judgements of value: no good and evil, no morality. The economic or, if you prefer, the quantitative factor, which is intimately linked to the pleasure principle, dominates all its processes. Instinctual cathexes seeking discharge—that, in our view, is all there is in the id.[8] It even seems that the energy of these instinctual impulses is in a state different from that in the other regions of the mind, far more mobile and capable of discharge; otherwise the displacements and condensations would not occur which are characteristic of the id and which so completely disregard the *quality* of what is cathected—what in the ego we should call an idea. We would give much to understand more about these things! You can see, incidentally, that we are in a position to attribute to the id characteristics other than that of its being unconscious, and you can recognize the possibility of portions of the ego and super-ego being unconscious without possessing the same primitive and irrational characteristics.

* * *

* * * We need scarcely look for a justification of the view that the ego is that portion of the id which was modified by the proximity and influence of the external world, which is adapted for the reception of stimuli and as a protective shield against stimuli, comparable to the cortical layer by which a small piece of living substance is surrounded. The relation to the external world has become the decisive factor for the ego; it has taken on the task of representing the external world to the id—fortunately for the id, which could not escape destruction if, in its blind efforts for the satisfaction of its instincts, it disregarded that supreme external power. In accomplishing this function, the ego must observe the external world, must lay down an accurate picture of it in the memory-traces of its perceptions, and by its exercise of the function of "reality-testing" must put aside whatever in this picture of the external world is an addition derived from internal sources of excitation. The ego controls the approaches to motility under the id's orders; but between a need

---

[8]In other words, the id seeks immediately to satisfy all "instinctual"—physical—desires.

and an action it has interposed a postponement in the form of the activity of thought, during which it makes use of the mnemic residues of experience. In that way it has dethroned the pleasure principle which dominates the course of events in the id without any restriction, and has replaced it by the reality principle, which promises more certainty and greater success.

∗ ∗ ∗

∗ ∗ ∗ To adopt a popular mode of speaking, we might say that the ego stands for reason and good sense while the id stands for the untamed passions.

So far we have allowed ourselves to be impressed by the merits and capabilities of the ego; it is now time to consider the other side as well. The ego is after all only a portion of the id, a portion that has been expediently modified by the proximity of the external world with its threat of danger. From a dynamic point of view it is weak, it has borrowed its energies from the id, and we are not entirely without insight into the methods —we might call them dodges—by which it extracts further amounts of energy from the id. One such method, for instance, is by identifying itself with actual or abandoned objects. The object-cathexes spring from the instinctual demands of the id. The ego has in the first instance to take note of them. But by identifying itself with the object it recommends itself to the id in place of the object and seeks to divert the id's libido on to itself. ∗ ∗ ∗ The ego must on the whole carry out the id's intentions, it fulfils its task by finding out the circumstances in which those intentions can best be achieved. The ego's relation to the id might be compared with that of a rider to his horse. The horse supplies the locomotive energy, while the rider has the privilege of deciding on the goal and of guiding the powerful animal's movement. But only too often there arises between the ego and the id the not precisely ideal situation of the rider being obliged to guide the horse along the path by which it itself wants to go.

∗ ∗ ∗

We are warned by a proverb against serving two masters at the same time. The poor ego has things even worse: it serves three severe masters and does what it can to bring their claims and demands into harmony with one another. These claims are always divergent and often seem incompatible. No wonder that the ego so often fails in its task. Its three tyrannical masters are the external world, the super-ego and the id. When we follow the ego's efforts to satisfy them simultaneously—or rather, to obey them simultaneously—we cannot feel any regret at having personified this ego and having set it up as a separate organism. It feels hemmed in on three sides, threatened by three kinds of danger, to which, if it is hard pressed, it reacts by generating anxiety. Owing to its origin from the experiences of the perceptual system, it is earmarked for representing the demands of the external world, but it strives too to be a loyal servant of the id, to remain on good terms with it, to recommend itself to it as an object and to attract its libido to itself. In its attempts to mediate between the id and reality, it is often obliged to cloak the *Ucs.* commands of the id with its own *Pcs.* [preconscious] rationalizations, to conceal the id's conflicts with reality, to profess, with diplomatic disingenuousness, to be taking notice of reality even when the id has remained rigid and unyielding. On the other hand it is observed at every step it takes by the strict super-ego, which lays down definite standards for its conduct, without taking any account of its difficulties from the direction of the id and the external world, and which, if those standards are not obeyed, punishes it with tense feelings of inferiority and of guilt. Thus the ego, driven by the id, confined by the super-ego, repulsed by reality, struggles to master its economic task of bringing about harmony among the forces and influences working in and upon it; and we can understand how it is that so often we cannot suppress a cry: "Life is not easy!" If the ego is obliged to admit its weakness, it breaks out in anxiety—realistic anxiety regarding the external world, moral anxiety regarding the super-ego and neurotic anxiety regarding the strength of the passions in the id.

I should like to portray the structural relations

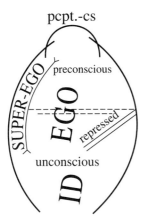

Figure 26.1 Freud's diagram of the structure of personality

of the mental personality, as I have described them to you, in the unassuming sketch which I now present you with:

As you see here, the super-ego merges into the id; indeed, as heir to the Oedipus complex it has intimate relations with the id; it is more remote than the ego from the perceptual system. The id has intercourse with the external world only through the ego—at least, according to this diagram. It is certainly hard to say to-day how far the drawing is correct. In one respect it is undoubtedly not. The space occupied by the unconscious id ought to have been incomparably greater than that of the ego or the preconscious. I must ask you to correct it in your thoughts.

And here is another warning, to conclude these remarks, which have certainly been exacting and not, perhaps, very illuminating. In thinking of this division of the personality into an ego, a super-ego and an id, you will not, of course, have pictured sharp frontiers like the artificial ones drawn in political geography. We cannot do jus-

tice to the characteristics of the mind by linear outlines like those in a drawing or in primitive painting, but rather by areas of colour melting into one another as they are presented by modern artists. After making the separation we must allow what we have separated to merge together once more. You must not judge too harshly a first attempt at giving a pictorial representation of something so intangible as psychical processes. It is highly probable that the development of these divisions is subject to great variations in different individuals; it is possible that in the course of actual functioning they may change and go through a temporary phase of involution. Particularly in the case of what is phylogenetically the last and most delicate of these divisions—the differentiation between the ego and the super-ego—something of the sort seems to be true. There is no question but that the same thing results from psychical illness. It is easy to imagine, too, that certain mystical practices may succeed in upsetting the normal relations between the different regions of the mind, so that, for instance, perception may be able to grasp happenings in the depths of the ego and in the id which were otherwise inaccessible to it. It may safely be doubted, however, whether this road will lead us to the ultimate truths from which salvation is to be expected. Nevertheless it may be admitted that the therapeutic efforts of psycho-analysis have chosen a similar line of approach. Its intention is, indeed, to strengthen the ego, to make it more independent of the super-ego, to widen its field of perception and enlarge its organization, so that it can appropriate fresh portions of the id. Where id was, there ego shall be. It is a work of culture—not unlike the draining of the Zuider Zee.[9]

---

[9]The Zuider Zee was a landlocked arm of the North Sea in the Netherlands. Its draining was a major land-reclamation project completed in 1932, about the time this essay was written.

LECTURE III: PARAPRAXES

Sigmund Freud

The following selection comes from one of the original series of introductory lectures that Freud delivered in Vienna about 15 years before writing the previous lecture. In this excerpt we see Freud doing his best to sell psychoanalysis to his audience, by answering their objections as he imagines them and illustrating his points with a large number of compelling examples.

Freud contributed many ideas that have entered everyday thought and speech. One of the most influential of those was his explanation of the phenomenon now popularly called the "Freudian slip." In the following selection, you can read in his own words what Freud thought about Freudian slips.

From *Introductory Lectures on Psycho-analysis*, by Sigmund Freud, in *The Standard Edition of the Complete Psychological Works of Sigmund Freud*, translated by James Strachey, pp. 48–72. Translation copyright © 1965, 1964, 1963 by James Strachey. Reprinted by permission of Liveright Publishing Corporation, Sigmund Freud Copyrights, the Institute of Psycho-Analysis, and the Hogarth Press.

Ladies and Gentlemen,—We arrived last time at the idea of considering parapraxes[1] not in relation to the intended function which they disturbed but on their own account; and we formed an impression that in particular cases they seemed to be betraying a sense of their own. We then reflected that if confirmation could be obtained on a wider scale that parapraxes have a sense, their sense would soon become more interesting than the investigation of the circumstances in which they come about.

Let us once more reach an agreement upon what is to be understood by the "sense" of a psychical process. We mean nothing other by it than the intention it serves and its position in a psychical continuity.[2] In most of our researches we can replace "sense" by "intention" or "purpose." Was it, then, merely a deceptive illusion or a poetic exaltation of parapraxes when we thought we recognized an intention in them?

We will take slips of the tongue as our examples. If we now look through a considerable number of observations of that kind, we shall find

---

[1]Freud used the German word "*Fehlleistungen*," which means "faulty acts" or "faulty functions." According to his translator, James Strachey, the concept did not exist before Freud and so a new word—*parapraxis*, the plural of which is *parapraxes*—was invented for use in English translations of Freud's writing (Freud, 1920/1989).

[2]By psychical continuity Freud means the interrelated functions of the different parts of the mind.

whole categories of cases in which the intention, the sense, of the slip is plainly visible. Above all there are those in which what was intended is replaced by its contrary. The President of the Lower House said in his opening speech: "I declare the sitting closed."[3] That is quite unambiguous. The sense and intention of his slip was that he wanted to close the sitting. ＊ ＊ ＊ We need only take him at his word. Do not interrupt me at this point by objecting that that is impossible, that we know that he did not want to close the sitting but to open it, and that he himself, whom we have just recognized as the supreme court of appeal, could confirm the fact that he wanted to open it. You are forgetting that we have come to an agreement that we will begin by regarding parapraxes on their own account; their relation to the intention which they have disturbed is not to be discussed till later. Otherwise you will be guilty of a logical error by simply evading the problem that is under discussion—by what is called in English "begging the question."

In other cases the slip of the tongue merely adds a second sense to the one intended. The sentence then sounds like a contraction, abbreviation, or condensation of several sentences. Thus, when the energetic lady said: "He can eat and drink what I want,"[4] it was just as though she had said: "He can eat and drink what he wants; but what has *he* to do with wanting? *I* will want instead of him." A slip of the tongue often gives the impression of being an abbreviation of this sort. For instance, a professor of anatomy at the end of a lecture on the nasal cavities asked whether his audience had understood what he said and, after general assent, went on: "I can hardly believe that, since even in a city with millions of inhabitants,

those who understand the nasal cavities can be counted *on one finger* . . . I beg your pardon, on the fingers of one hand." The abbreviated phrase has a sense too—namely, that there is only one person who understands them.

In contrast to these groups of cases, in which the parapraxis itself brings its sense to light, there are others in which the parapraxis produces nothing that has any sense of its own, and which therefore sharply contradict our expectations. If someone twists a proper name about by a slip of the tongue or puts an abnormal series of sounds together, these very common events alone seem to give a negative reply to our question whether all parapraxes have some sort of sense. Closer examination of such instances, however, shows that these distortions are easily understood and that there is by no means so great a distinction between these more obscure cases and the earlier straightforward ones.

A man who was asked about the health of his horse replied: "Well, it *draut* [a meaningless word] . . . it *dauert* [will last] another month perhaps." When he was asked what he had really meant to say, he explained that he had thought it was a "*traurige* [sad]" story. The combination of "*dauert*" and "*traurig*" had produced "*draut*."

＊ ＊ ＊

We seem now to have grasped the secret of a large number of slips of the tongue. If we bear this discovery in mind, we shall be able to understand other groups as well which have puzzled us hitherto. In cases of distortion of names, for instance, we cannot suppose that it is always a matter of competition between two similar but different names. It is not difficult, however, to guess the second intention. The distortion of a name occurs often enough apart from slips of the tongue; it seeks to give the name an offensive sound or to make it sound like something inferior, and it is a familiar practice (or malpractice) designed as an insult, which civilized people soon learn to abandon, but which they are *reluctant* to abandon. It is still often permitted as a "joke," though a pretty poor one. As a blatant and ugly example of this

---

[3]In his previous lecture, Freud had told of a politician who opened Parliament by saying, "Gentlemen, I take notice that a full quorum of members is present and herewith declare the sitting closed."

[4]The story referred to a woman who said, "My husband asked his doctor what diet he ought to follow; but the doctor told him he had no need to diet: he could eat and drink what I want."

way of distorting names, I may mention that in these days [of the first World War] the name of the President of the French Republic, Poincaré, has been changed into "*Schweinskarré*."[5] It is therefore plausible to suppose that the same insulting intention is present in these slips of the tongue and is trying to find expression in the distortion of a name. ✳ ✳ ✳

✳   ✳   ✳

Well, it looks now as though we have solved the problem of parapraxes, and with very little trouble! They are not chance events but serious mental acts; they have a sense; they arise from the concurrent action—or perhaps rather, the mutually opposing action—of two different intentions. But now I see too that you are preparing to overwhelm me with a mass of questions and doubts which will have to be answered and dealt with before we can enjoy this first outcome of our work. I certainly have no desire to force hasty decisions upon you. Let us take them all in due order, one after the other, and give them cool consideration.

What is it you want to ask me? Do I think that this explanation applies to *all* parapraxes or only to a certain number? Can this same point of view be extended to the many other kinds of parapraxis, to misreading, slips of the pen, forgetting, bungled actions, mislaying, and so on? In view of the psychical nature of parapraxes, what significance remains for the factors of fatigue, excitement, absent-mindedness and interference with the attention? Further, it is clear that of the two competing purposes in a parapraxis one is always manifest, but the other not always. What do we do, then, in order to discover the latter? And, if we think we have discovered it, how do we prove that it is not merely a probable one but the only correct one? Is there anything else you want to ask? If not, I will go on myself. You will recall that we do not set much store by parapraxes themselves, and that all we want is to learn from studying them something that may be turned to account for psycho-analysis. I therefore put this

question to you. What are these intentions or purposes which are able to disturb others in this way? And what are the relations between the disturbing purposes and the disturbed ones? Thus, no sooner is the problem solved than our work begins afresh.

First, then, is this the explanation of *all* cases of slips of the tongue? I am very much inclined to think so, and my reason is that every time one investigates an instance of a slip of the tongue an explanation of this kind is forthcoming. But it is also true that there is no way of proving that a slip of the tongue cannot occur without this mechanism. It may be so; but theoretically it is a matter of indifference to us, since the conclusions we want to draw for our introduction to psycho-analysis remain, even though—which is certainly not the case—our view holds good of only a minority of cases of slips of the tongue. The next question—whether we may extend our view to other sorts of parapraxis—I will answer in advance with a "yes." You will be able to convince yourselves of this when we come to examining instances of slips of the pen, bungled actions, and so on. ✳ ✳ ✳

A more detailed reply is called for by the question of what significance remains for the factors put forward by the authorities—disturbances of the circulation, fatigue, excitement, absent-mindedness and the theory of disturbed attention—if we accept the psychical mechanism of slips of the tongue which we have described. Observe that we are not denying these factors. It is in general not such a common thing for psycho-analysis to *deny* something asserted by other people; as a rule it merely adds something new—though no doubt it occasionally happens that this thing that has hitherto been overlooked and is now brought up as a fresh addition is in fact the essence of the matter. The influence on the production of slips of the tongue by physiological dispositions brought about by slight illness, disturbances of the circulation or states of exhaustion, must be recognized at once; daily and personal experience will convince you of it. But how little they explain! Above all, they are not necessary preconditions of parapraxes. Slips of the tongue are just as possible in

---

[5]"The Viennese term for a pork chop."—Translator

perfect health and in a normal state. These somatic factors only serve therefore, to facilitate and favour the peculiar mental mechanism of slips of the tongue. I once used an analogy to describe this relation, and I will repeat it here since I can think of none better to take its place. Suppose that one dark night I went to a lonely spot and was there attacked by a rough who took away my watch and purse. Since I did not see the robber's face clearly, I laid my complaint at the nearest police station with the words: "Loneliness and darkness have just robbed me of my valuables." The police officer might then say to me: "In what you say you seem to be unjustifiably adopting an extreme mechanistic view. It would be better to represent the facts in this way: 'Under the shield of darkness and favoured by loneliness, an unknown thief robbed you of your valuables.' In your case the essential task seems to me to be that we should find the thief. Perhaps we shall then be able to recover the booty."

Such psycho-physiological factors as excitement, absent-mindedness and disturbances of attention will clearly help us very little towards an explanation. They are only empty phrases, screens behind which we must not let ourselves be prevented from having a look. The question is rather what it is that has been brought about here by the excitement, the particular distracting of attention. And again, we must recognize the importance of the influence of sounds, the similarity of words and the familiar associations aroused by words. These facilitate slips of the tongue by pointing to the paths they can take. But if I have a path open to me, does that fact automatically decide that I shall take it? I need a motive in addition before I resolve in favour of it and furthermore a force to propel me along the path. So these relations of sounds and words are also, like the somatic dispositions, only things that *favour* slips of the tongue and cannot provide the true explanation of them. Only consider: in an immense majority of cases my speech is not disturbed by the circumstance that the words I am using recall others with a similar sound, that they are intimately linked with their contraries or that familiar associations

branch off from them. Perhaps we might still find a way out by following the philosopher Wundt, when he says that slips of the tongue arise if, as a result of physical exhaustion, the inclination to associate gains the upper hand over what the speaker otherwise intends to say. That would be most convincing if it were not contradicted by experience, which shows that in one set of cases the *somatic* factors favouring slips of the tongue are absent and in another set of cases the *associative* factors favouring them are equally absent.

I am particularly interested, however, in your next question: how does one discover the two mutually interfering purposes? You do not realize, probably, what a momentous question this is. One of the two, the purpose that is disturbed, is of course unmistakable: the person who makes the slip of the tongue knows it and admits to it. It is only the other, the disturbing purpose, that can give rise to doubt and hesitation. Now, we have already seen, and no doubt you have not forgotten, that in a number of cases this other purpose is equally evident. It is indicated by the *outcome* of the slip, if only we have the courage to grant that outcome a validity of its own. Take the President of the Lower House, whose slip of the tongue said the contrary of what he intended. It is clear that he wanted to open the sitting, but it is equally clear that he also wanted to close it. That is so obvious that it leaves us nothing to interpret. But in the other cases, in which the disturbing purpose only *distorts* the original one without itself achieving complete expression, how do we arrive at the disturbing purpose from the distortion?

In a first group of cases this is done quite simply and securely—in the same way, in fact, as with the *disturbed* purpose. We get the speaker to give us the information directly. After his slip of the tongue he at once produces the wording which he originally intended: "It *draut* . . . no, it *dauert* [will last] another month perhaps." [p. 257]. Well, in just the same way we get him to tell us the *disturbing* purpose. 'Why', we ask him, 'did you say "*draut*"?' He replies: 'I wanted to say "It's a *traurige* [sad] story".' * * * The speaker had to be asked why he had made the slip and what he could say about it. Otherwise he might perhaps have passed over his slip without wanting to explain it. But when he was asked he gave the explanation with the first thing that occurred to him. And now please observe that this small active step and its successful outcome are already a psycho-analysis and are a model for every psycho-analytic investigation which we shall embark upon later.

Am I too mistrustful, however, if I suspect that at the very moment at which psycho-analysis makes its appearance before your resistance to it simultaneously raises its head? Do you not feel inclined to object that the information given by the person of whom the question was asked—the person who made the slip of the tongue—is not completely conclusive? He was naturally anxious, you think, to fulfil the request to explain the slip, so he said the first thing that came into his head which seemed capable of providing such an explanation. But that is no proof that the slip did in fact take place in that way. It *may* have been so, but it may just as well have happened otherwise. And something else might have occurred to him which would have fitted in as well or perhaps even better.

It is strange how little respect you have at bottom for a psychical fact! Imagine that someone had undertaken the chemical analysis of a certain substance and had arrived at a particular weight for one component of it—so and so many milligrammes. Certain inferences could be drawn from this weight. Now do you suppose that it would ever occur to a chemist to criticize those inferences on the ground that the isolated substance might equally have had some other weight? Everyone will bow before the fact that this was the weight and none other and will confidently draw his further inferences from it. But when you are faced with the psychical fact that a particular thing occurred to the mind of the person questioned, you will not allow the fact's validity: something else might have occurred to him! You nourish the illusion of there being such a thing as psychical freedom, and you will not give it up. I am sorry to say I disagree with you categorically over this.

You will break off at that, but only to take up your resistance again at another point. You proceed: "It is the special technique of psycho-analysis, as we understand, to get people under analysis themselves to produce the solution of their problems. Now let us take another example —the one in which a speaker proposing the toast of honour on a ceremonial occasion called on his audience to hiccough [*aufzustossen*] to the health of the Chief. You say that the disturbing intention in this case was an insulting one: that was what was opposing the speaker's expression of respect. But this is pure interpretation on your part, based upon observations apart from the slip of the tongue. If in this instance you were to question the person responsible for the slip, he would not confirm your idea that he intended an insult; on the contrary, he would energetically repudiate it. Why, in view of this clear denial, do you not abandon your unprovable interpretation?"

Yes. You have lighted on a powerful argument this time. I can imagine the unknown proposer of the toast. He is probably a subordinate to the Chief of the Department who is being honoured —perhaps he himself is already an Assistant Lecturer, a young man with excellent prospects in life. I try to force him to admit that he may nevertheless have had a feeling that there was something in him opposing his toast in honour of the Chief. But this lands me in a nice mess. He gets impatient and suddenly breaks out: "Just you stop trying to cross-question me or I shall turn nasty. You're going to ruin my whole career with your suspicions. I simply said '*aufstossen* [hiccough to]' instead of '*anstossen* [drink to]' because I'd said '*auf*' twice before in the same sentence. That's what Meringer calls a perseveration and there's nothing more to be interpreted about it. D'you understand? *Basta!*"—H'm! That was a surprising reaction, a truly energetic denial. I see there's nothing more to be done with the young man. But I also reflect that he shows a strong personal interest in insisting on his parapraxis not having a sense. You may also feel that there was something wrong in his being quite so rude about a purely theoretical enquiry. But, you will think, when all is said and done he must know what he wanted to say and what he didn't.

But must he? Perhaps that may still be the question.

Now, however, you think you have me at your mercy. "So that's your technique," I hear you say. "When a person who has made a slip of the tongue says something about it that suits you, you pronounce him to be the final decisive authority on the subject. "He says so himself!" But when what he says doesn't suit your book, then all at once you say he's of no importance—there's no need to believe him."

That is quite true. But I can put a similar case to you in which the same monstrous event occurs. When someone charged with an offence confesses his deed to the judge, the judge believes his confession; but if he denies it, the judge does not believe him. If it were otherwise, there would be no administration of justice, and in spite of occasional errors we must allow that the system works.

"Are you a judge, then? And is a person who has made a slip of the tongue brought up before you on a charge? So making a slip of the tongue is an offence, is it?"

Perhaps we need not reject the comparison. But I would ask you to observe what profound differences of opinion we have reached after a little investigation of what seemed such innocent problems concerning the parapraxes—differences which at the moment we see no possible way of smoothing over. I propose a provisional compromise on the basis of the analogy with the judge and the defendant. I suggest that you shall grant me that there can be no doubt of a parapraxis having a sense if the subject himself admits it. *I will admit in return that we cannot arrive at a direct proof of the suspected sense if the subject refuses us information*, and equally, of course, if he is not at hand to give us the information. Then, as in the case of the administration of justice, we are obliged to turn to circumstantial evidence, which may make a decision more probable in some instances and less so in others. In the law courts it may be necessary for practical purposes

to find a defendant guilty on circumstantial evidence. We are under no such necessity; but neither are we obliged to disregard the circumstantial evidence. It would be a mistake to suppose that a science consists entirely of strictly proved theses, and it would be unjust to require this. Only a disposition with a passion for authority will raise such a demand, someone with a craving to replace his religious catechism by another, though it is a scientific one. Science has only a few apodeictic[6] propositions in its catechism: the rest are assertions promoted by it to some particular degree of probability. It is actually a sign of a scientific mode of thought to find satisfaction in these approximations to certainty and to be able to pursue constructive work further in spite of the absence of final confirmation.

But if the subject does not himself give us the explanation of the sense of a parapraxis, where are we to find the starting-points for our interpretation—the circumstantial evidence? In various directions. In the first place from analogies with phenomena apart from parapraxes: when, for instance, we assert that distorting a name when it occurs as a slip of the tongue has the same insulting sense as a deliberate twisting of a name. Further, from the psychical situation in which the parapraxis occurs, the character of the person who makes the parapraxis, and the impressions which he has received before the parapraxis and to which the parapraxis is perhaps a reaction. What happens as a rule is that the interpretation is carried out according to general principles: To begin with there is only a suspicion, a suggestion for an interpretation, and we then find a confirmation by examining the psychical situation. Sometimes we have to wait for subsequent events as well (which have, as it were, announced themselves by the parapraxis) before our suspicion is confirmed.

I cannot easily give you illustrations of this if I limit myself to the field of slips of the tongue, though even there some good instances are to be found. * * * The lady whose husband could eat and drink what *she* wanted is known to me as one

---

[6]Indisputable.

of those energetic women who wear the breeches in their home. ✶ ✶ ✶

But I can give you a large selection of circumstantial evidence of this kind if I pass over to the wide field of the other parapraxes.

If anyone forgets a proper name which is familiar to him normally or if, in spite of all his efforts, he finds it difficult to keep it in mind, it is plausible to suppose that he has something against the person who bears the name so that he prefers not to think of him. Consider, for instance, what we learn in the following cases about the psychical situation in which the parapraxis occurred.

"A Herr Y. fell in love with a lady, but he met with no success, and shortly afterward she married a Herr X. Thereafter, Herr Y., in spite of having known Herr X. for a long time and even having business dealings with him, forgot his name over and over again, so that several times he had to enquire what it was from other people when he wanted to correspond with Herr X." Herr Y. evidently wanted to know nothing of his more fortunate rival: "never thought of shall he be."

Or: A lady enquired from her doctor for news of a common acquaintance, but called her by her maiden name. She had forgotten her friend's married name. She admitted afterwards that she had been very unhappy about the marriage and disliked her friend's husband.

✶ ✶ ✶

The forgetting of intentions can in general be traced to an opposing current of thought, which is unwilling to carry out the intention. But this view is not only held by us psycho-analysts; it is the general opinion, accepted by everyone in their daily lives and only denied when it comes to theory. A patron who gives his protégé the excuse of having forgotten his request fails to justify himself. The protégé immediately thinks: "It means nothing to him; it's true he promised, but he doesn't really want to do it." For that reason forgetting is banned in certain circumstances of ordinary life; the distinction between the popular and the psycho-analytic view of these parapraxes seems to have disappeared. Imagine the lady of the house

receiving her guest with the words: "What? have you come today? I'd quite forgotten I invited you for today." Or imagine a young man confessing to his fiancée that he had forgotten to keep their last rendezvous. He will certainly not confess it; he will prefer to invent on the spur of the moment the most improbable obstacles which prevented his appearing at the time and afterwards made it impossible for him to let her know. We all know too that in military affairs the excuse of having forgotten something is of no help and is no protection against punishment, and we must all feel that that is justified. Here all at once everyone is united in thinking that a particular parapraxis has a sense and in knowing what that sense is. Why are they not consistent enough to extend this knowledge to the other parapraxes and to admit them fully? There is of course an answer to this question too.

✶ ✶ ✶

Cases of forgetting an intention are in general so clear that they are not of much use for our purpose of obtaining circumstantial evidence of the sense of a parapraxis from the psychical situation. Let us therefore turn to a particularly ambiguous and obscure kind of parapraxis—to losing and mislaying. You will no doubt find it incredible that we ourselves can play an intentional part in what is so often the painful accident of losing something. But there are plenty of observations like the following one. A young man lost a pencil of his of which he had been very fond. The day before, he had received a letter from his brother-in-law which ended with these words: "I have neither the inclination nor the time at present to encourage you in your frivolity and laziness." The pencil had actually been given to him by this brother-in-law. Without this coincidence we could not, of course, have asserted that a part was played in the loss by an intention to get rid of the thing. Similar cases are very common. We lose an object if we have quarreled with the person who gave it to us and do not want to be reminded of him; or if we no longer like the object itself and want to have an excuse for getting another and better one instead. The same intention directed against an object can also play a part, of course, in cases of dropping, breaking, or destroying things. Can we regard it as a matter of chance when a schoolchild immediately before his birthday loses, ruins or smashes some of his personal belongings, such as his satchel or his watch?

Nor will anyone who has sufficiently often experienced the torment of not being able to find something that he himself has put away feel inclined to believe that there is a purpose in mislaying things. Yet instances are far from rare in which the circumstances attendant on the mislaying point to an intention to get rid of the object temporarily or permanently.

Here is the best example, perhaps, of such an occasion. A youngish man told me the following story: "Some years ago there were misunderstandings between me and my wife. I found her too cold, and although I willingly recognized her excellent qualities we lived together without any tender feelings. One day, returning from a walk, she gave me a book which she had bought because she thought it would interest me. I thanked her for this mark of 'attention,' promised to read the book and put it on one side. After that I could never find it again. Months passed by, in which I occasionally remembered the lost book and made vain attempts to find it. About six months later my dear mother, who was not living with us, fell ill. My wife left home to nurse her mother-in-law. The patient's condition became serious and gave my wife an opportunity of showing the best side of herself. One evening I returned home full of enthusiasm and gratitude for what my wife had accomplished. I walked up to my desk, and without any definite intention but with a kind of somnambulistic certainty opened one of the drawers. On the very top I found the long-lost book I had mislaid." With the extinction of the motive the mislaying of the object ceased as well.

Ladies and Gentlemen, I could multiply this collection of examples indefinitely; but I will not do so here. You will in any case find a profusion of case material for the study of parapraxes in my *Psychopathology of Everyday Life* (first published in 1901). All these examples lead to the same result:

they make it probable that parapraxes have a sense, and they show you how that sense is discovered or confirmed by the attendant circumstances. I will be briefer to-day, because we have adopted the limited aim of using the study of these phenomena as a help towards a preparation for psychoanalysis. There are only two groups of observations into which I need enter more fully here: accumulated and combined parapraxes and the confirmation of our interpretations by subsequent events.

Accumulated and combined parapraxes are without doubt the finest flower of their kind. If we had only been concerned to prove that parapraxes have a sense we should have confined ourselves to them from the first, for in their case the sense is unmistakable even to the dull-witted and forces itself on the most critical judgement. An accumulation of these phenomena betrays an obstinacy that is scarcely ever a characteristic of chance events but fits in well with something intentional. Finally, the mutual interchangeability between different species of parapraxes demonstrates what it is in parapraxes that is important and characteristic: not their form or the method which they employ but the purpose which they serve and which can be achieved in the most various ways. For this reason I will give you an instance of repeated forgetting. Ernest Jones[7] tells us that once, for reasons unknown to him, he left a letter lying on his desk for several days. At last he decided to send it off, but he had it returned to him by the Dead Letter Office since he had forgotten to address it. After he had addressed it he took it to the post, but this time it had no stamp. And then at last he was obliged to admit his reluctance to sending the letter off at all.

In another case a bungled action is combined with an instance of mislaying. A lady travelled to Rome with her brother-in-law, who was a famous artist. The visitor was received with great honour by the German community in Rome, and among other presents he was given an antique gold medal. The lady was vexed that her brother-in-law

_____

[7]An English psychoanalyst.

did not appreciate the lovely object sufficiently. When she returned home (her place in Rome having been taken by her sister) she discovered while unpacking that she had brought the medal with her—how, she did not know. She at once sent a letter with the news to her brother-in-law, and announced that she would send the article she had walked off with back to Rome next day. But next day the medal had been so cleverly mislaid that it could not be found and sent off; and it was at this point, that the meaning of her "absent-mindedness" dawned on the lady: she wanted to keep the object for herself.

* * *

It would be agreeable to add further, similar examples. But I must proceed, and give you a glimpse of the cases in which our interpretation has to wait for the future for confirmation. The governing condition of these cases, it will be realized, is that the present psychical situation is unknown to us or inaccessible to our enquiries. Our interpretation is consequently no more than a suspicion to which we ourselves do not attach too much importance. Later, however, something happens which shows us how well-justified our interpretation had been. I was once the guest of a young married couple and heard the young woman laughingly describe her latest experience. The day after her return from the honeymoon she had called for her unmarried sister to go shopping with her as she used to do, while her husband went to his business. Suddenly she noticed a gentleman on the other side of the street, and nudging her sister had cried: "Look, there goes Herr L." She had forgotten that this gentleman had been her husband for some weeks. I shuddered as I heard the story, but I did not dare to draw the inference. The little incident only occurred to my mind some years later when the marriage had come to a most unhappy end.

Maeder tells of a lady who, on the eve of her wedding had forgotten to try on her wedding-dress and, to her dressmaker's despair, only re-membered it late in the evening. He connects this forgetfulness with the fact that she was soon divorced from her husband. I know a lady now divorced from her husband, who in managing her money affairs frequently signed documents in her maiden name, many years before she in fact resumed it.—I know of other women who have lost their wedding-rings during the honeymoon, and I know too that the history of their marriages has given a sense to the accident.—And now here is one more glaring example, but with a happier ending. The story is told of a famous German chemist that his marriage did not take place, because he forgot the hour of his wedding and went to the laboratory instead of to the church. He was wise enough to be satisfied with a single attempt and died at a great age unmarried.

The idea may possibly have occurred to you that in these examples parapraxes have taken the place of the omens or auguries of the ancients. And indeed some omens were nothing else than parapraxes, as, for instance, when someone stumbled or fell down. Others of them, it is true, had the character of objective happenings and not of subjective acts. But you would hardly believe how difficult it sometimes is to decide whether a particular event belongs to the one group or to the other. An act so often understands how to disguise itself as a passive experience.

All those of us who can look back on a comparatively long experience of life will probably admit that we should have spared ourselves many disappointments and painful surprises if we had found the courage and determination to interpret small parapraxes experienced in our human contacts as auguries and to make use of them as indications of intentions that were still concealed. As a rule we dare not do so; it would make us feel as though, after a detour through science, we were becoming superstitious again. Nor do all auguries come true, and you will understand from our theories that they do not all need to come true.

PSYCHOLOGICAL TYPES

Carl Jung

One mark of Freud's stature in intellectual history is the number of his adherents—and former adherents—who became major figures in their own right. Perhaps the best known of these is Carl Jung. Jung began his career in psychoanalysis as Freud's anointed "crown prince." Freud intended that Jung succeed him as president of International Psychoanalytic Association. The two carried on an intense correspondence for years and also traveled to the United States together in 1909.

When it came, the split between Freud and Jung was bitter. Jung felt that Freud overemphasized the role of sexuality and underemphasized the constructive role of the unconscious. But the conflict may have been deeper than that; Jung chafed under Freud's dominating role as his intellectual father figure and felt a need to achieve more independence. For his part, Freud regarded major departures from his theory simply as error, and was particularly alarmed by a turn Jung took in midlife toward a mystical view of the human psyche. Jung formulated ideas, still famous today, about a "collective unconscious" full of mysterious images and ideas shared by all members of the human race, and an "oceanic feeling" of being at one with the universe. Such ideas were anathema to the atheistic and hardheaded Freud.

In the following selection Jung explains one of the more down-to-earth of his theoretical ideas, his conception of introversion and extraversion and four related styles of thinking. These ideas have had an obvious and lasting influence. Recall, for example, that extraversion is one of the Big Five factors of personality espoused in the second section of this reader by Costa and McCrae. But Jung's conception is somewhat different from the behavioral styles labeled as extraversion and introversion today. Jung's introvert is someone who in a fundamental way has turned into himself or herself and away from the world; his extravert is wholly dependent on others for his or her intellectual and emotional life.

A widely used personality test, the Myers-Briggs Type Indicator (Myers & McCaulley, 1985), was designed to classify people as to their style of thinking, in Jungian terms. You might be classified as dominated by sensation, thinking, feeling, or intuition. This test is often used for vocational guidance. For example, the sensation style might be appropriate for an athlete, the thinking style for a lawyer, the feeling style for a poet, and the intuitive style for a clinical psychologist.

The following selection is an excerpt from a lecture Jung delivered in Territet, Switzerland in 1923. By this time Jung had split thoroughly from Freud and was well known for his own work.

From *Psychological Types*, by C. G. Jung, translated by R. Hull and H. Baynes, pp. 510–523. Copyright © 1971 by PUP. Reprinted by permission of Princeton University Press.

* * *

We shall discover, after a time, that in spite of the great variety of conscious motives and tendencies, certain groups of individuals can be distinguished who are characterized by a striking conformity of motivation. For example, we shall come upon individuals who in all their judgments, perceptions, feelings, affects, and actions feel external factors to be the predominant motivating force, or who at least give weight to them no matter whether causal or final motives are in question. I will give some examples of what I mean. St. Augustine: "I would not believe the Gospel if the authority of the Catholic Church did not compel it." A dutiful daughter: "I could not allow myself to think anything that would be displeasing to my father." One man finds a piece of modern music beautiful because everybody else pretends it is beautiful. Another marries in order to please his parents but very much against his own interests. There are people who contrive to make themselves ridiculous in order to amuse others; they even prefer to make butts of themselves rather than remain unnoticed. There are not a few who in everything they do or don't do have but one motive in mind: what will others think of them? "One need not be ashamed of a thing if nobody knows about it." There are some who can find happiness only when it excites the envy of others; some who make trouble for themselves in order to enjoy the sympathy of their friends.

Such examples could be multiplied indefinitely. They point to a psychological peculiarity that can be sharply distinguished from another attitude which, by contrast, is motivated chiefly by internal or subjective factors. A person of this type might say: "I know I could give my father the greatest pleasure if I did so and so, but I don't happen to think that way." Or: "I see that the weather has turned out bad, but in spite of it I shall carry out my plan." This type does not travel for pleasure but to execute a preconceived idea. Or: "My book is probably incomprehensible, but it is perfectly clear to me." Or, going to the other extreme: "Everybody thinks I could do something, but I know perfectly well I can do nothing." Such a man can be so ashamed of himself that he literally dares not meet people. There are some who feel happy only when they are quite sure nobody knows about it, and to them a thing is disagreeable just because it is pleasing to everyone else. They seek the good where no one would think of finding it. At every step the sanction of the subject must be obtained, and without it nothing can be undertaken or carried out. Such a person would have replied to St. Augustine: "I would believe the Gospel if the authority of the Catholic Church did *not* compel it." Always he has to prove that everything he does rests on his own decisions and convictions, and never because he is influenced by anyone, or desires to please or conciliate some person or opinion.

This attitude characterizes a group of individuals whose motivations are derived chiefly from the subject, from inner necessity. There is, finally, a third group, and here it is hard to say whether the motivation comes chiefly from within or without. This group is the most numerous and includes the less differentiated normal man, who is considered normal either because he allows himself no excesses or because he has no need of them. The normal man is, by definition, influenced as much from within as from without. He constitutes the extensive middle group, on one side of which are those whose motivations are determined mainly by the external object, and, on the other, those whose motivations are determined from within. I call the first group *extraverted*, and the second group *introverted*. The terms scarcely require elucidation as they explain themselves from what has already been said.

Although there are doubtless individuals whose type can be recognized at first glance, this is by no means always the case. As a rule, only careful observation and weighing of the evidence permit a sure classification. However simple and clear the fundamental principle of the two opposing attitudes may be, in actual reality they are complicated and hard to make out, because every individual is an exception to the rule. Hence one can never give a description of a type, no matter how complete, that would apply to more than one individual, despite the fact that in some ways it aptly characterizes thousands of others. Conformity is one side of a man, uniqueness is the other. Classification does not explain the individual psyche. Nevertheless, an understanding of psychological types opens the way to a better understanding of human psychology in general.

Type differentiation often begins very early, so early that in some cases one must speak of it as innate. The earliest sign of extraversion in a child is his quick adaptation to the environment, and the extraordinary attention he gives to objects and especially to the effect he has on them. Fear of objects is minimal; he lives and moves among them with confidence. His apprehension is quick but imprecise. He appears to develop more rapidly than the introverted child, since he is less reflective and usually without fear. He feels no barrier between himself and objects, and can therefore play with them freely and learn through them. He likes to carry his enterprises to the extreme and exposes himself to risks. Everything unknown is alluring.

To reverse the picture, one of the earliest signs of introversion in a child is a reflective, thoughtful manner, marked shyness and even fear of unknown objects. Very early there appears a ten-

dency to assert himself over familiar objects, and attempts are made to master them. Everything unknown is regarded with mistrust; outside influences are usually met with violent resistance. The child wants his own way, and under no circumstances will he submit to an alien rule he cannot understand. When he asks questions, it is not from curiosity or a desire to create a sensation, but because he wants names, meanings, explanations to give him subjective protection against the object. I have seen an introverted child who made his first attempts to walk only after he had learned the names of all the objects in the room he might touch. Thus very early in an introverted child the characteristic defensive attitude can be noted which the adult introvert displays towards the object; just as in an extraverted child one can very early observe a marked assurance and initiative, a happy trustfulness in his dealings with objects. This is indeed the basic feature of the extraverted attitude: psychic life is, as it were, enacted outside the individual in objects and objective relationships. In extreme cases there is even a sort of blindness for his own individuality. The introvert, on the contrary, always acts as though the object possessed a superior power over him against which he has to defend himself. His real world is the inner one.

Sad though it is, the two types are inclined to speak very badly of one another. This fact will immediately strike anyone who investigates the problem. And the reason is that the psychic values have a diametrically opposite localization for the two types. The introvert sees everything that is in any way valuable for him in the subject; the extravert sees it in the object. This dependence on the object seems to the introvert a mark of the greatest inferiority, while to the extravert the preoccupation with the subject seems nothing but infantile autoeroticism. So it is not surprising that the two types often come into conflict. This does not, however, prevent most men from marrying women of the opposite type. Such marriages are very valuable as psychological symbioses so long as the partners do not attempt a mutual "psychological" understanding. But this phase of understanding belongs to the normal development of every marriage provided the partners have the necessary leisure or the necessary urge to development—though even if both these are present real courage is needed to risk a rupture of the marital peace. In favourable circumstances this phase enters automatically into the lives of both types, for the reason that each type is an example of one-sided development. The one develops only external relations and neglects the inner; the other develops inwardly but remains outwardly at a standstill. In time the need arises for the individual to develop what has been neglected. The development takes the form of a differentiation of certain functions, to which I must now turn in view of their importance for the type problem.

The conscious psyche is an apparatus for adaptation and orientation, and consists of a number of different psychic functions. Among these we can distinguish four basic ones: *sensation, thinking, feeling, intuition.* Under sensation I include all perceptions by means of the sense organs; by thinking I mean the function of intellectual cognition and the forming of logical conclusions; feeling is a function of subjective valuation; intuition I take as perception by way of the unconscious, or perception of unconscious contents.

So far as my experience goes, these four basic functions seem to me sufficient to express and represent the various modes of conscious orientation. For complete orientation all four functions should contribute equally: thinking should facilitate cognition and judgment, feeling should tell us how and to what extent a thing is important or unimportant for us, sensation should convey concrete reality to us through seeing, hearing, tasting, etc., and intuition should enable us to divine the hidden possibilities in the background, since these too belong to the complete picture of a given situation.

In reality, however, these basic functions are seldom or never uniformly differentiated and equally at our disposal. As a rule one or the other function occupies the foreground, while the rest remain undifferentiated in the background. Thus there are many people who restrict themselves to the simple perception of concrete reality, without thinking about it or taking feeling values into account. They bother just as little about the possibilities hidden in a situation. I describe such people as *sensation types.* Others are exclusively oriented by what they think, and simply cannot adapt to a situation which they are unable to understand intellectually. I call such people *thinking types.* Others, again, are guided in everything entirely by feeling. They merely ask themselves whether a thing is pleasant or unpleasant, and orient themselves by their feeling impressions. These are the *feeling types.* Finally, the *intuitives* concern themselves neither with ideas nor with feeling reactions, nor yet with the reality of things, but surrender themselves wholly to the lure of possibilities, and abandon every situation in which no further possibilities can be scented.

Each of these types represents a different kind of one-sidedness, but one which is linked up with and complicated in a peculiar way by the introverted or extraverted attitude. It was because of this complication that I had to mention these function-types, and this brings us back to the question of the one-sidedness of the introverted and extraverted attitudes. This one-sidedness would lead to a complete loss of psychic balance if it were not compensated by an unconscious counterposition. Investigation of the unconscious has shown, for example, that alongside or behind the introvert's conscious attitude there is an unconscious extraverted attitude which automatically compensates his conscious one-sidedness.

* * *

The alteration of the conscious attitude is no light matter, because any habitual attitude is essentially a more or less conscious ideal, sanctified by custom and historical tradition, and founded on the bedrock of one's innate temperament. The conscious attitude is always in the nature of a *Weltanschauung,* if it is not explicitly a religion. It is this that makes the type problem so important. The opposition between the types is not merely an external conflict between men, it is the source of endless inner conflicts; the cause not only of external disputes and dislikes, but of nervous ills and psychic suffering. It is this fact, too, that obliges us physicians constantly to widen our medical horizon and to include within it not only general psychological standpoints but also questions concerning one's views of life and the world.

* * *

Recapitulating, I would like to stress that each of the two general attitudes, introversion and extraversion, manifests itself in a special way in an individual through the predominance of one of the four basic functions. Strictly speaking, there are no introverts and extraverts pure and simple, but only introverted and extraverted function-types, such as thinking types, sensation types, etc. There are thus at least eight clearly distinguishable types. Obviously one could increase this number at will if each of the functions were split into three subgroups, which would not be impossible em-

pirically. One could, for example, easily divide thinking into its three well-known forms: intuitive and speculative, logical and mathematical, empirical and positivist, the last being mainly dependent on sense perception. Similar subgroups could be made of the other functions, as in the case of intuition, which has an intellectual as well as an emotional and sensory aspect. In this way a large number of types could be established, each new division becoming increasingly subtle.

For the sake of completeness, I must add that I do not regard the classification of types according to introversion and extraversion and the four basic functions as the only possible one. Any other psychological criterion could serve just as well as a classifier, although, in my view, no other possesses so great a practical significance.

LOVE AND MARRIAGE

Alfred Adler

*Another brilliant and influential disciple of Freud who eventually broke away
was Alfred Adler. Adler succeeded Freud as president of the International Psychoanalytic Association in 1910, but resigned only a year later as he and Freud
parted ways. Like the dispute with Jung, the controversy between Freud and Adler became personal. But its intellectual basis seemed to lie in Adler's increasing
interest in the relationship between individual and society, and Freud's convic-
tion that Adler was not paying enough attention to the unconscious part of the
mind.*

*Adler introduced several ideas that became widespread in the way people
talk about personality. He believed that everyone has a powerful motivation to
overcome the feeling of powerlessness experienced in early childhood, and that in
some people this leads to a need to dominate others. The familiar term "inferiority complex" refers to the psychological state of someone driven to prove that
he or she is not inferior. Adler also introduced the term "life style" about the
time the following selection was written, as is mentioned in a note from the
translator. This term refers to the whole approach of a person to his or her life,
which permeates everything an individual feels and does.*

*These key Adlerian ideas are found in the following article. But the selection
does more than summarize tenets of Adler's theory. It demonstrates one of the
basic strengths of psychoanalytic approaches—that they often yield useful insights into everyday concerns. In this selection Adler mentions the three core
tasks of life, giving special attention to the problem of love and marriage. Written more than 70 years ago, much of the presentation has a contemporary ring.
The issues he discusses have been the grist for numerous best-selling self-help
books. It can make you wonder—if Adler were alive today, would his books be
sold in supermarkets?*

From "Love and Marriage," by A. Adler (1926/1982). In *Cooperation between the Sexes:
Writings on Women and Men, Love and Marriage, and Sexuality*, edited and translated by
H. L. Ansbacher and R. R. Ansbacher, pp. 104–116. New York: Norton. Reprinted with
permission of Estate of Sanford Greenberger and Northwestern University Press.

Love as a Life Task

To get to know a person completely, we must understand him also in his love relationships. We must be able to tell whether in matters of love he behaves correctly or incorrectly; and why in one case he may be suited, while in another case he would be unsuited. Quite naturally, the further problem arises: What can we do to prevent errors in love relationships? If we consider that human happiness depends perhaps to the largest part on the solution of the love and marriage problem, we will appreciate that these are most important questions.

One difficulty is brought up by most people right at the start. They say that people are not all alike and that two persons could perhaps have been happier, had each found a different partner. Granted this possibility, this consideration tells us only that the persons in question made a bad choice. But we do not know whether the foundering on the problem of love is due to the erroneous choice, or whether he or she would have foundered on this problem in any case for deeper reasons. An understanding of the human soul and its moving forces can often spare us from failures.

THE THREE LIFE TASKS The problem of love relationships is a part of the problem of human life. Its understanding is possible only if we regard the coherence with all other problems of life. Life poses three great task complexes, from the solution of which our future, our happiness depend.

Social task. The first life task is the social task in the broadest sense. Life demands of everybody a certain behavior and a very far-reaching ability for contact with our fellow men, a certain behavior within the family, and a formulation of his social attitude. It does matter for the fate of a person what kind of social order he sets as his direction-giving goal, to what extent he thinks in his actions of his own welfare, and to what extent of the welfare of others. His inner choice is often difficult to discern from his outward decisions; often he

cannot decide at all in questions of social attitude, and often his viewpoint must be understood in another sense than its outward appearance. What counts is always a person's behavior toward the human community, his fellow men in the widest sense, not what he or others think about it.

Occupation. A second life task is that of occupation—that is, the manner in which a person wants to make his abilities serve the general public. The solution of this question illuminates most clearly the essence of a person. For example, when a young man finds every occupation loathsome, we shall provisionally consider him not a suitable fellow man, because either he is not yet sufficiently mature for society, or he may never mature on his own. In most cases by far occupational choice is based on unconscious connections. They are unconscious in that at the time of choice nobody considers that he has taken a step for the benefit of the general public, that he has selected for himself a place in the general division of labor. Of course, what he does in his occupation also counts. One may reach an occupational choice but fail within the occupation, or recognize after a while that one really should have become something else. Frequent change of occupation permits the conclusion that the person in fact would prefer no occupation at all, or perhaps considers himself too good for any occupation—actually, not good enough—and only pretends to go along with it.

Love and Marriage. The third life task that every person must solve is the problem of love and marriage, to which we want to give here our special consideration. The child grows into this problem gradually. His entire surrounding is filled with love and marriage relationships. Unmistakably, the child, already in the very first years of life, attempts to take a stand and to give himself a direction toward this problem. What we hear about this in words is not decisive, because as soon as the child touches upon problems of love an enormous shyness often overcomes him. Some children express quite clearly that they cannot speak about this topic. Others are very devoted to their parents yet are not capable of being affectionate with them. A four-year-old boy returned proffered kisses with slaps in the face because the feeling of an affectionate impulse was uncanny to him, seemed to him frightening—one may even say humiliating.

Also in looking back on our own lives we notice that every affectionate impulse is accompanied by a sort of sense of shame and the impression that thereby one would become weaker or lose in value. This is very remarkable and requires an explanation. Our culture being generally oriented toward a masculine ideal, we grow up in the frame of mind that an affectionate impulse is a disgrace. Accordingly, in school, literature, and any environment, the children are continuously trained to see in love a kind of unmanliness. Sometimes they express this quite clearly, and some go so far that one may say they evade emotion.

THE LOGIC OF SOCIAL LIVING The child's first impulses of affection appear very early. As they develop, one can very easily note that they are all impulses of the social feeling. This is evidently innate, since it appears quite regularly. From the degree of its development we can appraise an individual's attitude to life.

The very concept of "human being" includes our entire understanding of social feeling. We cannot imagine that a human being could be designated as such after having lost it. Likewise, throughout history we find no human beings living in isolation. They always lived in groups, unless separated from one another artificially or through insanity. Darwin showed that animals with a less favorable position with regard to nature live in groups. Their vitality becomes effective by forming groups, unconsciously following a principle of self-preservation. Those that lived singly, in whose stepmotherly development social feeling was lacking, perished, victims of natural selection. The principle of natural selection is also dangerous for man, since, in facing nature, his physical equipment is most stepmotherly of all.

The situation of the inferiority and inadequacy of the human race develops in the whole race and in the individual a continuous drive and coercion that drive us on, until an approximate condition of rest is reached and some form of existence appears assured.[1]

We are still on this path, and today it is perhaps the best consolation for man to realize that our present situation is only a point of transition, a momentary phase of human development. He will naturally best pass through this phase, in reference to all problems of life, who is in accord with the actual conditions and does justice to the logic of the facts, whereas those who resist this logic, naturally will meet a merciless destiny. In the deepest sense, the feeling for the logic of human living together is social feeling.

The entire development of the child demands his embeddedness in a situation in which social feeling is present. His life and health are assured only if there are persons at hand who take his part. A newly born calf, for example, can very soon discriminate poisonous plants from others. The newly born human, however, due to the inferiority of his organism, depends on the social feeling of the adult. The child must for a long time be taken care of, taught, and trained until he can look after himself.

* * *

LOVE, PART OF SOCIAL FEELING The coherence of men among each other is necessitated not only by the pressing needs of the day, but also by our sexual organization. The division of humanity into two sexes, far from creating a separation, means an eternal compulsion toward one another. It creates the feeling of being mutually related, because in the veins of each a common blood flows, because each one is flesh from the flesh of another.

The marriage laws of the various peoples can be understood only from the viewpoint of love as a common bond of the entire group. Marriage and

---

[1]Adler saw this compensation for inferiority to be a basic drive in the human psyche.

sexual relations among members of the same family were interdicted because this would have led to an isolation of the families. Poetry, religions, the holy commandments are directed against incest and intended to eradicate it. While scholars have puzzled over the reason for the natural aversion of family members toward one another, we understand it quite easily on the basis of the social feeling that develops in each child and that eliminates all possibilities that could lead to an isolation of man.[2]

Now we can understand that love in its essential meaning, the relationship of the sexes, is always connected with social feeling and cannot be separated from it. Love, as a relationship of two, has, as a part of social feeling, its own laws and is a necessary component of the preservation of human society. One cannot think of a community without it. He who affirms the community necessarily also affirms love. He who has community feeling must favor marriage or a form of love of equal or higher value. On the other hand, a person whose social feeling is throttled, who has not arrived at a free development of his nature within humanity, will also show a strange form of love relationships.

Now we can draw a few conclusions that will facilitate an overview of this large area of love relationships and suddenly shed some light on it. A person whose social development is impaired, who has no friends, has not become a real fellow man, whose world view contradicts social feeling, and who perhaps has also not solved his occupational problem well—that is, one who is more or less completely lost to the community, is bound to have difficulties in his love relationships. Such persons will hardly be in a position to solve the erotic problem. They will take strange ways, will create difficulties, and will, where they actually find difficulties, reach for them as for a safeguarding excuse.

Disturbances of Love Relationships

Let us consider more closely the difficulties people create in their love relationships, and thereby gain a deeper insight into the entire problem. In a person's love relationships his entire personality is involved. We can understand his personality from his love relationships, as well as guess at his particular sexual aspirations from an understanding of his personality as a whole.[3]

SEEKING POWER OVER THE PARTNER

Obligating through love. Most frequently we find within the sexual relationship the erroneous assumption that love is an obligation for the other party. When we look around, and also observe ourselves, we will see that very often we commit the error of believing that the beloved person, by the mere fact of being loved, is obligated to us. This error seems somehow to be contained in our entire form of looking at things. It originates in childhood and the relationships with the family, where indeed the love of one is almost equal to the obligation of the other. In the adult, it is a remnant from childhood. The resulting excesses center around the thought: "Because I love you, you must do such and such." Thereby a much more severe tone is often introduced in the relationships of persons who are really devoted to each other. The need for power of the one who, on the strength of his own love, wants to draw the other into his schema, demands that the other's steps, expressions, achievements, etc., take place according to his wishes, "because he loves this person." This can easily turn into tyranny. A trace of this is found perhaps in every love relationship.

Thus we see the same factor permeating human love life that also otherwise leads always to

---

[2]Another reason for avoiding incest, not mentioned by Adler, is that interbreeding among relatives allows recessive genes to express themselves, leading to a higher frequency of birth defects.

[3]In the year in which this essay was published, Adler introduced the term "life style" into his writings. Thus we find here still the terms "entire personality," "personality," and "personality as a whole," which Adler subsequently equated with life style, while a few pages later he actually uses the term "life style."—Translator

disturbances of fellowship: the striving for power and personal superiority.[4]

In a human community, one must respect the freedom of the personal individuality to the extent of leaving the other person free choices. He who strives for personal superiority prevents his connection with a community. He does not want to fit into the whole, but wants the subordination of the others. Thereby he naturally disturbs the harmony in life, in society, among his fellow men. Since by nature no one wants permanently to have a yoke placed on him, those persons who, even in their love relationships are striving for power over the other, must meet with oversized difficulties. If they continue their inclination for presumption and superiority into their sex lives, they must seek a partner who appears to submit, or struggle with one who seeks superiority or victory on his own or in response to the situation. In the case of submission, love is transformed into slavery; in the second case, there will be a continuous, mutually destructive power struggle by which no harmony will ever be reached.

Selecting a subordinate partner. The ways of doing so vary greatly. Some domineering persons tremble so much for their ambition, their power, that they look only for a partner in whom there is no danger of superiority, who always appears to subordinate himself. These are by no means always worthless persons with high ambition. To be possessed by this striving for power is in our culture a generally prevalent trait causing immeasurable harm to the development of humanity.

In this light we can understand the relatively frequent strange phenomenon that people will in their love choice descend into a much lower and unsuitable social milieu. For example, a study of Goethe's love life would show that this ambitious man was extremely insecure in his love affairs. Concerned with the highest problem of humanity, he surprised his fellow men by marrying his cook. Emphasizing the equal worth of men, as we do, we are of course not indignant about this. But we

regard such action as out of keeping and want to understand it from that individual's viewpoint by examining his ultimate intention.

By our norm those persons will find each other who are socially and by their education and preparation for life best suited for each other. Suitors whose choices deviate from the general expectation are mostly persons who face the love problem with extreme hesitation and prejudices, are afraid of their sexual partner and, therefore are looking for a partner in whom they suspect less power and strength. It is of course possible that someone may deviate from the norm through a feeling of strength. But mostly it is done through weakness.

Such a choice appears to some of these careful individuals as an extremely happy solution, not understanding that their ultimate intention is to conceal their deeper motives through love and sexuality, and convinced that only Cupid is involved here. But as a rule such a relationship turns out poorly and has many disadvantages—not that the intellectually or socially "superior" partner would be disappointed, or that difficulties of a social nature would occur when the "inferior" partner would not satisfy certain requirements of family and social life. These and other external factors could be eliminated and bridged, if the ultimate intention of the "superior" partner could be realized. But strangely it is the "inferior" partner who does not tolerate for long seeing his weakness abused. Even if he does not understand what goes on, he nevertheless cannot get rid of the feeling that his shortcomings are being abused. From this feeling he takes to a kind of revenge; he will try to show that he is not less than the other.

There are many conspicuous cases of this kind. Often a young, cultured, outstandingly intelligent girl throws herself into the arms of an insignificant, often even immoral person, perhaps sometimes with the idea of saving a man whom she appears to love from the clutches of alcoholism, gambling, or indolence. Never yet have such people been saved through love. This action fails almost regularly. The "inferior" partner feels under all circumstances oppressed by his inferior classification. He does not let himself be loved and be

---

[4]This is one harmful result of the "inferiority complex."

saved, because the moving forces of his attitude to life are quite different and not recognizable by ordinary intelligence, the "common sense." He has perhaps long ago given up hope ever to amount to anything and sees in every situation that makes on him requirements as a fellow man a new danger that his presumed inferiority could become clearly apparent.

Many persons also are interested only in physically deficient or much older love partners. These cases rightfully attract our attention and call for an explanation. Sometimes we find a natural explanation arising from a particular situation. But even then this inclination always corresponds to a life style of taking the line of least resistance.

Predatory desire. Other persons fall in love almost only with partners who are already engaged. This strange fact may reveal various intentions. It may mean, "No," regarding the demands of love, striving for the impossible, or an unfulfillable ideal. But it may also mean, "wanting to take something away from another," a trait carried over into sexuality from the life style.

*   *   *

EVADING MARRIAGE Many people are not quite sufficiently mature for society, see in love and marriage relationships a danger zone, and express their immature views in various ways that are, on the surface, often unintelligible. Regarding these questions, which continuously bother them, they speak in generalities that, in some context, could be true and would not necessarily be a deception. For example, when somebody who is also otherwise timid believes he does not marry "because life these days is so difficult," each word is true enough. But it is also true for those who do marry. Such truths are expressed only by those who would have said "No" even without these truths. In that event they would have reached for another "truth." It would be undiplomatic to support a preconceived intention with a bad argument when good ones are available everywhere. Alarmingly, many people try to escape from the solution of

the life problems, and this also takes the guise of sex.

Unrequited love. This is the case in most instances of repeatedly unrequited love. It is a means for realizing, with a pretense of justification, the life goal of turning away from life, from the world. In such cases an unhappy love cannot be unhappy enough to fulfill its purpose. It strikes persons with a readiness to run away from the problems of life, especially those of love, which sometimes receives welcome reinforcement by a trick, a device. This is not always completely invented but is attached to some actual life relationship. Then it does not look like a device but resembles the obvious result of an experience.

We can also "make" a person unattainable. Often the suitor has, from the start, the impression that he will not be received well, but makes this an occasion for greater action. He believes he cannot live without the beloved person and courts her, although any objective observer would consider it improbable that his love would ever be requited. He even says so to himself. Often such courting takes a form apt to provoke resistance— for example, by being extremely vehement, or occurring at a time before any guarantees for living together are given. Such courtships are aimed at unrequited love. A surprisingly large number of persons steer toward this goal.

Some people have been infatuated even without knowing whether that person exists. This clearly expresses their ultimate intention not to have anything to do with love and marriage. Their infatuation can in all probability never be realized.

One should think, from the outside, that such behavior was not part of human nature. But such a person is an "escapist" throughout, and unrequited love provides him with an excellent hiding place. When he carries his unrequited love with him for five or ten years, he is during this entire time safe from all other solutions of this problem. Of course, he has suffered, paid the expenses for the realization of his intention. But his goal— which has remained unconscious to himself, which he himself did not understand—to stay away from the solution of the love and marriage problem, has thereby been reached with a good conscience and justification. Such a goal and solution are not compatible with the conditions of this earth and the logic of human living together. They are actually the deepest tragedy rather than a solution. Only by this ultimate deepest insight is corrective intervention possible.

High ideals. For the escapist, one frequently tested device is especially recommended. Let him create a new idea, a special ideal. Let him measure by this ideal all persons who cross his path in life. The consequence is that no one will prove suitable; they all deviate from the ideal. When he refuses and eliminates them, his action looks reasonable and well founded. But when we examine an individual case, we find that such a reasonably choosing person, even without his ideal, is willing from the start to say "No." The ideal contains desirable goals of frankness, honesty, courage, etc. But these concepts can be extended and stretched at will until they exceed any human measure. Thus we have at our disposal the love of something that we have previously "made" unattainable.

This device has various possibilities of concretization. We can love a person who was present once for a short time, made an impression, disappeared, and can now no longer be found. One would have to look all over the world to find him. At first we are touched by such fond and faithful love. However, the condition for the realization of such love on earth is superhuman and raises our suspicion.

FEAR AND LACK OF RESERVE Generally, the feeling of insecurity determines many forms of sexuality. There are young men who like only older women [as mentioned earlier], somehow in the erroneous opinion that in this case living together would be less difficult. They disclose their feelings of weakness also through a certain need for moth-

erly care. They are usually pampered persons who very much want to lean on somebody, who "still need a nursemaid." They can never have enough safeguards against the other sex, and become extremely disquieted when facing it.

There are in our culture alarmingly many such insecure persons with a strong blemish of our phase of development—the fear of love and marriage. It is a general trait of the times. Our society is full of escapists. Through some unhappy and erroneous attitude, they are always as if in flight, always chased and persecuted. Some men isolate themselves and hide. Some girls don't even dare to go on the street, convinced that all men are courting them and that they would always be only the object of attacks. This is pure vanity, capable of completely spoiling the life of a person.

Experiences and knowledge can be put to good use and to bad use. Among the bad uses is the exaggerated reversal of an error, which is equally an error. The opposite of keeping back and being taciturn is openness, and thus we find people who make errors by being open. They always offer themselves to others. Although it is very nice openly to confess one's love, we are firmly convinced that in our complex culture this is a serious mistake. The reason is that there is nobody who could simply tolerate this offer, and the one who made it so hastily will not only have to bear the pain of regret and the burden of resulting inhibitions, but will also disturb the partner in the spontaneous development of his love impulses. Because of the generally prevailing abuse of love and the existing tension and struggle between the sexes, the partner will never be quite sure whether the offer was genuine and true, or whether perhaps bad intentions were hidden behind it. There are no fixed rules—we must take the particularity of the partner into account and go by the given conditions of our culture. Today it appears rather advisable to hold back one's inclinations somewhat.

*   *   *

THE DISTRUST BETWEEN THE SEXES

Karen Horney

Like Jung and Adler, Karen Horney began her own psychoanalytic career as a follower and defender of Freud. But Horney was too much of an independent thinker to remain anyone's disciple for long. First practicing in Germany and then in America for most of her career, Horney invented a distinctly feminist form of psychoanalysis. The combination of a psychoanalytic style of thinking with ideas of the sort that it is difficult to imagine a male analyst propounding is well illustrated in the following selection.

The selection comes from a paper Horney delivered before the German Women's Medical Association in 1930. Like the previous selection by Adler, this paper also has a contemporary feel to it. Horney was ahead of her time, and her gentle critique of and subtle revisions to conventional psychoanalytic theory anticipated feminist objections that would be expressed over the following decades.

*　*　*

The relationship between men and women is quite similar to that between children and parents, in that we prefer to focus on the positive aspects of these relationships. We prefer to assume that love is the fundamentally given factor and that hostility is an accidental and avoidable occurrence. Although we are familiar with slogans such as "the battle of the sexes" and "hostility between the sexes," we must admit that they do not mean a great deal. They make us overfocus on sexual relations between men and women, which can very easily lead us to a too one-sided view. Actually, from our recollection of numerous case histories, we may conclude that love relationships are quite easily destroyed by overt or covert hostility. On the other hand we are only too ready to blame such difficulties on individual misfortune, on incompatibility of the partners, and on social or economic causes.

The individual factors, which we find causing poor relations between men and women, may be the pertinent ones. However, because of the great frequency, or better, the regular occurrence of disturbances in love relations, we have to ask ourselves whether the disturbances in the individual cases might not arise from a common background; whether there are common denominators for this easily and frequently arising suspiciousness between the sexes?

* * *

I would like to start with something very commonplace—namely, that a good deal of this atmosphere of suspiciousness is understandable and even justifiable. It apparently has nothing to do with the individual partner, but rather with the intensity of the affects and with the difficulty of taming them.

We know or may dimly sense that these affects can lead to ecstasy, to being beside oneself, to surrendering oneself, which means a leap into the unlimited and the boundless. This is perhaps why real passion is so rare. For like a good businessman, we are loath to put all our eggs in one basket. We are inclined to be reserved and ever ready to retreat. Be that as it may, because of our instinct for self-preservation, we all have a natural fear of losing ourselves in another person. That is why what happens to love, happens to education and psychoanalysis; everybody thinks he knows all about them, but few do. One is inclined to overlook how little one gives of oneself, but one feels all the more this same deficiency in the partner, the feeling of "You never really loved me." A wife who harbors suicidal thoughts because her husband does not give her all his love, time, and interest will not notice how much of her own hostility, hidden vindictiveness, and aggression are expressed through her attitude. She will feel only despair because of her abundant "love," while at the same time she will feel most intensely and see most clearly the lack of love in her partner. * * *

Here we are not dealing with pathological phenomena at all. In pathological cases we merely see a distortion and exaggeration of a general and normal occurrence. Anybody, to a certain extent, will be inclined to overlook his own hostile impulses, but under pressure of his own guilty conscience, may project them onto the partner. This process must, of necessity, cause some overt or covert distrust of the partner's love, fidelity, sincerity, or kindness. This is the reason why I prefer to speak of distrust between the sexes and not of hatred; for in keeping with our own experience we are more familiar with the feeling of distrust.

A further, almost unavoidable, source of dis-appointment and distrust in our normal love life derives from the fact that the very intensity of our feelings of love stirs up all of our secret expectations and longings for happiness, which slumber deep inside us. All our unconscious wishes, contradictory in their nature and expanding boundlessly on all sides, are waiting here for their fulfillment. The partner is supposed to be strong, and at the same time helpless, to dominate us and be dominated by us, to be ascetic and to be sensuous. He should rape us and be tender, have time for us exclusively and also be intensely involved in creative work. As long as we assume that he could actually fulfill all these expectations, we invest him with the glitter of sexual overestimation. We take the magnitude of such overvaluation for the measure of our love, while in reality it merely expresses the magnitude of our expectations. The very nature of our claims makes their fulfillment impossible. Herein lies the origin of the disappointments with which we may cope in a more or less effective way. Under favorable circumstances we do not even have to become aware of the great number of our disappointments, just as we have not been aware of the extent of our secret expectations. Yet there remain traces of distrust in us, as in a child who discovers that his father cannot get him the stars from the sky after all.

Thus far, our reflections certainly have been neither new nor specifically analytical and have often been better formulated in the past. The analytical approach begins with the question: What special factors in human development lead to the discrepancy between expectations and fulfillment and what causes them to be of special significance in particular cases? Let us start with a general consideration. There is a basic difference between human and animal development—namely, the long period of the infant's helplessness and dependency. The paradise of childhood is most often an illusion with which adults like to deceive themselves. For the child, however, this paradise is inhabited by too many dangerous monsters. Unpleasant experiences with the opposite sex seem to be unavoidable. We need only recall the capacity that children possess, even in their very early years, for passionate and instinctive sexual desires similar to those of adults and yet different from them. Children are different in the aims of their drives, but above all, in the pristine integrity of their demands. They find it hard to express their desires directly, and where they do, they are not taken seriously. Their seriousness sometimes is looked upon as being cute, or it may be overlooked or rejected. In short, children will undergo painful and humiliating experiences of being rebuffed, being betrayed, and being told lies. They also may have to take second place to a parent or sibling, and they are threatened and intimidated when they seek, in playing with their own bodies, those pleasures that are denied them by adults. The child is relatively powerless in the face of all this. He is not able to ventilate his fury at all, or only to a minor degree, nor can he come to grips with the experience by means of intellectual comprehension. Thus, anger and aggression are pent up within him in the form of extravagant fantasies, which hardly reach the daylight of awareness, fantasies that are criminal when viewed from the standpoint of the adult, fantasies that range from taking by force and stealing, to those about killing, burning, cutting to pieces, and choking. Since the child is vaguely aware of these destructive forces within him, he feels, according to the talion law,[1] equally threatened by the adults. Here is the origin of those infantile anxieties of which no child remains entirely free. This already enables us to understand better the fear of love of which I have spoken before. Just here, in this most irrational of all areas, the old childhood fears of a threatening father or mother are reawakened, putting us instinctively on the defensive. In other words, the fear of love will always be mixed with the fear of what we might do to the other person, or what the other person might do to us. A lover in the Aru Islands, for example, will never make a gift of a lock of hair to his beloved, because should an argument arise, the beloved might burn it, thus causing the partner to get sick.

---

[1]The law of retaliative justice, sometimes called "an eye for an eye."

I would like to sketch briefly how childhood conflicts may affect the relationship to the opposite sex in later life. Let us take as an example a typical situation: The little girl who was badly hurt through some great disappointment by her father will transform her innate instinctual wish to receive from the man into a vindictive one of taking from him by force. Thus the foundation is laid for a direct line of development to a later attitude, according to which she will not only deny her maternal instincts, but will have only one drive, i.e., to harm the male, to exploit him, and to suck him dry. She has become a vampire. Let us assume that there is a similar transformation from the wish to receive to the wish to take away. Let us further assume that the latter wish was repressed due to anxiety from a guilty conscience; then we have here the fundamental constellation for the formation of a certain type of woman who is unable to relate to the male because she fears that every male will suspect her of wanting something from him. This really means that she is afraid that he might guess her repressed desires. Or by completely projecting onto him her repressed wishes, she will imagine that every male merely intends to exploit her, that he wants from her only sexual satisfaction, after which he will discard her. Or let us assume that a reaction formation of excessive modesty will mask the repressed drive for power. We then have the type of woman who shies away from demanding or accepting anything from her husband. Such a woman, however, due to the return of the repressed, will react with depression to the nonfulfillment of her unexpressed, and often unformulated, wishes. She thus unwittingly jumps from the frying pan into the fire, as does her partner, because a depression will hit him much harder than direct aggression. Quite often the repression of aggression against the male drains all her vital energy. The woman then feels helpless to meet life. She will shift the entire responsibility for her helplessness onto the man, robbing him of the very breath of life. Here you have the type of woman who, under the guise of being helpless and childlike, dominates her man.

These are examples that demonstrate how the

fundamental attitude of women toward men can be disturbed by childhood conflicts. In an attempt to simplify matters, I have stressed only one point, which, however, seems crucial to me—the disturbance in the development of motherhood.

I shall now proceed to trace certain traits of male psychology. I do not wish to follow individual lines of development, though it might be very instructive to observe analytically how, for instance, even men who consciously have a very positive relationship with women and hold them in high esteem as human beings, harbor deep within themselves a secret distrust of them; and how this distrust relates back to feelings toward their mothers, which they experienced in their formative years. I shall focus rather on certain typical attitudes of men toward women and how they have appeared during various eras of history and in different cultures, not only as regards sexual relationships with women, but also, and often more so, in nonsexual situations, such as in their general evaluation of women.

I shall select some random examples, starting with Adam and Eve.[2] Jewish culture, as recorded in the Old Testament, is outspokenly patriarchal. This fact reflects itself in their religion, which has no maternal goddesses; in their morals and customs, which allow the husband the right to dissolve the marital bond simply by dismissing his wife. Only by being aware of this background can we recognize the male bias in two incidents of Adam's and Eve's history. First of all, woman's capacity to give birth is partly denied and partly devaluated: Eve was made of Adam's rib and a curse was put on her to bear children in sorrow. In the second place, by interpreting her tempting Adam to eat of the tree of knowledge as a sexual temptation, woman appears as the sexual temptress, who plunges man into misery. I believe that these two elements, one born out of resentment, the other out of anxiety, have damaged the rela-

tionship between the sexes from the earliest times to the present. Let us follow this up briefly. Man's fear of woman is deeply rooted in sex, as is shown by the simple fact that it is only the sexually attractive woman of whom he is afraid and who, although he strongly desires her, has to be kept in bondage. Old women, on the other hand, are held in high esteem, even by cultures in which the young woman is dreaded and therefore suppressed. In some primitive cultures the old woman may have the decisive voice in the affairs of the tribe; among Asian nations also she enjoys great power and prestige. On the other hand, in primitive tribes woman is surrounded by taboos during the entire period of her sexual maturity. Women of the Arunta tribe are able to magically influence the male genitals. If they sing to a blade of grass and then point it at a man or throw it at him, he becomes ill or loses his genitals altogether. Women lure him to his doom. In a certain East African tribe, husband and wife do not sleep together, because her breath might weaken him. If a woman of a South African tribe climbs over the leg of a sleeping man, he will be unable to run; hence the general rule of sexual abstinence two to five days prior to hunting, warfare, or fishing. Even greater is the fear of menstruation, pregnancy, and childbirth. Menstruating women are surrounded by extensive taboos—a man who touches a menstruating woman will die. There is one basic thought at the bottom of all this: Woman is a mysterious being who communicates with spirits and thus has magic powers that she can use to hurt the male. He must therefore protect himself against her powers by keeping her subjugated. Thus the Miri in Bengal do not permit their women to eat the flesh of the tiger, lest they become too strong. The Watawela of East Africa keep the art of making fire a secret from their women, lest women become their rulers. The Indians of California have ceremonies to keep their women in submission; a man is disguised as a devil to intimidate the women. The Arabs of Mecca exclude women from religious festivities to prevent familiarity between women and their

---

[2]The long paragraph that follows provides a good illustration of Horney's distinctly feminist style of psychoanalytic thinking.

overlords. We find similar customs during the Middle Ages—the Cult of the Virgin side by side with the burning of witches; the adoration of "pure" motherliness, completely divested of sexuality, next to the cruel destruction of the sexually seductive woman. Here again is the implication of underlying anxiety, for the witch is in communication with the devil. Nowadays, with our more humane forms of aggression, we burn women only figuratively, sometimes with undisguised hatred, sometimes with apparent friendliness. * * * In friendly and secret autos-da-fé, many nice things are said about women, but it is just unfortunate that in her God-given natural state, she is not the equal of the male. Moebius pointed out that the female brain weighs less than the male one, but the point need not be made in so crude a way. On the contrary, it can be stressed that woman is not at all inferior, only different, but that unfortunately she has fewer or none of those human or cultural qualities that man holds in such high esteem. She is said to be deeply rooted in the personal and emotional spheres, which is wonderful; but unfortunately, this makes her incapable of exercising justice and objectivity, therefore disqualifying her for positions in law and government and in the spiritual community. She is said to be at home only in the realm of eros. Spiritual matters are alien to her innermost being, and she is at odds with cultural trends. She therefore is, as Asians frankly state, a second-rate being. Woman may be industrious and useful but is, alas, incapable of productive and independent work. She is, indeed, prevented from real accomplishment by the deplorable, bloody tragedies of menstruation and childbirth. And so every man silently thanks his God, just as the pious Jew does in his prayers, that he was not created a woman.

Man's attitude toward motherhood is a large and complicated chapter. One is generally inclined to see no problem in this area. Even the misogynist is obviously willing to respect woman as a mother and to venerate her motherliness under certain conditions, as mentioned above regarding the Cult of the Virgin. In order to obtain a clearer

picture, we have to distinguish between two attitudes: men's attitudes toward motherliness, as represented in its purest form in the Cult of the Virgin, and their attitude toward motherhood as such, as we encounter it in the symbolism of the ancient mother goddesses. Males will always be in favor of motherliness, as expressed in certain spiritual qualities of women, i.e., the nurturing, selfless, self-sacrificing mother; for she is the ideal embodiment of the woman who could fulfill all his expectations and longings. In the ancient mother goddesses, man did not venerate motherliness in the spiritual sense, but rather motherhood in its most elemental meaning. Mother goddesses are earthy goddesses, fertile like the soil. They bring forth new life and they nurture it. It was this life-creating power of woman, an elemental force, that filled man with admiration. And this is exactly the point where problems arise. For it is contrary to human nature to sustain appreciation without resentment toward capabilities that one does not possess. Thus, a man's minute share in creating new life became, for him, an immense incitement to create something new on his part.[3] He has created values of which he might well be proud. State, religion, art, and science are essentially his creations, and our entire culture bears the masculine imprint.

However, as happens elsewhere, so it does here; even the greatest satisfactions or achievements, if born out of sublimation,[4] cannot fully make up for something for which we are not endowed by nature. Thus there has remained an obvious residue of general resentment of men against women. This resentment expresses itself, also in our times, in men's distrustful defensive maneuvers against the threat of women's invasion of their domains; hence their tendency to devalue

---

[3]Famously, Freud thought women suffered from "penis envy." In this passage, Horney seems to claim that men suffer from womb envy.

[4]Sublimation is the psychoanalytic mechanism by which a motivation to do one thing is turned to another purpose.

pregnancy and childbirth and to overemphasize male genitality. This attitude does not express itself in scientific theories alone, but is also of far-reaching consequence for the entire relationship between the sexes, and for sexual morality in general. Motherhood, especially illegitimate motherhood, is very insufficiently protected by law. * * * Conversely, there is ample opportunity for the fulfillment of the male's sexual needs. Emphasis on irresponsible sexual indulgence, and devaluation of women to an object of purely physical needs, are further consequences of this masculine attitude.

* * *

I do not want to be misunderstood as having implied that all disaster results from male supremacy and that relations between the sexes would improve if women were given the ascendency. However, we must ask ourselves why there should have to be any power struggle at all between the sexes. At any given time, the more powerful side will create an ideology suitable to help maintain its position and to make this position acceptable to the weaker one. In this ideology the differentness of the weaker one will be interpreted as inferiority, and it will be proven that these differences are unchangeable, basic, or God's will.[5] It is the function of such an ideology to deny or conceal the existence of a struggle. Here is one of the answers to the question raised initially as to why we have so little awareness of the fact that there is a struggle between the sexes. It is in the interest of men to obscure this fact; and the emphasis they place on their ideologies has caused women, also, to adopt these theories. Our attempt at resolving these rationalizations and at examining these ideologies as to their fundamental driving forces, is merely a step on the road taken by Freud.

* * *

That many-faceted thing called love succeeds in building bridges from the loneliness on this shore to the loneliness on the other one. These bridges can be of great beauty, but they are rarely built for eternity and frequently they cannot tolerate too heavy a burden without collapsing. Here is the other answer to the question posed initially of why we see love between the sexes more distinctly than we see hate—because the union of the sexes offers us the greatest possibilities for happiness. We therefore are naturally inclined to overlook how powerful are the destructive forces that continually work to destroy our chances for happiness.

We might ask in conclusion, how can analytical insights contribute to diminish the distrust between the sexes? There is no uniform answer to this problem. The fear of the power of the affects and the difficulty in controlling them in a love relationship, the resulting conflict between surrender and self-preservation, between the I and the Thou, is an entirely comprehensible, unmitigatable, and as it were, normal phenomenon. The same thing applies in essence to our readiness for distrust, which stems from unresolved childhood conflicts. These childhood conflicts, however, can vary greatly in intensity, and will leave behind traces of variable depth. Analysis not only can help in individual cases to improve the relationship with the opposite sex, but it can also attempt to improve the psychological conditions of childhood and forestall excessive conflicts. This, of course, is our hope for the future. In the momentous struggle for power, analysis can fulfill an important function by uncovering the real motives of this struggle. This uncovering will not eliminate the motives, but it may help to create a better chance for fighting the struggle on its own ground instead of relegating it to peripheral issues.

---

[5]Some modern, feminist critiques of evolutionary personality theory (see Part III) are suspicious of its account of sex differences on exactly these grounds.

EIGHT STAGES OF MAN

Erik Erikson

The last of the classic neo-Freudians to be included in these readings, Erik Erikson, was not really a contemporary of Freud. His career took place across the years following Freud's death in 1939, until Erikson's own death in 1994. But Erikson became the major figure among the neo-Freudians who never broke with the master. He considered himself a loyal disciple to the end, as many passages in the following selection demonstrate.

Despite his loyalty, Erikson's theory goes into territory far outside anything Freud ever seriously considered. The theoretical development for which he is best known, described in this selection, goes beyond Freud in a specific way. Freud viewed psychosexual development as a process that occurred in infancy and early childhood, and was essentially finished shortly after the attainment of puberty. For many years developmental psychology followed the same basic presumption.

But Erikson changed all that. Of his "eight stages of man," four take place during and after the final stage of development from a traditional Freudian perspective. Erikson viewed psychological development as something that occurs throughout life, as challenges, opportunities, and obligations change. At the very last stage, one comes to terms with one's impending death and the meaning of one's life past. The outcome of this stage is crucial for the next generation. In one of his most thought-provoking comments, Erikson writes "healthy children will not fear life if their parents have integrity enough not to fear death." So the last stage of one's own development intersects with the earlier stages in one's children, and the cycle begins again.

The entire field of developmental psychology—not just the part within psychoanalysis—was changed in a profound way as Erikson's framework became widely influential. Without ever using the term, Erikson invented what is today called "life-span developmental psychology," a psychology that studies the way people develop every step of the way from the first day of their life to the last. Erikson's most lasting contribution is the reminder that development is not aimed at an end point, but is a continuing process.

From *Childhood and Society*, by E. H. Erikson, pp. 219–234. Copyright © 1950, 1963 by W. W. Norton & Company, Inc., renewed 1978, 1991 by Erik H. Erikson. Reprinted by permission of W. W. Norton & Company, Inc.

1. Trust vs. Basic Mistrust

The first demonstration of social trust in the baby is the ease of his feeding, the depth of his sleep, the relaxation of his bowels. The experience of a mutual regulation of his increasingly receptive capacities with the maternal techniques of provision gradually helps him to balance the discomfort caused by the immaturity of homeostasis with which he was born. In his gradually increasing waking hours he finds that more and more adventures of the senses arouse a feeling of familiarity, of having coincided with a feeling of inner goodness. Forms of comfort, and people associated with them, become as familiar as the gnawing discomfort of the bowels. The infant's first social achievement, then, is his willingness to let the mother out of sight without undue anxiety or rage, because she has become an inner certainty as well as an outer predictability. Such consistency, continuity, and sameness of experience provide a rudimentary sense of ego identity which depends, I think, on the recognition that there is an inner population of remembered and anticipated sensations and images which are firmly correlated with the outer population of familiar and predictable things and people. Smiling crowns this development.

The constant tasting and testing of the relationship between inside and outside meets its crucial test during the rages of the biting stage, when the teeth cause pain from within and when outer friends either prove of no avail or withdraw from the only action which promises relief: biting. I would assume that this experience of an urge turning upon the self has much to do with the masochistic tendency of finding cruel and cold comfort in hurting oneself whenever an object has eluded one's grasp.

Out of this, therefore, comes that primary sense of badness, that original sense of evil and malevolence which signifies the potential loss of all that is good because we could not help destroying it inside, thus driving it away outside. This feeling persists in a universal homesickness, a nostalgia for familiar images undamaged by change. Tribes dealing with one segment of nature develop a collective magic which seems to treat the Supernatural Providers of food and fortune as if they were angry and must be appeased by prayer and self-torture. Primitive religions, the most primitive layer in all religions, and the religious layer in each individual, abound with efforts at atonement which try to make up for vague deeds against a maternal matrix and try to restore faith in the goodness of one's strivings and in the kindness of the powers of the universe.

* * * The general state of trust implies not only that one has learned to rely on the sameness and continuity of the outer providers, but also that one may trust oneself and the capacity of one's own organs to cope with urges; and that one is able to consider oneself trustworthy enough so that the providers will not need to be on guard lest they be nipped.

In psychopathology the absence of basic trust can best be studied in infantile schizophrenia, while weakness of such trust is apparent in adult personalities of schizoid and depressive character. The reestablishment of a state of trust has been found to be the basic requirement for therapy in these cases. For no matter what conditions may have caused a psychotic break, the bizarreness and withdrawal in the behavior of many very sick individuals hides an attempt to reconquer social mutuality by a testing of the borderlines between senses and physical reality, between words and social meanings.

Psychoanalysis assumes the early process of differentiation between inside and outside to be the origin of the mechanisms of projection and introjection which remain some of our deepest and most dangerous defense mechanisms. In introjection we feel and act as if an outer goodness had become an inner certainty. In projection, we experience an inner harm as an outer one: we endow significant people with the evil which actually is in us. These two mechanisms, then, projection and introjection, are assumed to be modeled after whatever goes on in infants when they would like to externalize pain and internalize pleasure, an intent which must yield to the testimony of the maturing senses and ultimately of reason. These mechanisms are, more or less normally, reinstated in acute crises of love, trust, and faith in the adult. Where they persist, they mark the "psychotic character."

The firm establishment of enduring patterns for the solution of the nuclear conflict of basic trust versus basic mistrust in mere existence is the first task of the ego, and thus first of all a task for maternal care. But let it be said here that the amount of trust derived from earliest infantile experience does not seem to depend on absolute quantities of food or demonstrations of love, but rather on the quality of the maternal relationship. Mothers, I think, create a sense of trust in their children by that kind of administration which in its quality combines sensitive care of the baby's individual needs and a firm sense of personal trustworthiness within the trusted framework of their culture's life style. This forms the basis in the child for a sense of identity which will later combine a sense of being "all right," of being oneself, and of becoming what other people trust one will become. ✳ ✳ ✳

2. Autonomy vs. Shame and Doubt

Anal-muscular maturation sets the stage for experimentation with two simultaneous sets of social modalities: holding on and letting go. As is the case with all of these modalities, their basic conflicts can lead in the end to either hostile or benign expectations and attitudes. Thus, to hold can become a destructive and cruel retaining or restraining, and it can become a pattern of care: to have and to hold. To let go, too, can turn into an inimical letting loose of destructive forces, or it can become a relaxed "to let pass" and "to let be." Culturally speaking, these attitudes are neither good nor bad; their value depends on whether their hostile implications are turned against enemy, or fellow man—or the self.

The latter danger is the one best known to us. For if denied the gradual and well-guided experi-

ence of the autonomy of free choice (or if, indeed, weakened by an initial loss of trust) the child will turn against himself all his urge to discriminate and to manipulate. He will overmanipulate himself, he will develop a precocious conscience. Instead of taking possession of things in order to test them by purposeful repetition, he will become obsessed by his own repetitiveness. By such obsessiveness, of course, he then learns to repossess the environment and to gain power by stubborn and minute control, where he could not find large-scale mutual regulation. Such hollow victory is the infantile model for a compulsion neurosis. It is also the infantile source of later attempts in adult life to govern by the letter, rather than by the spirit.

Outer control at this stage, therefore, must be firmly reassuring. The infant must come to feel that the basic faith in existence, which is the lasting treasure saved from the rages of the oral stage, will not be jeopardized by this about-face of his, this sudden violent wish to have a choice, to appropriate demandingly, and to eliminate stubbornly. Firmness must protect him against the potential anarchy of his as yet untrained sense of discrimination, his inability to hold on and to let go with discretion. As his environment encourages him to "stand on his own feet," it must protect him against meaningless and arbitrary experiences of shame and of early doubt.

Shame is an emotion insufficiently studied, because in our civilization it is so early and easily absorbed by guilt. Shame supposes that one is completely exposed and conscious of being looked at: in one word, self-conscious. One is visible and not ready to be visible; which is why we dream of shame as a situation in which we are stared at in a condition of incomplete dress, in night attire, "with one's pants down." Shame is early expressed in an impulse to bury one's face, or to sink, right then and there, into the ground. But this, I think, is essentially rage turned against the self. He who is ashamed would like to force the world not to look at him, not to notice his exposure. He would like to destroy the eyes of the world. Instead he must wish for his own invisibility. This potentiality is abundantly used in the educational method of "shaming" used so exclusively by some primitive peoples; its destructiveness is balanced in some civilizations by devices for "saving face." Visual shame precedes auditory guilt, which is a sense of badness to be had all by oneself when nobody watches and when everything is quiet—except the voice of the superego. Such shaming exploits an increasing sense of being small, which can develop only as the child stands up and as his awareness permits him to note the relative measures of size and power. ＊ ＊ ＊

Doubt is the brother of shame. Where shame is dependent on the consciousness of being upright and exposed, doubt, so clinical observation leads me to believe, has much to do with a consciousness of having a front and a back—and especially a "behind." For this reverse area of the body, with its aggressive and libidinal focus in the sphincters and in the buttocks, cannot be seen by the child, and yet it can be dominated by the will of others. The "behind" is thus the individual's dark continent, an area of the body which can be magically dominated and effectively invaded by those who would attack one's power of autonomy and who would designate as evil those products of the bowels which were felt to be all right when they were being passed. This basic sense of doubt in whatever one has left behind forms a substratum for later and more verbal forms of compulsive doubting; this finds its adult expression in paranoiac fears concerning hidden persecutors and secret persecutions threatening from behind and from within the behind.

3. Initiative vs. Guilt

The ambulatory stage and that of infantile genitality add to the inventory of basic social modalities that of "making," first in the sense of "being on the make." There is no simpler, stronger word to match the social modalities previously enumerated. The word suggests pleasure in attack and conquest. In the boy, the emphasis remains on phallic-intrusive modes; in the girl it turns to modes of "catching" in more aggressive forms of snatching and "bitchy" possessiveness, or in the milder form of making oneself attractive and endearing.

The danger of this stage is a sense of guilt over the goals contemplated and the acts initiated in one's exuberant enjoyment of new locomotor and mental power: acts of aggressive manipulation and coercion which go far beyond the executive capacity of organism and mind and therefore call for an energetic halt on one's contemplated initiative. While autonomy concentrates on keeping potential rivals out, and is therefore more an expression of jealous rage most often directed against encroachments by younger siblings, initiative brings with it anticipatory rivalry with those who have been there first and may, therefore, occupy with their superior equipment the field toward which one's initiative is directed. Jealousy and rivalry, those often embittered and yet essentially futile attempts at demarcating a sphere of unquestioned privilege, now come to a climax in a final contest for a favored position with the mother; the inevitable failure leads to resignation, guilt, and anxiety. The child indulges in fantasies of being a giant and a tiger, but in his dreams he runs in terror for dear life. This, then, is the stage of the "castration complex," the fear of losing the (now energetically eroticized) genitals as a punishment for the fantasies attached to their excitements.

Infantile sexuality and incest taboo, castration complex and superego all unite here to bring about that specifically human crisis during which the child must turn from an exclusive, pregenital attachment to his parents to the slow process of becoming a parent, a carrier of tradition. Here the most fateful split and transformation in the emotional powerhouse occurs, a split between potential human glory and potential total destruction. For here the child becomes forever divided in himself. The instinct fragments which before had enhanced the growth of his infantile body and mind now become divided into an infantile set which perpetuates the exuberance of growth potentials, and a parental set which supports and increases self-observation, self-guidance, and self-punishment.

Naturally, the parental set is at first infantile in nature: the fact that human conscience remains partially infantile throughout life is the core of human tragedy. For the superego of the child can be primitive, cruel, and uncompromising, as may be observed in instances where children overcontrol and overconstrict themselves to the point of self-obliteration; where they develop an over-obedience more literal than the one the parent has wished to exact; or where they develop deep regressions and lasting resentments because the parents themselves do not seem to live up to the new conscience which they have installed in the child. One of the deepest conflicts in life is the hate for a parent who served as the model and the executor of the superego, but who (in some form) was found trying to get away with the very transgressions which the child can no longer tolerate in himself. The suspiciousness and evasiveness which is thus mixed in with the all-or-nothing quality of the superego, this organ of tradition, makes moral (in the sense of moralistic) man a great potential danger to his own ego—and to that of his fellow men.

The problem, again, is one of mutual regulation. Where the child, now so ready to overmanipulate himself, can gradually develop a sense of paternal responsibility, where he can gain some insight into the institutions, functions, and roles which will permit his responsible participation, he will find pleasurable accomplishment in wielding tools and weapons, in manipulating meaningful toys—and in caring for younger children.

*   *   *

4. Industry vs. Inferiority

Before the child, psychologically already a rudimentary parent, can become a biological parent, he must begin to be a worker and potential provider. With the oncoming latency period,[1] the normally advanced child forgets, or rather sublimates, the necessity to "make" people by direct attack or to become papa and mama in a hurry: he now learns to win recognition by producing things. He has mastered the ambulatory field and the organ modes. He has experienced a sense of finality regarding the fact that there is no workable future within the womb of his family, and thus becomes ready to apply himself to given skills and tasks, which go far beyond the mere playful expression of his organ modes or the pleasure in the function of his limbs. He develops industry—i.e., he adjusts himself to the inorganic laws of the tool world. He can become an eager and absorbed unit of a productive situation. To bring a productive situation to completion is an aim which gradually supersedes the whims and wishes of his autonomous organism. His ego boundaries include his tools and skills: the work principle teaches him the pleasure of work completion by steady attention and persevering diligence.

His danger, at this stage, lies in a sense of inadequacy and inferiority. If he despairs of his tools and skills or of his status among his tool partners, his ego boundaries suffer, and he abandons hope for the ability to identify early with others who apply themselves to the same general section of the tool world. To lose the hope of such "industrial" association leads back to the more isolated, less tool-conscious "anatomical" rivalry of the Oedipal time.[2] The child despairs of his equipment in the tool world and in anatomy, and considers himself doomed to mediocrity or mutilation. It is at this point that wider society becomes significant in its ways of admitting the child to an understanding of meaningful roles in its total economy. Many a child's development is disrupted when family life may not have prepared him for school life, or when school life may fail to sustain the promises of earlier stages.

---

[1]At the end of the phallic period, around age 7, Freud described children as entering a "latency period" until the beginning of puberty a few years later. During this period issues of sexual development are temporarily set aside while the child learns important skills for later life.

[2]Part of the story of the Oedipal crisis told by Freud consists of the young boy comparing the size of his genitals with that of his father's, and feeling thoroughly inferior as a result.

5. Identity vs. Role Diffusion

With the establishment of a good relationship to the world of skills and tools, and with the advent of sexual maturity, childhood proper comes to an end. Youth begins. But in puberty and adolescence all samenesses and continuities relied on earlier are questioned again, because of a rapidity of body growth which equals that of early childhood and because of the entirely new addition of physical genital maturity. The growing and developing youths, faced with this physiological revolution within them, are now primarily concerned with what they appear to be in the eyes of others as compared with what they feel they are, and with the question of how to connect the roles and skills cultivated earlier with the occupational prototypes of the day. In their search for a new sense of continuity and sameness, adolescents have to refight many of the battles of earlier years, even though to do so they must artificially appoint perfectly well-meaning people to play the roles of enemies; and they are ever ready to install lasting idols and ideals as guardians of a final identity: here puberty rites "confirm" the inner design for life.

The integration now taking place in the form of ego identity is more than the sum of the childhood identifications. It is the accrued experience of the ego's ability to integrate these identifications with the vicissitudes of the libido, with the aptitudes developed out of endowment, and with the opportunities offered in social roles. The sense of ego identity, then, is the accrued confidence that the inner sameness and continuity are matched by the sameness and continuity of one's meaning for others, as evidenced in the tangible promise of a "career."

The danger of this stage is role diffusion. Where this is based on a strong previous doubt as to one's sexual identity, delinquent and outright psychotic incidents are not uncommon. If diagnosed and treated correctly, these incidents do not have the same fatal significance which they have at other ages. It is primarily the inability to settle on an occupational identity which disturbs young people. To keep themselves together they temporarily overidentify, to the point of apparent complete loss of identity, with the heroes of cliques and crowds. This initiates the stage of "falling in love," which is by no means entirely, or even primarily, a sexual matter—except where the mores demand it. To a considerable extent adolescent love is an attempt to arrive at a definition of one's identity by projecting one's diffused ego images on one another and by seeing them thus reflected and gradually clarified. This is why many a youth would rather converse, and settle matters of mutual identification, than embrace.

Puberty rites and confirmations help to integrate and to affirm the new identity. * * *

6. Intimacy vs. Isolation

It is only as young people emerge from their identity struggles that their egos can master the sixth stage, that of intimacy. What we have said about genitality now gradually comes into play. Body and ego must now be masters of the organ modes and of the nuclear conflicts, in order to be able to face the fear of ego loss in situations which call for self-abandon: in orgasms and sexual unions, in close friendships and in physical combat, in experiences of inspiration by teachers and of intuition from the recesses of the self. The avoidance of such experiences because of a fear of ego loss may lead to a deep sense of isolation and consequent self-absorption.

This, then, may be the place to complete our discussion of genitality.

For a basic orientation in the matter I shall quote what has come to me as Freud's shortest saying. It has often been claimed, and bad habits of conversation seem to sustain the claim, that psychoanalysis as a treatment attempts to convince the patient that before God and man he has only one obligation: to have good orgasms, with a fitting "object," and that regularly. This, of course, is not true. Freud was once asked what he thought a normal person should be able to do well. The questioner probably expected a complicated answer. But Freud, in the curt way of his old days, is reported to have said: "Lieben und arbeiten" (to love and to work). It pays to ponder on this simple formula; it gets deeper as you think about it. For when Freud said "love" he meant *genital* love, and genital *love*; when he said love *and* work, he meant a general work-productiveness which would not preoccupy the individual to the extent that he loses his right or capacity to be a genital and a loving being. Thus we may ponder, but we cannot improve on the formula which includes the doctor's prescription for human dignity—and for democratic living.

Genitality, then, consists in the unobstructed capacity to develop an orgastic potency so free of pregenital interferences that genital libido (not just the sex products discharged in Kinsey's "outlets"[3]) is expressed in heterosexual mutuality, with full sensitivity of both penis and vagina, and with a convulsion-like discharge of tension from the whole body. This is a rather concrete way of saying something about a process which we really do not understand. To put it more situationally: the total fact of finding, via the climactic turmoil of the orgasm, a supreme experience of the mutual regulation of two beings in some way breaks the point off the hostilities and potential rages caused by the oppositeness of male and female, of fact and fancy, of love and hate. Satisfactory sex relations thus make sex less obsessive, overcompensation less necessary, sadistic controls superfluous.

∗ ∗ ∗ The kind of mutuality in orgasm which psychoanalysis has in mind[4] is apparently easily obtained in classes and cultures which happen to make a leisurely institution of it. In more complex societies this mutuality is interfered with by so many factors of health, of tradition, of opportunity, and of temperament, that the proper formulation of sexual health would be rather this: A human being should be potentially able to accomplish mutuality of genital orgasm, but he should

also be so constituted as to bear frustration in the matter without undue regression wherever considerations of reality and loyalty call for it.

∗ ∗ ∗ In order to be of lasting social significance, the utopia of genitality should include:

1. mutuality of orgasm
2. with a loved partner
3. of the other sex[5]
4. with whom one is able and willing to share a mutual trust
5. and with whom one is able and willing to regulate the cycles of
   a. work
   b. procreation
   c. recreation
6. so as to secure to the offspring, too, a satisfactory development.

It is apparent that such utopian accomplishment on a large scale cannot be an individual or, indeed, a therapeutic task. Nor is it a purely sexual matter by any means.

7. Generativity vs. Stagnation

The discussion of intimacy versus isolation has already included a further nuclear conflict which, therefore, requires only a short explicit formulation: I mean generativity versus stagnation. I apologize for creating a new and not even pleasant term. Yet neither creativity nor productivity nor any other fashionable term seems to me to convey what must be conveyed—namely, that the ability to lose oneself in the meeting of bodies and minds leads to a gradual expansion of ego interests and of libidinal cathexis over that which has been thus generated and accepted as a responsibility. Generativity is primarily the interest in establishing and guiding the next generation or whatever in a given case may become the absorbing object of a parental kind of responsibility. Where this enrichment fails, a regression from generativity to an obsessive

---

[3]The reference here is to Alfred Kinsey, one of the first modern sex researchers. Kinsey focused closely on the nature and meaning of literal sex acts and "outlets," a term and approach Erikson obviously found limited and even distasteful.

[4]As the ideal outcome of a sexual relationship.

---

[5]Although Erikson obviously here expresses a different view, current psychology generally does not regard homosexuality as a neurosis or psychological failure.

need for pseudo intimacy, punctuated by moments of mutual repulsion, takes place, often with a pervading sense (and objective evidence) of individual stagnation and interpersonal impoverishment.

8. Ego Integrity vs. Despair

Only he who in some way has taken care of things and people and has adapted himself to the triumphs and disappointments adherent to being, by necessity, the originator of others and the generator of things and ideas—only he may gradually grow the fruit of these seven stages. I know no better word for it than ego integrity. Lacking a clear definition, I shall point to a few constituents of this state of mind. It is the ego's accrued assurance of its proclivity for order and meaning. It is a post-narcissistic love of the human ego—not of the self—as an experience which conveys some world order and spiritual sense, no matter how dearly paid for. It is the acceptance of one's one and only life cycle as something that had to be and that, by necessity, permitted of no substitutions; it thus means a new, a different love of one's parents. It is a comradeship with the ordering ways of distant times and different pursuits, as expressed in the simple products and sayings of such times and pursuits. Although aware of the relativity of all the various lifestyles which have given meaning to human striving, the possessor of integrity is ready to defend the dignity of his own life style against all physical and economic threats. For he knows that an individual life is the accidental coincidence of but one life cycle with but one segment of history; and that for him all human integrity stands or falls with the one style of integrity of which he partakes. The style of integrity developed by his culture or civilization thus becomes the "patrimony of his soul," the seal of his moral paternity of himself.[6] * * * Before this final solution, death loses its sting.

The lack or loss of this accrued ego integration is signified by fear of death: the one and only life cycle is not accepted as the ultimate of life. Despair expresses the feeling that the time is short, too short for the attempt to start another life and to try out alternate roads to integrity. Disgust hides despair.

Each individual, to become a mature adult, must to a sufficient degree develop all the ego qualities mentioned, so that a wise Indian, a true gentleman, and a mature peasant share and recognize in one another the final stage of integrity. But each cultural entity, to develop the particular style of integrity suggested by its historical place, utilizes a particular combination of these conflicts, along with specific provocations and prohibitions of infantile sexuality. Infantile conflicts become creative only if sustained by the firm support of cultural institutions and of the special leader classes representing them. In order to approach or experience integrity, the individual must know how to be a follower of image bearers in religion and in politics, in the economic order and in technology, in aristocratic living and in the arts and sciences. Ego integrity, therefore, implies an emotional integration which permits participation by followership as well as acceptance of the responsibility of leadership.

Webster's dictionary is kind enough to help us complete this outline in a circular fashion. Trust (the first of our ego values) is here defined as "the assured reliance on another's integrity," the last of our values. I suspect that Webster had business in mind rather than babies, credit rather than faith. But the formulation stands. And it seems possible to further paraphrase the relation of adult integrity and infantile trust by saying that healthy children will not fear life if their parents have integrity enough not to fear death.

* * * In order to indicate the whole conceptual area which is awaiting systematic treatment, I shall conclude this chapter with a diagram.[7] In

---

[6]Erikson seemed to take this advice to heart. He never knew his father and in midlife abandoned his stepfather's name and took instead the name Erikson, as a way of claiming his own moral paternity of himself.

[7]The meaning of this diagram, reproduced in many textbooks, is not made entirely clear by Erikson. But Franz and White (1985) "fill in" the rows and columns

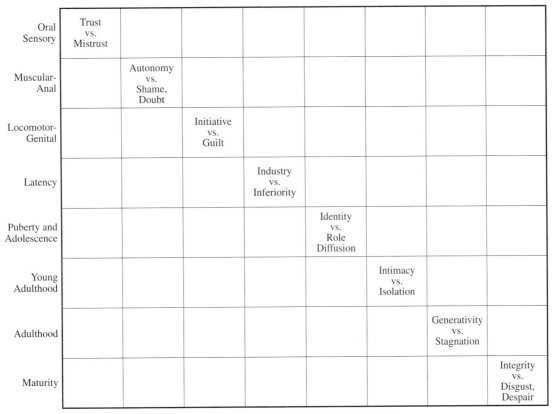

Oral Sensory	Trust vs. Mistrust						
Muscular-Anal		Autonomy vs. Shame, Doubt					
Locomotor-Genital			Initiative vs. Guilt				
Latency				Industry vs. Inferiority			
Puberty and Adolescence					Identity vs. Role Diffusion		
Young Adulthood						Intimacy vs. Isolation	
Adulthood							Generativity vs. Stagnation
Maturity							Integrity vs. Disgust, Despair

Figure 31.1

this, as in the diagram of pregenital zones and modes, the diagonal represents the sequence of enduring solutions, each of which is based on the integration of the earlier ones. At any given stage of the life cycle the solution of one more nuclear conflict adds a new ego quality, a new criterion of increasing strength. The criteria proposed in this chart are to be treated in analogy to the criteria for health and illness in general—i.e., by ascer-

taining whether or not there is "a pervading subjective sense of" the criterion in question, and whether or not "objective evidence of the dominance of" the criterion can be established by indirect examination (by means of depth psychology). Above the diagonal there is space for a future elaboration of the precursors of each of these solutions, all of which begin with the beginning; below the diagonal there is space for the designation of the derivatives of these solutions in the maturing and the mature personality.

associated with identity and intimacy, showing the heuristic power of Erikson's theory even as they seek to offer their own revision of it.

MOMMY AND I ARE ONE:
IMPLICATIONS FOR PSYCHOTHERAPY

Lloyd H. Silverman and Joel Weinberger

Psychoanalytic ideas continue to influence modern research in various ways. First, some psychoanalytic thinkers continue to develop variations on the Freudian theme, based on their clinical experience and introspection. This enterprise seems the wave of the past, however; certainly no modern neo-Freudian of the stature of Jung, Adler, Horney, or Erikson seems to be practicing it.

A second way in which psychoanalytic ideas influence modern research is indirectly. It has been claimed that research examining the effects of contradictory motivations within an individual, or the effect of parenting styles on psychological development, or the processes of emotional attachment across the life span all are "a little bit psychoanalytic" because they embody ideas that can be traced to Freud (Westen, 1990). This claim implies that some researchers are conducting psychoanalytic studies without knowing it!

A third influence is more direct. A small but determined band of modern researchers are attempting to bring Freudian thought into the modern age by subjecting psychoanalytic ideas to empirical tests that match exacting standards of methodological rigor. The third paragraph of the following selection rapidly lists a large number of such investigations.

Many of these studies test intriguing hypotheses, but the research focused on in the following selection, by the psychoanalytic researchers Lloyd Silverman and Joel Weinberger, may be the most remarkable of all. Silverman and Weinberger theorize that people have a basic tendency to seek "oneness" with others, particularly parents and loved ones. They use this idea to explain their astonishing experimental result, that flashing a phrase like "Mommy and I are one" too quickly to be consciously perceived can have beneficial effects on psychological well-being.

The community of research psychology has not exactly received this finding with open arms. Although the article was published in American Psychologist, *the journal of record of the mainstream American Psychological Association, the attitude of most researchers to this day can probably be accurately described as intrigued but suspicious. Unfortunately, as this article describes, relevant research is extremely difficult to conduct and, even more unfortunately, Silverman died soon after this article appeared.*

While the ultimate status of "Mommy and I are one" remains uncertain, the studies described in the following selection provide a good example of the kind of efforts a few modern researchers are willing to make to provide empirical evidence for psychoanalytic ideas.

* * *

The "clinical theory" of psychoanalysis is composed of dynamic and genetic propositions (Hartmann & Kris, 1945). Genetic propositions account for current behavior in terms of earlier events and experiences. Dynamic propositions explain the same behavior from the standpoint of the "here and now," that is, the unconscious wishes, anxieties, fantasies, and beliefs that are motivating the behavior.

Dynamic propositions, in particular, have long served as a potent stimulus for research studies. In recent reviews by Fisher and Greenberg (1977) and by Kline (1982), several hundred studies have been cited that bear on various psychoanalytic dynamic propositions. However, until about 25 years ago, this research was limited in two ways: (a) It was unsystematic, in that, typically, an investigator (or a team of investigators) engaged in one or two studies without investigating anything in depth; (b) studies were limited to validation attempts; thus, results, even when positive (and often they were not), merely supported an aspect of clinically derived psychoanalytic thinking and did not go beyond what was consensually agreed upon within the "psychoanalytic community."

In the 1960s, this picture began to change. A number of research programs (in contrast to isolated studies) were initiated in which psychoanalytic dynamic issues were examined systematically and in depth, the results of which often contrib-

uted to, rather than merely validated, clinically derived ideas. A partial list would include (a) the investigations of Sampson, Weiss, and their co-workers (e.g., Sampson & Weiss, 1984), in which transcripts of treatment sessions were used to study the role of unconscious beliefs on pathogenesis[1] and the effects of the disconfirmation of these beliefs on the therapeutic process; (b) the studies of Blatt and colleagues (e.g., Blatt, Wein, Chevron, & Quinlan, 1979), in which questionnaire, projective test, and observational data were used to investigate different types of depressive experiences in terms of such variables as guilt and loss dynamics and level of "object representation"; (c) the studies by Masling and his associates (e.g., Masling, Johnson, & Saturansky, 1974) of persons high and low on oral dynamics (as expressed in Rorschach responses) with regard to overt behavior, physiological responsivity, and symptom vulnerability; (d) the work of Reyher and his colleagues (e.g., Reyher, 1967), in which symptom formation has been studied through the hypnotic implantation of false memories (paramnesias) involving the conflictual expression of sexual and aggressive wishes; (e) our own work involving the "subliminal psychodynamic activation method" (see summaries in Silverman, 1976, 1983; Weinberger & Silverman, 1986), in which tachistoscopically pre-

---

[1]Pathogenesis is the development of disease, in this context, mental illness.

sented subliminal stimuli[2] have been used to investigate a variety of psychoanalytic dynamic propositions. In this article, we will limit ourselves to experiments that bear on a particular dynamic proposition—one that we believe has implications for understanding positive change in psychotherapy.

Overview of Thesis

Our thesis, which is composed of two parts, proposes first that there are powerful wishes, typically unconscious, in many adults, for a state of oneness with another person: in the terminology of psychoanalysis, a state in which representations of self and other are fused or merged. These wishes are often referred to in the psychoanalytic literature as "symbiotic" and are believed to originate in the infant's experience with the "good mother of early childhood," that is, the mother when she was experienced very early in life as comforting, protective, and nurturing (see Mahler, Pine, & Bergman, 1975, for elaboration). The second part of the thesis states that when these oneness or symbiotic-like wishes are gratified, adaptation can be enhanced if simultaneously a sense of self is preserved.

We shall cite two kinds of data that support the proposed thesis, one "soft" and one "hard." The soft data come from unsystematic observations, mainly of clinicians. The hard data come from laboratory experiments. Although we consider the latter as the main support for our thesis, we view the soft data as complementing the hard data in an important way. Data from the laboratory, because of their artificiality (especially when a thesis about complex human behavior is under consideration) are helped to "come alive" by the soft data of real life.

---

[2]In a technique borrowed from cognitive psychology, stimuli are presented on a machine called a tachistoscope with very brief flashes of light (a few milliseconds in duration). A "subliminal" stimulus is one that a subject is not consciously aware of having perceived. In some studies, stimuli (such as pictures or words) shown with a tachistoscope too quickly to be consciously perceived have nonetheless been shown to have psychological effects.

The Soft Data

As far back as 1902, William James described how a state of oneness can be sought through mystical experiences:

> In mystic states we . . . become one with the Absolute. . . . This is the everlasting and triumphant mystical tradition, hardly altered by differences of clime or creed. . . . The me and . . . the thou are not (separate). . . . In the One, there can be no distinction. (pp. 410–411)

In a related vein, Fierman (1965) has described why spectators often become fascinated by performers who execute acts in perfect unison:

> The source of the . . . fascination . . . [is the illusion that the performers] are not wholly separate personalities, but have only one mind between them. That means that [people] have a secret desire that "fusion" be possible. (pp. 119–120)

Bergmann (1971), quoting from the myth described in Plato's *Symposium*, has noted how this same state of oneness (or fusion) can be sought through the experience of being in love:

> The intense yearning which each of them had for the other does not appear to be the desire of lover's intercourse, but of something else which the soul of either evidently desires and cannot tell and of which she has only a dark and doubtful presentiment. Suppose Hephaestus, with his instruments, [was] to come to the pair who are lying side by side . . . and said to them . . . "do you desire to be wholly one: always day and night to be in one another's company? For if this is what you desire I am ready to melt you into one and let you grow together." . . . There is not a man . . . who when he heard the proposal would deny that this meeting and melting into one another, this becoming one instead of two, was the very expression of his ancient needs (*Symposium*, 192, Jowett translation).

From this and other citations Bergmann concluded that "love revives, if not direct memories, then feelings and archaic . . . states that were once active in the symbiotic phase" (p. 32).

More recently, jogging also has been viewed as providing oneness gratifications. Thus, Sacks

(1979) quoted well-known runners such as Bannister: "[running produces] a feeling of being one with the seashore" and Sheehan: "I felt at the beginning of the run . . . [as if] I take the universe around me and wrap myself in it and become one with it" and concluded that "the current popularity of running may be due, in part, to the relative ease with which the runner . . . can obtain [symbiotic-like] experiences" (1979, pp. 132–133). (See Silverman, Lachmann, & Milich, 1982, pp. 231–256, for other ways that people seek oneness.)

In addition to the just-cited soft data bearing on what can be called "the search for oneness," there are other soft data—that is, unsystematic observations—supporting the second part of the thesis, that the attainment of oneness gratifications can have positive effects on people. That attaining a state of oneness can lead to subjective pleasure is implicit in Bergmann's (1971) comment about love, cited above. It also was attested to by James (1902) in his discussion of religious experience, when he quoted Suso (a German mystic), who declared that in experiencing oneness with God, "the highest bliss is to be found" (p. 411).

Rose (1972) saw value in oneness experiences beyond subjective pleasure:

> Throughout life [a person] may temporarily suspend the distinction between self and others and thus momentarily experience a state of mind similar to the early unity with mother. . . . Such operations may result in nothing more remarkable than normally creative adaptation to circumstance. At the least it affords . . . a return from the solitude of individuation refreshed to meet the moment. At the most, it may result in transcending the limitations of earlier stages . . . to simplify, unify anew and recreate an expanded reality. . . . To merge in order to re-emerge may be part of the fundamental process of psychological growth. (p. 185)

*   *   *

The Hard Data

Our main support for the proposition that the gratification of symbiotic-like wishes enhances adaptation comes from the laboratory. It consists of data from experiments involving the subliminal psychodynamic activation method referred to above. As has been described elsewhere in a detailing of the history of this method (Silverman, Lachmann, & Milich, 1982, pp. 20–22), serendipitous findings from experiments conducted in the early 1960s on subliminal "recovery effects" led to the inference that psychoanalytic dynamic propositions could be studied in subliminal perception experiments. (*Subliminal recovery effects* refer to the emergence of aspects of a subliminally presented stimulus in a subject's productions—usually drawings or associations; in contrast, *subliminal psychodynamic effects* refer to changes in adaptive behaviors, usually increases or decreases in psychopathology, after the exposure of subliminal stimuli with dynamic content.)

During the next two decades, this lead was systematically pursued. Over 60 studies have been carried out—more than half in laboratories independent of our own—that have demonstrated subliminal psychodynamic activation effects (see summaries in Silverman, 1976, 1983; Weinberger & Silverman, 1986). Under double-blind conditions (i.e., with both subjects and investigators unaware of the stimulus conditions), the subliminal (four milliseconds) exposure of stimuli with psychodynamic content affected behavior in a way that subliminal exposure of neutral stimuli did not and supported psychoanalytically based hypotheses of various kinds.

Moreover, in several of these studies (e.g., Garske, 1984; Rutstein & Goldberger, 1973; Silverman & Spiro, 1968), when the same psychodynamic stimuli that produced subliminal effects were presented supraliminally (usually at exposures of five seconds), typically there were no effects. These findings are in keeping with the psychoanalytic supposition that when psychodynamic content is brought into awareness, its links with psychopathology can be severed. (See Silverman, 1972, for elaboration.)

STUDIES OF SCHIZOPHRENICS The initial exploration of the thesis that there could be salutary effects of oneness gratifications began with experiments with schizophrenics. There were a few clinical reports (e.g., Limentani, 1956; Searles, 1965) that schizophrenics often showed diminished pathology when symbiotic-like wishes were gratified. Because other clinicians challenged this view (e.g., Des Lauriers, 1962; Lidz, 1973), it seemed particularly worthwhile to subject this proposition to an experimental test. Although it hardly seemed feasible to directly gratify symbiotic-like wishes in the laboratory, it did seem feasible, using the subliminal psychodynamic activation method, to stimulate an (unconscious) fantasy of such wishes being gratified.

This was attempted in the following experiment (Silverman, R. H. Spiro, Weissberg, & Candell, 1969). Twenty-four hospitalized schizophrenic men were seen individually for three sessions, in each of which a baseline and "critical" assessment was made of the level of psychopathology before and after subliminal stimulation. The assessments—both in this experiment and in the others with schizophrenics that will be cited —consisted of the administration of psychological tests (such as the Word Association) that had been found in clinical psychodiagnostic testing to reveal schizophrenic disturbances (Rapaport, Gill, & Schafer, 1945; Schafer, 1948). Two dependent variables were examined. One was "thought disorder"—instances of peculiar verbalizations, autistic concepts, illogical reasoning, and so on. The other was "nonverbal pathology" emerging during test administration—for example, inappropriate smiling or laughing, peculiar gestures, and speech blocking.

Between the pre- and postassessments, the subjects received several subliminal exposures of one of three verbal–pictorial stimuli: (a) the message MOMMY AND I ARE ONE, accompanied by a picture of a man and woman merged at the shoulders like Siamese twins; (b) the message PEOPLE ARE THINKING, accompanied by a picture of two men in a contemplative pose; (c) the message DESTROY MOTHER accompanied by a picture of a man attacking a woman with a knife. The first of these stimuli was intended to provide symbiotic-like gratifications by activating the fantasy that a state of oneness already existed, thus providing an experimental test of the controversial proposition under consideration. The second stimulus was intended as a (relatively) neutral control stimulus. The third stimulus was intended to activate aggressive wishes, thus building into the experiment a replication of a finding from a number of earlier studies in which such activation was found to intensify pathology in schizophrenics. (As is discussed in Silverman, 1977, with respect to ethical issues, the effects of stimuli such as this are fleeting, typically dissipating within 15 minutes.)

As had been found in over a dozen previous studies (summarized in Mendelsohn & Silverman, 1982), the aggressive stimulus, when compared with the control, increased pathology. The effects of the "symbiotic stimulus," however, were more complicated. The predicted pathology reduction turned out to depend on an individual-difference variable related to the preservation of sense of self, alluded to in the statement of our thesis. * * *

The introduction of new stimuli. After a number of replications of the MOMMY AND I ARE ONE effect on differentiated schizophrenics were carried out, several investigators asked themselves the following question: What would happen if certain key words in the MOMMY AND I ARE ONE stimulus were changed? Would the outcome be the same or would the pathology-reducing effects vanish? This was an important question to address, for two reasons. First, on the basis of the results reported thus far, a critic could justifiably argue that the effects obtained might simply have been a function of a fantasy involving "mommy" rather than a specific fantasy involving oneness. Second, even if it could be demonstrated more definitively that a oneness fantasy was involved, the question could be asked regarding whether the fantasized oneness had to be with mommy in order for it to be ameliorative. To address the first question, other words were substituted for ONE in the message, and for the second question, the word MOMMY was changed.

Three studies (Bronstein & Rodin, 1983; Kaplan, Thornton, & Silverman, in press; Silbert,

1982) found that activating the theme of oneness produced ameliorative effects for (relatively differentiated) schizophrenics that were not produced when other, even very similar, themes were activated. In Bronstein and Rodin's (1983) experiment, for example, the MOMMY AND I ARE ONE stimulus was compared with other stimuli that were psychoanalytically conceptualized (following Schafer, 1968) as involving other ways of "internalizing" mommy: MOMMY AND I ARE THE SAME, MOMMY AND I ARE ALIKE, and MOMMY IS INSIDE ME (as well as a control stimulus). Only the oneness stimulus reduced pathology.

Three other studies involving schizophrenic individuals (Cohen, 1977; Jackson, 1983; Kaye, 1975) have been carried out that have focused on a second key word in the symbiotic stimulus, MOMMY. Jackson (1983) for example, working with groups of both male and female schizophrenics, asked the question of whether a oneness fantasy involving some important figure other than "mommy" would be ameliorative. (All other studies of schizophrenics except Cohen, 1977, have been with males, because the original studies were carried out in Veterans Administration hospitals, and later investigators felt obliged to use male subjects in their replication attempts.) Jackson found that the males, although responsive in the usual way to MOMMY AND I ARE ONE, showed no effect when subliminally presented with the message DADDY AND I ARE ONE. (This replicated a finding by Kaye, 1975.)

When Jackson examined the results for his female schizophrenics, however, the converse was found. The schizophrenic women were unaffected by the MOMMY AND I ARE ONE stimulus but showed reduced pathology after DADDY AND I ARE ONE. (This replicated an earlier finding by Cohen, 1977.) We will return to these sex differences after citing parallel data from studies with nonschizophrenics.

* * *

STUDIES OF NONSCHIZOPHRENICS In the early 1970s, after having completed several studies in which the MOMMY AND I ARE ONE stimulus had lowered pathology in schizophrenic patients, researchers considered the possibility that its ameliorative effects might not be limited to this group. The rationale for thus expanding the research resides in the general importance that many psychoanalytic writers (e.g., M. Bergmann, 1971; Mahler, Pine, & A. Bergmann, 1975; Rose, 1972; Shafhi, 1973) have accorded symbiotic needs during childhood. Their writings suggest not only that symbiotic-like wishes can persist into adulthood in nonschizophrenics but that when these wishes are gratified, they can bring about positive behavior change. We thus reasoned that nonschizophrenics also might respond positively to the subliminal activation of oneness fantasies. A number of investigations were therefore conducted in which it was hypothesized that people other than schizophrenic patients would respond to the MOMMY AND I ARE ONE stimulus with improved adaptation.

In contrast to the studies with schizophrenics, the majority of studies with nonschizophrenics used a between-subjects design; instead of being administered the experimental and control conditions in a single sitting, subjects were assigned to an experimental or control group, and subliminal stimulation was repeated over many days. The reasoning in these investigations was that large "doses" of subliminal oneness stimulation might produce more substantive adaptation-enhancing effects than could be produced when this stimulation was administered on a single occasion.

In one group of these studies, the stimulation of symbiotic-like fantasies was used as a treatment adjunct with groups of persons with a particular kind of problematic behavior that they wanted to change. Subjects received an accepted therapy for their problem, accompanied by subliminal stimulation. Sessions ranged from one to four times a week, and treatment duration was anywhere from 2 to 12 weeks. Subjects were randomly assigned to a group that received MOMMY AND I ARE ONE and a control group that received a relatively neutral stimulus such as PEOPLE ARE WALKING.

Palmatier and Bornstein (1980), for example, used this design with smokers receiving the behavior modification technique of "rapid smoking." Subjects were seen for 12 therapy sessions, and at the end of that time all subjects, in both experimental and control groups, became abstainers, a result that obviously was due to the rapid smoking rather than to subliminal oneness stimulation. However, at a one-month follow-up, 67% of those who had received MOMMY AND I ARE ONE, compared to only 13% of the controls, were still abstainers. (Abstinence was evaluated from self-reports and was "independently verified by contacting someone who knew the subject's smoking habits," p. 718.) This substantive as well as statistically significant result could be confidently attributed to the experimental stimulus, because (as in all subliminal psychodynamic activation studies) double-blind conditions were maintained to counter the influence of experimenter bias (Rosenthal, 1966) and demand characteristics (Orne, 1962).[3]

Similar results have been found for groups receiving the symbiotic stimulus (when compared with control groups receiving a neutral message) in studies of adolescents with personality disorders who were receiving psychotherapy in a residential treatment setting (Bryant-Tuckett & Silverman, 1984), college students in group therapy (Linehan & O'Toole, 1982), persons with assertiveness difficulties receiving behavior assertiveness training (Packer, 1984), alcoholics in Alcoholics Anonymous (AA) counseling (Schurtman, Palmatier, & E. Martin, 1982), insect phobic people receiving a variant of systematic desensitization (Silverman, Frank, & Dachinger, 1974), and obese persons receiving behavior modification techniques for reducing food intake (Silverman, A. Martin, Ungaro, & Mendelsohn, 1978). For example, in the Schurtman et al. (1982) study, those in the MOMMY AND I ARE ONE group showed greater improvement on the Tennessee Self-Concept Scale

(Fitts, 1965) and on the Multiple Affect Adjective Checklist (MAACL; Zuckerman & Lubin, 1965) anxiety and depression scales; and in the Packer (1984) investigation, those in the symbiotic group showed a greater increment in assertiveness, as reflected both in ratings by the behavior assertiveness "trainer" (who was unaware of the tachistoscopic conditions) and in their performance on a videotaped behavior assessment test (patterned after an audiotaped test developed by McFall & Lillesand, 1971).

In another group of studies, this same intervention was used in an educational rather than a treatment setting. Ariam and Siller (1982), for example, in a study in Israel, translated MOMMY AND I ARE ONE into two Hebrew versions, one a more literal and the other a more poetic translation. They found that Israeli high school students who received either of these stimuli four days a week for six weeks fared considerably better in a mathematics course than students who received either of two subliminal control stimuli. (The marks for the experimental students were over a full grade higher than the controls.) In five other educational adjunct studies—four in the United States and one in Pakistan—the MOMMY AND I ARE ONE group also did better academically than a control group. This academic improvement, we believe, was most likely attributable to the oneness stimulus either lowering anxiety level or strengthening the students' bond with their teachers, possibilities that we shall return to shortly.

VARIABLES AFFECTING OUTCOME IN ONENESS EXPERIMENTS

* * *

Regarding sex differences, whereas almost all male groups showed greater adaptive behavior after the MOMMY AND I ARE ONE stimulus than the control groups with which they were compared, for about half of the female groups (regardless of diagnostic category), there were no differences between experimental and control conditions. How can these differential results for males and females be understood? Silverman, Lachmann, and Milich (1982) have proposed the following:

---

[3]Rosenthal and Orne are influential methodologists who have warned about the possibility that experimenters can extract from subjects the results they expect or implicitly demand of them. A routine safeguard against this process is the "double blind," in which neither the subject *nor* the experimenter knows which condition a given subject has been assigned to.

(The) less reliable positive responses (of women) to MOMMY AND I ARE ONE . . . we suspect [are] related to differences between men and women in the degree to which they are differentiated from their mothers. Bernstein (1980), after considering both the clinical literature and case material of her own, concludes that women tend to be less differentiated from their mothers than men. Her conclusion seems particularly warranted given the following considerations. First, as Maccoby and Jacklin (1974) have noted, many kinds of observations support the proposition that females are notably less aggressive than males, and it has been posited by such psychoanalytic writers as Jacobson (1964) that aggression aids infants in differentiating from their mothers. Moreover, because daughters are the same gender as their mothers, they have less of a basis for differentiating themselves from their mothers than do sons. (pp. 112–113)

If these suppositions are correct, the proviso formulated earlier—that oneness fantasies will be adaptation enhancing only if a sense of self can be preserved—is less apt to be met in women if oneness is with mother. Consistent with this formulation is Jackson's (1983) finding cited earlier—that although MOMMY AND I ARE ONE was not ameliorative for female schizophrenics, DADDY AND I ARE ONE was ameliorative. A similar result has emerged from a study of college women (Silverman & Grabowski, 1982), in which it was found that whereas MOMMY AND I ARE ONE did not reduce anxiety (as it did for college men), the message MY LOVER AND I ARE ONE had this effect. It would appear that unconscious oneness fantasies involving someone other than "mommy" are less apt to threaten a woman's sense of self and thus are more likely to have adaptation-enhancing consequences.

Possible Mediating Processes

Why does behavior become more adaptive after symbiotic-like fantasies are activated? We propose that (at least) three processes are at work, for each of which there are some supporting data. First, such fantasies can allay anxiety and mobilize positive affects, perhaps because the idea of being one with "mommy" leaves the person feeling protected and comforted. Several investigators (e.g., Fulford, 1980; Garske, 1984; Silverman, Kwawer, Wolitzky, & Coron, 1973) have reported that the subliminal presentation of MOMMY AND I ARE ONE diminishes anxiety. Garske (1984), for example, found in three experiments that unselected college students, after being subliminally exposed to this stimulus, had lower anxiety scores on the Spielberger State Anxiety Scale (Spielberger, Gorsuch, & Lushene, 1970) than students receiving a subliminal neutral message. That positive affect can be mobilized by subliminal oneness stimulation was demonstrated in a recent study by Frauman, Lynn, Hardaway, and Molteni (1984). After being subjected to subliminal stimulation, an experimental and a control group of college students were hypnotized and asked to select topics that they wished to talk about. Those who had received the MOMMY AND I ARE ONE stimulus chose topics with more positive affective valence.

A second way in which the activation of symbiotic-like fantasies may enhance adaptation is by gratifying dependency-related needs, perhaps because the fantasy of being at one with mommy can connote an in utero existence where the fetus is constantly fed and nurtured. (See Silverman, Lachmann & Milich, 1982, p. 126, where this speculation is considered.) This then can reduce the necessity for a person to seek dependency gratifications in maladaptive ways. Thus, in keeping with the general clinical supposition that addictive behaviors are miscarried attempts at seeking dependency gratifications, in studies of alcoholics (Schurtman, Palmatier, & E. Martin, 1982), cigarette smokers (Palmatier & Bornstein, 1980), and obese individuals (Silverman, A. Martin, Ungaro, & Mendelsohn, 1978), subjects who received the MOMMY AND I ARE ONE stimulus were better able to give up their "habit" than subjects who received a subliminal neutral stimulus.

More direct evidence that activating unconscious symbiotic-like fantasies can reduce dependency needs comes from a recent study by Bryant-Tuckett and Silverman (1984). Adolescents at a residential treatment center received either

MOMMY AND I ARE ONE or PEOPLE ARE WALKING five times a week for six weeks. Although the main purpose of the study was to examine the effect of the experimental intervention on achievement test scores (with the experimental group showing considerably more improvement than the controls), teachers also rated the students for their ability to perform independently in the classroom. Those in the experimental group showed greater independent functioning.

A third way that activating symbiotic-like fantasies may enhance adaptive behavior is that the person can become more receptive to the interventions offered by helping persons who may be unconsciously perceived (in part) as "mommy," the prototypic helping figure. This factor could have played a role in the therapy and educational adjunct studies already cited, particularly in two of them in which there was direct evidence that the tie to the therapist became stronger as a result of MOMMY AND I ARE ONE stimulation. In the study by Schurtman et al. (1982), alcoholics in the experimental group were rated by their counselors as more involved in the AA counseling they were receiving than those in the control group. And in the study by Linehan and O'Toole (1982), students who were receiving group counseling disclosed more to their counselors when the counseling was accompanied by MOMMY AND I ARE ONE stimulation than when it was accompanied by PEOPLE ARE WALKING stimulation. Because the ability to disclose during counseling can be viewed as a sign that a good alliance exists between counselee and counselor, here, too, we have evidence that the activation of symbiotic-like fantasies allowed for greater receptivity to what a helping figure was offering.

* * *

Concluding Comment

The fact that positive results have been obtained when the MOMMY AND I ARE ONE stimulus has been administered to various populations in a variety of settings and with different dependent variables attests to the general adaptation-enhancing consequences of gratifying unconscious oneness fantasies. One can ask, however, how valid is our extrapolation from these laboratory experiments to the psychotherapy situation? A confident answer to this question must await the kinds of direct tests of our formulation that we outlined in the last section.[4] But we think it fair to characterize this formulation as at least plausible, given that it is consistent with both the research data and a number of clinical commentaries.

For those readers who feel sufficiently impressed to take our formulation seriously at this point, we would like to sound a caution concerning the activation of unconscious oneness fantasies in psychotherapy. Recall that the second part of our thesis proposed that unconscious oneness fantasies enhance adaptive functioning only if, simultaneously, a sense of self is preserved. Both rational considerations and data (cited earlier and detailed in Silverman, Lachmann, & Milich, 1982, pp. 72–76, 88) suggest this qualification and point to the possibility that activating such fantasies can have deleterious effects in some cases. (The generally negative effects of cults—see Conway and Siegelman, 1978—exemplify the harmful consequences of an abundance of opportunities to experience oneness in the context of compromising the sense of self.) Dangers such as this suggest that therapists should ask themselves whether their manner and techniques are as supportive of patient efforts to sustain a strong sense of self as they are of activating oneness fantasies. Only when the answer to this question is affirmative can the therapist feel confident that the activation of oneness fantasies is likely to prove beneficial. In addition, there are individual differences to be considered. Different people require different weightings of oneness gratifications and encouragement of self experience (see Silverman, Lachmann, & Milich, 1982, pp. 61–75, 199–222). Furthermore, people vary in terms of whether and to what extent par-

---

[4]In a lengthy passage omitted from this excerpt, Silverman and Weinberg explained the implications of their findings for the practice of psychotherapy and suggested some directions for further research.

ticular interventions will activate oneness fantasies and/or an enhanced sense of self. It is up to the therapist to make these determinations for each of his or her patients and to act accordingly.

References

Ariam, S., & Siller, J. (1982). Effects of subliminal oneness stimuli in Hebrew on academic performance of Israeli high school students; further evidence of the adaptation-enhancing effects of symbiotic fantasies in another culture using another language. *Journal of Abnormal Psychology, 91,* 343–349.

Bergmann, M. S. (1971). On the capacity to love. In J. B. McDevitt & C. S. Settlage (Eds.), *Separation-individuation: Essays in honor of Margaret S. Mahler* (pp. 15–40). New York: International Universities Press.

Blatt, S. J., Wein, S., Chevron, E., & Quinlan, D. (1979). Parental representations and depression in normal young adults. *Journal of Abnormal Psychology, 88,* 388–397.

Bronstein, A., & Rodin, G. (1983). An experimental study of internalization fantasies in schizophrenic men. *Psychotherapy: Theory, Research and Practice, 20,* 408–416.

Bryant-Tuckett, R., & Silverman, L. H. (1984). Effects of the subliminal stimulation of symbiotic fantasies on the academic performance of emotionally handicapped students. *Journal of Counseling Psychology, 31,* 295–305.

Cohen, R. (1977). *The effects of four subliminally introduced merging stimuli on the psychopathology of schizophrenic women.* Unpublished doctoral dissertation, Columbia University.

Conway, F., & Siegelman, J. (1978). *Snapping.* New York: Delta.

Des Lauriers, A. M. (1962). *The experience of reality in childhood schizophrenia.* New York: International Universities Press.

Fierman, S. (Ed.). (1965). *Effective psychotherapy—The contribution of Hellmuth Kaiser.* New York: Free Press.

Fisher, S., & Greenberg, R. P. (1977). *The scientific credibility of Freud's theories and therapy.* New York: Basic Books.

Fitts, W. H. (1965). *Tennessee Self-Concept Scale.* Nashville, TN: Counselor Recordings and Tests.

Frauman, D. C., Lynn, S. J., Hardaway, R., & Molteni, A. (1984). Effect of subliminal symbiotic activation on hypnotic rapport and susceptibility. *Journal of Abnormal Psychology, 93,* 481–483.

Fulford, P. F. (1980). *The effect of subliminal merging stimuli on test anxiety.* Unpublished doctoral dissertation, St. John's University.

Garske, J. (1984, August). *Effects of subliminal activation on affective states.* Paper presented at the meeting of the American Psychological Association, Toronto. (Available from Department of Psychology, Ohio University, Athens, OH)

Hartmann, H., & Kris, E. (1945). The genetic approach in psychoanalysis. *Psychoanalytic Study of the Child, 1,* 11–30.

Jackson, J. (1983). The effects of subliminally activated fantasies of merger with each parent on the pathology of male and female schizophrenics. *Journal of Nervous and Mental Disease, 171,* 280–289.

James, W. (1902). *The varieties of religious experience.* New York: The Modern Library.

Kaplan, R., Thornton, P., & Silverman, L. H. (in press). Further data on the effects of subliminal symbiotic stimulation on schizophrenics. *Journal of Nervous and Mental Disease.*

Kaye, M. (1975). *The therapeutic value of three merging stimuli for male schizophrenics.* Unpublished doctoral dissertation, Yeshiva University.

Kline, P. (1982). *Fact and fantasy in Freudian theory.* London: Methuen.

Lidz, T. (1973). *The origin and treatment of schizophrenic disorders.* New York: Basic Books.

Limentani, D. (1956). Symbiotic identification in schizophrenia. *Psychiatry, 19,* 231–236.

Linehan, E., & O'Toole, J. (1982). The effect of subliminal stimulation of symbiotic fantasy on college students' self-disclosures in group counseling. *Journal of Counseling Psychology, 29,* 151–157.

Mahler, M. S., Pine, F., & Bergman, A. (1975). *The psychological birth of the human infant.* New York: Basic Books.

Masling, J., Johnson, C., & Saturansky, C. (1974). Oral imagery, accuracy of perceiving others, and performance in Peace Corps training. *Journal of Personality and Social Psychology, 30,* 414–419.

McFall, R. M., & Lillesand, D. B. (1971). Behavior rehearsal with modeling and coaching in assertiveness training. *Journal of Abnormal Psychology, 81,* 199–218.

Mendelsohn, E., & Silverman, L. H. (1982). Effects of stimulating psychodynamically relevant unconscious fantasies on schizophrenic psychopathology. *Schizophrenia Bulletin, 8,* 532–547.

Orne, M. (1962). On the social psychology of the psychological experiment. *American Psychologist, 17,* 776–783.

Packer, S. (1984, August). *Subliminal activation of unconscious fantasies as an adjunct in behavior assertiveness training.* Paper presented at the meeting of the American Psychological Association, Toronto, Canada. (Available from Counseling Center, Princeton University, Princeton, NJ)

Palmatier, J. R., & Bornstein, P. H. (1980). The effects of subliminal stimulation of symbiotic merging fantasies on behavioral treatment of smokers. *Journal of Nervous and Mental Disease, 168,* 715–720.

Rapaport, D., Gill, M. G., & Schafer, R. (1945). *Diagnostic psychological testing.* Chicago: The Year Book Publishers.

Reyher, J. (1967). Hypnosis in research on psychopathology. In J. E. Gordon (Ed.), *Handbook of clinical and experimental hypnosis.* New York: Macmillan.

Rose, G. (1972). Fusion states. In P. L. Giovacchini (Ed.), *Tactics and techniques in psychoanalytic therapy* (pp. 137–169). New York: Aronson.

Rosenthal, R. (1966). *Experimenter effects in behavioral research.* Englewood Cliffs, NJ: Prentice-Hall.

Rutstein, E. H., & Goldberger, L. (1973). The effects of aggressive stimulation on suicidal patients: An experimental study of the psychoanalytic theory of suicide. In B. Rubinstein (Ed.), *Psychoanalysis and contemporary science* (Vol. 2, pp. 157–174). New York: Macmillan.

Sacks, M. (1979). A psychodynamic overview of sports. *Runners World, 9,* 13–22.

Sampson, H., & Weiss, J. (1984). Testing hypotheses: The approach of the Mount Zion Psychotherapy Research Group. In L. Greenberg & W. Pinsof (Eds.), *The psychotherapeutic process: A research handbook.* New York: Guilford.

Schafer, R. (1948). *The clinical application of psychological tests.* New York: International Universities Press.

Schafer, R. (1968). *Aspects of internalization.* New York: International Universities Press.

Schurtman, R., Palmatier, J. R., & Martin, E. S. (1982). On the activation of symbiotic gratification fantasies as an aid in the treatment of alcoholics. *International Journal of the Addictions, 17,* 1157–1174.

Searles, H. F. (1965). *Collected papers on schizophrenia and related subjects.* New York: International Universities Press.

Shafii, M. (1973). Silence in the service of the ego: Psychoanalytic study of meditation. *International Journal of Psychoanalysis, 54,* 431–443.

Silbert, J. (1982). *Human symbiosis, the holding environment and schizophrenia: An experimental study.* Unpublished doctoral dissertation, New York University.

Silverman, L. H. (1972). Drive stimulation and psychopathology: On the conditions under which drive-related external events evoke pathological reactions. In R. R. Holt & E. Peterfreund (Eds.), *Psychoanalysis and contemporary science* (Vol. 1, pp. 306–326). New York: Macmillan.

Silverman, L. H. (1976). Psychoanalytic theory: The reports of my death are greatly exaggerated. *American Psychologist, 31,* 621–637.

Silverman, L. H. (1977). *Ethical considerations and guidelines in the use of subliminal psychodynamic activation.* Unpublished manuscript, Research Center for Mental Health, New York University.

Silverman, L. H. (1983). The subliminal psychodynamic activation method: Overview and comprehensive listing of studies. In J. Masling (Ed.), *Empirical studies of psychoanalytic theories* (Vol. 1, pp. 69–100). Hillsboro, NJ: Erlbaum.

Silverman, L. H., Frank, S., & Dachinger, P. (1974). Psychoanalytic reinterpretation of the effectiveness of systematic desensitization: Experimental data bearing on the role of merging fantasies. *Journal of Abnormal Psychology, 83,* 313–318.

Silverman, L. H., & Grabowski, R. (1982). *The effects of activating oneness fantasies on the anxiety level of male and female college students.* Unpublished manuscript, Research Center for Mental Health, New York University.

Silverman, L. H., Kwawer, J. S., Wolitzky, C., & Coron, M. (1973). An experimental study of aspects of the psychoanalytic theory of male homosexuality. *Journal of Abnormal Psychology, 82,* 178–188.

Silverman, L. H., Lachmann, F., & Milich, R. (1982). *The search for oneness.* New York: International Universities Press.

Silverman, L. H., Martin, A., Ungaro, R., & Mendelsohn, E. (1978). Effect of subliminal stimulation of symbiotic fantasies on behavior modification treatment of obesity. *Journal of Consulting Psychology, 46,* 432–441.

Silverman, L. H., & Spiro, R. H. (1968). The effects of subliminal, supraliminal, and vocalized aggression on the ego functioning of schizophrenics. *Journal of Nervous and Mental Disease, 146,* 50–61.

Silverman, L. H., & Spiro, R. H., Weissberg, J. S., & Candell, P. (1969). The effects of aggressive activation and the need to merge on pathological thinking in schizophrenia. *Journal of Nervous and Mental Disease, 148,* 39–51.

Spielberger, C. D., Gorsuch, R. L., & Lushene, R. E. (1970). *Manual for the state-trait anxiety inventory.* Palo Alto, CA: Consulting Psychologists Press.

Weinberger, J., & Silverman, L. H. (1986). Subliminal psychodynamic activation: An approach to testing psychoanalytic propositions. In R. Hogan & W. Jones (Eds.), *Perspectives in personality: Theory, measurement and interpersonal dynamics* (Vol. 2). Greenwich, CT: JAI Press.

Zuckerman, M., & Lubin, B. (1965). *Manual for the Multiple Affect Adjective Checklist.* San Diego, CA: Educational and Industrial Testing Service.

Womb Envy, Testyria, and Breast Castration Anxiety: What If Freud Were Female?

Gloria Steinem

*Over the century since its introduction, both psychoanalysis and Freud person-
ally have been the subject of numerous criticisms. Freud has been pilloried for
being a plagiarist, liar, and sexist. His theory has been denounced as immoral,
dirty, unscientific, and politically incorrect. During his lifetime Freud complained
about the criticism he received, but also seemed to revel in it somewhat (Gay,
1988). He expected his theory to upset people. In fact, Freud believed that because psychoanalysis exposes essential but uncomfortable truths, it* should *upset*
people.

*It is astonishing to see how often modern critics attack psychoanalysis by
attacking Freud himself. The underlying assumption seems to be that if Freud
was a scoundrel, then his theory must be wrong. (It is tempting to wonder if
this very unscientific style of argument is at all related to modern trends in political reporting, where the desperate race to uncover "scandal" in politicians'
lives increasingly pushes out analysis of the policies they pursue.)*

*Other, more legitimate criticisms of Freud have some degree of merit. For
example, there is no question that the empirical base of psychoanalytic theory
would not be considered even marginally sufficient for a new theory today.
Freud based his theory on introspection and his experience with patients; he reported very little that would today be considered "data." Modern research, such
as seen in the preceding selection, only begins to rectify this shortcoming. But
other kinds of information besides controlled research—such as the degree to
which therapists and people in general have found the theory useful over the
years—may also be relevant.*

*The most difficult charge from which to defend Freud and psychoanalysis is
that of sexism. Unlike so many other areas of his thought, Freud's view of
women seems to have been influenced by the conventional attitudes of his time.
As a result, some of his ideas appear strange by contemporary standards. Freud*

thought women experienced "penis envy," and in general seemed to describe men as normal humans, and women as damaged men.

In the final selection in this section, the prominent feminist writer Gloria Steinem (writing in Ms. *magazine) attacks without mercy Freud's most vulnerable point. She invents a fictitious psychoanalyst named Dr. Phyllis Freud. The Madame Doctor expounds a famous theory that takes everything psychoanalysis says about women, and says it about men instead. Steinem appends footnotes to this paper documenting some astonishing statements about women uttered by psychoanalysts over the years. Steinem's article also demonstrates the continuing truth of an aspect of Freud's theory that he expected, and even seemed to relish, from the beginning—psychoanalysis makes people mad.*

Freud will perhaps always be a controversial figure, and psychoanalysis is a highly imperfect creation. It is a challenging task to balance what the theory has to offer with the things that are clearly wrong about it. Similarly, when reading pieces such as the one that follows, it is difficult to separate out serious criticisms from outspoken indignation. And it is worth pondering just what it is about psychoanalysis that makes it still worth attacking, again and again, more than half a century after its founder's death.*

From "Womb Envy, Testyria, and Breast Castration Anxiety: What If Freud Were Female?" by G. Steinem (1994). In *Ms.*, 49–56. Adapted with permission.

T o sense the difference between *what is* and *what could be*, we may badly need the "Aha!" that comes from exchanging subject for object; the flash of recognition that starts with a smile. I've grown to have a lot of faith in this technique of reversal. It not only produces empathy, but it's a great detector of bias, in ourselves as well as in others. In fact, the deeper the bias, the more helpful it is to make a similar statement about the other gender—or a different race, class, sexuality, physical ability, whatever—and see how it sounds.

* * *

In pursuit of the reasons why Sigmund Freud is still with us, and, most important, how it feels to be on the wrong side of his ubiquitous presence, I propose that male human beings in general, as well as everyone in the psychological trade, male or female, imagine themselves on the receiving end of a profession—indeed, a popular culture—suffused with the work and worship of one of the most enduring, influential, and fiercely defended thinkers in Western civilization: Dr. Phyllis Freud.

You will come to know her here through the words of her biographer, a scholar who is a little defensive because of criticisms of Freud, but still starstruck, and very sure of being right—in other words, a typical Freudian. Every detail of Phyllis' biography springs from Sigmund's, with only first names, pronouns, and anything else related to gender changed in order to create a gender-reversed world.

As in so much of life, the fun is in the text, but the truth is in the footnotes. Read both.

It's important to understand that when little Phyllis was growing up in Vienna in the mid-1800s, women were considered superior because

---

* All footnotes are by the author (Gloria Steinem) and appeared in the original.

of their ability to give birth. This belief in female superiority was so easily mistaken for an immutable fact of life that conditions like *womb envy* had become endemic among males.[1]

Indeed, the belief in women's natural right to dominate was the very foundation of matriarchal Western civilization. At the drop of a hat, wise women would explain that, while men might dabble in the arts, they could never become truly *great* painters, sculptors, musicians, poets, or anything else that demanded creativity, for they lacked the womb, which was the very source of creativity. Similarly, since men had only odd, castrated breasts that created no sustenance, they might become adequate family cooks, but certainly they could never become great chefs, vintners, herbalists, nutritionists, or anything else that required a flair for food, a knowledge of nutrition, or a natural instinct for gustatory nuance. And because childbirth caused women to use the health care system more than men did, making childbirth its natural focus,[2] there was little point in encouraging young men to become physicians, surgeons, researchers, or anything other than low-paid health care helpers.

Even designing their own clothes was left to men only at the risk of unfortunate results. When allowed to dress themselves, they could never get beyond the envy of wombs and female genitals that condemned them to an endless repetition of female sexual symbolism. Thus, the open button-to-neck "V" of men's jackets was a recapitulation of the "V" of female genitalia; the knot in men's ties replicated the clitoris while the long ends of the tie took the shape of labia; and men's bow ties were the clitoris *erecta* in all its glory. They were, to use Phyllis Freud's technical term, "representations."[3]

In addition, men's lack of firsthand experience with birth and nonbirth—with choosing between conception and contraception, existence and nonexistence, as women did so wisely for all their fertile years—also reduced any sense of justice and ethics they might develop.[4] This tended to disqualify them as philosophers, whose very purview was the question of existence versus nonexistence plus all the calibrations in between. Certainly, it also lessened men's ability to make life-and-death judgments, which explained—and perhaps still does—their absence from decision-making positions in the law, law enforcement, the military, or other such professions.

After life-giving wombs and sustenance-giving breasts, women's ability to menstruate was the most obvious proof of their superiority. Only women could bleed without injury or death; only they rose from the gore each month like a phoenix; only their bodies were in tune with the ulu-

---

[1]Modern Freudians *still* won't give up on penis envy. In 1981, *Freud and Women*, by Lucy Freeman and Dr. Herbert S. Strean (Continuum), contained this typical defense: "Contemporary psychoanalysts . . . agree penis envy is a universal fantasy of little girls at the age of four, [but . . .] if a little girl's emotional needs are understood by a loving mother and protective father, the normal fantasies of penis envy that occur during her phallic stage of sexual development will be accepted, then suppressed . . . and she will be able to love a man not for the physical attribute which, as a little girl, she envied and unconsciously wished to possess, but out of her feelings for him as a total person. She will want him not as a possessor of the desired phallus, but as mate and father of her child. In Freud's words, her original wish for a penis has changed into the wish for a baby."—Author

[2]Actually, this is true—women do use the health-care system about 30 percent more than men do—but you'd never know it from who's in charge. Logic is in the eye of the logician.—Author

[3]Here are Freeman and Strean: "In her unconscious envy of the penis, many a woman adorns herself with feathers, sequins, furs, glistening silver and gold ornaments that 'hang down'—what psychoanalysts call 'representations' of the penis." I rest my case.—Author

[4]At the age of 76, with all the wisdom of his career to guide him, Freud wrote: "We also regard women as weaker in their social interests and as having less capacity for sublimating their instincts than men." His assumption that women were incapable of reaching the highest stage of ethical development—which was, in masculinist thought, the subordination of the individual to an abstract principle—became the foundation of the field of ethics. For an antidote, see Carol Gilligan's *In a Different Voice* (Harvard University Press). —Author

lations of the universe and the timing of the tides. Without this innate lunar cycle, how could men have a sense of time, tides, space, seasons, the movement of the universe, or the ability to measure anything at all? How could men mistress the skills of measurement for mathematics, engineering, architecture, surveying—and many other fields? In Christian churches, how could males serve the Daughter of the Goddess with no monthly evidence of Her death and resurrection? In Judaism, how could they honor the Matriarchal God without the symbol of Her sacrifices recorded in the Old Ovariment? Thus insensible to the movements of the planets and the turning of the universe, how could men become astronomers, naturalists, scientists—or much of anything at all?[5]

It was simply accepted for males to be homemakers, ornaments, devoted sons, and sexual companions (providing they were well trained, of course, for, though abortion was well accepted, it was painful and to be avoided, and a careless impregnation could be punished by imprisonment).[6]

Once Phyllis Freud got into brilliant theorizing that went far beyond her training as a nineteenth-

century neurologist, however, her greatest impact was to come not from phrases like *womb envy* and *anatomy is destiny*. No, those truths were already part of the culture. It was her interest in and treatment of *testyria*, a disease marked by uncontrollable fits of emotion and mysterious physical symptoms so peculiar to males that most experts assumed the condition to be related to the testicles. Though testyrical males were often thought to be perverse, pretending, or otherwise untreatable, some treatments had been devised. They ranged from simple water cures, bed rest, mild electric shock, or, for the well-to-do, trips to a spa, to circumcision, the removal of the testicles, cauterization of the penis, and other remedies that may seem draconian now, but were sometimes successful in subduing testyrical fits, and, in any case, were a product of their times.[7] In Paris, Phyllis Freud had also been among the hundreds of women who assembled in lecture halls to see demonstrations of hypnosis—a new technique for treating these mysterious symptoms by reaching into the unconscious—on male testyrics brought in for the purpose.

In fact, that sight had coalesced in Freud's mind with a case of testyria she had heard about in Vienna. A neurologist colleague, Dr. Josephine Breuer, had discussed her progress in relieving testyrical symptoms by encouraging a patient to explore the memories of earlier painful experiences with which the symptoms seemed associated—first with the aid of hypnosis, later by just talking them out through free association. Actually, this method had been improvised and named the "talking cure" by the young patient in question, Bert Pappenheim.

---

[5]As another antidote to antimenstruation bias, try this argument: Since in women's "difficult" days before the onset of the menstrual period, the female hormone is at its lowest ebb, women are in those few days the most like what men are like *all month long.*—Author

[6]Yes, abortion was punishable by imprisonment at that time, and yes, the other reversals are also true. Descriptions of the era's sexism have been used to make Sigmund's attitude toward women seem understandable, even enlightened. Ignoring the many advances of his day flattens the ground around him to make him look taller. Here are a few other realities: George Sand was born a half century before Freud, and was one of many women who managed to live a life more free and unconventional than Freud could imagine even for himself. U.S. suffragists had issued the Declaration of Sentiments at Seneca Falls eight years before Freud was born. Throughout his formative years, Austrian suffragists, socialists, and reformers were working on every area of women's social and political rights—as were their counterparts in other countries. And there was an active movement in Austria for homosexual rights at the turn of the century.—Author

[7]For from-the-horse's-mouth documents of the period on the sadistic treatment of female patients—from electrical shocks to clitoridectomy and other sex-related surgeries—see Jeffrey Moussaieff Masson's *A Dark Science: Women, Sexuality, and Psychiatry in the Nineteenth Century* (Farrar, Straus & Giroux). For this tradition as adapted in the Freudian era, see Phyllis Chesler's *Women and Madness* (Harcourt Brace Jovanovich). —Author

When Freud began her practice in the study of her Vienna apartment, hypnosis and Pappenheim's "talking cure" combined in her courageous focus on testyria. The symptoms she saw included depression, hallucinations, and a whole array of ailments, from paralysis, incapacitating headaches, chronic vomiting and coughing, and difficulty in swallowing, to full-scale testyrical fits, imitative pregnancies, and self-injury that included "couvade," or slitting the skin of the penis—an extreme form of womb and menstruation envy that was an imitation of female functions.[8]

Even as Freud worked first with hypnosis, then more and more with psychoanalysis (for she had honored Pappenheim's "talking cure" with that new and scientific name), she theorized about what might be the cause. Because testyria was particularly common among men in their teens and twenties, she surmised that homemaking, childrearing, sexual service, sperm production, and other parts of men's natural sphere had not yet yielded their mature satisfactions. Since some young men were also indulging in the dangerous practice of masturbation, they were subject to severe neurosis and sexual dysfunction per se. Among older and more rebellious or intellectual men, there was also the problem of being too womb-envying to attract a mate. Finally, there were those husbands who were married to women who had no regard for their sexual satisfaction; who, for example, practiced coitus interruptus either as a form of contraception, or from simple disregard.[9]

Extreme gratitude from her patients was understandable. Not only was Phyllis Freud the rare woman who listened to men, but she took what they said seriously and made it the subject of her own brilliant theories, even of science. This advanced attitude joins other evidence in exposing the gratuitous hostility of masculinists who accuse Freud of androphobia.[10] As a young woman, Phyllis had even translated into German Harriet Taylor Mill's *The Emancipation of Men*, a tract on male equality that a less enlightened woman would never have read.[11] Later, she supported the idea that men could also become psychoanalysts—provided, of course, they subscribed to Freudian theory, just as any female analyst would do. (Certainly, Freud would not have approved of the current school of equality that demands "men's history" and other special treatment.)

I'm sure that if you read carefully each of Freud's case histories, you will see the true depth of her understanding for the opposite sex.[12]

Freud wisely screened all she heard from testyrical men through her understanding, well accepted to this day, that men are sexually passive, just as they are intellectually and ethically. The libido was intrinsically feminine, or, as she put it

---

[8]I couldn't resist *couvade*, a pregnancy-imitating ritual among men in tribal cultures where pregnancy and birth are worshiped. Women are made out to be the "naturally" masochistic ones in patriarchal cultures, but doesn't slitting the penis sound pretty masochistic to you?

In the case of Freud and his colleagues, however, the self-cutting and other mutilations they were seeing in their practices were probably what has now been traced to real events of sexual and other sadistic abuse in childhood: females (and males when they are similarly abused) repeat what was done to them, punishing the body that "attracted" or "deserved" such abuse, and anesthetizing themselves against pain, just as they were forced to do in the past.—Author

[9]Interesting—this one works both ways. Since "coitus interruptus" could be defined as an "interruptus" by whichever half of the pair has finished coitus—if you see what I mean—it needs no reversal.—Author

[10]O.K., maybe it's not perfect, but you try making up a word for man-hating. Also try figuring out why there isn't one.—Author

[11]Freud picked up a little extra money by translating John Stuart Mill's *The Emancipation of Women* while doing peacetime military service. What this mostly proves is that he was exposed to ideas of equality early—and rejected them. As he wrote to his wife, Martha: "Am I to think of my delicate sweet girl as a competitor?. . . . the position of woman cannot be other than what it is: to be an adored sweetheart in youth, and a beloved wife in maturity."—Author

[12]You bet.—Author

with her genius for laywoman's terms, "man possesses a weaker sexual instinct."

This was proved by man's mono-orgasmic nature. No serious authority disputed the fact that females, being multiorgasmic, were well adapted to pleasure, and thus were the natural sexual aggressors; in fact, "envelopment," the legal term for intercourse, was an expression of this active/passive understanding.[13] It was also acted out in microcosm in the act of conception itself. Think about it: the large ovum expends no energy, waits for the sperm to seek out its own destruction in typically masculine and masochistic fashion, and then simply envelops the infinitesimal sperm. As the sperm disappears into the ovum, it is literally eaten alive—much like the male spider eaten by his mate. Even the most quixotic male liberationist would have to agree that biology leaves no room for doubt about an intrinsic female dominance.[14]

What intrigued Freud was not these biological facts, however, but their psychological impact: for instance, the way males were rendered incurably narcissistic, anxious, and fragile by having their genitals so precariously perched and visibly exposed on the outside of their bodies. Men's wombl essness and loss of all but vestigial breasts and useless nipples were the end of a long evolutionary journey toward the sole functions of sperm production, sperm carrying, and sperm delivery. Women were responsible for all the other processes of reproduction. Female behavior, health, and psychology governed gestation and birth. Since time immemorial, this disproportionate share in reproductive influence had unbalanced the sexes. (Freud realized the consequences for women as well, among them *breast castration anxiety*: a woman who looks at the flattened male chest with its odd extraneous nipples fears deep in her psyche that she will return to that breast castrated state.)

Finally, there was the physiological fact of the penis. It confirmed the initial bisexuality of all humans.[15] After all, life begins as female, in the womb as elsewhere[16] (the explanation for men's residual nipples). Penile tissue has its origin in, and thus has retained a comparable number of nerve endings as, the clitoris.[17] But somewhere along the evolutionary line, the penis acquired a double function: excretion of urine and sperm delivery. (Indeed, during boys' feminine, masturbatory, clitoral stage of development—before they had seen female genitals and realized that their penises were endangered and grotesque compared to the compact, well-protected clitoris—the penis had a third, albeit immature, function of masturbatory pleasure.)[18] All this resulted in an organ suffering from functional overload. The most obvious, painful, diurnal, nocturnal (indeed, even multidiurnal and multinocturnal) outcome for this residual clitoral tissue was clear: *men were forced to urinate through their clitorises.*

No doubt, this was the evolutionary cause for the grotesque enlargement and exposure of the pe-

---

[13]Try replacing "penetration" with "envelopment" and see what happens to your head.—Author

[14]Let's face it. Biology can be used to prove anything. Phyllis describes fertilization in terms of female dominance. Sigmund's terms are better suited to rape: "The male sex cell is actively mobile and searches out the female one, and the latter, the ovum, is immobile and waits passively," he wrote in "Femininity." "This behavior of the elementary sexual organisms is indeed a model for the conduct of sexual individuals during intercourse. The male pursues the female for the purpose of sexual union, seizes hold of her, and penetrates into her." What feminism asks—and I hope science, too, will ask one day—is, why do we have to assume domination? How about cooperation?—Author

[15]Actually, S. F. did believe in bisexuality—especially in young children, for they hadn't yet figured out how precious the penis was.—Author

[16]True.—Author

[17]Also true. *Somebody* had equality in mind.—Author

[18]Here is Sigmund in "Some Psychological Consequences of the Anatomical Distinction Between the Sexes": There is "a momentous discovery which little girls are destined to make. They notice the penis of a brother or playmate, strikingly visible and of large proportions, at once recognize it as the superior counterpart of their own small and inconspicuous organ, and from that time forward fall a victim to envy for the penis. . . . She has seen it and knows that she is without it and wants to have it."—Author

nis, and for its resulting insensitivity due to lack of protection. Though the nerve endings in the female's clitoris remained exquisitely sensitive and close to the surface—carefully carried, as they were, in delicate mucous membranes, which were protected by the labia—the exposed penile versions of the same nerve endings had gradually become encased in a protective, deadening epidermis; a fact that deprived men of the intense, radiating, whole-body pleasure that only the clitoris could provide. Men's lesser sex drive and diminished capacity for orgasm followed, as day follows night.

As Phyllis Freud proved in clinical studies that would become both widely accepted and tremendously influential, male sexuality became mature only when pleasure was transferred from the penis to the mature and appropriate area: the fingers and tongue. Freud reasoned brilliantly that since insemination and pregnancy could not accompany every orgasm experienced by multiorgasmic females, it must also be the case for males that sexual maturity would be measured by their ability to reach climax in a nonprocreative way. Immature *penile* orgasms had to be replaced by *lingual* and *digital* ones. In "Masculinity" as elsewhere, Phyllis Freud was very clear: "In the clitoral phase of boys, the penis is the leading erotogenic zone. But it is not, of course, going to remain so. . . . The penis should . . . hand over its sensitivity, and at the same time its importance, to the lingual/digital areas."[19]

[19]In "Femininity," Sigmund explained: "In the phallic phase of girls the clitoris is the leading erotogenic zone. But it is not, of course, going to remain so. . . . The clitoris should . . . hand over its sensitivity, and at the same time, its importance, to the vagina."

Should we excuse him as a man of his time? Here's the conclusion of Lisa Appignanesi and John Forrester in *Freud's Women* (HarperCollins): "It is almost inconceivable that Freud was not aware of the orthodox views of contemporary anatomists and physiologists, who had, from well before the early nineteenth century, demonstrated that the clitoris was the specific site of female sexual pleasure, and who, in the medical writing of his time, had asserted that the vagina had virtually no erotic functions at all. Nineteenth-century medical encyclopedia writers closed the file on the vagina in the same way Alfred Kinsey [did] in the mid-20th century, with a flourish of definitively and chillingly rank-pulling medical rhetoric: virtually the entire vagina could be operated on without the need of an anesthetic."

Still think the digital/lingual reversal is too outrageous? Maybe—but it allows men a lot more nerve endings than Freud allowed us.—Author

PART V

Humanistic Approaches to Personality

The humanistic approaches to personality emphasize that which is uniquely human about psychology's object of study. Studying people is not the same as studying rocks, trees, or animals, because people are fundamentally different. The unique aspects on which humanistic approaches focus are experience, awareness, free will, dignity, and the meaning of life. None of these mean much to rocks, trees, or animals, but they are all crucial to the human condition.

Our first selection, by the philosopher Jean-Paul Sartre, describes the existential philosophy that forms the bedrock of humanistic psychology. Existential analysis begins with the concrete and specific analysis of a single human being existing in a particular moment in time and space. It leads directly to concerns with phenomenology (the study of experience), free will, and the meaning of life. All of these existential issues are important for humanistic psychologists.

Sartre seems to view free will as a burden—it leaves one "forlorn," without external guidance about the right way to live. But the humanistic psychologists who borrowed so much of existential philosophy instead view free will as an opportunity. In the second selection, Abraham Maslow briefly describes what he sees as the implications of existential philosophy for psychology, and argues that an existential viewpoint not only reclaims free will but offers new opportunities for personal growth and fulfillment.

This message is echoed by Gordon Allport, another pioneering humanistic psychologist, in the next selection. Allport focuses on the need in psychology for a "self," by which he means a psychological construct that has purpose, identity, experience, and a will to live and to grow. Nonhumanistic areas of psychology ignore these, Allport claims, but each is essential.

The next selection is another article by Maslow. This one presents his well-known theory of motivation, often referred to as the "hierarchy of needs." What is humanistic about this theory is that motivation begins rather than ends with the basic needs for survival and safety. After those are satisfied, Maslow pro-

poses, uniquely human needs for understanding, beauty, and self-actualization become important.

Existentialism claims that one's experience of reality is more important than reality itself; this message is echoed in the fifth selection, by the psychologist George Kelly. Kelly's theory proposes that each person builds his or her experience of reality out of a set of uniquely individual ideas called "personal constructs." An important corollary to this proposal is that to understand another person, one needs to understand his or her view of reality and the personal constructs that comprise it. The article is not a summary of Kelly's theory, however. Rather, it uses his theory to analyze threat, aggression, and hostility, and to understand why (in his estimation) only the last of these necessarily causes problems.

The best known of the humanistic psychologists surely was Carl Rogers. Rogers' theory begins with the existential observation that people have free will, then adds the assumption that when left alone people will always freely choose life and growth. This faith leads him to develop the most optimistic of all the humanistic psychologies.

The final selection is by the modern humanistic psychologist Mihalyi Csikszentmihalyi. Like Rogers, Csikszentmihalyi combines two ideas with an important result. The two ideas he combines are the existentialist postulation of free will and the accompanying postulation that the momentary experience of reality overwhelms the importance of reality itself (whatever that might be). Putting them together, he concludes that one might as well choose to experience happiness. He is then led to ask, what is happiness? He concludes that true happiness consists not of ecstasy but rather a state of calm absorption he calls "flow."

The psychologist Ernest Hilgard once warned of the example of the entomologist who found a bug he couldn't classify, so he stepped on it. The largest contribution of the humanistic psychologists is their sustained focus on issues—such as experience, free will, and the meaning of life—that other areas of psychology are content to ignore.

THE HUMANISM OF EXISTENTIALISM

Jean-Paul Sartre

The philosophical basis of humanistic psychology is existentialism. And the lead-ing exponent of existentialism has been Jean-Paul Sartre. Sartre was a French philosopher, dramatist, and novelist. He was a person of high principles. He was imprisoned by the Germans when they invaded France in 1940, and after his release he became active in the French Resistance. He was awarded the 1964 Nobel Prize in Literature but rejected it, saying that to accept such an award would compromise his integrity as a writer.

Existentialism is a philosophy that claims that "existence precedes essence." This means that first one exists—this is the only given—and then one must de-cide what such existence means. Since a person's existence occurs only a moment at a time, the experience of life in each moment is all-important. Any influence from the environment, the past, or the future can only affect one to the degree one is aware of it now. *Sartre derives from these postulates an ethical code that emphasizes the freedom of oneself and others, and an accompanying, inescapa-ble, total responsibility for everything one thinks and does.*

We will see in later selections how humanistic psychologists integrate several key observations of existential philosophy into their theories. For now, note how Sartre argues that

- *the experience of each moment of existence is the basis for all else;*
- *each individual must interpret what reality is and what it means;*
- *people have complete freedom and total responsibility for their actions;*
- *there is no moral or ethical code beyond that which each individual must invent —with the one exception that it is essential to take responsibility for our own free choices, whatever they are; and*
- *it is in accepting freedom and taking responsibility—despite everything—that hu-mans achieve dignity.*

From *Essays in Existentialism*, edited by W. Baskin, pp. 31–62. Copyright © 1965 by Phil-osophical Library, Inc. Published by arrangement with Carol Publishing Group.

* * *

What is meant by the term *existentialism?*

* * *

It is the most austere of doctrines. It is intended strictly for specialists and philosophers. Yet it can be defined easily. * * * What [existentialists] have in common is that they think that existence precedes essence, or, if you prefer, that subjectivity must be the starting point.

* * *

Atheistic existentialism, which I represent, states that if God does not exist, there is at least one being in whom existence precedes essence, a being who exists before he can be defined by any concept, and that this being is man, or, as Heidegger[1] says, human reality. What is meant here by saying that existence precedes essence? It means that, first of all, man exists, turns up, appears on the scene, and, only afterwards, defines himself. If man, as the existentialist conceives him, is indefinable, it is because at first he is nothing. Only afterward will he be something, and he himself will have made what he will be. Thus, there is no human nature, since there is no God to conceive it. Not only is man what he conceives himself to be, but he is also only what he wills himself to be after this thrust toward existence.

Man is nothing else but what he makes of himself. Such is the first principle of existentialism. It is also what is called subjectivity. * * * [By this,] we mean that man first exists, that is, that man first of all is the being who hurls himself toward a future and who is conscious of imagining himself as being in the future. Man is at the start a plan which is aware of itself, rather than a patch of moss, a piece of garbage, or a cauliflower; nothing exists prior to this plan; there is nothing in heaven; man will be what he will have planned to be. Not what he will want to be. Because by the word "will" we generally mean a conscious decision, which is subsequent to what

we have already made of ourselves. I may want to belong to a political party, write a book, get married; but all that is only a manifestation of an earlier, more spontaneous choice that is called "will." But if existence really does precede essence, man is responsible for what he is. Thus, existentialism's first move is to make every man aware of what he is and to make the full responsibility of his existence rest on him. And when we say that a man is responsible for himself, we do not only mean that he is responsible for his own individuality, but that he is responsible for all men.

* * * When we say that man chooses his own self, we mean that every one of us does likewise; but we also mean by that that in making this choice he also chooses all men. In fact, in creating the man that we want to be, there is not a single one of our acts which does not at the same time create an image of man as we think he ought to be. To choose to be this or that is to affirm at the same time the value of what we choose, because we can never choose evil. We always choose the good, and nothing can be good for us without being good for all.

If, on the other hand, existence precedes essence, and if we grant that we exist and fashion our image at one and the same time, the image is valid for everybody and for our whole age. Thus, our responsibility is much greater than we might have supposed, because it involves all mankind. * * * If I want to marry, to have children; even if this marriage depends solely on my own circumstances or passion or wish, I am involving all humanity in monogamy and not merely myself. Therefore, I am responsible for myself and for everyone else. I am creating a certain image of man of my own choosing. In choosing myself, I choose man.

This helps us understand what the actual content is of such rather grandiloquent words as anguish, forlornness, despair.[2] As you will see, it's all quite simple.

---

[1]A German existentialist philosopher whose thinking underlies much of the theory that Sartre espouses in this article.

[2]Gloomy-sounding words like these are a staple of existentialist philosophy.

First, what is meant by anguish? The existentialists say at once that man is anguish. What that means is this: the man who involves himself and who realizes that he is not only the person he chooses to be, but also a lawmaker who is, at the same time, choosing all mankind as well as himself, can not help escape the feeling of his total and deep responsibility. Of course, there are many people who are not anxious; but we claim that they are hiding their anxiety, that they are fleeing from it. Certainly, many people believe that when they do something, they themselves are the only ones involved, and when someone says to them, "What if everyone acted that way?" they shrug their shoulders and answer, "Everyone doesn't act that way." But really, one should always ask himself, "What would happen if everybody looked at things that way?" There is no escaping this disturbing thought except by a kind of double-dealing. A man who lies and makes excuses for himself by saying "Not everybody does that," is someone with an uneasy conscience, because the act of lying implies that a universal value is conferred upon the lie.

Anguish is evident even when it conceals itself. This is the anguish that Kierkegaard called the anguish of Abraham. You know the story: an angel has ordered Abraham to sacrifice his son; if it really were an angel who has come and said, "You are Abraham, you shall sacrifice your son," everything would be all right. But everyone might first wonder, "Is it really an angel, and am I really Abraham? What proof do I have?"

There was a madwoman who had hallucinations; someone used to speak to her on the telephone and give her orders. Her doctor asked her, "Who is it who talks to you?" She answered, "He says it's God." What proof did she really have that it was God? If an angel comes to me, what proof is there that it's an angel? And if I hear voices, what proof is there that they come from heaven and not from hell, or from the subconscious, or a pathological condition? What proves that they are addressed to me? What proof is there that I have been appointed to impose my choice and my conception of man on humanity? I'll never find any

proof or sign to convince me of that. If a voice addresses me, it is always for me to decide that this is the angel's voice; if I consider that such an act is a good one, it is I who will choose to say that it is good rather than bad.

Now, I'm not being singled out as an Abraham, and yet at every moment I'm obliged to perform exemplary acts. For every man, everything happens as if all mankind had its eyes fixed on him and were guiding itself by what he does. And every man ought to say to himself, "Am I really the kind of man who has the right to act in such a way that humanity might guide itself by my actions?" And if he does not say that to himself, he is masking his anguish.

There is no question here of the kind of anguish which would lead to quietism, to inaction. It is a matter of a simple sort of anguish that anybody who has had responsibilities is familiar with. For example, when a military officer takes the responsibility for an attack and sends a certain number of men to death, he chooses to do so, and in the main he alone makes the choice. Doubtless, orders come from above, but they are too broad; he interprets them, and on this interpretation depend the lives of ten or fourteen or twenty men. In making a decision he can not help having a certain anguish. All leaders know this anguish. That doesn't keep them from acting; on the contrary, it is the very condition of their action. For it implies that they envisage a number of possibilities, and when they choose one, they realize that it has value only because it is chosen. We shall see that this kind of anguish, which is the kind that existentialism describes, is explained, in addition, by a direct responsibility to the other men whom it involves. It is not a curtain separating us from action, but is part of action itself.

When we speak of forlornness, a term Heidegger was fond of, we mean only that God does not exist and that we have to face all the consequences of this. The existentialist is strongly opposed to a certain kind of secular ethics which would like to abolish God with the least possible expense. About 1880, some French teachers tried to set up a secular ethics which went something like this: God is a useless and costly hypothesis; we are discarding it; but, meanwhile, in order for there to be an ethics, a society, a civilization, it is essential that certain values be taken seriously and that they be considered as having an *a priori* existence. It must be obligatory, *a priori*, to be honest, not to lie, not to beat your wife, to have children, etc., etc. So we're going to try a little device which will make it possible to show that values exist all the same, inscribed in a heaven of ideas, though otherwise God does not exist. In other words—and this, I believe, is the tendency of everything called reformism in France—nothing will be changed if God does not exist. We shall find ourselves with the same norms of honesty, progress, and humanism, and we shall have made of God an outdated hypothesis which will peacefully die off by itself.

The existentialist, on the contrary, thinks it very distressing that God does not exist, because all possibility of finding values in a heaven of ideas disappears along with Him; there can no longer be an *a priori* Good, since there is no infinite and perfect consciousness to think it. Nowhere is it written that the Good exists, that we must be honest, that we must not lie; because the fact is we are on a plane where there are only men. Dostoievsky[3] said, "If God didn't exist, everything would be possible." That is the very starting point of existentialism. Indeed, everything is permissible if God does not exist, and as a result man is forlorn, because neither within him nor without does he find anything to cling to. He can't start making excuses for himself.

If existence really does precede essence, there is no explaining things away by reference to a fixed and given human nature. In other words, there is no determinism, man is free, man is freedom. On the other hand, if God does not exist, we find no values or commands to turn to which legitimize our conduct. So, in the bright realm of values, we have no excuse behind us, nor justification before us. We are alone, with no excuses.

That is the idea I shall try to convey when I say that man is condemned to be free. Condemned, because he did not create himself, yet, in other respects is free; because, once thrown into the world, he is responsible for everything he does. The existentialist does not believe in the power of passion. He will never agree that a sweeping passion is a ravaging torrent which fatally leads a man to certain acts and is therefore an excuse. He thinks that man is responsible for his passion.

The existentialist does not think that man is going to help himself by finding in the world some omen by which to orient himself. Because he thinks that man will interpret the omen to suit himself. Therefore, he thinks that man, with no support and no aid, is condemned every moment to invent man. * * *

To give you an example which will enable you to understand forlornness better, I shall cite the case of one of my students who came to see me under the following circumstances: his father was on bad terms with his mother, and, moreover, was inclined to be a collaborationist;[4] his older brother had been killed in the German offensive of 1940, and the young man, with somewhat immature but generous feelings, wanted to avenge him. His mother lived alone with him, very much upset by the half-treason of her husband and the death of her older son; the boy was her only consolation.

The boy was faced with the choice of leaving for England and joining the Free French Forces—that is, leaving his mother behind—or remaining with his mother and helping her to carry on. He was fully aware that the woman lived only for him and that his going-off—and perhaps his death—would plunge her into despair. He was also aware that every act that he did for his mother's sake was a sure thing, in the sense that it was helping

---

[3]Fyodor Dostoyevsky (the more common English spelling) was a 19th-century Russian novelist.

[4]A collaborationist was a resident of a country occupied by Germany in World War II who cooperated with the invaders. Germany conquered France, where Sartre lived, in 1940. Sartre was imprisoned by the Germans for a year, then freed. Upon his release, at great personal risk, Sartre became active in the French Resistance.

her to carry on, whereas every effort he made toward going off and fighting was an uncertain move which might run aground and prove completely useless; for example, on his way to England he might, while passing through Spain, be detained indefinitely in a Spanish camp; he might reach England or Algiers and be stuck in an office at a desk job. As a result, he was faced with two very different kinds of action: one, concrete, immediate, but concerning only one individual; the other concerned an incomparably vaster group, a national collectivity, but for that very reason was dubious, and might be interrupted en route. And, at the same time, he was wavering between two kinds of ethics. On the one hand, an ethics of sympathy, of personal devotion; on the other, a broader ethics, but one whose efficacy was more dubious. He had to choose between the two.

Who could help him choose? Christian doctrine? No. Christian doctrine says, "Be charitable, love your neighbor, take the more rugged path, etc., etc." But which is the more rugged path? Whom should he love as a brother? The fighting man or his mother? Which does the greater good, the vague act of fighting in a group, or the concrete one of helping a particular human being to go on living? Who can decide *a priori*? Nobody. No book of ethics can tell him. The Kantian ethics says, "Never treat any person as a means, but as an end." Very well, if I stay with mother, I'll treat her as an end and not as a means; but by virtue of this very fact, I'm running the risk of treating the people around me who are fighting, as means; and, conversely, if I go to join those who are fighting, I'll be treating them as an end, and, by doing that, I run the risk of treating my mother as a means.

If values are vague, and if they are always too broad for the concrete and specific case that we are considering, the only thing left for us is to trust our instincts. That's what this young man tried to do; and when I saw him, he said, "In the end, feeling is what counts. I ought to choose whichever pushes me in one direction. If I feel that I love my mother enough to sacrifice everything else

for her—my desire for vengeance, for action, for adventure—then I'll stay with her. If, on the contrary, I feel that my love for my mother isn't enough, I'll leave."

But how is the value of a feeling determined? What gives his feeling for his mother value? Precisely the fact that he remained with her. I may say that I like so-and-so well enough to sacrifice a certain amount of money for him, but I may say so only if I've done it. I may say "I love my mother well enough to remain with her" if I have remained with her. The only way to determine the value of this affection is, precisely, to perform an act which confirms and defines it. But, since I require this affection to justify my act, I find myself caught in a vicious circle.

On the other hand, a mock feeling and a true feeling are almost indistinguishable; to decide that I love my mother and will remain with her, or to remain with her by putting on an act, amount somewhat to the same thing. In other words, the feeling is formed by the acts one performs; so, I can not refer to it in order to act upon it. Which means that I can neither seek within myself the true condition which will impel me to act, nor apply to a system of ethics for concepts which will permit me to act. You will say, "At least, he did go to a teacher for advice." But if you seek advice from a priest, for example, you have chosen this priest; you already knew, more or less, just about what advice he was going to give you. In other words, choosing your adviser is involving yourself. The proof of this is that if you are a Christian, you will say, "Consult a priest." But some priests are collaborating, some are just marking time, some are resisting. Which to choose? If the young man chooses a priest who is resisting or collaborating, he has already decided on the kind of advice he's going to get. Therefore, in coming to see me he knew the answer I was going to give him, and I had only one answer to give: "You're free, choose, that is, invent." No general ethics can show you what is to be done; there are no omens in the world. The Catholics will reply, "But there are." Granted—but, in any case, I myself choose the meaning they have.

When I was a prisoner,[5] I knew a rather remarkable young man who was a Jesuit. He had entered the Jesuit order in the following way: he had had a number of very bad breaks; in childhood, his father died, leaving him in poverty, and he was a scholarship student at a religious institution where he was constantly made to feel that he was being kept out of charity; then, he failed to get any of the honors and distinctions that children like; later on, at about eighteen, he bungled a love affair; finally, at twenty-two, he failed in military training, a childish enough matter, but it was the last straw.

This young fellow might well have felt that he had botched everything. It was a sign of something, but of what? He might have taken refuge in bitterness or despair. But he very wisely looked upon all this as a sign that he was not made for secular triumphs, and that only the triumphs of religion, holiness, and faith were open to him. He saw the hand of God in all this, and so he entered the order. Who can help seeing that he alone decided what the sign meant?

Some other interpretation might have been drawn from this series of setbacks; for example, that he might have done better to turn carpenter or revolutionist. Therefore, he is fully responsible for the interpretation. Forlornness implies that we ourselves choose our being. Forlornness and anguish go together.

As for despair, the term has a very simple meaning. It means that we shall confine ourselves to reckoning only with what depends upon our will, or on the ensemble of probabilities which make our action possible. When we want something, we always have to reckon with probabilities. I may be counting on the arrival of a friend. The friend is coming by rail or street-car; this supposes that the train will arrive on schedule, or that the street-car will not jump the track. I am left in the realm of possibility; but possibilities are to be reckoned with only to the point where my action comports with the ensemble of these possibilities, and no further. The moment the possibilities I am

considering are not rigorously involved by my action, I ought to disengage myself from them, because no God, no scheme, can adapt the world and its possibilities to my will. When Descartes said, "Conquer yourself rather than the world," he meant essentially the same thing.

* * *

Things will be as man will have decided they are to be. Does that mean that I should abandon myself to quietism? No. First, I should involve myself; then, act on the old saw "Nothing ventured, nothing gained." Nor does it mean that I shouldn't belong to a party, but rather that I shall have no illusions and shall do what I can. For example, suppose I ask myself, "Will socialization, as such, ever come about?" I know nothing about it. All I know is that I'm going to do everything in my power to bring it about. Beyond that, I can't count on anything. Quietism is the attitude of people who say, "Let others do what I can't do." The doctrine I am presenting is the very opposite of quietism, since it declares, "There is no reality except in action." Moreover, it goes further, since it adds, "Man is nothing else than his plan; he exists only to the extent that he fulfills himself; he is therefore nothing else than the ensemble of his acts, nothing else than his life."

According to this, we can understand why our doctrine horrifies certain people. Because often the only way they can bear their wretchedness is to think, "Circumstances have been against me. What I've been and done doesn't show my true worth. To be sure, I've had no great love, no great friendship, but that's because I haven't met a man or woman who was worthy. The books I've written haven't been very good because I haven't had the proper leisure. I haven't had children to devote myself to because I didn't find a man with whom I could have spent my life. So there remains within me, unused and quite viable, a host of propensities, inclinations, possibilities, that one wouldn't guess from the mere series of things I've done."

Now, for the existentialist there is really no love other than one which manifests itself in a person's being in love. There is no genius other than one which is expressed in works of art; the

---

[5]That is, a prisoner of the Germans in 1940–1941.

genius of Proust is the sum of Proust's works; the genius of Racine is his series of tragedies. Outside of that, there is nothing. Why say that Racine could have written another tragedy, when he didn't write it? A man is involved in life, leaves his impress on it, and outside of that there is nothing. To be sure, this may seem a harsh thought to someone whose life hasn't been a success. But, on the other hand, it prompts people to understand that reality alone is what counts, that dreams, expectations, and hopes warrant no more than to define a man as a disappointed dream, as miscarried hopes, as vain expectations. In other words, to define him negatively and not positively. However, when we say, "You are nothing else than your life," that does not imply that the artist will be judged solely on the basis of his works of art; a thousand other things will contribute toward summing him up. What we mean is that a man is nothing else than a series of undertakings, that he is the sum, the organization, the ensemble of the relationships which make up these undertakings.

When all is said and done, what we are accused of, at bottom, is not our pessimism, but an optimistic toughness. If people throw up to us our works of fiction[6] in which we write about people who are soft, weak, cowardly, and sometimes even downright bad, it's not because these people are soft, weak, cowardly, or bad; because if we were to say that they are that way because of heredity, the workings of environment, society, because of biological or psychological determinism, people would be reassured. They would say, "Well, that's what we're like, no one can do anything about it." But when the existentialist writes about a coward, he says that this coward is responsible for his cowardice. He's not like that because he has a cowardly heart or lung or brain; he's not like that on account of his physiological make-up; but he's like that because he has made himself a coward by his acts. There's no such thing as a cowardly constitution; there are nervous constitutions; there is

poor blood, as the common people say, or there are strong constitutions. But the man whose blood is poor is not a coward on that account, for what makes cowardice is the act of renouncing or yielding. A constitution is not an act; the coward is defined on the basis of the acts he performs. People feel, in a vague sort of way, that this coward we're talking about is guilty of being a coward, and the thought frightens them. What people would like is that a coward or a hero be born that way.

*   *   *

[Existentialism] is the only [theory] which gives man dignity, the only one which does not reduce him to an object. The effect of all materialism is to treat every man, including the one philosophizing, as an object, that is, as an ensemble of determined reactions in no way distinguished from the ensemble of qualities and phenomena which constitute a table or a chair or a stone. We definitely wish to establish the human realm as an ensemble of values distinct from the material realm. But the subjectivity that we have thus arrived at, and which we have claimed to be truth, is not a strictly individual subjectivity, for we have demonstrated that one discovers in the *cogito*[7] not only himself, but others as well.

*   *   *

If it is impossible to find in every man some universal essence which would be human nature, yet there does exist a universal human condition. It's not by chance that today's thinkers speak more readily of man's condition than of his nature. By condition they mean, more or less definitely, the *a priori* limits which outline man's fundamental situation in the universe. Historical situations vary; a man may be born a slave in a pagan society or a feudal lord or a proletarian. What does not vary is the necessity for him to exist in the world, to be at work there, to be there in the midst of other people, and to be mortal there. The limits are neither subjective nor objective, or, rather,

---

[6]Sartre wrote novels and plays about the human condition, including the novel *Nausea* (published in 1938) and the play *No Exit* (1944).

[7]The reference here is to *cogito ergo sum*, "I think, therefore I am." This is the famous existentialist pronouncement by the philosopher Descartes.

they have an objective and a subjective side. Objective because they are to be found everywhere and are recognizable everywhere; subjective because they are *lived* and are nothing if man does not live them, that is, freely determine his existence with reference to them. And though the configurations may differ, at least none of them are completely strange to me, because they all appear as attempts either to pass beyond these limits or recede from them or deny them or adapt to them. Consequently, every configuration, however individual it may be, has a universal value.

* * *

* * * One may choose anything if it is on the grounds of free involvement.

* * *

* * * Fundamentally [humanism means] this: man is constantly outside of himself; in projecting himself, in losing himself outside of himself, he makes for man's existing; and, on the other hand, it is by pursuing transcendent goals that he is able to exist; man, being this state of passing-beyond, and seizing upon things only as they bear upon this passing-beyond, is at the heart, at the center of this passing-beyond. There is no universe other than a human universe, the universe of human subjectivity. This connection between transcendency, as a constituent element of man—not in the sense that God is transcendent, but in the sense of passing beyond—and subjectivity, in the sense that man is not closed in on himself but is always present in a human universe, is what we call existentialist humanism. Humanism, because we remind man that there is no lawmaker other than himself, and that in his forlornness he will decide by himself; because we point out that man will fulfill himself as man, not in turning toward himself, but in seeking outside of himself a goal which is just this liberation, just this particular fulfillment.

* * *

Existential Psychology— What's in It for Us?

Abraham H. Maslow

One of the founders of American humanistic psychology was Abraham Maslow. In the following brief article Maslow specifically addresses the ways in which European existentialist philosophy, of the sort described by Sartre in the previous selection, is relevant to psychology. At the very end, Maslow also demonstrates the manner in which American psychologists typically have drawn a more optimistic message from existentialism than did the existentialists themselves. Dismissing the existentialist obsession with anguish, forlornness, and despair as so much "high-IQ whimpering," Maslow claims that the loss of illusions is always, in the end, exhilarating and strengthening.

From "Existential Philosophy—What's in It for Us?" By A. H. Maslow. In *Existential Philosophy*, 2d ed., edited by R. May, pp. 49–57. New York: Random House. Copyright © 1969 by the McGraw-Hill Companies. Adapted with permission.

I am not an existentialist, nor am I even a careful and thorough student of this movement. There is much in the existentialist writings that I find extremely difficult, or even impossible, to understand and that I have not made much effort to struggle with.

I must confess also that I have studied existentialism not so much for its own sake as in the spirit of, "What's in it for me as a psychologist?" trying all the time to translate it into terms I could use. Perhaps this is why I have found it to be not so much a totally new revelation as a stressing, confirming, sharpening, and rediscovering of trends already existing in American psychology (the various self psychologies, growth psychologies, self-actualization psychologies, organismic psychologies, certain neo-Freudian psychologies,

the Jungian psychology, not to mention some of the psychoanalytic ego psychologists, the Gestalt therapists, and I don't know how many more).

For this and other reasons, reading the existentialists has been for me a very interesting, gratifying, and instructive experience. And I think this will also be true for many other psychologists, especially those who are interested in personality theory and in clinical psychology. It has enriched, enlarged, corrected, and strengthened my thinking about the human personality, even though it has not necessitated any fundamental reconstruction.

First of all, permit me to define existentialism in a personal way, in terms of "what's in it for me." To me it means essentially a radical stress on the concept of identity and the experience of identity as a *sine qua non* of human nature and of any philosophy or science of human nature. I choose this concept as *the* basic one partly because I understand it better than terms like essence, existence, and ontology and partly because I also feel that it can be worked with empirically, if not now, then soon.

But then a paradox results, for the Americans have *also* been impressed with the quest for identity (Allport, Rogers, Goldstein, Fromm, Wheelis, Erikson, Horney, May, *et al.*). And I must say that these writers are a lot clearer and a lot closer to raw fact, that is, more empirical than are, e.g., the Germans Heidegger and Jaspers.[1]

1. Conclusion number one is, then, that the Europeans and Americans are not so far apart as appears at first. We Americans have been "talking prose all the time and didn't know it." Partly, of course, this simultaneous development in different countries is itself an indication that the people who have independently been coming to the same conclusions are all responding to something real outside themselves.

2. This something real is, I believe, the total collapse of all sources of values outside the individual. Many European existentialists are largely reacting to Nietzsche's conclusion that God is dead and perhaps to the fact that Marx also is dead. The Americans have learned that political democracy and economic prosperity do not in themselves solve any of the basic value problems. There is no place else to turn but inward, to the self, as the locus of values.[2] Paradoxically, even some of the religious existentialists will go along with this conclusion part of the way.

3. It is extremely important for psychologists that the existentialists may supply psychology with the underlying philosophy that it now lacks. Log-

ical positivism has been a failure, especially for clinical and personality psychologists.[3] At any rate, the basic philosophical problems will surely be opened up for discussion again, and perhaps psychologists will stop relying on pseudosolutions or on unconscious, unexamined philosophies that they picked up as children.

4. An alternative phrasing of the core (for us Americans) of European existentialism is that it deals radically with that human predicament presented by the gap between human aspirations and human limitations (between what the human being *is*, what he would *like* to be, and what he *could* be). This is not so far off from the identity problem as it might at first sound. A person is both actuality *and* potentiality.

That serious concern with this discrepancy could revolutionize psychology, there is no doubt in my mind. Various literatures already support such a conclusion, e.g., projective testing, self-actualization, the various peak experiences (in which this gap is bridged), the Jungian psychologies, various theological thinkers.

Not only this, but they raise also the problems and techniques of integration of this twofold nature of man, his lower and his higher, his creatureliness and his Godlikeness. On the whole, most philosophies and religions, Eastern as well as Western, have dichotomized them, teaching that the way to become "higher" is to renounce and master "the lower." The existentialists however, teach that *both* are simultaneously defining characteristics of human nature. Neither can be repudiated; they can only be integrated. But we already know something of these integration techniques—of insight, of intellect in the broader sense, of love, of creativeness, of humor and tragedy, of play, of art. I suspect we will focus our studies on these integrative techniques more than

---

[1]The psychologists listed were identified with humanistic or humanistic-psychoanalytic positions; the Germans were speculative philosophers.

[2]This was a key point in the previous selection by Sartre.

[3]In this context, Maslow is using the term "logical positivism" to refer to the position that truth can be known with certainty if correct methods are used. In psychology this leads to a superscientific outlook that emphasizes operational definitions and precise measurements over deeper meanings.

we have in the past. Another consequence for my thinking of this stress on the twofold nature of man is the realization that some problems must remain eternally insoluble.

5. From this flows naturally a concern with the ideal, authentic, or perfect, or Godlike human being, a study of human potentialities as *now* existing in a certain sense, as *current* knowable reality. This, too, may sound merely literary, but it is not. I remind you that this is just a fancy way of asking the old, unanswered questions, "What are the goals of therapy, of education, of bringing up children?"

It also implies another truth and another problem that calls urgently for attention. Practically every serious description of the "authentic person" extant implies that such a person, by virtue of what he has become, assumes a new relation to his society and, indeed, to society in general. He not only transcends himself in various ways; he also transcends his culture. He resists enculturation. He becomes more detached from his culture and from his society. He becomes a little more a member of his species and a little less a member of his local group. My feeling is that most sociologists and anthropologists will take this hard.[4] I therefore confidently expect controversy in this area.

6. From the European writers, we can and should pick up their greater emphasis on what they call "philosophical anthropology," that is, the attempt to define man, and the differences between man and any other species, between man and objects, and between man and robots. What are his unique and defining characteristics? What is as essential to man that without it he would no longer be defined as a man?

On the whole, this is a task from which American psychology has abdicated. The various behaviorisms do not generate any such definition, at least none that can be taken seriously. (What *would* an S-R man be like?) Freud's picture of man was clearly unsuitable, leaving out as it did his aspirations, his realizable hopes, his Godlike qualities. ✳ ✳ ✳

7. The Europeans are stressing the self-making of the self, in a way that the Americans do not. Both the Freudians and the self-actualization and growth theorists in this country talk more about discovering the *self* (as if it were there waiting to be found) and of *uncovering* therapy (shovel away the top layers and you will see what has been always lying there, hidden). To say, however, that the self is a project and is *altogether* created by the continual choices of the person himself is almost surely an overstatement in view of what we know of, e.g., the constitutional and genetic determinants of personality. This clash of opinion is a problem that can be settled empirically.

8. A problem we psychologists have been ducking is the problem of responsibility and, necessarily tied in with it, the concepts of courage and of will in the personality. Perhaps this is close to what the psychoanalysts are now calling "ego strength."

9. American psychologists have listened to Allport's call for an idiographic psychology[5] but have not done much about it. Not even the clinical psychologists have. We now have an added push from the phenomenologists and existentialists in this direction, one that will be *very* hard to resist, indeed, I think, theoretically *impossible* to resist. If the study of the uniqueness of the individual does not fit into what we know of science, then so much the worse for the conception of science. It, too, will have to endure re-creation.

10. Phenomenology[6] has a history in American psychological thinking, but on the whole I

---

[4]Many anthropologists work from the assumption that members of different cultures are basically and even irreducibly different. But Sartre spoke of the "universal human condition," a viewpoint Maslow here seems to endorse.

[5]At times Gordon Allport called for an "idiographic" approach that treated each person as a unique case rather than as a point on a continuum. But neither Allport nor his successors ever seemed entirely clear about how to do this, as Maslow mentions.

[6]Phenomenology is the study of experience; in psychology it treats an individual's perception of reality as the essential fact about him or her.

think it has languished. The European phenomenologists, with their excruciatingly careful and laborious demonstrations, can reteach us that the best way of understanding another human being, or at least *a* way necessary for some purposes, is to get into *his Weltanschauung*[7] and to be able to see *his* world through *his* eyes. Of course such a conclusion is rough on any positivistic philosophy of science.

11. The existentialist stress on the ultimate aloneness of the individual is a useful reminder for us not only to work out further the concepts of decision, of responsibility, of choice, of self-creation, of autonomy, of identity itself. It also makes more problematic and more fascinating the mystery of communication between alonenesses via, e.g., intuition and empathy, love and altruism, identification with others, and homonomy in general. We take these for granted. It would be better if we regarded them as miracles to be explained.

12. Another preoccupation of existentialist writers can be phrased very simply, I think. It is the dimension of seriousness and profundity of living (or perhaps the "tragic sense of life") contrasted with the shallow and superficial life, which is a kind of diminished living, a defense against the ultimate problems of life. This is not just a literary concept. It has real operational meaning, for instance, in psychotherapy. I (and others) have been increasingly impressed with the fact that tragedy can sometimes be therapeutic and that therapy often seems to work best when people are *driven* into it by pain. It is when the shallow life does not work that it is questioned and that there occurs a call to fundamentals. Shallowness in psychology does not work either, as the existentialists are demonstrating very clearly.

13. The existentialists, along with many other groups, are helping to teach us about the limits of verbal, analytic, conceptual rationality. They are part of the current call back to raw experience as prior to any concepts or abstractions. This amounts to what I believe to be a justified critique of the whole way of thinking of the Western world

---

[7]World view.

in the twentieth century, including orthodox positivistic science and philosophy, both of which badly need reexamination.

14. Possibly most important of all the changes to be wrought by phenomenologists and existentialists is an overdue revolution in the theory of science. I should not say "wrought by," but rather "helped along by," because there are many other forces helping to destroy the official philosophy of science or "scientism." It is not only the Cartesian split between subject and object that needs to be overcome. There are other radical changes made necessary by the inclusion of the psyche and of raw experience in reality, and such a change will affect not only the science of psychology but all other sciences as well. For example, parsimony, simplicity, precision, orderliness, logic, elegance, definition are all of the realm of abstraction.

15. I close with the stimulus that has most powerfully affected me in the existentialist literature, namely, the problem of future time in psychology. Not that this, like all the other problems or pushes I have mentioned up to this point, was totally unfamiliar to me, nor, I imagine, to *any* serious student of the theory of personality. * * * Growth and becoming and possibility necessarily point toward the future, as do the concepts of potentiality and hoping and of wishing and imagining; reduction to the concrete is a loss of future; threat and apprehension point to the future (no future = no neurosis); self-actualization is meaningless without reference to a currently active future; life can be a gestalt in time, etc., etc.

And yet the *basic and central* importance of this problem for the existentialists has something to teach us. * * * I think it fair to say that no theory of psychology will ever be complete that does not centrally incorporate the concept that man has his future within him, dynamically active at this present moment. * * * Also we must realize that *only* the future is *in principle* unknown and unknowable, which means that all habits, defenses, and coping mechanisms are doubtful and ambiguous because they are based on past experience. Only the flexibly creative person can really manage [the] future, *only* the one who can face novelty with confidence and without fear. I am convinced that much of what we now call psychology is the study of the tricks we use to avoid the anxiety of absolute novelty by making believe the future will be like the past.

* * *

It is possible that existentialism will not only enrich psychology. It may also be an additional push toward the establishment of another *branch* of psychology, the psychology of the fully evolved and authentic self and its ways of being. * * *

Certainly it seems more and more clear that what we call "normal" in psychology is really a psychopathology of the average, so undramatic and so widely spread that we do not even notice it ordinarily. The existentialist's study of the authentic person and of authentic living helps to throw this general phoniness, this living by illusions and by fear, into a harsh, clear light which reveals it clearly as sickness, even though widely shared.

I do not think we need take too seriously the European existentialists' harping on dread, on anguish, on despair, and the like, for which their only remedy seems to be to keep a stiff upper lip.[8] This high-IQ whimpering on a cosmic scale occurs whenever an external source of values fails to work. They should have learned from the psychotherapists that the loss of illusions and the discovery of identity, though painful at first, can be ultimately exhilarating and strengthening.

---

[8]This is Maslow's sarcastic construal of Sartre's call for existential courage.

Is the Concept of Self Necessary?

Gordon W. Allport

Gordon Allport is usually remembered as a trait psychologist, and we have already seen one of his important articles in the trait section of this reader (Part II). But Allport was also one of the early humanistic psychologists. He was deeply interested in the process of personal growth (a process he called "becoming") and believed that personality was much more than the collection of instincts, habits, and reflexes represented in the behaviorist psychology dominant in America in the early twentieth century. Allport had the very humanistic concern that such descriptions leave out something essential. In the following essay Allport argues that the central concept for psychology should be that of the self.

Allport describes eight functions of the self that cannot easily be subsumed by other kinds of psychological concepts. For example, the self has purpose, identity, experience, and a will to live. These are not complex learned reflexes, but essential aspects of human existence. Allport further points out that some things we do—such as speak English or obey traffic laws—are experienced as matters of mere fact rather than matters of importance. Other things we do, however, seem "to be vital and central in becoming." For example, for the explorer Raold Amundsen the quest to see the North and South Poles dominated his entire life. Allport observes that we feel a certain "warm" ownership of the central aspects of our selves, and so uses the term "proprium" to refer to that feeling of proprietariness.

Allport's description of the self had a wide influence on later generations of humanistic psychologists. And its roots can be seen in existential philosophy of the sort described by Sartre. Allport's "propriate striving" is a seeking after goals one has freely and consciously chosen; Sartre believed that such conscious choice is the essence of existence.

From "Is the Concept of Self Necessary? The Proprium." In *Becoming: Basic Consideration for a Psychology of Personality*, by G. W. Allport (1955), pp. 36–65. New Haven, CT: Yale University Press. Copyright © 1955 by Yale University Press.

* * *

The first thing an adequate psychology of growth should do is to draw a distinction between what are matters of *importance* to the individual and what are merely matters of *fact* to him; that is, between what he feels to be vital and central in becoming and what belongs to the periphery of his being.

Many facets of our life-style are not ordinarily felt to have strong personal relevance. Each of us, for example, has innumerable tribal habits that mark our life-style but are nothing more than opportunistic modes of adjusting. The same holds true for many of our physiological habits. We keep to the right in traffic, obey the rules of etiquette, and make countless unconscious or semiconscious adjustments, all of which characterize our life-style but are not *propriate*, i.e., not really central to our sense of existence. Consider, for example, the English language habits that envelop our thinking and communication. Nothing could be of more pervasive influence in our lives than the store of concepts available to us in our ancestral tongue and the frames of discourse under which our social contacts proceed. And yet the use of English is ordinarily felt to be quite peripheral to the core of our existence. It would not be so if some foreign invader should forbid us to use our native language. At such a time our vocabulary and accent and our freedom to employ them would become very precious and involved with our sense of self. So it is with the myriad of social and physiological habits we have developed that are never, unless interfered with, regarded as essential to our existence as a separate being.

Personality includes these habits and skills, frames of reference, matters of fact and cultural values, that seldom or never seem warm and important. But personality includes what is warm and important also—all the regions of our life that we regard as peculiarly ours, and which for the time being I suggest we call the *proprium*. The proprium includes all aspects of personality that make for inward unity.

Psychologists who allow for the proprium use both the term "self" and "ego"—often interchangeably; and both terms are defined with varying degrees of narrowness or of comprehensiveness. Whatever name we use for it, this sense of what is "peculiarly ours" merits close scrutiny. The principal functions and properties of the proprium need to be distinguished.

To this end William James over sixty years ago proposed a simple taxonomic scheme (James, 1890). There are, he maintained, two possible orders of self: an empirical self (the *Me*) and a knowing self (the *I*). Three subsidiary types comprise the empirical Me: the material self, the social self, and the spiritual self. Within this simple framework he fits his famous and subtle description of the various states of mind that are "peculiarly ours." His scheme, however, viewed in the perspective of modern psychoanalytic and experimental research, seems scarcely adequate. In particular it lacks the full psychodynamic flavor of modern thinking. With some trepidation, therefore, I offer what I hope is an improved outline for analyzing the propriate aspects of personality. Later we shall return to the question, Is the concept of *self* necessary?

The Proprium

1. BODILY SENSE   The first aspect we encounter is the bodily *me*. It seems to be composed of streams of sensations that arise within the organism —from viscera, muscles, tendons, joints, vestibular canals, and other regions of the body. The technical name for the bodily sense is *coenesthesis*. Usually this sensory stream is experienced dimly; often we are totally unaware of it. At times, however, it is well configured in consciousness in the exhilaration that accompanies physical exercise, or in moments of sensory delight or pain. The infant, apparently, does not know that such experiences are "his." But they surely form a necessary foundation for his emerging sense of self. The baby who at first cries from unlocalized discomfort will,

in the course of growth, show progressive ability to identify the distress as his own.

The bodily sense remains a lifelong anchor for our self-awareness, though it never alone accounts for the entire sense of self, probably not even in the young child who has his memories, social cues, and strivings to help in the definition. Psychologists have paid a great deal of attention, however, to this particular component of self-awareness, rather more than to other equally important ingredients. One special line of investigation has been surprisingly popular: the attempt to locate self in relation to specific bodily sensations. When asked, some people will say that they *feel* the self in their right hands, or in the viscera. Most, however, seem to agree with Claparède that a center midway between the eyes, slightly behind them within the head, is the focus. It is from this cyclopean eye that we estimate what lies before and behind ourselves, to the right or left, and above and below. Here, phenomenologically speaking, is the locus of the ego (Claporède, 1924). ∗ ∗ ∗

How very intimate (propriate) the bodily sense is can be seen by performing a little experiment in your imagination. Think first of swallowing the saliva in your mouth, or do so. Then imagine expectorating it into a tumbler and drinking it! What seemed natural and "mine" suddenly becomes disgusting and alien. Or picture yourself sucking blood from a prick in your finger; then imagine sucking blood from a bandage around your finger! What I perceive as belonging intimately to my body is warm and welcome; what I perceive as separate from my body becomes, in the twinkling of an eye, cold and foreign.

Certainly organic sensations, their localization and recognition, composing as they do the bodily *me*, are a core of becoming. But it would be a serious mistake to think, as some writers do, that they alone account for our sense of what is "peculiarly ours."

2. SELF-IDENTITY   Today I remember some of my thoughts of yesterday; and tomorrow I shall remember some of my thoughts of both yesterday and today; and I am subjectively certain that they are the thoughts of the same person. In this situation, no doubt, the organic continuity of the neuromuscular system is the leading factor. Yet the process involves more than reminiscence made possible by our retentive nerves. The young infant has retentive capacity during the first months of life but in all probability no sense of self-identity. This sense seems to grow gradually, partly as a result of being clothed and named, and otherwise marked off from the surrounding environment. Social interaction is an important factor. It is the actions of the other to which he differentially adjusts that force upon a child the realization that he is not the other, but a being in his own right. The difficulty of developing self-identity in childhood is shown by the ease with which a child depersonalizes himself in play and in speech (Allport, 1937). Until the age of four or five we have good reason to believe that as perceived by the child personal identity is unstable. Beginning at about this age, however, it becomes the surest attest a human being has of his own existence.

3. EGO-ENHANCEMENT   We come now to the most notorious property of the proprium, to its unabashed self-seeking. Scores of writers have featured this clamorous trait in human personality. It is tied to the need for survival, for it is easy to see that we are endowed by nature with the impulses of self-assertion and with the emotions of self-satisfaction and pride. Our language is laden with evidence. The commonest compound of self is *selfish*, and of ego *egoism*. Pride, humiliation, self-esteem, narcissism are such prominent factors that when we speak of ego or self we often have in mind only this aspect of personality. And yet, self-love may be prominent in our natures without necessarily being sovereign. The proprium, as we shall see, has other facets and functions.

4. EGO-EXTENSION   The three facets we have discussed—coenesthesis, self-identity, ego-enhancement—are relatively early developments in personality, characterizing the whole of the child's proprium. Their solicitations have a heavily bio-

logical quality and seem to be contained within the organism itself. But soon the process of learning brings with it a high regard for possessions, for loved objects, and later, for ideal causes and loyalties. We are speaking here of whatever objects a person calls "mine." They must at the same time be objects of *importance*, for sometimes our sense of "having" has no affective tone and hence no place in the proprium. A child, however, who identifies with his parent is definitely extending his sense of self, as he does likewise through his love for pets, dolls, or other possessions, animate or inanimate.

As we grow older we identify with groups, neighborhood, and nation as well as with possessions, clothes, home. They become matters of importance to us in a sense that other people's families, nations, or possessions are not. Later in life the process of extension may go to great lengths, through the development of loyalties and of interests focused on abstractions and on moral and religious values. Indeed, a mark of maturity seems to be the range and extent of one's feeling of self-involvement in abstract ideals.

5. RATIONAL AGENT The ego, according to Freud, has the task of keeping the organism as a whole in touch with reality, of intermediating between unconscious impulses and the outer world. Often the rational ego can do little else than invent and employ defenses to forestall or diminish anxiety. These protective devices shape the development of personality to an extent unrealized sixty years ago. It is thanks to Freud that we understand the strategies of denial, repression, displacement, reaction formation, rationalization, and the like better than did our ancestors.

We have become so convinced of the validity of these defense mechanisms, and so impressed with their frequency of operation, that we are inclined to forget that the rational functioning of the proprium is capable also of yielding true solutions, appropriate adjustments, accurate planning, and a relatively faultless solving of the equations of life.

Many philosophers, dating as far back as Boethius in the sixth century, have seen the rational

nature of personality as its most distinctive property. * * * It may seem odd to credit Freud, the supreme irrationalist of our age, with helping preserve for psychology the emphasis upon the ego as the rational agent in personality, but such is the case. For whether the ego reasons or merely rationalizes, it has the property of synthesizing inner needs and outer reality. Freud [has] not let us forget this fact, and [has] thus made it easier for modern cognitive theories to deal with this central function of the proprium.

6. SELF-IMAGE A propriate function of special interest today is the self-image, or as some writers call it, the phenomenal self. Present-day therapy is chiefly devoted to leading the patient to examine, correct, or expand this self-image. The image has two aspects: the way the patient regards his present abilities, status, and roles; and what he would like to become, his *aspirations* for himself. The latter aspect, which Karen Horney calls the "idealized self-image," (Horney, 1950) is of especial importance in therapy. On the one hand it may be compulsive, compensatory, and unrealistic, blinding its possessor to his true situation in life. On the other hand, it may be an insightful cognitive map, closely geared to reality and defining a wholesome ambition. The ideal self-image is the imaginative aspect of the proprium, and whether accurate or distorted, attainable or unattainable, it plots a course by which much propriate movement is guided and therapeutic progress achieved.

There are, of course, many forms of becoming that require no self-image, including automatic cultural learning and our whole repertoire of opportunistic adjustments to our environment. Yet there is also much growth that takes place only with the aid of, and because of, a self-image. This image helps us bring our view of the present into line with our view of the future. * * *

7. PROPRIATE STRIVING We come now to the nature of motivation. Unfortunately we often fail to distinguish between propriate and peripheral motives. The reason is that at the rudimentary levels of becoming, which up to now have been the chief

levels investigated, it *is* the impulses and drives, the immediate satisfaction and tension reduction, that are the determinants of conduct. Hence a psychology of opportunistic adjustment seems basic and adequate, especially to psychologists accustomed to working with animals. At low levels of behavior the familiar formula of drives and their conditioning appears to suffice. But as soon as the personality enters the stage of ego-extension, and develops a self-image with visions of self-perfection, we are, I think, forced to postulate motives of a different order, motives that reflect propriate striving. Within experimental psychology itself there is now plenty of evidence that conduct that is "ego involved" (propriate) differs markedly from behavior that is not (Allport, 1943).

* * *

In his autobiography Raold Amundsen tells how from the age of fifteen he had one dominant passion—to become a polar explorer. The obstacles seemed insurmountable, and all through his life the temptations to reduce the tensions engendered were great. But the propriate striving persisted. While he welcomed each success, it acted to raise his level of aspiration, to maintain an over-all commitment. Having sailed the Northwest Passage, he embarked upon the painful project that led to the discovery of the South Pole. Having discovered the South Pole, he planned for years, against extreme discouragement, to fly over the North Pole, a task he finally accomplished. But his commitment never wavered until at the end he lost his life in attempting to rescue a less gifted explorer, Nobile, from death in the Arctic. Not only did he maintain one style of life, without ceasing, but this central commitment enabled him to withstand the temptation to reduce the segmental tensions continually engendered by fatigue, hunger, ridicule, and danger (Amundsen, 1928).

* * *

Propriate striving distinguishes itself from other forms of motivation in that, however beset by conflicts, it makes for unification of personality. There is evidence that the lives of mental patients are marked by the proliferation of unrelated subsystems, and by the loss of more homogeneous

systems of motivation (McQuitty, 1950). When the individual is dominated by segmental drives, by compulsions, or by the winds of circumstance, he has lost the integrity that comes only from maintaining major directions of striving. The possession of long-range goals, regarded as central to one's personal existence, distinguishes the human being from the animal, the adult from the child, and in many cases the healthy personality from the sick.[1]

Striving, it is apparent, always has a future reference. As a matter of fact, a great many states of mind are adequately described only in terms of their futurity. Along with *striving*, we may mention *interest*, *tendency*, *disposition*, *expectation*, *planning*, *problem solving*, and *intention*. While not all future-directedness is phenomenally propriate, it all requires a type of psychology that transcends the prevalent tendency to explain mental states exclusively in terms of past occurrences. People, it seems, are busy leading their lives into the future, whereas psychology, for the most part, is busy tracing them into the past.

8. THE KNOWER Now that we have isolated these various propriate functions—all of which we regard as peculiarly ours—the question arises whether we are yet at an end. Do we not have in addition a cognizing self—a knower, that transcends all other functions of the proprium and holds them in view? In a famous passage, William James wrestles with this question, and concludes that we have not. There is, he thinks, no such thing as a substantive self distinguishable from the sum total, or stream, of experiences. Each moment of consciousness, he says, appropriates each previous moment, and the knower is thus somehow embedded in what is known. "The thoughts themselves are the thinker."

Opponents of James argue that no mere series of experiences can possibly turn themselves into

---

[1]Compare this to Sartre's prescription for authentic existence. It is the choosing of one's own goals in life that is uniquely human; thus a concern with such choices is "humanistic."

an awareness of that series as a unit. Nor can "passing thoughts" possibly regard themselves as important or interesting. To whom is the series important or interesting if not to *me*? I am the ultimate monitor. The self as *knower* emerges as a final and inescapable postulate.

* * *

We not only know *things*, but we know (i.e., are acquainted with) the empirical features of our own proprium. It is I who have bodily sensations, I who recognize my self-identity from day to day; I who note and reflect upon my self-assertion, self-extension, my own rationalizations, as well as upon my interests and strivings. When I thus think about my own propriate functions I am likely to perceive their essential togetherness, and feel them intimately bound in some way to the knowing function itself.

Since such knowing is, beyond any shadow of doubt, a state that is peculiarly ours, we admit it as the eighth clear function of the proprium. (In other words, as an eighth valid meaning of "self" or "ego.") But it is surely one of nature's perversities that so central a function should be so little understood by science, and should remain a perpetual bone of contention among philosophers. Many, like Kant, set this function (the "pure ego") aside as something qualitatively apart from other propriate functions (the latter being assigned to the "empirical me"). Others, like James, say that the ego *qua* knower is somehow contained within the ego *qua* known. Still others, personalistically inclined, find it necessary to postulate a single self as knower, thinker, feeler, and doer—all in one blended unit of a sort that guarantees the continuance of all becoming (Bertocci, 1945).

We return now to our unanswered question: Is the concept of self necessary in the psychology of personality? Our answer cannot be categorical since all depends upon the particular usage of "self" that is proposed. Certainly all legitimate phenomena that have been, and can be ascribed, to the self or ego must be admitted as data indispensable to a psychology of personal becoming. All eight functions of the "proprium" (our temporary neutral term for central interlocking operations of personality) must be admitted and included. In particular the unifying act of perceiving and knowing (of comprehending propriate states at belonging together and belonging to me) must be fully admitted.

At the same time, the danger is very real that a homunculus[2] may creep into our discussions of personality, and be expected to solve all our problems without in reality solving any. Thus, if we ask "What determines our moral conduct?" the answer may be "The self does it." Or, if we pose the problem of choice, we say "The self chooses." Such question-begging would immeasurably weaken the scientific study of personality by providing an illegitimate regressus. There are, to be sure, ultimate problems of philosophy and of theology that psychology cannot even attempt to solve, and for the solution of such problems "self" in some restricted and technical meaning may be a necessity.

But so far as psychology is concerned our position, in brief, is this: all psychological functions commonly ascribed to a self or ego must be admitted as data in the scientific study of personality. These functions are not, however, coextensive with personality as a whole. They are rather the special aspects of personality that have to do with warmth, with unity, with a sense of personal importance. In this exposition I have called them "propriate" functions. If the reader prefers, he may call them self-functions, and in this sense self may be said to be a necessary psychological concept. * * *

* * *

References

Allport, G. W. (1937). *Personality: A Psychological Interpretation.* New York: Henry Holt.

---

[2]A "homunculus theory" is one that posits a "little man in the head" that does all the thinking for a person. Such a theory explains nothing because the question of why the little man does what he does remains unanswered.

Allport, G. W. (1943). The ego in contemporary psychology. *Psychological Review, 50*, 451–478.

Amundsen, R. (1928). *My Life as an Explorer.* Garden City, NY: Doubleday, Doran.

Bertocci, P. A. (1945). The psychological self, the ego, and personality. *Psychological Review, 52*, 91–99.

Claparède, E. (1924). Note sur la localisation du moi. *Archives de psychologie, 19*, 172–182.

Horney, K. (1950). *Neurosis and Human Growth: The Struggle toward Self-realization.* New York: Norton.

James, W. (1890). *Principles of Psychology* (Vol. 1). New York: Henry Holt.

McQuitty, L. (1950). A measure of personality integration in relation to the concept of self. *Journal of Personality, 18*, 461–482.

A Theory of Human Motivation

Abraham H. Maslow

*Maslow's best-known contribution to psychology is his proposal that human mo-
tivation is organized by a hierarchy of needs. Lower, physiological and safety
needs must be satisfied before higher needs can emerge. These include the need
for esteem, the need for self-actualization, the need to know and understand,
and aesthetic needs. None of these latter needs are directly tied to survival; they
become potent only after the survival needs are taken care of.*

*Maslow's theory, described in the following selection, is humanistic in two
ways. First, he explicitly states that the study of human motivation does not
need to be based on findings from research with animals. "It is no more necessary to study animals before one can study man than it is to study mathematics
before one can study geology or psychology or biology." Second and more important, Maslow's higher needs are uniquely human. The needs to experience
beauty, to understand the world, and to fulfill one's potential all stem from the
quest for authentic existence at the core of existential philosophy and humanistic
psychology.*

*Maslow's theory leads him to write a couple of prescriptions for human de-
velopment. First, he observes that a child satisfied in basic needs early in life
becomes relatively tolerant of deprivation in later life, and better able to focus
on higher goals. Therefore, children should be raised to feel satisfied and safe.
Second, "a man who is thwarted in any of his basic needs may fairly be envisaged as a sick man." Maslow concludes that a society that thwarts the basic
needs of individuals is therefore itself sick. On the other hand, "the good or
healthy society would then be defined as one that permitted man's highest purposes to emerge by satisfying all his basic needs."*

From "A Theory of Human Motivation," in *Motivation and Personality*, 3d ed., by A. H.
Maslow, revised by R. Frager, J. Fadiman, C. McReynolds, and R. Cox, pp. 80–106. Copy-
right © 1954, 1987 by Harper & Row, Publishers, Inc. Copyright © 1970 by Abraham H.
Maslow. Reprinted by permission of Addison-Wesley Educational Publishers Inc.

* * *

The Basic Needs

THE PHYSIOLOGICAL NEEDS The needs that are usually taken as the starting point for motivation theory are the so-called physiological drives. Two recent lines of research make it necessary to revise our customary notions about these needs: first, the development of the concept of homeostasis, and second, the finding that appetites (preferential choices among foods) are a fairly efficient indication of actual needs or lacks in the body.

Homeostasis refers to the body's automatic efforts to maintain a constant, normal state of the blood stream. * * *

* * * If the body lacks some chemical, the individual will tend (in an imperfect way) to develop a specific appetite or partial hunger for that food element.

Thus it seems impossible as well as useless to make any list of fundamental physiological needs, for they can come to almost any number one might wish, depending on the degree of specificity of description. We cannot identify all physiological needs as homeostatic. That sexual desire, sleepiness, sheer activity, and maternal behavior in animals are homeostatic has not yet been demonstrated. Furthermore, this list would not include the various sensory pleasure (tastes, smells, tickling, stroking), which are probably physiological and which may become the goals of motivated behavior.

These physiological drives or needs are to be considered unusual rather than typical because they are isolable, and because they are localizable somatically. That is to say, they are relatively independent of each other, of other motivations, and of the organism as a whole, and second, in many cases, it is possible to demonstrate a localized, underlying somatic base for the drive. This is true less generally than has been thought (exceptions are fatigue, sleepiness, maternal responses) but it is still true in the classic instances of hunger, sex, and thirst.

It should be pointed out again that any of the physiological needs and the consummatory behavior involved with them serve as channels for all sorts of other needs as well. That is to say, the person who thinks he is hungry may actually be seeking more for comfort, or dependence, than for vitamins or proteins. Conversely, it is possible to satisfy the hunger need in part by other activities such as drinking water or smoking cigarettes. In other words, relatively isolable as these physiological needs are, they are not completely so.

Undoubtedly these physiological needs are the most prepotent of all needs. What this means specifically is that in the human being who is missing everything in life in an extreme fashion, it is most likely that the major motivation would be the physiological needs rather than any others. A person who is lacking food, safety, love, and esteem would most probably hunger for food more strongly than for anything else.

If all the needs are unsatisfied, and the organism is then dominated by the physiological needs, all other needs may become simply nonexistent or be pushed into the background. It is then fair to characterize the whole organism by saying simply that it is hungry, for consciousness is almost completely preëmpted by hunger. All capacities are put into the service of hunger-satisfaction, and the organization of these capacities is almost entirely determined by the one purpose of satisfying hunger. The receptors and effectors, the intelligence, memory, habits, all may now be defined simply as hunger-gratifying tools. Capacities that are not useful for this purpose lie dormant, or are pushed into the background. The urge to write poetry, the desire to acquire an automobile, the interest in American history, the desire for a new pair of shoes are, in the extreme case, forgotten or become of secondary importance. For the man who is extremely and dangerously hungry, no other interests exist but food. He dreams food, he remembers food, he thinks about food, he emotes only about food, he perceives only food, and he wants only food. The more subtle determinants that ordinarily fuse with the physiological drives in organizing even feeding, drinking, or sexual behavior, may now be so completely overwhelmed as to allow us to speak at this time (but *only* at this time) of pure hunger drive and behavior, with the one unqualified aim of relief.

Another peculiar characteristic of the human organism when it is dominated by a certain need is that the whole philosophy of the future tends also to change. For our chronically and extremely hungry man, Utopia can be defined simply as a place where there is plenty of food. He tends to think that, if only he is guaranteed food for the rest of his life, he will be perfectly happy and will never want anything more. Life itself tends to be defined in terms of eating. Anything else will be defined as unimportant. Freedom, love, community feeling, respect, philosophy, may all be waved aside as fripperies that are useless, since they fail to fill the stomach. Such a man may fairly be said to live by bread alone.

It cannot possibly be denied that such things are true, but their *generality* can be denied. Emergency conditions are, almost by definition, rare in the normally functioning peaceful society. That this truism can be forgotten is attributable mainly to two reasons. First, rats have few motivations other than physiological ones, and since so much of the research upon motivation has been made with these animals, it is easy to carry the rat picture over to the human being. Second, it is too often not realized that culture itself is an adaptive tool, one of whose main functions is to make the physiological emergencies come less and less often. In most of the known societies, chronic extreme hunger of the emergency type is rare, rather than common. In any case, this is still true in the United States. The average American citizen is experiencing appetite rather than hunger when he says, "I am hungry." He is apt to experience sheer life-and-death hunger only by accident and then only a few times through his entire life.

Obviously a good way to obscure the higher motivations, and to get a lopsided view of human capacities and human nature, is to make the organism extremely and chronically hungry or thirsty. Anyone who attempts to make an emer-

gency picture into a typical one, and who will measure all of man's goals and desires by his behavior during extreme physiological deprivation is certainly being blind to many things. It is quite true that man lives by bread alone—when there is no bread. But what happens to man's desires when there *is* plenty of bread and when his belly is chronically filled?

At once other (and higher) needs emerge and these, rather than physiological hungers, dominate the organism. And when these in turn are satisfied, again new (and still higher) needs emerge, and so on. This is what we mean by saying that the basic human needs are organized into a hierarchy of relative prepotency.

One main implication of this phrasing is that gratification becomes as important a concept as deprivation in motivation theory, for it releases the organism from the domination of a relatively more physiological need, permitting thereby the emergence of other more social goals. The physiological needs, along with their partial goals, when chronically gratified cease to exist as active determinants or organizers of behavior. They now exist only in a potential fashion in the sense that they may emerge again to dominate the organism if they are thwarted. But a want that is satisfied is no longer a want. The organism is dominated and its behavior organized only by unsatisfied needs. If hunger is satisfied, it becomes unimportant in the current dynamics of the individual.

This statement is somewhat qualified by a hypothesis to be discussed more fully later, namely, that it is precisely those individuals in whom a certain need has always been satisfied who are best equipped to tolerate deprivation of that need in the future, and that furthermore, those who have been deprived in the past will react differently to current satisfactions than the one who has never been deprived.

THE SAFETY NEEDS If the physiological needs are relatively well gratified, there then emerges a new set of needs, which we may categorize roughly as the safety needs. All that has been said of the physiological needs is equally true, although in less degree, of these desires. The organism may equally well be wholly dominated by them. They may serve as the almost exclusive organizers of behavior, recruiting all the capacities of the organism in their service, and we may then fairly describe the whole organism as a safety-seeking mechanism. Again we may say of the receptors, the effectors, of the intellect, and of the other capacities that they are primarily safety-seeking tools. Again, as in the hungry man, we find that the dominating goal is a strong determinant not only of his current world outlook and philosophy but also of his philosophy of the future. Practically everything looks less important than safety (even sometimes the physiological needs, which being satisfied are now underestimated). A man in this state, if it is extreme enough and chronic enough, may be characterized as living almost for safety alone.

Although in this chapter we are interested primarily in the needs of the adult, we can approach an understanding of his safety needs perhaps more efficiently by observation of infants and children, in whom these needs are much more simple and obvious. One reason for the clearer appearance of the threat or danger reaction in infants is that they do not inhibit this reaction at all, whereas adults in our society have been taught to inhibit it at all costs. Thus even when adults do feel their safety to be threatened, we may not be able to see this on the surface. Infants will react in a total fashion and as if they were endangered, if they are disturbed or dropped suddenly, startled by loud noises, flashing light, or other unusual sensory stimulation, by rough handling, by general loss of support in the mother's arms, or by inadequate support.

Another indication of the child's need for safety is his preference for some kind of undisrupted routine or rhythm. He seems to want a predictable, orderly world. For instance, injustice, unfairness, or inconsistency in the parents seems to make a child feel anxious and unsafe. This attitude may be not so much because of the injustice *per se* or any particular pains involved, but rather because this treatment threatens to make the world look unreliable, or unsafe, or unpredictable. Young children seem to thrive better under a system that has at least a skeletal outline of rigidity, in which there is a schedule of a kind, some sort of routine, something that can be counted upon, not only for the present but also far into the future. Child psychologists, teachers, and psychotherapists have found that permissiveness within limits, rather than unrestricted permissiveness is preferred as well as *needed* by children. Perhaps one could express this more accurately by saying that the child needs an organized world rather than an unorganized or unstructured one.

The central role of the parents and the normal family setup are indisputable. Quarreling, physical assault, separation, divorce, or death within the family may be particularly terrifying. Also parental outbursts of rage or threats of punishment directed to the child, calling him names, speaking to him harshly, handling him roughly, or actual physical punishment sometimes elicit such total panic and terror that we must assume more is involved than the physical pain alone. While it is true that in some children this terror may represent also a fear of loss of parental love, it can also occur in completely rejected children, who seem to cling to the hating parents more for sheer safety and protection than because of hope of love.

Confronting the average child with new, unfamiliar, strange, unmanageable stimuli or situations will too frequently elicit the danger or terror reaction, as for example, getting lost or even being separated from the parents for a short time, being confronted with new faces, new situations, or new tasks, the sight of strange, unfamiliar, or uncontrollable objects, illness, or death. Particularly at such times, the child's frantic clinging to his parents is eloquent testimony to their role as protectors (quite apart from their roles as food givers and love givers).

From these and similar observations, we may generalize and say that the average child in our society generally prefers a safe, orderly, predictable, organized world, which he can count on, and in which unexpected, unmanageable, or other dangerous things do not happen, and in which, in any case, he has all-powerful parents who protect and shield him from harm.

* * *

The healthy, normal, fortunate adult in our culture is largely satisfied in his safety needs. The peaceful, smoothly running, good society ordinarily makes its members feel safe enough from wild animals, extremes of temperature, criminal assault, murder, tyranny, etc. Therefore, in a very real sense, he no longer has any safety needs as active motivators. Just as a sated man no longer feels hungry, a safe man no longer feels endangered. If we wish to see these needs directly and clearly we must turn to neurotic or near-neurotic individuals, and to the economic and social underdogs. In between these extremes, we can perceive the expressions of safety needs only in such phenomena as, for instance, the common preference for a job with tenure and protection the desire for a savings account and for insurance of various kinds (medical, dental, unemployment, disability, old age).

Other broader aspects of the attempt to seek safety and stability in the world are seen in the very common preference for familiar rather than unfamiliar things, or for the known rather than the unknown. The tendency to have some religion or world philosophy that organizes the universe and the men in it into some sort of satisfactorily coherent, meaningful whole is also in part motivated by safety seeking. Here too we may list science and philosophy in general as partially motivated by the safety needs (we shall see later that there are also other motivations to scientific, philosophical, or religious endeavor).

Otherwise the need for safety is seen as an active and dominant mobilizer of the organism's resources only in emergencies, e.g., war, disease, natural catastrophes, crime waves, societal disorganization, neurosis, brain injury, chronically bad situations.

Some neurotic adults in our society are, in many ways, like the unsafe child in their desire for safety, although in the former it takes on a somewhat special appearance. Their reaction is often to unknown, psychological dangers in a world that is perceived to be hostile, overwhelming, and threatening. Such a person behaves as if a great catastrophe were almost always impending, i.e., he is usually responding as if to an emergency. His safety needs often find specific expression in a search for a protector, or a stronger person on whom he may depend, perhaps a fuehrer.

* * *

The neurosis in which the search for safety takes its clearest form is in the compulsive-obsessive neurosis. Compulsive-obsessives try frantically to order and stabilize the world so that no unmanageable, unexpected, or unfamiliar dangers will ever appear. They hedge themselves about with all sorts of ceremonials, rules, and formulas so that every possible contingency may be provided for and so that no new contingencies may appear. They are much like the brain-injured cases, described by Goldstein[1] who manage to maintain their equilibrium by avoiding everything unfamiliar and strange and by ordering their restricted world in such a neat, disciplined, orderly fashion that everything in the world can be counted on. They try to arrange the world so that anything unexpected (dangers) cannot possibly occur. If, through no fault of their own, something unexpected does occur, they go into a panic reaction as if this unexpected occurrence constituted a grave danger. What we can see only as a none-too-strong preference in the healthy person, e.g., preference for the familiar, becomes a life-and-death necessity in abnormal cases. The healthy taste for the novel and unknown is missing or at a minimum in the average neurotic.

THE BELONGINGNESS AND LOVE NEEDS If both the physiological and the safety needs are fairly well gratified, there will emerge the love and affection and belongingness needs, and the whole cycle already described will repeat itself with this new center. Now the person will feel keenly, as never before, the absence of friends, or a sweet-

---

[1]Kurt Goldstein was a neurologist and psychiatrist who wrote on clinical psychology, human nature, and language.

heart, or a wife, or children. He will hunger for affectionate relations with people in general, namely, for a place in his group, and he will strive with great intensity to achieve this goal. He will want to attain such a place more than anything else in the world and may even forget that once, when he was hungry, he sneered at love as unreal or unnecessary or unimportant.

In our society the thwarting of these needs is the most commonly found core in cases of maladjustment and more severe psychopathology. Love and affection, as well as their possible expression in sexuality, are generally looked upon with ambivalence and are customarily hedged about with many restrictions and inhibitions. Practically all theorists of psychopathology have stressed thwarting of the love needs as basic in the picture of maladjustment. ✶ ✶ ✶

One thing that must be stressed at this point is that love is not synonymous with sex. Sex may be studied as a purely physiological need. Ordinarily sexual behavior is multidetermined, that is to say, determined not only by sexual but also by other needs, chief among which are the love and affection needs. Also not to be overlooked is the fact that the love needs involve both giving *and* receiving love.

THE ESTEEM NEEDS All people in our society (with a few pathological exceptions) have a need or desire for a stable, firmly based, usually high evaluation of themselves, for self-respect, or self-esteem, and for the esteem of others. These needs may therefore be classified into two subsidiary sets. These are, first, the desire for strength, for achievement, for adequacy, for mastery and competence, for confidence in the face of the world, and for independence and freedom.[2] Second, we

have what we may call the desire for reputation or prestige (defining it as respect or esteem from other people), status, dominance, recognition, attention, importance, or appreciation. These needs have been relatively stressed by Alfred Adler and his followers, and have been relatively neglected by Freud. More and more today, however, there is appearing wide-spread appreciation of their central importance, among psychoanalysts as well as among clinical psychologists.

Satisfaction of the self-esteem need leads to feelings of self-confidence, worth, strength, capability, and adequacy, of being useful and necessary in the world. But thwarting of these needs produces feelings of inferiority, of weakness, and of helplessness. These feelings in turn give rise to either basic discouragement or else compensatory or neurotic trends. ✶ ✶ ✶

✶ ✶ ✶ We have been learning more and more of the dangers of basing self-esteem on the opinions of others rather than on real capacity, competence, and adequacy to the task. The most stable and therefore most healthy self-esteem is based on *deserved* respect from others rather than on external fame or celebrity and unwarranted adulation.

THE NEED FOR SELF-ACTUALIZATION Even if all these needs are satisfied, we may still often (if not always) expect that a new discontent and restlessness will soon develop, unless the individual is doing what he is fitted for. A musician must make music, an artist must paint, a poet must write, if he is to be ultimately at peace with himself. What a man *can* be, he *must* be. This need we may call self-actualization.

✶ ✶ ✶ [This term] refers to a man's desire for self-fulfillment, namely, to the tendency for him to become actualized in what he is potentially. This tendency might be phrased as the desire to

---

[2]Whether or not this particular desire is universal we do not know. The crucial question, especially important today, is, Will men who are enslaved and dominated inevitably feel dissatisfied and rebellious? We may assume on the basis of commonly known clinical data that a man who has known true freedom (not paid for

by giving up safety and security but rather built on the basis of adequate safety and security) will not willingly or easily allow his freedom to be taken away from him. But we do not know that this is true for the person born into slavery.—Author become more and more what one is, to become everything that one is capable of becoming.

The specific form that these needs will take will of course vary greatly from person to person. In one individual it may take the form of the desire to be an ideal mother, in another it may be expressed athletically, and in still another it may be expressed in painting pictures or in inventions.

The clear emergence of these needs usually rests upon prior satisfaction of the physiological, safety, love, and esteem needs.

* * *

THE DESIRES TO KNOW AND TO UNDERSTAND
The main reason we know little about the cognitive impulses, their dynamics, or their pathology, is that they are not important in the clinic, and certainly not in the clinic dominated by the medical-therapeutic tradition, i.e., getting rid of disease. The florid, exciting, and mysterious symptoms found in the classical neuroses are lacking here. Cognitive psychopathology is pale, subtle, and easily overlooked, or defined as normal. It does not cry for help. As a consequence we find nothing on the subject in the writings of the great inventors of psychotherapy and psychodynamics, Freud, Adler, Jung, etc. Nor has anyone yet made any systematic attempts at constructing cognitive psychotherapies.

* * *

* * * There are some reasonable grounds for postulating positive *per se* impulses to satisfy curiosity, to know, to explain, and to understand.

1. Something like human curiosity can easily be observed in the higher animals. The monkey will pick things apart, will poke his finger into holes, will explore in all sorts of situations where it is improbable that hunger, fear, sex, comfort status, etc., are involved. Harlow's experiments (1950) have amply demonstrated this in an acceptably experimental way.

2. The history of mankind supplies us with a satisfactory number of instances in which man looked for facts and created explanations in the face of the greatest danger, even to life itself. There have been innumerable humbler Galileos.

3. Studies of psychologically healthy people indicate that they are, as a defining characteristic, attracted to the mysterious, to the unknown, to the chaotic, unorganized, and unexplained. This seems to be a *per se* attractiveness; these areas are in themselves and of their own right interesting. The contrasting reaction to the well known is one of boredom.

4. It may be found valid to extrapolate from the psychopathological. The compulsive-obsessive neurotic (and neurotic in general), Goldstein's brain-injured soldiers, Maier's fixated rats (1939), all show (at the clinical level of observation) a compulsive and anxious clinging to the familiar and a dread of the unfamiliar, the anarchic, the unexpected, the undomesticated. On the other hand, there are some phenomena that may turn out to nullify this possibility. Among these are forced unconventionality, a chronic rebellion against any authority whatsoever, Bohemianism, the desire to shock and to startle, all of which may be found in certain neurotic individuals, as well as in those in the process of deacculturation.

* * *

5. Probably there are true psychopathological effects when the cognitive needs are frustrated. For the moment, though, we have no really sound data available. The following clinical impressions are pertinent.

6. I have seen a few cases in which it seemed clear to me that the pathology (boredom, loss of zest in life, self-dislike, general depression of the bodily functions, steady deterioration of the intellectual life, of tastes, etc.) were produced in intelligent people leading stupid lives in stupid jobs. I have at least one case in which the appropriate cognitive therapy (resuming part-time studies, getting a position that was more intellectually demanding, insight) removed the symptoms.

I have seen *many* women, intelligent, prosperous, and unoccupied, slowly develop these same symptoms of intellectual inanition. Those who followed my recommendation to immerse themselves in something worthy of them showed improvement or cure often enough to impress me with the reality of the cognitive needs. In those countries in which access to the news, to information, and to the facts [was] cut off, and in those where official theories were profoundly contradicted by obvious facts, at least some people responded with generalized cynicism, mistrust of *all* values, suspicion even of the obvious, a profound disruption of ordinary interpersonal relationships, hopelessness, loss of morale, etc. Others seem to have responded in the more passive direction with dullness, submission, loss of capacity, coarctation, and loss of initiative.

7. The needs to know and to understand are seen in late infancy and childhood, perhaps even more strongly than in adulthood. Furthermore this seems to be a spontaneous product of maturation rather than of learning, however defined. Children do not have to be taught to be curious. But they *may* be taught, as by institutionalization, *not* to be curious.

8. Finally, the gratification of the cognitive impulses is subjectively satisfying and yields end-experience. Though this aspect of insight and understanding has been neglected in favor of achieved results, learning, etc., it nevertheless remains true that insight is usually a bright, happy, emotional spot in any person's life, perhaps even a high spot in the life span.

The overcoming of obstacles, the occurrence of pathology upon thwarting, the widespread occurrence (cross-species, cross-cultural), the never-dying (though weak) insistent pressure, the need of gratification of this need as a prerequisite for the fullest development of human potentialities, the spontaneous appearance in the early history of the individual, all these point to a basic cognitive need.

This postulation, however, is not enough. Even after we know, we are impelled to know more and more minutely and microscopically on the one hand, and on the other, more and more extensively in the direction of a world philosophy, theology, etc. The facts that we acquire, if they are isolated or atomistic, inevitably get theorized about, and either analyzed or organized or both.

This process has been phrased by some as the search for meaning. We shall then postulate a desire to understand, to systematize, to organize, to analyze, to look for relations and meanings, to construct a system of values.

Once these desires are accepted for discussion, we see that they too form themselves into a small hierarchy in which the desire to know is prepotent over the desire to understand. All the characteristics of a hierarchy of prepotency that we have described above seem to hold for this one as well.

We must guard ourselves against the too easy tendency to separate these desires from the basic needs we have discussed above, i.e., to make a sharp dichotomy between cognitive and conative needs. The desire to know and to understand are themselves conative, i.e., having a striving character, and are as much personality needs as the basic needs we have already discussed. Furthermore, as we have seen, the two hierarchies are interrelated rather than sharply separated; and as we shall see below, they are synergic rather than antagonistic.

THE AESTHETIC NEEDS We know even less about these than about the others, and yet the testimony of history, of the humanities, and of aestheticians forbids us to bypass this uncomfortable (to the scientist) area. I have attempted to study this phenomenon on a clinical-personological basis with selected individuals, and have at least convinced myself that in *some* individuals there is a truly basic aesthetic need. They get sick (in special ways) from ugliness, and are cured by beautiful surroundings; they *crave* actively, and their cravings can be satisfied *only* by beauty. It is seen almost universally in healthy children. Some evidence of such an impulse is found in every culture and in every age as far back as the cavemen.

Much overlapping with conative and cognitive needs makes it impossible to separate them sharply. The needs for order, for symmetry, for closure, for completion of the act, for system, and for structure may be indiscriminately assigned to *either* cognitive, conative, or aesthetic, or even to neurotic needs. ✳ ✳ ✳ What, for instance, does it mean when a man feels a strong conscious impulse to straighten the crookedly hung picture on the wall?

Further Characteristics of the Basic Needs

THE DEGREE OF FIXITY OF THE HIERARCHY OF BASIC NEEDS We have spoken so far as if this hierarchy were a fixed order, but actually it is not nearly so rigid as we may have implied. It is true that most of the people with whom we have worked have seemed to have these basic needs in about the order that has been indicated. However, there have been a number of exceptions.

1. There are some people in whom, for instance, self-esteem seems to be more important than love. This most common reversal in the hierarchy is usually due to the development of the notion that the person who is most likely to be loved is a strong or powerful person, one who inspires respect or fear, and who is self-confident or aggressive. Therefore such people who lack love and seek it may try hard to put on a front of aggressive, confident behavior. But essentially they seek high self-esteem and its behavior expressions more as a means to an end than for its own sake; they seek self-assertion for the sake of love rather than for self-esteem itself.

2. There are other apparently innately creative people in whom the drive to creativeness seems to be more important than any other counterdeterminant. Their creativeness might appear not as self-actualization released by basic satisfaction, but in spite of lack of basic satisfaction.

3. In certain people the level of aspiration may be permanently deadened or lowered. That is to say, the less prepotent goals may simply be lost, and may disappear forever, so that the person who has experienced life at a very low level, e.g., chronic unemployment, may continue to be satisfied for the rest of his life if only he can get enough food.

4. The so-called psychopathic personality is another example of permanent loss of the love needs. These are people who, according to the best data available, have been starved for love in the earliest months of their lives and have simply lost forever the desire and the ability to give and to receive affection (as animals lose sucking or pecking reflexes that are not exercised soon enough after birth).

5. Another cause of reversal of the hierarchy is that when a need has been satisfied for a long time, this need may be underevaluated. People who have never experienced chronic hunger are apt to underestimate its effects and to look upon food as a rather unimportant thing. If they are dominated by a higher need, this higher need will seem to be the most important of all. It then becomes possible, and indeed does actually happen, that they may, for the sake of this higher need, put themselves into the position of being deprived in a more basic need. We may expect that after a longtime deprivation of the more basic need there will be a tendency to reevaluate both needs so that the more prepotent need will actually become consciously prepotent for the individual who may have given it up lightly. Thus a man who has given up his job rather than lose his self-respect, and who then starves for six months or so, may be willing to take his job back even at the price of losing his self-respect.

6. Another partial explanation of *apparent* reversals is seen in the fact that we have been talking about the hierarchy of prepotency in terms of consciously felt wants or desires rather than of behavior. Looking at behavior itself may give us the wrong impression. What we have claimed is that the person will *want* the more basic of two needs when deprived in both. There is no necessary implication here that he will act upon his desires. Let us stress again that there are many determinants of behavior other than the needs and desires.

7. Perhaps more important than all these exceptions are the ones that involve ideals, high social standards, high values, and the like. With such values people become martyrs; they will give up everything for the sake of a particular ideal, or value. These people may be understood, at least

in part, by reference to one basic concept (or hypothesis), which may be called increased frustration-tolerance through early gratification. People who have been satisfied in their basic needs throughout their lives, particularly in their earlier years, seem to develop exceptional power to withstand present or future thwarting of these needs simply because they have strong, healthy character structure as a result of basic satisfaction. They are the strong people who can easily weather disagreement or opposition, who can swim against the stream of public opinion, and who can stand up for the truth at great personal cost. It is just the ones who have loved and been well loved, and who have had many deep friendships who can hold out against hatred, rejection, or persecution.

I say all this in spite of the fact that a certain amount of sheer habituation is also involved in any full discussion of frustration tolerance. For instance, it is likely that those persons who have been accustomed to relative starvation for a long time are partially enabled thereby to withstand food deprivation. What sort of balance must be made between these two tendencies, of habituation on the one hand, and of past satisfaction breeding present frustration tolerance on the other hand, remains to be worked out by further research. Meanwhile we may assume that both are operative, side by side, since they do not contradict each other. In respect to this phenomenon of increased frustration tolerance, it seems probable that the most important gratifications come in the first two years of life. That is to say, people who have been made secure and strong in the earliest years, tend to remain secure and strong thereafter in the face of whatever threatens.

DEGREES OF RELATIVE SATISFACTION So far, our theoretical discussion may have given the impression that these five sets of needs are somehow in such terms as the following: If one need is satisfied, then another emerges. This statement might give the false impression that a need must be satisfied 100 percent before the next need emerges. In actual fact, most members of our society who are normal are partially satisfied in all their basic needs and partially unsatisfied in all their basic needs at the same time. A more realistic description of the hierarchy would be in terms of decreasing percentages of satisfaction as we go up the hierarchy of prepotency. For instance, if I may assign arbitrary figures for the sake of illustration, it is as if the average citizen is satisfied perhaps 85 percent in his physiological needs, 70 percent in his safety needs, 50 percent in his love needs, 40 percent in his self-esteem needs, and 10 percent in his self-actualization needs.

As for the concept of emergence of a new need after satisfaction of the prepotent need, this emergence is not a sudden, saltatory phenomenon, but rather a gradual emergence by slow degrees from nothingness. For instance, if prepotent need A is satisfied only 10 percent, then need B may not be visible at all. However, as this need A becomes satisfied 25 percent, need B may emerge 5 percent; as need A becomes satisfied 75 percent, need B may emerge 50 percent, and so on.

* * *

ANIMAL AND HUMAN CENTERING This theory starts with the human being rather than any lower and presumably simpler animal. Too many of the findings that have been made in animals have been proved to be true for animals but not for the human being. There is no reason whatsoever why we should start with animals in order to study human motivation. The logic or rather illogic behind this general fallacy of pseudosimplicity has been exposed often enough by philosophers and logicians as well as by scientists in each of the various fields. It is no more necessary to study animals before one can study man than it is to study mathematics *before* one can study geology or psychology or biology.

* * *

THE ROLE OF GRATIFIED NEEDS It has been pointed out above several times that our needs usually emerge only when more prepotent needs have been gratified. Thus gratification has an important role in motivation theory. Apart from this, however, needs cease to play an active determining or organizing role as soon as they are gratified.

What this means is that, e.g., a basically satisfied person no longer has the needs for esteem, love, safety, etc. The only sense in which he might be said to have them is in the almost metaphysical sense that a sated man has hunger, or a filled bottle has emptiness. If we are interested in what *actually* motivates us, and not in what has, will, or might motivate us, then a satisfied need is not a motivator. It must be considered for all practical purposes simply not to exist, to have disappeared. This point should be emphasized because it has been either overlooked or contradicted in every theory of motivation I know. The perfectly healthy, normal, fortunate man has no sex needs or hunger needs, or needs for safety, or for love, or for prestige, or self-esteem, except in stray moments of quickly passing threat. * * *

It is such considerations as these that suggest the bold postulation that a man who is thwarted in any of his basic needs may fairly be envisaged simply as a sick man. This is a fair parallel to our designation as sick of the man who lacks vitamins or minerals. Who will say that a lack of love is less important than a lack of vitamins? Since we know the pathogenic effects of love starvation, who is to say that we are invoking value questions in an unscientific or illegitimate way, any more

than the physician does who diagnoses and treats pellagra or scurvy? If I were permitted this usage, I should then say simply that a healthy man is primarily motivated by his needs to develop and actualize his fullest potentialities and capacities. If a man has any other basic needs in any active, chronic sense, he is simply an unhealthy man. He is as surely sick as if he had suddenly developed a strong salt hunger or calcium hunger. If we were to use the word *sick* in this way, we should then also have to face squarely the relations of man to his society. One clear implication of our definition would be that (1) since a man is to be called sick who is basically thwarted, and (2) since such basic thwarting is made possible ultimately only by forces outside the individual, then (3) sickness in the individual must come ultimately from a sickness in the society. The good or healthy society would then be defined as one that permitted man's highest purposes to emerge by satisfying all his basic needs.

* * *

References

Harlow, H. F. (1950). Learning motivated by a manipulation drive. *Journal of Experimental Psychology, 40,* 228–234.

Maier, N. R. F. (1939). *Studies of abnormal behavior in the rat.* New York: Harper.

THE THREAT OF AGGRESSION

George Kelly

We have seen that a central tenet of the existential philosophy and humanistic psychology is that an individual's experience of the world is all-important. This idea was developed most fully by George Kelly, the author of the following selection. Kelly theorized that each person builds his or her unique view of the world out of a set of ideas, or "personal constructs." To understand another person, one needs to understand the way that person views reality. To do that, you need to understand the person's construct system.

The following selection, a paper delivered at a humanistic psychology conference in 1964, represents Kelley's attempt to use personal construct theory to resolve a humanist dilemma. The dilemma is this: If the purpose of existence is for everybody to express themselves, what happens when one person's self-expression gets in the way of the goals of another? Kelly rejects the notion that if everybody were truly self-expressive everybody would get along. Instead, he provides a uniquely Kellyan perspective.

Kelly proposes that threat is the experience of expecting something to happen that will require a revision in one's personal construct system. Aggression is the attempt to change something and is not necessarily bad. But hostility is harmful because, by Kelly's definition, it is the attempt to "extort" confirming evidence out of the environment.

For example, in an intellectual debate you might feel the threat of being wrong. You then aggressively present the best counterargument you can muster. So far so good. But if your argument is met with a convincing reply, then you are in a difficult situation. You either must conclude you were wrong and revise your personal construct system—always a difficult thing to do—or respond in a hostile fashion. You might scream at your opponent, or stalk out of the room, or do any number of other hostile acts, all of which serve the purpose of avoiding the self-confrontation of your own error. The purpose of hostility, therefore, is to avoid corrective feedback and that, Kelly argues, is what makes it a problem. The only hope for personal growth is to profit from experience. That is why Kelly claims "the acknowledgment of defeat or tragedy is not a destructive step." On the contrary, it may be a sign that you have learned something.

From "The Threat of Aggression," by G. Kelly. In *Clinical Psychology and Personality: The Selected Papers of George Kelly*, edited by B. Maher (1969/1964), pp. 281–288. Copyright © 1969 by John Wiley & Sons, Inc. Reprinted with permission of John Wiley & Sons, Inc.

This conference has been convened to consider the topic of humanism in psychology. But I am not sure I have a very clear idea of what humanism is. Ostensibly it has something to do with man, though I have often doubted that it had to do with anyone I know. Nevertheless, I suppose that when psychologists get together and say that we ought to revive humanism it is because they are alarmed by the tendency of their disciplines to ignore man, except as an inexhaustible source of data, and to become preoccupied, instead, with their own bibliographies, expendable animals, and the rituals of laboratory science. A *humanistic* turn of events would, then, be one, I presume, in which the focal importance of living man would be reaffirmed, and psychology would no longer be pursued for its own sake.

*   *   *

Humanism is, as I see it, not something we revive. Humanism has to do with the present, the novel, the defiant, [and] the alive. * * * The true humanist fumbles with present uncertainties. * * * The humanist continually risks being historically wrong in order to set something right. The humanist is aggressive, and hopes thus to achieve better things. * * *

The Humanist Paradox

*   *   *

* * * [Humanism asserts] that whatever is truly characteristic of man is good and should therefore be preserved and protected against any distorting influence. Man, in the light of his audacious achievements, should be encouraged to go on being the kind of person he has so aptly proved himself to be; he should express himself; he should go right ahead and be audacious. But he should not be permitted to tamper with human nature; that is carrying audacity too far!

It is this theme—a theme sometimes identified as permissiveness, sometimes as nonaggression, sometimes as respect for the dignity of man—that often colors the meaning of humanism. Thus, humanism appears to have created for itself a paradox. The audacity of man in general has proved to be so valuable a human asset that the audacity of any particular man must be restrained from impinging upon it. Man must express himself—that is very very important—but never, never must he express himself in such a way that anything human will be affected.

One way out of this paradox is to believe that the nature of man is such that if he does express himself—his true self—he will harmonize with all other men who truly express themselves. This is to say that the intrinsic nature of man is intrinsically compatible with its collective self, and that disharmonies arise only out of extrinsic distortions, or, possibly, out of temporary immaturities.

Another way out is to say that man cannot be manipulated except as his nature conspires. Whatever he does, it is he who does it. And the fact that he does it under certain imposed conditions in no way denies his dignity, but, instead, stands as a credit to his personal achievement ("under optimal psychological conditions," as we sometimes say). A child learns to play the piano well by being forced to practice four hours a day. That is not suppression; that is a human accomplishment. When he grows up he will probably be proud of it—and perhaps think of himself as a first-class humanist. A depressed person is disciplined to a hospital routine of scrubbing floors and scouring toilets. As a result he finds himself too busy to worry. So, again, man prevails! See how the organism's ingenious adaptability has contrived to substitute reality for imagination? How fortunate! Not everyone is able to do that!

But it is difficult for me to see how either of these constructions can provide an escape from the humanist's paradox. The interpretation of man as a naturally harmonious being, who likes other people in proportion to his admiration of himself, seems to ignore the fact of human tyranny. Whether he can rise above this unpleasant fact is another question. But it appears to me to be as presumptuous to regard man as naturally good as it is to label him as inherently evil. Moreover, we are still much too busy sorting out good from evil to be altogether clear about which is which, or whether man is wholly one or the other.

The other construction of man—the construction of him as an ingenious conformist, a slave who is smart enough to know his place—is not very encouraging to the fellow who doesn't want to be a slave, or practice his music lessons, or live in Levittown, but on the banks of Walden Pond.[1] He persists in thinking that under other circumstances he might accomplish a lot more. He may be right. And then, again, he may be wrong, for some men do accomplish more under a reinforcement schedule than when left to their own devices. And what is the humanist going to say about that?

The Meaning of Threat

The human enterprise is, at best, a touch-and-go proposition. Any assumptions we make about what is good, or what is evil, or what will open the door to the future, are best regarded as only temporary, and any conclusions we draw from our experiences are best seen as approximations of what we may eventually understand. The human quest is not about to be concluded, nor is truth already partly packaged for distribution and consumption. Instead, it seems likely that whatever may now appear to be the most obvious fact will look quite different when regarded from the vantage point of tomorrow's fresh theoretical positions. Yet it is a misfortune that man should be so set on being right at the very outset that he dares not risk stupidities in an effort to devise something better than what he has.

This brings us back to the audacity of man, which, as you already know, I have come to regard as the primary humanistic theme. I like that theme. But let us not overlook the fact that this audacity is the very thing that men fear when they see it about to be expressed—and as often admire when it has run its course. In a world where vast

[1]Levittown is an infamous suburb of identical, mass-produced houses. Walden Pond is where Thoreau, a freethinker, went to get in touch with nature and himself.

experiments are being undertaken, where new psychological devices are being employed, and strange societies are being constituted, we dread the far-reaching implications of what is about to happen to us.

This is threat. To feel that one is on the threshold of deep changes in himself and his way of life is, I think, its essential feature. Threat is, from this point of view, an impending personal experience, not a set of ominous circumstances. Moreover, it is in the context of threat—or dread—that the two terms, aggression and hostility, become subjectively synonymous. This is to say that to encounter either in the actions of another person is to raise the specter of transformation in oneself. And may I point out also the curious fact that the two terms have become synonyms both in the language that diplomats use and in the language that psychologists use—as well, it seems, as in the language that humanists speak.

So how do we encourage human audacity without inviting one man's initiative to suppress another's? This is the humanist's dilemma. It is also the dilemma of democracy—how do you give political sovereignty to a people, or a state, bent on suppressing its minorities? So, also, it is the problem of the economist—how can you have a free enterprise system that produces the Bell Telephone Company, and still claim that you have anything that even remotely resembles free enterprise? * * *

Aggression

Before trying to find a humanistic answer to these questions, let me turn to a psychological matter. We call aggressive men hostile because what they do seems destructive, especially when it is pointed in our direction. We don't want them to meddle with our lives. Thus we judge them not so much by the character of their acts as by our own characteristic response to their initiative.

But what happens to us is not to be confounded with what is happening within them. What they undertake is not measured by what we experience. If one is to have an adequate psychology of man, it must be a psychology of the actor, not the victim.[2] This is to say that behavior needs to be explained within the fact, not before or after the fact. Our own reaction to what another person attempts is scarcely enough to account for what he is trying to accomplish. Nor do our hurt feelings constitute a psychological analysis of his behavior.

Now may I go on to say that this equating of aggression with our projection of destructive intent is the outcome of nineteenth century notions about scientific determinism. To think scientifically about the psychology of man has seemed to mean that we must regard him as an intervening variable—called an "organism"—in a stimulus-response couplet. Our ventures collapse when challenged by an aggressive colleague. How shall we explain it? Simple! The collapse is the observed response; he is the obvious stimulus; and we are the organismic victim caught in the S-R squeeze. His aggression caused our downfall; and what more do you need to explain what the rascal was up to?

A stimulus-response psychology is, of course, one in which human responses are explained in terms of their external antecedents—their stimuli. And stimuli, in such a system, are reciprocally explained in terms of what they produce—their responses. That is the solipsism, or "equation," as we prefer to call it in mathematics. If I am threatened, then the person whom I see as the stimulus explains my experience. If I can cope with his aggression only by contemplating a profound change in myself, then the scoundrel must be hostile. Psychotherapists will recognize this as something that turns up rather frequently among their patients. But it is much more widespread than that; it is a conclusion commonly reached by all those who live out their lives according to the formula of stimulus-response.

---

[2]This is a key tenet of Kelly's personal construct theory. To understand a person, you need to understand how the world looks from his or her perspective. A common error, according to Kelly, is to evaluate other people in terms of our reactions to them.

But stimulus-response psychology is not the only possible kind of psychology. We can, if we wish, employ a psychology which casts its explanations in terms of what the person himself is doing, not what others do to him or what they think he has done to them. Aggression, in such a psychological system, is more akin to initiative. It is an expression of the audacity of man, even as he ventures into the realm of psychology. The aggressive man—like the humanist—may be one who risks being wrong in order to set something right—or in order to find out what rightly explains his fellow man.

Hostility

Now hostility, in this way of thinking, may, or may not, involve aggression, and aggression may, or may not, involve hostility. The two constructs are propositionally independent of each other. If we are to employ a notion of hostility within this kind of psychological system we must understand the hostile person's enterprise in terms of his own outlook, not merely in terms of the threat that others experience when they seek to come to terms with him.

Since any system of psychology must provide some explanation of the means by which a person checks up on himself, it becomes important to understand how the implications of such a checkup are incorporated. In stimulus-response theory the checkup is cast in terms of reinforcement, that is to say, by ascribing some kind of stimulus quality to the response itself, or to its consequences, which will feed back into the system. But in personal construct theory the checkup is provided by confirmation of expectations. This is to say that if the expectations that follow from one's construction of events continually fail to materialize, a revision of the construction system is called for. This means that defeat must be recognized, failure identified, and even tragedy experienced if man is to survive, and all the more so if man is to achieve anything of epic proportions.

But a major revision of one's construct system can threaten him with immediate change, or chaos, or anxiety. Thus it often seems better to extort confirmation of one's anticipations—and therefore of the system that produced them—rather than to risk the utter confusion of those moments of transition. It is this extortion of confirmation that characterizes hostility.

A nation, before admitting that its long leap forward in the defense of human life has proved invalid, may destroy millions of lives when they disclose evidence of the failure of the system. A country may go to war to displace responsibility for its mistakes. A man may commit murder to discredit what has proved him wrong. And, since hostility may as easily employ passivity as aggression, we may resort either to spiteful "obedience" or "respect for law" to simulate the missing validity in a crumbling societal system. Or, in a family whose structure is no longer viable, we may offer indulgence to replace affection and to smother a child's unexpected independence.

Nevertheless, whether undertaken by aggressive or passive means, hostility is, in a personal construct theoretical system, an extortional undertaking designed by the person to protect a heavy investment in his own construction of life. And if, perchance, his hostility proves destructive of others, then that, unfortunately, is the way it must be. The economy must be preserved; the fact that the elderly starve in India or on the other side of town is incidental. Heresy must be controlled; too bad that intellectual curiosity on the campus must be denied. Bombs must be dropped; to be sure, children will die, but who can say it was we who put them in the target area? From our point of view, it is a precious way of life that we defend—Cadillacs and all. But what the hostile man does not know is that it is he who is the eventual victim of his own extortion. With the adoption of hostility he surrenders his capacity to judge the outcome of his way of life, and without that capacity he must inevitably go astray.

The acknowledgment of defeat or tragedy is not a destructive step for man to take. It characterizes, instead, the negative outcome of any crucial test of our way of life, and it is, therefore, an essential feature of human progress toward more positive outcomes. Hostility does not, for this very reason, contribute to human achievement. Primarily because it denies failure it leads, instead, to the abatement of human enterprise, and substitutes for nobler undertakings a mask of complacency.

A Step for the Humanist

In this way of thinking, which I have proposed for the humanistically inclined psychologist, there are three key notions that must be lifted from the context of stimulus-response psychology and recast in the light of a psychology of the man himself. They are *threat*, *aggression*, and *hostility*. Threat, for the man himself, is the experience of being on the brink of a major shift in his core construct system. Aggression, for the man himself, is one's own initiative, not what that initiative may lead another to do or feel. And so with hostility, too; hostility is the extortion of confirming evidence to present to oneself when there seems too much at stake to undertake the personal changes that natural evidence requires.

The humanistic psychologist's dilemma—how to protect human audacity from human audacity without stifling human audacity—finds another kind of solution when we manage to step outside the stimulus-response solipsism. It is the hostile, and not necessarily the aggressive enterprise, that must be guarded against. The aggressive effort to understand man, or to experiment with ways of accomplishing psychological feats never before achieved, is not intrinsically destructive. It may, of course, be hazardous. It does become destructive, however, when one tries to make it appear that disconfirming events did not actually arise, or that what failed to occur actually happened. And this, in turn, is generated by the notion that we ought always to be right before we commit ourselves, a notion that later makes it very hard to concede our mistakes, or to revise our construction of the world when our heavily invested anticipations fail to materialize.

Humanism reflects audacity in man. But this audacity, when it substitutes extortion for disconfirmation, disengages itself from the world and abandons the future of mankind. Humanism, while it openly experiences defeat, does not succumb to it, for to do that would be to give up man's aggressive undertakings altogether, and, with them, all the aspirations that arise from being tragically human. Thus, the experience of tragedy, and not the sense of certainty, is the basis of all hope, and is indeed the most essential step in the bold pursuit of better things. And that, I submit, is a notion that lies close to the heart of the human enterprise.

A Theory of Personality and Behavior

Carl R. Rogers

Certainly the best-known humanist, and among the best-known American psy-chologists of the 20th century, was Carl Rogers. Rogers developed a view of psy-chology that managed to combine the seemingly incompatible basic tenets of existentialism and optimism. He did this by combining the existentialist premise that people are free to choose with a faith that—when left alone—they are in-clined to choose life and growth.

The problem, Rogers believed, is that people are so seldom left alone. Throughout their development they become saddled with the unrealistic expecta-tions of others. These "conditions of worth," as Rogers called them, lead you to distort your view of experience and of yourself. The result can be a negative self-image and self-defeating choices.

Rogers also offered a cure. If you can believe yourself to be worthy no mat-ter what—and thus remove conditions of worth—you are then freed to think clearly about the world, and enabled to make the correct choices in life. Nothing further is necessary. In particular, there is no need to tell patients—Rogers called them "clients," a labeling that many therapists have now adopted—what to do. Their own decisions will be the right ones, if only they can be helped to think without distortion.

The technique for accomplishing this Rogers called "client-centered therapy." The therapist's job is not to impose her own views on the client, but to allow the client to draw his own conclusions in an atmosphere of safety and uncondi-tional regard. To this end, the therapist "reflects" or clarifies the client's thoughts, and expresses a deeply emotional approval of everything the client says and does. The result, Rogers claimed, is not only a greater self-acceptance by the client, but the client's greater acceptance of the other people in his life.

The following excerpt from a much longer work lays out some of the key propositions of Rogers' theory. Rogers gave these propositions Roman numerals (there were 19 (XIX) in all). The more essential ones—in our judgment—are included in what follows.

---

*   *   *

The statement which follows been molded by a score of years of first hand contact with clinical problems, and more particularly and more deeply by the decade of struggle to formulate an effective and consistent psychotherapy, the process of that effort being the changing formulations of the client-centered approach.[1] The increased entrance into the thinking and feeling of the other person, characteristic of client-centered therapy, has necessitated profound changes in the author's whole theoretical ideation. Like Maslow, the writer would confess that in the early portion of his professional life he held a theoretical view opposed at almost every point to the view he has gradually come to adopt as a result of clinical experience and clinically oriented research.

In order to present the thinking as clearly as possible, and also in order to make possible the detection of flaws or inconsistencies, the material which follows is offered as a series of propositions, with a brief explanation and exposition of each proposition. Since the theory is regarded as tentative, questions are raised in regard to various propositions, particularly where it seems uncertain that they adequately account for all the phenomena. Some of these propositions must be regarded as assumptions, while the majority may be regarded as hypotheses subject to proof or disproof. Taken as a whole, the series of propositions presents a theory of behavior which attempts to account for the phenomena previously known, and also for the facts regarding personality and behavior which have more recently been observed in therapy.

*   *   *

---

[1]The "client-centered approach" is the Rogerian technique of psychotherapy, in which the therapist helps the client to make, accept, and understand his or her own choices.

The Propositions

1) EVERY INDIVIDUAL EXISTS IN A CONTINUALLY CHANGING WORLD OF EXPERIENCE OF WHICH HE IS THE CENTER. This private world may be called the phenomenal field, the experiential field, or described in other terms. It includes all that is experienced by the organism, whether or not these experiences are consciously perceived. Thus the pressure of the chair seat against my buttocks is something I have been experiencing for an hour, but only as I think and write about it does the symbolization of that experience become present in consciousness. * * *

It should be recognized that in this private world of experience of the individual, only a portion of that experience, and probably a very small portion, is *consciously* experienced. Many of our sensory and visceral sensations are not symbolized. It is also true, however, that a large portion of this world of experience is *available* to consciousness, and may become conscious if the need of the individual causes certain sensations to come into focus because they are associated with the satisfaction of a need. In other words, most of the individual's experiences constitute the ground of the perceptual field, but they can easily become figure, while other experiences slip back into ground. * * *

An important truth in regard to this private world of the individual is that it can only be known, in any genuine or complete sense, to the individual himself. No matter how adequately we attempt to measure the stimulus—whether it be a beam of light, a pinprick, a failure on an examination, or some more complex situation—and no matter how much we attempt to measure the perceiving organism—whether by psychometric tests or physiological calibrations—it is still true that the individual is the only one who can know how the experience was perceived. I can never know with vividness or completeness how a pinprick or a failure on an examination is experienced by you.

The world of experience is for each individual, in a very significant sense, a private world.

*   *   *

II) THE ORGANISM REACTS TO THE FIELD AS IT IS EXPERIENCED AND PERCEIVED. THIS PERCEPTUAL FIELD IS, FOR THE INDIVIDUAL, "REALITY." This is a simple proposition, one of which we are all aware in our own experience, yet it is a point which is often overlooked. I do not react to some absolute reality, but to my perception of this reality. It is this perception which for me *is* reality. [Consider] the example of two men driving at night on a western road. An object looms up in the middle of the road ahead. One of the men sees a large boulder, and reacts with fright. The other, a native of the country, sees a tumbleweed and reacts with nonchalance. Each reacts to the reality as perceived.

This proposition could be illustrated from the daily experience of everyone. Two individuals listen to a radio speech made by a political candidate about whom they have no previous knowledge. They are both subjected to the same auditory stimulation. Yet one perceives the candidate as a demagogue, a trickster, a false prophet, and reacts accordingly. The other perceives him as a leader of the people, a person of high aims and purposes. Each is reacting to the reality as he has perceived it. In the same way, two young parents each perceive differently the behavior of their offspring. The son and daughter have differing perceptions of their parents. And the behavior in all these instances is appropriate to the reality-as-perceived. This same proposition is exemplified in so-called abnormal conditions as well. The psychotic who perceives that his food is poisoned, or that some malevolent group is out to "get" him, reacts to his reality-as-perceived in much the same fashion that you or I would respond if we (more "realistically") perceived our food as contaminated, or our enemies as plotting against us.

*   *   *

To the present writer it seems unnecessary to posit or try to explain any concept of "true" reality. For purposes of understanding psychological

phenomena, reality is, for the individual, his perceptions. Unless we wish to involve ourselves in philosophical questions, we do not need to attempt to solve the question as to what *really* constitutes reality. For psychological purposes, reality is basically the private world of individual perceptions, though for social purposes reality consists of those perceptions which have a high degree of commonality among various individuals. Thus this desk is "real" because most people in our culture would have a perception of it which is very similar to my own.

*   *   *

That the perceptual field is the reality to which the individual reacts is often strikingly illustrated in therapy, where it is frequently evident that when the perception changes, the reaction of the individual changes. As long as a parent is perceived as a domineering individual, that is the reality to which the individual reacts. When he is perceived as a rather pathetic individual trying to maintain his status, then the reaction to this new "reality" is quite different.

III) THE ORGANISM REACTS AS AN ORGANIZED WHOLE TO THIS PHENOMENAL FIELD.

*   *   *

In the psychological realm, any simple S-R[2] type of explanation of behavior seems almost impossible. A young woman talks for an hour about her antagonism to her mother. She finds, following this, that a persistent asthmatic condition, which she has not even mentioned to the counselor, is greatly improved. On the other hand a man who feels that his security in his work is being seriously threatened, develops ulcers. It is extremely cumbersome to try to account for such phenomena on the basis of an atomistic chain of events. The outstanding fact which must be taken into theoretical account is that the organism is at all times a total organized system, in which alteration of any part may produce changes in any

---

[2]S-R stands for "stimulus-response," and refers to the positivistic behaviorism to which humanists like Rogers typically set themselves in opposition.

other part. Our study of such part phenomena must start from this central fact of consistent, goal-directed organization.

IV) THE ORGANISM HAS ONE BASIC TENDENCY AND STRIVING—TO ACTUALIZE, MAINTAIN, AND ENHANCE THE EXPERIENCING ORGANISM. Rather than many needs and motives, it seems entirely possible that all organic and psychological needs may be described as partial aspects of this one fundamental need. * * *

We are talking here about the tendency of the organism to maintain itself—to assimilate food, to behave defensively in the face of threat, to achieve the goal of self-maintenance even when the usual pathway to that goal is blocked. We are speaking of the tendency of the organism to move in the direction of maturation, as maturation is defined for each species. This involves self-actualization, though it should be understood that this is a directional term. The organism does not develop to the full its capacity for suffering pain, nor does the human individual develop or actualize his capacity for terror or, on the physiological level, his capacity for vomiting. The organism actualizes itself in the direction of greater differentiation of organs and of function. It moves in the direction of limited expansion through growth, expansion through extending itself by means of its tools, and expansion through reproduction. It moves in the direction of greater independence or self-responsibility. Its movement is in the direction of an increasing self-government, self-regulation, and autonomy, and away from heteronymous control, or control by external forces. This is true whether we are speaking of entirely unconscious organic processes, such as the regulation of body heat, or such uniquely human and intellectual functions as the choice of life goals. Finally, the self-actualization of the organism appears to be in the direction of socialization,[3] broadly defined.

* * *

It is our experience in therapy which has brought us to the point of giving this proposition a central place. The therapist becomes very much aware that the forward-moving tendency of the human organism is the basis upon which he relies most deeply and fundamentally. It is evident not only in the general tendency of clients to move in the direction of growth when the factors in the situation are clear, but is most dramatically shown in very serious cases where the individual is on the brink of psychosis or suicide. Here the therapist is very keenly aware that the only force upon which he can basically rely is the organic tendency toward ongoing growth and enhancement. Something of our experience has been summarized by the writer in an earlier paper.

> As I study, as deeply as I am able, the recorded clinical cases which have been so revealing of personal dynamics, I find what seems to me to be a very significant thing. I find that the urge for a greater degree of independence, the desire for a self-determined integration, the tendency to strive, even through much pain, toward a socialized maturity, is as strong as—no, is stronger than—the desire for comfortable dependence, the need to rely upon external authority for assurance. . . . Clinically I find it to be true that though an individual may remain dependent because he has always been so, or may drift into dependence without realizing what he is doing, or may temporarily wish to be dependent because his situation appears desperate, I have yet to find the individual who, when he examines his situation deeply, and feels that he perceives it clearly, deliberately chooses dependence, deliberately chooses to have the integrated direction of himself undertaken by another. When all the elements are clearly perceived, the balance seems invariably in the direction of the painful but ultimately rewarding path of self-actualization or growth.

It would be grossly inaccurate to suppose that the organism operates smoothly in the direction of self-enhancement and growth. It would be perhaps more correct to say that the organism moves through struggle and pain toward enhancement and growth. The whole process may be symbolized and illustrated by the child's learning to walk. The first steps involve struggle, and usually pain. Often it is true that the immediate reward involved in

---

[3]Integration into society.

taking a few steps is in no way commensurate with the pain of falls and bumps. The child may, because of the pain, revert to crawling for a time. Yet in the overwhelming majority of individuals, the forward direction of growth is more powerful than the satisfactions of remaining infantile. The child will actualize himself, in spite of the painful experiences in so doing. In the same way, he will become independent, responsible, self-governing, socialized, in spite of the pain which is often involved in these steps. Even where he does not, because of a variety of circumstances, exhibit growth of these more complex sorts, one may still rely on the fact that the tendency is present. Given the opportunity for clear-cut choice between forward-moving and regressive behavior, the tendency will operate.

* * *

V) BEHAVIOR IS BASICALLY THE GOAL-DIRECTED ATTEMPT OF THE ORGANISM TO SATISFY ITS NEEDS AS EXPERIENCED, IN THE FIELD AS PERCEIVED.

* * *

It is noted that behavior is postulated as a reaction to the field as perceived. This point, like some of the other propositions, is proved every day in our experience, but is often overlooked. The reaction is not to reality, but to the perception of reality. A horse, sensing danger, will try to reach the safety and security which he perceives in his stall, even though the barn may be in flames. A man in the desert will struggle just as hard to reach the "lake" which he perceives in a mirage, as to reach a real water hole. At a more complex level, a man may strive for money because he perceives money as the source of emotional security, even though in fact it may not satisfy his need. Often, of course, the perception has a high degree of correspondence with reality, but it is important to recognize that it is the perception, not the reality, which is crucial in determining behavior.

It should also be mentioned that in this concept of motivation all the effective elements exist in the present. Behavior is not "caused" by something which occurred in the past. Present tensions and present needs are the only ones which the organism endeavors to reduce or satisfy. While it is true that past experience has certainly served to modify the meaning which will be perceived in present experiences, yet there is no behavior except to meet a present need.

* * *

VII) THE BEST VANTAGE POINT FOR UNDERSTANDING BEHAVIOR IS FROM THE INTERNAL FRAME OF REFERENCE OF THE INDIVIDUAL HIMSELF. It was mentioned in Proposition I that the only person who could fully know his field of experience was the individual himself. Behavior is a reaction to the field as perceived. It would therefore appear that behavior might be best understood by gaining, in so far as possible, the internal frame of reference of the person himself, and seeing the world of experience as nearly as possible through his eyes.[4]

What we have been doing for the most part in psychology may be likened to the early studies of primitive societies. The observer reported that these primitive peoples ate various ridiculous foods, held fantastic and meaningless ceremonies, and behaved in ways that were a mixture of virtue and depravity. The thing that he did not see was that he was observing from his own frame of reference and placing his own values upon their modes of behavior. We do the same thing in psychology when we speak of "trial-and-error behavior," "delusions," "abnormal behavior," and so on. We fail to see that we are evaluating the person from our own, or from some fairly general, frame of reference, but that the only way to understand his behavior meaningfully is to understand it as he perceives it himself, just as the only way to understand another culture is to assume the frame of reference of that culture. When that is done, the various meaningless and strange behaviors are seen to be part of a meaningful and goal-directed activity. There is then no such thing as random trial-and-error behavior, no such thing as a

---

[4]Recall that this was also a fundamental premise of Kelly's personal construct theory.

delusion, except as the individual may apply these terms to his past behavior. In the present, the behavior is always purposeful, and in response to reality as it is perceived.

*   *   *

To point out the advantages of viewing behavior from the internal frame of reference is not to say that this is the royal road to learning. There are many drawbacks. For one thing, we are largely limited to gaining an acquaintance with the phenomenal field as it is experienced in consciousness. This means that the greater the area of experience not in consciousness, the more incomplete will be the picture. The more we try to infer what is present in the phenomenal field but not conscious (as in interpreting projective techniques), the more complex grow the inferences until the interpretation of the client's projections may become merely an illustration of the clinician's projections.

Furthermore our knowledge of the person's frame of reference depends primarily upon communication of one sort or another from the individual. Communication is at all times faulty and imperfect. Hence only in clouded fashion can we see the world of experience as it appears to this individual.

We may state the whole situation logically thus:

It is possible to achieve, to some extent, the other person's frame of reference, because many of the perceptual objects—self, parents, teachers, employers, and so on—have counterparts in our own perceptual field, and practically all the attitudes toward these perceptual objects—such as fear, anger, annoyance, love, jealousy, satisfaction—have been present in our own world of experience.

Hence we can infer, quite directly, from the communication of the individual, or less accurately from observation of his behavior, a portion of his perceptual and experiential field.

The more all his experiences are available to his consciousness, the more is it possible for him to convey a total picture of his phenomenal field.

The more his communication is a free expression, unmodified by a need or desire to be defensive, the more adequate will be the communication of the field. (Thus a diary is apt to be a better communication of the perceptual field than a court utterance where the individual is on trial.)

It is probably for the reasons just stated that client-centered counseling has proved to be such a valuable method for viewing behavior from the person's frame of reference. The situation minimizes any need of defensiveness.[5] The counselor's behavior minimizes any prejudicial influence on the attitudes expressed. The person is usually motivated to some degree to communicate his own special world, and the procedures used encourage him to do so. The increasing communication gradually brings more of experience into the realm of awareness, and thus a more accurate and total picture of this individual's world of experience is conveyed. On this basis a much more understandable picture of behavior emerges.

*   *   *

VIII) A Portion of the Total Perceptual Field Gradually Becomes Differentiated as the Self. * * * We shall have much to say about various aspects of the operation of the self. For the present the point is made that gradually, as the infant develops, a portion of the total private world becomes recognized as "me," "I," "myself." There are many puzzling and unanswered questions in regard to the dawning concept of the self. We shall try to point out some of these.

Is social interaction necessary in order for a self to develop? Would the hypothetical person reared alone upon a desert island have a self? Is the self primarily a product of the process of symbolization? Is it the fact that experiences may be not only directly experienced, but symbolized and manipulated in thought, that makes the self pos-

---

[5]The therapist's job is to make the client feel appreciated and approved of "unconditionally," and thereby remove conditions of worth. The therapist does this by reflecting back to the client, as approvingly as possible, everything he or she says.

sible? Is the self simply the symbolized portion of experience? These are some of the questions which shrewd research may be able to answer.

Another point which needs to be made in regard to the development of a conscious self is the fact that it is not necessarily coexistent with the physical organism.[6] There is no possibility of a sharp line between organism and environment, and that there is likewise no sharp limit between the experience of the self and of the outside world. Whether or not an object or an experience is regarded as a part of the self depends to a considerable extent upon whether or not it is perceived as within the control of the self. Those elements which we control are regarded as a part of self, but when even such an object as a part of our body is out of control, it is experienced as being less a part of the self. The way in which, when a foot "goes to sleep" from lack of circulation, it becomes an object to us rather than a part of self, may be a sufficient illustration. Perhaps it is this "gradient of autonomy" which first gives the infant the awareness of self, as he is for the first time aware of a feeling of control over some aspect of his world of experience.

* * *

IX) AS A RESULT OF INTERACTION WITH THE EN-VIRONMENT, AND PARTICULARLY AS A RESULT OF EVALUATIONAL INTERACTION WITH OTHERS, THE STRUCTURE OF SELF IS FORMED—AN ORGANIZED, FLUID, BUT CONSISTENT CONCEPTUAL PATTERN OF PERCEPTIONS OF CHARACTERISTICS AND RELATIONSHIPS OF THE "I" OR THE "ME," TOGETHER WITH VALUES ATTACHED TO THESE CONCEPTS.

X) THE VALUES ATTACHED TO EXPERIENCES, AND THE VALUES WHICH ARE A PART OF THE SELF STRUCTURE, IN SOME INSTANCES ARE VALUES EX-PERIENCED DIRECTLY BY THE ORGANISM, AND IN SOME INSTANCES ARE VALUES INTROJECTED OR TAKEN OVER FROM OTHERS, BUT PERCEIVED IN

DISTORTED FASHION, AS IF THEY HAD BEEN EX-PERIENCED DIRECTLY. It will probably be best to discuss these two important propositions together. In the past few years they have been revised and reworded so many different times by the author that it is quite certain the present statement is inadequate also. Yet within the range of experience which these propositions attempt to symbolize, there seem clearly to be some highly important learnings for the personality theorist.

As the infant interacts with his environment he gradually builds up concepts about himself, about the environment, and about himself in relation to the environment. * * * The very young infant has little uncertainty in valuing. At the same time that there is the dawning awareness of "I experience," there is also the awareness that "I like," "I dislike." "I am cold, and I dislike it," "I am cuddled and I like it," "I can reach my toes and find this enjoyable"—these statements appear to be adequate descriptions of the infant's experience, though he does not have the verbal symbols which we have used. He appears to value those experiences which he perceives as enhancing himself, and to place a negative value on those experiences which seem to threaten himself or which do not maintain or enhance himself.

There soon enters into this picture the evaluation of self by others. "You're a good child," "You're a naughty boy"—these and similar evaluations of himself and of his behavior by his parents and others come to form a large and significant part of the infant's perceptual field. Social experiences, social evaluations by others, become a part of his phenomenal field along with experiences not involving others—for example, that radiators are hot, stairs are dangerous, and candy tastes good.

It is at this stage of development, it would seem, that there takes place a type of distorted symbolization of experience, and a denial of experience to awareness, which has much significance for the later development of psychological maladjustment. Let us try to put this in general and schematic terms.

One of the first and most important aspects of

---

[6]Recall that Allport said much the same thing about the self, or "proprium."

the self-experience of the ordinary child is that he is loved by his parents. He perceives himself as lovable, worthy of love, and his relationship to his parents as one of affection. He experiences all this with satisfaction. This is a significant and core element of the structure of self as it begins to form.

At this same time he is experiencing positive sensory values, [he] is experiencing enhancement in other ways. It is enjoyable to have a bowel movement at any time or place that the physiological tension is experienced. It is satisfying and enhancing to hit, or to try to do away with, baby brother. As these things are initially experienced, they are not necessarily inconsistent with the concept of self as a lovable person.

But then to our schematic child comes a serious threat to self. He experiences words and actions of his parents in regard to these satisfying behaviors, and the words and actions add up to the feeling "You are bad, the behavior is bad, and you are not loved or lovable when you behave in this way." This constitutes a deep threat to the nascent structure of self. The child's dilemma might be schematized in these terms: "If I admit to awareness the satisfactions of these behaviors and the values I apprehend in these experiences, then this is inconsistent with my self as being loved or lovable."[7]

Certain results then follow in the development of the ordinary child. One result is a denial in awareness of the satisfactions that were experienced. The other is to distort the symbolization of the experience of the parents. The accurate symbolization would be: "I perceive my parents as experiencing this behavior as unsatisfying to them." The distorted symbolization, distorted to preserve the threatened concept of self, is: "I perceive this behavior as unsatisfying."

It is in this way, it would seem, that parental attitudes are not only introjected,[8] but what is much more important, are experienced not as the attitude of another, but in distorted fashion, *as if* based on the evidence of one's own sensory and visceral equipment. Thus, through distorted symbolization, expression of anger comes to be "experienced" as bad, even though the more accurate symbolization would be that the expression of anger is often experienced as satisfying or enhancing. The more accurate representation is not, however, permitted to enter awareness, or if it does enter, the child is anxious because of the inconsistency he is entertaining within himself. Consequently, "I like baby brother" remains as the pattern belonging in the concept of the self, because it is the concept of the relationship which is introjected from others through the distortion of symbolization, even when the primary experience contains many gradations of value in the relationship, from "I like baby brother" to "I hate him!" In this way the values which the infant attaches to experience become divorced from his own organismic functioning, and experience is valued in terms of the attitudes held by his parents, or by others who are in intimate association with him. These values come to be accepted as being just as "real" as the values which are connected with direct experience. The "self" which is formed on this basis of distorting the sensory and visceral evidence to fit the already present structure acquires an organization and integration which the individual endeavors to preserve. Behavior is regarded as enhancing this self when no such value is apprehended through sensory or visceral reactions; behavior is regarded as opposed to the maintenance or enhancement of the self when there is no negative sensory or visceral reaction. It is here, it seems, that the individual begins on a pathway which he later describes as "I don't really know myself." The primary sensory and visceral reactions are ignored, or not permitted into consciousness, except in distorted form. The values which might be built upon them cannot be admitted to awareness. A concept of self based in part upon a distorted symbolization has taken their place.

Out of these dual sources—the direct experiencing by the individual, and the distorted symbolization of sensory reactions resulting in the

[7]This is the process by which conditions of worth end up requiring people to distort their self-views in order to protect their self-esteem.

[8]Integrated into the child's own personality.

introjection of values and concepts *as if* experienced—there grows the structure of the self. Drawing upon the evidence and upon clinical experience, it would appear that the most useful definition of the self-concept, or self-structure, would be along these lines. The self-structure is an organized configuration of perceptions of the self which are admissible to awareness. It is composed of such elements as the perceptions of one's characteristics and abilities; the percepts and concepts of the self in relation to others and to the environment; the value qualities which are perceived as associated with experiences and objects; and the goals and ideals which are perceived as having positive or negative valence. It is, then, the organized picture, existing in awareness either as figure or ground, of the self and the self-in-relationship, together with the positive or negative values which are associated with those qualities and relationships, as they are perceived as existing in the past, present, or future.

It may be worth while to consider for a moment the way in which the self-structure might be formed without the element of distortion and denial of experience. ⋆ ⋆ ⋆

If we ask ourselves how an infant might develop a self-structure which did not have within it the seeds of later psychological difficulty, our experience in client-centered therapy offers some fruitful ideas. Let us consider, very briefly, and again in schematic form, the type of early experience which would lay a basis for a psychologically healthy development of the self. The beginning is the same as we have just described. The child experiences, and values his experiences positively or negatively. He begins to perceive himself as a psychological object, and one of the most basic elements is the perception of himself as a person who is loved. As in our first description he experiences satisfaction in such behaviors as hitting baby brother. But at this point there is a crucial difference. The parent who is able (1) genuinely to accept these feelings of satisfaction experienced by the child, and (2) fully to accept the child who experiences them, and (3) at the same time to accept his or her own feeling that

such behavior is unacceptable in the family, creates a situation for the child very different from the usual one. The child in this relationship experiences no threat to his concept of himself as a loved person. He can experience fully and accept within himself and as a part of himself his aggressive feelings toward his baby brother. He can experience fully the perception that his hitting behavior is not liked by the person who loves him. What he then does depends upon his conscious balancing of the elements in the situation—the strength of his feeling of aggression, the satisfactions he would gain from hitting the baby, the satisfactions he would gain from pleasing his parent. The behavior which would result would probably be at times social and at other times aggressive. It would not necessarily conform entirely to the parent's wishes, nor would it always be socially "good." It would be the adaptive behavior of a separate, unique, self-governing individual. Its great advantage, as far as psychological health is concerned, is that it would be realistic, based upon an accurate symbolization of all the evidence given by the child's sensory and visceral equipment in this situation. It may seem to differ only very slightly from the description given earlier, but the difference is an extremely important one. Because the budding structure of the self is not threatened by loss of love, because feelings are accepted by his parent, the child in this instance does not need to deny to awareness the satisfactions which he is experiencing, nor does he need to distort his experience of the parental reaction and regard it as his own. He retains instead a secure self which can serve to guide his behavior by freely admitting to awareness, in accurately symbolized form, all the relevant evidence of his experience in terms of its organismic satisfactions, both immediate and longer range. He is thus developing a soundly structured self in which there is neither denial nor distortion of experience.

⋆ ⋆ ⋆

XIV) PSYCHOLOGICAL MALADJUSTMENT EXISTS WHEN THE ORGANISM DENIES TO AWARENESS SIGNIFICANT SENSORY AND VISCERAL EXPERI-

ENCES, WHICH CONSEQUENTLY ARE NOT SYMBO-
LIZED AND ORGANIZED INTO THE GESTALT OF THE
SELF-STRUCTURE. WHEN THIS SITUATION EXISTS,
THERE IS A BASIC OR POTENTIAL PSYCHOLOGICAL
TENSION. ＊ ＊ ＊ If we think of the structure of
the self as being a symbolic elaboration of a portion of the private experiential world of the organism, we may realize that when much of this
private world is denied symbolization, certain basic tensions result. We find, then, that there is a
very real discrepancy between the experiencing organism as it exists, and the concept of self which
exerts such a governing influence upon behavior.
This self is now very inadequately representative
of the experience of the organism. Conscious control becomes more difficult as the organism strives
to satisfy needs which are not consciously admitted, and to react to experiences which are denied
by the conscious self. Tension then exists, and if
the individual becomes to any degree aware of this
tension or discrepancy, he feels anxious, feels that
he is not united or integrated, that he is unsure
of his direction. Such statements may not be the
surface account of the maladjustment, such surface account having more often to do with the
environmental difficulties being faced, but the
feeling of inner lack of integration is usually communicated as the individual feels free to reveal
more of the field of perception which is available
to his consciousness. Thus, such statements as "I
don't know what I'm afraid of," "I don't know
what I want," "I can't decide on anything," "I
don't have any real goal" are very frequent in
counseling cases and indicate the lack of any integrated purposeful direction in which the individual is moving.

＊ ＊ ＊

In other instances, the individual feels, as he
explores his maladjustment, that he has no self,
that he is a zero, that his only self consists of en-
deavoring to do what others believe he should do.
The concept of self, in other words, is based almost entirely upon valuations of experience which
are taken over from others and contains a minimum of accurate symbolization of experience, and
a minimum of direct organismic valuing of ex-

perience.[9] Since the values held by others have no
necessary relationship to one's actual organic ex-
periencings, the discrepancy between the self
structure and the experiential world gradually
comes to be expressed as a feeling of tension and
distress. One young woman, after slowly permitting her own experiences to come into awareness
and form the basis of her concept of self, puts it
very briefly and accurately thus: "I've always tried
to be what the others thought I should be, but
now I'm wondering whether I shouldn't just see
that I am what I am."

＊ ＊ ＊

XVIII) WHEN THE INDIVIDUAL PERCEIVES AND
ACCEPTS INTO ONE CONSISTENT AND INTEGRATED
SYSTEM ALL HIS SENSORY AND VISCERAL EXPE-
RIENCES, THEN HE IS NECESSARILY MORE UNDER-
STANDING OF OTHERS AND IS MORE ACCEPTING
OF OTHERS AS SEPARATE INDIVIDUALS. This
proposition has been felt to be true in our clinical
therapeutic work. It is one of the unexpected findings that have grown out of the client-centered
approach. To the person not familiar with therapeutic experience, it may seem like wishful thinking to assert that the person who accepts himself
will, because of this self-acceptance, have better
interpersonal relations with others.

We find clinically, however, that the person
who completes therapy is more relaxed in being
himself, more sure of himself, more realistic in his
relations with others, and develops notably better
interpersonal relationships. One client, discussing
the results which therapy has had for her, states
something of this fact in these words: "I am myself, and I am different from others. I am getting
more happiness in being myself, and I find myself
more and more letting other people assume the
responsibility for being selves."

If we try to understand the theoretical basis
upon which this takes place, it appears to be as
follows:

---

[9]Recall that Sartre saw this as the worst existential mistake you could make—to decide to allow your decisions to be made by others.

The person who denies some experiences must continually defend himself against the symbolization of those experiences.

As a consequence, all experiences are viewed defensively as potential threats, rather than for what they really are.

Thus in interpersonal relationships, words or behaviors are experienced and perceived as threatening, which were not so intended.

Also, words and behaviors in others are attacked because they represent or resemble the feared experiences.

There is then no real understanding of the other as a separate person, since he is perceived mostly in terms of threat or nonthreat to the self.

But when all experiences are available to consciousness and are integrated, then defensiveness is minimized. When there is no need to defend, there is no need to attack.

When there is no need to attack, the other person is perceived for what he really is, a separate individual, operating in terms of his own meanings, based on his own perceptual field.

While this may sound abstruse, it is corroborated by much everyday evidence, as well as by clinical experience. Who are the individuals, in any neighborhood, or in any group, that inspire confidential relationships, seem able to be understanding of others? They tend to be individuals with a high degree of acceptance of all aspects of self. In clinical experience, how do better interpersonal relationships emerge? It is on this same basis. The rejecting mother who accepts her own negative attitudes toward her child finds that this acceptance, which at first she has feared, makes her more relaxed with her child. She is able to observe him for what he is, not simply through a screen of defensive reactions. Doing so, she perceives that he is an interesting person, with bad features, but also good ones, toward whom she feels at times hostile, but toward whom she also feels at times affectionate. On this comfortable and realistic and spontaneous basis a *real* relationship develops out of her real experiencing, a satisfying

relationship to both. It may not be composed entirely of sweetness and light, but it is far more comfortable than any artificial relationship could possibly be. It is based primarily upon an acceptance of the fact that her child is a separate person.

The woman who hated her mother comes, after she has accepted all her feelings of affection as well as hate, to see her mother as a person with a variety of characteristics: interesting, good, vulgar, and bad. With this much more accurate perception she understands her mother, accepts her for what she is, and builds a real rather than a defensive relationship with her.

The implications of this aspect of our theory are such as to stretch the imagination. Here is a theoretical basis for sound interpersonal, intergroup, and international relationships. Stated in terms of social psychology, this proposition becomes the statement that the person (or persons or group) who accepts himself thoroughly, will necessarily improve his relationship with those with whom he has personal contact, because of his greater understanding and acceptance of them. This atmosphere of understanding and acceptance is the very climate most likely to create a therapeutic experience and consequent self-acceptance in the person who is exposed to it. Thus we have, in effect, a psychological "chain reaction" which appears to have tremendous potentialities for the handling of problems of social relationships.

XIX) AS THE INDIVIDUAL PERCEIVES AND ACCEPTS INTO HIS SELF-STRUCTURE MORE OF HIS ORGANIC EXPERIENCES, HE FINDS THAT HE IS REPLACING HIS PRESENT VALUE *SYSTEM*—BASED SO LARGELY UPON INTROJECTIONS WHICH HAVE BEEN DISTORTEDLY SYMBOLIZED—WITH A CONTINUING ORGANISMIC VALUING *PROCESS*. In therapy, as the person explores his phenomenal field, he comes to examine the values which he has introjected and which he has used as if they were based upon his own experience. (See Proposition X.) He is dissatisfied with them, often expressing the attitude that he has just been doing what others thought he should do. But what does *he* think he should do? There he is puzzled and lost. If one gives up the guidance of an introjected system of values, what is to take its place? He often feels quite incompetent to discover or build any alternative system. If he cannot longer accept the "ought" and "should," the "right" and "wrong" of the introjected system, how can he know what values take their place?[10]

Gradually he comes to experience the fact that he is making value judgments in a way that is new to him, and yet a way that was also known to him in his infancy. Just as the infant places an assured value upon an experience, relying on the evidence of his own senses, as described in Proposition X, so too the client finds that it is his own organism which supplies the evidence upon which value judgments may be made. He discovers that his own senses, his own physiological equipment, can provide the data for making value judgments and for continuously revising them. No one needs to tell him that it is good to act in a freer and more spontaneous fashion, rather than in the rigid way to which he has been accustomed. He senses, he feels that it is satisfying and enhancing. Or when he acts in a defensive fashion, it is his own organism that feels the immediate and short-term satisfaction of being protected and that also senses the longer-range dissatisfaction of having to remain on guard. He makes a choice between two courses of action, fearfully and hesitantly, not knowing whether he has weighed their values accurately. But then he discovers that he may let the evidence of his own experience indicate whether he has chosen satisfyingly. He discovers that he does not need to *know* what are the correct values; through the data supplied by his own organism, he can experience what is satisfying and enhancing. He can put his confidence in a valuing *process*, rather than in some rigid, introjected *system* of values.

Let us look at this proposition in a slightly different way. Values are always accepted because they are perceived as principles making for the maintenance, actualization, and enhancement of the organism. It is on this basis that social values are introjected from the culture. In therapy it would seem that the reorganization which takes place is on the basis that those values are retained which are *experienced* as maintaining or enhancing the organism as distinguished from those which are said by others to be for the good of the organism. For example, an individual accepts from the culture the value, "One should neither have nor express feelings of jealous aggressiveness toward siblings." The value is accepted because it is presumed to make for the enhancement of the individual—a better, more satisfied person. But in therapy this person, as a client, examines this value in terms of a more basic criterion—namely, his own sensory and visceral experiences: "Have I felt the denial of aggressive attitudes as something enhancing myself?" The value is tested in the light of personal organic evidence.

It is in the outcome of this valuing of values that we strike the possibility of very basic similarities in all human experience. For as the individual tests such values, and arrives at his own personal values, he appears to come to conclusions which can be formulated in a generalized way: that the greatest values for the enhancement of the organism accrue when all experiences and all attitudes are permitted conscious symbolization, and when behavior becomes the meaningful and balanced satisfaction of *all* needs, these needs being available to consciousness. The behavior which thus ensues will satisfy the need for social approval, the need to express positive affectional feelings, the need for sexual expression, the need to avoid guilt and regret as well as the need to express aggression. Thus, while the establishment of values by each individual may seem to suggest a complete anarchy of values, experience indicates that quite the opposite is true. Since all individuals have basically the same needs, including the need for acceptance by others, it appears that when each individual formulates his own values, in terms of his own direct experience, it is not anarchy which results, but a high degree of commonality and a genuinely socialized system of values. One of the

---

[10]Recall that Sartre saw this as the fundamental existential dilemma. If no external authority can tell us what is right and wrong, on what basis can we choose?

ultimate ends, then, of an hypothesis of confidence in the individual, and in his capacity to resolve his own conflicts, is the emergence of value systems which are unique and personal for each individual, and which are changed by the changing evidence of organic experience, yet which are at the same time deeply socialized, possessing a high degree of similarity in their essentials.

* * *

Conclusion

This chapter has endeavored to present a theory of personality and behavior which is consistent with our experience and research in client-centered therapy. This theory is basically phenom-enological in character, and relies heavily upon the concept of the self as an explanatory construct. It pictures the end point of personality development as being a basic congruence between the phenomenal field of experience and the conceptual structure of the self—a situation which, if achieved, would represent freedom from internal strain and anxiety, and freedom from potential strain; which would represent the maximum in realistically oriented adaptation; which would mean the establishment of an individualized value system having considerable identity with the value system of any other equally well-adjusted member of the human race.

* * *

FROM *FLOW: THE PSYCHOLOGY OF OPTIMAL EXPERIENCE*

Mihalyi Csikszentmihalyi

An important part of both existentialism and humanism is phenomenology, the idea that one's experience of reality, a moment at a time, is all-important. Sartre wrote that "there is no universe other than a human universe, the universe of human subjectivity." And we have seen that Rogers' first proposition was that "every individual exists in a continually changing world of experience"; his second, that "this perceptual field is, for the individual, 'reality.'"

The modern American psychologist Mihalyi Csikszentmihalyi begins the following selection by noting the same dilemma described so vividly by Sartre. It is difficult to find meaning in life because every individual is ultimately doomed to decay and death, and neither religion nor science offers any certain guidelines on how one should live in the meantime. As Maslow noted in an earlier selection, existentialists like Sartre offer little help out of this dilemma, just advice to face it directly and "keep a stiff upper lip." But Csikszentmihalyi has a different— and uniquely humanistic—idea.

He combines two aspects of existentialism: the despair at the meaningless of life and the emphasis on phenomenology as the central aspect of existence. He suggests that the way out of the existential dilemma is to take matters into one's own hands. Rather than despair at one's ultimate fate, instead learn to make the most of the momentary experience of existence that is, in the final phenomenological analysis, all that one has. Specifically, spend as much time as possible in a state of what Csikszentmihalyi calls "flow."

Flow is a state of unselfconscious concentration, in which one focuses on a task or activity while losing track of time. By being in flow, Csikszentmihalyi proposes, one can cast off the shackles of mortal existence, because no matter what has happened to you in the past, and regardless of what awaits you in the future, you can be in flow now.

By emphasizing the choice to be in flow, Csikszentmihalyi brings in another idea that we have seen throughout the existentialist and humanist writings in this section: free will. Sartre saw free will as a duty and a burden. But Csikszentmihalyi views it more as an opportunity. Since you can freely choose what to experience, why not experience flow? In this way, rather than leading to forlorn-ness and despair, free will can produce happiness of the only sort an existential-ist could ever believe in: happiness experienced one moment at a time.

* * *

As people move through life, passing from the hopeful ignorance of youth into sober-ing adulthood, they sooner or later face an increasingly nagging question: "Is this all there is?" Childhood can be painful, adolescence con-fusing, but for most people, behind it all there is the expectation that after one grows up, things will get better. During the years of early adulthood the future still looks promising, the hope remains that one's goals will be realized. But inevitably the bathroom mirror shows the first white hairs and confirms the fact that those extra pounds are not about to leave; inevitably eyesight begins to fail and mysterious pains begin to shoot through the body. Like waiters in a restaurant starting to place breakfast settings on the surrounding tables while one is still having dinner, these intimations of mortality plainly communicate the message: Your time is up, it's time to move on. When this hap-pens, few people are ready. "Wait a minute, this can't be happening to me. I haven't even begun to live. Where's all that money I was supposed to have made? Where are all the good times I was going to have?"

A feeling of having been led on, of being cheated, is an understandable consequence of this realization. From the earliest years we have been conditioned to believe that a benign fate would provide for us. After all, everybody seemed to agree that we had the great fortune of living in the richest country that ever was, in the most sci-entifically advanced period of human history, surrounded by the most efficient technology, protected by the wisest constitution. Therefore, it made sense to expect that we would have a richer, more meaningful life than any earlier members of

the human race. If our grandparents, living in that ridiculously primitive past, could be content, just imagine how happy we would be! Scientists told us this was so, it was preached from the pulpits of churches, and it was confirmed by thousands of TV commercials celebrating the good life. Yet despite all these assurances, sooner or later we wake up alone, sensing that there is no way this affluent, scientific, and sophisticated world is go-ing to provide us with happiness.

As this realization slowly sets in, different peo-ple react to it differently. Some try to ignore it, and renew their efforts to acquire more of the things that were supposed to make life good—bigger cars and homes, more power on the job, a more glamorous life style. They renew their ef-forts, determined still to achieve the satisfaction that up until then has eluded them. Sometimes this solution works, simply because one is so drawn into the competitive struggle that there is no time to realize that the goal has not come any nearer. But if a person does take the time out to reflect, the disillusionment returns: After each suc-cess it becomes clearer that money, power, status, and possessions do not, by themselves, necessarily add one iota to the quality of life.

Others decide to attack directly the threatening symptoms. If it is a body going to seed that rings the first alarm, they will go on diets, join health clubs, do aerobics, buy a Nautilus, or undergo plastic surgery. If the problem seems to be that nobody pays much attention, they buy books about how to get power or how to make friends, or they enroll in assertiveness training courses and have power lunches. After a while, however, it be-comes obvious that these piecemeal solutions won't work either. No matter how much energy we devote to its care, the body will eventually give out. If we are learning to be more assertive, we might inadvertently alienate our friends. And if we devote too much time to cultivating new friends, we might threaten relationships with our spouse and family. There are just so many dams about to burst and so little time to tend to them all.

Daunted by the futility of trying to keep up with all the demands they cannot possibly meet, some will just surrender and retire gracefully into relative oblivion. They will give up on the world and cultivate their little gardens. They might dabble in genteel forms of escape such as developing a harmless hobby or accumulating a collection of abstract paintings or porcelain figurines. Or they might lose themselves in alcohol or the dream-world of drugs. While exotic pleasures and expensive recreations temporarily take the mind off the basic question "Is this all there is?" few claim to have ever found an answer that way.

Traditionally, the problem of existence has been most directly confronted through religion, and an increasing number of the disillusioned are turning back to it, choosing either one of the standard creeds or a more esoteric Eastern variety. But religions are only temporarily successful attempts to cope with the lack of meaning in life; they are not permanent answers.[1] At some moments in history, they have explained convincingly what was wrong with human existence and have given credible answers. From the fourth to the eighth century of our era Christianity spread throughout Europe, Islam arose in the Middle East, and Buddhism conquered Asia. For hundreds of years these religions provided satisfying goals for people to spend their lives pursuing. But today it is more difficult to accept their worldviews as definitive. The form in which religions have presented their truths—myths, revelations, holy texts—no longer compels belief in an era of scientific rationality, even though the substance of the truths may have remained unchanged. A vital new religion may

one day arise again. In the meantime, those who seek consolation in existing churches often pay for their peace of mind with a tacit agreement to ignore a great deal of what is known about the way the world works.

The evidence that none of these solutions is any longer very effective is irrefutable. In the heyday of its material splendor, our society is suffering from an astonishing variety of strange ills. The profits made from the widespread dependence on illicit drugs are enriching murderers and terrorists. It seems possible that in the near future we shall be ruled by an oligarchy of former drug dealers, who are rapidly gaining wealth and power at the expense of law-abiding citizens. And in our sexual lives, by shedding the shackles of "hypocritical" morality, we have unleashed destructive viruses upon one another.

* * *

Why is it that, despite having achieved previously undreamed-of miracles of progress, we seem more helpless in facing life than our less privileged ancestors were? The answer seems clear: while humankind collectively has increased its material powers a thousandfold, it has not advanced very far in terms of improving the content of experience.

Reclaiming Experience

There is no way out of this predicament except for an individual to take things in hand personally. If values and institutions no longer provide as supportive a framework as they once did, each person must use whatever tools are available to carve out a meaningful, enjoyable life. One of the most important tools in this quest is provided by psychology. Up to now the main contribution of this fledgling science has been to discover how past events shed light on present behavior. It has made us aware that adult irrationality is often the result of childhood frustrations. But there is another way that the discipline of psychology can be put to use. It is in helping answer the question: Given that we are who we are, with whatever hang-ups and repressions, what can we do to improve our future?

---

[1]Sartre made a very similar point in the selection earlier in this section.

To overcome the anxieties and depressions of contemporary life, individuals must become independent of the social environment to the degree that they no longer respond exclusively in terms of its rewards and punishments. To achieve such autonomy, a person has to learn to provide rewards to herself. She has to develop the ability to find enjoyment and purpose regardless of external circumstances. This challenge is both easier and more difficult than it sounds: easier because the ability to do so is entirely within each person's hands; difficult because it requires a discipline and perseverance that are relatively rare in any era, and perhaps especially in the present. And before all else, achieving control over experience requires a drastic change in attitude about what is important and what is not.

We grow up believing that what counts most in our lives is that which will occur in the future. Parents teach children that if they learn good habits now, they will be better off as adults. Teachers assure pupils that the boring classes will benefit them later, when the students are going to be looking for jobs. The company vice president tells junior employees to have patience and work hard, because one of these days they will be promoted to the executive ranks. At the end of the long struggle for advancement, the golden years of retirement beckon. "We are always getting to live," as Ralph Waldo Emerson used to say, "but never living." Or as poor Frances learned in the children's story, it is always bread and jam tomorrow, never bread and jam today.

* * *

There is no question that to survive, and especially to survive in a complex society, it is necessary to work for external goals and to postpone immediate gratifications. But a person does not have to be turned into a puppet jerked about by social controls. The solution is to gradually become free of societal rewards and learn how to substitute for them rewards that are under one's own powers. This is not to say that we should abandon every goal endorsed by society; rather, it means that, in addition to or instead of the goals

others use to bribe us with, we develop a set of our own.

The most important step in emancipating oneself from social controls is the ability to find rewards in the events of each moment. If a person learns to enjoy and find meaning in the ongoing stream of experience, in the process of living itself, the burden of social controls automatically falls from one's shoulders. Power returns to the person when rewards are no longer relegated to outside forces. It is no longer necessary to struggle for goals that always seem to recede into the future, to end each boring day with the hope that tomorrow, perhaps, something good will happen. Instead of forever straining for the tantalizing prize dangled just out of reach, one begins to harvest the genuine rewards of living. But it is not by abandoning ourselves to instinctual desires that we become free of social controls. We must also become independent from the dictates of the body, and learn to take charge of what happens in the mind. Pain and pleasure occur in consciousness and exist only there.[2] As long as we obey the socially conditioned stimulus-response patterns that exploit our biological inclinations, we are controlled from the outside. To the extent that a glamorous ad makes us salivate for the product sold or that a frown from the boss spoils the day, we are not free to determine the content of experience.[3] Since what we experience *is* reality, as far as we are concerned, we can transform reality to the extent that we influence what happens in consciousness and thus free ourselves from the threats and blandishments of the outside world. "Men are not afraid of things, but of how they view them," said Epictetus a long time ago. And the great emperor Marcus Aurelius wrote: "If you

---

[2]This is a classic phenomenological observation. The Watergate burglar G. Gordon Liddy is said to have held his hand above a candle while his flesh burned. "Doesn't that hurt?" he was asked. "Of course it hurts," he replied. "The trick is not to care." This viewpoint is probably the only thing Liddy and Csikszentmihalyi have in common.

[3]This is what the existentialists called living in bad faith.

are pained by external things, it is not they that disturb you, but your own judgment of them. And it is in your power to wipe out that judgment now."

* * *

The rest of this chapter provides an overview of what makes experience enjoyable. This description is based on long interviews, questionnaires, and other data collected over a dozen years from several thousand respondents. Initially we interviewed only people who spent a great amount of time and effort in activities that were difficult, yet provided no obvious rewards such as money or prestige: rock climbers, composers of music, chess players, amateur athletes. Our later studies included interviews with ordinary people, leading ordinary existences; we asked them to describe how it felt when their lives were at their fullest, when what they did was most enjoyable. These people included urban Americans—surgeons, professors, clerical and assembly-line workers, young mothers, retired people, and teenagers. They also included respondents from Korea, Japan, Thailand, Australia, various European cultures, and a Navajo reservation. On the basis of these interviews we can now describe what makes an experience enjoyable, and thus provide examples that all of us can use to enhance the quality of life.

The Elements of Enjoyment

The first surprise we encountered in our study was how similarly very different activities were described when they were going especially well. Apparently the way a long-distance swimmer felt when crossing the English Channel was almost identical to the way a chess player felt during a tournament or a climber progressing up a difficult rock face. All these feelings were shared, in important respects, by subjects ranging from musicians composing a new quartet to teenagers from the ghetto involved in a championship basketball game.

The second surprise was that, regardless of cul-ture, stage of modernization, social class, age, or gender, the respondents described enjoyment in very much the same way. *What* they did to experience enjoyment varied enormously—the elderly Koreans liked to meditate, the teenage Japanese liked to swarm around in motorcycle gangs—but they described *how* it felt when they enjoyed themselves in almost identical terms. Moreover, the *reasons* the activity was enjoyed shared many more similarities than differences. In sum, optimal experience, and the psychological conditions that make it possible, seem to be the same the world over.[4]

As our studies have suggested, the phenomenology of enjoyment has eight major components. When people reflect on how it feels when their experience is most positive, they mention at least one, and often all, of the following. First, the experience usually occurs when we confront tasks we have a chance of completing. Second, we must be able to concentrate on what we are doing. Third and fourth, the concentration is usually possible because the task undertaken has clear goals and provides immediate feedback. Fifth, one acts with a deep but effortless involvement that removes from awareness the worries and frustrations of everyday life. Sixth, enjoyable experiences allow people to exercise a sense of control over their actions. Seventh, concern for the self disappears, yet paradoxically the sense of self emerges stronger after the flow experience is over. Finally, the sense of the duration of time is altered; hours pass by in minutes, and minutes can stretch out to seem like hours. The combination of all these elements causes a sense of deep enjoyment that is so rewarding people feel that expending a great deal of energy is worthwhile simply to be able to feel it.

* * *

A Challenging Activity That Requires Skills * * * By far the overwhelming propor-

---

[4]This is reminiscent of Sartre's universal human condition and the claim we have seen the humanists make that people are basically the same the world over.

tion of optimal experiences are reported to occur within sequences of activities that are goal-directed and bounded by rules—activities that require the investment of psychic energy, and that could not be done without the appropriate skills. * * *

* * *

Any activity contains a bundle of opportunities for action, or "challenges," that require appropriate skills to realize. For those who don't have the right skills, the activity is not challenging; it is simply meaningless. Setting up a chessboard gets the juices of a chess player flowing, but leaves cold anyone who does not know the rules of the game. To most people, the sheer wall of El Capitan in Yosemite valley is just a huge chunk of featureless rock. But to the climber it is an arena offering an endlessly complex symphony of mental and physical challenges.

One simple way to find challenges is to enter a competitive situation. Hence the great appeal of all games and sports that pit a person or team against another. In many ways, competition is a quick way of developing complexity: "He who wrestles with us," wrote Edmund Burke, "strengthens our nerves, and sharpens our skill. Our antagonist is our helper." The challenges of competition can be stimulating and enjoyable. But when beating the opponent takes precedence in the mind over performing as well as possible, enjoyment tends to disappear. Competition is enjoyable only when it is a means to perfect one's skills; when it becomes an end in itself, it ceases to be fun.

* * *

In all the activities people in our study reported engaging in, enjoyment comes at a very specific point: whenever the opportunities for action perceived by the individual are equal to his or her capabilities. Playing tennis, for instance, is not enjoyable if the two opponents are mismatched. The less skilled player will feel anxious, and the better player will feel bored. The same is true of every other activity: a piece of music that is too simple relative to one's listening skills will be boring, while music that is too complex will be frustrating. Enjoyment appears at the boundary between boredom and anxiety, when the challenges are just balanced with the person's capacity to act.

The golden ratio between challenges and skills does not only hold true for human activities. Whenever I took our hunting dog, Hussar, for a walk in the open fields he liked to play a very simple game—the prototype of the most culturally widespread game of human children, escape and pursuit. He would run circles around me at top speed, with his tongue hanging out and his eyes warily watching every move I made, daring me to catch him. Occasionally I would take a lunge, and if I was lucky I got to touch him. Now the interesting part is that whenever I was tired, and moved halfheartedly, Hussar would run much tighter circles, making it relatively easy for me to catch him; on the other hand, if I was in good shape and willing to extend myself, he would enlarge the diameter of his circle. In this way, the difficulty of the game was kept constant. With an uncanny sense for the fine balancing of challenges and skills, he would make sure that the game would yield the maximum of enjoyment for us both.

THE MERGING OF ACTION AND AWARENESS
When all a person's relevant skills are needed to cope with the challenges of a situation, that person's attention is completely absorbed by the activity. There is no excess psychic energy left over to process any information but what the activity offers. All the attention is concentrated on the relevant stimuli.

As a result, one of the most universal and distinctive features of optimal experience takes place: people become so involved in what they are doing that the activity becomes spontaneous, almost automatic; they stop being aware of themselves as separate from the actions they are performing.

A dancer describes how it feels when a performance is going well: "Your concentration is very complete. Your mind isn't wandering, you are not thinking of something else; you are totally involved in what you are doing. . . . Your energy is flowing very smoothly. You feel relaxed, comfortable, and energetic."

A rock climber explains how it feels when he is scaling a mountain: "You are so involved in what you are doing [that] you aren't thinking of yourself as separate from the immediate activity. . . . You don't see yourself as separate from what you are doing."

A mother who enjoys the time spent with her small daughter: "Her reading is the one thing that she's really into, and we read together. She reads to me, and I read to her, and that's a time when I sort of lose touch with the rest of the world, I'm totally absorbed in what I'm doing."

A chess player tells of playing in a tournament: ". . . the concentration is like breathing—you never think of it. The roof could fall in and, if it missed you, you would be unaware of it."

It is for this reason that we called the optimal experience "flow." The short and simple word describes well the sense of seemingly effortless movement. The following words from a poet and rock climber apply to all the thousands of interviews collected by us and by others over the years: "The mystique of rock climbing is climbing; you get to the top of a rock glad it's over but really wish it would go on forever. The justification of climbing is climbing, like the justification of poetry is writing; you don't conquer anything except things in yourself. . . . The act of writing justifies poetry. Climbing is the same: recognizing that you are a flow. The purpose of the flow is to keep on flowing, not looking for a peak or utopia but staying in the flow. It is not a moving up but a continuous flowing; you move up to keep the flow going. There is no possible reason for climbing except the climbing itself; it is a self-communication."

Although the flow experience appears to be effortless, it is far from being so. It often requires strenuous physical exertion, or highly disciplined mental activity. It does not happen without the application of skilled performance. Any lapse in concentration will erase it. And yet while it lasts consciousness works smoothly, action follows action seamlessly. In normal life, we keep interrupting what we do with doubts and questions. "Why am I doing this? Should I perhaps be doing something else?" Repeatedly we question the necessity of our actions, and evaluate critically the reasons for carrying them out. But in flow there is no need to reflect, because the action carries us forward as if by magic.

CLEAR GOALS AND FEEDBACK The reason it is possible to achieve such complete involvement in a flow experience is that goals are usually clear and feedback immediate. A tennis player always knows what she has to do: return the ball into the opponent's court. And each time she hits the ball she knows whether she has done well or not. The chess player's goals are equally obvious: to mate the opponent's king before his own is mated. With each move, he can calculate whether he has come closer to this objective. The climber inching up a vertical wall of rock has a very simple goal in mind: to complete the climb without falling. Every second, hour after hour, he receives information that he is meeting that basic goal.

* * *

In some creative activities, where goals are not clearly set in advance, a person must develop a strong personal sense of what she intends to do. The artist might not have a visual image of what the finished painting should look like, but when the picture has progressed to a certain point, she should know whether this is what she wanted to achieve or not. And a painter who enjoys painting must have internalized criteria for "good" or "bad" so that after each brush stroke she can say: "Yes, this works; no, this doesn't." Without such internal guidelines, it is impossible to experience flow.

Sometimes the goals and the rules governing an activity are invented or negotiated on the spot. For example, teenagers enjoy impromptu interactions in which they try to "gross each other out," or tell tall stories, or make fun of their teachers. The goal of such sessions emerges by trial and error, and is rarely made explicit; often it remains below the participants' level of awareness. Yet it is clear that these activities develop their own rules and that those who take part have a clear idea of what constitutes a successful "move," and of who is doing well. In many ways this is the pattern of a good jazz band or any improvisational group. Scholars or debaters obtain similar satisfaction when the "moves" in their arguments mesh smoothly, and produce the desired result.

What constitutes feedback varies considerably in different activities. Some people are indifferent to things that others cannot get enough of. For instance, surgeons who love doing operations claim that they wouldn't switch to internal medicine even if they were paid ten times as much as they are for doing surgery, because an internist never knows exactly how well he is doing. In an operation, on the other hand, the status of the patient is almost always clear: as long as there is no blood in the incision, for example, a specific procedure has been successful. When the diseased organ is cut out, the surgeon's task is accomplished; after that there is the suture that gives a gratifying sense of closure to the activity. And the surgeon's disdain for psychiatry is even greater than that for internal medicine: To hear surgeons talk, the psychiatrist might spend ten years with a patient without knowing whether the cure is helping him.

Yet the psychiatrist who enjoys his trade is also receiving constant feedback: the way the patient holds himself, the expression on his face, the hesitation in his voice, the content of the material he brings up in the therapeutic hour—all these bits of information are important clues the psychiatrist uses to monitor the progress of the therapy. The difference between a surgeon and a psychiatrist is that the former considers blood and excision the only feedback worth attending to, whereas the latter considers the signals reflecting a patient's state of mind to be significant information. The surgeon judges the psychiatrist to be soft because he is interested in such ephemeral goals; the psychiatrist thinks the surgeon crude for his concentration on mechanics.

The *kind* of feedback we work toward is in and of itself often unimportant: What difference does it make if I hit the tennis ball between the white lines, if I immobilize the enemy king on the chessboard, or if I notice a glimmer of understanding in my patient's eyes at the end of the therapeutic hour? What makes this information valuable is the symbolic message it contains: that I have succeeded in my goal. Such knowledge creates order in consciousness, and strengthens the structure of the self.

* * *

CONCENTRATION ON THE TASK AT HAND One of the most frequently mentioned dimensions of the flow experience is that, while it lasts, one is able to forget all the unpleasant aspects of life. This feature of flow is an important by-product of the fact that enjoyable activities require a complete focusing of attention on the task at hand—thus leaving no room in the mind for irrelevant information.

In normal everyday existence, we are the prey of thoughts and worries intruding unwanted in consciousness. Because most jobs, and home life in general, lack the pressing demands of flow experiences, concentration is rarely so intense that preoccupations and anxieties can be automatically ruled out. Consequently the ordinary state of mind involves unexpected and frequent episodes of entropy interfering with the smooth run of psychic energy. This is one reason why flow improves the quality of experience: the clearly structured demands of the activity impose order and exclude the interference of disorder in consciousness.

A professor of physics who was an avid rock climber described his state of mind while climbing as follows: "It is as if my memory input has been cut off. All I can remember is the last thirty seconds, and all I can think ahead is the next five minutes." In fact, any activity that requires concentration has a similarly narrow window of time.

But it is not only the temporal focus that counts. What is even more significant is that only a very select range of information can be allowed into awareness. Therefore all the troubling thoughts that ordinarily keep passing through the mind are temporarily kept in abeyance. As a young basketball player explains: "The court—that's all that matters. . . . Sometimes out on the court I think of a problem, like fighting with my steady girl, and I think that's nothing compared to the game. You can think about a problem all day but as soon as you get in the game, the hell with it!" And another: "Kids my age, they think a lot . . . but when you are playing basketball, that's all there is on your mind—just basketball. . . . Everything seems to follow right along."

A mountaineer expands on the same theme: "When you're [climbing] you're not aware of other problematic life situations. It becomes a world unto its own, significant only to itself. It's a concentration thing. Once you're into the situation, it's incredibly real, and you're very much in charge of it. It becomes your total world."

A similar sensation is reported by a dancer: "I get a feeling that I don't get anywhere else. . . . I have more confidence in myself than any other time. Maybe an effort to forget my problems. Dance is like therapy. If I am troubled about something, I leave it out of the door as I go in [the dance studio]."

*   *   *

THE PARADOX OF CONTROL   Enjoyment often occurs in games, sports, and other leisure activities that are distinct from ordinary life, where any number of bad things can happen. If a person loses a chess game or botches his hobby he need not worry; in "real" life, however, a person who mishandles a business deal may get fired, lose the mortgage on the house, and end up on public assistance. Thus the flow experience is typically described as involving a sense of control—or, more precisely, as lacking the sense of worry about losing control that is typical in many situations of normal life.

Here is how a dancer expresses this dimension of the flow experience: "A strong relaxation and calmness comes over me. I have no worries of failure. What a powerful and warm feeling it is! I want to expand, to hug the world. I feel enormous power to effect something of grace and beauty." And a chess player: ". . . I have a general feeling of well-being, and that I am in complete control of my world."

What these respondents are actually describing is the *possibility*, rather than the *actuality*, of control. The ballet dancer may fall, break her leg, and never make the perfect turn, and the chess player may be defeated and never become a champion. But at least in principle in the world of flow perfection is attainable.

This sense of control is also reported in enjoyable activities that involve serious risks, activities that to an outsider would seem to be much more potentially dangerous than the affairs of normal life. People who practice hang gliding, spelunking, rock climbing, race-car driving, deep-sea diving, and many similar sports for fun are purposefully placing themselves in situations that lack the safety nets of civilized life. Yet all these individuals report flow experiences in which a heightened sense of control plays an important part.

It is usual to explain the motivation of those who enjoy dangerous activities as some sort of pathological need: they are trying to exorcise a deep-seated fear, they are compensating, they are compulsively reenacting an Oedipal fixation, they are "sensation seekers." While such motives may be occasionally involved, what is most striking, when one actually speaks to specialists in risk, is how their enjoyment derives not from the danger itself but from their ability to minimize it. So rather than a pathological thrill that comes from courting disaster, the positive emotion they enjoy is the perfectly healthy feeling of being able to control potentially dangerous forces.

The important thing to realize here is that activities that produce flow experiences, even the seemingly most risky ones, are so constructed as to allow the practitioner to develop sufficient skills to reduce the margin of error to as close to zero as possible. Rock climbers, for instance, recognize two sets of dangers: "objective" and "subjective" ones. The first kind are the unpredictable physical events that might confront a person on the mountain: a sudden storm, an avalanche, a falling rock, a drastic drop in temperature. One can prepare oneself against these threats, but they can never be completely foreseen. Subjective dangers are those that arise from the climber's lack of skill—including the inability to estimate correctly the difficulty of a climb in relation to one's ability.

The whole point of climbing is to avoid objective dangers as much as possible and to eliminate subjective dangers entirely by rigorous discipline and sound preparation. As a result, climbers genuinely believe that climbing the Matterhorn is safer than crossing a street in Manhattan, where the objective dangers—taxi drivers, bicycle messengers, buses, muggers—are far less predictable than those on the mountain, and where personal skills have less chance to ensure the pedestrian's safety.

As this example illustrates, what people enjoy is not the sense of *being* in control, but the sense of *exercising* control in difficult situations. It is not possible to experience a feeling of control unless one is willing to give up the safety of protective routines. Only when a doubtful outcome is at stake, and one is able to influence that outcome, can a person really know whether she is in control.

*　*　*

When a person becomes so dependent on the ability to control an enjoyable activity that he cannot pay attention to anything else, then he loses the ultimate control: the freedom to determine the content of consciousness. Thus enjoyable activities that produce flow have a potentially negative aspect: while they are capable of improving the quality of existence by creating order in the mind, they can become addictive, at which point the self becomes captive of a certain kind of order, and is then unwilling to cope with the ambiguities of life.

THE LOSS OF SELF-CONSCIOUSNESS We have seen earlier that when an activity is thoroughly engrossing, there is not enough attention left over to allow a person to consider either the past or the future, or any other temporarily irrelevant stimuli. One item that disappears from awareness deserves special mention, because in normal life we spend so much time thinking about it: our own self. Here is a climber describing this aspect of the experience: "It's a Zen feeling, like meditation or concentration. One thing you're after is the one-pointedness of mind. You can get your ego

mixed up with climbing in all sorts of ways and it isn't necessarily enlightening. But when things become automatic, it's like an egoless thing, in a way. Somehow the right thing is done without you ever thinking about it or doing anything at all. . . . It just happens. And yet you're more concentrated." *　*　*

*　*　*

Preoccupation with the self consumes psychic energy because in everyday life we often feel threatened. Whenever we are threatened we need to bring the image we have of ourselves back into awareness, so we can find out whether or not the threat is serious, and how we should meet it. For instance, if walking down the street I notice some people turning back and looking at me with grins on their faces, the normal thing to do is immediately to start worrying: "Is there something wrong? Do I look funny? Is it the way I walk, or is my face smudged?" Hundreds of times every day we are reminded of the vulnerability of our self. And every time this happens psychic energy is lost trying to restore order to consciousness.

But in flow there is no room for self-scrutiny. Because enjoyable activities have clear goals, stable rules, and challenges well matched to skills, there is little opportunity for the self to be threatened. When a climber is making a difficult ascent, he is totally taken up in the mountaineering role. He is 100 percent a climber, or he would not survive. There is no way for anything or anybody to bring into question any other aspect of his self. Whether his face is smudged makes absolutely no difference. The only possible threat is the one that comes from the mountain—but a good climber is well trained to face that threat, and does not need to bring the self into play in the process.

The absence of the self from consciousness does not mean that a person in flow has given up the control of his psychic energy, or that she is unaware of what happens in her body or in her mind. In fact the opposite is usually true. When people first learn about the flow experience they sometimes assume that lack of self-consciousness has something to do with a passive obliteration of the self, a "going with the flow" Southern

California–style. But in fact the optimal experience involves a very active role for the self. A violinist must be extremely aware of every movement of her fingers, as well as of the sound entering her ears, and of the total form of the piece she is playing, both analytically, note by note, and holistically, in terms of its overall design. A good runner is usually aware of every relevant muscle in his body, of the rhythm of his breathing, as well as of the performance of his competitors within the overall strategy of the race. A chess player could not enjoy the game if he were unable to retrieve from his memory, at will, previous positions, past combinations.

So loss of self-consciousness does not involve a loss of self, and certainly not a loss of consciousness, but rather, only a loss of consciousness *of* the self. What slips below the threshold of awareness is the *concept* of self, the information we use to represent to ourselves who we are. And being able to forget temporarily who we are seems to be very enjoyable. When not preoccupied with our selves, we actually have a chance to expand the concept of who we are. Loss of self-consciousness can lead to self-transcendence, to a feeling that the boundaries of our being have been pushed forward.

⋆   ⋆   ⋆

THE TRANSFORMATION OF TIME   One of the most common descriptions of optimal experience is that time no longer seems to pass the way it ordinarily does. The objective, external duration we measure with reference to outside events like night and day, or the orderly progression of clocks, is rendered irrelevant by the rhythms dictated by the activity. Often hours seem to pass by in minutes; in general, most people report that time seems to pass much faster. But occasionally the reverse occurs: Ballet dancers describe how a difficult turn that takes less than a second in real time stretches out for what seems like minutes: "Two things happen. One is that it seems to pass really fast in one sense. After it's passed, it seems to have passed really fast. I see that it's 1:00 in the morning, and I say: 'Aha, just a few minutes ago it was 8:00.' But then while

I'm dancing . . . it seems like it's been much longer than maybe it really was." The safest generalization to make about this phenomenon is to say that during the flow experience the sense of time bears little relation to the passage of time as measured by the absolute convention of the clock.

⋆   ⋆   ⋆

⋆ ⋆ ⋆ It is not clear whether this dimension of flow is just an epiphenomenon—a by-product of the intense concentration required for the activity at hand—or whether it is something that contributes in its own right to the positive quality of the experience. Although it seems likely that losing track of the clock is not one of the major elements of enjoyment, freedom from the tyranny of time does add to the exhilaration we feel during a state of complete involvement.

The Autotelic Experience

The key element of an optimal experience is that it is an end in itself. Even if initially undertaken for other reasons, the activity that consumes us becomes intrinsically rewarding. Surgeons speak of their work: "It is so enjoyable that I would do it even if I didn't have to." Sailors say: "I am spending a lot of money and time on this boat, but it is worth it—nothing quite compares with the feeling I get when I am out sailing."

The term *autotelic* derives from two Greek words, *auto* meaning self, and *telos* meaning goal. It refers to a self-contained activity, one that is done not with the expectation of some future benefit, but simply because the doing itself is the reward. Playing the stock market in order to make money is not an autotelic experience; but playing it in order to prove one's skill at foretelling future trends is—even though the outcome in terms of dollars and cents is exactly the same. Teaching children in order to turn them into good citizens is not autotelic, whereas teaching them because one enjoys interacting with children is. What transpires in the two situations is ostensibly identical; what differs is that when the experience is autotelic, the person is paying attention to the activity for its own sake; when it is not, the attention is focused on its consequences.

Most things we do are neither purely autotelic nor purely exotelic (as we shall call activities done for external reasons only), but are a combination of the two. Surgeons usually enter into their long period of training because of exotelic expectations: to help people, to make money, to achieve prestige. If they are lucky, after a while they begin to enjoy their work, and then surgery becomes to a large extent also autotelic.

＊ ＊ ＊

An autotelic experience is very different from the feelings we typically have in the course of life. So much of what we ordinarily do has no value in itself, and we do it only because we have to do it, or because we expect some future benefit from it. Many people feel that the time they spend at work is essentially wasted—they are alienated from it, and the psychic energy invested in the job does nothing to strengthen their self. For quite a few people free time is also wasted. Leisure provides a relaxing respite from work, but it generally consists of passively absorbing information, without using any skills or exploring new opportunities for action. As a result life passes in a sequence of boring and anxious experiences over which a person has little control.

The autotelic experience, or flow, lifts the course of life to a different level. Alienation gives way to involvement, enjoyment replaces boredom, helplessness turns into a feeling of control, and psychic energy works to reinforce the sense of self, instead of being lost in the service of external goals. When experience is intrinsically rewarding life is justified in the present, instead of being held hostage to a hypothetical future gain.

＊ ＊ ＊

PART VI

Cross-cultural Approaches to Personality

Migrations and technological advances have caused many cultures around the world to become both increasingly diverse and increasingly interconnected. This is perhaps nowhere more true than in America, where subcultures of European, African, Latin, and Asian origin all live within the same borders. But elsewhere in the world as well, cultural diversity is becoming more the rule than the exception.

It is only natural, therefore, that recent years have seen an increasing and international interest in the way psychological processes and personality might differ across cultures. Sometimes this interest has led to broad claims that psychology is culturally specific and nothing can be said about people in general. But more often psychologists interested in culture have tried to draw general lessons from comparing the personalities of people who live in different cultural contexts.

The first selection in this section, by the anthropologist John Caughey, exemplifies one very common approach to cross-cultural research in personality. Caughey lived for a time on a South Pacific island and reported back as to the three personality traits he observed to be most important in that culture. The second selection, by the psychologists Kuo-shu Yang and Michael Bond, exemplifies a different approach to the same problem. Yang and Bond use questionnaires and psychometric methodology to investigate whether personality descriptions in Chinese can be reduced to the same "Big Five" traits many psychologists believe to be useful in English.

In the third selection, Enrico Jones and Avril Thorne point out that the comparison of cultures is not necessarily an international enterprise. Many nations, including the United States, contain within them important and distinct subcultures. They argue against the common practice of imposing the dominant culture's view of reality and of psychological adjustment upon members of minority cultures. Going further, they also argue against the imposition of standard psychometric methods of the sort used by Yang and Bond, and instead ad-

vocate a qualitative methodology in which the subject and researcher engage in a true collaboration to understand each other's view of reality.

In the fourth selection, Hazel Markus and Shinobu Kitayama seem to go even further. They argue that the self as an independent, bounded entity that can be described by personality traits of any sort is itself a cultural construction —specifically, a construction of Western culture. Asian cultures, they assert, view the self as much more interconnected with other selves and with the culture at large.

The following brief piece, an excerpt from a novel by David Lodge, illustrates how the views of Jones, Thorne, Markus, and Kitayama concerning the social construction of reality and of selfhood are consistent with modern deconstructionist trends in literary criticism.

The final selection, by the important cross-cultural psychologist Harry Triandis, seeks a middle ground between the idea of a "one size fits all" psychology and the radical deconstructionist idea that members of different cultures simply cannot be compared, and instead must be understood in their own terms. Triandis proposes a triad of traits that can be used to characterize both individuals and whole cultures. Through the use of many examples, Triandis demonstrates how the dimensions of collectivism-individualism, tightness-looseness, and complexity can account for an important part of the ways in which the psychologies of different cultures both differ from and are similar to one another.

PERSONAL IDENTITY ON FÁÁNAKKAR

John L. Caughey

When members of different cultures talk about personality, what terms do they use? This is a long-standing and central issue for the cross-cultural study of personality. Just as investigators such as Costa and McCrae (Part II) have searched for the key terms for describing personality in English, anthropologists and cross-cultural psychologists for years have visited other cultures and reported back about the terms for describing personality in those languages.

This enterprise involves much more than looking up trait words in a dictionary and doing a translation. For one thing, some cultures have no dictionaries. More importantly, although the words used in one language may be translatable into another language, this fact does not necessarily imply that the two words serve the same function or have the same importance in their respective cultural contexts. Deeper research is required to find out what the most important concepts are for describing personality within a particular culture.

Two styles of such research can be identified. The first, anthropological style is for a researcher to visit a culture, immerse himself or herself in its life, and report back how its denizens talk about people. This kind of study yields a detailed—anthropologists use the term "thick"—description of life in another culture, but all the conclusions seem to rest ultimately in the perceptions of the individual researcher. A second, more psychological style is to construct personality questionnaires, using the accepted techniques of psychometrics, in different cultures and languages. Then an attempt is made to compare the results in the two cultures.

The following selection, by the anthropologist John Caughey, is an example of the first kind of research. (The next selection will illustrate the other kind.) Caughey visited an isolated island culture in the South Pacific, and reports back on the basic traits they use to describe personality. He reports that the three most important traits—perhaps, though he does not mention it, comparable to the "Big Five" in English—can be roughly translated as respectfulness, bravery, and "strong thought." He presents a chart that represents the interrelations of these and other terms important in the culture, and provides some vivid examples of particular individuals described in these terms.

One is left to ponder a couple of questions. First, if another researcher visited this culture, would he or she report back the same terms as the most important ones? Caughey does not describe in this article exactly how he drew his conclusions; they came from a personal immersion in the culture that would not be easy to duplicate. Second, assuming Caughey's description is accurate, to what degree is the manner of describing personality that he describes different from the ways of our own culture?

From "Personality Identity and Social Organization," by J. L. Caughey (1980). In *Ethos*, 8, 173–203. Reproduced by permission of the American Anthropological Association. Not for further reproduction.

* * *

Identity approaches to social organization depend upon the discovery and description of the systems of classification with which the people of a particular society sort themselves out into *kinds of persons*, and upon the ways in which these classifications are connected to the conduct of social interactions. Identity theorists have suggested that in many, and possibly all, cultures two distinct systems of classification are employed; one set of categories for social roles or *social identities* and a second set of categories for personality types of *personal identities* (Goodenough, 1965; Robbins, 1973). Labels for social identities, such as "lawyer," "professor," or "uncle" refer to social positions (e.g., occupational, age/sex, and kinship categories) which carry rights and duties vis-à-vis the occupants of matching social positions (Goodenough, 1965, pp. 3–4). Social identities are based on rules of conduct which specify what someone in one social capacity (e.g., "bartender") owes to and can demand from someone in another social capacity (e.g., "waitress," "customer," "owner") (Goodenough, 1965, p. 8; cf. Spradley Mann, 1975). On the other hand, labels for personal identity, such as "jealous," "shy," or "aggressive," are understood to refer not to social roles but to what someone is like "as a person." Taken as "personal and independent of one's social or occupational station in life" (Goodenough, 1963, p. 178; cf. Goodenough 1965, p. 4), they are considered to refer to an individual's "personality," "temperament," or "character."

* * *

Personal Identity on Fáánakkar

My study of personal identity and social organization was carried out on the Trukese island of Fáánakkar in the Eastern Caroline Islands of Micronesia.[1] Fáánakkar lies across the lagoon from Romónum, the island where most of the previous fieldwork on Truk had been carried out, and it is considerably larger than Romónum. My fieldwork was done mainly in two districts of Fáánakkar, an area similar to Romónum in both size (approximately .4 square miles) and population (346 people). While there are differences in detail, the social systems of the two islands are also similar. On Fáánakkar as on Romónum, the population is divided up into named "districts" (*sóópw*), each of which is composed of eight to ten "matrilineages" (*eterekes*). The members of such groups control valuables such as land and magical knowledge in common, and stand together against outsiders. Marriages are arranged between members of the same or adjacent districts, and couples reside in extended family groupings at clusters of dwelling houses at one of the lineage centers where they have kin ties. Within a given lineage, brothers have authority over sisters and elder persons have authority over younger members. The eldest male is usually the "lineage leader" (*mmwenó*), and the

---

[1]The name "Fáánakkar" is a pseudonym for the island in eastern Truk which I studied during eleven months of fieldwork in 1968. For a discussion of that research see Caughey, (1977, pp. 1–7).—Author.

leader of the chiefly lineage is also the "district chief" (*samwoonum sóópw*) (Caughey, 1977; cf. Goodenough, 1951, 1974).

Given these arrangements, people regularly interact with one another in terms of social identities based on lineage and district membership, kinship categories, age/sex categories, magical specializations, and leadership roles. However, people are also much concerned with assessing one another's *personal* identity or "character" (*napanap*, literally "shape"). In the Fáánakkar theory of the self, "character" is understood to refer to the style or "shape" of an individual's thoughts and emotions. Taxonomically, "character" is a cover term for a series of expressions which may be appropriately employed in describing an individual's personal style. The most significant character descriptors are contained within a system of classification based on the interrelationships of three pairs of terms. Each pair consists of one expression designating a positive character quality and a second designating the negative opposite attribute. These terms are listed below with preliminary English glosses:[2]

1. *mosonoson*: "respectfulness," "humility," "kindness" *namanam tekiya*: "arrogance," "haughtiness"
2. *pwara*: "bravery," "mastery," "power" *nissimwa*: "cowardice," "weakness," "subservience"
3. *ekiyek péchékkún*: "strong thought," "competitive thought" *ekiyek pwoteete*: "weak thought," "lazy thought"

An understanding of the meaning of these terms depends on relating them to certain assumptions about character inherent in the Fáánakkar theory of the self. First of all, it is taken for granted that character is an object for critical evaluation. The combination of the three admirable traits, "respectfulness," "bravery," and "strong thought" defines the ideal type. This combination constitutes an emotionally charged and highly significant image within this culture and a

person who approximates it is viewed with the greatest admiration. The combination of *namanam tekiya* and *pwara* ("arrogant bravery" or *mwááneson*, "man lowering") is viewed with ambivalence. "Arrogance" usually carries a strong negative evaluation but it intensifies an aspect of bravery in a way which is sometimes admirable. Other possible character types are considered progressively less desirable (see Figure 41.1). The worst character type combines the three negative traits, "arrogance," "cowardice," and "weak thought" and each of these terms evokes strong feelings of hatred and contempt (Caughey, 1977, pp. 25–40).

A second important assumption is that character is unstable. The readiness with which they characterize their fellows shows that people have a more or less distinct impression of the current personal identity of all those with whom they regularly interact, but all such impressions are considered tentative.

> Although he has been a leading figure on Fáánakkar, D. O. got drunk and cursed many people including some in his own district. He also got into a fight with one of his kinsmen. The next day another man commented as follows: "A long time ago D.O. stopped drinking. He wanted to be a man, he wanted to be a good person, he wanted to be respectful. And he *was* extremely respectful. But yesterday he was wounded by his drinking. People liked him until yesterday but now some will think, 'What is this? Is he turning into an evil person?' They will be undecided about him."

As this text suggests, the maintenance or transformation of character is thought to be due in major part, to the individual's inner desire to achieve good character. It also relates to an individual's "understanding." As individuals get older, their understanding and hence their character sometimes improves. A lineage leader described his sister's son as follows:

> I despise the arrogance of B.Q. He is brave, but he lacks strong thought, His thinking is womanly. He has not reached the age of manhood, however, and his character may change.

---

[2]Translations.

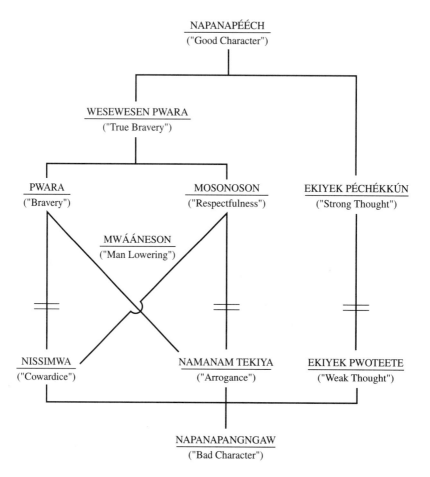

Figure 41.1 Dimensions of character on Fáánakkar

Character is also considered subject to alteration by a variety of other factors including magical forces. Spells and magical medicines may be used to improve a child's character. Sometimes adults are also affected, as is evident in a neighbor's characterization of A. W.

> A. W. *used* to be arrogant. He was strong and he thought he could beat up all the men of his district. . . . *Now* A. W. is very respectful. His wife put the medicine of love magic called "gluing" on him.

It is also assumed that certain individuals may feign (*mwaaken*) positive character they do not truly possess.

These assumptions are important for the con-duct of social interactions; they are also important for the appraisal of personal identity. They mean that the character of others cannot be taken for granted; rather, character is something which has to be carefully monitored. One must be ready to radically reassess the character of another person, either because the apparent character was fraud-ulent or because the individual has, in fact, changed. As Gladwin and Sarason indicate (1953, p. 149), the people of Truk are quite ready to re-vise their opinions of others, even those with whom they are closely related.

When directly asked about the meaning of their character terms, the people of Fáánakkar readily offer brief definitions. "A person of respectfulness," it may be said, "has sympathy for other people" or "truly understands etiquette." "True bravery," they say, "does not mean looking for fights, it does not mean being arrogant and starting fights, it means being respectful until someone wants a fight." A person of "strong thought" is one who "thinks in terms of the three stones, to envy, to equal, and to surpass," and so forth. While such definitions are crucial in getting a feel for the orientation of this framework of personality evaluation, they are rough, rule of thumb generalizations about the thought and behavior of people with given character attributes. As such they do not fully encompass the meaning of these personality terms because they do not provide the information necessary to determine when a particular person will be judged by the people of Fáánakkar to have the qualities to which the character terms refer. This is a problem for the understanding of any system of personal identity including that of American culture.

The meanings of personality terms are much less obvious than is often assumed—as suggested by the fact that neither our folk nor dictionary definitions specify criteria which would allow an outsider to make culturally appropriate character assessments in American society. As Williams (1968) points out, "unless we know what behavior qualifies as honest in various circumstances we have no real guide to particular conduct; we know only that something called 'honesty' is regarded as a desirable thing" (pp. 284–285).

* * *

While the general meaning of character terms is partially revealed in the definitions offered by the people of Fáánakkar, and while their character terms can be roughly glossed with English personality terms, neither of these strategies effectively specifies the meaning of Fáánakkar character terms. This is because neither provides the information necessary to determine when a particular person will be judged by the people of Fáánakkar to have a given character quality.

In the Fáánakkar theory of the self, as in most anthropological approaches, personality is assumed to be intrapsychic, but this assumption ob-

scures the actual process of personality appraisal. In practice personality judgments depend on interpretations of observable behavior based on a systematic connection between personal identity and the rules of social identity relationships. The only way one can tell whether an individual "has" (i.e., has displayed) a given character quality—say, *namanam tekiya*—is by knowing the rights and duties governing the particular social identities the person is operating in. This means, first of all, that superficially similar English glosses cannot be treated as equivalent to the Trukese terms. It is not only that the two sets of terms are embedded in fundamentally different theories of the self, it is also that an act which is *namanam tekiya* in terms of Trukese culture may not be "arrogant" in terms of American culture. Even more important, an act which might be *namanam tekiya* in terms of the rules of one Fáánakkar social identity relationship may be *mosonoson* in another relationship, because the rules governing both substantive and ceremonial aspects of conduct vary significantly from one social relationship to another. Maps specifying the expectations and obligations of particular social identity relationships are not just guides to appropriate conduct; they also provide the frame of reference through which personality is defined and assessed.

* * * Because it is taken for granted that personal worth is measured by character, and because of various aspects of their enculturation, including inculcation and identification, people on Fáánakkar are deeply concerned about character appraisal. From the point of view of the individual actor, the positive terms represent ideal self-images and the negative terms represent feared self-images. In order to maintain their own self-esteem, in order to influence others to judge their character favorably, and in order to avoid the consequences that are expected to befall a person of negative character, people seek to play the rules of their social roles in ways which will allow them to achieve and maintain positive character. Concern with character often functions as a means of social control, but it does not always have this effect. Because "strong thought" and "bravery" are more important than "respectfulness," people sometimes violate the rules of their social identity relationships—as by stealing openly—in order to enhance their reputations. * * * It is necessary to understand how concern with character leads people sometimes to follow these rules and sometimes to break them. Here as elsewhere an understanding of social behavior on Fáánakkar demands attention to *personal* as well as social identity.

Anthropologists have frequently expressed dissatisfaction with culture and personality studies which employ Western psychological categories to appraise the modal personality and "explain" the social behavior of people in other societies. Such studies have been strongly criticized from a variety of different perspectives (cf. Shweder, 1979, p. 257). As Kiefer (1977, p. 106) observes, some writers have questioned the utility of "personality" as an explanatory concept, while others have predicted the demise of research in culture and personality. Ethnopsychological approaches offer a promising and relatively little explored alternative. By focusing on the conceptions of personal identity employed in the culture studied, by considering how the meanings of personality terms are connected to the rules of social identity relationships, and by examining how such terms come to represent positive and negative goals for the self, we can begin to formulate detailed ethnographic answers to questions about the relationships between the individual and culture which were fundamental to the development of culture and personality studies and which are basic to psychological anthropology generally (cf. Langness and Kennedy, 1979, p. 101; Bourguignon, 1973, p. 1109). That is, we can get at the motivations of individual actors and the ways in which these motivations influence the conduct of social relationships.

References

Bourguignon, E. (1973). Psychological anthropology. In J. Honigmann (Ed.), *Handbook of social and cultural anthropology.* Chicago: Rand McNally.

Caughey, J. L. (1977). *Fáánakkar: Cultural values in a micronesian society.* Philadelphia: University of Pennsylvania Publications in Anthropology, No. 2.

Gladwin, T., & Sarason, S. (1953). *Truk: Man in paradise.* New York: Wenner-Gren.

Goodenough, W. H. (1951). *Property, kin, and community on Truk.* New Haven: Yale University Publications in Anthropology, No. 46.

Goodenough, W. H. (1963). *Cooperation in change.* New York: Wiley.

Goodenough, W. H. (1965). Rethinking "status" and "role": Toward a general model of the cultural organization of social relationships. In M. Banton (Ed.), *The relevance of models for social anthropology.* London: Tavistock.

Goodenough, W. H. (1974). Changing social organization on Romónum, Truk, 1947–1965. In R. Smith (Ed.), *Social organization and the applications of anthropology.* New York: Harper & Row.

Kiefer, C. (1977). Psychological anthropology. In B.J Siegal, A. R. Beals, & S. A. Tyler (Eds.), *Annual review of anthropology.* Palo Alto, CA: Annual Reviews.

Langness, L. L., & Kennedy, J. G. (1979). Editorial. *Ethos, 7,* 95–103.

Robbins, R. (1973). Identity, culture, and behavior. In J. Honigmann (Ed.), *Handbook of social and cultural anthropology.* Chicago: Rand McNally.

Shweder, R. A. (1979). Rethinking culture and personality theory, Part I. *Ethos, 7,* 255–278.

Spradley, J., & Mann, B. (1975). *The cocktail waitress.* New York: Wiley.

Williams, R. M. (1968). The concept of values. In D. Sills (Ed.), *International encyclopedia of the social sciences* (Vol. 16). New York: Macmillan and the Free Press.

EXPLORING IMPLICIT PERSONALITY THEORIES WITH INDIGENOUS OR IMPORTED CONSTRUCTS: THE CHINESE CASE

Kuo-shu Yang and Michael Harris Bond

The next selection illustrates the way cross-cultural psychologists go about examining the terms used to describe personality in different cultures. Kuo-shu Yang, a psychologist based in Taiwan, and Michael Bond, a psychologist who has lived and worked for many years in Hong Kong, collaborate on a comparison of "indigenous" versus "imported" constructs to describe personality in a Chinese culture. To this end, they apply an arsenal of psychometric techniques. You will see that the methodological technique of Yang and Bond is very different from the more impressionist approach illustrated in the previous selection.

Yang and Bond begin with the observation that some cross-cultural research has made the mistake of beginning with Western or English terms, then assessing their applicability in other cultures. This approach reminds them of colonialism, in which an outside power imposes its view on a native culture. They argue that a preferable approach is to begin one's investigation within a culture, just as investigations of the Big Five began within English.

Yang and Bond began by culling 150 personality-trait adjectives from Chinese-language books and newspapers. They then had a sample of residents of Taiwan use these adjectives to describe six persons on a scale from 0 to 3. For purposes of comparison, they also had these same subjects use translations of 20 terms used, in English, to assess the Big Five.

Yang and Bond then did a factor analysis—a statistical technique for assessing correlations among variables and reducing many down to a few—of the Chinese adjectives and came up with five factors. They then correlated the "Chinese Big Five" with the English Big Five.

Perhaps inevitably, the conclusion they reached was less than crystal clear. There seems to be some overlap between the Chinese and English five factors, and some important differences. The lesson of this research, therefore, may be that to ask "are the five factors universal?" is to ask the wrong question. A better question is, what are the important terms for understanding personality within each of the major cultures of the world? Yang and Bond provide a good start toward the answer to this question for the Chinese culture of Taiwan.

From "Exploring Implicit Personality Theories with Indigenous or Imported Constructs: The Chinese Case," by K. Yang and M. H. Bond. In *Journal of Personality and Social Psychology*, *58*, 1087–1095. Copyright © 1990 by the American Psychological Association. Adapted with permission.

The semantic repertoire of a language has been treated as a repository for those constructs that its community of users has found useful in parceling their natural and human world (Dixon, 1977). For this reason, psychologists have often turned to the trait lexicon of a language in their search for the fundamental dimensions used by that language community in perceiving persons. As John, Goldberg, and Angleitner (1984) have argued,

> A taxonomy of these personality descriptors can provide us with a systematic account of how people who speak that language conceive of personality, especially which kinds of individual differences they regard as most important in their daily transactions. (p. 86)

The typical procedure involves a number of steps: First, a representative selection of the descriptors for personality functioning is taken; second, this subset is further refined to eliminate synonyms, and occasionally to group similar items into clusters; third, the resulting list is presented to speakers of that language to rate the applicability of each trait or trait scale to a target person, usually peers; and fourth, these ratings are intercorrelated across targets and dimensions of person perception are then extracted, usually by factor analysis (e.g., Goldberg, 1981).

In an earlier study, Tupes and Christal (1961) isolated five orthogonal factors used by Americans to perceive one another, namely, Surgency, Agreeableness, Conscientiousness, Emotional Stability, and Culture (also, see Norman, 1963). These five dimensions have also been unearthed by Goldberg (1981), using variations in procedure and subject populations. There is still considerable debate over the number and nature of such dimensions (Peabody & Goldberg, 1989), but for our purposes, it seemed safe to conclude that these Big Five dimensions of personality variation may represent the basic ways in which persons from the United States construct their interpersonal world (Digman & Takemoto-Chock, 1981), that is, one representation of the implicit personality theory of Americans.

How strongly may one claim that these five dimensions are universal or pancultural? To date, the descriptions used by Norman (1963) have been imported into three very different cultures, namely, those of the Philippines (Guthrie & Bennett, 1971), Japan (Bond, Nakazato, & Shiraishi, 1975), and Hong Kong (Bond, 1979). Broadly, the results may be synthesized to indicate that university students in all three societies use at least the first four of these dimensions and construe them in roughly similar ways.

The shortfall of this research approach, however, is that raters outside the United States have been invited to use personality descriptors taken from the English language and then interpreted by Americans. It has not yet been determined how dimensions derived by this use of the American materials might overlap with those derived from that culture's own language system. Do users of the Chinese language, for example, blend conscientiousness and agreeableness to form a broader dimension of social morality, as Yang and Bond (1985) asserted? Nor is it certain how successfully the imported American materials allow researchers to detect the full range of dimensions for perception available in the host culture's legacy of personality language. So, does the failure to detect a separable dimension of Culture in the Philippines

(Guthrie & Bennett, 1971) reflect its absence in Tagalog or merely the insensitivity of the American descriptors for this language community?

A small but growing number of studies have begun appearing that examine the dimensions of personality perception available to users of languages other than English (e.g., Brokken, 1978; Nakazato, Bond, & Shiraishi, 1976; Yang & Bond, 1985). In many cases the dimensions so elicited bear a striking resemblance to those originally found in the United States. So, for example, Brokken's Agreeableness appears to correspond with the American. In other cases, some interpretive leap to assert equivalence is made by psychologists fluent in both linguistic and cultural systems. So, for example, Yang and Bond maintained that their Extraversion corresponds with Norman's (1963) Extraversion. In yet other cases, dimensions emerge for which no clear parallel with the Big Five appears obvious. So, for example, Nakazato et al.'s Volition is difficult to relate to any of the American dimensions.

A more objective solution to this equivalence issue could be achieved by including the 20 bipolar descriptors[1] used by Norman (1963) along with the pool of descriptors gleaned from the indigenous language. The resulting pattern of intercorrelations would then indicate how the items defining the American Big Five align themselves with respect to native dimensions. One could determine, for example, whether the American clusters are divided or combined when associating with local factors, whether the American groupings define unique dimensions of perceptual space, and whether the indigenous language isolates novel factors immune to the American probes. Any of these results would have important implications for cross-cultural person perception, and hence interaction (Bond & Forgas, 1984).

The issue of importing measuring tools versus developing indigenous materials enjoys a classic status in cross-cultural psychology, where it is related to the emic-etic issue (Berry, 1969).[2] The law of least effort combined with psychology's origin in the West has meant that many cultures elsewhere have been studied through a foreign looking glass. Psychologists interested in a particular construct, say locus of control (Hui, 1982), translate the relevant test into the local language, administer it to comparable groups, and then make comparative statements about psychological process. Because this approach assumes the universal or etic status of the underlying construct and applies it in cultures where its status is uncertain, this approach to research has been labeled *imposed etic*.

This ubiquitous procedure has obvious parallels in the colonial experience that many of these now liberated countries have struggled to put behind them, and understandably draws considerable fire (see e.g., Yang, 1986). In the midst of these political and social debates, however, the scientific issue is easy to overlook, namely, are the imposed etics in fact tapping culture-general processes, as hoped, or pasting one culture's emic or particular processes over another's checkerboard of constructs, as feared? In the area of intelligence, for example, there is evidence of considerable construct equivalence from culture to culture (Vandenburg, 1959, 1967). With one or two exceptions, however, there is much less research on this problem in the area of social processes (Bond, 1988b; Triandis & Marin, 1983). This study enables the examination of this volatile issue in the area of person perception, because its design involves the rating of common target persons with both imported and indigenous constructs, using their attendant measurement scales.

In this case, we are examining the rich legacy of the Chinese language, as used by inhabitants of Taiwan. This would appear to be a useful group to compare with the American for a number of reasons. There is a substantial body of empirical

---

[1]This refers to pairs of opposite traits used in earlier research by Norman to measure the Big Five traits of personality. These included "talkative-silent," "adventurous-cautious," and others.

[2]The emic-etic issue refers to the distinction between aspects of thought that are universal, or "etic," versus those that are local, or "emic."

knowledge about the Chinese (Bond, 1986) to which the findings may be linked, and growing evidence that the Chinese will modernize in ways different from cultures in the West (Bond & King, 1985; Chinese Culture Connection, 1987; Yang, 1988). Furthermore, the Chinese are activated by collectivist concerns (Hsu, 1953). This cultural dimension of collectivism-individualism is receiving considerable theoretical (Triandis, 1988) and empirical (Triandis et al., 1986) attention these days, and may provide a fulcrum for prying the psychological mainstream loose from its Western center of gravity (Bond, 1988a). Results of the research linking Chinese and American dimensions of personality perception should thus command more than local interest.

Method

INSTRUMENTS In the present study, two major assessment instruments were used for data collection. The first had six versions specifically designed to use the same set of 150 personality-trait adjectives in the Chinese language to describe six different target persons significant in one's life. The 150 personality-trait adjectives used in each questionnaire were drawn from a pool of 557 Chinese personality-trait adjectives that had earlier been collected by Yang and Lee (1971) to form a compendium representative of the most widely used personality-descriptive predicates of the Chinese language. This breadth was ensured by selecting trait descriptors from a variety of printed media, including books and newspapers.

To choose the best adjectives for use in the present study, Yang and Lee's (1971) 557 entries were first classified into three groups:

1. Other-oriented adjectives, which describe personality traits that concern mainly behavior involving some other person or group; examples are *considerate, gregarious, obedient,* and *patriotic.*

2. Thing-oriented adjectives, which describe personality traits that concern mainly behavior involving some external thing or things; examples are *greedy, punctual, superstitious,* and *thrifty.*

3. Self-oriented adjectives, which describe personality traits that concern behavior that involves neither other persons nor groups, nor an external thing or things; examples are *changeable, clever, moody,* and *self-respectful.*

Adjectives in each of these three groups were further divided into three subgroups in terms of their average ratings on social desirability (SD) provided in Yang and Lee's list. Adjectives with an SD average greater than 5.28 (on a 7-step rating scale that ranged from 1 to 7) were considered positive, those with an SD value smaller than 2.87 were considered negative, and those with an SD value between these were considered neutral.

The semantic meanings of the adjectives in each of nine subgroups were carefully examined and compared, and those whose meanings were vague, ambiguous, or similar to some other adjective in the same subgroup were discarded. From the remaining pool, about one third of all adjectives were randomly chosen in proportion to the percentages of adjectives in the nine subgroups. The 150 adjectives so obtained were considered an unbiased sample representative of the most frequently used trait adjectives in the Chinese language. It is in this sense that such adjectives may be said to be emic or indigenous in nature.

Given that the adjectives were culled from newspapers, they represent Chinese written talk about personality. This written talk is identical to that used in other Chinese communities, however, as virtually the same written script is used in China and in Hong Kong, Singapore, and elsewhere.

The same 150 adjectives with a fixed randomized order were used to construct six separate versions for the assessment of the emic dimensions of Chinese person perception with respect to the six most familiar persons in one's life. Specifically, the same adjectives were used to describe the following six target persons in six different questionnaires: (a) your own father, (b) your own mother, (c) your best known teacher, (d) your most familiar neighbor, (e) your best friend of the same sex, and (f) yourself.

In each questionnaire the subject was supposed to use the adjectives to describe the specific target person on a four-step rating scale ranging from 0 to 3. He or she was required to indicate how much the target person possessed the personality trait described by each adjective: *definitely not at all* (0), *just a little* (1), *substantially* (2), or *very much* (3). To raise the validity of the subject's responses, the instructions in the questionnaire reminded the subject that he or she should describe the personality of the rated target person as objectively as possible without being influenced by his or her affect, no matter how strong it was toward that person, that he or she should do each rating as independently as possible without letting the rating of one trait be affected by that of the others, and that data collected from all subjects would be statistically analyzed on a group basis, rather than on an individual basis.

Another major assessment tool in this study was composed of the 20 bipolar rating scales drawn from Cattell's (1947) reduced personality sphere set on the basis of the results of several analyses presented by Tupes and Christal (1958). The four scales with the highest median factor loadings for each of the following five factors identified in these earlier analyses were chosen: Extraversion (or Surgency), Agreeableness, Conscientiousness, Emotional Stability, and Culture (see Norman, 1963).[3] The bipolar descriptions of the 20 personality traits were first translated into Chinese and then checked using the back-translation procedure (Brislin, 1970).[4] The 20 anchored rating scales in the final Chinese version were converted into a seven-step format with a labeled neutral point, rather than the original peer-nomination, forced-choice format used in the studies by Tupes and Christal (1958) and Nor-

man (1961, 1963). All 20 scales were printed in the same randomized order in the six different questionnaires for those six target persons. When applied to Chinese subjects, these translated scales would provide empirical measures of person perception that are obviously imposed etic in Berry's (1969) sense.

The inventory of adjectives and of bipolar descriptions for the same target person were put together in that order to form a questionnaire for that person. The six questionnaires so constructed were labeled Questionnaire A (*father*), B (*mother*), C (*teacher*), D (*neighbor*), E (*friend*), and F (*self*).

SUBJECTS Adequate comprehension of the exact meanings of the instructions, adjectives, and descriptions in each questionnaire requires a rather high level of Chinese literacy. For this reason, only university and college students were used as subjects. In total, more than 2,000 Chinese students were drawn from 60 different departments of seven universities and four colleges in northern Taiwan (mostly in Taipei). Each subject had to complete two of the six questionnaires as a set, and different students in each class received different sets of questionnaires according to a prearranged systematic order to ensure that the obtained samples would be sufficiently equivalent or comparable in their composition.

After eliminating those few subjects who were unable to complete their questionnaires, the following sizes of the samples for the various target persons were obtained, that is. Questionnaire A (*father*), 718; B (*mother*), 692; C (*teacher*), 636; D (*neighbor*), 633; E (*friend*), 670; and F (*self*), 668. In each of the six samples, approximately half of the subjects were male and half were female. Each sample was composed of more first- and second-year students than third- and fourth-year students.

PROCEDURE The six questionnaires were divided into three sets of two each, namely, *AD, BE,* and *CF.* About 800 copies of each set were printed and thoroughly mixed with copies of the other two sets. More than 2,000 copies of questionnaire sets were administered to the subjects on a group basis

---

[3]Yang and Bond have just described how they chose the 20 trait terms to serve, in translation, as measures of the Big Five for comparison purposes.

[4]Back-translation is a procedure for ensuring the accuracy of translation from one language to another. A translated word or phrase is translated back to its original language, and a native speaker of the original language compares the translation with the original.

TABLE 42.1

Most Salient Variables and Their Average Varimax Loadings on the Five Factors

Salient variable	Average loading	Salient variable	Average loading	Salient variable	Average loading	Salient variable	Average loading
Social Orientation–Self-Centeredness				**Expressiveness–Conservatism (continued)**			
Honest	.61	Untruthful	−.53	Straightforward	.43	Rigid	−.45
Good and gentle	.57	Selfish	−.50	Humorous	.43	Solemn	−.43
Loyal	.55	Opportunistic	−.49	Talkative	.43	Awkward	−.41
Cordial	.55	Sly	−.49	Mischievous	.41	Introverted	−.41
Kind	.54	Greedy	−.47	Optimistic	.39	Stubborn	−.35
Friendly	.48	Naughty	−.47	Broad-minded	.38	Indifferent	−.35
Frank	.48	Ruthless	−.45	Gracious	.37		
Morally clean	.47	Merciless	−.44	Generous	.36		
Responsible	.45	Hostile	−.44				
Gracious	.43	Harsh	−.44	**Self-Control–Impulsiveness**			
Competence–Impotence				Quiet and refined	.42	Impulsive	−.55
				Cultured	.41	Irritable	−.53
Determined	.46	Dependent	−.49	Modest	.40	Frivolous	−.42
Resolute and firm	.46	Fearful	−.48	Upright and correct	.38	Bad-tempered	−.42
Capable	.46	Timid	−.48	Self-possessed	.37	Headstrong	−.39
Tactful	.46	Childish	−.43	Steady	.36	Stubborn	−.38
Brave	.44	Foolish	−.41	Objective	.35	Opinionated	−.37
Smart	.43	Dull	−.40			Extreme	−.37
Rational	.43	Shallow	−.39				
Independent	.42	Vulgar	−.36	**Optimism–Neuroticism**			
Wise	.42	Shy	−.35				
Quick and sharp	.41	Self-disdainful	−.34	Optimistic	.47	Moody	−.67
Expressiveness–Conservatism				Pleasant	.38	Worrying	−.64
				Self-confident	.34	Pessimistic	−.55
Vivacious	.56	Old-fashioned	−.46			Anxious	−.50
Passionate	.47	Conservative	−.46			Sensitive	−.42
						Self-pitying	−.38

Note. Data is derived from the 150 adjective scales for the six target persons (i.e., father, mother, teacher, neighbor, friend, and self).

in their classrooms. Care was taken to make the final sample for each target person consist of students with approximately equal proportions by sex, from all four years, and from such major colleges as agriculture, engineering, law, liberal arts, medicine, science, and social sciences.

Each time the questionnaires were given to the subjects by one of the research assistants experienced in test administration, without the teacher's being present. Each subject was allowed to take as

much time as he or she needed to complete the anonymous questionnaire.

The final samples for the six target persons were composed of about four times as many respondents as the total number of variables (150 + 20 = 170). The dimensions of Chinese person perception were identified by separately factor analyzing the data collected by the adjective inventory and those collected by the bipolar descriptions, one pair of such analyses for each of the six target persons. The emic dimensions were then related to the imposed etic dimensions for the same target person by correlational analysis.

Results

EMIC DIMENSIONS

✷ ✷ ✷

✷ ✷ ✷ [For each of the six target persons,] a transformation procedure was adopted to standardize each subject's raw scores on the 150 adjective scales into *z* scores with the mean of the 150 raw scores as the origin and the standard deviation as the unit. We then carried out separate factor analyses for the six target persons, starting with correlational matrices computed from standardized scores. The principal-axis and varimax procedures were used as the methods for factoring and rotation, respectively, and the number of extracted factors was determined simultaneously by the scree test and the examination of the salient variables and their loadings obtained in several trial factor analyses.[5]

THE CHINESE BIG FIVE. For each target person, five–six bipolar[6] factors were finally identified to represent the emic dimensions of Chinese person perception. ✷ ✷ ✷ Although the number of factors extracted varied slightly, five were common to all the targets. The most salient variables, and their average loadings, for each of these five common factors are given in Table 42.1. The semantic meanings of the salient adjectives for the various factors justify the use of the following verbal titles for factor labeling: *Social Orientation–Self-Centeredness, Competence–Impotence, Expressiveness–Conservatism, Self-Control–Impulsiveness,* and *Optimism–Neuroticism.* These five bipolar factors

---

[5]This is a description of the standard technical procedure for deciding how many factors serve as an adequate summary of a longer list of adjectives.

[6]Factors each labeled by a pair of opposite terms.

may be regarded as the basic emic dimensions of Chinese person perception.[7]

✷ ✷ ✷

OVERLAP OF INDIGENOUS AND IMPORTED FACTORS Five-factor solutions have been proposed for both the indigenous and the imported descriptors of personality. In terms of the relation between these two sets of factors, a number of questions can be asked.

First, are there any indigenous factors that are not represented in the perceptual space defined by the imported factors? The answer to this question addresses the issue of whether imported instruments overlook dimensions that are used and tapped by local descriptors.

Second, for those indigenous factors that can be so defined, is there a one-to-one correspondence between an imported factor and an indigenous factor? The answer to this question addresses the issue of whether the imported instrument cuts the perceptual pie into the same segments as does the indigenous instrument.

Third, what is the overall degree of overlap between the indigenous set of personality trait dimensions and the imported set? This global question summarizes the preceding, more specific questions.

To address these three questions we computed approximate factor scores for each subject's rating of the six target persons, using the five indigenous and five imported dimensions. For the indigenous items, we calculated a factor score by summing the scores of the salient variables defining the factors as listed in Table 42.1; for the imported items, we calculated it by summing scores on bipolar descriptions with loadings greater than .50.

We computed an intercorrelation matrix of the indigenous and imported factor scores for each of the six targets. An average of these cor-

---

[7]The numbers in Table 42.1 can be interpreted as correlations between each term and the factor with which it is associated.

TABLE 42.2

AVERAGE CORRELATIONS BETWEEN THE EMIC AND IMPOSED ETIC FACTORS

Imposed etic factor	Emic factors				
	S-S	C-I	E-C	S-I	O-N
Extraversion	.21	.09	.51	.01	.16
Agreeableness	.66	.29	.30	.56	.14
Conscientiousness	.28	.31	−.09	.43	.01
Emotional Stability	.35	.55	.36	.43	.44
Culture	.29	.50	.37	.28	.11

Note. Data derived from the six target persons (i.e., father, mother, teacher, neighbor, friend, and self).
S-S = Social Orientation-Self-Centeredness, C-I = Competence-Importance,
E-C = Expressiveness-Conservatism, S-I = Self-Control-Impulsiveness,
O-N = Optimism-Neuroticism, respectively.

relations was then taken, based on their Z score transformations (see Table 42.2).[8]

* * *

Discussion

The purpose of this study was to examine the relation between indigenous and imported descriptors of personality. We argued that a fair examination of both emics and imposed etics would help address the tempestuous issue of cultural imperialism in psychology (Bond, 1988a, 1988b; Enriquez, 1988; Sampson, 1985; Yang, 1986). There are, of course, important personal, social, and political dimensions underlying this concern. The intellectual component of the con-

---

[8]Yang and Bond reported several other, more technical analyses that have been omitted from this excerpt. Their results are presented most clearly in Table 42.2. This table shows the correlations between the English Big Five, down the rows, and the Chinese Big Five, across the columns. The two schemes clearly overlap, and equally clearly are not perfectly equivalent.

cern, however, is that the importation of foreign instrumentation and theorizing results in an incomplete and distorted science. This study was conducted to provide some empirical ballast that is in short supply.

For the area of person perception, this debate can be focused on the concern about whether salient constructs in the local culture will be overlooked by the foreign scales, and how close the degree of overlap is, both overall and for specific dimensions.

To address these questions, Chinese personality descriptors were gathered in a manner that ensured that the resulting sample would be both comprehensive and representative of terms in use. Although a culling was not made from the dictionary, it is extremely unlikely that any personality dimension of importance has been neglected by sampling from newspapers. Indeed, the five factors extracted from the Chinese terms have a breadth and validity that [are] readily apparent to any Chinese psychologist. They constitute obvious starting points for anyone exploring the functional relations between these dimensions of personality perception and social behavior (e.g., Bond & Forgas, 1984) or personality itself (e.g., McCrae & Costa, 1987).

If only these indigenous materials had been used, many cross-culturalists would probably have detected some apparent universals. Optimism–Neuroticism would have been tied to Emotional Stability, Expressiveness to Extraversion, and so forth. Indeed, in our earlier report (Yang & Bond, 1985), we asserted that Social Orientation was a blend of Agreeableness and Conscientiousness. By actually including the original markers for these American dimensions, however, a more reliable and sobering pattern emerges.

So, Optimism does indeed relate to Emotional Stability, but Emotional Stability is in fact correlated more highly with Competence. Expressiveness does indeed relate to Extraversion, but it is also significantly related to Culture and Emotional Stability and is negatively related to Conscientiousness. Social Orientation does indeed relate strongly to Agreeableness, but its connection to Conscientiousness is dramatically smaller. In fact, the addition of the other four imported factors to Agreeableness only increased the variance explained in Social Orientation by 3.4%, from 43.6% to 47.0%.

Overall, the imported dimensions do a reasonable job of identifying four of the five indigenous factors. There is, however, a one-to-one correspondence for only one of these four factors. Even there, only 43.6% of the variance was shared. Of course, reliability issues may lower the estimate of overlap, but one could well ask if construct identity has been established; even in this one case it is unlikely that Social Orientation and Agreeableness ratings would bear the same relation to other criterion variables (as, for example, in Bond & Forgas, 1984). McCrae and Costa (1987) have argued the case that Norman's Big Five represent fundamental dimensions of personality and are perceived because they map a reality inherent in other people. As such, these dimensions are in the targets and hence need to be assessed with some degree of accuracy for effective social functioning. This assessment will then be tied to various dimensions of interpersonal behavior. Consistent with this reasoning is Bond's (1983) study, animated by Gibson's (1979) dictum that "Perception is for doing" (p. 143).[9] Bond argued that each dimension of personality perception functioned to guide the perceiver's responses toward the target across the fundamental dimensions of interpersonal behavior (Triandis, 1978), reasoning that has been confirmed cross-culturally (Bond & Forgas, 1984). We hope that more research energy will be directed to this interpersonal aspect of the perception issue (Tagiuri, 1969).

Returning to this study, we must acknowledge an inevitable arbitrariness in our conclusions about overlap in the indigenous and imported measures. There is no scientific rule to help us answer the question of how much similarity is enough. The bottom line is variance explained and how much slippage one is willing to tolerate. Although we believe that indigenous instruments will evidence more powerful relation to criterion variables than will imports, this empirical issue has not been addressed in the present study. We hope that future research will grasp this fascinating nettle (e.g., Triandis & Marin, 1983).

Even if our confidence in local instruments is vindicated, they will only be relatively better than imports. There will always be an obvious trade-off, as considerable time and energy can be saved by importing instruments as compared with developing them locally. Many social scientists will sacrifice and have sacrificed the putative power of indigenous instruments for the convenience of using ready-made imports.

As we have discovered, however, the pattern of interrelations between imported and indigenous factors is complex. The construct validation of the imported and indigenous instruments is likely to yield somewhat different theories about the local reality (often construed as reality) even if they are both true (i.e., useful). And it is this broader area of indigenous theory development that the use of imported instruments may especially compromise.

References

Berry, J. W. (1969). On cross-cultural comparability. *International Journal of Psychology, 4,* 119–128.

Bond, M. H. (1979). Dimensions of personality used in perceiving peers: Cross-cultural comparisons of Hong Kong, Japanese, American, and Filipino university students. *International Journal of Psychology, 14,* 47–56.

Bond, M. H. (1983). Linking person perception dimensions to behavioral intention dimensions: The Chinese connection. *Journal of Cross-Cultural Psychology, 14,* 41–63.

Bond, M. H. (Ed.). (1986). *The psychology of the Chinese people.* Hong Kong: Oxford University Press.

Bond, M. H. (Ed.). (1988a). *The cross-cultural challenge to social psychology.* Newbury Park, CA: Sage.

Bond, M. H. (1988b). Finding universal dimensions of individual variation in multicultural studies of values: The Rokeach and Chinese value surveys. *Journal of Personality and Social Psychology, 55,* 1009–1015.

Bond, M. H., & Forgas, J. P. (1984). Linking person perception to behavioral intention across cultures. The role of cultural collectivism. *Journal of Cross-Cultural Psychology, 15,* 337–352.

---

[9]This is an oft-quoted maxim of the psychologist J. J. Gibson, who studied visual perception.

Bond, M. H., & King, A. Y. C. (1985). Coping with the threat of Westernization in Hong Kong. *International Journal of Intercultural Relations, 9*, 351–364.

Bond, M. H., Nakazato, H., & Shiraishi, D. (1975). Universality and distinctiveness in dimensions of Japanese person perception. *Journal of Cross-Cultural Psychology, 6*, 346–57.

Brislin, R. W. (1970). Back-translation for cross-cultural research. *Journal of Cross-Cultural Psychology, 1*, 185–216.

Brokken, F. B. (1978). *The language of personality.* Unpublished doctoral dissertation, University of Groningen, The Netherlands.

Cattell, R. B. (1947). Confirmation and clarification of primary personality traits. *Psychometrica, 42*, 402–421.

Chinese Culture Connection. (1987). Chinese values and the search for culture-free dimensions of culture. *Journal of Cross-Cultural Psychology, 18*, 143–164.

Digman, J. M., & Takemoto-Chock, N. K. (1981). Factors in the natural language of personality: Reanalysis, comparison and interpretation of six major studies. *Multivariate Behavioral Research, 16*, 149–170.

Dixon, R. M. W. (1977). Where have all the adjectives gone? *Studies in Language, 1*, 19–80.

Enriquez, V. (1988). The structure of Philippine social values: Towards integrating indigenous values and appropriate technology. In D. Sinha & H. S. R. Kao (Eds.), *Social values and development: Asian perspectives* (pp. 124–148). New Delhi, India: Sage.

Gibson, J. J. (1979). *The ecological approach to visual perception.* Boston: Houghton Mifflin.

Goldberg, L. R. (1981). Language and individual differences: The search for universals in personality lexicons. In L. Wheeler (Ed.), *Review of personality and social psychology* (Vol. 2, pp. 141–165). Beverly Hills, CA: Sage.

Guthrie, G. M., & Bennett, A. B. (1971). Cultural differences in implicit personality theory. *International Journal of Psychology, 6*, 305–312.

Hsu, F. L. K. (1953). *Americans and Chinese: Two ways of life.* New York: Abelard-Schuman.

Hui, C. C. H. (1982). Locus of control: A review of cross-cultural research. *International Journal of Intercultural Relations, 6*, 301–323.

John, O. P., Goldberg, L. R., & Angleitner, A. (1984). Better than the alphabet: Taxonomics of personality descriptive terms in English, Dutch, and German. In H. Bonarius, G. van Heck, & N. Smid (Eds.), *Personality psychology in Europe: Theoretical and empirical developments* (pp. 83–100). Lisse, The Netherlands: Swets & Zeitlinger.

McCrae, R. R., & Costa, P. T. Jr. (1987). Validation of the five-factor model of personality across instruments and observers. *Journal of Personality and Social Psychology, 52*, 81–90.

Nakazato, H., Bond, M. H., & Shiraishi, D. (1976). Dimensions of personality perception: An examination of Norman's hypothesis. *Japanese Journal of Psychology, 47*, 139–148. (In Japanese)

Norman, W. T. (1961). Development of self-report tests to measure personality factors identified from peer nominations (USAF ASD *Technical Note* No. 61-44).

Norman, W. T. (1963). Toward an adequate taxonomy of personality attributes: Replicated factor structure in peer nomination personality ratings. *Journal of Abnormal and Social Psychology, 66*, 574–583.

Peabody, D., & Goldberg, L. R. (1989). Some determinants of factor structures from personality-trait descriptors. *Journal of Personality and Social Psychology, 57*, 552–567.

Sampson, E. E. (1985). The decentralization of identity: Toward a revised concept of personal and social order. *American Psychologist, 40*, 1203–1211.

Tagiuri, R. (1969). Person perception. In G. Lindzey & E. Aronson (Eds.), *The handbook of social psychology* (2nd ed., Vol. 3, pp. 395–449). Reading, MA: Addison-Wesley.

Triandis, H. C. (1978). Some universals of social behavior. *Personality and Social Psychology Bulletin, 4*, 1–16.

Triandis, H. C., Bontempo, R., Betancourt, H., Bond, M. H., Leung, K., Brenes, A., Georgas, J., Hui, H. C., Marin, G., Setiadi, B., Sinha, J. B. P., Verma, J., Spangenberg, J., Touzard, H., & de Montmollin, G. (1986). The measurement of the etic aspects of individualism and collectivism across cultures. *Australian Journal of Psychology, 38*, 257–267.

Triandis, H. C., & Marin, G. (1983). Etic plus emic versus pseudo etic: A test of a basic assumption of contemporary cross-cultural psychology. *Journal of Cross-Cultural Psychology, 14*, 489–499.

Tupes, E. C., & Christal, R. E. (1958). Stability of personality trait rating factors obtained under diverse conditions (USAF WADC *Technical Note* No. 58-61).

Tupes, E. C., & Christal, R. E. (1961). Recurrent personality factors based on trait ratings. (USAF ASD *Technical Report* No. 61-97).

Vandenberg, S. G. (1959). The primary mental abilities of Chinese students: A comparative study of the stability of a factor structure. *Annals of the New York Academy of Sciences, 79*, 257–304.

Vandenberg, S. G. (1967). The primary mental abilities of South American students: A second comparative study of the generality of a cognitive factor structure. *Multivariate Behavioral Research, 2*, 175–198.

Yang, K. S. (1986). Chinese personality and its change. In M. H. Bond (Ed.), *The psychology of the Chinese people* (pp. 106–170). Hong Kong: Oxford University Press.

Yang, K. S. (1988). Will societal modernization eventually eliminate cross-cultural psychological differences? In M. H. Bond (Ed.), *The cross-cultural challenge to social psychology* (pp. 67–85). Newbury Park, CA: Sage.

Yang, K. S., & Bond, M. H. (1985). Dimensions of Chinese person perception: An emic approach. In C. Chiao (Ed.), *Proceedings of the conference on modernization and Chinese culture* (pp. 309–325). Hong Kong: Institute of Social Studies, Chinese University of Hong Kong. (In Chinese)

Yang, K. S., & Lee, P. H. (1971). Likeability, meaningfulness, and familiarity of 557 Chinese adjectives for personality trait description. *Acta Psychologica Taiwanica, 13*, 36–37. (In Chinese)

Rediscovery of the Subject: Intercultural Approaches to Clinical Assessment

Enrico E. Jones and Avril Thorne

*Human cultures vary not just across international boundaries, but within them.
The United States, for example, contains within it large and vibrant cultures
with roots that extend back to Europe, Africa, Asia, and Latin America.
Many of the same issues involved in comparing one culture to another
apply with equal urgency to the comparison between subcultures such as these.
A mistake often made in this context, argue the authors of the next selection, is
to view members of minority cultures as deficient or even damaged in comparison to members of the majority culture. This mistake stems from the habit of
judging subcultures in terms applicable to and dictated by the dominant culture
and the attendant failure to understand minority cultures in their own
terms.*

*The authors of the next selection are the clinical psychologist Enrico Jones
and the personality psychologist Avril Thorne. They review some of the motivations and techniques for, and difficulties of, developing a psychology that is relevant to members of different cultures. They point out that the same issues arise
whether one is comparing two cultures that are physically located on different
continents or within the same city. The central issue, they argue, is the phenomenological one raised by the humanists in the preceding section: Does our psychology sufficiently comprehend and appreciate the different ways in which
different people experience reality?*

*Jones and Thorne argue that it is insufficient simply to adjust standard per-
sonality tests for different cultures, or to make the kind of comparison performed
by Yang and Bond in the preceding selection, because both methods fail to "reflect the dynamic, changing nature of our social world." They also object to the
development of new measures specific to particular cultures because this practice
treats all members of a single culture as equivalent and seems to wall off cultures from each other. Their prescription is for a more subjective method, in
which the researcher and the subject join into a mutual quest for understanding,*

393

and the result is a narrative account that eschews most of the usual conventions of scientific presentation.

This is a radical prescription, one that most psychologists have yet to endorse and that places Jones and Thorne squarely within the humanist and phenomenological tradition. Jones and Thorne know well the research practices that they criticize here. Their viewpoint is worth taking seriously as a clear discussion of just how difficult it is for members of one culture to understand another. The problem, Jones and Thorne suggest, stems from—and is not really different from —the fundamental difficulty that always arises when one individual tries to understand another.

In recent years, the many problems attendant to the psychological assessment of cultural and ethnic minority groups have been widely acknowledged (Butcher, 1982; E. E. Jones & Korchin, 1982). For a number of decades, psychology and the social sciences in general have labored within the confines of the assumption that ethnic minorities are frequently deficient in important ways. The 'deficit hypothesis' (Katz, 1974), briefly stated, posits that minority communities have historically experienced isolation and continued economic and cultural deprivation and that impoverishment, powerlessness, and disorganization find expression in psychological deficits in such realms as intellectual performance (Guthrie, 1976; Kamin, 1974), personality functioning (Proshansky & Newton, 1974), and mental health (Baughman & Dahlstrom, 1972; Kardiner & Ovesey, 1951). Deficit conceptions of the psychological and social functioning of cultural minorities arose in part from a "psychology of race differences" tradition. Studies in this tradition typically compared minority and majority groups on measures standardized on White samples. Cultural, linguistic, and social-status differences were typically minimized or overlooked, and in these and other ways the psychological import of obtained differences was obscured.

By now, of course, serious questions have been raised concerning the methodological adequacy of ethnic and multicultural research in the United States (Cole & Bruner, 1971; Gynther, 1972). An important step forward occurred when traditional research strategies and assessment techniques began to be seriously applied cross-culturally. The obvious linguistic and cultural differences between researchers, their assessment methods, and indigenous target populations evoked an appreciation for context and for local meanings that had been missing from efforts at studying minority groups within our society. There has been a growing awareness that ethnic minorities, although physically proximate to the majority culture, cannot be readily or effectively compared with dominant culture group members on conventional assessment measures. Increasingly, inquiry into the psychological functioning of minority group members has been recast in a cross-cultural paradigm that is sensitive to the cultural loading in our measures and to problems in the interpretation of information derived from such assessment methods.

A pivotal issue for intercultural assessment is construct definition (Irvine & Carroll, 1980), that is, what it is that our procedures and measures actually allow us to know and understand. A case in point is the study of personality in Black populations, an important focus of which has been the construct *self-concept.* Inquiry about Black self-concept has centered on the notion of White preference, the hypothesis being that especially Black children reject themselves and express self-identification and evaluative preference for physical characteristics (represented by dolls, puppets, drawings, or photographs) that are not Black. This research was initially undertaken to substantiate the deleterious effect of school segregation among Black children (Clark & Clark, 1950), but it has subsequently been impugned by minority social scientists as a damaging example of the deficit hypothesis. The construct validity of the White-preference paradigm and the assumptions underlying it were subjected to an important critique by Banks (1982), who argued that preference for dominant culture artifacts among some Black children has not been convincingly linked to a tendency toward self-rejection and low self-esteem. This view has recently been supported by McAdoo's (1985) work demonstrating that measures of racial attitude are unrelated to Black children's self-concept and that, among many Black youth, an out-group orientation is directly related not to self-hatred but to positive self-concept. It is quite possible that in a multicultural society such as ours, a too exclusive own-group preference among minorities may reflect a defensive use of ethnic identity[1] (DeVos, 1982).

Another instructive example is the construct, Internal-External Locus of Control, (I-E scale; Rotter, 1966), which measures the extent to which people report they exercise control over their lives and destinies. The I-E scale has become a frequently used measure in studies of minority populations and of gender differences as well as in cross-cultural investigations. The scale is popular in this kind of research because the control construct intersects social, clinical, and political realms with its relevance to such experiences as social alienation, feelings of powerlessness, lack of personal control, and desire for self-determination. Cross-cultural studies have found differences among samples from a variety of nations and cultures. The most consistent findings have shown a higher degree of externality among women than among men and among people from developing nations than those from industrialized societies (McGinnies, Nordholm, Ward, & Bhanthumnavin, 1974; Nagelschmidt & Jakob, 1977). However, important inconsistencies have also emerged. Several studies of United States Blacks, for example, found that young, non-college-educated, lower-class samples tended to score more externally than White samples (Battle & Rotter, 1963; Lefcourt, 1965). The meaning of this difference was called into question by Gurin, Gurin, Lao, and Beattie's (1969) study of Black college students. Contrary to what might be predicted on the basis of Rotter's theory, it was discovered that Blacks who were willing to participate in social protest action obtained low scores on internal control, suggesting that external scorers believed they could influence their destinies.

Factor analytic studies, considered an important means for establishing a measure's validity, have also raised serious questions about the meaning of the I-E scale in different populations. Studies of I-E scale item responses among Brazilians, Jamaicans, United States Blacks, and women (E. E. Jones & Zoppel, 1979; Nagelschmidt & Jakob, 1977; Sanger & Alker, 1972) have not supported Rotter's (1975) claim that the scale is unidimensional; instead they have suggested that attitude structures in these groups vary and that the comparison of summary I-E scale scores across samples is consequently inappropriate. This tendency for the factor structure of the I-E scale to differ as a function of the population under study leaves few researchers at ease when confronted with the problem of understanding the meaning and implications of differences across population groups. The use of the locus of control construct cross-culturally or with minority groups may constitute an *imposed etic* (Berry, 1969), a culture-specific schema erroneously presumed to be universal in nature.[2]

---

[1] A use of identity to distort reality so as to protect one's self-esteem.

[2] Recall the use of the term "imposed etic" in the selection by Yang and Bond. A "schema" is an idea or construct.

New Norms for Minority Groups?

The pitfalls in intercultural assessment are also illustrated in the evaluation of psychological dysfunction, especially as measured through inventory-type indices.[3] Minority status or ethnicity as an important source of variance on such assessment instruments has been well-documented, especially in relation to the Minnesota Multiphasic Personality Inventory[4] (MMPI; E. E. Jones, 1978). Subgroup differences on the MMPI were, until relatively recently, construed as demonstrating lower levels of personal adjustments among Blacks, or Chicanos, or Native Americans (e.g., Baughman & Dahlstrom, 1972). Gynther's (1972) comprehensive review and reinterpretation of such data suggests a number of alternate explanations to the old deficit hypothesis, primary among them being the impact of cultural differences on values, perceptions, and expectations. Although Blacks and other United States minorities, for example, tend to score quite a bit higher on the MMPI Schizophrenia (Sc) scale, recent cross-cultural work has demonstrated that subjects from countries ranging from Israel to Japan have similarly elevated Sc scale scores (Butcher & Pancheri, 1976).

Fairly extensive cross-national and cross-cultural work has been conducted with the MMPI. Butcher and Pancheri (1976) argued for the cross-language generality and comparability of the MMPI factor structure. It appears that conventional inventory-type measures can be adapted to different cultural groups if careful work is carried out to determine such matters as equivalence of factor structures and intercultural generality of test constructs, and if renorming[5] and validation studies are conducted. There is also some evidence that

the diagnostic classification system, from which the MMPI scales are derived, is applicable cross-culturally (Dohrenwend & Dohrenwend, 1974), although this remains a controversial topic. Because new norms are being developed for the MMPI in several nations, the call for renorming the instrument for United States ethnic groups (e.g., Gynther, 1972) appears to be a natural application of an increasingly accepted cross-cultural framework for psychological inquiry.

Still, the problems in adapting such measures for minority groups are far from being thoroughly worked out, and it is difficult to imagine that they ever entirely will be. One persistent problem is the percentage of items endorsed[6] differently by ethnic and dominant culture groups. Studies have consistently shown that the endorsement rate for MMPI items among, for example, Black and White subjects is different for a very high percentage (40%–80%) of items and that the content of these items suggests that they are culturally sensitive (E. E. Jones, 1978). Indeed, there is evidence that the well-known MMPI scale score differences between Blacks and Whites would be even greater if it were not for a cancelling-out process within scales. The effect of item-endorsement differences of such magnitude remains a serious problem for the validity of traditional clinical interpretations.

It may be more difficult to adapt conventional standardized measures to United States ethnic minority populations than to foreign populations contained within national boundaries because minority groups can be extraordinarily heterogeneous, and they reside within an ever-changing sociocultural context. Renorming the MMPI for Blacks would require, at the very least, an adequate sampling of regional differences (e.g., north vs. south, urban vs. rural). But would the new norms be valid for distinct subgroups, such as Jamaican and Haitian immigrants? The problem is an even larger one for Hispanics, who include sizable populations of Puerto Ricans and Cubans as

---

[3]Such as self-report personality tests.

[4]The most widely used personality test in the world, the MMPI was developed to measure several categories of psychopathology.

[5]Adjusting for the different means and variabilities of different groups.

[6]Answered in the direction (true or false) that indicates the subject has the trait being measured.

well as Mexican Americans and Central Americans. Although some Hispanics are recent arrivals, many have resided in the United States for generations, and there are important differences in language use, culture, and ethnic identity among the various groups (Muñoz, 1982). Should such variation be recognized, we would be confronted with an array of new norms for many different population subgroups and with a growing proliferation of a psychotechnology that places us at an ever increasing distance from the subject of our inquiry.

It is true that the construction of new norms acknowledges the pluralistic nature of our society. However, it also reflects a kind of static view of society and rests on the assumption that ethnic communities maintain their culture in a stable, enduring fashion. It fails to consider important processes of acculturation or, as some prefer, cultural interpenetration; nor does it reflect the dynamic, changing nature of our social world in whose continuing evolution minority groups play an important role. Individuals are considered only as members of a category, and the extent to which they share the values and perceptions of their particular ethnic group is obscured. Such a strategy must ultimately run afoul of an important egalitarian ethos in American society that views formal recognition of questionable distinctions among individuals with distaste.

Culture-Specific Measures: Remedy or Ideological Reaction?

Another proposal for remedying the problems of assessment of cultural minorities goes beyond establishing different norms and instead advocates the construction of entirely new, culture-specific measures. This solution foregoes intercultural assessments entirely and, indeed, challenges the soundness of applying any assessment procedure in culture comparisons. A recent volume (R. L. Jones, 1996), for example, provided tests and measures expressly developed for Black popula-

tions. Instruments included personality assessment questionnaires, self-esteem scales, and ethnic identity measures. The rationale behind the construction of these new, culture-specific instruments is that they more accurately reflect minority experiences, values, and personality characteristics than do conventional measures. Such instruments are still in nascent form and, admittedly, require a great deal more work to establish their validity and utility.

There is a question, though, whether these culture-specific instruments are truly useful remedies to the problem of etic instruments or whether they are primarily products of an ideology. There has been a tendency among minority social scientists to emphasize the differences, cultural and otherwise, between the majority group and ethnic minorities. Their motives have been influenced, at least in part, by social movements of recent decades that have had as important themes ethnic identity and pride and a renewed interest in cultural and historical roots. Minority researchers have often been at the forefront in recognizing the importance of cultural diversity for psychological inquiry and of challenging the inequity associated with the deficit hypothesis. A parallel development has occurred among some feminist scholars, who emphasize differences between the male-dominated culture and women's culture.

Such thinking, motivated by concern for social justice and human equality, has contributed to an appreciation of the cultural pluralism of our society and has defined the ways in which psychological theories and procedures can contribute to the maintenance of an inequitable status quo. The question remains, however, whether ethnic-specific measures enlarge our understanding of personality functioning and psychopathology. Communities of scholars will find it difficult to develop comprehensive understandings if assessment procedures are highly specialized and are not comparable across samples and if they obstruct communication and inquiry across cultural boundaries.

In some ways, these culture-specific methods seem to repeat the problems of the conventional measures they will presumably supplant. To date, such measures have considered a given ethnic group as homogeneous, without consideration of geographic, religious, generational or social-status differences. There are undeniably common qualities in the experience of ethnicity: certain mutually shared experiences that are the result of more-or-less shared culture and like conditions. However, there are also important differences within ethnicity, and for that matter, within gender. Such differences have perhaps more often been recognized by feminist scholars than by minority researchers. Feminist scholars, for example, have called for a more refined understanding of women of color and women of working class background, whose experiences are not well represented in prevailing psychological theories (Eisenstein, 1983). What all members of a minority group share and what is likely to be different (and in what degree) remains largely unspecified; within-group variability[7] is enormous.

There has been a longstanding debate about whether ethnic groups in the United States have separate and distinct cultures. The case for Spanish-speaking and Asian Americans is, at least for the more recently arrived, readily made, although the argument for distinct cultural elements among Black Americans has also been advanced (DuBois, 1908; Herskovitz, 1958; Price-Williams, 1975). The question of whether or not minorities have distinct cultures can in part be addressed through the notion of *subjective culture* (Osgood, 1965; Triandis, 1972). Subjective culture is a group's characteristic way of perceiving its social environment. People who live near one another, speak the same dialect, and engage in similar activities are likely to share the same subjective culture. Particularly relevant to the discussion here is that the assumption of heterogeneity (what is similar and what is different) is essential even to the concept of subjective culture.

An instructive example of inattention to in-group variability by those who are keen on culture-specific instruments is the disregard of education or socioeconomic status as an important mediator of cultural experience. Any analysis of ethnic culture must, in fact, address socioeconomics because it is not always clear whether the characteristics presumed to be distinctive are attributable to cultural differences or to social status and educational level. Although some ethnic characteristics may persist as minority group members advance educationally and economically, others may not. It is likely that standard assessment instruments are more valid for minorities who have achieved middle-class status than for those who are working class or poor (E. E. Jones & Zoppel, 1979), and one wonders whether those researchers who advocate culture-specific instruments are actually referring to the latter subgroup, significant as it may be within the minority population. Education is closely associated with acculturation processes, and the concern in many minority communities that school curricula include ethnic history or related topics can be understood in this light. It is clear that some of the same problems attending the creation of new norms for ethnic groups on conventional measures—group heterogeneity and acculturation—also apply to the construction of culture-specific assessment procedures.

We must seriously question whether culture-specific methods really provide an answer to the problems of psychological inquiry with ethnic minority populations in a society as diverse as our own, where cultures transform one another and where minority individuals often aspire strongly to educational and economic advancement and not infrequently reside long distances from their communities of origin. With the exclusionary note they strike, such methods reflect in part an attempt to assert the existence of ethnic culture, which is sometimes perceived as in danger of being devitalized, and reflect in part an expression of a need among minority group individuals to maintain a distinctive identity.

---

[7]The differences between members of the same group.

Primacy of the Subjective in Clinical Assessment

The problems of intercultural and multiethnic assessment and research readily direct attention to a larger problem concerning the nature of psychological and social inquiry itself. Traditional positivist and empiricist methods of inquiry have been targets of a growing crescendo of criticism, with chords struck by interpretive or hermeneutic approaches (Packer, 1985; Rabinow & Sullivan, 1979), feminist commentary on science (Keller, 1985; Vickers, 1982), and social constructionist perspectives (Gergen, 1985). Although these critical analyses differ in interesting ways among themselves, they have joined with longstanding phenomenological critiques of research methods in psychology[8] (Giorgi, 1976; Valle & King, 1978).

These various perspectives challenge the often-held view that scientific theory and empirical method serve to reflect or map reality in a direct and transparent manner. The interpretive critique, for example, posits that the web of meaning that constitutes human existence cannot be meaningfully or accurately reduced to narrow categories such as "behaviors" or "acts" or, for that matter, personality test scores. This approach recognizes that issues of understanding and interpretation arise in the very construction of categories and in the identification of data (Packer, 1985). Not incidentally, those who attempt to apply psychological methods interculturally have long grappled with these very concerns.

Traditional assessment relies on documenting the co-occurrences of observables. In contrast, the interpretive approach attempts to elucidate and make explicit understandings of observed actions. The approach uses a detailed, progressive description of episodes of social interchange and gradually articulates more of their organization. Accounts are given by both the subject and the observer of events and actions, principally in a narrative, natural language form. Especially rele-

vant to intercultural assessment, interpretations are rendered in the context of the historical and cultural situation under study. The co-occurrences that are often presumed to be universal in traditional research are viewed as being more temporary, situated in the vicissitudes of particular social processes. Constructionism's affinity with hermeneutic approaches is clear in its concern with elaborating human system meanings. Of particular importance for the present discussion is the considerable ethnomethodological work that has been carried out from this perspective, especially the emphasis on methods used by persons in various cultures to render the world sensible (Geertz, 1979).

Many contemporary social scientists have not found the empiricist orientation a congenial perspective because it advocates manipulation of, and removal from, the persons one wishes to understand. Indeed, both minority (E. E. Jones & Korchin, 1982) and feminist (e.g., Wittig, 1985) investigators have struggled with the tension between scholarly inquiry and advocacy and with the tension between scientific and humanistic values in the choice of methods and procedures. Feminists have searched for alternative methods of inquiry and have occasionally noted the extent to which other perspectives share their concern for more contextualized and intersubjectively valid processes of interpretation (Vickers, 1982). Minority scholars, on their part, have largely overlooked the interpretive, constructionist alternative and have instead either confined themselves to all-out attacks on conventional methods (c.f. Banks's, 1982, "deconstructive falsification") or have attempted to develop ever more careful, and questionable, culture-specific refinements and adaptations of existing empirical methods (see R. L. Jones, 1996). This is an unfortunate oversight because constructionism invites the view that prevailing categories of understanding are historically and culturally situated and are therefore subject to critique and transformation. In contrast with the claimed moral neutrality of the empiricist tradition, constructionism is sensitive to moral criteria for scientific practice. Gergen (1985), for example,

---

[8]Critiques that claim the usual methods of psychology fail to tap into the subject's experience of reality.

argued that the extent to which psychological theory and practice enter into the life of a culture to sustain certain patterns of conduct and alter others, it must be evaluated in terms of its social benefits: "The practitioner can no longer justify a socially reprehensible conclusion on the ground of being a victim of facts; the pragmatic implications of such a conclusion within society must be confronted" (p. 273). It is this kind of ethically accountable vision of psychological research and practice that many in our field have sought.

The phenomenological tradition within psychology shares with the relatively more recent interpretive, feminist, and constructionist perspectives a critique of experimentation and of its deemphasis of the subject's experience (Colaizzi, 1978). The focus of the phenomenological perspective is the subject's apprehension and understanding of his or her own world. Phenomena and situations are defined principally by the subject rather than by the investigator. The emphasis is on describing a phenomenon rather than imposing what we presume to know about it; in the language of cross-cultural psychology, this is akin to emic exploration. The investigator not only obtains information about the subject's understanding of the objective situation but also, and more important, obtains a shared experience to which the subjects of the study have contributed as communication partners (Giorgi, 1976).

Few would argue with the proposition that clinical assessment must in some way be oriented toward understanding the understandings of individuals: how they construe their experiences, their predicaments, their lives. All theoretical frameworks concede that one cannot adequately comprehend psychological disturbances through exclusive reliance on procedures that remain outside the disturbance as it is lived and experienced. Psychological problems cannot be studied, let alone treated, without a fundamental respect for the person and without a constant effort to grasp the experience of the person. This is true even for medically oriented approaches, despite their emphasis on diagnostic signs and symptomology. Behavioral approaches, especially the newer

cognitive-behavioral treatments, have increasingly emphasized the importance of the inner thought processes of the subject. Psychodynamically oriented practitioners have traditionally underscored the importance of personal interviews to provide background data that will contextualize and personalize the results of other, often more structured, tests and procedures. Although clinical assessment must somehow be grounded in experience and introspection, subjective experience is often deemphasized in contemporary procedures. And although neglect of personal meanings is pervasive in much standardized assessment, the problem is even more critical in intercultural assessment. Especially here there is a need to move beyond form, for example, diagnostic category or scale score, and to reemphasize underlying meaning.

Subject as Collaborator: Narrative Accounts

Interpretive, constructionist, and experiential methods all favor obtaining some form of introspective, narrative account from the subject. In particular, they emphasize the elaboration of meaning through joint inquiry with the subject. The inquiry is open-ended and reflective and has the quality of critical dialogue (Von Eckartsberg, 1971). An example is Levinson's (1978) biographical interviewing method, which aimed to reconstruct an individual's life story. The biographical interview combined aspects of the research interview, the clinical interview, and a conversation between acquaintances. As a research interview, certain topics had to be covered; however, the interviewer was also sensitive to the feelings expressed by the subject and followed themes through diverse topics. As a conversation between acquaintances, the relationship was egalitarian, and the interviewer could respond with his or her personal experiences. The result was not "simply an interviewing technique or procedure, but a relationship of some intimacy, intensity, and duration; significant work [was] involved in forming and maintaining and terminating the relationship" (Levinson, 1978, p. 15). Oakley's (1981) discussion of her interviews with pregnant women provided another example. Whereas traditional textbook formulas for interviewing define the interview situation as a one-way process in which the interviewer asks questions and the respondent provides answers, Oakley revealed the poverty of this framework through a study of the questions that respondents asked back. These questions signified a good deal about important concerns of the respondents, including their unanticipated need for medical information and psychological support. This kind of assessment approach construes the investigative encounter as an unfolding relationship, in process rather than static. Its effectiveness relies in large part on the capacity of the examiner to ask discerning questions, to interpret responses skillfully, and to perspicaciously decide which responses should be further pursued. Its success also depends in part on the capacity of the subject, with the help of the interviewer, to begin to elaborate or articulate what is meant by a particular response.

The more psychometrically oriented investigator or clinician might ponder how such concepts as test validity and reliability, which have long anchored traditional assessment techniques, are to be considered within approaches that view the subject as collaborator. Validity (in the sense of how we know we are identifying and assessing that which we wish) and reliability (the extent of unsystematic variation of a subject's responses or scores from one assessment occasion to another) have, at least in their technical meaning, a more direct reference to empirical models. These models are formal, quantitatively oriented systems of description and explanation that use categorization and operations by which categories are established and related to one another (as with personality inventories). They make use of procedures to assure a verifiable reference and are regulated by requirements of consistency (e.g., test reliability) and noncontradiction. As we have already discussed briefly (see Bruner, 1986, for a more complete statement of this important topic), con-

structivism, and related work in theories of meaning, has shifted the focus in our scientific dialogue away from the products of scientific inquiry toward the processes of inquiry themselves. Social science, especially, has begun to move away from the traditional positivist stance toward a more interpretive stance in which meaning becomes the central focus (e.g., how speech is interpreted and by what codes meaning is regulated; Bruner, 1986). The emphasis in narrative accounts, then, is not on procedures for establishing formal and empirical proof but on verisimilitude (or face validity). The narrative method attempts to achieve believable accounts that involve action, intention, and goals. Language is viewed as an expression of culture, and narratives are conceptualized as constituting a psychological and cultural reality that is alive. We should not lose sight of the fact that it is precisely a deep disquiet about the validity (in the broad sense) of conventional assessment methods cross-culturally that has led to efforts at developing alternative procedures.

*   *   *

Conclusion

Many problems of clinical assessment and research with cultural and ethnic minorities stem from the tendency of psychologists and others interested in social inquiry to presume that a priori hypotheses and standard measures adequately map the experience, reality, and meanings of a particular people. Proposed alternatives to conventional assessment procedures—renorming standard measures or constructing entirely new, culture-specific instruments—attempt to move closer to particular populations. Such approaches, however, do not focally address one of the most difficult and persistent problems in intercultural assessment: how to ensure that assessment techniques adequately reflect the experience of a cultural group and at the same time facilitate the cross-communication of findings to other groups. The collaborative and flexible nature of narrative accounts promotes ecologically valid interpretations and invites attempts to replicate and verify findings with other populations. The collection of accounts furthers an appreciation of the understandings subjects of cultural minority groups have about their behavior and their world. As a method, it encourages a suspension of skepticism about subjects' willingness to communicate their experience. A genuine interest in the individual is a precondition for the successful use of this collaborative method, as is the establishment of trust and rapport. By failing to include the subject's viewpoint in various aspects of assessment and psychological inquiry, we have often obscured the meaning of our findings and have promoted the attitude that cultural differences are boundaries to be crossed rather than relationships to be entered into.

References

Banks, W. C. (1982). Deconstructive falsification: Foundations of a critical method in Black psychology. In E. E. Jones & S. J. Korchin (Eds.), *Minority mental health* (pp. 59–73). New York: Praeger.

Battle, E., & Rotter, J. (1963). Children's feelings of personal control as related to social class and ethnic group. *Journal of Personality, 31*, 482–491.

Baughman, E., & Dahlstrom, W. G. (1972). Racial differences on the MMPI. In S. Guterman (Ed.), *Black psyche: The modal personality pattern of Black Americans* (pp. 166–188). Berkeley, CA: Glendessary Press.

Berry, J. W. (1969). On cross-cultural comparability. *International Journal of Psychology, 4*, 119–128.

Bruner, J. (1986). *Actual minds, possible worlds.* Cambridge, MA: Harvard University Press.

Butcher, J. N. (1982). Cross-cultural research methods in clinical psychology. In P. C. Kendall & J. N. Butcher (Eds.), *Handbook of research methods in clinical psychology* (pp. 273–308). New York: Wiley.

Butcher, J. N., & Pancheri, P. (1976). *A handbook of cross-national MMPI research.* Minneapolis: University of Minnesota Press.

Clark, K. B., & Clark, M. P. (1950). Emotional factors in racial identification and preference in Negro children. *Journal of Negro Education, 19*, 341–350.

Colaizzi, P. F. (1978). Psychological research as the phenomenologist views it. In R. S. Valle & M. King (Eds.), *Existential-phenomenological alternatives for psychology* (pp. 48–71). New York: Oxford University Press.

Cole, M., & Bruner, J. S. (1971). Cultural differences and inferences about psychological processes. *American Psychologist, 26*, 867–876.

DeVos, G. A. (1982). Adaptive strategies in U.S. minorities. In E. E. Jones & S. J. Korchin (Eds.), *Minority mental health* (pp. 74–117). New York: Praeger.

Dohrenwend, B. P., & Dohrenwend, B. S. (1974). Social and cultural influences on psychopathology. *Annual Review of Psychology, 25*, 417–453.

DuBois, W. E. B. (1908). *The Negro American family.* Atlanta, GA: Atlanta University Press.

Eisenstein, H. (1983). *Contemporary feminist thought.* Boston: Hall.

Geertz, C. (1979). From the native's point of view: On the nature of anthropological understanding. In P. Rabinow & W. M. Sullivan, (Eds.), *Interpretive social science: A reader* (pp. 225–241). Berkeley: University of California Press.

Gergen, K. J. (1985). The social constructionist movement in modern psychology. *American Psychologist, 40*, 266–275.

Giorgi, A. (1976). Phenomenology and the foundations of psychology. In W. J. Arnold (Ed.), *1975 Nebraska symposium on motivation* (pp. 281–348). Lincoln: University of Nebraska Press.

Gurin, P., Gurin, R., Lao, R., & Beattie, M. (1969). Internal-external control in the motivational dynamics of Negro youth. *Journal of Social Issues, 25*, 29–53.

Guthrie, R. (1976). *Even the rat was white.* New York: Harper & Row.

Gynther, M. (1972). White norms and black MMPIs: A prescription for discrimination? *Psychological Bulletin, 78*, 386–402.

Herskovitz, M. L. (1958). *The myth of the Negro past.* Boston: Beacon Press.

Irvine, S. H., & Carroll, W. K. (1980). Testing and assessment across cultures. In H. C. Triandis & J. W. Berry (Eds.), *Handbook of cross-cultural psychology: Methodology* (Vol. 2, pp. 181–244). Boston: Allyn & Bacon.

Jones, E. E. (1978). Black-white personality differences: Another look. *Journal of Personality Assessment, 42*, 244–252.

Jones, E. E., & Korchin, S. J. (1982). Minority mental health: Perspectives. In E. E. Jones & S. J. Korchin (Eds.), *Minority mental health* (pp. 3–36). New York: Praeger.

Jones, E. E., & Zoppel, C. L. (1979). Personality differences among blacks in Jamaica and the United States. *Journal of Cross-Cultural Psychology, 10*, 435–456.

Jones, R. L. (Ed.). (1996). *Handbook of tests and measurements for Black populations* (Vols. 1–2). Hampton, VA: Cobb & Henry.

Kamin, L. (1974). *The science and politics of IQ.* Potomac, MD: Erlbaum.

Kardiner, A., & Ovesey, L. (1951). *The mark of oppression.* Cleveland, OH: The World.

Katz, I. (1974). Alternatives to a personality-deficit interpretation of Negro underachievement. In P. Watson (Ed.), *Psychology and race* (pp. 377–391). Chicago: Aldine.

Keller, E. F. (1985). *Reflections on gender and science.* New Haven, CT: Yale University Press.

Lefcourt, H. (1965). Risk-taking in Negro and white adults. *Journal of Personality and Social Psychology, 2*, 765–770.

Levinson, D. J. (1978). *The seasons of a man's life.* New York: Knopf.

McAdoo, H. P. (1985). Racial attitude and self-concept of young black children over time. In H. P. McAdoo & J. L. McAdoo (Eds.), *Black children: Social, educational and parental environments* (pp. 213–242). Beverly Hills, CA: Sage.

McGinnies, E., Nordholm, L. A., Ward, C. D., & Bhanthumnavin, D. L. (1974). Sex and cultural differences in perceived locus of control among students in five countries. *Journal of Consulting and Clinical Psychology, 42,* 451–455.

Muñoz, R. F. (1982). The Spanish-speaking consumer and the community mental health center. In E. E. Jones & S. J. Korchin (Eds.), *Minority mental health* (pp. 362–398). New York: Praeger.

Nagelschmidt, A., & Jakob, R. (1977). Dimensionality of Rotter's I-E Scale in a society in the process of modernization. *Journal of Cross-Cultural Psychology, 8,* 101–111.

Oakley, A. (1981). Interviewing women: A contradiction in terms. In H. Roberts (Ed.), *Doing feminist research* (pp. 30–61). London: Routledge & Kegan Paul.

Osgood, C. E. (1965). Cross-cultural comparability in attitude measurements via multilingual semantic differentials. In I. D. Steiner & M. Fishbein (Eds.), *Current studies in social psychology* (pp. 95–107). Chicago: Holt, Rinehart & Winston.

Packer, M. J. (1985). Hermeneutic inquiry in the study of human conduct. *American Psychologist, 40,* 1081–1093.

Price-Williams, D. R. (1975). *Explorations in cross-cultural psychology.* San Francisco: Chandler & Sharp.

Proshansky, H., & Newton, P. (1974). Colour: The nature and meaning of Negro self-identity. In P. Watson (Ed.), *Psychology and race* (pp. 176–212). Chicago: Aldine.

Rabinow, P., & Sullivan, W. M. (1979). The interpretive turn: Emergence of an approach. In P. Rabinow & W. M. Sullivan (Eds.), *Interpretive social science: A reader* (pp. 1–21). Berkeley, University of California Press.

Rotter, J. (1966). Generalized expectancies for internal versus external control of reinforcement. *Psychological Monographs, 80* (1, Whole No. 609).

Rotter, J. B. (1975). Some problems and misconceptions related to the construct of internal versus external control of reinforcement. *Journal of Consulting and Clinical Psychology, 43,* 56–67.

Sanger, S., & Alker, H. (1972). Dimensions of internal-external locus of control and the women's liberation movement. *Journal of Social Issues, 28,* 115–129.

Triandis, H. C. (1972). *The analysis of subjective culture.* New York: Wiley.

Valle, R. S., & King, M. (Eds.). (1978). *Existential-phenomenological alternatives for psychology.* New York: Oxford University Press.

Vickers, J. M. (1982). Memoirs of an ontological exile: The methodological rebellions of feminist research. In G. Finn & A. Miles (Eds.), *Feminism in Canada* (pp. 27–46). Montreal, Quebec, Canada: Black Rose Books.

Von Eckartsberg, R. (1971). On experiential methodology. In A. Giorgi, W. F. Fischer, & R. von Eckartsberg (Eds.), *Duquesne studies in phenomenological psychology* (Vol. 1, pp. 66–79). Pittsburgh, PA: Duquesne University Press.

Wittig, M. A. (1985). Metatheoretical dilemmas in the psychology of gender. *American Psychologist, 40,* 800–811.

A Collective Fear of the Collective: Implications for Selves and Theories of Selves

Hazel Rose Markus and Shinobu Kitayama

The preceding selections by Caughey and by Yang and Bond, although they acknowledge important differences among cultures, take one universal fact for granted: They both assume that human beings are individuals who can be meaningfully characterized, one at a time, using personality traits. Even Jones and Thorne assume that it is useful to understand and to characterize particular individuals. This assumption, "that people are independent, bounded, autonomous entities," is precisely what the authors of the next selection bring into question. The well-known American social psychologist Hazel Markus and her Japanese colleague Shinobu Kitayama describe the idea of the autonomous individual as a notion that is peculiar to Western, Euro-American culture. Japanese and other Asian cultures, they claim, have a very different view of what a person is all about.

Cultures outside Europe and North American emphasize the interdependence of the person with the larger culture, which Markus and Kitayama call the "the collective." Habitual Western modes of thought as well as political ideology combine to see people as essentially separate from each other and emphasize independence, autonomy, and individual differences. However, this seemingly obvious idea may be a cultural artifact. In the East, individuals are seen as part of a greater whole, and it is not so important for one person to compete with or dominate another.

Perhaps because they are arguing against what they see as the conventional wisdom, Markus and Kitayama somewhat romanticize the Eastern view of the self. For example, they write that Asian child-rearing "places a continual emphasis on understanding and relating to others," and that the collective view is characterized by caring, responsibility, and love. But of course there is a trade-off of advantages and disadvantages between the Eastern and Western way of life. For example, in collectivist cultures one's spouse is commonly chosen by others on the basis of a negotiation between families. Perhaps as a result of cultural conditioning, most Europeans and Americans would rather choose their own spouses! As Markus and Kitayama point out, individual rights of all sorts are not given a high priority in collectivist cultures.

Two aspects of the following article are of particular value. First, the article urges us to reexamine an assumption about human psychology held so deeply that few people in our culture are probably even aware of holding it. Second, Markus and Kitayama present, in their Figure 1, a comprehensive model of the relationship between a culture's collective reality, social processes, individual reality, habitual psychological tendencies, and action. This model has the potential to be useful for the analysis of psychological differences among cultures on many different dimensions, not just collectivism vs. individualism.

Our cultural nightmare is that the individual throb of growth will be sucked dry in slavish social conformity. All life long, our central struggle is to defend the individual from the collective.

—Plath, 1980, p. 216

Selves, as well as theories of selves, that have been constructed within a European-American cultural frame show the influence of one powerful notion—the idea that people are independent, bounded, autonomous entities who must strive to remain unshackled by their ties to various groups and collectives (Bellah, Madsen, Sullivan, Swidler, & Tipton, 1985; Farr, 1991; Sampson, 1985; Shweder & Bourne, 1984). This culturally shared idea of the self is a pervasive, taken-for-granted assumption that is held in place by language, by the mundane rituals and social practices of daily life, by the law, the media, the foundational texts like the Declaration of Independence and the Bill of Rights, and by virtually all social institutions. The individualist ideal as sketched in its extreme form in the opening quotation might not be explicitly endorsed by many Americans and Europeans. Some version of this view is, however, the basis of social science's persistent belief in the person as a rational, self-interested actor, and it occasions a desire not to be defined by others and a deep-seated wariness,

in some instances even a fear, of the influence of the generalized other, of the social, and of the collective.

* * *

Recent analyses of the self in cultures other than the European-American (e.g., Daniels, 1984; Derné, 1992; Markus & Kitayama, 1991; Triandis, 1990; White & Kirkpatrick, 1985) reveal some very different perspectives on the relation between the self and the collective. Japanese culture, for example, emphasizes the *inter*dependence of the individual with the collective rather than independence from it. The analysis of non–European-American views of self has two notable benefits. First, such an analysis can illuminate some central characteristics of these non-Western cultures themselves. Second, and more important for our purposes, it can help uncover some aspects of European-American social behavior that are not well captured in the current social psychological theories.

Culture and Self

INDEPENDENCE OF SELF FROM THE COLLECTIVE— A CULTURAL FRAME The model that underlies virtually all current social science views the self as an entity that (a) comprises a unique, bounded configuration of internal attributes (e.g., preferences, traits, abilities, motives, values, and rights) and (b) behaves primarily as a consequence of these internal attributes. It is the individual level of reality—the thoughts and feelings of the single individual—that is highlighted and privileged in the explanation and analysis of behavior; the collective level of reality recedes and remains secondary. The major normative task is to maintain the independence of the individual as a self-contained entity or, more specifically, to be true to one's own internal structures of preferences, rights, convictions, and goals and, further, to be confident and to be efficacious. According to this *independent* view of the self, there is an enduring concern with expressing one's internal attributes both in public and in private. Other people are crucial in maintaining this construal of the self, but they are primarily crucial for their role in evaluating and appraising the self or as standards of comparison (see Markus & Kitayama, 1991; Triandis, 1990, for a discussion of the independent or individualist self). Others do not, however, *participate* in the individual's own subjectivity.

*　*　*

INTERDEPENDENCE OF THE SELF AND THE COLLECTIVE—AN ALTERNATIVE FRAME The pervasive influence of the individualist ideal in many aspects of European-American social behavior has appeared in high relief as we have carried out a set of studies on the self and its functioning in a variety of Asian countries, including Japan, Thailand, and Korea (Kitayama & Markus, 1993; Kitayama, Markus, & Kurokawa, 1991; Markus & Kitayama, 1991, 1992). What has become apparent is that the European-American view of the self and its relation to the collective is only *one* view. There are other, equally powerful but strikingly different, collective notions about the self and its relation to the collective.

From one such alternative view, the self is viewed not as an independent entity separate from the collective but instead as a priori fundamentally interdependent with others. Individuals do not stand in opposition to the confines and constraints of the external collective, nor do they voluntarily choose to become parts of this external collective. Instead, the self *is* inherently social—an integral part of the collective. This interdependent view grants primacy to the *relationship* between self and others. The self derives only from the individual's relationships with specific others in the collective. There is no self without the collective; the self is a part that becomes whole only in interaction with others (e.g., Kondo, 1990; Kumagai & Kumagai, 1985; Lebra, 1992). It is defined and experienced as inherently connected with others. In contrast to the European-American orientation, there is an abiding fear of being on one's own, of being separated or disconnected from the collective. A desire for independence is cast as unnatural and immature.

The major normative task of such a self is not to maintain the independence of the individual as a self-contained entity but instead to maintain *inter*dependence with others. Rather than as an independent decision maker, the self is cast as "a single thread in a richly textured fabric of relationships" (Kondo, 1990, p. 33). This view of the self and of the collective requires adjusting and fitting to important relationships, occupying one's proper place in the group, engaging in collectively appropriate actions, and promoting the goals of others. One's thoughts, feelings, and actions are made meaningful only in reference to the thoughts, feelings, and actions of others in the relationship, and consequently others are crucially important in the very definition of the self. (For more detailed descriptions of the interdependent self, see Hsu, 1953; Kondo, 1990; Markus & Kitayama, 1991.)

Interdependence in this sense is theoretically distinct from social identity (e.g., Tajfel & Turner, 1985; Turner & Oakes, 1989), which refers to social categorizations that define a person as a member of particular social categories (e.g., American, male, Protestant, engineer). Social identity, in the framework of Turner and colleagues, is always defined in counterpoint to personal identity, which is all the ways a person is *different* from his or her in-groups. The key feature of interdependence is not distinctiveness or uniqueness but a heightened awareness of the other, and of the nature of one's relation to the other, and an expectation of some mutuality in this regard across all behavioral domains, even those that can be designated as private or personal.

DIFFERENCES IN THE ENCULTURATION OF THE "BASIC" TASKS Although both European-American and Asian cultural groups recognize that independence from others and interdependence with others are essential human tendencies or tasks, these two tasks are weighted and organized quite differently in the two groups. The notion of the autonomous individual in continuous tension with the external collective is "natural" only from a particular cultural perspective. From an alternative perspective, such an arrangement appears somewhat unnatural and contrived. In Japan, for example, the culture in its dominant ideology, patterns of social customs, practices, and institutions emphasizes and foregrounds not independence from others but interdependence with others. Interdependence is the first goal to be taken care of; it is crafted and nurtured in the social episodes and scripted actions of everyday social life, so that it becomes spontaneous, automatic, and taken for granted. Although independence is also essential for social functioning, it remains a tacit and less culturally elaborated pursuit. It is left to the intentions and initiatives of each individual member, and so its pursuit is relatively optional and is the focus of personal and unofficial discourse because it is not strongly constrained or widely supported by socially sanctioned cultural practices.

THE CULTURAL SHAPING OF PSYCHOLOGICAL PROCESSES In Figure 44.1, we have illustrated how the "reality" of independence is created and maintained in selves, as well as in theories of selves. According to this view, a cultural group's way of self-understanding is simultaneously related to a set of macrolevel phenomena, such as cultural views of personhood and their supporting collective practices, and to a set of microlevel phe-

nomena, like individual lives and their constituent cognitive, emotional, and motivational processes.

Collective reality. Under the heading "collective reality" we have included cultural values and their related ecological, historical, economic, and sociopolitical factors. For example, the United States is a nation with a rich tradition of moral imperatives, but the most well elaborated is the need to protect the "natural rights" of each individual. This core cultural ideal is rooted most directly in the Declaration of Independence and the Bill of Rights, which protect certain inalienable rights, including life, liberty, and the pursuit of happiness. This high-lighting of individuals and their rights is objectified and reified in a variety of democratic political institutions and free-market capitalism. In Japan, as throughout Asia, the prevalent ideological and moral discourses are not tied to individual rights but to the inevitability of a strict hierarchical order and to the achievement of virtue through cultivation of the individual into a "social man" (Yu, 1992). This core cultural ideal is anchored in the works of Confucius and Mencius and finds expression in an array of economic, political, and social institutions.

Sociopsychological products and processes—transmitting the core ideas. The cultural ideals and moral imperatives of a given cultural group are given life by a diverse set of customs, norms, scripts, practices, and institutions that carry out the transformation of the collective reality into the largely personal or psychological reality. These sociopsychological products and processes objectify and make "real" the core ideas of the society (Bourdieu, 1972; D'Andrade, 1984; Durkheim, 1898/1953; Farr & Moscovici, 1984; Geertz, 1973; Oyserman & Markus, in press). For example, in the United States, the idea of human rights (including liberty from the thrall of the collective) as inherent and God-given gains its force from a large array of legal statutes protecting individual rights. In this way the individual gains superiority to the collective.

Child-rearing practices in the United States,

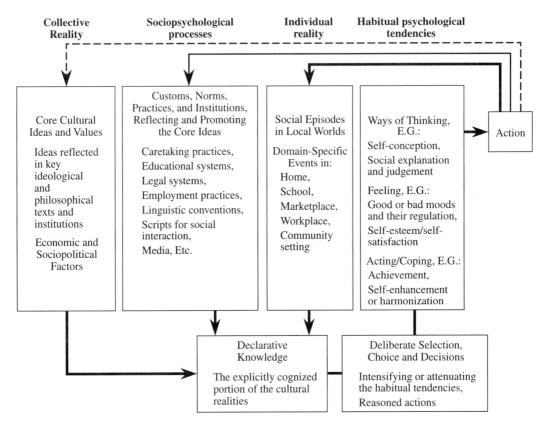

Figure 44.1 Cultural shaping of psychological reality

rooted in Freudian theory and filtered through Dr. Spock and most recently the self-esteem movement, also work to develop the constituent elements of the self and to reinforce the importance of having a distinct self that the individual can feel good about. A recent study (Chao, 1993), for example, found that 64% of European-American mothers, in comparison with 8% of Chinese mothers, stressed building children's "sense of themselves" as an important goal of child rearing. Many American mothers take every opportunity to praise children and to help them realize the ways in which they are positively unique or different from their peers. Training in autonomy and the development of the appreciation of being alone also comes early. Day-old children sleep alone in their cribs, often in separate rooms from

their parents (Shweder, Jensen, & Goldstein, 1995). On the playground, children are taught to stand up for themselves and fight back if necessary (Kashiwagi, 1989).

Another important quality of personhood, from the independent perspective, is the capacity to make one's own choice. In much of Western culture, but especially in North America, there are numerous examples of everyday scripts that presuppose the actor's right to make a choice. It is common for American hosts to instruct their guests, "Help yourself." With this suggestion, the host invites the guest to affirm the self by expressing some of those preferences that are thought to constitute the "real self." American children, then, are socialized to have distinct preferences. Long before the child is old enough to answer, caretakers pose questions like "Do you want the red cup or the blue cup?" With such questions, mothers signal to children that the capacity for independent choice is an important and desirable attribute. And the availability of choice gives rise to the need for preferences by which to make choices.

The practices of the media further create and foster the objectivity of the autonomous, independent self. Advertising in the United States makes appeals to nonconformity, originality, and uniqueness. A hard-sell approach is common in which the product is presented as the best or the leader of its kind, and purchasing it is claimed to reveal that the consumer has the "right" preferences or attitudes (Mueller, 1987; Zandpour, Chang, & Catalano, 1992). For example, Chanel recently marketed, in both the United States and Europe, a men's cologne with the strikingly unsubtle name of *Egoïste* and the slogan "For the man who walks on the right side of the fine line between arrogance and awareness of self-worth."

Perhaps the most powerful practice of all for the purpose of creating a shared concern with independence is that of advancing, promoting, and compensating people according to their "merit." This practice places a lifelong emphasis on inner attributes, capacities, and abilities as the "real" measure of the self and encourages people to define and develop these attributes.

In many Asian cultures, there is an equally diverse and powerful set of sociopsychological processes in each of these corresponding domains, but these practices are rooted in a view of the self as an interdependent entity. For example, in place of (or, to a certain extent, in addition to) the emphasis on human rights, there exist dense systems of rules and norms that highlight the duties of each individual to the pertinent collective, whether it is the company, school, or nation. Moreover, there are many fewer statutes protecting individual rights, and the Japanese resort to court suits to secure their rights far less readily than European-Americans (Hideo, 1988).

In the course of interpersonal interaction, the Japanese are encouraged to try to read the partner's mind and to satisfy what is taken as the partner's expectations or desires. A Japanese mother does not ask for a child's preference but instead tries to determine what is best for the child and to arrange it. Rather than asking a guest to make a choice, Japanese hosts do their best to prepare and offer what they infer to be the best possible meal for the guest, saying, for example, "Here's a turkey sandwich for you. I thought you said you like turkey better than beef last time we met."

Child rearing in many Asian cultures places a continual emphasis on understanding and relating to others, first to the mother and then to a wide range of others. The rules of interdependence are explicitly modeled, and the goal is to maintain harmonious relationships (Hsu, 1953). Interdependence can be found in all domains. In stark opposition to American practices and Freudian wisdom, cosleeping and cobathing are common in Japanese families. The emphasis is not on developing a good, private sense of self but on tuning in to and being sensitive to others. Punishing or reprimanding Japanese children often involves not the withholding of rights and privileges but a threat to the relationship. Mothers will say, "I don't like children like you" or "People will laugh at you" (Okimoto & Rohlen, 1988).

With respect to media practices, Japanese advertising often uses soft-sell appeals that focus on harmony or connection with nature or with others (Mueller, 1987). In classified ads, employers explicitly seek individuals with good interpersonal relations, as opposed to self-starters or innovators (Caproni, Rafaeli, & Carlile, 1993). A focus on relationships is also evident in all types of business practices. Japan stands out from all countries in the West because of its emphasis on durable and pervasive ties between government and industry, between banks and businesses, and among corporations. Okimoto and Rohlen (1988) contend that the emphasis on organizational networks and human relationships is so strong that Japanese capitalism can be labeled *relational capitalism*. In the pursuit of long-term relationships and mutual trust, Japanese corporations operate quite differently, often, for example, forgoing the maximization of short-term profits with the hope of gaining a long-term market share. And in contrast to the European-American emphasis on merit for promotion and compensation, wages and advancement in the majority of Japanese companies and institutions are tied to seniority in the system. In addition, employment in large corporations is typically permanent, and there is little lateral entry from the outside—all publicly scripted collective practices that foster and promote a view of the self as inherently relational and interdependent.

Beyond the caretaking, legal, business, and media practices we have alluded to are a host of others, including educational and linguistic practices, and all the scripts and institutions that structure everyday social interactions. An important element in understanding which practices will become socially established is how the practices reflect and carry the group's underlying cultural values. Americans, for example, will be particularly susceptible to ideas and practices that directly follow from individualism (Sperber, 1985). Other practices—welfare and universal health care programs are good examples—will have a more difficult time taking hold in the United States.

Local worlds—living the core ideas. The third segment of Figure 44.1 represents the specific settings, circumstances, and situations of everyday life that make up an individual's immediate social environment and in which particular customs, norms, and practices become lived experience. The local worlds—home, school, the workplace, the community center, the church, the restaurant, bar, or café, the marketplace—and the specific activities or episodes they support—helping a child with homework, shopping for a gift, drinking with friends, discussing politics, playing baseball, working with others to meet a deadline—demand specific, culturally appropriate responses if a person is to become a valued member of the family, school, workplace, or community.

It is within the demands and expectations of these domain-specific, recurrent social episodes that people, often quite unknowingly, live out the core cultural values. So Americans are likely to create and live within settings that elicit and pro-

mote the sense that one is a positively unique individual who is separate and independent from others. For example, in many American schools, each child in the class has the opportunity to be a "star" or a "Very Special Person" for a week during the school year. Likewise, Japanese will create and live with situations that promote the sense of self as interdependent with others. In Japanese schools, children routinely produce group pictures or story boards, and no child leaves to go to the playground or lunch until all members of the group are ready to leave.

Habitual psychological tendencies reflecting the core ideas. As a result of efforts to respond or adjust to the set of specific episodes that constitute the individual's life space, episodes that have themselves been shaped by norms, practices, and institutions supporting the cultural group's core ideas, a set of habitual psychological tendencies is likely to develop. The final segment of Figure 44.1 represents the individual's "authentic" subjective experience—particular, proceduralized ways of thinking, feeling, striving, knowing, understanding, deciding, managing, adjusting, adapting, which are, in some large part, structured, reinforced, and maintained by the constraints and affordances of the particular social episodes of the individual's local worlds. In this way, people who live within a society whose daily practices and formal institutions all promote independence will come not just to believe that they are, but to experience themselves as, autonomous, bounded selves who are distinct from other members of the collective. This will be evident in many ways of thinking, feeling, and acting, but it is particularly evident when people are asked to characterize themselves.

For example, by the time they are young adults, many Americans will seek an optimal distinctiveness from others (Brewer, 1990) and will "naturally" experience an ambivalence about their collective nature and a deep concern with being categorically perceived or socially determined. The journalist Barbara Ehrenreich (1992) describes an interchange with an acquaintance who has just rediscovered her own ethnic and religious heritage and now feels in contact with her 2000-year ancestral traditions. The acquaintance asks about Ehrenreich's ethnic background. The first word to come out of Ehrenreich's mouth in answer to the question is "None." She is surprised at how natural and right her answer seems, yet slightly embarrassed. She reflects and decides that her response when asked the nature of her ethnicity was quite correct. Her identity, she claims, comes from the realization that "we are the kind of people that whatever our distant ancestors' religions —we do not believe, we do not carry on traditions, we do not do things just because someone has done them before." Her ethnicity, she contends, is rooted not in a given group but in the ideas "Think for yourself" and "Try new things." In conclusion, Ehrenreich tells of asking her own children whether they ever had any stirring of "ethnic or religious identity." "None," they all conclude, and she reports, "My chest swelled with pride as would my mother's to know that the race of 'None' marches on."

A tendency to define one's "real" self as distinct from one's social groups and obligations is characteristic of both younger and older cohorts of Americans as well. In a series of studies with young children, Hart and his colleagues (Hart, 1988; Hart & Edelstein, 1992) asked American children to imagine a "person machine" that makes the original person disappear but at the same time manufactures other people, copies of the original, which receive some but not all of the original person's characteristics. The respondent's task is to judge which new manufactured person —the one with the same physical attributes (looks like you), the one with the same social attributes (has the same friends and family), or the one with the same psychological attributes (same thoughts and feelings)—will be most like the original person. By ninth grade, Hart et al. (Hart, Fegley, Hung Chan, Mulvey, & Fischer, 1993) finds that most respondents believe it is the copy with the original's psychological characteristics that is the most similar to the original.

These findings are consistent with those of several other studies of cultural variation in self-

categorization (Cousins, 1989; Triandis, 1990) and suggest that, for American students, it is the internal features of the self—the traits, attributes, and attitudes—that are privileged and regarded as critical to self-definition. From this perspective, the significant aspects of the self are those that are the inside, the private property—one's characteristic ways of behaving, one's habitual thoughts, feelings, and beliefs (e.g., think for yourself, try new things)—the elements that do not explicitly reference others or the social world. Such internal attributes are also mentioned by the Japanese, but they appear to be understood as relatively situation specific and therefore elusive and unreliable (Cousins, 1989) as defining features of self. For the Japanese, the critical features are those attributes—social roles, duties, obligations—that connect one to the larger world of social relationships. (For other detailed examples of the cultural shaping of judgment, self, and emotion, see Kitayama & Markus, 1993, 1995; Markus & Kitayama, 1994.) In a study examining response time for self-description,[1] Kitayama et al. (1991) find that Japanese respondents are decidedly slower to characterize themselves than American respondents and that this is particularly true for positive attributes.

The top level of Figure 44.1 indicates feedback loops from each individual's action. The most immediate and frequent feedback occurs at the micro level. Most obviously, what an individual does influences the very nature of the situation in which he or she has acted. There are, however, people who at times contribute, through their actions, not just to the micro level but also to the more macro level. The bottom level of Figure 44.1 represents a more cognitive influence. Some portion of the social realities—both macro and micro—can be represented cognitively. This cognized portion of

---

[1]In such a study personality adjectives are presented on a screen, and subjects must respond "me" or "not me" by pressing a key. The time taken to respond is measured in milliseconds. A slower response implies that a particular attribute is a less central aspect of the self-concept.

culture is shaded in each segment of the figure. The articulated, declarative knowledge of cultural values, practices, and conventions may be recruited in modulating social action, either facilitating or inhibiting the automatized psychological tendencies. Importantly, however, psychological tendencies can develop independently of this second, articulated route of cultural influence. In this way, cultural values and beliefs can cause differences in psychological processes even when these beliefs (e.g., a fear of influence by the collective) are not cognitively encoded and overtly articulated. Of course, the values and beliefs often are encoded cognitively, but this current analysis implies that cognitive representations need not be central in the cultural shaping of psychological processes. Instead, we suggest that psychological processes and behavior can be best understood as an important, but only partial, element of the dynamic cultural and historical process that involves the systematic (though by no means error-free or "faxlike") transmission of cultural imperatives to shape and define the nature of the specific, immediate life space—the microlevel reality—for each individual.

Implications of a Collective Fear of the Collective for Psychological Theorizing

Using Asian cultures, particularly Japan, as a point of reference and standard, we have sketched how the European-American fear of the collective may arise and how it is naturalized, enacted, and embodied so that people rarely see or feel the collective nature or source of their behavior and instead experience themselves as separate and self-contained entities. A large set of mutually reinforcing everyday rituals, social practices, and institutions work together to elaborate and objectify the culture's view of what the self is and what it should be. Independence and autonomy are thus the "natural" mode of being—in Geertz's (1975) terms, they become "experience near" phenomena. The subjective authenticity or "naturalness"

of this mode, however, is a function of the degree of fit between habitual psychological tendencies and the cultural and social systems that are grounded in these cultural imperatives.

Theorists of European-American behavior have also been extremely influenced by the prevailing ideology of individualism. They have often viewed the self as in tension, or even as in opposition, to the "ruck of society" (Plath, 1980) or the "thrall of society" (Hewitt, 1989). The source of all important behavior is typically "found" in the unique configuration of internal attributes—thoughts, feelings, motives, abilities—that form the bounded, autonomous whole. As a consequence, the ways in which the self is, in fact, quite interdependent with the collective have been underanalyzed and undertheorized. It is our view that there are a number of important reasons for theorists to go beyond theories that are directly shaped by the cultural ideal of individualism and to consider a broader view of the self.

First, and most obviously, although current descriptions of the largely independent and autonomous self could be argued to be reasonably adequate for European-American selves, a growing body of evidence suggests that they are simply not valid for many other cultural groups (see extended discussions of this point in Markus & Kitayama, 1991; Triandis, 1990; Triandis, Bontempo, & Villareal, 1988). Second, although the cultural ideal of independence is very influential in the nature and functioning of the European-American self, it does not determine it completely. For example, with respect to the bounded or fixed nature of the self, there are a variety of studies that reveal the self as decidedly malleable and its content and functioning as dependent on the social context. Typically these studies are not integrated with the literature that suggests stability of the self (e.g., Fazio, Effrein, & Falender, 1981; James, 1993; Jones & Pittman, 1982; Markus & Kunda, 1986; McGuire & McGuire, 1982; Schlenker, 1980).

Third, at least in the United States, the analysis of the selves of those groups in society that are somewhat marginalized—women, members of nondominant ethnic groups, the poor, the unschooled, and the elderly—reveals a more obvious interdependence between the self and the collective. For example, women describe themselves in relational terms (Gilligan, 1982; Jordan, Kaplan, Miller, Stivey, & Surrey, 1991), and they do not reveal the "typical" preference for being positively unique or different from others (Josephs, Markus, & Tafarodi, 1992). Other studies reveal that those groups that are in the minority with respect to language, skin color, or religion are decidedly more likely to define themselves in collective terms (Allen, Dawson, & Brown, 1989; Bowman, 1987; Husain, 1992). Further, Americans with less schooling are more likely to describe themselves in terms of habitual actions and roles, and less likely to characterize themselves in terms of psychological attributes, than those with more schooling (Markus, Herzog, Holmberg, & Dielman, 1992). And those with low self-esteem show a marked tendency to describe themselves as similar to others (Josephs et al., 1992). These findings suggest that those with power and privilege are those most likely to internalize the prevailing European-American cultural frame to achieve Ehrenreich's "ethnicity of none" and to "naturally" experience themselves as autonomous individuals.

Fourth, a number of recent studies show many Americans to be extremely concerned about others and the public good (Bellah et al., 1985; Bellah, Madsen, Sullivan, Swidler, & Tipton, 1991; Hewitt, 1989; Withnow, 1992) and to characterize themselves in interdependent terms. For example, a recent representative sample of 1,500 adults, aged 30 or over, found that although Americans indeed characterized themselves in terms of trait attributes and not social roles or obligations, the most frequently used attributes were *caring, responsible, loved*—all terms that imply some concern with a connection to the collective (Markus et al., 1992). Even if, as we have suggested, this connection is clearly voluntary and done on one's own terms, the prevailing model of the self could be modified.

And finally, increasingly throughout social psychology, there are indications that the individualist model of the self is too narrow and fails to take account of some important aspects of psychological reality. For example, within social psychology specifically, there is a great deal of evidence that people are exquisitely sensitive to others and to social pressure. People conform, obey, diffuse responsibility in a group, allow themselves to be easily persuaded about all manner of things, and become powerfully committed to others on the basis of minimal action (Myers, 1993). Despite the powerful cultural sanctions against allowing the collective to influence one's thoughts and actions, most people are still much less self-reliant, self-contained, or self-sufficient than the ideology of individualism suggests they should be. It appears in these cases that the European-American model of self is somewhat at odds with observed individual behavior and that it might be reformulated to reflect the substantial interdependence that characterizes even Western individualists.

Alternative Views of the Self and the Collective

In trying to formulate the collective sources of the self among Europeans or Americans, models of the self and the collective "Asian style" may be particularly informative.[2] If we assume, as does Shweder (1991), that every group can be considered an expert on some features of human expe-

---

[2]Some of the most important work suggesting the need for alternative models of the self comes from feminist theorists who have argued in the last 15 years that relations have a power and significance in women's lives that has gone unrecognized (Belenky, Clinchy, Goldberger, & Tarule, 1986; Gilligan, 1982; Jordan et al., 1991). The development of a psychology of women has shown that the "Lone Ranger" model of the self simply does not fit many women's experience because women's sense of self seems to involve connection and engagement with relationships and collective. In this work, being dependent does not invariably mean being helpless, powerless, or without control. It often means being interdependent—having a sense that one is able to have an effect on others and is willing to be responsive to others and become engaged with them (Jordan, 1991).—Author

rience and that different cultural groups "light up" different aspects of this experience, then Asian cultures may be an important source of conceptual resources in the form of concepts, frameworks, theories, or methods that can be employed to "see" interdependence. Even though interdependence American style will doubtlessly look quite different from interdependence Japanese style, an analysis of divergent cultural groups may further any theorist's understanding of the possibilities, potential, and consequences, both positive and negative, for socialness, for engagement, for interdependence, and for the ties that bind.

* * *

We have argued here that the cultural frame of individualism has put a very strong stamp on how social psychologists view the individual and his or her relation to the collective. Although this individualist view has provided a powerful framework for the analysis of social behavior, it has also, necessarily, constrained theories, methods, and dominant interpretations of social behavior. Because individualism is not just a matter of belief or value but also one of everyday practice, including scientific practice, it is not easy for theorists to view social behavior from another cultural frame, and it is probably harder still to reflect a different frame in empirical work. But the comparative approach that is characteristic of the developing cultural psychology (e.g., Cole, 1990; Stigler, Shweder, & Herdt, 1990) may eventually open new and productive possibilities for the understanding and analysis of behavior.

For example, just as social influence, from the perspective of an interdependent cultural frame, can be seen as the mutual negotiation of social reality, helping can be seen as a result of obligation, duty, or morality, rather than as voluntary or intentional (e.g., Miller, Bersoff, & Harwood, 1990). Similarly, emotion can be viewed as an enacted interpersonal process (Rosaldo, 1984) or as an interpersonal atmosphere, as it is characterized in some non-Western theories (White, 1990). Further, cognition can be seen as an internalized aspect of communication (Zajonc, 1992), and the

early idea of the social and interactive nature of the mind (e.g., Asch, 1952; Bruner, 1990; Vygotsky, 1978) can be taken much more seriously than it has been. In general, viewing the self and social behavior from alternative perspectives may enable theorists to see and elaborate at least one important and powerful universal that might otherwise be quite invisible—the ways in which psychological functioning (in this case, the nature of the self), as well as theories about psychological functioning (here, theories of the nature of the self), are in many ways culture specific and conditioned by particular, but tacit and taken-for-granted, meaning systems, values, and ideals.

References

Allen, R. L., Dawson, M. C., & Brown, R. E. (1989). A schema based approach to modeling an African American racial belief system. *American Political Science Review, 83*, 421–442.

Asch, S. E. (1952). *Social psychology.* Englewood Cliffs, NJ: Prentice-Hall.

Belenky, M. F., Clinchy, B. M., Goldberger, N. R., & Tarule, J. M. (1986). *Women's ways of knowing: The development of self, voice, and mind.* New York: Basic Books.

Bellah, R. N., Madsen, R., Sullivan, W. M., Swidler, A., & Tipton, S. M. (1985). *Habits of the heart: Individualism and commitment in American life.* Berkeley: University of California Press.

Bellah, R. N., Madsen, R., Sullivan, W. M., Swidler, A., & Tipton, S. M. (1991). *The good society.* New York: Knopf.

Bourdieu, P. (1972). *Outline of a theory of practice.* Cambridge: Cambridge University Press.

Bowman, P. J. (1987). Post-industrial displacement and family role strains: Challenges to the Black family. In P. Voydanoff & L. C. Majka (Eds.), *Families and economic distress.* Newbury Park, CA: Sage.

Brewer, M. B. (1990, August). *The social self: On being the same and different at the same time.* Presidential address to the Society for Personality and Social Psychology presented at the annual meeting of the American Psychological Association, Boston.

Bruner, J. (1990). *Acts of meaning.* Cambridge, MA: Harvard University Press.

Caproni, P., Rafaeli, A., & Carlile, P. (1993, July). *The social construction of organized work: The role of newspaper employment advertising.* Paper presented at the European Group on Organization Studies conference, Paris, France.

Chao, R. K. (1993). *East and West: Concepts of the self reflected in mothers' reports of their child-rearing.* Unpublished manuscript, University of California, Los Angeles.

Cole, M. (1990). Cultural psychology: A once and future discipline? In J. J. Berman (Ed.), *Nebraska Symposium on Mo-*

tivation, 1989 (Vol. 37, pp. 279–336). Lincoln: University of Nebraska Press.

Cousins, S. (1989). Culture and selfhood in Japan and the U.S. *Journal of Personality and Social Psychology, 56,* 124–131.

D'Andrade, R. (1984). Cultural meaning systems. In R. A. Shweder & R. A. LeVine (Eds.), *Cultural theories: Essays on mind, self, and emotion* (pp. 88–119). New York: Cambridge University Press.

Daniels, E. V. (1984). *Fluid signs; Being a person the Tamil way.* Berkeley: University of California Press.

Derné, S. (1992). Beyond institutional and impulsive conceptions of self: Family structure and the socially anchored real self. *Ethos, 20,* 259–288.

Durkheim, E. (1953). Individual representations and collective representations. In E. Durkheim (Ed.), *Sociology and philosophy* (D. F. Pocok, Trans.) (pp. 1–38). New York: Free Press. (Original work published 1898)

Ehrenreich, B. (1992, March). The race of none. *Sunday New York Times Magazine,* pp. 5–6.

Farr, R. M. (1991). Individualism as a collective representation. In V. Aebischer, J. P. Deconchy, & M. Lipiansky (Eds.), *Idéologies et représentations sociales* (pp. 129–143). Cousset (Fribourg), Switzerland: Delval.

Farr, R. M., & Moscovici, S. (Eds.). (1984). *Social representations.* Cambridge: Cambridge University Press.

Fazio, R. H., Effrein, E. A., & Falender, Y. J. (1981). Self-perceptions following social interactions. *Journal of Personality and Social Psychology, 41,* 232–242.

Geertz, C. (1973). *The interpretation of cultures.* New York: Basic Books.

Geertz, C. (1975). On the nature of anthropological understanding. *American Scientist, 63,* 47–53.

Gilligan, C. (1982). *In a different voice: Psychological theory and women's development.* Cambridge, MA: Harvard University Press.

Hart, D. (1988). The adolescent self-concept in social context. In D. Lapsley & F. Power (Eds.), *Self, ego, and identity: Integrative approaches* (pp. 71–90). New York: Springer-Verlag.

Hart, D., & Edelstein, W. (1992). Self understanding development in cultural context. In T. M. Brinthaupt & R. P. Lipka (Eds.), *The self: Definitional and methodological issues.* Albany: State University of New York Press.

Hart, D., Fegley, S., Hung Chan, Y., Mulvey, D., & Fischer, L. (1993). *Judgment about personal identity in childhood and adolescence.* Unpublished manuscript.

Hewitt, J. P. (1989). *Dilemmas of the American self.* Philadelphia: Temple University Press.

Hideo, T. (1988). The role of law and lawyers in Japanese society. In D. I. Okimoto & T. P. Rohlen (Eds.), *Inside the Japanese system: Readings on contemporary society and political economy* (pp. 194–196). Stanford, CA: Stanford University Press.

Hsu, F. L. K. (1953). *Americans and Chinese: Two ways of life.* New York: H. Schuman.

Husain, M. G. (1992, July). *Ethnic uprising and identity.* Paper presented at the 11th Congress of the International Association for Cross-Cultural Psychology, Liege, Belgium.

James, K. (1993). Conceptualizing self with in-group stereotypes: Context and esteem precursors. *Personality and Social Psychology Bulletin, 19,* 117–121.

Jones, E. E., & Pittman, T. S. (1982). Towards a general theory of strategic self-preservation. In J. Suls (Ed.), *Psychological perspectives on the self* (Vol. 1, pp. 231–262). Hillsdale, NJ: Lawrence Erlbaum.

Jordan, J. V. (1991). Empathy and self boundaries. In J. V. Jordan, A. G. Kaplan, J. B. Miller, I. P. Stivey, & J. L. Surrey (Eds.), *Women's growth in connection* (pp. 67–80). New York: Guilford.

Jordan, J. V., Kaplan, A. G., Miller, J. B., Stivey, I. P., & Surrey, J. L. (Eds.). (1991). *Women's growth in connection.* New York: Guilford.

Josephs, R. A., Markus, H., & Tafarodi, R. W. (1992). Gender differences in the source of self-esteem. *Journal of Personality and Social Psychology, 63,* 391–402.

Kashiwagi, K. (1989, July). *Development of self-regulation in Japanese children.* Paper presented at the tenth annual meeting of the International Society for the Study of Behavioral Development, Jyväskylä, Finland.

Kitayama, S., & Markus, H. (1993). Construal of the self as a cultural frame: Implications for internationalizing psychology. In J. D'Arms, R. G. Hastie, S. E. Hoelscher, & H. K. Jacobson (Eds.), *Becoming more international and global: Challenges for American higher education.* Manuscript submitted for publication.

Kitayama, S., & Markus, H. (1995). A cultural perspective on self-conscious emotions. In J. P. Tangney & K. W. Fisher (Eds.), *Shame, guilt, embarrassment and pride: Empirical studies of self-conscious emotions.* New York: Guilford.

Kitayama, S., Markus, H., & Kurokawa, M. (1991, October). *Culture, self, and emotion: The structure and frequency of emotional experience.* Paper presented at the biannual meeting of the Society for Psychological Anthropology, Chicago.

Kondo, D. (1990). *Crafting selves: Power, gender, and discourses of identity in a Japanese work place.* Chicago: University of Chicago Press.

Kumagai, H. A., & Kumagai, A. K. (1985). The hidden "I" in *amae*: "Passive love" and Japanese social perception. *Ethos, 14,* 305–321.

Lebra, T. S. (1976). *Japanese patterns of behavior.* Honolulu: University of Hawaii Press.

Lebra, T. S. (1992, June). *Culture, self, and communication.* Paper presented at the University of Michigan, Ann Arbor.

Markus, H., Herzog, A. R., Holmberg, D. E., & Dielman, L. (1992). *Constructing the self across the life span.* Unpublished manuscript, University of Michigan, Ann Arbor.

Markus, H., & Kitayama, S. (1991). Culture and the self: Implications for cognition, emotion, and motivation. *Psychological Review, 98,* 224–253.

Markus, H., & Kitayama, S. (1992). The what, why and how of cultural psychology: A review of R. Shweder's *Thinking through cultures. Psychological Inquiry, 3,* 357–364.

Markus, H., & Kitayama, S. (1994). The cultural construction of self and emotion: Implications for social behavior. In S. Kitayama & H. R. Markus (Eds.), *Emotion and culture: Empirical studies of mutual influence* (pp. 89–130). Washington, DC: American Psychological Association.

Markus, H., & Kunda, Z. (1986). Stability and malleability in the self-concept in the perception of others. *Journal of Personality and Social Psychology, 51,* 1–9.

McGuire, W. J., & McGuire, C. V. (1982). Significant others

in self space: Sex differences and developmental trends in social self. In J. Suls (Ed.), *Psychological perspectives on the self* (Vol. 1, pp. 71–96). Hillsdale, NJ: Lawrence Erlbaum.

Miller, J. G., Bersoff, D. M., & Harwood, R. L. (1990). Perceptions of social responsibilities in India and in the United States: Moral imperatives or personal decisions? *Journal of Personality and Social Psychology, 58,* 33–46.

Mueller, B. (1987, June/July). Reflections of culture: An analysis of Japanese and American advertising appeals. *Journal of Advertising Research,* pp. 51–59.

Myers, D. (1993). *Social psychology* (4th ed.). New York: McGraw-Hill.

Okimoto, D. I., & Rohlen, T. P. (Eds.). (1988). *Inside the Japanese system: Readings on contemporary society and political economy.* Stanford, CA: Stanford University Press.

Oyserman, D., & Markus, H. R. (in press). Self as social representation. In S. Moscovici and U. Flick (Eds.), *Psychology of the social.* Berlin: Rowohlt Taschenbuch Verlag Gmbh.

Plath, D. W. (1980). *Long engagements: Maturity in modern Japan.* Stanford, CA: Stanford University Press.

Rosaldo, M. (1984). Toward an anthropology of self and feeling. In R. A. Shweder & R. A. LeVine (Eds.), *Culture theory: Essays on mind, self, and emotion* (pp. 137–157). Cambridge: Cambridge University Press.

Sampson, E. E. (1985). The decentralization of identity: Toward a revised concept of personal and social order. *American Psychologist, 40,* 1203–1211.

Schlenker, B. R. (1980). *Impression management.* Pacific Grove, CA: Brooks/Cole.

Shweder, R. A. (1991). *Thinking through cultures: Expeditions in cultural psychology.* Cambridge, MA: Harvard University Press.

Shweder, R. A., & Bourne, E. (1984). Does the concept of the person vary cross-culturally? In R. A. Shweder & R. A. LeVine (Eds.), *Culture theory: Essays on mind, self, and emotion* (pp. 158–199). Cambridge: Cambridge University Press.

Shweder, R. A., Jensen, L. A., & Goldstein, W. M. (1995). Who sleeps by whom revisted: A method for extracting the moral goods implicit in practice. In J. Goodnow, P. Miller, & F. Kessel (Eds.), *Cultural practices as contexts for development.* San Francisco: Jossey-Bass.

Sperber, D. (1985). Anthropology and psychology: Towards an epidemiology of representations. *MAN, 20,* 73–89.

Stigler, J. W., Shweder, R. A., & Herdt, G. (Eds.). (1990). *Cultural psychology: Essays on comparative human development.* London: Cambridge University Press.

Tajfel, H., & Turner, J. C. (1985). The social identity theory of intergroup behavior. In S. Worchel & W. G. Austin (Eds.), *Psychology of intergroup relations* (pp. 7–24). Chicago: Nelson-Hall.

Triandis, H. C. (1990). Cross-cultural studies of individualism and collectivism. In J. J. Berman (Ed.), *Nebraska Symposium on Motivation, 1989* (Vol. 37, pp. 41–143).

Triandis, H. C., Bontempo, R., & Villareal, M. (1988). Individualism and collectivism: Cross-cultural perspectives on self-ingroup relationships. *Journal of Personality and Social Psychology, 54,* 323–338.

Turner, J. C., & Oakes, P. J. (1989). Self-categorization theory and social influence. In P. B. Paulus (Ed.), *The psychology of group influence* (2nd ed.). Hillsdale, NJ: Lawrence Erlbaum.

Vygotsky, L. S. (1978). *Mind in society: The development of higher psychological processes* (M. Cole, V. John-Steiner, S. Scribner, & E. Souberman, Eds.). Cambridge, MA: Harvard University Press.

White, G. M. (1990). Moral discourse and the rhetoric of emotion. In C. Lutz & L. Abu-Lughod (Eds.), *Language and the politics of emotion.* Cambridge: Cambridge University Press.

White, G. M., & Kirkpatrick, J. (Eds.). (1985). *Person, self, and experience: Exploring Pacific ethnopsychologies.* Berkeley and Los Angeles: University of California Press.

Withnow, R. (1992). *Acts of compassion.* Princeton, NJ: Princeton University Press.

Yu, A. B. (1992, July). *The self and life goals of traditional Chinese: A philosophical and cultural analysis.* Paper presented at the 11th Congress of the International Association for Cross-Cultural Psychology, Liege, Belgium.

Zajonc, R. B. (1992, April). *Cognition, communication, consciousness: A social psychological perspective.* Invited address at the 20th Katz-Newcomb Lecture at the University of Michigan, Ann Arbor.

Zandpour, F., Chang, C., & Catalano, J. (1992, January/February). Stories, symbols, and straight talk: A comparative analysis of French, Taiwanese, and U.S. TV commercials. *Journal of Advertising Research,* pp. 25–38.

FROM *NICE WORK*

David Lodge

Not all psychologists are aware that proposals such as those by Markus and Ki-tayama are part of a broader intellectual trend that, so far, has only brushed psychology. In recent years, a school of literary criticism called "deconstruction-ism" has dominated many university English departments. As the following se-lection notes, deconstructionism holds that "there is no such thing as the 'self' on which capitalism and the classic novel are founded"—a point of view that is remarkably similar to the view espoused by Markus and Kitayama that the self is an arbitrary idea constructed by culture.

The following selection is a brief excerpt from the novel Nice Work, *written by a British professor of English named David Lodge. Lodge knows his decon-structionism, and in the excerpted passage he puts this trendy viewpoint into the mind of a fictitious academic named Robyn Penrose. He notes that his character Robyn does not herself believe in the idea of character, seeing the idea of the autonomous self as a Western cultural invention that not only permeates litera-ture but is an integral part of capitalism.*

The most valuable part of Robyn's view, as of that of Markus and Kitay-ama, is that it leads us to rethink assumptions about reality that we are used to taking for granted. Still, at the end of the day Lodge notes that—despite her ideological viewpoint—Robyn still has anxieties, frustrations, desires, and ambi-tions, all of which seem to belong to her individually. Perhaps the same is true about the authors of the preceding selection!

And there, for the time being, let us leave Vic Wilcox, while we travel back an hour or two in time, a few miles in space, to meet a very different character. A character who, rather awkwardly for me, doesn't herself believe in the concept of character. That is to say (a favourite phrase of her own), Robyn Penrose, Temporary Lecturer in English Literature at the University of Rummidge, holds that "character" is a bourgeois myth, an illusion created to reinforce the ideology of capitalism. As evidence for this assertion she will point to the fact that the rise of the novel (the literary genre of "character" *par excellence*) in the eighteenth century coincided with the rise of capitalism; that the triumph of the novel over all other literary genres in the nineteenth century coincided with the triumph of capitalism; and that the modernist and postmodernist deconstruction of the classic novel in the twentieth century has coincided with the terminal crisis of capitalism.

Why the classic novel should have collaborated with the spirit of capitalism is perfectly obvious to Robyn. Both are expressions of a secularised Protestant ethic, both dependent on the idea of an autonomous individual self who is responsible for and in control of his/her own destiny, seeking happiness and fortune in competition with other autonomous selves. This is true of the novel considered both as commodity and as mode of representation. (Thus Robyn in full seminar spate.) That is to say, it applies to novelists themselves as well as to their heroes and heroines. The novelist is a capitalist of the imagination. He or she invents a product which consumers didn't know they wanted until it was made available, manufactures it with the assistance of purveyors of risk capital known as publishers, and sells it in competition with makers of marginally differentiated products of the same kind. The first major English novelist, Daniel Defoe, was a merchant. The second, Samuel Richardson, was a printer. The novel was the first mass-produced cultural artefact. (At this point Robyn, with elbows tucked into her sides, would spread her hands outwards from the wrist, as if to imply that there is no need to say more. But of course she always has much more to say.)

According to Robyn (or, more precisely, according to the writers who have influenced her thinking on these matters) there is no such thing as the "self" on which capitalism and the classic novel are founded—that is to say, a finite, unique soul or essence that constitutes a person's identity; there is only a subject position in an infinite web of discourses—the discourses of power, sex, family, science, religion, poetry, etc. And by the same token, there is no such thing as an author, that is to say, one who originates a work of fiction *ab nihilo*. Every text is a product of intertextuality, a tissue of allusions to and citations of other texts; and, in the famous words of Jacques Derrida (famous to people like Robyn, anyway), "*il n'y a pas de hors-texte*," there is nothing outside the text. There are no origins, there is only production, and we produce our "selves" in language. Not "*you are what you eat*" but "*you are what you speak*" or, rather "*you are what speaks you*," is the axiomatic basis of Robyn's philosophy, which she would call, if required to give it a name, "semiotic materialism." It might seem a bit bleak, a bit inhuman ("antihumanist, yes; inhuman, no," she would interject), somewhat deterministic ("not at all; the truly determined subject is he who is not aware of the discursive formations that determine him. Or her," she would add scrupulously, being among other things a feminist), but in practice this doesn't seem to affect her behaviour very noticeably—she seems to have ordinary human feelings, ambitions, desires, to suffer anxieties, frustrations, fears, like anyone else in this imperfect world, and to have a natural inclination to try and make it a better place. I shall therefore take the liberty of treating her as a character, not utterly different in kind, though of course belonging to a very different social species, from Vic Wilcox.

* * *

The Self and Social Behavior in Differing Cultural Contexts

Harry C. Triandis

We have seen that some cultural psychologists are fond of citing the phenomenological idea that it is one's experience of reality—not reality itself—that is all-important. This is sometimes taken to imply that it is not meaningful to compare one culture's view of reality with that of another, because no common frame of reference is possible. But recall that in Part V Jean-Paul Sartre argued not only that each individual's view of reality is distinct, but that there is also a universal human condition. This idea implies that the ultimate goal of cultural psychology should be to reconcile cultural variety with common humanity.

Few psychologists have achieved this goal so well as Harry Triandis. Born in Greece, for the past several decades Triandis has had a steady influence on the development of cross-cultural psychology from his base at the University of Illinois. In his research Triandis has consistently tried to describe the ways in which different cultures are both the same and different, and to formulate a set of dimensions along which all cultures can be characterized.

In the following selection, an excerpt from one of his major theoretical papers, Triandis proposes that cultures vary along three dimensions that are psychologically important. Some cultures are collectivist while others are relatively individualist; this is the dimension that was discussed in detail in the earlier selection by Markus and Kitayama. In addition, cultures vary in the degree to which they do or do not tolerate deviations from social norms (a dimension called looseness vs. tightness) and in their complexity. Triandis describes the relations between these variables and the development of the self. For example, North American culture is individualist, loose, and complex, which may produce a uniquely American kind of personality. He also describes how these dimensions are related to aspects of the environment, child-rearing patterns, and social behavior.

Notice how Triandis manages to sidestep a couple of common pitfalls of cultural psychology. First, he avoids the trap of being painted into one or another extreme corner on the question of whether human nature is universal or variable. He consistently expresses the view that cultures all have aspects they share

with each other (called etics) and aspects that are locally unique (called emics).
Second, he never implies—as do other writers such as Markus and Kitayama—
that some positions on the dimensions of cultural variation are better than oth-
ers. It is neither good nor bad to be collectivist, individualist, tight, loose, com-
plex or simple. It is always a matter of trade-offs; the disadvantages of one
position are compensated for by advantages of the other. For example, members
of collectivist cultures gain in group support what they lose in individual free-
dom; the reverse could be said about members of individualistic cultures.

In the end, what Triandis describes could be called a "Big Three" for cul-
tures. The traits of collectivism-individualism, tightness-looseness, and complexity
are a group of psychologically relevant attributes that, Triandis demonstrates,
can provide a sort of personality profile for an entire culture.

From "The Self and Social Behavior in Differing Cultural Contexts," by H. C. Triandis. In
Psychological Review, 96, 506–520. Copyright © 1989 by the American Psychological Association. Adapted with permission.

The study of the self has a long tradition in psychology (e.g., Allport, 1943, 1955; Baumeister, 1987; Gordon & Gergen, 1968; James, 1890/1950; Murphy, 1947; Schlenker, 1985; Smith, 1980; Ziller, 1973), anthropology (e.g., Shweder & LeVine, 1984), and sociology (e.g., Cooley, 1902; Mead, 1934; Rosenberg, 1979). There is a recognition in most of these discussions that the self is shaped, in part, through interaction with groups. However, although there is evidence about variations of the self across cultures (Marsella, DeVos, & Hsu, 1985; Shweder & LeVine, 1984), the specification of the way the self determines aspects of social behavior in different cultures is undeveloped.

This article will examine first, aspects of the self; second, dimensions of variation of cultural contexts that have direct relevance to the way the self is defined; and third, the link between culture and self.

Definitions

THE SELF For purposes of this article, the self consists of all statements made by a person, overtly or covertly, that include the words "I," "me," "mine," and "myself" (Cooley, 1902). This broad definition indicates that all aspects of social motivation are linked to the self. Attitudes (e.g., *I* like X), beliefs (e.g., *I* think that X results in Y), intentions (e.g., *I* plan to do X), norms (e.g., in *my* group, people should act this way), roles (e.g., in *my* family, fathers act this way), and values (e.g., *I* think equality is very important) are aspects of the self.

The statements that people make that constitute the self have implications for the way people sample information (sampling information that is self-relevant more frequently than information that is not self-relevant), the way they process information (sampling more quickly information that is self-relevant than information that is not self-relevant), and the way they assess information (assessing more positively information that supports their current self-structure than information that challenges their self-structure). Thus, for instance, a self-instruction such as "I must do X" is more likely to be evaluated positively, and therefore accepted, if it maintains the current self-structure than if it changes this structure. This has implications for behavior because such self-instructions are among the several processes that lead to behavior (Triandis, 1977, 1980).

In other words, the self is an active agent that

promotes differential sampling, processing, and evaluation of information from the environment, and thus leads to differences in social behavior. Empirical evidence about the link of measures of the self to behavior is too abundant to review here. A sample will suffice: People whose self-concept was manipulated so that they thought of themselves (a) as "charitable" gave more to charity (Kraut, 1973), (b) as "neat and tidy" threw less garbage on the floor (Miller, Brickman, & Bolen, 1975), and (c) as "honest" were more likely to return a pencil (Shotland & Berger, 1970). Self-definition results in behaviors consistent with that definition (Wicklund & Gollwitzer, 1982). People who defined themselves as doers of a particular behavior were more likely to do that behavior (Greenwald, Carnot, Beach, & Young, 1987). Identity salience leads to behaviors consistent with that identity (Stryker & Serpe (1982). Self-monitoring (Snyder, 1974) has been linked to numerous behaviors (e.g., Snyder, 1987; Snyder, Simpson, & Gangestad, 1986). The more an attitude (an aspect of the self) is accessible to memory, the more likely it is to determine behavior (Fazio & Williams, 1986). Those with high self-esteem were found to be more likely to behave independently of group norms (Ziller, 1973).

* * *

To the extent such aspects are *shared* by people who speak a common language and who are able to interact because they live in adjacent locations during the same historical period, we can refer to all of these elements as a cultural group's *subjective culture* (Triandis, 1972). This implies that people who speak different languages (e.g., English and Chinese) or live in nonadjacent locations (e.g., England and Australia) or who have lived in different time periods (e.g., 19th and 20th centuries) may have different subjective cultures.

Some aspects of the self may be universal. "I am hungry" may well be an element with much the same meaning worldwide and across time. Other elements are extremely culture-specific. For instance, they depend on the particular mythology-religion-worldview and language of a culture. "My soul will be reincarnated" is culture-specific.

Some elements of the self imply action. For example, "I should be a high achiever" implies specific actions under conditions in which standards of excellence are present. Other elements do not imply action (e.g., I am tall).

* * *

One major distinction among aspects of the self is between the private, public, and collective self (Baumeister, 1986b; Greenwald & Pratkanis, 1984). Thus, we have the following: *the private self*—cognitions that involve traits, states, or behaviors of the person (e.g., "I am introverted," "I am honest," "I will buy X"); *the public self*—cognitions concerning the *generalized other*'s view of the self, such as "People think I am introverted" or "People think I will buy X"; and *the collective self*—cognitions concerning a view of the self that is found in some collective (e.g., family, coworkers, tribe, scientific society); for instance, "My family thinks I am introverted" or "My coworkers believe I travel too much."

The argument of this article is that people sample these three kinds of selves with different probabilities, in different cultures, and that has specific consequences for social behavior.

The private self is an assessment of the self by the self. The public self corresponds to an assessment of the self by the generalized other. The collective self corresponds to an assessment of the self by a specific reference group. Tajfel's (1978) notion of a *social identity*, "that part of the individual's self-concept which derives from his (or her) knowledge of his (her) membership in a social group (or groups) together with the values and emotional significance attached to that membership," (p. 63) is part of the collective self. Tajfel's theory is that people choose ingroups that maximize their positive social identity. However, that notion reflects an individualistic emphasis, because in many collectivist cultures people do not have a choice of ingroups. For instance, even though the Indian constitution has banned castes, caste is still an important aspect of social identity in that culture. Historical factors shape different identities (Baumeister, 1986a).

The notion of sampling has two elements: a

universe of units to be sampled and a *probability* of choice of a unit from that universe. The universe can be more or less complex. By complexity is meant that the number of distinguishable elements might be few versus many, the differentiation within the elements may be small or large, and the integration of the elements may be small or large. The number of nonoverlapping elements (e.g., I am bold; I am sensitive) is clearly relevant to complexity. The differentiation of the elements refer to the number of distinctions made within the element. For example, in the case of the social class element, a person may have a simple conception with little differentiation (e.g., people who are unemployed vs. working vs. leading the society) or a complex conception with much differentiation (e.g., rich, with new money, well educated vs. rich with new money, poorly educated). *Integration* refers to the extent a change in one element changes few versus many elements. Self-structures in which changes in one element result in changes in many elements are more complex than self-structures in which such changes result in changes of only a few elements (Rokeach, 1960).

In families in which children are urged to be themselves, in which "finding yourself" is valued, or in which self-actualization is emphasized, the private self is likely to be complex. In cultures in which families emphasize "what other people will think about you," the public self is likely to be complex. In cultures in which specific groups are emphasized during socialization (e.g., "remember you are a member of this family," ". . . you are a Christian"), the collective self is likely to be complex, and the norms, roles, and values of that group acquire especially great emotional significance.

* * *

One of many methods that are available to study the self requires writing 20 sentence completions that begin with "I am . . ." (Kuhn & McPartland, 1954). The answers can be content-analyzed to determine whether they correspond to the private, public, or collective self. If a social group is part of the answer (e.g., I am a son =

family; I am a student = educational institution; I am Roman Catholic = religion), one can classify the response as part of the collective self. If the generalized other is mentioned (e.g., I am liked by most people), it is part of the public self. If there is no reference to an entity outside the person (e.g., I am bold), it can be considered a part of the private self. Experience with this scoring method shows that coders can reach interrater reliabilities in the .9+ range. The percentage of the collective responses varies from 0 to 100, with sample means in Asian cultures in the 20% to 52% range and in European and North American samples between 15% and 19%. Public-self responses are relatively rare, so sample means of private-self responses (with student samples) are commonly in the 81% to 85% range. In addition to such content analyses, one can examine the availability (how frequently a particular group, e.g., the family, is mentioned) and the accessibility (when is a particular group mentioned for the first time in the rank-order) of responses (Higgins & King, 1981).

This method is useful because it provides an operational definition of the three kinds of selves under discussion. Also, salience is reflected directly in the measure of accessibility, and the complexity of particular self is suggested by the availability measure.

Although this method has many advantages, a multimethod strategy for the study of the self is highly recommended, because every method has some limitations and convergence across methods increases the validity of our measurements. Furthermore, when methods are used in different cultures in which people have different expectations about what can be observed, asked, or analyzed, there is an interaction between culture and method. But when methods converge similarly in different cultures and when the antecedents and consequences of the self-construct in each culture are similar, one can have greater confidence that the construct has similar or equivalent meanings across cultures.

Other methods that can tap aspects of the self have included interviews (e.g., Lobel, 1984),

Q-sorts of potentially self-descriptive attributes (e.g., Block, 1986), the Multistage Social Identity Inquirer (Zavalloni, 1975; Zavalloni & Louis-Guerin, 1984), and reaction times when responding to whether a specific attribute is self-descriptive (Rogers, 1981).

* * *

I have defined the self as one element of subjective culture (when it is shared by members of a culture) and distinguished the private, public, and collective selves, and indicated that the complexity of these selves will depend on cultural variables. The more complex a particular self, the more probable it is that it will be sampled. Sampling of a particular self will increase the probability that behaviors implicated in this aspect of the self will occur, when situations favor such occurrence. For example, data suggest that people from East Asia sample their collective self more frequently than do Europeans or North Americans. This means that elements of their reference groups, such as group norms or group goals, will be more salient among Asians than among Europeans or North Americans. In the next section I will describe cultural variation along certain theoretical dimensions that are useful for organizing the information about the sampling of different selves, and hence can account for differences in social behavior across cultures.

CULTURAL PATTERNS There is evidence of different selves across cultures (Marsella et al., 1985). However, the evidence has not been linked systematically to particular dimensions of cultural variation. This section will define three of these dimensions.

Cultural complexity. A major difference across cultures is in cultural complexity. Consider the contrast between the human bands that existed on earth up to about 15,000 years ago and the life of a major metropolitan city today. According to archaeological evidence, the bands rarely included more than 30 individuals. The number of relationships among 30 individuals is relatively small; the number of relationships in a major metropolitan area is potentially almost infinite. The number of potential relationships is one measure of cultural complexity. Students of this construct have used many others. One can get reliable rank orders by using information about whether cultures have writing and records, fixity of residence, agriculture, urban settlements, technical specialization, land transport other than walking, money, high population densities, many levels of political integration, and many levels of social stratification. Cultures that have all of these attributes (e.g., the Romans, the Chinese of the 5th century B.C., modern industrial cultures) are quite complex. As one or more of the aforementioned attributes are missing, the cultures are more simple, the simplest including the contemporary food gathering cultures (e.g., the nomads of the Kalahari desert).

Additional measures of complexity can be obtained by examining various domains of culture. Culture includes language, technology, economic, political, and educational systems, religious and aesthetic patterns, social structures, and so on. One can analyze each of these domains by considering the number of distinct elements that can be identified in it. For example, (a) language can be examined by noting the number of terms that are available (e.g., 600 camel-related terms in Arabic; many terms about automobiles in English), (b) economics by noting the number of occupations (the U.S. Employment and Training Administration's *Dictionary of Occupational Titles* contains more than 250,000), and (c) religion by noting the number of different functions (e.g., 6,000 priests in one temple in Orissa, India, each having a different function).

One of the consequences of increased complexity is that individuals have more and more potential ingroups toward whom they may or may not be loyal. As the number of potential ingroups increases, the loyalty of individuals to any one ingroup decreases. Individuals have the option of giving priority to their personal goals rather than to the goals of an ingroup. Also, the greater the affluence of a society, the more financial independence can be turned into social and emotional independence, with the individual giving priority to personal rather than in-group goals. Thus, as societies become more complex and affluent, they also can become more individualistic. However, there are some moderator variables that modify this simple picture, that will be discussed later, after I examine more closely the dimension of individualism-collectivism.

Individualism-collectivism. Individualists give priority to personal goals over the goals of collectives; collectivists either make no distinctions between personal and collective goals, or if they do make such distinctions, they subordinate their personal goals to the collective goals (Triandis, Bontempo, Villareal, Asai, & Lucca, 1988). Closely related to this dimension, in the work of Hofstede (1980), is *power distance* (the tendency to see a large difference between those with power and those without power). Collectivists tend to be high in power distance.

Although the terms *individualism* and *collectivism* should be used to characterize cultures and societies, the terms *idiocentric* and *allocentric* should be used to characterize individuals. Triandis, Leung, Villareal, and Clack (1985) have shown that within culture (Illinois) there are individuals who differ on this dimension, and the idiocentrics report that they are concerned with achievement, but are lonely, whereas the allocentrics report low alienation and receiving much social support. These findings were replicated in Puerto Rico (Triandis et al., 1988). The distinction of terms at the cultural and individual levels of analysis is useful because it is convenient when discussing the behavior of allocentrics in individualist cultures and idiocentrics in collectivist cultures (e.g., Bontempo, Lobel, & Triandis, 1989).

In addition to subordinating personal to collective goals, collectivists tend to be concerned about the results of their actions on members of their ingroups, tend to share resources with ingroup members, feel interdependent with ingroup members, and feel involved in the lives of ingroup members (Hui & Triandis, 1986). They emphasize the integrity of in-groups over time and de-

emphasize their independence from ingroups (Triandis et al., 1986).

Shweder's data (see Shweder & LeVine, 1984) suggest that collectivists perceive ingroup norms as universally valid (a form of ethnocentrism). A considerable literature suggests that collectivists automatically obey ingroup authorities and are willing to fight and die to maintain the integrity of the ingroup, whereas they distrust and are unwilling to cooperate with members of outgroups (Triandis, 1972). However, the definition of the ingroup keeps shifting with the situation. Common fate, common outside threat, and proximity (which is often linked to common fate) appear to be important determinants of the ingroup/outgroup boundary. Although the family is usually the most important ingroup, tribe, coworkers, coreligionists, and members of the same political or social collective or the same aesthetic or scientific persuasion can also function as important ingroups. When the state is under threat, it becomes the ingroup.

Ingroups can also be defined on the basis of similarity (in demographic attributes, activities, preferences, or institutions) and do influence social behavior to a greater extent when they are stable and impermeable (difficult to gain membership or difficult to leave). Social behavior is a function of ingroup norms to a greater extent in collectivist than individualist cultures. (Davidson, Jaccard, Triandis, Morales, and Diaz-Guerrero, 1976).

In collectivist cultures, ingroups influence a wide range of social situations (e.g., during the cultural revolution in China, the state had what was perceived as "legitimate influence" on every collective). In some cases, the influence is extreme (e.g., the Rev. Jones's People's Temple influenced 911 members of that collective to commit suicide in 1978).

* * *

As discussed earlier, over the course of cultural evolution there has been a shift toward individualism. Content analyses of social behaviors recorded in written texts (Adamopoulos & Bontempo, 1986) across historical periods show a shift from communal to exchange relationships. Behaviors related to trading are characteristic of individualistic cultures, and contracts emancipated individuals from the bonds of tribalism (Pearson, 1977).

The distribution of collectivism-individualism, according to Hofstede's (1980) data, contrasts most of the Latin American, Asian, and African cultures with most of the North American and Northern and Western European cultures. However, many cultures are close to the middle of the dimension, and other variables are also relevant. Urban samples tend to be individualistic, and traditional-rural samples tend toward collectivism within the same culture (e.g., Greece in the work of Doumanis, 1983; Georgas, 1989; and Katakis, 1984). Within the United States one can find a good deal of range on this variable, with Hispanic samples much more collectivist than samples of Northern and Western European backgrounds (G. Marin & Triandis, 1985).

The major antecedents of individualism appear to be cultural complexity and affluence. The more complex the culture, the greater the number of ingroups that one may have, so that a person has the option of joining ingroups or even forming new ingroups. Affluence means that the individual can be independent of ingroups. If the ingroup makes excessive demands, the individual can leave it. Mobility is also important. As individuals move (migration, changes in social class) they join new in-groups, and they have the opportunity to join ingroups whose goals they find compatible with their own. Furthermore, the more costly it is in a particular ecology for an ingroup to reject ingroup members who behave according to their own goals rather than according to ingroup goals, the more likely are people to act in accordance with their personal goals, and thus the more individualistic is the culture. Such costs are high when the ecology is thinly populated. One can scarcely afford to reject a neighbor if one has only one neighbor. Conversely, densely populated ecologies are characterized by collectivism, not only because those who behave inappropriately can be excluded, but also because it is necessary to regulate behavior more strictly to overcome problems of crowding.

As rewards from ingroup membership increase, the more likely it is that a person will use ingroup goals as guides for behavior. Thus, when ingroups provide many rewards (e.g., emotional security, status, income, information, services, willingness to spend time with the person) they tend to increase the person's commitment to the ingroup and to the culture's collectivism.

The size of ingroups tends to be different in the two kinds of cultures. In collectivist cultures, ingroups tend to be small (e.g., family), whereas in individualist cultures they can be large (e.g., people who agree with me on important attitudes).

Child-rearing patterns are different in collectivist and individualist cultures. The primary concern of parents in collectivist cultures is obedience, reliability, and proper behavior. The primary concern of parents in individualistic cultures is self-reliance, independence, and creativity. Thus, we find that in simple, agricultural societies, socialization is severe and conformity is demanded and obtained (Berry, 1967, 1979). Similarly, in working-class families in industrial societies, the socialization pattern leads to conformity (Kohn, 1969, 1987). In more individualist cultures such as food gatherers (Berry, 1979) and very individualistic cultures such as the United States, the child-rearing pattern emphasizes self-reliance and independence; children are allowed a good deal of autonomy and are encouraged to explore their environment. Similarly, creativity and self-actualization are more important traits and are emphasized in child-rearing in the professional social classes (Kohn, 1987).

It is clear that conformity is functional in simple, agricultural cultures (if one is to make an irrigation system, each person should do part of the job in a well-coordinated plan) and in working-class jobs (the boss does not want subordinates who do their own thing). Conversely, it is dysfunctional in hunting cultures, in which one must be ingenious, and in professional jobs, in which one must be creative. The greater the cultural complexity, the more is conformity to one ingroup dysfunctional, inasmuch as one cannot take advantage of new opportunities available in other parts of the society.

The smaller the family size, the more the child is allowed to do his or her own thing. In large families, rules must be imposed, otherwise chaos will occur. As societies become more affluent (individualistic), they also reduce the size of the family, which increases the opportunity to raise children to be individualists. Autonomy in childrearing also leads to individualism. Exposure to other cultures (e.g., through travel or because of societal heterogeneity) also increases individualism, inasmuch as the child becomes aware of different norms and has to choose his or her own standards of behavior.

* * *

Tight versus loose cultures. In collectivist cultures, ingroups demand that individuals conform to ingroup norms, role definitions, and values. When a society is relatively homogeneous, the norms and values of ingroups are similar. But heterogeneous societies have groups with dissimilar norms. If an ingroup member deviates from ingroup norms, ingroup members may have to make the painful decision of excluding that individual from the ingroup. Because rejection of ingroup members is emotionally draining, cultures develop tolerance for deviation from group norms. As a result, homogeneous cultures are often rigid in requiring that ingroup members behave according to the ingroup norms. Such cultures are *tight*. Heterogeneous cultures and cultures in marginal positions between two major cultural patterns are flexible in dealing with ingroup members who deviate from ingroup norms. For example, Japan is considered tight, and it is relatively homogeneous. Thailand is considered loose, and it is in a marginal position between the major cultures of India and China; people are pulled in different directions by sometimes contrasting norms, and hence they must be more flexible in imposing their norms. In short, tight cultures (Pelto, 1968) have clear norms that are reliably imposed. Little deviation from normative behavior is tolerated, and severe sanctions

are administered to those who deviate. *Loose* cultures either have unclear norms about most social situations or tolerate deviance from the norms. For example, it is widely reported in the press that Japanese children who return to Japan after a period of residence in the West, are criticized most severely by teachers because their behavior is not "proper." Japan is a tight culture in which deviations that would be considered trivial in the West (such as bringing Western food rather than Japanese food for lunch) are noted and criticized. In loose cultures, deviations from "proper" behavior are tolerated, and in many cases there are no standards of "proper" behavior. Theocracies[1] are prototypical of tight cultures, but some contemporary relatively homogeneous cultures (e.g., the Greeks, the Japanese) are also relatively tight. In a heterogeneous culture, such as the United States, it is more difficult for people to agree on specific norms, and even more difficult to impose severe sanctions. Geographic mobility allows people to leave the offended communities in ways that are not available in more stable cultures. Urban environments are more loose than rural environments, in which norms are clearer and sanctions can be imposed more easily. Prototypical of loose cultures are the Lapps and the Thais. In very tight cultures, according to Pelto, one finds corporate control of property, corporate ownership of stored food and production power, religious figures as leaders, hereditary recruitment into priesthood, and high levels of taxation.

* * *

The intolerance of inappropriate behavior characteristic of tight cultures does not extend to all situations. In fact, tight cultures are quite tolerant of foreigners (they do not know better), and of drunk, and mentally ill persons. They may even have rituals in which inappropriate behavior is expected. For example, in a tight culture such as Japan one finds the office beer party as a ritual institution, where one is expected to get drunk and to tell the boss what one "really" thinks of him (it is rarely her). Similarly, in loose cultures,

---

[1]Nations run by religious rule.

there are specific situations in which deviance is not tolerated. For example, in Orissa (India), a son who cuts his hair the day after his father dies is bound to be severely criticized, although the culture is generally loose.

* * *

Culture and Self

Culture is to society what memory is to the person. It specifies designs for living that have proven effective in the past, ways of dealing with social situations, and ways to think about the self and social behavior that have been reinforced in the past. It includes systems of symbols that facilitate interaction (Geertz, 1973), rules of the game of life that have been shown to "work" in the past. When a person is socialized in a given culture, the person can use custom as a substitute for thought, and save time.

The three dimensions of cultural variation just described reflect variations in culture that have emerged because of different ecologies, such as ways of surviving. Specifically, in cultures that survive through hunting or food gathering, in which people are more likely to survive if they work alone or in small groups because game is dispersed, individualism emerges as a good design for living. In agricultural cultures, in which cooperation in the building of irrigation systems and food storage and distribution facilities is reinforced, collectivist designs for living emerge. In complex, industrial cultures, in which loosely linked ingroups produce the thousands of parts of modern machines (e.g., a 747 airplane), individuals often find themselves in situations in which they have to choose ingroups or even form their own ingroups (e.g., new corporation). Again, individualistic designs for living become more functional. In homogeneous cultures, one can insist on tight norm enforcement; in heterogeneous, or fast changing, or marginal (e.g., confluence of two major cultural traditions) cultures, the imposition of tight norms is difficult because it is unclear whose norms are to be used. A loose culture is more likely in such ecologies.

Over time, cultures become more complex, as new differentiations prove effective. However, once complexity reaches very high levels, moves toward simplification emerge as reactions to too much complexity. For example, in art styles, the pendulum has been swinging between the "less is more" view of Oriental art and the "more is better" view of the rococo period in Europe. Similarly, excessive individualism may create a reaction toward collectivism, and excessive collectivism, a reaction toward individualism; or tightness may result from too much looseness, and looseness from too much tightness. Thus, culture is dynamic, ever changing.

* * *

The three dimensions of cultural variation described earlier are systematically linked to different kinds of self. In this section I provide hypotheses linking culture and self.

INDIVIDUALISM-COLLECTIVISM Child-rearing patterns in individualistic cultures tend to emphasize self-reliance, independence, finding yourself, and self-actualization. As discussed earlier, such child-rearing increases the complexity of the private self, and because there are more elements of the private self to be sampled, more are sampled. Thus, the probability that the private rather than the other selves will be sampled increases with individualism. Conversely, in collectivist cultures, child-rearing emphasizes the importance of the collective; the collective self is more complex and more likely to be sampled.

* * *

Such patterns are usually associated with rewards for conformity to ingroup goals, which leads to internalization of the ingroup goals. Thus, people do what is expected of them, even if that is not enjoyable. Bontempo et al. (1989) randomly assigned subjects from a collectivist (Brazil) and an individualist (U.S.) culture to two conditions of questionnaire administration: public and private. The questionnaire contained questions about how the subject was likely to act when the ingroup expected a behavior that was costly to the individual (e.g., visit a friend in the hospital, when this was time consuming). Both of the questions How should the person act? and How enjoyable would it be to act? were measured. It was found that Brazilians gave the same answers under both the anonymous and public conditions. Under both conditions they indicated that they would do what was expected of them. The U.S. sample indicated they would do what was expected of them in the public but not in the private condition. The U.S. group's private answers indicated that the subjects thought that doing the costly behaviors was unlikely, and certainly not enjoyable. Under the very same conditions the Brazilians indicated that they thought the costly prosocial behaviors were likely and enjoyable. In short, the Brazilians had internalized[2] the ingroup norms so that conformity to the ingroup appeared enjoyable to them.

* * *

Observations indicate that the extent to which an ingroup makes demands on individuals in few or in many areas shows considerable variance. For example, in the United States, states make very few demands (e.g., pay your income tax), whereas in China during the cultural revolution, the Communist Party made demands in many areas (artistic expression, family life, political behavior, civic action, education, athletics, work groups, even location, such as where to live). It seems plausible that the more areas of one's life that are affected by an ingroup, the more likely the individual is to sample the collective self.

* * *

TIGHT-LOOSE CULTURES Homogeneous, relatively isolated cultures tend to be tight, and they will sample the collective self more than will heterogeneous, centrally located cultures. The more homogeneous the culture, the more the norms will be clear and deviation from normative behavior can be punished. Cultural heterogeneity increases the confusion regarding what is correct and

proper behavior. Also, cultural marginality[3] tends to result in norm and role conflict and pressures individuals toward adopting different norms. Because rejection of the ingroup members who have adopted norms of a different culture can be costly, individuals moderate their need to make their ingroup members conform to their ideas of proper behavior. So, the culture becomes loose (i.e., tolerant of deviations from norms).

The looser the culture, the more the individual can choose what self to sample. If several kinds of collective self are available, one may choose to avoid norm and role conflict by rejecting all of them and developing individual conceptions of proper behavior. Thus, sampling of the private self is more likely in loose cultures and sampling of the collective self is more likely in tight cultures. Also, tight cultures tend to socialize their children by emphasizing the expectations of the generalized other. Hence, the public self will be complex and will be more likely to be sampled. In other words, tight cultures tend to sample the public and collective self, whereas loose cultures tend to sample the private self.

When the culture is both collectivist and tight, then the public self is extremely likely to be sampled. That means people act "properly," as that is defined by society, and are extremely anxious [about not acting] correctly. Their private self does not matter. As a result, the private and public selves are often different. Doi (1986) discussed this point extensively, comparing the Japanese public self (*tatemae*) with the private self (*honne*). He suggested that in the United States there is virtue in keeping public and private consistent (not being a hypocrite). In Japan, proper action matters. What you feel about such action is irrelevant. Thus, the Japanese do not like to state their personal opinions, but rather seek consensus.

Consistently with Doi's (1986) arguments is Iwao's (1988) research. She presented scenarios to Japanese and Americans and asked them to judge

---

[2]Made a part of themselves.

[3]Not being part of the mainstream of a culture and feeling that one or one's group is at the "margins."

various actions that could be appropriate responses to these situations. For example, one scenario (daughter brings home person from another race) included as a possible response "thought that he would never allow them to marry but told them he was in favor of their marriage." This response was endorsed as the *best* by 44% of the Japanese sample but by only 2% of the Americans; it was the *worst* in the opinion of 48% of the Americans and 7% of the Japanese.

Although the private self may be complex, this does not mean that it will be communicated to others if one can avoid such communication. In fact, in tight cultures people avoid disclosing much of the self, because by disclosing they may reveal some aspect of the self that others might criticize. In other words, they may be aware of the demands of the generalized other and avoid being vulnerable to criticism by presenting little of this complex self to others. Barlund (1975) reported studies of the self-disclosure to same-sex friend, opposite-sex friend, mother, father, stranger, and untrusted acquaintance in Japan and in the United States. The pattern of self-disclosure was the same—that is, more to same-sex friend, and progressively less to opposite-sex friend, mother, father, stranger, and least to the untrusted acquaintance. However, the amount disclosed in each relationship was about 50% more in the United States than in Japan.

CULTURAL COMPLEXITY The more complex the culture, the more confused is likely to be the individual's identity. Dragonas (1983) sampled the self-concepts of 11- and 12-year-olds in Greek small villages (simple), traditional cities (medium), and large cities (complex) cultures. She found that the more complex the culture, the more confusing was the identity. Similarly, Katakis (1976, 1978, 1984) found that the children of farmers and fishermen, when asked what they would be when they are old, unhesitatingly said "farmer" or "fisherman," whereas in the large cities the responses frequently were of the "I will find myself" variety. Given the large number of in-

groups that are available in a complex environment and following the logic presented here, individuals may well opt for sampling their private self and neglect the public or collective selves.

CONTENT OF SELF IN DIFFERENT CULTURES The specific content of the self in particular cultures will reflect the language and availability of mythological constructs of that culture. Myths often provide ideal types that are incorporated in the self forged in a given culture (Roland, 1984a). For example, peace of mind and being free of worries have been emphasized as aspects of the self in India (Roland, 1984b) and reflect Indian values that are early recognizable in Hinduism and Buddhism (which emerged in India). Mythological, culture specific constructs become incorporated in the self (Sinha, 1982, 1987). Roland (1984b) claimed that the private self is more "organized around 'we', 'our' and 'us' . . ." (p. 178) in India than in the West. But particular life events may be linked to more than one kind of self. For example, Sinha (1987b) found that the important goals of Indian managers are their own good health and the good health of their family (i.e., have both private and collective self-elements).

Sinha (personal communication, November 1985) believes the public self is different in collectivist and individualist cultures. In individualistic cultures it is assumed that the generalized other will value autonomy, independence, and self-reliance, and thus individuals will attempt to act in ways that will impress others (i.e., indicate that they have these attributes). To be distinct and different are highly valued, and people find innumerable ways to show themselves to others as different (in dress, possessions, speech patterns). By contrast, in collectivist cultures, conformity to the other in public settings is valued. Thus, in a restaurant, everyone orders the same food (in traditional restaurants, only the visible leader gets a menu and orders for all). The small inconvenience of eating nonoptimal food is more than compensated by the sense of solidarity that such actions generate. In collectivist cultures, being "nice" to ingroup others is a high value, so that one expects in most situations extreme politeness and a display of harmony (Triandis, Marin, Lisansky, & Betancourt, 1984). Thus, in collectivist cultures, the public self is an extension of the collective self. One must make a good impression by means of prosocial behaviors toward ingroup members, acquaintances, and others who may become ingroup members. At the same time, one can be quite rude to outgroup members, and there is no concern about displaying hostility, exploitation, or avoidance of outgroup members.

* * *

The collective self in collectivist cultures includes elements such as "I am philotimos" (traditional Greece, meaning "I must act as is expected of me by my family and friends"; see Triandis, 1972), "I must sacrifice myself for my ingroup," "I feel good when I display affection toward my ingroup," and "I must maintain harmony with my ingroup even when that is very disagreeable." The person is less self-contained in collectivist than in individualistic cultures (Roland, 1984b, p. 176).

Identity is defined on the basis of different elements in individualistic and collectivist cultures. Individualistic cultures tend to emphasize elements of identity that reflect possessions—what do I own, what experiences have I had, what are my accomplishments (for scientists, what is my list of publications). In collectivist cultures, identity is defined more in terms of relationships—I am the mother of X, I am a member of family Y, and I am a resident of Z. Furthermore, the qualities that are most important in forming an identity can be quite different. In Europe and North America, being logical, rational, balanced, and fair are important attributes; in Africa, personal style, ways of moving, the unique spontaneous self, sincere self-expression, unpredictability, and emotional expression are most valued. The contrast between classical music (e.g., Bach or Mozart) and jazz reflects this difference musically.

CONSEQUENCES OF SAMPLING THE PRIVATE AND COLLECTIVE SELF In the previous section I examined the relationship between the three dimensions of cultural variation and the probabilities of differential sampling of the private, public, and collective selves. In this section I review some of the empirical literature that is relevant to the theoretical ideas just presented.

An important consequence of sampling the collective self is that many of the elements of the collective become salient. Norms, roles, and values (i.e., proper ways of acting as defined by the collective) become the "obviously" correct ways to act. Behavioral intentions reflect such processes. Thus, the status of the other person in the social interaction—for example, is the other an ingroup or an outgroup member—becomes quite salient. Consequently, in collectivist cultures, individuals pay more attention to ingroups and outgroups and moderate their behavior accordingly, than is the case in individualistic cultures (Triandis, 1972).

* * *

Who is placed in the ingroup is culture specific. For example, ratings of the "intimacy" of relationships on a 9-point scale suggest that in Japan there is more intimacy with acquaintances, coworkers, colleagues, best friends, and close friends than in the United States (Gudykunst & Nishida, 1986).

Atsumi (1980) argued that understanding Japanese social behavior requires distinguishing relationships with benefactors, true friends, coworkers, acquaintances, and outsiders (strangers). The determinants of social behavior shift depending on this classification. Behavior toward benefactors requires that the person go out of his way to benefit them. Behavior toward true friends is largely determined by the extent the behavior is enjoyable in itself, and the presence of these friends makes it enjoyable. Behavior toward coworkers is determined by both norms and cost/benefit considerations. Finally, behavior toward outsiders is totally determined by cost/benefit ratios.

* * *

The behavioral intentions of persons in collectivist cultures appear to be determined by cognitions that are related to the survival and benefit of their collective. In individualist cultures, the concerns are personal. An example comes from a study of smoking. A collectivist sample (Hispanics in the U.S.) showed significantly more concern than an individualist sample (non-Hispanics) about smoking affecting the health of others, giving a bad example to children, harming children, and bothering others with the bad smell of cigarettes, bad breath, and bad smell on clothes and belongings, whereas the individualist sample was more concerned about the physiological symptoms they might experience during withdrawal from cigarette smoking (G. V. Marin, Marin, Otero-Sabogal, Sabogal, & Perez-Stable, 1987).

The emphasis on harmony within the ingroup, found more strongly in collectivist than in individualist cultures, results in the more positive evaluation of group-serving partners (Bond, Chiu, & Wan, 1984), the choice of conflict resolution techniques that minimize animosity (Leung, 1985, 1987), the greater giving of social support (Triandis et al., 1985), and the greater support of ingroup goals (Nadler, 1986). The emphasis on harmony may be, in part, the explanation of the lower heart-attack rates among unacculturated than among acculturated Japanese-Americans (Marmot & Syme, 1976). Clearly, a society in which confrontation is common is more likely to increase the blood pressure of those in such situations, and hence the probability of heart attacks; avoiding conflict and saving face must be linked to lower probabilities that blood pressure will become elevated. The probability of receiving social support in collectivist cultures may be another factor reducing the levels of stress produced by unpleasant life events and hence the probabilities of heart attacks (Triandis et al., 1988).

Although ideal ingroup relationships are expected to be smoother, more intimate, and easier in collectivist cultures, outgroup relationships can be quite difficult. Because the ideal social behaviors often cannot be attained, one finds many splits of the ingroup in collectivist cultures. Avoidance relationships are frequent and, in some cases, required by norms (e.g., mother-in-law avoidance

in some cultures). Fights over property are common and result in redefinitions of the ingroup. However, once the ingroup is defined, relationships tend to be very supportive and intimate within the ingroup, whereas there is little trust and often hostility toward outgroup members. Gabrenya and Barba (1987) found that collectivists are not as effective in meeting strangers as are individualists. Triandis (1967) found unusually poor communication among members of the same corporation who were not ingroup members (close friends) in a collectivist culture. Bureaucracies in collectivist cultures function especially badly because people hoard information (Kaiser, 1984). Manipulation and exploitation of outgroups is common (Pandey, 1986) in collectivist cultures. When competing with outgroups, collectivists are more competitive than individualists (Espinoza & Garza, 1985) even under conditions when competitiveness is counterproductive.

In individualistic cultures, people exchange compliments more frequently than in collectivist cultures (Barlund & Araki, 1985). They meet people easily and are able to cooperate with them even if they do not know them well (Gabrenya & Barba, 1987). Because individualists have more of a choice concerning ingroup memberships, they stay in those groups with whom they can have relatively good relationships and leave groups with whom they disagree too frequently (Verma, 1985).

Competition tends to be interpersonal in individualistic and intergroup in collectivist cultures (Hsu, 1983; Triandis et al., 1988). Conflict is frequently found in family relationships in individualistic cultures and between families in collectivist cultures (Katakis, 1978).

There is a substantial literature (e.g., Berman, Murphy-Berman, & Singh, 1985; Berman, Murphy-Berman, Singh, & Kumar, 1984; Hui, 1984; G. Marin, 1985; Triandis et al., 1985) indicating that individualists are more likely to use equity, and collectivists to use equality or need, as the norms for the distribution of resources (Yang, 1981). This is consistent with the emphasis on trading discussed earlier. By contrast, the emphasis on communal relationships (Mills & Clark, 1982) found in collectivist cultures leads to emphases on equality and need. The parallel with gender differences, where men emphasize exchange and women emphasize communal relationships (i.e., equity and need; Major & Adams, 1983; Brockner & Adsit, 1986), respectively, is quite striking. ⋆ ⋆ ⋆

⋆　⋆　⋆

Conclusions

Aspects of the self (private, public, and collective) are differentially sampled in different cultures, depending on the complexity, level of individualism, and looseness of the culture. The more complex, individualistic, and loose the culture, the more likely it is that people will sample the private self and the less likely it is that they will sample the collective self. When people sample the collective self, they are more likely to be influenced by the norms, role definitions, and values of the particular collective, than when they do not sample the collective self. When they are so influenced by a collective, they are likely to behave in ways considered appropriate by members of that collective. The more they sample the private self, the more their behavior can be accounted for by exchange theory and can be described as an exchange relationship. The more they sample the collective self, the less their behavior can be accounted for by exchange theory; it can be described as a communal relationship. However, social behavior is more likely to be communal when the target of that behavior is an ingroup member than when the target is an outgroup member. Ingroups are defined by common goals, common fate, the presence of an external threat, and/or the need to distribute resources to all ingroup members for the optimal survival of the ingroup. Outgroups consist of people with whom one is in competition or whom one does not trust. The ingroup-outgroup distinction determines social behavior more strongly in collectivist than in individualist cultures. When the culture is both collectivist and tight, the public self is particularly likely to be sampled. In short, a major determinant of social behavior is the kind of self that operates in the particular culture.

References

Adamopoulos, J., & Bontempo, R. N. (1986). Diachronic universals in interpersonal structures. *Journal of Cross-Cultural Psychology, 17,* 169–189.

Allport, G. W. (1943). The ego in contemporary psychology. *Psychological Review, 50,* 451–478.

Allport, G. W. (1955). *Becoming.* New Haven, CT: Yale University Press.

Atsumi, R. (1980). Patterns of personal relationships: A key to understanding Japanese thought and behavior. *Social Analysis, 6,* 63–78.

Barlund, D. C. (1975). *Public and private self in Japan and the United States.* Tokyo: Simul Press.

Barlund, D. C., & Araki, S. (1985). Intercultural encounters: The management of compliments by Japanese and Americans. *Journal of Cross-Cultural Psychology, 16,* 9–26.

Baumeister, R. F. (1986a). *Identity: Cultural change and the struggle for self.* New York: Oxford University Press.

Baumeister, R. F. (1986b). *Public self and private self.* New York: Springer.

Baumeister, R. F. (1987). How the self became a problem: A psychological review of historical research. *Journal of Personality and Social Psychology, 52,* 163–176.

Berman, J. J., Murphy-Berman, V., & Singh, P. (1985). Cross-cultural similarities and differences in perceptions of fairness. *Journal of Cross Cultural Psychology, 16,* 55–67.

Berman, J. J., Murphy-Berman, V., Singh, P., & Kumar, P. (1984, September). *Cross-cultural similarities and differences in perceptions of fairness.* Paper presented at the International Congress of Psychology, in Acapulco, Mexico.

Berry, J. W. (1967). Independence and conformity in subsistence level societies. *Journal of Personality and Social Psychology, 7,* 415–418.

Berry, J. W. (1979). A cultural ecology of social behavior. In L. Berkowitz (Ed.), *Advances in experimental social psychology* (Vol. 12, pp. 177–207). New York: Academic Press.

Block, J. (1986, March). *Longitudinal studies of personality.* Colloquium given at the University of Illinois, Psychology Department.

Bond, M. H., Chiu, C., & Wan, K. (1984). When modesty fails: The social impact of group effacing attributions following success or failure. *European Journal of Social Psychology, 16,* 111–127.

Bontempo, R., Lobel, S. A., & Triandis, H. C. (1989). *Compliance and value internalization among Brazilian and U.S. students.* Manuscript submitted for publication.

Brockner, J., & Adsit, L. (1986). The moderating impact of sex on the equity satisfaction relationship: A field study. *Journal of Applied Psychology, 71,* 585–590.

Cooley, C. H. (1902). *Human nature and the social order.* New York: Scribner.

Davidson, A. R., Jaccard, J. J., Triandis, H. C., Morales, M. L., & Diaz-Guerrero, R. (1976). Cross-cultural model testing:

Toward a solution of the etic-emic dilemma. *International Journal of Psychology, 11,* 1–13.

Doumanis, M. (1983). *Mothering in Greece: From collectivism to individualism.* New York: Academic Press.

Doi, T. (1986). *The anatomy of conformity: The individual versus society.* Tokyo: Kodansha.

Dragonas, T. (1983). *The self-concept of preadolescents in the Hellenic context.* Unpublished doctoral dissertation, University of Ashton, Birmingham, England.

Espinoza, J. A., & Garza, R. T. (1985). Social group salience and interethnic cooperation. *Journal of Experimental Social Psychology, 231,* 380–392.

Fazio, R. H., & Williams, C. J. (1986). Attitude accessibility as a moderator of the attitude-perception and attitude-behavior relations: An investigation of the 1984 presidential election. *Journal of Personality and Social Psychology, 51,* 505–514.

Gabrenya, W. K., & Barba, L. (1987, March). *Cultural differences in social interaction during group problem solving.* Paper presented at the meetings of the Southeastern Psychological Association, Atlanta.

Geertz, C. (1973). *The interpretation of cultures.* New York: Basic Books.

Georgas, J. (1989). Changing family values in Greece: From collectivist to individualist. *Journal of Cross-Cultural Psychology, 20,* 80–91.

Gordon, C., & Gergen, K. J. (1968). (Eds.), *The self in social interaction.* New York: Wiley.

Greenwald, A. G., Carnot, C. G., Beach, R., & Young, B. (1987). Increasing voting behavior by asking people if they expect to vote. *Journal of Applied Psychology, 71,* 315–318.

Greenwald, A. G., & Pratkanis, A. R. (1984). The self. In R. S. Wyer & T. K. Srull (Eds.), *Handbook of social cognition* (Vol. 3, pp. 129–178). Hillsdale, NJ: Erlbaum.

Gudykunst, W. B., & Nishida. T. (1986). The influence of cultural variability on perceptions of communication behavior associated with relationship terms. *Human Communication Research, 13,* 147–166.

Higgins, E. T., & King, G. (1981). Accessibility of social constructs: Information-processing consequences of individual and contextual variability. In N. Cantor & J. F. Kihlstrom (Eds.), *Personality, cognition and social interaction* (pp. 69–121). Hillsdale, NJ: Erlbaum.

Hofstede, G. (1980). *Culture's consequences.* Beverly Hills, CA: Sage.

Hsu, F. L. K. (1983). *Rugged individualism reconsidered.* Knoxville: University of Tennessee Press.

Hui, C. H. (1984). *Individualism-collectivism: Theory, measurement and its relationship to reward allocation.* Unpublished doctoral dissertation, Department of Psychology, University of Illinois at Champaign-Urbana.

Hui, C. H., & Triandis, H. C. (1986). Individualism-collectivism: A study of cross-cultural researchers. *Journal of Cross Cultural Psychology, 17,* 225–248.

Iwao, S. (1988, August). *Social psychology's models of man: Isn't it time for East to meet West?* Invited address to the International Congress of Scientific Psychology, Sydney, Australia.

James, W. (1950). *The principles of psychology.* New York: Dover. (Original work published 1890)

Katakis, C. D. (1976). An exploratory multilevel attempt to investigate interpersonal and intrapersonal patterns of 20 Athenian families. *Mental Health and Society, 3,* 1–9.

Katakis, C. D. (1978). On the transaction of social change processes and the perception of self in relation to others. *Mental Health and Society, 5,* 275–283.

Katakis, C. D. (1984). Oi tris tautotites tis Ellinikis oikogenoias [The three identities of the Greek family]. Athens, Greece: Kedros.

Kohn, M. L. (1969). *Class and conformity.* Homewood, IL: Dorsey.

Kohn, M. L. (1987). Cross-national research as an analytic strategy. *American Sociological Review, 52,* 713–731.

Kraut, R. E. (1973). Effects of social labeling on giving to charity. *Journal of Experimental Social Psychology, 9,* 551–562.

Kuhn, M. H., & McPartland, T. (1954). An empirical investigation of self-attitudes. *American Sociological Review, 19,* 68–76.

Leung, K. (1985). *Cross-cultural study of procedural fairness and disputing behavior.* Unpublished doctoral dissertation, Department of Psychology, University of Illinois, Champaign-Urbana.

Leung, K. (1987). Some determinants of reactions to procedural models for conflict resolution: A cross-national study. *Journal of Personality and Social Psychology, 53,* 898–908.

Lobel, S. A. (1984). *Effects of sojourn to the United States. A SYMLOG content analysis of in-depth interviews.* Unpublished doctoral dissertation, Harvard University.

Major, B., & Adams, J. B. (1983). Role of gender, interpersonal orientation, and self-presentation in distributive justice behavior. *Journal of Personality and Social Psychology, 45,* 598–608.

Marin, G. (1985). Validez transcultural del principio de equidad: El colectivismo-individualismo como una variable moderatora [Transcultural validity of the principle of equity: Collectivism–individualism as a moderating variable]. *Revista Interamericana de Psicologia Occupational, 4,* 7–20.

Marin, G., & Triandis, H. C. (1985). Allocentrism as an important characteristic of the behavior of Latin Americans and Hispanics. In R. Diaz-Guerrero (Ed.), *Cross-cultural and national studies in social psychology* (69–80). Amsterdam, The Netherlands: North Holland.

Marin, G. V., Marin, G., Otero-Sabogal, R., Sabogal, F., & Perez-Stable, E. (1987). *Cultural differences in attitudes toward smoking: Developing messages using the theory of reasoned action* (Tech. Rep.). (Available from Box 0320, 400 Parnassus Ave., San Francisco, CA 94117)

Marmot, M. G., & Syme, S. L. (1976). Acculturation and coronary heart disease in Japanese Americans. *American Journal of Epidemiology, 104,* 225–247.

Marsella, A. J., DeVos, G., & Hsu, F. L. K. (1985). *Culture and self.* New York: Tavistock.

Mead, G. H. (1934). *Mind, self, and society.* Chicago: University of Chicago Press.

Miller, R. L., Brickman, P., & Bolen, D. (1975). Attribution versus persuasion as a means of modifying behavior. *Journal of Personality and Social Psychology, 31,* 430–441.

Mills, J., & Clark, E. S. (1982). Exchange and communal relationships. In L. Wheeler (Ed.), *Review of personality and social psychology* (Vol. 3, pp. 121–144). Beverly Hills, CA: Sage.

Murphy, G. (1947). *Personality.* New York: Harper.

Nadler, A. (1986). Help seeking as a cultural phenomenon: Differences between city and kibbutz dwellers. *Journal of Personality and Social Psychology, 51*, 976–982.

Pandey, J. (1986). Sociocultural perspectives on ingratiation. *Progress in Experimental Personality Research, 14*, 205–229.

Pearson, H. W. (Ed.). (1977). *The livelihood of man: Karl Polanyi*. New York: Academic Press.

Pelto, P. J. (1968, April). The difference between "tight" and "loose" societies. *Transaction*, 37–40.

Rogers, T. B. (1981). A model of the self as an aspect of the human information processing system. In N. Cantor & J. F. Kihlstrom (Eds.), *Personality, cognition and social interaction* (pp. 193–214). Hillsdale, NJ: Erlbaum.

Rokeach, M. (1960). *The open and closed mind*. New York: Basic Books.

Roland, A. (1984a). Psychoanalysis in civilization perspective. *Psychoanalytic Review, 7*, 569–590.

Roland, A. (1984b). The self in India and America: Toward a psychoanalysis of social and cultural contexts. In V. Kovolis (Ed.), *Designs of selfhood* (pp. 123–130). New Jersey: Associated University Press.

Rosenberg, M. (1979). *Conceiving the self*. New York: Basic Books.

Schlenker, B. R. (1985). Introduction. In B. R. Schlenker (Ed.). *Foundations of the self in social life* (pp. 1–28). New York: McGraw-Hill.

Shotland, R. L., & Berger, W. G. (1970). Behavioral validation of several values from the Rokeach value scale as an index of honesty. *Journal of Applied Psychology, 54*, 433–435.

Shweder, R. A., & LeVine, R. A. (1984). *Cultural theory: Essays on mind, self and emotion*. New York: Cambridge University Press.

Sinha, J. B. P. (1982). The Hindu (Indian) identity. *Dynamische Psychiatrie, 15*, 148–160.

Sinha, J. B. P. (1987). *Work cultures in Indian Organizations* (ICSSR Report). New Delhi, India: Concept Publications House.

Smith, M. B. (1980). Attitudes, values and selfhood. In H. E. Howe & M. M. Page (Eds.), *Nebraska Symposium on Motivation, 1979* (pp. 305–358). Lincoln: University of Nebraska Press.

Snyder, M. (1974). Self-monitoring and expressive behavior. *Journal of Personality and Social Psychology, 30*, 526–537.

Snyder, M. (1987). *Public appearances as private realities: The psychology of self-monitoring*. New York: Freeman.

Snyder, M., Simpson, J. A., & Gangestad, S. (1986). Personality and sexual relations. *Journal of Personality and Social Psychology, 51*, 181–190.

Stryker, S., & Serpe, R. T. (1982). Commitment, identity salience, and role behavior: Theory and research example. In W. Ickes & E. S. Knowles (Eds.), *Personality, roles and social behavior* (pp. 199–218). New York: Springer.

Tajfel, H. (1978). *Differentiation between social groups*. London: Academic Press.

Triandis, H. C. (1967). Interpersonal relations in international organizations. *Journal of Organizational Behavior and Human Performance, 2*, 26–55.

Triandis, H. C. (1972). *The analysis of subjective culture*. New York: Wiley.

Triandis, H. C. (1977). *Interpersonal behavior*. Monterey, CA: Brooks/Cole.

Triandis, H. C. (1980). Values, attitudes, and interpersonal behavior. In H. Howe & M. Page (Eds.), *Nebraska Symposium on Motivation, 1979* (pp. 195–260). Lincoln: University of Nebraska Press.

Triandis, H. C., Bontempo, R., Betancourt, H., Bond, M., Leung, K., Brenes, A., Georgas, J., Hui, C. H., Marin, G., Setiadi, B., Sinha, J. B. P., Verma, J., Spangenberg, J., Touzard, H., & de Montmollin, G. (1986). The measurement of etic aspects of individualism and collectivism across cultures. *Australian Journal of Psychology* (Special issue on cross-cultural psychology), *38*, 257–267.

Triandis, H. C., Bontempo, R., Villareal, M. J., Asai, M., & Lucca, N. (1988). Individualism and collectivism: Cross-cultural perspectives on self-ingroup relationships. *Journal of Personality and Social Psychology, 54*, 323–338.

Triandis, H. C., Leung, K., Villareal, M. J., & Clack, F. L. (1985). Allocentric versus idiocentric tendencies: Convergent and discriminant validation. *Journal of Research in Personality, 19*, 395–415.

Triandis, H. C., Marin, G., Lisansky, J., & Betancourt, H. (1984). *Simpatia* as a cultural script of Hispanics. *Journal of Personality and Social Psychology, 47*, 1363–1375.

United States Employment and Training Administration. *Dictionary of occupational titles*. Washington, DC: Government Printing Office.

Verma, J. (1985). The ingroup and its relevance to individual behaviour: A study of collectivism and individualism. *Psychologia, 28*, 173–181.

Wicklund, R. A., & Gollwitzer, P. M. (1982). *Symbolic self-completion*. Hillsdale, NJ: Erlbaum.

Yang, K. S. (1981). Social orientation and individual modernity among Chinese students in Taiwan. *Journal of Social Psychology, 113*, 159–170.

Zavalloni, M. (1975). Social identity and the recoding of reality. *International Journal of Psychology, 10*, 197–217.

Zavalloni, M., & Louis-Guerin, C. (1984). *Identité sociale et conscience: Introduction á l'égo-écologie* [Social identity and conscience: Introduction to the ego ecology]. Montréal, Canada: Les presses de l'université de Montreal.

Ziller, R. C. (1973). *The social self*. New York: Pergamon.

PART VII

Behaviorist, Social Learning, and Cognitive Approaches to Personality

Behavioristic psychology treats behavior as a product solely of the immediate environment and the individual's history of rewards and punishments. In its original version, behaviorism avoided assuming the existence of any "inner," mental states or traits at all. For a "functional analysis" of behavior, it was sufficient to connect visible rewards and punishments with visible behaviors.

This point of view has evolved in an interesting way over the years. The social learning and cognitive theorists have added to behaviorism one more assumption, that one's beliefs about, or "representations," of the rewards and punishments in the environment are more important than what the environment actually contains. For example, if you believe a behavior will be rewarded you will probably do it, even if in fact the behavior will be punished. But of course your representation of a belief like this is a nonvisible, internal state, which means that modern, cognitive approaches to personality have grown a long distance from their behaviorist roots.

The first selection in this section was written by the key figure in modern behaviorism and one of the most important social scientists of the century. In "Why Organisms Behave" B. F. Skinner introduces the idea of functional analysis, and dismisses neural causes, psychic causes, and everything else that "radical" behaviorists find irrelevant to a sufficient understanding of behavior. Instead, he proposes that the answer to why organisms behave is always to be found in the external variables—rewards and punishments—of which behavior is always a function, and expresses optimism that this approach will solve all of the basic issues of psychology. In the second selection, published almost 35 years later, Skinner takes a more pessimistic tack as he laments the failure of behaviorism to, in fact, take over all of psychology. He blames humanistic psychology, cognitive psychology, and the sloppy habits of everyday speech, and warns that a psychology that neglects functional analysis will find itself dealing in myth or— just as bad—discover that it has been rendered obsolete by biology.

Despite Skinner's urgent and consistent pleading over the years, many psychologists with behaviorist sympathies nonetheless found the strict limits of classic behaviorism to be just too confining. Several different psychologists developed "social learning" theories that attempted to combine behaviorism's empirical rigor with a renewed concern with defense mechanisms, social interaction, mental life, and other phenomena that behaviorism neglected. One of the most important of these psychologists is Julian Rotter, whose primer on the key elements of social learning theory is the third selection. Another important social learning theorist is Albert Bandura, the author of the fourth selection. Bandura displays some fundamentally behavioristic leanings, but goes way beyond behaviorism by describing the operation of what he calls the "self system." Through a process Bandura calls "reciprocal determinism," an individual's self system develops as a result of experience, but also determines future behavior and the future environment. Thus, the environment may determine the person, as behaviorists would maintain, but the person also determines the environment.

The fifth selection is by Walter Mischel, whose influential attack on trait psychology we saw in Part II. Mischel presents a social learning theory that is similar in many respects to those of Rotter and Bandura. He adds a distinctively cognitive orientation, in which the person's beliefs about and representations of the environment become more important than the environment itself (in this we see an echo of the phenomenological ideas of Mischel's teacher, George Kelly). Mischel also describes five "cognitive social learning person variables" that, he argues, present a reconceptualization of individual differences in personality that goes beyond trait theory.

One of Mischel's cognitive social learning person variables is the "strategy." That is, different people use different strategies to attain their goals. In the sixth selection, Julie Norem describes the differences between students who employ an optimistic versus a pessimistic strategy in motivating themselves to do academic work. Interestingly, both strategies work, though optimists seem to lead a more pleasant life. Norem's point is that different people can and often do use different strategies in pursuit of the very same goal.

The final selection, by Carol Dweck and Ellen Leggett, takes cognitive social learning theory one step further by explicitly tying together cognition, motivation, and behavior. They describe a difference in outlook on the world (being what they call an "entity" versus an "incremental" theorist) that produces a difference in goals (which they call "performance" versus "learning" goals), which produce different patterns of behavior in response to failure (which they call "mastery-oriented" and "helpless" patterns).

As you shall see, behaviorism has evolved a long way from the classic behaviorists to the social learning theorists to the cognitive theorists. The most recent developments offer a promise for the reintegration of personality psychology. The modern cognitive social learning theorists are renewing their attention to in-

dividual differences and describing patterns of thought, motivation, and behavior of the sort that have long been of interest to some trait theorists. This development opens the possibility for cognitive and trait theorists to begin again to take one another's work seriously and develop a personality psychology that draws on the strengths of both approaches.

WHY ORGANISMS BEHAVE

B. F. Skinner

The major historical figure in behaviorism, and one of the best-known social scientists of the 20th century, is B. F. Skinner. Over a career that spanned more than 60 years (he died in 1990), Skinner argued strenuously and consistently that behavior was a scientific topic no different, in principle, from any other. That is, behavior is best studied through experimental methods, and the best way to demonstrate that you understand a behavior is to show that you can control it. Skinner always expressed annoyance with theories that located causes of behavior in the mind or even in the physical brain. He felt this practice merely postponed understanding, because the mind cannot be observed and the brain is poorly understood. Instead, Skinner argued, psychology should address the powerful causes of behavior that can *be both seen and experimentally manipulated: the rewards and punishments in the environment of the "organism."*

The first selection in this section, an excerpt from a basic text on behaviorism Skinner published at the height of his career in 1953, clearly sets forth the behaviorist manifesto. Skinner argues that locating causes of behavior in the stars, the physique, genetics, or even the nervous system offers nothing to psychological understanding. Each only misleads or—at best—distracts analysis away from the causes of behavior that ought to be the real business of psychologists.

Skinner's model for a science of psychology is "functional analysis." Such an analysis entails identifying—and, in many cases, controlling—the environmental causes of which behavior is a "function." Skinner further urges that these causes be conceptualized in concrete, physical terms. Rather than abstract social forces, for example, Skinner urges us to pay attention to the specific, immediate, concrete rewards and punishments in the social environment that affect what a person does. This focus on specifics, he believed, could enable people to design environments that would elicit behaviors leading to better outcomes for all.

From *Science and Human Behavior*, by B. F. Skinner, © 1953, pp. 23–42. Adapted by permission of Prentice-Hall, Inc., Upper Saddle River, NJ.

We are concerned with the causes of human behavior. We want to know why men behave as they do. Any condition or event which can be shown to have an effect upon behavior must be taken into account. By discovering and analyzing these causes we can predict behavior; to the extent that we can manipulate them, we can control behavior.

There is a curious inconsistency in the zeal with which the doctrine of personal freedom has been defended,[1] because men have always been fascinated by the search for causes. The spontaneity of human behavior is apparently no more challenging than its "why and wherefore." So strong is the urge to explain behavior that men have been led to anticipate legitimate scientific inquiry and to construct highly implausible theories of causation. This practice is not unusual in the history of science. The study of any subject begins in the realm of superstition. The fanciful explanation precedes the valid. Astronomy began as astrology; chemistry as alchemy. The field of behavior has had, and still has, its astrologers and alchemists. A long history of prescientific explanation furnishes us with a fantastic array of causes which have no function other than to supply spurious answers to questions which must otherwise go unanswered in the early stages of a science.

Some Popular "Causes" of Behavior

Any conspicuous event which coincides with human behavior is likely to be seized upon as a cause. The position of the planets at the birth of the individual is an example. Usually astrologers do not try to predict specific actions from such causes, but when they tell us that a man will be impetuous, careless, or thoughtful, we must suppose that specific actions are assumed to be affected. Numerology finds a different set of causes —for example, in the numbers which compose the street address of the individual or in the number of letters in his name. Millions of people turn to these spurious causes every year in their desperate need to understand human behavior and to deal with it effectively.

The predictions of astrologers, numerologists, and the like are usually so vague that they cannot be confirmed or disproved properly. Failures are easily overlooked, while an occasional chance hit is dramatic enough to maintain the behavior of the devotee in considerable strength. * * *

Another common practice is to explain behavior in terms of the structure of the individual. The proportions of the body, the shape of the head, the color of the eyes, skin, or hair, the marks on the palms of the hands, and the features of the face have all been said to determine what a man will do.[2] The "jovial fat man," Cassius with his "lean and hungry look," and thousands of other characters or types thoroughly embedded in our language affect our practices in dealing with human behavior. A specific act may never be predicted from physique, but different types of personality imply predispositions to behave in different ways, so that specific acts are presumed to be affected. This practice resembles the mistake we all make when we expect someone who looks like an old acquaintance to behave like him also. When a "type" is once established, it survives in everyday use because the predictions which are made with it, like those of astrology, are vague, and occasional hits may be startling.

* * *

When we find, or think we have found, that conspicuous physical features explain part of a man's behavior, it is tempting to suppose that inconspicuous features explain other parts. This is implied in the assertion that a man shows certain behavior because he was "born that way." To object to this is not to argue that behavior is never determined by hereditary factors. Behavior requires a behaving organism which is the product

---

[1]For example, by the humanists in Part V.

[2]Recall the selection by Wells in Part III.

of a genetic process. Gross differences in the behavior of different species show that the genetic constitution, whether observed in the body structure of the individual or inferred from a genetic history, is important. But the doctrine of "being born that way" has little to do with demonstrated facts. It is usually an appeal to ignorance. "Heredity," as the layman uses the term, is a fictional explanation of the behavior attributed to it.

Even when it can be shown that some aspect of behavior is due to season of birth, gross body type, or genetic constitution, the fact is of limited use. It may help us in predicting behavior, but it is of little value in an experimental analysis or in practical control because such a condition cannot be manipulated after the individual has been conceived. The most that can be said is that the knowledge of the genetic factor may enable us to make better use of other causes. If we know that an individual has certain inherent limitations, we may use our techniques of control more intelligently, but we cannot alter the genetic factor.[3]

The practical deficiencies of programs involving causes of this sort may explain some of the vehemence with which they are commonly debated. Many people study human behavior because they want to do something about it—they want to make men happier, more efficient and productive, less aggressive, and so on. To these people, inherited determiners—as epitomized in various "racial types"—appear to be insurmountable barriers, since they leave no course of action but the slow and doubtful program of eugenics.[4]

---

[3]It is unclear why Skinner here portrays the inability to alter the genotype as an important limitation. In terms of Skinner's own analysis alteration of the phenotype (overt behavior) should be a sufficient goal.

[4]Skinner is referring to writings early in the 20th century that identified "national" or "racial" characters. For example, southern Europeans were held to be emotional and northern Europeans to be cold and analytical. Skinner expresses (well-taken) doubts that such descriptions are accurate, and further argues that even if they were accurate the only prescription they offer is to "improve" the human species through selective breeding (eugenics). Skinner calls such a eugenic strategy "doubtful," surely an understatement.

The evidence for genetic traits is therefore closely scrutinized, and any indication that it is weak or inconsistent is received with enthusiasm. But the practical issue must not be allowed to interfere in determining the extent to which behavioral dispositions are inherited. The matter is not so crucial as is often supposed, for we shall see that there are other types of causes available for those who want quicker results.

Inner "Causes"

Every science has at some time or other looked for causes of action inside the things it has studied. Sometimes the practice has proved useful, sometimes it has not. There is nothing wrong with an inner explanation as such, but events which are located inside a system are likely to be difficult to observe. For this reason we are encouraged to assign properties to them without justification. Worse still, we can invent causes of this sort without fear of contradiction. The motion of a rolling stone was once attributed to its *vis viva*. The chemical properties of bodies were thought to be derived from the *principles* or *essences* of which they were composed. Combustion was explained by the *phlogiston* inside the combustible object. Wounds healed and bodies grew well because of a *vis medicatrix*. It has been especially tempting to attribute the behavior of a living organism to the behavior of an inner agent, as the following examples may suggest.

NEURAL CAUSES The layman uses the nervous system as a ready explanation of behavior. The English language contains hundreds of expressions which imply such a causal relationship. At the end of a long trial we read that the *nerves* of the accused are *on edge*, that the wife of the accused is on the verge of a *nervous breakdown*, and that his lawyer is generally thought to have lacked the *brains* needed to stand up to the prosecution. Obviously, no direct observations have been made of the nervous systems of any of these people. Their "brains" and "nerves" have been invented on the spur of the moment to lend substance to what might otherwise seem a superficial account of their behavior.

The sciences of neurology and physiology have not divested themselves entirely of a similar practice. Since techniques for observing the electrical and chemical processes in nervous tissue had not yet been developed, early information about the nervous system was limited to its gross anatomy. Neural processes could only be inferred from the behavior which was said to result from them. Such inferences were legitimate enough as scientific theories, but they could not justifiably be used to explain the very behavior upon which they were based. The hypotheses of the early physiologist may have been sounder than those of the layman, but until independent evidence could be obtained, they were no more satisfactory as explanations of behavior. Direct information about many of the chemical and electrical processes in the nervous system is now available. Statements about the nervous system are no longer necessarily inferential or fictional. But there is still a measure of circularity in much physiological explanation, even in the writings of specialists. In World War I a familiar disorder was called "shell shock." Disturbances in behavior were explained by arguing that violent explosions had damaged the structure of the nervous system, though no direct evidence of such damage was available. In World War II the same disorder was classified as "neuropsychiatric." The prefix seems to show a continuing unwillingness to abandon explanations in terms of hypothetical neural damage.[5]

Eventually a science of the nervous system based upon direct observation rather than inference will describe the neural states and events which immediately precede instances of behavior. We shall know the precise neurological conditions which immediately precede, say, the response, "No, thank you." These events in turn will be found to be preceded by other neurological events, and these in turn by others. This series will lead us back to events outside the nervous system and, eventually, outside the organism. * * * We do not have and may never have this sort of neurological information at the moment it is needed in order to predict a specific instance of behavior. It is even more unlikely that we shall be able to alter the nervous system directly in order to set up the antecedent conditions of a particular instance. The causes to be sought in the nervous system are, therefore, of limited usefulness in the prediction and control of specific behavior.

PSYCHIC INNER CAUSES An even more common practice is to explain behavior in terms of an inner agent which lacks physical dimensions and is called "mental" or "psychic." The purest form of the psychic explanation is seen in the animism of primitive peoples. From the immobility of the body after death it is inferred that a spirit responsible for movement has departed. The *enthusiastic* person is, as the etymology of the word implies, energized by a "god within." It is only a modest refinement to attribute every feature of the behavior of the physical organism to a corresponding feature of the "mind" or of some inner "personality." The inner man is regarded as driving the body very much as the man at the steering wheel drives a car. The inner man wills an action, the outer executes it. The inner loses his appetite, the outer stops eating. The inner man wants and the outer gets. The inner has the impulse which the outer obeys.

It is not the layman alone who resorts to these practices, for many reputable psychologists use a similar dualistic system of explanation. The inner man[6] is sometimes personified clearly, as when delinquent behavior is attributed to a "disordered personality," or he may be dealt with in fragments, as when behavior is attributed to mental processes, faculties, and traits. Since the inner man does not occupy space, he may be multiplied at will. It has been argued that a single physical organism is controlled by several psychic agents and that its behavior is the resultant of their several wills. The

---

[5]The current label for this syndrome, post-traumatic stress disorder, is more in line with Skinner's descriptive preference without attributing cause.

[6]Sometimes called the "homunculus."

Freudian concepts of the ego, superego, and id are often used in this way. They are frequently regarded as nonsubstantial creatures, often in violent conflict, whose defeats or victories lead to the adjusted or maladjusted behavior of the physical organism in which they reside.

Direct observation of the mind comparable with the observation of the nervous system has not proved feasible. It is true that many people believe that they observe their "mental states" just as the physiologist observes neural events, but another interpretation of what they observe is possible. Introspective psychology[7] no longer pretends to supply direct information about events which are the causal antecedents, rather than the mere accompaniments, of behavior. It defines its "subjective" events in ways which strip them of any usefulness in a causal analysis. The events appealed to in early mentalistic explanations of behavior have remained beyond the reach of observation. Freud insisted upon this by emphasizing the role of the unconscious—a frank recognition that important mental processes are not directly observable. The Freudian literature supplies many examples of behavior from which unconscious wishes, impulses, instincts, and emotions are inferred. Unconscious thought-processes have also been used to explain intellectual achievements. Though the mathematician may feel that he knows "how he thinks," he is often unable to give a coherent account of the mental processes leading to the solution of a specific problem. But any mental event which is unconscious is necessarily inferential, and the explanation is therefore not based upon independent observations of a valid cause.

The fictional nature of this form of inner cause is shown by the ease with which the mental process is discovered to have just the properties needed to account for the behavior. When a professor turns up in the wrong classroom or gives the wrong lecture, it is because his *mind* is, at least for the moment, *absent*. If he forgets to give a reading assignment, it is because it has slipped his *mind* (a hint from the class may re*mind* him of it). He begins to tell an old joke but pauses for a moment, and it is evident to everyone that he is trying to make up his *mind* whether or not he has already used the joke that term. His lectures grow more tedious with the years, and questions from the class confuse him more and more, because his *mind* is failing. What he says is often disorganized because his *ideas* are confused. He is occasionally unnecessarily emphatic because of the force of his *ideas*. When he repeats himself, it is because he has an *idée fixe;* and when he repeats what others have said, it is because he borrows his *ideas*. Upon occasion there is nothing in what he says because he lacks *ideas*. In all this it is obvious that the mind and the ideas, together with their special characteristics, are being invented on the spot to provide spurious explanations. A science of behavior can hope to gain very little from so cavalier a practice. Since mental or psychic events are asserted to lack the dimensions of physical science, we have an additional reason for rejecting them.

CONCEPTUAL INNER CAUSES The commonest inner causes have no specific dimensions at all, either neurological or psychic. When we say that a man eats *because* he is hungry, smokes a great deal *because* he has the tobacco habit, fights *because* of the instinct of pugnacity, behaves brilliantly *because* of his intelligence, or plays the piano well *because* of his musical ability, we seem to be referring to causes. But on analysis these phrases prove to be merely redundant descriptions. A single set of facts is described by the two statements: "He eats" and "He is hungry." A single set of facts is described by the two statements: "He smokes a great deal" and "He has the smoking habit." A single set of facts is described by the two statements: "He plays well" and "He has musical ability." The practice of explaining one statement in terms of the other is dangerous because it suggests that we have found the cause and therefore need search no further. Moreover, such terms as "hunger," "habit," and "intelligence" convert what are essentially the properties of a process or relation

---

[7]A kind of psychology, prominent in the field's early days, in which trained "introspectionists" tried to observe their own mental processes.

into what appear to be things. Thus we are unprepared for the properties eventually to be discovered in the behavior itself and continue to look for something which may not exist.

The Variables of Which Behavior Is a Function

The practice of looking inside the organism for an explanation of behavior has tended to obscure the variables which are immediately available for a scientific analysis. These variables lie outside the organism, in its immediate environment and in its environmental history. They have a physical status to which the usual techniques of science are adapted, and they make it possible to explain behavior as other subjects are explained in science. These independent variables are of many sorts and their relations to behavior are often subtle and complex, but we cannot hope to give an adequate account of behavior without analyzing them.

Consider the act of drinking a glass of water. This is not likely to be an important bit of behavior in anyone's life, but it supplies a convenient example. We may describe the topography of the behavior in such a way that a given instance may be identified quite accurately by any qualified observer. Suppose now we bring someone into a room and place a glass of water before him. Will he drink? There appear to be only two possibilities: either he will or he will not. But we speak of the *chances* that he will drink, and this notion may be refined for scientific use. What we want to evaluate is the *probability* that he will drink. This may range from virtual certainty that drinking will occur to virtual certainty that it will not. The very considerable problem of how to measure such a probability will be discussed later. For the moment, we are interested in how the probability may be increased or decreased.

Everyday experience suggests several possibilities, and laboratory and clinical observations have added others. It is decidedly not true that a horse may be led to water but cannot be made to drink.

By arranging a history of severe deprivation we could be "absolutely sure" that drinking would occur. In the same way we may be sure that the glass of water in our experiment will be drunk. Although we are not likely to arrange them experimentally, deprivations of the necessary magnitude sometimes occur outside the laboratory. We may obtain an effect similar to that of deprivation by speeding up the excretion of water. For example, we may induce sweating by raising the temperature of the room or by forcing heavy exercise, or we may increase the excretion of urine by mixing salt or urea in food taken prior to the experiment. It is also well known that loss of blood, as on a battlefield, sharply increases the probability of drinking. On the other hand, we may set the probability at virtually zero by inducing or forcing our subject to drink a large quantity of water before the experiment.

If we are to predict whether or not our subject will drink, we must know as much as possible about these variables. If we are to induce him to drink, we must be able to manipulate them. In both cases, moreover, either for accurate prediction or control, we must investigate the effect of each variable quantitatively with the methods and techniques of a laboratory science.

Other variables may, of course, affect the result. Our subject may be "afraid" that something has been added to the water as a practical joke or for experimental purposes. He may even "suspect" that the water has been poisoned. He may have grown up in a culture in which water is drunk only when no one is watching. He may refuse to drink simply to prove that we cannot predict or control his behavior. These possibilities do not disprove the relations between drinking and the variables listed in the preceding paragraphs; they simply remind us that other variables may have to be taken into account. We must know the history of our subject with respect to the behavior of drinking water, and if we cannot eliminate social factors from the situation, then we must know the history of his personal relations to people resembling the experimenter. Adequate prediction in any science requires information about all relevant variables, and the control of a subject matter for practical purposes makes the same demands.

Other types of "explanation" do not permit us to dispense with these requirements or to fulfill them in any easier way. It is of no help to be told that our subject will drink provided he was born under a particular sign of the zodiac which shows a preoccupation with water or provided he is the lean and thirsty type or was, in short, "born thirsty." Explanations in terms of inner states or agents, however, may require some further comment. To what extent is it helpful to be told, "He drinks because he is thirsty"? If to be thirsty means nothing more than to have a tendency to drink, this is mere redundancy. If it means that he drinks because of a state of thirst, an inner causal event is invoked. If this state is purely inferential—if no dimensions are assigned to it which would make direct observation possible—it cannot serve as an explanation. But if it has physiological or psychic properties, what role can it play in a science of behavior?

The physiologist may point out that several ways of raising the probability of drinking have a common effect: they increase the concentration of solutions in the body. Through some mechanism not yet well understood, this may bring about a corresponding change in the nervous system which in turn makes drinking more probable. In the same way, it may be argued that all these operations make the organism "feel thirsty" or "want a drink" and that such a psychic state also acts upon the nervous system in some unexplained way to induce drinking. In each case we have a causal chain consisting of three links: (1) an operation performed upon the organism from without—for example, water deprivation; (2) an inner condition—for example, physiological or psychic thirst; and (3) a kind of behavior—for example, drinking. Independent information about the second link would obviously permit us to predict the third without recourse to the first. It would be a preferred type of variable because it would be nonhistoric; the first link may lie in the

past history of the organism, but the second is a current condition. Direct information about the second link is, however, seldom, if ever, available. Sometimes we infer the second link from the third: an animal is judged to be thirsty if it drinks. In that case, the explanation is spurious. Sometimes we infer the second link from the first: an animal is said to be thirsty if it has not drunk for a long time. In that case, we obviously cannot dispense with the prior history.

The second link is useless in the *control* of behavior unless we can manipulate it. At the moment, we have no way of directly altering neural processes at appropriate moments in the life of a behaving organism, nor has any way been discovered to alter a psychic process. We usually set up the second link through the first: we make an animal thirsty, in either the physiological or the psychic sense, by depriving it of water, feeding it salt, and so on. In that case, the second link obviously does not permit us to dispense with the first. Even if some new technical discovery were to enable us to set up or change the second link directly, we should still have to deal with those enormous areas in which human behavior is controlled through manipulation of the first link. A technique of operating upon the second link would increase our control of behavior, but the techniques which have already been developed would still remain to be analyzed.

The most objectionable practice is to follow the causal sequence back only as far as a hypothetical second link. This is a serious handicap both in a theoretical science and in the practical control of behavior. It is no help to be told that to get an organism to drink we are simply to "make it thirsty" unless we are also told how this is to be done. When we have obtained the necessary prescription for thirst, the whole proposal is more complex than it need be. Similarly, when an example of maladjusted behavior is explained by saying that the individual is "suffering from anxiety," we have still to be told the cause of the anxiety. But the external conditions which are then invoked could have been directly related to the maladjusted behavior. Again, when we are told that a man stole a loaf of bread because "he was hungry," we have still to learn of the external conditions responsible for the "hunger." These conditions would have sufficed to explain the theft.

The objection to inner states is not that they do not exist, but that they are not relevant in a functional analysis.[8] We cannot account for the behavior of any system while staying wholly inside it; eventually we must turn to forces operating upon the organism from without. Unless there is a weak spot in our causal chain so that the second link is not lawfully determined by the first, or the third by the second, then the first and third links must be lawfully related. If we must always go back beyond the second link for prediction and control, we may avoid many tiresome and exhausting digressions by examining the third link as a function of the first. Valid information about the second link may throw light upon this relationship but can in no way alter it.

A Functional Analysis

The external variables of which behavior is a function provide for what may be called a causal or functional analysis. We undertake to predict and control the behavior of the individual organism. This is our "dependent variable"—the effect for which we are to find the cause. Our "independent variables"—the causes of behavior—are the external conditions of which behavior is a function. Relations between the two—the "cause-and-effect relationships" in behavior—are the laws of a science. A synthesis of these laws expressed in quantitative terms yields a comprehensive picture of the organism as a behaving system.

This must be done within the bounds of a natural science. We cannot assume that behavior has

any peculiar properties which require unique methods or special kinds of knowledge. It is often argued[9] that an act is not so important as the "intent" which lies behind it, or that it can be described only in terms of what it "means" to the behaving individual or to others whom it may affect. If statements of this sort are useful for scientific purposes, they must be based upon observable events, and we may confine ourselves to such events exclusively in a functional analysis. Although such terms as "meaning" and "intent" appear to refer to properties of behavior, they usually conceal references to independent variables. This is also true of "aggressive," "friendly," "disorganized," "intelligent," and other terms which appear to describe properties of behavior but in reality refer to its controlling relations.

The independent variables must also be described in physical terms. An effort is often made to avoid the labor of analyzing a physical situation by guessing what it "means" to an organism or by distinguishing between the physical world and a psychological world of "experience." This practice also reflects a confusion between dependent and independent variables. The events affecting an organism must be capable of description in the language of physical science. It is sometimes argued that certain "social forces" or the "influences" of culture or tradition are exceptions. But we cannot appeal to entities of this sort without explaining how they can affect both the scientist and the individual under observation. The physical events which must then be appealed to in such an explanation will supply us with alternative material suitable for a physical analysis.

By confining ourselves to these observable events, we gain a considerable advantage, not only in theory, but in practice. A "social force" is no more useful in manipulating behavior than an inner state of hunger, anxiety, or skepticism. Just as we must trace these inner events to the manipulable variables of which they are said to be func-

---

[8]This important clarification of and qualification of Skinner's position has often been neglected by his critics over the years.

[9]For example, by humanistic, phenomenological, and cognitive psychologists.

tions before we may put them to practical use, so we must identify the physical events through which a "social force" is said to affect the organism before we can manipulate it for purposes of control. In dealing with the directly observable data we need not refer to either the inner state or the outer force.

* * *

Whatever Happened to Psychology as the Science of Behavior?

B. F. Skinner

By the time the following selection was first published, in 1987, Skinner was near the end of his very long career. Behaviorism had established itself as one of the major paradigms of psychology, and Skinner himself was world-famous. Yet in this article you will see both the same general ideas and a very different tone from the unbounded optimism in the previous selection. Skinner expresses a surprising amount of disappointment and even bitterness. The heyday of behaviorism had come and gone, and the "cognitive revolution" and psychology's rediscovery of the mind had become a dominant theme of the field. So although behaviorism had been dominant for a time and remains an important paradigm, Skinner asks why it did not *become* psychology.*

Skinner identifies three villains. One is humanistic psychology, a longtime foe of behaviorism, and its insistence that people have the capacity for free choice. The second he labels "psychotherapy," but he really seems have in mind the various and to Skinner, sloppy habits of speech that obscure functional analysis. For example, we just referred to something Skinner seemed to "have in mind," a phrase Skinner would have regarded as a potentially misleading verbal shorthand for what Skinner was really doing. It turned out to be difficult, even for behaviorists, to expunge from the language terms such as mind, intention, knowledge, and desire. The third culprit is cognitive psychology, which Skinner regards as no more scientific than humanistic psychology. Cognitive psychology's emphasis on the mind and its description of unobservable mental processes has distracted psychologists from their real business, which is the prediction and control of behavior. Skinner makes the further interesting point that when cognitive psychologists describe mental processes that they expect ultimately to be explained in neurological terms, they are entering risky terrain. "Once you tell the world that another science will explain what your key terms really mean," he warns, "you must forgive the world if it decides the other science is doing the important work."

In our view, the reason behaviorism did not completely and permanently take over psychology was that—despite Skinner's cogent critique—psychologists became convinced that mentalistic terms do refer to something important. Most psychologists came to believe (as do nearly all nonpsychologists) that thoughts and feelings (the inner states Skinner omitted from functional analysis) are interesting and consequential. Even as Skinner penned the words of this, one of his final essays, the social learning theorists had already bent and stretched behaviorism to include nonbehavioral phenomena, and the cognitive social learning theorists were taking those developments even further, as we shall see later in this section.

There can scarcely be anything more familiar than human behavior. We are always in the presence of at least one behaving person. Nor can there be anything more important, whether it is our own behavior or that of those whom we see every day or who are responsible for what is happening in the world at large. Nevertheless it is certainly not the thing we understand best. Granted that it is possibly the most difficult subject ever submitted to scientific analysis, it is still puzzling that so little has been done with the instruments and methods that have been so productive in the other sciences. * * *

* * *

For more than half a century the experimental analysis of behavior as a function of environmental variables and the use of that analysis in the interpretation and modification of behavior in the world at large have reached into every field of traditional psychology. Yet they have not *become* psychology, and the question is, Why not? Perhaps answers can be found in looking at three formidable obstacles that have stood in the path of an experimental analysis of behavior.

Obstacle 1: Humanistic Psychology

Many people find the implications of a behavioral analysis disturbing. The traditional direction of action of organism and environment seems to be reversed. Instead of saying that the organism sees, attends to, perceives, "processes," or otherwise acts upon stimuli, an operant analysis holds that stimuli acquire control of behavior through the part they play in contingencies of reinforcement. Instead of saying that an organism stores copies of the contingencies to which it is exposed and later retrieves and responds to them again, it says that the organism is changed by the contingencies and later responds as a changed organism, the contingencies having passed into history. The environment takes over the control formerly assigned to an internal, originating agent.

Some long-admired features of human behavior are then threatened. Following the lead of evolutionary theory, an operant analysis replaces creation with variation and selection.[1] There is no longer any need for a creative mind or plan, or for purpose or goal direction. Just as we say that species-specific behavior did not evolve *in order that* a species could adapt to the environment but rather evolved *when* it adapted, so we say that operant behavior is not strengthened by reinforcement *in order that* the individual can adjust to the

---

[1]Evolutionary theory assumes that random variation creates a variety of organisms in each generation, of which some survive and reproduce more successfully than others. Similarly, Skinner's operant behavior theory assumes that organisms begin by behaving more or less randomly, but processes of reinforcement cause some behaviors to "survive" and others to drop out of the repertoire.

environment but is strengthened *when* the individual adjusts (where "adapt" and "adjust" mean "behave effectively with respect to").

The disenthronement of a creator seems to threaten personal freedom (Can we be free if the environment is in control?) and personal worth (Can we take credit for our achievements if they are nothing more than the effects of circumstances?). It also seems to threaten ethical, religious, and governmental systems that hold people responsible for their conduct. Who or what is responsible if unethical, immoral, or illegal behavior is due to heredity or personal history? Humanistic psychologists have attacked behavioral science along these lines. Like creationists in their attack on secular humanists (with the humanists on the other side), they often challenge the content or selection of textbooks, the appointment of teachers and administrators, the design of curricula, and the allocation of funds.

Obstacle 2: Psychotherapy

Certain exigencies of the helping professions are another obstacle in the path of a scientific analysis of behavior. Psychotherapists must talk with their clients and, with rare exceptions, do so in everyday English, which is heavy laden with references to internal causes—"I ate because I was *hungry*," "I could do it because I *knew* how to do it," and so on. All fields of science tend to have two languages, of course. Scientists speak one with casual acquaintances and the other with colleagues. In a relatively young science, such as psychology, the use of the vernacular may be challenged. How often have behaviorists heard, "You just said 'It crossed my mind!' I thought there wasn't supposed to be any mind." It has been a long time since anyone challenged a physicist who said, "That desk is made of solid oak," by protesting, "But I thought you said that matter was mostly empty space."

The two languages of psychology raise a special problem. What we feel when we are hungry or when we know how to do something are states of our bodies. We do not have very good ways of observing them, and those who teach us to observe them usually have no way at all. We were taught to say "I'm hungry," for example, by persons who knew perhaps only that we had not eaten for some time ("You missed your lunch; you must be *hungry*") or had observed something about our behavior ("You are eating ravenously. You must be *hungry*"). Similarly, we were taught to say "I know" by persons who had perhaps only seen us doing something ("Oh, you *know* how to do that!") or had told us how to do something and then said "Now you *know*." The trouble is that private states are almost always poorly correlated with the public evidence.

References to private events are, nevertheless, often accurate enough to be useful. If we are preparing a meal for a friend, we are not likely to ask, "How long has it been since you last ate?" or "Will you probably eat a great deal?" We simply ask, "How *hungry* are you?" If a friend is driving us to an appointment, we are not likely to ask, "Have you driven there before?" or "Has anyone told you where it is?" Instead we ask, "Do you *know* where it is?" Being hungry and knowing where something is are states of the body resulting from personal histories, and what is said about them may be the only available evidence of those histories. Nevertheless, how much a person eats does depend upon a history of deprivation, not upon how a deprived body feels, and whether a person reaches a given destination does depend upon whether he or she has driven there before or has been told how to get there, not upon introspective evidence of the effects.

Psychotherapists must ask people what has happened to them and how they feel because the confidential relationship of therapist and client prevents direct inquiry. (It is sometimes argued that what a person remembers may be more important than what actually happened, but that is true only if something else has happened, of which it would also be better to have independent evidence.[2]) But although the use of reports of feelings

---

[2]This is a succinct rebuttal to the phenomenological position.

and states of mind can be justified on practical grounds, there is no justification for their use in theory making. The temptation, however, is great. Psychoanalysts, for example, specialize in feelings. Instead of investigating the early lives of their patients or watching them with their families, friends, or business associates, they ask them what has happened and how they feel about it. It is not surprising that they should then construct theories in terms of memories, feelings, and states of mind or that they should say that an analysis of behavior in terms of environmental events lacks "depth."

Obstacle 3: Cognitive Psychology

A curve showing the appearance of the word *cognitive* in the psychological literature would be interesting. A first rise could probably be seen around 1960; the subsequent acceleration would be exponential. Is there any field of psychology today in which something does not seem to be gained by adding that charming adjective to the occasional noun? The popularity may not be hard to explain. When we became psychologists, we learned new ways of talking about human behavior. If they were "behavioristic," they were not very much like the old ways. The old terms were taboo, and eyebrows were raised when we used them. But when certain developments seemed to show that the old ways might be right after all, everyone could relax. Mind was back.

Information theory was one of those developments, computer technology another. Troublesome problems seemed to vanish like magic. A detailed study of sensation and perception was no longer needed; one could simply speak of processing information. It was no longer necessary to construct settings in which to observe behavior; one could simply describe them. Rather than observe what people actually did, one could simply ask them what they would probably do.

That mentalistic psychologists are uneasy about these uses of introspection is clear from the desperation with which they are turning to brain science, asking it to tell them what perceptions, feelings, ideas, and intentions "really are." And brain scientists are happy to accept the assignment. To complete the account of an episode of behavior (for example, to explain what happens when a reinforcement brings an organism under the control of a given stimulus) is not only beyond the present range of brain science, it would lack the glamour of a revelation about the nature of mind. But psychology may find it dangerous to turn to neurology for help. Once you tell the world that another science will explain what your key terms really mean, you must forgive the world if it decides that the other science is doing the important work.

Cognitive psychologists like to say that "the mind is what the brain does," but surely the rest of the body plays a part. The mind is what the *body* does. It is what the *person* does. In other words, it is behavior, and that is what behaviorists have been saying for more than half a century. ∗ ∗ ∗

∗   ∗   ∗

Damage and Repair

By their very nature, the antiscience stance of humanistic psychology, the practical exigencies of the helping professions, and the cognitive restoration of the royal House of Mind have worked against the definition of psychology as the science of behavior. Perhaps that could be justified if something more valuable had been achieved, but has that happened? Is there a better conception of psychology? To judge from the psychological literature, there are either many conceptions, largely incompatible, or no clear conception at all. Introductory textbooks do not help because, with an eye on their books' being adopted, the authors call their subject the "science of behavior *and* mental life" and make sure that every field of interest is covered. What the public learns from the media is equally confusing.

Is there a rapidly expanding body of facts and principles? Of our three obstacles, only cognitive psychology offers itself as an experimental science. It usually does so with a certain éclat, but have its promises been kept? When the journal *Psychology*

Today celebrated its 15th anniversary, it asked 10 psychologists to name the most important discoveries made during that period of time. As Nicolas Wade (1982) has pointed out, no 2 of the 10 agreed on a single achievement that could properly be called psychology. For more than two years *Science* has not published a single article on psychology, except one on memory citing work on brain-operated and brain-damaged people and one on the neurological basis of memory retrieval. Apparently the editors of *Science* no longer regard psychology itself as a member of the scientific community.

Nor has psychology developed a strong technology. Internal determiners get in the way of effective action. An article on "Energy Conservation Behavior" in the *American Psychologist* (Costanzo, Archer, Aronson, & Pettigrew, 1986), carries the significant subtitle, "The Difficult Path From Information to Action." If you take the "rational economic" path and tell people about the consequences of what they are doing or of what they might do instead, they are not likely to change. (And for good reason: Information is not enough; people seldom take advice unless taking other advice has been reinforced.) If, on the other hand, you adopt the "attitude-change" approach, people are also not likely to change. Attitudes are inferences from the behavior that is said to show their presence and are not directly accessible. If I turn off unnecessary lights and appliances in my home, it is not because I have a "positive attitude" toward conservation, but because doing so has had some kind of reinforcing consequence. To induce people to conserve energy, one must change contingencies of reinforcement, not attitudes. No one should try to beat a "path from information to action," because action is the problem and contingencies the solution. * * *

* * *

Beyond the current reach of all of the sciences lies an issue that cannot be safely neglected by any of them—the future of the world. For a variety of reasons all three of our "obstacles" have had special reasons for neglecting it. Humanistic psychologists are unwilling to sacrifice feelings of freedom

and worth for the sake of a future, and when cognitive psychologists turn to feelings and states of mind for theoretical purposes and psychotherapists for practical ones, they emphasize the here and now. Behavior modification, in contrast, is more often preventive than remedial. In both instruction and therapy, current reinforcers (often contrived) are arranged to strengthen behavior that student and client will find useful *in the future.*

When Gandhi was asked, "What are we to do?" he is said to have replied, "Think of the poorest man you have ever met and then ask if what you are doing is of any benefit to him." But he must have meant "of any benefit to the many people who, without your help, will be like him." To feed the hungry and clothe the naked are remedial acts. We can easily see what is wrong and what needs to be done. It is much harder to see and do something about the fact that world agriculture must feed and clothe billions of people, most of them yet unborn. It is not enough to *advise* people how to behave in ways that will make a future possible; they must be given effective reasons for behaving in those ways, and that means effective contingencies of reinforcement now.

Unfortunately, references to feelings and states of mind have an emotional appeal that behavioral alternatives usually lack. Here is an example: "If the world is to be saved, people must learn to be noble without being cruel, to be filled with faith, yet open to truth, to be inspired by great purposes without hating those who thwart them." That is an "inspiring" sentence. We like nobility, faith, truth, and great purposes and dislike cruelty and hatred. But what does it inspire us to *do*? What must be changed if people are to behave in noble rather than cruel ways, to accept the word of others but never without questioning it, to do things that have consequences too remote to serve as reinforcers, and to refrain from attacking those who oppose them? The fault, dear Brutus, is not in our stars *nor in ourselves* that we are underlings. The fault is in the world. It is a world that we have made and one that we must change if the species is to survive.

For at least 2,500 years philosophers and psychologists have proceeded on the assumption that because they were themselves behaving organisms, they had privileged access to the causes of their behavior. But has any introspectively observed feeling or state of mind yet been unambiguously identified in either mental or physical terms? Has any ability or trait of character been statistically established to the satisfaction of everyone? Do we know how anxiety changes intention, how memories alter decisions, how intelligence changes emotion, and so on? And, of course, has anyone ever explained how the mind works on the body or the body on the mind?

Questions of that sort should never have been asked. Psychology should confine itself to its accessible subject matter and leave the rest of the story of human behavior to physiology.

References

Costanzo, M., Archer, D., Aronson, E., & Pettigrew, T. (1986). Energy conservation behavior: The difficult path from information to action. *American Psychologist, 41,* 521–528.

Wade, N. (1982, April 30). Smart apes or dumb? *New York Times,* p. 28.

An Introduction to Social Learning Theory

Julian Rotter

Although many psychologists were attracted to the precision and empirical rigor of Skinner's empirical analysis of behavior, some also found classic behaviorism to be overly limiting of what could be studied. So they tried to find a way to keep behaviorism's scientific virtues while addressing new and complex topics such as cognition (thought), individual differences, and even defense mechanisms. These efforts to extend behaviorism were called the social learning theories.

One of the important and early developers of a social learning theory was Julian Rotter. In the next selection, published in 1972, after Rotter and his theory had attained a considerable amount of prominence, Rotter describes some of the basic tenets of his theory. While his focus remains on observable behavior and variables in the environment (which he calls the "situation") that control it, Rotter reveals he is no behaviorist with his discussion of "implicit behaviors" such as rationalizing, repressing, considering alternatives, planning, and reclassifying. Rotter seems to be trying simultaneously to move behaviorism onto the turf of both psychoanalytic theory and its consideration of defense mechanisms, and also cognitive psychology and its consideration of strategies and mental categories. Later on, Rotter also tries to account for individual differences in personality, particularly along a construct he calls "locus of control"—still a widely used construct today.

The later social learning theorists, such as Albert Bandura, turned their attention away from defense mechanisms and individual differences and focused on the relation between cognition and behavior. So Rotter's approach is not as influential today as it once was. But his concept of locus of control continues in wide use. And his theory stands as the high-water mark of attempts to extend behavioristic analysis to as many psychological phenomena as possible.

From "An Introduction to Social Learning Theory," by J. B. Rotter (1972). In *Applications of a Social Learning Theory of Personality*, edited by J. B. Rotter, J. E. Chance and E. J. Phares, pp. 1–46. New York: Holt, Rinehart & Winston. Reprinted with permission of the authors.

* * *

Basic Concepts

In SLT[1], four basic concepts are utilized in the prediction of behavior. These concepts are *behavior potential, expectancy, reinforcement value*, and the *psychological situation.* * * *

BEHAVIOR POTENTIAL Behavior potential may be defined as the potentiality of any behavior's occurring in any given situation or situations as calculated in relation to any single reinforcement or set of reinforcements.

Behavior potential is a relative concept. That is, one calculates the potentiality of any behavior's occurring in relation to the other alternatives open to the individual. Thus, it is possible to say only that in a specific situation the potentiality for occurrence of behavior x is greater than that for behavior z.

The SLT concept of behavior is quite broad. Indeed, behavior may be that which is directly observed but also that which is indirect or implicit. This notion includes a broad spectrum of possibilities—swearing, running, crying, fighting, smiling, choosing, and so on, are all included. These are all observable behaviors, but implicit behaviors that can only be measured indirectly, such as rationalizing, repressing, considering alternatives, planning, and reclassifying, would also be included. The objective study of cognitive activity is a difficult but important aspect of social learning theory. Principles governing the occurrence of such cognitive activities are not considered different from those that might apply to any observable behavior.

EXPECTANCY Expectancy may be defined as the probability held by the individual that a particular reinforcement will occur as a function of a specific behavior on his part in a specific situation or sit-

uations. Expectancy is systematically independent of the value or importance of the reinforcement.

In SLT the concept of expectancy is defined as a subjective probability, but this definition does not imply inaccessibility to objective measurement. People's probability statements, and other behaviors relating to the probability of occurrence of an event, often differ systematically from their actuarial experience with the event in the past. A variety of other factors operate in specific instances to influence one's probability estimates. Such factors may include the nature or the categorization of a situation, patterning and sequential considerations, uniqueness of events, generalization, and the perception of causality.

REINFORCEMENT VALUE The reinforcement value of any one of a group of potential external reinforcements may be ideally defined as the degree of the person's preference for that reinforcement to occur if the possibilities of occurrence of all alternatives were equal.

Again, reinforcement value is a relative term. Measurement of reinforcement value occurs in a choice situation. That is, reinforcement value refers to a preference, and preference indicates that one favors something over something else. Such preferences show consistency and reliability within our culture and also, generally speaking, can be shown to be systematically independent of expectancy. * * *

THE PSYCHOLOGICAL SITUATION Behavior does not occur in a vacuum. A person is continuously reacting to aspects of his external and internal environment. Since he reacts selectively to many kinds of stimulation, internal and external simultaneously, in a way consistent with his unique experience and because the different aspects of his environment mutually affect each other, we choose to speak of the psychological situation rather than the stimulus. * * *

Several writers have pointed out the difficulty of identifying situations independently of behav-

---

[1]Social learning theory.

ior. That is, how can one describe a situation, as one might a physical stimulus, independently of the particular S's[2] response? However, the problem is not really so different from that of describing stimuli along dimensions of color, although it is perhaps vastly more complicated in social situations. In the case of color stimuli, ultimately the criterion is a response made by an observer, sometimes aided by an intermediate instrument. The response is one that is at the level of sensory discrimination and thus leads to high observer agreement. In the case of social situations, the level of discrimination is common sense based on an understanding of a culture rather than a reading from an instrument. As such, reliability of discrimination may be limited but still be sufficiently high to make practical predictions possible. Specific situations can be identified as school situations, employment situations, girl friend situations, and so on. For the purpose of generality, various kinds of psychological constructs can be devised to arrive at broader classes of situations having similar meaning to S. The utility of such classes would have to be empirically determined, depending on the S's response. The objective referents for these situations, which provide the basis for prediction, however, can be independent of the specific S. That is, they can be reliably identified by cultural, common sense terms.

BASIC FORMULAS The preceding variables and their relations may be conveniently stated in the formulas that follow. It should be remembered, however, that these formulas do not at this time imply any precise mathematical relations. Indeed, although the relation between expectancy and reinforcement value is probably a multiplicative one, there is little systematic data at this point that would allow one to evolve any precise mathematical statement.

The basic formula is stated thus:

$$BP_{x,s_1,R_a} = f(E_{x,R_a,s_1} \ \& \ RV_{a,s_1}) \quad (1)$$

---

[2]Subject's.

Formula (1) says, The potential for behavior x to occur, in situation 1 in relation to reinforcement a, is a function of the expectancy of the occurrence of reinforcement a, following behavior x in situation 1, and the value of reinforcement a in situation 1.

Formula (1) is obviously limited, inasmuch as it deals only with the potential for a given behavior to occur in relation to a single reinforcement. As noted earlier, description at the level of personality constructs usually demands a broader, more generalized concept of behavior, reflected in the following formula:

$$BP_{(x-n),s_{(1-n)},R_{(a-n)}}$$
$$= f(E_{(x-n),s_{(1-n)},R_{(a-n)}} \ \& \ RV_{(a-n),s_{(1-n)}}) \quad (2)$$

Formula (2) says, The potentiality of functionally related behaviors x to n to occur, in specified situations 1 to n in relation to potential reinforcements a to n, is a function of the expectancies of these behaviors leading to these reinforcements in these situations and the values of these reinforcements in these situations. To enhance communication by reducing verbal complexity, three terms—*need potential, freedom of movement,* and *need value*—have been introduced. A formula incorporating these latter terms is:

$$NP = f(FM \ \& \ NV) \quad (3)$$

Thus, need potential is a function of freedom of movement and need value. In broader predictive or clinical situations, formula (3) would more likely be used, while formula (2) would be more appropriate in testing more specific, experimental hypotheses.

The fourth variable, *situation*, is left implicit in formula (3). SLT is highly committed to the importance of the psychological situation. It is emphasized that behavior varies as the situation does. But obviously, there is also transituational generality in behavior. If there were not, there would be no point in discussing personality as a construct or as a field of study. However, along with generality there is also situational specificity. While it may be true that person A is generally more aggressive than person B, nonetheless there can arise many occasions on which person B behaves more aggressively than does person A. Predictions based solely on internal characteristics of the individual are not sufficient to account for the complexities of human behavior.

*   *   *

Need Potential

The concept *need potential* is the broader analogue of behavior potential. The difference is that need potential refers to groups of functionally related behaviors rather than single behaviors. Functional relatedness of behaviors exists when several behaviors all lead to, or are directed toward, obtaining the same or similar reinforcements. The process of generalization occurring among functionally related behaviors allows for better than chance prediction from one specific referent of the category to another. (Similarity of reinforcement is not the only basis for functional relatedness of behaviors.) Need potential, then, describes the mean potentiality of a group of functionally related behaviors, directed at obtaining the same or a set of similar reinforcements, occurring in any segment of the individual's life.

The kinds of behaviors that can be grouped into functional categories may range from very molecular physical or objectively defined acts to implicit behaviors such as identifying with authority figures. Such categories may be progressively more inclusive depending upon one's predictive goal and the level of predictive accuracy required. For example, *need potential for recognition is more inclusive than need potential for recognition in psychology.*[3]

In practice, estimates of need potential are made utilizing some sampling procedure. Perhaps, observations are made of how *S* behaves in selected or specified situations. Normally, the determination of the relation between behaviors and reinforcements is made on a cultural basis. That is, on a cultural basis we know that studying is related to a group of reinforcements called academic recognition. At this point a brief discussion of some need concepts used in social learning theory will be helpful in understanding the sections to follow.

It is crucial to the development of a theory of personality that a descriptive language be established which deals with the content of personality. One difficulty with many learning theories is their almost exclusive emphasis on the processes of acquisition of behavior and of performance and their almost total neglect of the content of personality.[4] In contrast, many personality theories suffer from the reverse situation, emphasizing content (needs, traits, and so on) while neglecting process.

In developing content terms, SLT began by attempting to profit from the experience of clinicians, psychotherapists, and students of the culture generally. Development of a reliable, communicable, and valid language of description is an ever-evolving process. Furthermore, it is an empirical process, wherein the final test is predictive utility of the terms and not armchair rumination.

Based on the foregoing considerations, six need descriptions were developed at a fairly broad level of abstraction. From these relatively broad categories, more specific abstractions can be developed. Some of these can be included almost entirely within one of the broad categories, while some others might be related as well to one category as to another. The six broad categories arrived at and their definitions are the following:

> *Recognition-Status:* Need to be considered competent or good in a professional, social, occupational, or play activity. Need to gain social or vocational position—that is, to be more skilled or better than others.

---

[3]That is, the need to be famous is more general than the need to be a famous psychologist.

[4]Here is an explicit statement of Rotter's disagreement with Skinner.

Protection-Dependency: Need to have another person or group of people prevent frustration or punishment, or to provide for the satisfaction of other needs.

Dominance: Need to direct or to control the actions of other people, including members of family and friends. To have any action taken be that which he suggests.

Independence: Need to make own decisions, to rely on oneself, together with the need to develop skills for obtaining satisfactions directly without the mediation of other people.

Love and Affection: Need for acceptance and indication of liking by other individuals. In contrast to recognition-status, *not* concerned with social or professional positions, but seeks persons' warm regard.

Physical Comfort: Learned need for physical satisfaction that has become associated with gaining security.

All of these categories were presumed to be at about the same general level of inclusiveness.

The general term *need* used in this context refers to the entire complex of *need potential, freedom of movement,* and *need value.* The term refers to a set of constructs describing directionality of behavior, *not* to a state of deprivation or arousal in the organism. Used in this way the concept *need* is neither the equivalent of need value (or preference for certain kinds of goals) only nor the equivalent of *need potential* only.

To return to the discussion of need potential, it should be apparent that relying exclusively on cultural definitions of terms can lead to problems in individual prediction. For example, even though many people may study in order to achieve academic reinforcements, it may be true that a few people study in order to attain affectional responses from their girl friends. Therefore, the latter kind of individual would not be demonstrating a high need potential for academic recognition, but rather, for love and affection from opposite sex peers.

* * *

Need Value

Need value is defined as mean preference value of a set of functionally related reinforcements. Where reinforcement value indicates preference for one reinforcement over others, need value indicates preference for one set of functionally related reinforcements over another set (always assuming that expectancy for occurrence is held constant). Recall that functionality of reinforcements comes about either through stimulus generalization or through an extension of the principle of mediated stimulus generalization. Occurrence of functionality among reinforcements has been demonstrated empirically on a substitution basis, as well as in terms of generalization of expectancies among functionally related behaviors. Demonstration of functionality by substitution involves a situation where behavior toward a goal is blocked, and it is then noted which behavior is adopted as a substitute.

Earlier, when need potential was discussed, it was emphasized that descriptions of need categories based on functionally related behaviors must ultimately be arrived at on an empirical basis. Likewise, given a workable culture-based definition, one is cautioned about generalizing beyond the confines of one's own culture. Similarly, one must be cognizant of individual development of idiosyncratic need structures which may not follow those of the larger culture.

* * *

Freedom of Movement

Freedom of movement is defined as mean expectancy of obtaining positive satisfactions as a result of a set of related behaviors directed toward obtaining a group of functionally related reinforcements. Thus, when an individual has a high expectancy of attaining reinforcements that define a given need area for him, he is said to have high freedom of movement in that need area. In short, he feels that his behavioral techniques will be successful for his goals. When freedom of movement is low, particularly in relation to a need area of high value, the individual may anticipate punishment or failure. Thus, the concept of freedom of movement bears a relation to the concept of anxiety as described by other theories. * * *

* * *

* * * When freedom of movement is low while need value is high, we have a situation of conflict. To escape punishment and failure in an area of great importance to him, the individual adopts various avoidant behaviors. He may also try to reach his goals in irreal or symbolic ways, such as fantasy, which do not run the risk of incurring failure or punishment. Most behavior regarded as psychopathological is avoidant or irreal behavior. * * *

In summary, defensive behaviors provide an indirect measure of freedom of movement because such behaviors suggest the degree to which the individual expects negative reinforcement in a given need area. It is crucial in using this method that it first be established that the individual places a high value on the need in question. Otherwise, what seems avoidant may turn out to be an uncomplicated lack of interest.

Minimal Goal Level

Related to the concept of low freedom of movement is another SLT concept—*minimal goal level.* Specifically defined, minimal goal level refers to the lowest goal in a continuum of potential reinforcements for some life situation which will be perceived by the person as satisfactory to him. This definition suggests that reinforcements may be ordered from highly positive to highly negative. The point along this dimension at which reinforcements change from positive to negative in value for the person is his minimal goal level. Internalized minimal goals are responsible for the often observed instance where a person attains many goals that appear highly desirable to others and yet he, nonetheless, experiences a sense of failure or low freedom of movement. From his point of view, he is failing. When someone has extremely high minimal goals, whether in achievement, dominance, or love and affection, and is not

obtaining reinforcements at or above this level, then by definition he has low freedom of movement.

The same analysis, in reverse, supplies the reason that a person may be contented, even though observers perceive his level of goal achievement to be exceedingly low. To the extent that problems in living often derive from a too high minimal goal level (or, more infrequently, from a very low minimal goal level), psychotherapy may concentrate on changing minimal goals by changing the value of reinforcements. As discussed in the preceding section on reinforcement values, value changes are accomplished by pairing the reinforcements in question with others of either a higher or lower value. For example, the individual is led to develop the expectancy that a previously negatively valued reinforcement—such as a grade of B—can lead to the positive reinforcements of praise and acceptance. * * *

* * *

The Situation

Implicit in all the preceding discussions has been the idea that the *psychological situation* is an extremely important determinant of behavior. This view is in sharp contrast to those positions that adopt a "core" approach to personality and assert that once the basic elements of personality are identified, reliable prediction follows. Core views are inherent in both psychoanalytic theories of dynamics and in trait and typological descriptive schemes. In short, many theories are so preoccupied with identifying highly stable aspects of personality that they fail to make systematic use of the psychological situation in the prediction of behavior.[5] The SLT approach contends that such a posture severely limits prediction by permitting only global statements about future behavior which are limited to a very low level of accuracy in prediction.

From the SLT view, each situation is com-

---

[5]Notice that this complaint is very similar to that voiced by Skinner, and on this point social learning theory is allied with behaviorism.

posed of cues serving to arouse in the individual certain expectancies for reinforcement of specific behaviors. For example, even though an individual may be described as possessing an extremely strong predisposition to aggressive behavior, he will not behave aggressively in a given situation if the latter contains cues suggesting to him that aggressive behavior is very likely to result in strong punishment. Meanings that cues acquire for the individual are based on prior learning history and can be determined in advance in order to help us predictively. Again, some of these meanings can be assumed on a cultural basis, but the possibilities raised by idiosyncratic life experiences must be recognized also.

Recognition that behavior is not determined solely by personal characteristics but also by situational considerations specifies the necessity for descriptive categories for different situations. Psychology can be accurately said to have made less progress in devising classifications for situations than in almost any other area. * * *

* * *

Generalized Expectancies: Problem-Solving Skills

Man is a categorizing animal. He continuously forms concepts, changes concepts, and discovers new dimensions of similarity. While similarity of reinforcements is an extremely important basis for his conceptualizations, there are also other dimensions along which he perceives similarity. Within SLT any part of the environment to which the individual responds, or its totality, is referred to as a situational determinant. When an individual perceives that a number of people are alike because they are of the same sex, color, occupation, or age, he develops expectations about these people. Experience with one of them generalizes to others of the same class. When generalization takes place, we have the basis for believing that functional relations exist. That is, prediction of one referent from another referent of the same class can be made at a better than chance level.

Generalized expectancies about people, and the behaviors and reinforcements connected with them, are part of the basis for what has been traditionally called social attitudes in psychology. * * *

Situations, both social and nonsocial, may also be perceived as similar in that they present similar problems. For example, all of us are faced continuously with the problem of deciding whether what happens to us is contingent on our own behavior and can be controlled by our own actions, or whether it depends upon luck, the intervention of powerful others, or influences we cannot understand. We develop a generalized expectancy across situations which may differ in needs satisfied or reinforcements expected, but which are similar with respect to perception of control that we can exercise to change or maintain these situations. As with social attitudes, when generalization occurs from one situation to another, individual differences may develop in how the situations themselves are perceived or categorized. In such a case, generalized expectancies may deal with properties of situational stimuli. That is, the basis for similarity does not lie, in this instance, in the nature of reinforcements but in the nature of the situation. Behaviors relevant to these situationally mediated expectancies are also functionally related because of similarity of the problems to be solved.

When a behavior directed toward a goal is blocked, or fails to achieve the goal, the failure itself may be regarded as a property of a new situation involving a problem to be solved. A generalized expectancy that problems can be solved by a technique of looking for alternatives may also be developed regardless of the specific need or reinforcement involved. The degree to which a generalized problem-solving expectancy is developed may be an important source of individual differences in behavior.

Another common human experience is that of being provided with information from other people—either promises of reinforcements to come or merely statements of presumed fact. Implicit in all these situations is the problem of whether to believe or not to believe the other person. A generalized expectancy of trust or distrust can be an important determinant of behavior.

The mature human can probably perceive an extremely large number of dimensions of similarities in problem characteristics in complex social situations. Some dimensions, however, are broader than others and some, undoubtedly, are far more relevant for particular kinds of psychological predictions than others. In recent years, many SLT investigations have concerned some of these dimensions. Two of these are the dimension of internal versus external control of reinforcement[6] and the dimension of interpersonal trust. * * *

* * *

Positive and Negative Reinforcements as Situational Cues

Reinforcements, whether words, acts, or tangible objects, are also parts of the psychological situation, as are cues closely associated with occurrence of reinforcements. Content categories based on perceived similarities of reinforcement (needs), perceived similarities of social cues (social attitudes), and perceived similarities of the nature of the problems to be solved (generalized expectancies) have been discussed. There may also be similarities in situations based on the sign (whether positive or negative) or intensity of reinforcements, or combinations of these along with the circumstances in which they occur.

Occurrence of a negative reinforcement,[7] or its anticipation, as already indicated, may lead to defensive or avoidant behaviors; and such behaviors

can be understood as having a potential for a particular class of reinforcements. It may be characteristic of some people, however, that they respond with aggression, repression, withdrawal, projection, depression, and so on, somewhat independently of the kind (need category) of reinforcement. These responses may be a function of the sign or strength of the reinforcement rather than its particular form. In other words, we can talk not only about a behavior potential to repress competitive failures but a behavior potential to repress all strong negative reinforcements. How functional or general such potentials are across need areas is an empirical matter. Mild failure in an achievement-related task may increase the potential for some individuals to narrow their attention, increase concentration, and so on. However, mild failure might not have the same effect should it occur in initiating a social relationship.

* * *

Part 1: Summary

This chapter describes a molar learning theory of complex behavior with special reference to behavior in which the reinforcements depend on the behavior of other people. The purpose of the theory is prediction of behavior and the internal or cognitive processes related to behavior. While the same principles may also be important in early acquisition of more simple behaviors, the theory is not primarily concerned with more molecular principles which explain why one thing in a complex situation is associated with another, nor how very simple responses are built up into complex patterns of response. It is not that such principles are unimportant; they simply are not the focus of this theory. Once the basic patterns of behavior have been developed, the problem is to determine when one is chosen over another in a specific situation. This is the focus of this theory.

In addition to the principles governing the processes of choice behavior, social learning theory attempts to describe various ways in which generality of behavior may be described. In other words, bases for a content theory of individual dif-

---

[6]This concept, also called "locus of control," is a dimension of personality that distinguishes between people who believe their actions control the important outcomes in their life (internal locus of control) and those who believe these outcomes are controlled by other forces such as luck and powerful others (external locus of control). Of all of Rotter's ideas the concept of locus of control is probably the most influential today.

[7]Here by "negative reinforcement" Rotter means punishment.

ferences are developed. The most important of these bases is the similarity of reinforcements. Other categories of content are based upon the similarity of social objects (social attitudes) and similarities in the type of problem to be solved in a particular situation (generalized expectancies). A fourth category of behaviors may be based upon similarities in the sign and strength of reinforce-ments. Finally, the need for functional categories of situations characterized in common sense social terms is described. Such categories are prerequisite to prediction of behavior in a manner that attends to both its generality and its situational specificity.

*   *   *

The Self System in Reciprocal Determinism

Albert Bandura

The most prominent of the social learning theorists is Stanford psychologist Albert Bandura. Indeed, even though Bandura's theory was developed after that of Julian Rotter, it is sometimes forgotten that both are called "social learning theory." Bandura's version shares many elements with Rotter's, most importantly the common goal of stretching an essentially behavioristic analysis to cover topics neglected—or even forbidden—by the behaviorists. Both theories also give a prominent role to "expectancies," a cognitive concept that refers to a person's beliefs about the probable results of his or her actions.

The following selection, published at the height of Bandura's career, goes beyond Rotter in an interesting way. Bandura tackles the heavy philosophical issues that surround "basic conceptions of human nature." He points out that the behaviorists and the humanists, seemingly opposite in viewpoint, share one basic idea: the unidirectional causation of behavior. That is, behaviorists see behavior as a function of reinforcements in the environment or (in Rotter's term) the situation. At the opposite end, humanists see behavior as a function of the person, his or her characteristics and, most importantly, his or her free choice. In the following selection, Bandura seeks a middle ground between these seemingly irreconcilable viewpoints.

Bandura does this by proposing the existence of a "self system." This cognitive system, consisting of thoughts and feelings about the self, arises as a result of experience but, once constructed, has its own important effects on behavior. For example, the self system sets goals and evaluates one's own progress toward those goals. Just as importantly, the self system affects one's own environment by administering rewards and punishments to the self (such as promising oneself an ice cream as soon as one finishes reading Bandura's chapter), and by selecting the environments that one enters. For example, once one enrolls at college, one is buffeted by all sorts of environmental pressures—rewards and punishments— that coerce one to study for exams, write term papers, live in the library, and so on. But whether to enroll in college in the first place is a choice made by the self system. Similarly, one's activities and the way one evaluates oneself are critically influenced by the people one is surrounded with. But to an important degree a person chooses his or her companions, and so chooses who to be influenced by.

Bandura seems to be a behaviorist at heart, despite his advocacy for the self system. This is because he views the self system as being, in the final analysis, a result of the environment. But by viewing the self system as something that— once constructed—can shape behavior and even shape the environment (through a process Bandura calls "reciprocal determinism"), Bandura opens up possibilities for the analysis and prediction of behavior that go beyond anything envisaged by classical behaviorism.

Recent years have witnessed a heightened interest in the basic conceptions of human nature underlying different psychological theories. This interest stems in part from growing recognition of how such conceptions delimit research to selected processes and are in turn shaped by findings of paradigms embodying the particular view. As psychological knowledge is converted to behavioral technologies, the models of human behavior on which research is premised have important social as well as theoretical implications (Bandura, 1974).

Explanations of human behavior have generally been couched in terms of a limited set of determinants, usually portrayed as operating in a unidirectional manner. Exponents of environmental determinism study and theorize about how behavior is controlled by situational influences. Those favoring personal determinism seek the causes of human behavior in dispositional sources in the form of instincts, drives, traits, and other motivational forces within the individual. ⋆ ⋆ ⋆

⋆ ⋆ ⋆ The present article analyzes the various causal models and the role of self influences in behavior from the perspective of reciprocal determinism.

Unidirectional environmental determinism is carried to its extreme in the more radical forms of behaviorism. ⋆ ⋆ ⋆ ([For example] "A person

does not act upon the world, the world acts upon him," Skinner, 1971, p. 211). The environment thus becomes an autonomous force that automatically shapes, orchestrates, and controls behavior. ⋆ ⋆ ⋆

⋆ ⋆ ⋆

There exists no shortage of advocates of alternative theories emphasizing the personal determination of environments. Humanists and existentialists,[1] who stress the human capacity for conscious judgment and intentional action, contend that individuals determine what they become by their own free choices. Most psychologists find conceptions of human behavior in terms of unidirectional personal determinism as unsatisfying as those espousing unidirectional environmental determinism. To contend that mind creates reality fails to acknowledge that environmental influences partly determine what people attend to, perceive, and think. To contend further that the methods of natural science are incapable of dealing with personal determinants of behavior does not enlist many supporters from the ranks of those who are moved more by empirical evidence than by philosophic discourse.

Social learning theory (Bandura, 1974, 1977b) analyzes behavior in terms of reciprocal determin-

---

[1]Such as represented in Part V.

ism. The term *determinism* is used here to signify the production of effects by events, rather than in the doctrinal sense that actions are completely determined by a prior sequence of causes independent of the individual. Because of the complexity of interacting factors, events produce effects probabilistically rather than inevitably. In their transactions with the environment, people are not simply reactors to external stimulation. Most external influences affect behavior through intermediary cognitive processes. Cognitive factors partly determine which external events will be observed, how they will be perceived, whether they have any lasting effects, what valence and efficacy they have, and how the information they convey will be organized for future use. The extraordinary capacity of humans to use symbols enables them to engage in reflective thought, to create, and to plan foresightful courses of action in thought rather than having to perform possible options and suffer the consequences of thoughtless action. By altering their immediate environment, by creating cognitive self-inducements, and by arranging conditional incentives for themselves, people can exercise some influence over their own behavior. An act therefore includes among its determinants self-produced influences.

It is true that behavior is influenced by the environment, but the environment is partly of a person's own making. By their actions, people play a role in creating the social milieu and other circumstances that arise in their daily transactions. Thus, from the social learning perspective, psychological functioning involves a continuous reciprocal interaction between behavioral, cognitive, and environmental influences.

Reciprocal Determinism and Interactionism

* * *

Interaction processes have been conceptualized in three fundamentally different ways. These alternative formulations are summarized schematically in Figure 50.1. In the unidirectional notion of interaction, persons and situations are treated as independent entities that combine to produce behavior. This commonly held view can be called into question on both conceptual and empirical grounds. Personal and environmental factors do not function as independent determinants; rather, they determine each other. Nor can "persons" be considered causes independent of their behavior. It is largely through their actions that people produce the environmental conditions that affect their behavior in a reciprocal fashion. The experiences generated by behavior also partly determine what individuals think, expect, and can do, which in turn, affect their subsequent behavior.

A second conception of interaction acknowledges that personal and environmental influences are bidirectional, but it retains a unidirectional view of behavior. In this analysis, persons and situations are considered to be interdependent causes of behavior, but behavior is treated as though it were only a by-product that does not figure at all in the causal process. * * *

* * *

In the social learning view of interaction, which is analyzed as a process of reciprocal determinism (Bandura, 1977b), behavior, internal personal factors, and environmental influences all operate as interlocking determinants of each other. As shown in Figure 50.1, the process involves a triadic reciprocal interaction rather than a dyadic conjoint or a dyadic bidirectional one. We have already noted that behavior and environmental conditions function as reciprocally interacting determinants. Internal personal factors (e.g., conceptions, beliefs, self-perceptions) and behavior also operate as reciprocal determinants of each other. For example, people's efficacy and outcome expectations influence how they behave, and the environmental effects created by their actions in turn alter their expectations. People activate different environmental reactions, apart from their behavior, by their physical characteristics (e.g., size, physiognomy, race, sex, attractiveness) and socially conferred attributes, roles, and status. The

Unidirectional

B = f (P, E)

Partially Bidirectional

B = f (P ⇌ E)

Figure 50.1 Schematic representation of three alternative conceptions of interaction: *B* signifies behavior, *P* the cognitive and other internal events that can affect perceptions and actions, and *E* the external environment

differential social treatment affects recipients' self-conceptions and actions in ways that either maintain or alter the environmental biases.

The relative influence exerted by these three sets of interlocking factors will vary in different individuals and under different circumstances. In some cases, environmental conditions exercise such powerful constraints on behavior that they emerge as the overriding determinants. If, for example, people are dropped in deep water they will all promptly engage in swimming activities, however uniquely varied they might be in their cognitive and behavioral repertoires. There are times when behavior is the central factor in the interlocking system. One example of this is persons who play familiar piano selections for themselves that create a pleasing sensory environment. The behavior is self-regulated over a long period by the sensory effects it produces, whereas cognitive activities and contextual environmental events are not much involved in the process.

In other instances, cognitive factors serve as the predominant influence in the regulatory system. The activation and maintenance of defensive behavior is a good case in point. False beliefs activate avoidance responses that keep individuals out of touch with prevailing environmental conditions, thus creating a strong reciprocal interaction between beliefs and action that is protected from corrective environmental influence. In extreme cases, behavior is so powerfully controlled by bizarre internal contingencies that neither the beliefs nor the accompanying actions are much affected even by extremely punishing environmental consequences (Bateson, 1961).

In still other instances, the development and activation of the three interlocking factors are all highly interdependent. Television-viewing behavior provides an everyday example. Personal preferences influence when and which programs, from among the available alternatives, individuals choose to watch on television. Although the potential televised environment is identical for all viewers, the actual televised environment that impinges on given individuals depends on what they select to watch. Through their viewing behavior, they partly shape the nature of the future televised environment. Because production costs and commercial requirements also determine what people are shown, the options provided in the televised environment partly shape the viewers' preferences. Here, all three factors—viewer preferences, viewing behavior, and televised offerings—reciprocally affect each other.

The methodology for elucidating psychological processes requires analysis of sequential interactions between the triadic, interdependent factors within the interlocking system. Investigations of reciprocal processes have thus far rarely, if ever, examined more than two of the interacting factors simultaneously. Some studies analyze how cognitions and behavior affect each other in a reciprocal fashion (Bandura, 1977a; Bandura & Adams, 1977). More often, however, the sequential analysis centers on how social behavior and environment determine each other. In these studies of dyadic exchanges, behavior creates certain conditions and is, in turn, altered by the very conditions it creates (Bandura, Lipsher, & Miller, 1960; Patterson, 1975; Raush, Barry, Hertel, & Swain, 1974; Thomas & Martin, 1976).

From the perspective of reciprocal determinism, the common practice of searching for the ultimate environmental cause of behavior is an idle exercise because, in an interactional process, one and the same event can be a stimulus, a response, or an environmental reinforcer, depending on where in the sequence the analysis arbitrarily begins.

* * *

* * * Regulatory processes are not governed solely by the reciprocal influence of antecedent and consequent acts. While behaving, people are also cognitively appraising the progression of events. Their thoughts about the probable effects of prospective actions partly determine how acts are affected by their immediate environmental consequences. Consider, for example, investigations of reciprocal coercive behavior in an ongoing dyadic interaction. In discordant families, coercive behavior by one member tends to elicit coercive counteractions from recipients in a mutual escalation of aggression (Patterson, 1975). However, coercion often does not produce coercive counteractions. To increase the predictive power of a theory of behavior, it is necessary to broaden the analysis to include cognitive factors that operate in the interlocking system. Counterresponses to antecedent acts are influenced not only by their immediate effects but also by judgments of later consequences for a given course of action. Thus, aggressive children will continue, or even escalate, coercive behavior in the face of immediate punishment when they expect persistence eventually to gain them what they seek. But the same momentary punishment will serve as an inhibitor rather than as an enhancer of coercion when they expect continuance of the aversive conduct to be ineffective. * * *

Cognitions do not arise in a vacuum, nor do they function as autonomous determinants of behavior. In the social learning analysis of cognitive development, conceptions about oneself and the nature of the environment are developed and verified through four different processes (Bandura, 1977b). People derive much of their knowledge from direct experience of the effects produced by their actions. Indeed, most theories of cognitive

development, whether they favor behavioristic, information-processing, or Piagetian[2] orientations, focus almost exclusively on cognitive change through feedback from direct experimentation. However, results of one's own actions are not the sole source of knowledge. Information about the nature of things is frequently extracted from vicarious experience. In this mode of verification, observation of the effects produced by somebody else's actions serves as the source and authentication of thoughts.

There are many things we cannot come to know by direct or vicarious experience because of limited accessibility or because the matters involve metaphysical ideas that are not subject to objective confirmation. When experiential verification is either difficult or impossible, people develop and evaluate their conceptions of things in terms of the judgments voiced by others. In addition to enactive, vicarious, and social sources of thought verification, all of which rely on external influences, logical verification also enters into the process, especially in later phases of development. After people acquire some rules of inference, they can evaluate the soundness of their reasoning and derive from what they already know new knowledge about things that extend beyond their experiences.

External influences play a role not only in the development of cognitions but in their activation as well. Different sights, smells, and sounds will elicit quite different trains of thought. Thus, while it is true that conceptions govern behavior, the conceptions themselves are partly fashioned from direct or mediated transactions with the environment. A complete analysis of reciprocal determinism therefore requires investigation of how all three sets of factors—cognitive, behavioral, and environmental—interact reciprocally among themselves. Contrary to common misconception,

---

[2]Jean Piaget was a Swiss psychologist whose ideas have had an important influence on developmental psychology. The idea referred to here concerns Piaget's description of how the mind develops through an interaction between knowledge and experience.

social learning theory does not disregard personal determinants of behavior. Within this perspective, such determinants are treated as integral, dynamic factors in causal processes rather than as static trait dimensions.

Self-regulatory Functions of the Self System

The differences between unidirectional and reciprocal analyses of behavior have been drawn most sharply in the area of self-regulatory phenomena. Exponents of radical behaviorism have always disavowed any construct of self for fear that it would usher in psychic agents and divert attention from physical to experiential reality.[3] While this approach encompasses a large set of environmental factors, it assumes that self-generated influences either do not exist or, if they do, that they have no effect upon behavior. Internal events are treated simply as an intermediate link in a causal chain. Since environmental conditions presumably create the intermediate link, one can explain behavior in terms of external factors without recourse to any internal determinants. Through a conceptual bypass, cognitive determinants are thus excised from the analysis of causal processes.

In contrast to the latter view, internal determinants of behavior are gaining increasing attention in contemporary theorizing and research. Indeed, self-referent processes occupy a central position in social learning theory (Bandura, 1977b). As will be shown later, self-generated events cannot be relegated to a redundant explanatory link. In the triadic reciprocal system, they not only operate as reciprocal determinants of behavior but they play a role in the perception and formation of the environmental influences themselves.

* * *

In social learning theory, a self system is not a psychic agent that controls behavior. Rather, it refers to cognitive structures that provide reference

mechanisms and to a set of subfunctions for the perception, evaluation, and regulation of behavior. Before proceeding to a reciprocal analysis of self influences, the processes by which people exercise some control over their own behavior will be reviewed briefly.

COMPONENT PROCESSES IN SELF-REGULATION
Figure 50.2 summarizes the different component processes in the self-regulation of behavior through self-prescribed contingencies. Behavior typically varies on a number of dimensions, some of which are listed in the self-observation component. Depending on value orientations and the functional significance of given activities, people attend selectively to certain aspects of their behavior and ignore variations on nonrelevant dimensions.

Simply observing variations in one's performances yields some relevant information, but such data, in themselves, do not provide any basis for personal reactions. Behavior produces self-reactions through a judgmental function that includes several subsidiary processes. Whether a given performance will be regarded as commendable or dissatisfying depends upon the personal standards against which it is evaluated. Actions that measure up to internal standards are appraised favorably; those that fall short are judged unsatisfactory.

For most activities, there are no absolute measures of adequacy. The time in which a given distance is run, the number of points obtained on an achievement test, or the size of charitable contributions often do not convey sufficient information for self-appraisal even when compared with an internal standard. When adequacy is defined relationally, performances are evaluated by comparing them with those of others. The referential comparisons may involve standard norms, the performances of particular individuals, or the accomplishments of reference groups.

One's previous behavior is continuously used as the reference against which ongoing performance is judged. In this referential process, it is self-comparison that supplies the measure of

---

[3]We saw Skinner raise exactly this worry in the selections earlier in this section.

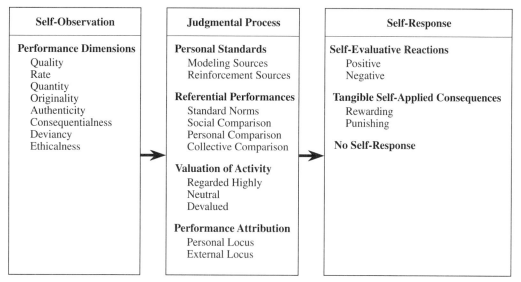

Figure 50.2 Component processes in the self-regulation of behavior by self-prescribed contingencies

adequacy. Past attainments influence performance appraisals mainly through their effects on standard setting. After a given level of performance is attained, it is no longer challenging, and new self-satisfactions are often sought through progressive improvement.

Another important factor in the judgmental component of self-regulation concerns the evaluation of the activities. People do not much care how they perform on tasks that have little or no significance for them. And little effort is expended on devalued activities. It is mainly in areas affecting one's welfare and self-esteem that favorable performance appraisals activate personal consequences (Simon, 1978).

Self-reactions also vary depending on how people perceive the determinants of their behavior. They take pride in their accomplishments when they ascribe their successes to their own abilities and efforts. They do not derive much self-satisfaction, however, when they view their performances as heavily dependent on external factors. The same is true for judgments of failure and blameworthy conduct. People respond self-critically to inadequate performances for which they hold themselves responsible but not to those

which they perceive are due to unusual circumstances or to insufficient capabilities. Performance appraisals set the occasion for self-produced consequences. Favorable judgments give rise to rewarding self-reactions, whereas unfavorable appraisals activate negative self-reactions. Performances that are judged to have no personal significance do not generate any reactions one way or another.

In the social learning view, self-regulated incentives alter performance mainly through their motivational function (Bandura, 1976). Contingent self-reward improves performance not because it strengthens preceding responses. When people make self-satisfaction or tangible gratifications conditional upon certain accomplishments, they motivate themselves to expend the effort needed to attain the desired performances. Both the anticipated satisfactions of desired accomplishments and the dissatisfactions with insufficient ones provide incentives for actions that increase the likelihood of performance attainments.

Much human behavior is regulated through self-evaluative consequences in the form of self-satisfaction, self-pride, self-dissatisfaction, and self-criticism. The act of writing is a familiar example of a behavior that is continuously self-regulated through evaluative self-reactions. Writers adopt a standard of what constitutes an acceptable piece of work. Ideas are generated and rephrased in thought before they are committed to paper. Provisional contructions are successively revised until authors are satisfied with what they have written. The more exacting the personal standards, the more extensive are the corrective improvements.

People also get themselves to do things they would otherwise put off by making tangible outcomes conditional upon completing a specified level of performance. In programs of self-directed change, individuals improve and maintain behavior on their own over long periods by arranging incentives for themselves (Bandura, 1976; Goldfried & Merbaum, 1973; Mahoney & Thoresen, 1974). In many instances, activities are regulated through self-prescribed contingencies involving both evaluative and tangible self-rewards. Authors influence how much they write by making breaks, recreational activities, and other tangible rewards contingent on completing a certain amount of work (Wallace, 1977), but they revise and improve what they write by their self-evaluative reactions.

* * *

Reciprocal Influence of External Factors on Self-regulatory Functions

Social learning theory regards self-generated influences not as automonous regulators of behavior but as contributory influences in a reciprocally interacting system. A variety of external factors serve as reciprocal influences on the operation of a self system. They can affect self-regulatory processes in at least three major ways: They are involved in the development of the component functions in self-regulatory systems; they provide partial support for adherence to self-prescribed contingencies; and they facilitate selective activation and disen-

gagement of internal contingencies governing conduct.

DEVELOPMENT OF SELF-REGULATORY FUNCTIONS The development of capabilities for self-reaction requires adoption of standards against which performances can be evaluated. These internal criteria do not emerge in a vacuum. Behavioral standards are established by precept, evaluative consequences accompanying different performances, and exposure to the self-evaluative standards modeled by others (Bandura, 1976, 1977b; Masters & Mokros, 1974). People do not passively absorb behavioral standards from the environmental stimuli that happen to impinge upon them. They extract generic standards from the multiplicity of evaluative reactions that are exemplified and taught by different individuals or by the same individuals on different activities and in different settings (Bandura, 1976; Lepper, Sagotsky, & Mailer, 1975). People must therefore process the divergent information and eventually arrive at personal standards against which to measure their own behavior.

Associational preferences add another reciprocal element to the acquisition process. The people with whom one regularly associates partly influence the standards of behavior that are adopted. Value orientations, in turn, exercise selective influence on choices of activities and associates (Bandura & Walters, 1959; Krauss, 1964).

EXTERNAL SUPPORTS FOR SELF-REGULATORY SYSTEMS In analyzing regulation of behavior through self-produced consequences, one must distinguish between two different sources of incentives that operate in the system. First, there is the arrangement of self-reward contingent upon designated performances to create proximal incentives for oneself to engage in the activities. Second, there are the more distal incentives for adhering to the self-prescribed contingencies.

Adherence to performance requirements for self-reward is partly sustained by periodic environmental influences that take a variety of forms (Bandura, 1977b). First, there are the negative sanctions for unmerited self-reward. When standards are being acquired or when they are later applied inconsistently, rewarding oneself for undeserving performances is more likely than not to evoke critical reactions from others. Occasional sanctions for unmerited self-reward influence the likelihood that people will withhold rewards from themselves until their behavior matches their standards (Bandura, Mahoney, & Dirks, 1976). Personal sanctions operate as well in fostering such adherence. After people adopt codes of conduct, when they perform inadequately or violate their standards they tend to engage in self-critical and other distressing trains of thought. Anticipated, thought-produced distress over faulty behavior provides an internal incentive to abide by personal standards of performance (Bandura, 1977b).

Negative inducements, whether personal or social, are not the most reliable basis upon which to rest a system of self-regulation. Fortunately, there are more advantageous reasons for exercising some influence over one's own behavior through self-arranged incentives. Some of these personal benefits are extrinsic to the behavior; others derive from the behavior itself.

People are motivated to institute performance contingencies for themselves when the behavior they seek to change is aversive. To overweight persons, the discomforts, maladies, and social costs of obesity create inducements to control their overeating. Similarly, students are prompted to improve their study behavior when failures in course work make academic life sufficiently distressing. By making self-reward conditional upon performance attainments, individuals can reduce aversive behavior, thereby creating natural benefits for their efforts.

The benefits of self-regulated change may provide natural incentives for adherence to personal prescriptions for valued activities as well as for unpleasant ones. People often motivate themselves by conditional incentives to enhance their skills in activities they aspire to master. Here the personal benefits derived from improved proficiency support self-prescription of contingencies. Self-generated inducements are especially important in ensuring continual progress in creative endeavors, because people have to develop their own work schedules for themselves. There are no clocks to punch or supervisors to issue directives. In analyzing the writing habits and self-discipline of novelists, Wallace (1977) documents how famous novelists regulate their writing output by making self-reward contingent upon completion of a certain amount of writing each day whether the spirit moves them or not.

If societies relied solely on inherent benefits to sustain personal contingencies, many activities that are tiresome and uninteresting until proficiency in them is acquired would never be mastered. Upholding standards is therefore socially promoted by a vast system of rewards including praise, social recognition, and honors. Few accolades are bestowed on people for self-rewarding their mediocre performances. Direct praise or seeing others publicly recognized for upholding excellence fosters adherence to high performance standards (Bandura, Grusec, & Menlove, 1967).

* * *

Because personal and environmental determinants affect each other in a reciprocal fashion, attempts to assign causal priority to these two sources of influence reduce to the "chicken-or-egg" debate. The quest for the ultimate environmental determinant of activities regulated by self-influence becomes a regressive exercise that can yield no victors in explanatory contests, because for every ultimate environmental cause that is invoked, one can find prior actions that helped to produce it.

SELECTIVE ACTIVATION AND DISENGAGEMENT OF SELF-REACTIVE INFLUENCES The third area of research on the role of external factors in self-regulation centers on the selective activation and disengagement of self-reactive influences (Bandura, 1977b). Theories of internalization that portray incorporated entities (e.g., the conscience or superego, moral codes) as continuous internal overseers of conduct are usually at a loss to explain the variable operation of internal control and the perpetration of inhumanities by otherwise humane people.

In the social learning analysis, considerate people perform culpable acts because of the reciprocal dynamics between personal and situational determinants of behavior rather than because of defects in their moral structures. Development of self-regulatory capabilities does not create an invariant control mechanism within a person. Self-evaluative influences do not operate unless activated, and many situational dynamics influence their selective activation.

After ethical and moral standards of conduct are adopted, anticipatory self-censuring reactions for violating personal standards ordinarily serve as self-deterrents against reprehensible acts (Bandura & Walters, 1959).[4] Self-deterring consequences are likely to be activated most strongly when the causal connection between conduct and the detrimental effects it produces is unambiguous. There are various means, however, by which self-evaluative consequences can be dissociated from reprehensible behavior. ✳ ✳ ✳

One set of disengagement practices operates at the level of the behavior. What is culpable can be made honorable through moral justifications and palliative characterizations (Gambino, 1973; Kelman, 1973). In this process, reprehensible conduct is made personally and socially acceptable by portraying it in the service of beneficial or moral ends. Such cognitive restructuring of behavior is an especially effective disinhibitor because it not only eliminates self-generated deterrents but engages self-reward in the service of the behavior.

Another set of dissociative practices operates by obscuring or distorting the relationship between actions and the effects they cause. By displacing and diffusing responsibility, people do not see themselves as personally accountable for their actions and are thus spared self-prohibiting reactions (Bandura, Underwood, & Fromson, 1975; Milgram, 1974). Additional ways of weakening self-deterring reactions operate by disregarding or obscuring the consequences of actions. When people embark on a self-disapproved course of action for personal gain, or because of other inducements, they avoid facing the harm they cause. Self-censuring reactions are unlikely to be activated as long as the detrimental effects of conduct are disregarded.

The final set of disengagement practices operates at the level of the recipients of injurious effects. The strength of self-evaluative reactions partly depends on how the people toward whom actions are directed are viewed. Maltreatment of individuals who are regarded as subhuman or debased is less apt to arouse self-reproof than if they are seen as human beings with dignifying qualities (Zimbardo, 1969). Detrimental interactions usually involve a series of reciprocally escalative actions in which the victims are rarely faultless. One can always select from the chain of events an instance of defensive behavior by the adversary as the original instigation. By blaming victims, one's own actions are excusable. The disengagement of internal control, whatever the means, is not achieved solely through personal deliberation. People are socially aided in this process by indoctrination, scapegoating, and pejorative stereotyping of people held in disfavor.

As is evident from preceding discussion, the development of self-regulatory functions does not create an automatic control system, nor do situational influences exercise mechanical control. Personal judgments operating at each subfunction preclude the automaticity of the process. There is leeway in judging whether a given behavioral standard is applicable. Because of the complexity and inherent ambiguity of most events, there is even greater leeway in the judgment of behavior and its effects. To add further to the variability of the control process, most activities are performed under collective arrangements that obscure responsibility, thus permitting leeway in judging the degree of personal agency in the effects that are socially produced. In short, there exists considerable latitude for personal judgmental factors to affect whether or not self-regulatory influences will be activated in any given activity.

---

[4]That is, you know you will feel guilty if you do it.

Reciprocal Influence of Personal Factors on Reinforcement Effects

Reinforcement has commonly been viewed as a mechanistic process in which responses are shaped automatically and unconsciously by their immediate consequences. The assumption of automaticity of reinforcement is crucial to the argument of unidirectional environmental control of behavior. One can dispense with the so-called internal link in causal chains only if persons are conceived of as mechanical respondents to external stimuli. The empirical evidence does not support such a view (Bandura, 1977b; Bower, 1975; Mischel, 1973; Neisser, 1976). External influences operate largely through cognitive processes.

During ongoing reinforcement, respondents are doing more than simply emitting responses. They develop expectations from observed regularities about the outcomes likely to result from their actions under given situational circumstances. Contrary to claims that behavior is controlled by its immediate consequences, behavior is related to its outcomes at the level of aggregate consequences rather than momentary effects (Baum, 1973). People process and synthesize contextual and outcome information from sequences of events over long intervals about the action patterns that are necessary to produce given outcomes.

The notion that behavior is governed by its consequences fares better for anticipated than for actual consequences (Bandura, 1977b). We have already reviewed research demonstrating how the same environmental consequences have markedly different effects on behavior depending on respondents' beliefs about the nature of the relationships between actions and outcomes and the meaning of the outcomes. When belief differs from actuality, which is not uncommon, behavior is weakly influenced by its actual consequences until more realistic expectations are developed through repeated experience. But it is not always expectations that change in the direction of social reality. Acting on erroneous expectations can alter how others behave, thus shaping the social reality in the direction of the expectations.

While undergoing reinforcing experiences, people are doing more than learning the probabilistic contingencies between actions and outcomes. They observe the progress they are making and tend to set themselves goals of progressive improvement. Investigators who have measured personal goal setting as well as changes in performance find that external incentives influence behavior partly through their effects on goal setting (Locke, Bryan, & Kendall, 1968). When variations in personal goals are partialed out, the effects of incentives on performance are reduced. Performance attainments also provide an important source of efficacy information for judging one's personal capabilities. Changes in perceived self-efficacy, in turn, affect people's choices of activities, how much effort they expend, and how long they will persist in the face of obstacles and aversive experiences (Bandura, 1977a; Brown & Inouye, 1978).

Because of the personal determinants of reinforcement effects, to trace behavior back to environmental "reinforcers" by no means completes the explanatory regress. To predict how outcomes will affect behavior, one must know how they are cognitively processed. To understand fully the mechanisms through which consequences change behavior, one must analyze the reciprocally contributory influences of cognitive factors.

Reciprocal Determinism as a Generic Analytic Principle

The discussion thus far has primarily addressed issues regarding the reciprocal interactions between behavior, thought, and environmental events as they occur at the individual level. Social learning theory treats reciprocal determinism as a basic principle for analyzing psychosocial phenomena at varying levels of complexity, ranging from intrapersonal development, to interpersonal behavior, to the interactive functioning of organizational and societal systems. At the intrapersonal level, people's conceptions influence what they perceive and do, and their conceptions are in turn altered by the effects of their actions and the observed consequences accruing to others (Bandura, 1977a; Bower, 1975). Information-processing models are concerned mainly with internal mental operations. A comprehensive theory must also analyze how conceptions are converted to actions, which furnish some of the data for conceptions. In social learning theory, people play an active role in creating information-generating experiences as well as in processing and transforming informative stimuli that happen to impinge upon them. This involves reciprocal transactions between thought, behavior, and environmental events which are not fully encompassed by a computer metaphor. People are not only perceivers, knowers, and actors. They are also self-reactors with capacities for reflective self-awareness that are generally neglected in information-processing theories based on computer models of human functioning.

At the level of interpersonal behavior, we have previously examined how people reciprocally determine each others' actions (Bandura et al., 1960; Patterson, 1975; Raush et al., 1974). Although the mutuality of behavior may be the focus of study, the reciprocal processes involve cognition as well as action. At the broader societal level, reciprocal processes are reflected in the interdependence of organizational elements, social subsystems, and transnational relations (Bandura, 1973; Keohane & Nye, 1977). Here the matters of interest are the patterns of interdependence between systems, the criteria and means used for gauging systemic performances, the mechanisms that exist for exercising reciprocal influence, and the conditions that alter the degree and type of reciprocal control that one system can exert on another.

It is within the framework of reciprocal determinism that the concept of freedom assumes meaning (Bandura, 1977b). Because people's conceptions, their behavior, and their environments are reciprocal determinants of each other, individuals are neither powerless objects controlled by environmental forces nor entirely free agents who can do whatever they choose. People can be considered partially free insofar as they shape future conditions by influencing their courses of action. By creating structural mechanisms for reciprocal influence, such as organizational systems of checks and balances, legal systems, and due process and elective procedures, people can bring their influence to bear on each other. Institutional reciprocal mechanisms thus provide not only safeguards against unilateral social control but the means for changing institutions and the conditions of life. Within the process of reciprocal determinism lies the opportunity for people to shape their destinies as well as the limits of self-direction.

References

Bandura, A. (1973). *Aggression: A social learning analysis.* Englewood Cliffs, NJ: Prentice-Hall.

Bandura, A. (1974). Behavior theory and the models of man. *American Psychologist, 29,* 859–869.

Bandura, A. (1976). Self-reinforcement: Theoretical and methodological considerations. *Behaviorism, 4,* 135–155.

Bandura, A. (1977a). Self-efficacy: Toward a unifying theory of behavioral change. *Psychological Review, 84,* 191–215.

Bandura, A. (1977b). *Social learning theory.* Englewood Cliffs, NJ: Prentice-Hall.

Bandura, A., & Adams, N. E. (1977). Analysis of self-efficacy theory of behavioral change. *Cognitive Therapy and Research, 1,* 287–308.

Bandura, A., Grusec, J. E., & Menlove, F. L. (1967). Some social determinants of self-monitoring reinforcement systems. *Journal of Personality and Social Psychology, 5,* 449–455.

Bandura, A., Lipsher, D. H., & Miller, P. E. (1960). Psychotherapists' approach-avoidance reactions to patients' expression of hostility. *Journal of Consulting Psychology, 1960,* 1–8.

Bandura, A., Mahoney, M. J., & Dirks, S. J. (1976). Discriminative activation and maintenance of contingent self-reinforcement. *Behaviour Research and Therapy, 14,* 1–6.

Bandura, A., Underwood, B., & Fromson, M. E. (1975). Disinhibition of aggression through diffusion of responsibility and dehumanization of victims. *Journal of Research in Personality, 9,* 253–269.

Bandura, A., & Walters, R. H. (1959). *Adolescent aggression.* New York: Ronald.

Bateson, G. (Ed.). (1961). *Perceval's narrative: A patient's account of his psychosis, 1830–1832.* Stanford, CA: Stanford University Press.

Baum, W. M. (1973). The correlation-based law of effect. *Journal of the Experimental Analysis of Behavior, 20,* 137–153.

Bower, G. H. (1975). Cognitive psychology: An introduction. In W. K. Estes (Ed.), *Handbook of learning and cognition.* Hillsdale, NJ: Erlbaum.

Brown, I., Jr., & Inouye, D. K. (1978). Learned helplessness through modeling: The role of perceived similarity in competence. *Journal of Personality and Social Psychology, 36*, 900–908.

Gambino, R. (1973). Watergate lingo: A language of non-responsibility. *Freedom at Issue*, No. 22.

Goldfried, M. R., & Merbaum, M. (Eds.). (1973). *Behavior change through self-control.* New York: Holt, Rinehart & Winston.

Kelman, H. C. (1973). Violence without moral restraint: Reflections on the dehumanization of victims and victimizers. *Journal of Social Issues, 29*, 25–61.

Keohane, R. O., & Nye, J. S. (1977). *Power and interdependence: World politics in transition.* Boston: Little, Brown.

Krauss, I. (1964). Sources of educational aspirations among working-class youth. *American Sociological Review, 29*, 867–879.

Lepper, M. R., Sagotsky, J., & Mailer, J. (1975). Generalization and persistence of effects of exposure to self-reinforcement models. *Child Development, 46*, 618–630.

Locke, E. A., Bryan, J. F., & Kendall, L. M. (1968). Goals and intentions as mediators of the effects of monetary incentives on behavior. *Journal of Applied Psychology, 52*(2), 104–121.

Mahoney, M. J., & Thoresen, C. E. (1974). *Self-control: Power to the person.* Monterey, CA: Brooks/Cole.

Masters, J. C., & Mokros, J. R. (1974). Self-reinforcement processes in children. In H. W. Reese (Ed.), *Advances in child development and behavior* (Vol. 9). New York: Academic Press.

Milgram, S. (1974). *Obedience to authority: An experimental view.* New York: Harper & Row.

Mischel, W. (1973). Toward a cognitive social learning reconceptualization of personality. *Psychological Review, 80*, 252–283.

Neisser, U. (1976). *Cognition and reality: Principles and implications of cognitive psychology.* San Francisco: W. H. Freeman.

Patterson, G. R. (1975). The aggressive child: Victim and architect of a coercive system. In L. A. Hamerlynck, E. J. Mash, & L. C. Handy (Eds.), *Behavior modification and families.* New York: Brunner/Mazel.

Raush, H. L., Barry, W. A., Hertel, R. K., & Swain, M. A. (1974). *Communication conflict and marriage.* San Francisco: Jossey-Bass.

Simon, K. M. (1978). *Self-evaluative reactions to one's own performances: The role of personal significance of performance attainments.* Unpublished manuscript, Stanford University.

Skinner, B. F. (1971). *Beyond freedom and dignity.* New York: Knopf.

Thomas, E. A. C., & Martin, J. A. (1976). Analyses of parent-child interaction. *Psychological Review, 83*, 141–156.

Wallace, I. (1977). Self-control techniques of famous novelists. *Journal of Applied Behavior Analysis, 10*, 515–525.

Zimbardo, P. G. (1969). The human choice: Individuation, reason, and order versus deindividuation, impulse, and chaos. In W. J. Arnold & D. Levine (Eds.), *Nebraska Symposium on Motivation* (Vol. 17). Lincoln: University of Nebraska Press.

TOWARD A COGNITIVE SOCIAL LEARNING RECONCEPTUALIZATION OF PERSONALITY

Walter Mischel

Another important social learning theorist is Walter Mischel, whose critique of personality traits we saw in Part II. His ideas overlap considerably with those of Rotter and Bandura, but take a distinctively more cognitive cast. Mischel is centrally concerned with the mental processes by which people interpret their worlds, and so labels his theory a "cognitive social learning reconceptualization of personality." The "reconceptualization" part of this label refers to his rejection of the psychology of personality traits and his desire to formulate an alternative way of thinking about people.

The following selection is Mischel's most influential theoretical article, published in 1973 (he and his student Yuichi Shoda published an update of this perspective in 1995). In it, Mischel presents a conceptualization of the self that overlaps in many ways with the one by Bandura in the preceding selection. Mischel breaks the self system into five components, which he labels "cognitive social learning person variables." These variables, meant to replace personality traits as ways of thinking about individual differences, are cognitive and behavioral construction competencies, encoding strategies and personal constructs, expectancies, subjective stimulus values, and self-regulatory systems and plans.

We have already seen that self-regulatory systems are an important part of Bandura's theory, that subjective stimulus values are an important part of Rotter's, and that expectancies play a prominent role in both. Mischel's unique contribution—influenced by his teacher, the phenomenologist George Kelly—is a close focus on the cognitive processes by which people interpret their worlds and act accordingly.

---

* * *

Cognitive Social Learning Person Variables

* * *

A set of person variables is proposed, based on theoretical developments in the fields of social learning and cognition.

Given the overall findings on the discriminativeness of behavior[1] and on the complexity of the interactions between the individual and the situation, it seems reasonable in the search for person variables to look more specifically at what the person *constructs* in particular conditions, rather than trying to infer what broad traits he generally *has*, and to incorporate in descriptions of what he does the specific psychological conditions in which the behavior will and will not be expected to occur. What people do, of course, includes much more than motor acts and requires us to consider what they do cognitively and affectively as well as motorically.

The proposed cognitive social learning approach to personality shifts the unit of study from global traits inferred from behavioral signs to the individual's cognitive activities and behavior patterns, studied in relation to the specific conditions that evoke, maintain, and modify them and which they, in turn, change (Mischel, 1968). The focus shifts from attempting to compare and generalize about what different individuals "are like" to an assessment of what they *do*—behaviorally and cognitively—in relation to the psychological conditions in which they do it. The focus shifts from describing situation-free people with broad trait adjectives to analyzing the specific interactions between conditions and the cognitions and behaviors of interest.

Personality research on social behavior and cognition in recent years has focused mainly on

the processes through which behaviors are acquired, evoked, maintained, and modified (e.g., Bandura, 1969; Mischel, 1968). Much less attention has been given to the psychological products within the individual of cognitive development and social learning experiences. Yet a viable psychology of personality demands attention to person variables that are the products of the individual's total history and that in turn mediate the manner in which new experiences affect him.

The proposed person variables are a synthesis of seemingly promising constructs in the areas of cognition and social learning. The selections should be seen as suggestive and open to progressive revision rather than as final. These tentative person variables are not expected to provide ways to accurately predict broadly cross-situational behavioral differences between persons: the discriminativeness and idiosyncratic organization of behavior are facts of nature, not limitations unique to trait theories. But these variables should serve to demonstrate that a social behavior approach to persons does not imply an empty organism. They should suggest useful ways of conceptualizing and studying specifically how persons mediate the impact of stimuli and generate distinctive complex molar behavior patterns. And they should help to conceptualize person-situation interactions in a theoretical framework based on contributions from both cognitive and behavioral psychology.

The proposed cognitive social learning person variables deal first with the individual's *competencies* to construct (generate) diverse behaviors under appropriate conditions. Next, one must consider the individual's *encoding* and *categorization* of events. Furthermore, a comprehensive analysis of the behaviors a person performs in particular situations requires attention to his *expectancies* about outcomes, the *subjective values* of such outcomes, and his *self-regulatory systems and plans*. The following five sections discuss each of these proposed person variables. While these variables obviously overlap and interact, each may provide distinctive information about the individ-

---

[1] The variability of an individual's behavior from one situation to another.

ual and each may be measured objectively and varied systematically.

COGNITIVE AND BEHAVIORAL CONSTRUCTION COMPETENCIES Through direct and observational learning the individual acquires information about the world and his relationship to it. As a result of observing events and attending to the behavior of live and symbolic models (through direct and film-mediated observation, reading, and instruction) in the course of cognitive development the perceiver acquires the potential to generate vast repertoires of organized behavior. While the pervasive occurrence and important consequences of such observational learning have been convincingly demonstrated (e.g., Bandura, 1969; Campbell, 1961), it is less clear how to conceptualize just what gets learned. The phenomena to be encompassed must include such diverse learnings as the nature of sexual gender identity (e.g., Kohlberg, 1966), the structure (or construction) of the physical world (e.g., Piaget, 1954), the social rules and conventions that guide conduct (e.g., Aronfreed, 1968), the personal constructs generated about self and others (e.g., Kelly, 1955), the rehearsal strategies of the observer (Bandura, 1971a). Some theorists have discussed these acquisitions in terms of the products of information processing and of information integration (e.g., Anderson, 1972; Bandura, 1971a; Rumelhart, Lindsey, & Norman, 1971), others in terms of schemata and cognitive templates (e.g., Aronfreed, 1968).

The concept of *cognitive and behavioral construction competencies* seems sufficiently broad to include the vast array of psychological acquisitions of organized information that must be encompassed. The term "constructions" also emphasizes the constructive manner in which information seems to be retrieved (e.g., Neisser, 1967) and the active organization through which it is categorized and transformed (Bower, 1970; Mandler, 1967, 1968). It has become plain that rather than mimicking observed responses or returning memory traces from undisturbed storage vaults, the ob-

server selectively *constructs* (generates) his renditions of "reality." Indeed, research on modeling effects has long recognized that the products of observational learning involve a novel, highly organized synthesis of information rather than a photocopy of specific observed responses (e.g., Bandura, 1971b; Mischel & Grusec, 1966). The present concept of construction competencies should call attention to the person's cognitive activities—the operations and transformations that he performs on information—rather than to a store of finite cognitions and responses that he "has."

Although the exact cognitive processes are far from clear, it is apparent that each individual acquires the capacity to construct a great range of potential behaviors, and different individuals acquire different behavior construction capabilities. The enormous differences between persons in the range and quality of the cognitive and behavioral patterns that they can generate is evident from even casual comparison of the construction potentials of any given individual with those, for example, of an Olympic athlete, a Nobel Prize winner, a retardate, an experienced forger, or a successful actor.

* * *

For many purposes, it is valuable to assess the quality and range of the cognitive constructions and behavioral enactments of which the individual is capable. In this vein, rather than assess "typical" behavior, one assesses *potential* behaviors or achievements. One tests what the person *can* do (e.g., Wallace, 1966) rather than what he "usually" does. Indeed one of the most recurrent and promising dimensions of individual differences in research seems to involve the person's *cognitive and behavioral (social) competencies* (e.g., White, 1959; Zigler & Phillips, 1961, 1962). These competencies presumably reflect the degree to which the person can generate adaptive, skillful behaviors that will have beneficial consequences for him. Personality psychology can profit from much greater attention to cognitive and intellectual competencies since these "mental abilities" seem to have much better temporal and cross-situational stability and influence than most of the social traits and motivations traditionally favored in personality research (e.g., Mischel, 1968, 1969).

* * *

The relative stability of the person's construction capacities may be one of the important contributors to the impression of consistency in personality. The fact that cognitive skills and behavior-generating capacities tend to be relatively enduring is reflected in the relatively high stability found in performances closely related to cognitive and intellectual variables, as has been stressed before (Mischel, 1968, 1969). The individual who knows how to be assertive with waiters, for example, or who knows how to solve certain kinds of interpersonal problems competently, or who excels in singing, is *capable* of such performances enduringly.

ENCODING STRATEGIES AND PERSONAL CONSTRUCTS   From the perspective of personality psychology, an especially important component of information processing concerns the perceiver's ways of encoding and grouping information from stimulus inputs. People can readily perform *cognitive transformations* on stimuli (Mischel & Moore, 1973), focusing on selected aspects of the objective stimulus (e.g., the taste versus the shape of a food object): such selective attention, interpretation, and categorization substantially alter the impact the stimulus exerts on behavior (see also Geer, Davison, & Gatchel, 1970; Schachter, 1964). Likewise, the manner in which perceivers encode and selectively attend to observed behavioral sequences greatly influences what they learn and subsequently can do (Bandura, 1971a, 1971b). Clearly, different persons may group and encode the same events and behaviors in different ways. At a molar level, such individual differences are especially evident in the personal constructs individuals employ (e.g., Argyle & Little, 1972; Kelly, 1955) and in the kinds of information to which they selectively attend (Mischel, Ebbesen, & Zeiss, 1973).

The behaviorally oriented psychologist eschews inferences about global dispositions and focuses instead on the particular stimuli and behaviors of interest. But what are "the stimuli and behaviors of interest?" Early versions of behaviorism attempted to circumvent this question by simplistic definitions in terms of clearly delineated motor "acts" (such as bar press) in response to clicks and lights. As long as the behaviors studied were those of lower animals in experimenter-arranged laboratory situations, the units of "behavior" and "stimuli" remained manageable with fairly simple operational definitions. More recent versions of behavior theory, moving from cat, rat, and pigeon confined in the experimenter's apparatus to people in exceedingly complex social situations, have extended the domain of studied behavior much beyond motor acts and muscle twitches; they seek to encompass what people do cognitively, emotionally, and interpersonally, not merely their arm, leg, and mouth movements. Now the term "behavior" has been expanded to include virtually anything that an organism does, overtly or covertly, in relation to extremely complex social and interpersonal events. Consider, for example, "aggression," "anxiety," "defense," "dependency," "self-concepts," "self-control," "self-reinforcement." Such categories go considerably beyond self-evident behavior descriptions. A category like aggression involves inferences about the subject's intentions (e.g., harming another versus accidental injury) and abstractions about behavior, rather than mere physical description of actions and utterances.

* * *

There is considerable evidence that people categorize their own personal qualities in relatively stable trait terms (e.g., on self-ratings and self-report questionnaires). These self-categorizations, while often only complexly and tenuously related to nonverbal behavior, may be relatively durable and generalized (Mischel, 1968, 1969). * * * While traditional personality research has focused primarily on exploring the correlates of such self-categorizations, in the present view they comprise merely one kind of person variable.

EXPECTANCIES So far the person variables considered deal with what the individual is capable of doing and how he categorizes events. To move from potential behaviors to actual performance, from construction capacity and constructs to the construction of behavior in specific situations, requires attention to the determinants of performance. For this purpose, the person variables of greatest interest are the subject's expectancies. While it is often informative to know what an individual *can* do and how he construes events and himself, for purposes of specific prediction of behavior in a particular situation it is essential to consider his specific expectancies about the consequences of different behavioral possibilities in that situation. For many years personality research has searched for individual differences on the psychologist's hypothesized dimensions while neglecting the subject's own expectancies (hypotheses). More recently, it seems increasingly clear that the expectancies of the subject are central units for psychology (e.g., Bolles, 1972; Estes, 1972; Irwin, 1971; Rotter, 1954). These hypotheses guide the person's selection (choice) of behaviors from among the enormous number which he is capable of constructing within any situation.

On the basis of direct experience, instructions, and observational learning, people develop expectancies about environmental contingencies (e.g., Bandura, 1969). Since the expectancies that are learned within a given situation presumably reflect the objective contingencies in that situation, an expectancy construct may seem superfluous. The need for the expectancy construct as a person variable becomes evident, however, when one considers individual differences in response to the same situational contingencies due to the different expectancies that each person brings to the situation. An expectancy construct is justified by the fact that the person's expectancies (inferred from statements) may not be in agreement with the objective contingencies in the situation. Yet behavior

may be generated in light of such expectancies, as seen, for example, in any verbal conditioning study when a subject says plural nouns on the erroneous hypothesis that the experimenter is reinforcing them.[2]

* * *

One type of expectancy concerns *behavior-outcome relations* under particular conditions. These *behavior-outcome expectancies* (hypotheses, contingency rules) represent the "if____, then____" relations between behavioral alternatives and probable outcomes anticipated with regard to particular behavioral possibilities in particular situations. In any given situation, the person will generate the response pattern which he expects is most likely to lead to the most subjectively valuable outcomes (consequences) in that situation (e.g., Mischel, 1966; Rotter, 1954). In the absence of new information about the behavior-outcome expectancies in any situation the individual's performance will depend on his previous behavior-outcome expectancies in similar situations. This point is illustrated in a study (Mischel & Staub, 1965) which showed that presituational expectancies significantly affect choice behavior in the absence of situational information concerning probable performance-outcome relationships. But the Mischel and Staub study also showed that new information about behavior-outcome relations in the particular situation may quickly overcome the effects of presituational expectancies, so that highly specific situational expectancies become the dominant influences on performance.

When the expected consequences for performance change, so does behavior, as seen in the discriminative nature of responding which was elaborated in earlier sections and documented

---

[2]In a verbal conditioning study, a subject talks while an experimenter reinforces certain verbalizations by saying "good." If the subject believes that he or she is being rewarded for saying plural nouns, the subject will say more of them, even if in fact the experimenter is reinforcing something else. This is a simple demonstration that it is the subject's beliefs about reinforcement, not the reinforcment itself, that controls behavior.

elsewhere (Mischel, 1968). But in order for changes in behavior-outcome relations to affect behavior substantially, the person must recognize them. In the context of operant conditioning,[3] it has become evident that the subject's awareness of the behavior-outcome relationship crucially affects the ability of response consequences (reinforcements) to modify his complex performances (e.g., Spielberger & DeNike, 1966). The essence of adaptive performance is the recognition and appreciation of new contingencies. To cope with the environment effectively, the individual must recognize new contingencies as quickly as possible and reorganize his behavior in the light of the new expectancies. Strongly established behavior-outcome expectancies with respect to a response pattern may constrain an individual's ability to adapt to changes in contingencies. Indeed, "defensive reactions" may be seen in part as a failure to adapt to new contingencies because the individual is still behaving in response to old contingencies that are no longer valid. The "maladaptive" individual is behaving in accord with expectancies that do not adequately represent the actual behavior-outcome rules in his current life situation.

In the present view, the effectiveness of response-contingent reinforcements (i.e., operant conditioning) rests on their ability to modify behavior-outcome expectancies. When information about the response pattern required for reinforcement is conveyed to the subject by instructions, "conditioning" tends to occur much more readily than when the subject must experience directly the reinforcing contingencies actually present in the operant training situation. For example, accurate instructions about the required response and the reinforcement schedule to which subjects would be exposed exerted far more powerful effects on performance than did the reinforcing contingencies (Kaufman, Baron, & Kopp, 1966). Presumably, such instructions exert their effects by altering response-outcome expectancies. To the extent that information about new response-reinforcement

contingencies can be conveyed to motivated human beings more parsimoniously through instructions or observational experiences than through operant conditioning procedures (e.g., Kaufman et al., 1966), an insistence upon direct "shaping" may reflect an unfortunate (and wasteful) failure to discriminate between the animal laboratory and the human condition.

A closely related second type of expectancy concerns *stimulus-outcome relations*. As noted previously in the discussion of generalization and discrimination, the outcomes expected for any behavior hinge on a multitude of stimulus conditions that moderate the probable consequences of any pattern of behavior. These stimuli ("signs") essentially "predict" for the person other events that are likely to occur. More precisely, the individual learns (through direct and observational experiences) that certain events (cues, stimuli) predict certain other events. * * *

Stimulus-outcome expectancies seem especially important person variables for understanding the phenomena of classical conditioning. For example, through the contiguous association of a light and painful electric shock in aversive classical conditioning the subject learns that the light predicts shock. If the product of classical conditioning is construed as a stimulus-outcome expectancy, it follows that any information which negates that expectancy will eliminate the conditioned response. In fact, when subjects are informed that the "conditioned stimuli" will no longer be followed by pain-producing events, their conditioned emotional reactions are quickly eliminated (e.g., Grings & Lockhart, 1963). Conversely, when subjects were told that a particular word would be followed by shock, they promptly developed conditioned heart-rate responses (Chatterjee & Eriksen, 1962). In the same vein, but beyond the conditioning paradigm, if subjects learn to generate "happy thoughts" when faced by stimuli that otherwise would frustrate them beyond endurance, they can manage to tolerate the "aversive" situation with equanimity (Mischel, Ebbesen, & Zeiss, 1972). Outside the artificial confines of the

---

[3]Skinner's explanation of behavior change.

laboratory in the human interactions of life, the "stimuli" that predict outcomes often are the social behaviors of others in particular contexts. The meanings attributed to those stimuli hinge on a multitude of learned correlations between behavioral signs and outcomes.

* * *

In the present view, the person's expectancies mediate the degree to which his behavior shows cross-situational consistency or discriminativeness. When the expected consequences for the performance of responses across situations are not highly correlated, the responses themselves should not covary strongly[4] (Mischel, 1968). Since most social behaviors lead to positive consequences in some situations but not in other contexts, highly discriminative specific expectancies tend to be developed and the relatively low correlations typically found among a person's response patterns across situations become understandable (Mischel, 1968). Expectancies also will not become generalized across response modes[5] when the consequences for similar content expressed in different response modes are sharply different, as they are in most life circumstances (Mischel, 1968). Hence expectancies tend to become relatively specific, rather than broadly generalized. Although a person's expectancies (and hence performances) tend to be highly discriminative, there certainly is some generalization of expectancies, but their patterning in the individual tends to be idiosyncratically organized to the extent that the individual's history is unique. * * *

While behavior-outcome and stimulus-outcome expectancies seem viable person variables, it would be both tempting and hazardous to transform them into generalized trait-like dispositions by endowing them with broad cross-situational consistency or removing them from the context of the specific stimulus conditions on which they depend. At the empirical level, "generalized expectancies" tend to be generalized only within relatively narrow, restricted limits (e.g., Mischel & Staub, 1965; Mischel, Ebbesen, & Zeiss, 1973). For example, the generality of "locus of control" is in fact limited, with distinct, unrelated expectancies found for positive and negative outcomes and with highly specific behavioral correlates for each (Mischel, Zeiss, & Zeiss, 1973). If expectancies are converted into global trait-like dispositions and extracted from their close interaction with situational conditions, they are likely to become just as useless as their many theoretical predecessors. On the other hand, if they are construed as relatively specific (and modifiable) "if ____, then ____" hypotheses about contingencies, it becomes evident that they exert important effects on behavior (e.g., Mischel & Staub, 1965).

SUBJECTIVE STIMULUS VALUES Even if individuals have similar expectancies, they may select to perform different behaviors because of differences in the *subjective values* of the outcomes which they expect. For example, given that all persons expect that approval from a therapist depends on verbalizing particular kinds of self-references, there may be differences in the frequency of such verbalizations due to differences in the perceived value of obtaining the therapist's approval. Such differences reflect the degree to which different individuals value the response-contingent outcome. Therefore it is necessary to consider still another person variable: the subjective (perceived) value for the individual of particular classes of events, that is, his stimulus preferences and aversions. This unit refers to stimuli that have acquired the power to induce positive or negative emotional states in the person and to function as incentives or reinforcers for his behavior. The subjective value of any stimulus pattern may be acquired and modified through instructions and observational experiences as well as through direct experiences (Bandura, 1969).

---

[4]That is, when a person expects that a given behavior will have different consequences in two different situations, what he or she does in one of those situations will have little relation to what he or she does in the other.

[5]That is, an expectancy about the result of one behavior will not necessarily influence another behavior.

* * *

SELF-REGULATORY SYSTEMS AND PLANS While behavior is controlled to a considerable extent by externally administered consequences for actions, the individual also regulates his own behavior by self-imposed goals (standards) and self-produced consequences. Even in the absence of external constraints and social monitors, persons set performance goals for themselves and react with self-criticism or self-satisfaction to their behavior depending on how well it matches their expectations and criteria. The concept of self-imposed achievement standards is seen in Rotter's (1954) "minimal goal" construct and in more recent formulations of self-reinforcing functions (e.g., Bandura, 1971c; Kanfer, 1971; Kanfer & Marston, 1963; Mischel, 1968, 1973).

The essence of self-regulatory systems is the subject's adoption of *contingency rules* that guide his behavior in the absence of, and sometimes in spite of, immediate external situational pressures. Such rules specify the kinds of behavior appropriate (expected) under particular conditions, the performance levels (standards, goals) which the behavior must achieve, and the consequences (positive and negative) of attaining or failing to reach those standards. Each of these components of self-regulation may be different for different individuals, depending on their unique earlier histories or on more recently varied instructions or other situational information.

Some of the components in self-regulation have been demonstrated in studies of goal setting and self-reinforcement (e.g., Bandura & Whalen, 1966; Bandura & Perloff, 1967; Mischel & Liebert, 1966). Perhaps the most dramatic finding from these studies is that even young children will not indulge themselves with freely available immediate gratifications but, instead, follow rules that regulate conditions under which they may reinforce themselves. Thus, children, like adults, far from being simply hedonistic, make substantial demands of themselves and impose complex contingencies upon their own behavior. The stringency or severity of self-imposed criteria is rooted in the observed standards displayed by salient models as well as in the individual's direct socialization history (e.g., Mischel & Liebert, 1966), although after they have been adopted, the standards may be retained with considerable persistence.

After the standards (terminal goals) for conduct in a particular situation have been selected, the often long and difficult route to self-reinforcement and external reinforcement with material rewards is probably mediated extensively by covert symbolic activities, such as praise and self-instructions, as the individual reaches subgoals. When individuals imagine reinforcing and noxious stimuli, their behavior appears to be influenced in the same manner as when such stimuli are externally presented (e.g., Cautela, 1971). These covert activities serve to maintain goal-directed work until the performance matches or exceeds the person's terminal standards (e.g., Meichenbaum, 1971). Progress along the route to a goal is also mediated by self-generated distractions and cognitive operations through which the person can transform the aversive "self-control" situation into one which he can master effectively (e.g., Mischel et al., 1972; Mischel & Moore, 1973a, 1973b). While achievement of important goals leads to positive self-appraisal and self-reinforcement, failure to reach significant self-imposed standards may lead the individual to indulge in psychological self-lacerations (e.g., self-condemnation). The anticipation of such failure probably leads to extensive anxiety, while the anticipation of success may help to sustain performance, although the exact mechanisms of self-regulation still require much empirical study.

* * *

OVERVIEW OF PERSON VARIABLES In sum, individual differences in behavior may reflect differences in each of the foregoing person variables and in their interactions, summarized in Table 51.1.

First, people differ in their *construction competencies*. Even if people have similar expectancies about the most appropriate response pattern in a particular situation and are uniformly motivated to make it, they may differ in whether or not (and

---

TABLE 51.1

SUMMARY OF COGNITIVE SOCIAL LEARNING PERSON VARIABLES

1. Construction competencies: ability to construct (generate) particular cognitions and behaviors. Related to measures of IQ, social and cognitive (mental) maturity and competence, ego development, social-intellectual achievements and skills. Refers to what the subject knows and *can* do.
2. Encoding strategies and personal constructs: units for categorizing events and for self-descriptions.
3. Behavior-outcome and stimulus-outcome expectancies in particular situations.
4. Subjective stimulus values: motivating and arousing stimuli, incentives, and aversions.
5. Self-regulatory systems and plans: rules and self-reactions for performance and for the organization of complex behavior sequences.

---

how well) they *can* do it, that is, in their ability to construct the preferred response. For example, due to differences in skill and prior learning, individual differences may arise in interpersonal problem solving, empathy and role taking, or cognitive-intellective achievements. Response differences also may reflect differences in how individuals *categorize* a particular situation (i.e., in how they encode, group, and label the events that comprise it) and in how they construe themselves and others. Differences between persons in their performance in any situation depend on their behavior-outcome and stimulus-outcome *expectancies*, that is, differences in the expected outcomes associated with particular responses or stimuli in particular situations. Performance differences also may be due to differences in the subjective *values* of the outcomes expected in the situation. Finally, individual differences may be due to differences in the *self-regulatory systems* and plans that each person brings to the situation.

* * *

THREE PERSPECTIVES IN PERSONALITY STUDY

The study of persons may be construed alternatively from three complementary perspectives. Construed from the viewpoint of the psychologist seeking procedures or operations necessary to produce changes in performance, it may be most useful to focus on the environmental *conditions* necessary to modify the subject's behavior and therefore to speak of "stimulus control," "operant conditioning," "classical conditioning," "reinforcement control," "modeling" and so on. Construed from the viewpoint of the theorist concerned with how these operations produce their effects in the subject who undergoes them, it may be more useful to speak of alterations in processed information and specifically in constructs, expectancies, subjective values, rules, and other theoretical *person variables* that mediate the effects of conditions upon behavior. Construed from the viewpoint of the experiencing subject, it may be more useful to speak of the same events in terms of their *phenomenological impact* as thoughts, feelings, wishes, and other subjective (but communicable) internal states of experience. Confusion arises when one fails to recognize that the same events (e.g., the "operant conditioning" of a child's behavior at nursery school) may be alternatively construed from each of these perspectives and that the choice of constructions (or their combinations) depends on the construer's purpose. Ultimately, conceptualizations of the field of personality will have to be large enough to encompass the phenomena seen from all three perspectives. The present cognitive social learning approach to persons hopefully is a step in that direction.

References

Anderson, N. H. (1972). Information integration theory: A brief survey. (Tech. Rep. No. 24) La Jolla: University of California at San Diego, Center for Human Information Processing.

Argyle, M., & Little, B. R. (1972). Do personality traits apply to social behavior? *Journal of Theory of Social Behavior, 2*, 1–35.

Aronfreed, J. (1968). *Conduct and conscience: The socialization of internalized control over behavior.* New York: Academic Press.

Bandura, A. (1969). *Principles of behavior modification.* New York: Holt, Rinehart & Winston.

Bandura, A. (1971a). Analysis of modeling processes. In A. Bandura (Ed.), *Psychological modeling: Conflicting theories.* Chicago: Aldine-Atherton.

Bandura, A. (1971b). *Social learning theory.* New York: General Learning Press.

Bandura, A. (1971c). Vicarious and self-reinforcement processes. In R. Glaser (Ed.), *The nature of reinforcement.* New York: Academic Press.

Bandura, A., & Perloff, B. (1967). Relative efficacy of self-monitored and externally imposed reinforcement systems. *Journal of Personality and Social Psychology, 7,* 111–116.

Bandura, A., & Whalen, C. K. (1966). The influence of antecedent reinforcement and divergent modeling cues on patterns of self-reward. *Journal of Personality and Social Psychology, 3,* 373–382.

Bolles, R. C. (1972). Reinforcement, expectancy, and learning. *Psychological Review, 79,* 394–409.

Bower, G. H. (1970). Organizational factors in memory. *Cognitive Psychology, 1,* 18–46.

Campbell, D. T. (1961). Conformity in psychology's theories of acquired behavioral dispositions. In I. A. Berg & B. M. Bass (Eds.), *Conformity and deviation.* New York: Harper.

Cautela, J. R. (1971). Covert conditioning. In A. Jacobs & L. B. Sachs (Eds.), *The psychology of private events.* New York: Academic Press.

Chatterjee, B. B., & Eriksen, C. W. (1962). Cognitive factors in heart rate conditioning. *Journal of Experimental Psychology, 64,* 272–279.

Estes, W. K. (1972). Reinforcement in human behavior. *American Scientist, 60,* 723–729.

Geer, J. H., Davison, G. C., & Gatchel, R. K. (1970). Reduction of stress in humans through nonveridical perceived control of aversive stimulation. *Journal of Personality and Social Psychology, 16,* 731–738.

Grings, W. W., & Lockhart, R. A. (1963). Effects of anxiety-lessening instructions and differential set development on the extinction of GSR. *Journal of Experimental Psychology, 66,* 292–299.

Irwin, F. W. (1971). *Intentional behavior and motivation.* New York: Lippincott.

Kanfer, F. H. (1971). The maintenance of behavior by self-generated stimuli and reinforcement. In A. Jacobs & L. B. Sachs (Eds.), *The psychology of private events.* New York: Academic Press.

Kanfer, F. H., & Marston, A. R. (1963). Determinants of self-reinforcement in human learning. *Journal of Experimental Psychology, 66,* 245–254.

Kaufman, A., Baron, A., & Kopp, R. E. (1966). Some effects of instructions on human operant behavior. *Psychonomic Monograph Supplements, 1,* 243–250.

Kelly, G. (1955). *The psychology of personal constructs.* New York: Basic Books.

Kohlberg, A. (1966). A cognitive-developmental analysis of children's sex-role concepts and attitudes. In E. E. Maccoby (Ed.), *The development of sex differences.* Stanford: Stanford University Press.

Mandler, G. (1967). Organization and memory. In K. W. Spence & J. T. Spence (Eds.), *The psychology of learning and motivation: Advances in research and theory.* New York: Academic Press.

Mandler, G. (1968). Association and organization: Facts, fancies and theories. In T. R. Dixon & D. L. Horton (Eds.), *Verbal behavior and general behavior theory.* Englewood Cliffs, NJ: Prentice-Hall.

Meichenbaum, D. H. (1971). *Cognitive factors in behavior modification: Modifying what clients say to themselves.* (Research Report No. 25) Waterloo: University of Waterloo.

Mischel, W. (1966). Theory and research on the antecedents of self-imposed delay of reward. In B. A. Maher (Ed.), *Progress in experimental personality research.* Vol. 3. New York: Academic Press.

Mischel, W. (1968). *Personality and assessment.* New York: Wiley.

Mischel, W. Continuity and change in personality. *American Psychologist,* 1969, *24,* 1012–1018.

Mischel, W. (1973). Processes in delay of gratification. In L. Berkowitz (Ed.), *Advances in social psychology* (Vol. 7). New York: Academic Press.

Mischel, W., Ebbesen, E. B., & Zeiss, A. R. (1972). Cognitive and attentional mechanisms in delay of gratification. *Journal of Personality and Social Psychology, 21,* 204–218.

Mischel, W., Ebbesen, E. B., & Zeiss, A. R. (1973). Selective attention to the self: Situational and dispositional determinants. *Journal of Personality and Social Psychology, 27,* 129–142.

Mischel, W., & Grusec, J. (1966). Determinants of the rehearsal and transmission of neutral and aversive behaviors. *Journal of Personality and Social Psychology, 3,* 197–205.

Mischel, W., & Liebert, R. M. (1966). Effects of discrepancies between observed and imposed reward criteria on their acquisition and transmission. *Journal of Personality and Social Psychology, 3,* 45–53.

Mischel, W., & Moore, B. (1973a). Effects of attention to symbolically presented rewards upon self-control. *Journal of Personality and Social Psychology,* in press.

Mischel, W., & Moore, B. (1973b). Cognitive transformations of the stimulus in delay of gratification. Unpublished manuscript, Stanford University.

Mischel, W., & Staub, E. (1965). Effects of expectancy on working and waiting for larger rewards. *Journal of Personality and Social Psychology, 2,* 625–633.

Neisser, U. (1967). *Cognitive psychology.* New York: Appleton-Century-Crofts.

Piaget, J. (1954). *The construction of reality in the child.* New York: Basic Books.

Rotter, J. B. (1954). *Social learning and clinical psychology.* Englewood Cliffs, N. J.: Prentice-Hall.

Rummelhart, D. E., Lindsey, P. H., & Norman, D. A. (1971). A process model for long-term memory. (Tech. Rep. No. 17). La Jolla: University of California at San Diego, Center for Human Information Processing.

Schachter, S. (1964). The interaction of cognitive and physiological determinants of emotional state. In L. Berkowitz (Ed.), *Advances in experimental social psychology* (Vol. 1). New York: Academic Press.

Spielberger, D. C., & DeNike, L. D. (1966). Descriptive behaviorism versus cognitive theory in verbal operant conditioning. *Psychological Review, 73,* 306–326.

Wallace, J. (1966). An abilities conception of personality: Some implications for personality measurement. *American Psychologist, 21,* 132–138.

White, R. W. (1959). Motivation reconsidered: The concept of competence. *Psychological Review, 66,* 297–333.

Zigler, E., & Phillips, L. (1961). Social competence and outcome in psychiatric disorder. *Journal of Abnormal and Social Psychology, 63,* 264–271.

Zigler, E., & Phillips, L. (1962). Social competence and the process-reactive distinction in psychopathology. *Journal of Abnormal and Social Psychology, 65,* 215–222.

COGNITIVE STRATEGIES AS PERSONALITY: EFFECTIVENESS, SPECIFICITY, FLEXIBILITY, AND CHANGE

Julie K. Norem

In the previous selection, Walter Mischel made the point that personality is not just something one "has," but also something one "does." One thing a person does, he proposed, is to formulate strategies by which to live life and fulfill goals. The following selection is by Julie Norem (who was a student of Mischel's student Nancy Cantor). Norem describes research that examines two particular strategies, which she calls defensive pessimism and "illusory glow" optimism.

In a study of college students, Norem found that optimists, who motivate themselves by expecting the best, and pessimists, who motivate themselves by fearing the worst, seemed to do about equally well in college. And Norem claims both groups did better than subjects with no strategy at all.

A couple of fundamental principles are demonstrated by this research. First, different people often use different routes to the same goal. Although the pessimists and optimists followed very different strategies, they both pursued academic success and seemed to achieve that goal about equally often. Second, a strategy that works in one domain may not work in another. Students who were pessimists about their schoolwork were not necessarily pessimists about their social life; those who were seemed to have difficulty. Pessimism seems to be a strategy that can help you get work done, but does not make you popular.

The purpose of the research in the next selection is to bring one of Mischel's cognitive social learning variables to life by showing how people develop and implement strategies for attaining their important goals in life.

From "Cognitive Strategies as Personality: Effectiveness, Specificity, Flexibility, and Change," by J. K. Norem (1989). In *Personality Psychology: Recent Trends and Emerging Directions*, edited by D. M. Buss and N. Cantor, pp. 45–60. New York: Springer-Verlag. Adapted with permission.

As units of personality, *cognitive strategies* describe how individuals use self-knowledge and knowledge about the social world to translate their goals into behavior. The concept of a strategy captures coherent patterns of appraisal, planning, retrospection, and effort (Bruner, Goodnow, & Austin, 1956; Cantor & Kihlstrom, 1987; Norem, 1987; Showers & Cantor, 1985). Strategies focus on *process*: the ways people direct their attention, construct expectations and goals, allocate their time and effort, protect their self-esteem, and react emotionally. Thus, strategies elaborate on the *instantiation* of traits and motives. Analysis of personality and individual differences in terms of strategies shifts emphasis away from general dispositions towards the cognitive links between motives and actions.

This perspective on personality assumes that a general trait, disposition, or motive has many potential manifestations. * * * Need for achievement, for example, may be expressed in cutthroat competition among brokers on Wall Street, or through dedication to improving on a "personal best" in a marathon. Similarly, specific behaviors may represent a number of diverse general characteristics when performed by different individuals in different situations. Organizing departmental colloquia could be an expression of affiliative motives for one person and an expression of power motives for another (Winter, 1988). The contention here is that *personality* is embodied at least as much in the different ways nAch[1] (or introversion or aggression) might be expressed by different individuals, as in differences in those characteristics themselves. Individual differences are expressed in the interpretations of situations and pursuit of specific goals: e.g., beating others vs. improving one's self, or promoting collegial discourse vs. controlling people and resources.

These assumptions, then, locate personality in the specific goals individuals construct for themselves, in the form of "life tasks" (Cantor & Kihl-

strom, 1987), "personal projects" (Palys & Little, 1983), "personal strivings" (Emmons, 1986), or even situationally specific expectations; and in the strategies individuals develop to pursue these goals (e.g. Buss, 1987; Cantor, Norem, Niedenthal, Langston & Brower, 1987). There are several important implications of personality conceived of in this way. In this chapter, I plan to discuss these implications, review some recent data that support hypotheses derived from this perspective, and conclude with a consideration of future directions in personality research that build on current data and theory.

Examples of Strategies: Defensive Pessimism and "Illusory Glow" Optimism

Throughout this discussion, research on two particular strategies will serve to illustrate the central tenets of this approach. These strategies are "illusory glow" optimism and defensive pessimism (Norem & Cantor, 1986a). The defensive pessimism strategy involves individuals with acknowledged positive performance histories in a particular domain, who, nevertheless, set unrealistically low expectations when anticipating new situations within that domain. Individuals using the strategy feel anxious and out of control, and play through a "worst-case" analysis—dwelling on possible negative outcomes—even when those outcomes seem improbable.

Data from experimental and field research on defensive pessimism in the achievement domain indicate that these negative expectations do not become self-fulfilling prophecies, or lead to effort withdrawal. Nor do they necessarily have the emotional consequences associated with more generalized pessimistic or depressive attributional style (Peterson & Seligman, 1984; Showers & Ruben, 1988). Instead, individuals using the defensive pessimist strategy invest considerable effort in tasks they see as important (Norem & Cantor, 1986b).

---

[1]Need for achievement.

Moreover, in the short-run at least, individuals using the strategy perform as well as subjects using an optimistic strategy, and feel just as satisfied with their performance. Unlike optimistic subjects, defensive pessimists do not seem to "revise" their understanding of a performance after the fact in order to protect their self-esteem. For example, in an experimental setting, they did not deny having control when given failure feedback relative to when given success feedback (Norem & Cantor, 1986a).

In contrast, individuals using "illusory glow" optimism do not anticipate negative outcomes; nor do they typically feel anxious or out of control prior to performance situations. Optimists set realistically high expectations, based on their past successes. They then protect or enhance their positive self-image using the battery of positive illusions and biases documented by researchers investigating the differences between depressive and non-depressive cognition (see Taylor & Brown, 1988, for a review). In the study cited in the paragraph above, optimistic subjects showed a typical "illusion of control" for success, while denying control for failure.

It is important to note that individuals using these two different strategies have constructed somewhat different goals for themselves, which follow from their appraisal of relevant situations. Research comparing these groups has focused on situations that both optimists and defensive pessimists see as important, rewarding, and absorbing. The defensive pessimists, however, also see these same situations as more stressful and less within their control than the optimists (Cantor et al., 1987). For the defensive pessimist group, therefore, there is an additional crucial dimension to the "problem" presented by these situations: dealing with anxiety and "taking control" of a situation in order to perform well.

For the optimist group, remaining in control and staying "up" is part of the challenge. Indeed, there is some evidence from the studies cited above that their performance may suffer if they confront negative information or do experience

anxiety, (Cantor et al., 1987). This suggests that their goal may include avoiding negative information and contemplation of the possibility of failure (Miller, 1987).

Another way of understanding the different goals of the two groups is to consider combinations of motives. Both groups resemble, in background, aspiration and cumulative performance, high need for achievement subjects (Atkinson, 1957). Both groups come from families that emphasize achievement-related activities (Norem & Cantor, 1990). The high anxiety and low expectations among defensive pessimists, however, resemble that found among high fear of failure subjects in traditional achievement research. (Atkinson & Litwin, 1960). There is some reason to think that individuals using defensive pessimism might be high in nAch and high fear of failure: a motive constellation that Atkinson and his colleagues predict should cause immobilization. Indeed, Self (1988) finds that academic optimists and defensive pessimists do not differ in the satisfaction they expect to derive from success, but that pessimists expect significantly greater unhappiness from failure than the optimists. This fits with the emphasis on "working through" the implications of bad outcomes found in the defensive pessimist group, who, apparently, actively attempt to fight immobilization in order to take control of or "harness" their anxiety so that they may concentrate on the task at hand (Norem & Cantor, 1986b).

The emphasis on these two strategies throughout this chapter is, of course, not meant to suggest that they in any way exhaust the category of strategies individuals may use, even within the context of performance situations. Various emotional and behavioral self-handicapping strategies come quickly to mind as alternative ways, for example, to approach performance situations, based on somewhat differently constructed goals. There are numerous other strategies individuals may use, especially when one considers different domains of human activity (Folkman & Lazarus, 1985; Frese, Stewart & Hannover, 1987; Kuhl, 1985; Langston

& Cantor, 1989; Miller, 1987; Paulhus & Martin, 1987; Pyszczynski & Greenberg, 1987; Snyder & Smith, 1986; Zirkel & Cantor, 1988). Aside from the author's convenience, however, there are two reasons why these particular strategies are especially useful examples for the purposes of this chapter. First, research on these strategies includes experimental work, questionnaire studies, and a longitudinal project. There are data from contrived laboratory contexts, and from "messier" real-life situations. There are self-report data, objective-performance data, experience-sampling data, and observer ratings. Although the subjects in these studies have all been college students, they are students drawn from quite different populations, demographically and otherwise. The research reviewed below has been conducted using subjects from the general undergraduate population at the University of Michigan and from a somewhat more select sample of Honors College students. In addition, there are data from undergraduate subjects at Northeastern University, who represent different demographic characteristics, who encounter a different academic environment while attending an urban school known for its cooperative education program, and who arrive at college with a much greater diversity in preparation and aptitude than students at Michigan. The convergence of these different data sources lends substantial support to the argument that strategies provide a powerful tool for exploring personality function.

Second, optimism and defensive pessimism are strategies used by individuals who *do not* appear to differ in other ways, which might suggest that differences in strategy are merely epiphenomena.[2] Among college students, there are no significant demographic or SES differences between those using optimism and those using defensive pessimism. Nor do they differ significantly in high school rank, high school grade point average, SAT scores, or number of family members in college. There is no reason to suspect that the difference in strategies among these individuals is a simple

function of intelligence, past performance, scholastic aptitude, preparation for college, or some readily identifiable influence from their social structure. Therefore, they provide a clear opportunity to contrast the expression of personality via different strategies with relatively less "noise" from other variables.

Theoretical Implications of a Strategy-Based Approach to Personality

STRATEGY EFFECTIVENESS One implication of considering personality in terms of strategies is an emphasis on the *effectiveness* of different strategies. Adaptation and coping are thus seen as a function of individual goals, the manner in which individuals pursue their goals, and the probable consequences of various goal-strategy combinations. Strategy effectiveness involves: (a) the extent to which a strategy leads to successful outcomes; (b) the "costs" of using the strategy, in terms of emotional wear and tear, the response of others, and/or lost opportunities; (c) the potential costs of *not* using the strategy (or being without a coherent strategy for pursuing a particular goal). Effectiveness may also be a function of the indirect consequences that using a strategy in one domain has for other domains.

Research on the effectiveness of defensive pessimism and optimism within the academic domain highlights the importance of considering all of the above points when attempting to evaluate the effectiveness of a strategy. Norem and Cantor (1986a, b) found that, when left to use their habitual strategy on anagram and puzzle tasks (presented as tests of "different kinds of abilities"), subjects prescreened for self-reported use of defensive pessimism or optimism performed equivalently well.[3] They were also equivalently satisfied

---

[2]Phenomena that play no causal role.

[3]Prescreening for individuals using defensive pessimism and optimism is done using a nine-item, face valid questionnaire. Subjects indicate the extent to which each item is characteristic of them. The items include questions such as "I generally go into academic situa-

with their performances after the fact. This was so even though the defensive pessimism group reported feeling significantly more anxious and out of control prior to the test. When, however, the experimenter interfered with the defensive pessimists' strategy by encouraging them, their performance suffered, relative to optimists in the same condition (whose performance improved) and defensive pessimists in the control condition.

Cantor et al., (1987), as part of an ongoing longitudinal study[4] of the transition to college life, studied academic optimism and defensive pessimism among freshmen in the Honors College at the University of Michigan. Their results converged with the experimental data in that the students using defensive pessimism appraised their academic tasks significantly more negatively than the students using optimism: they felt less in control, more stressed, found academic tasks more difficult, more important, and more time consuming. They also expected to do more poorly than the optimists expected to do.

A similar pattern of emotions and appraisal appeared in data from an experience-sampling study in which a subsample of the Honors students carried electronic pagers that "beeped" on a random schedule several times a day for ten days. At each "beep," the students filled out a report of

what they were doing and how they were feeling (Cantor & Norem, 1989; Norem, 1987). In these data, defensive pessimist subjects reported feeling significantly less control, less enjoyment, less progress, and more stress than optimists during academic situations, especially in "anticipatory" situations, such as when they were studying for a test. Their reports from other situations, however, were just as positive as the optimists'. As a consequence, their reported feelings of control are significantly more variable across situations than the optimists'.

Just as in the laboratory studies, the negative appraisal and lack of control reported by the defensive pessimists did not impair their performance over the short-run, (although there are suggestions of relatively greater "costs" over the long-run; see below). Defensive pessimists and optimists both performed quite well academically during their first and second years in college (GPAs above 3.30), and there were no differences in average GPA between the two groups. There were also no differences between the two groups in social satisfaction or in an overall measure of perceived stress during their first two years in college.

From these studies, it seems reasonable to conclude that the defensive pessimist and optimist strategies are both *effective* insofar as the individuals using them perform well on academic tasks. It is also important to understand that the characteristic ways in which information about tasks and the self is used by the two strategy groups is not incidental to their performance. Playing through contingency plans is significantly negatively related to GPA for the optimists in the Honors College sample. In contrast, it is significantly positively related for the defensive pessimists, for whom it is an integral part of "dealing with" the problems presented by academic tasks. Negativity about the academic domain and negative beliefs about the self are negatively related to performance for the optimists—a pattern that contrasts markedly with relationships found for the defensive pessimist. Negativity of academic plans is not related to GPA for the latter group (whose plans

---

tions expecting the worst, even though things usually turn out OK," and "I usually go into academic situations with positive expectations." There are four questions describing aspects of the defensive pessimist strategy and four describing aspects of the optimistic strategy. There is also a question that asks subjects to indicate the extent to which they believe they have done well in the past. The sum of the pessimistic items is subtracted from the sum of the optimistic items. Subjects in the bottom and top thirds of the distribution of answers are selected for use of defensive pessimism and optimism respectively, *providing* that they strongly endorse the item about positive past experience (6 or higher on a 9-point scale). This is done to select for *defensively* pessimistic subjects, as opposed to those whose pessimism is realistic, or based on distortion of past experience.—Author

[4]A longitudinal study is one that follows a single group of subjects for an extended period of time, sometimes years.

progress from very negative possible outcomes to successful resolution of those outcomes), and negative beliefs about the academic self are strongly positively related to GPA.

Another way of assessing the effectiveness of optimism and defensive pessimism is to compare the outcomes of those using these strategies with the outcomes of other individuals. Norem and Cantor (1990) looked at the performance of a group of individuals, labelled "aschematics," who, initially, did not seem to have a coherent strategy for the academic domain. These are individuals who are in the middle third of the academic optimism-pessimism prescreening distribution,[5] and who sometimes resemble optimists, sometimes resemble pessimists, but are, characteristically, neither.

The aschematics in the Honors College sample were less absorbed in and anxious about academic tasks than the pessimists, but also felt less in control than the optimists. They were somewhat less reflective than the other two groups, and had significantly fewer mismatches between their actual and ideal self-concepts in the academic domain (Higgins, Klein & Strauman, 1985). Data from the experience-sampling study show that a subgroup of the aschematics spend 29% of their time on academic tasks (relative to 38% and 35% for optimists and defensive pessimists), felt significantly less in control across situations than optimists, and were more lonely, angry, and more in conflict in virtually every situation sampled than the other two strategy groups. For the aschematics, *unlike* the defensive pessimists who seem able to "take control" by using their strategy, feeling out of control is negatively related to GPA performance and academic satisfaction. Finally, the aschematics achieve marginally lower GPAs than the other two groups during their first year in college, and significantly lower GPAs during their second year.

These data show the aschematic group "floundering" in their approach to academic tasks—re-

sults interpreted by Norem and Cantor as a consequence of poorly articulated goals within the achievement domain and a resultant lack of a coherent strategy for that domain. * * *

As will be seen below, the aschematics were eventually able to develop effective approaches to dealing with their academic tasks, once their goals within that domain crystallized. Initially, however, it seems clear that both the defensive pessimist strategy and the optimistic strategy were considerably more effective than no strategy at all.

The data reviewed so far strongly support the contention that defensive pessimism and optimism can be effective strategies, at least within the academic domain and with respect to performance outcomes. Consideration of strategy effectiveness should, however, also include assessment of the relative "costs" of a strategy to the individual using it. There are no current data showing significant short-term costs to the use of either optimism or defensive pessimism in the academic domain —especially when the use of those strategies is contrasted with the absence of a strategy. Looking in depth at how the strategies of optimism and defensive pessimism unfold over time, however, reveals important differences between the strategies apt to be related to differences in the longer term costs of each. The experience-sampling data reveal much greater variance in emotions—especially in feelings of control—for the pessimists than for the other two groups. Over the course of a few years, the emotional ups and downs of academic defensive pessimism may accumulate and take a heavy toll on well-being. In addition, the pessimists seem to rely heavily on a small group of close friends: they spend more time with a relatively small group of "best friends," while the optimists spend more time with a larger group of "friends." It may be that the pessimists' best friends find themselves wearying of the pessimists' worry and anxiety.

In fact, the costs or "side effects" of defensive pessimism show up strongly in data from the Honors College sample during their third year in college (Cantor & Norem, 1989). A telephone sur-

---

[5]That is, individuals who scored in the middle on the optimist-pessimist questionnaire.

vey assessed reports of physical and psychological symptoms, satisfaction with academic and social performance, and junior year GPA among this sample. Results indicate that the defensive pessimists, although not doing badly in any absolute sense, were suffering somewhat relative to the optimists. They reported experiencing greater frequencies of psychological and physical symptoms, felt less satisfied with their academic and social performances, and had lower GPAs than the optimists. (Again, it is important to note that, although below the optimists' GPA, the pessimists were still performing quite well: mean GPA = 3.35). In this case, the indirect consequences of using a strategy repeatedly over time are clearly important to assessment of the effectiveness of the strategy. Of course, we do not know from these data what would have happened to the defensive pessimists if they had not been using their strategy. Recall from previous research that defensive pessimists who were "deprived" of their strategy in a performance situation were relatively debilitated (Norem & Cantor, 1986b). The pessimists' appraisal of academic situations focuses on their anxiety and feelings of being out of control. Although it may be stressful to recognize and continually experience those feelings, the pessimists are at least able to "work through" them to some extent by using their strategy. Even though defensive pessimism is apparently not "cost-free" over time, it may be preferable to feeling anxious and out of control, and to having no way of coping with those feelings.

These data about the short- and long-term consequences of different strategies within the academic domain highlight the complexity of the process by which individuals pursue their goals. So far, we have only considered these strategies within one domain—that of academic achievement activities. Another aspect of the effectiveness of strategies, however, concerns the relative fit between strategy and domain. Simply put, some strategies may be better suited to some domains than to others. This raises the question of how domain-specific an individual's strategies are and the extent to which people can adjust the strategies they use to fit particular contexts.

Domain Specificity, Flexibility, and Strategy Change

Strategies stem from appraising a situation and activating relevant goals. One of the reasons that a strategy may not be equally effective in all situations is that all situations do not provide the same opportunities to realize a given goal. Nor, in the absence of monomania, are individuals likely to interpret all situations in the same way. Therefore, there is no a priori reason to assume that individuals will use the same kind of strategy in different kinds of situations.

Moreover, there is no assumption that strategies that characterize an individual at one period in his/her life will continue to do so throughout the passing years. The concept of a strategy explicitly recognizes the potential—indeed, the probability—of change as an individual's goals change. As goals are successfully realized, as cumulative feedback indicates a strategy is unsuccessful or exacts too high a cost, or as tasks in a domain are abandoned or transformed and new goals formulated, one would expect to find corresponding strategy change.

In research to date, the academic and social versions of the defensive pessimism prescreening questionnaire show average correlations of .30 across several samples of University of Michigan students (Norem & Cantor, 1986b, Norem, 1987; Showers, 1986), and .23 for two samples of Northeastern students (Norem, 1988). Both correlations are significant, but modest: it is clear that once categorization into strategy group is made for both domains, not everyone who uses defensive pessimism academically also uses it socially, and that not all academic optimists are social optimists. There is some potential, then, for domain specificity in the application of defensive pessimism. This is also reflected in the academic defensive pessimists' appraisal of the social domain: they do not generalize their negative perspective from the academic to the social domain. Academic pessimists feel just as much control over and have just as high expectations for the social domain as academic optimists, *and* as social optimists (Cantor et al., 1987). Similarly, social defensive pessimists neither set low expectations for their academic performance nor appraise academic tasks negatively (Norem & Illingworth, 1989).

Furthermore, when the self-knowledge of social and academic defensive pessimists and optimists is compared within and across each domain, clear domain specificity appears. Academic defensive pessimists have more negative academic selves than academic optimists, but have equivalently positive social selves. The comparable pattern of domain-specific self-knowledge is found among social optimists and defensive pessimists: the latter have more negative beliefs about their social selves, but not about their academic selves (Cantor et al., 1987; Norem, 1987; Norem & Illingworth, 1989).

In addition to providing support for the idea that use of a given strategy is potentially domain-specific, social defensive pessimism provides an informative look at issues of strategy-situation fit. Recall that defensive pessimism involves setting low expectations, focusing on anxiety, reflecting extensively on negative outcomes, and working very hard on a task. Although academic defensive pessimists experience reasonable success using these procedures, the strategy might be less effective in the social domain.

First, academic situations such as those studied in the research above may differ from many social situations in that, for the most part, there are externally provided, explicit evaluations of performance. Typically, students receive grades, scores, and/or other feedback about their scholastic performance. Even if not entirely "objective," this feedback comes from outside sources and provides easy comparison to past performance and the performance of others. Rarely, in social interactions, are performance outcomes so unequivocal. It may be that in situations where there is relatively less objective positive information about past perfor-

mance, the defensive pessimist strategy flounders, since it depends on contrasting defensively low expectations with realistically high past performance.

Second, the correlation between the amount of time and effort spent in preparation and eventual performance is probably quite strong and positive within academic situations. In other words, despite what students might say, there is some positive relationship between the amount of time spent studying and final exam grades in most classrooms. The same contingencies, however, may not operate as clearly in the social domain. One can hardly help but think of the prototypical adolescent repeating his/her carefully thought out greeting while waiting for a prospective date to answer the phone—only to find that every word gets jumbled on the way out, and the result is an embarrassing squeak or mumble. It is easy to come up with examples of when "trying too hard" (or being seen that way) can lead to social failure. Indeed, one might even speculate that extensive planning reflection, and effort prior to a social occasion increases the risk of bumbling, stilted interactions, emotional anticlimax, and disappointment.

Data from the Honors College sample do show that social pessimism is less effective than academic pessimism: social pessimists are less satisfied and feel significantly more stressed than social optimists during their first and third years in college (Norem, 1987). Observers of interviews with social pessimists and optimists rate them as less satisfied with their social performance, less interested in trying new things, less apt to try to make new affiliations, more reluctant to think about good social outcomes, more stressed by social tasks, and more apt to ruminate obsessively about problems than are social optimists (see Norem, 1987 for details).

The picture that emerges from these data is not one of individuals *using* defensive pessimism to work through anxiety and motivate themselves; rather, it resembles a picture of unmotivated, mildly depressed subjects, stuck in a repetitive cycle of negativity. It is interesting to note in this context that, among the academic defensive pessimists from the Honors College sample, those who were also defensively pessimistic in the social domain exhibited the most psychological and physical symptoms, the most stress, and the greatest dissatisfaction with their lives (by their junior year) of any group. Indeed, most of the long-term negative consequences found among academic defensive pessimists (relative to optimists) are a function of the low scores of the "pan-domain" pessimists. Defensive pessimism, in other words, may leave a lot to be desired as a social strategy. Those within this sample who use it only within the academic domain seem to fare better than those who overgeneralize or misapply the strategy to tasks in the social domain.

These data have at least two important implications. The first is that the effectiveness of any strategy is apt to vary from situation to situation. One can, therefore, generate a number of testable hypotheses about the relative effectiveness of different strategies in different contexts, which, in turn, have implications for the successful adjustment of people using those strategies in those contexts. Thus, for example, the greater emotional "cost" of defensive pessimism (compared to optimism) would seem to imply that it is relatively inappropriate or ineffective for situations where potential negative outcomes are not strongly influenced by individual effort or not very consequential in and of themselves. Becoming anxious about and planning several different routes for weekly trips to the grocery store is probably not going to result in benefits that compensate for the strain. (It may be that spending time and energy worrying may be more aversive than the actual negative consequences about which one is concerned.) When, however, careful reflection, mental rehearsal, and effort do significantly increase the probability of good outcomes, positive outcomes are especially attractive, and/or when negative outcomes are especially disastrous, defensive pessimism may be "worth it"—i.e., highly effective. In contrast, especially to the extent that "illusory glow" optimism involves active avoidance of negative information, there are situations where it may not be a particularly effective strategy. When

careful attention to feedback about errors is necessary for learning, when potential negative consequences are extreme, and/or when there are significant risks associated with overconfidence, an optimistic strategy could prove costly. One might hope, for example, that defensive pessimists, as opposed to "illusory glow" optimists, are overrepresented among individuals designing and operating nuclear power plants.[6]

This discussion also suggests that a potentially important aspect of the effectiveness of a given strategy may be the sensitivity with which it is employed from situation to situation. If strategies become overlearned, automatic, or overgeneralized, they may also be relatively less effective. There are corresponding implications: 1) individuals with more strategies available in their repertoire may be better able to adapt to a variety of situations, and may choose to become involved in more different kinds of situations than those with fewer strategies; 2) individuals who are flexible in the way they use the strategies in their repertoire may be better off—especially over time—than those who employ the same strategy over and over.

Recent data provide some support for these hypotheses. A subsample of the Honors College subjects participated in "problem-solving" interviews during their sophomore year, in which they were asked to respond to hypothetical problem situations in different domains, and specific attempts were made by the interviewers to "throw a curve" to each interviewee: i.e., after describing their initial plan, subjects were presented with objections to the plans and asked what they would do if the plans did not work. Among other things, the videotapes of these interviews were coded for "flexibility" of response in each situation (see Norem, 1987, for details). These flexibility ratings correlated positively with sophomore GPA ($r = .39$, $p < .05$), junior year GPA ($r = .24$, $p < .10$), and negatively with physical symptoms ($r = -.37$, $p < .05$) and psychological symptoms ($r = -.43$, $p < .01$) during the junior year.

---

[6]The word "glow" was not intended—initially—as a pun in this context.—Author

In addition, data from the Honors College sample collected during their senior year indicate that the academic defensive pessimists have, to a large extent, recovered from their junior year "slump"—*and*, that many of them have begun to use the optimistic strategy within the academic domain (Norem, 1989; see Showers, 1986, for data showing that this change is unlikely to be due to unreliability of the prescreening). The defensive pessimists no longer have lower satisfaction or grade point averages, and they no longer construe the academic domain more negatively than the optimists. Closer analyses of these results reveal that the mean improvement shown by the defensive pessimist group is primarily a function of those academic pessimists who have switched to an optimistic strategy. It is impossible, of course, to tell from these data whether or not this group's improved functioning is a result of their switch to optimism, whether their switch is a function of improved outcomes, or whether some third variable(s) is behind each. Nevertheless, it does seem that individuals have some potential to change their strategies in response to feedback. It is tempting to speculate that the subjects who change strategy do so in response to changes in their primary goals, either within the academic domain, or in other domains which have an impact on their approach to academic tasks.

*   *   *

Conclusion

A strategy-based approach to the study of personality attempts to illuminate how individuals accomplish (or fail to accomplish) the things that are important to them. Strategies capture the coherence of people's approaches to different domains and highlight important differences between those approaches. A given strategy is part of an individual's personality for as long as he/she is using it to work on current life tasks, or for as long as it remains a viable part of his/her repertoire of strategies. Strategies are, theoretically, among the most malleable units of personality—although, at this point, we know relatively little about the actual limits on flexibility in strategy use, the typical extent of people's strategy repertoires, or how difficult it is to accomplish strategy change. We do, however, have the basis of a model for predicting change. As people move from one set of life tasks to another, we would predict more strategy change than when they remain within the same context over time (Stewart & Healy, 1985). Similarly, consideration of the effectiveness of different strategies in different domains provides the basis for predictions about better and worse coping. Personality adjustment can be considered in terms of the short- and long-term effectiveness of the strategies people employ, and the extent to which they are flexible and sensitive in response to different situations.

From this perspective, personality is the set of goals and strategies that organize an individual's thoughts, feelings and actions, and comprise the tools with which people adapt to their worlds. Personality includes both the tasks that a given group of individuals may have in common (e.g., their desire to get good grades and make new friends during their freshman year in college), and that which distinguishes individuals within that group (e.g., their unique interpretations of those situations in terms of opportunity, challenge, stress, and control). As an instrument of adaptation, personality's potential for change over time is as important as its consistency. Looking at how people articulate their tasks, and the limits and advantages of the strategies they use to work on them should help clarify the conditions under which change is embraced, expected, or resisted.

References

Atkinson, J. W. (1957). Motivational determinants of risk-taking. *Psychological Review, 64,* 359–372.

Atkinson, J. W. & Litwin, C. H. (1960). Achievement motive and test anxiety conceived as motive to approach success and motive to avoid failure. *Journal of Abnormal and Social Psychology, 60,* 52–63.

Bruner, J. S., Goodnow, J. J., & Austin, G. A. (1956). *A study of thinking.* New York: Wiley.

Buss, D. M. (1987). Selection, evocation, and manipulation.

Journal of Personality and Social Psychology, 53, 1214–1221.

Cantor, N. & Kihlstrom, J. F. (1987). *Personality and social intelligence.* New York: Prentice-Hall.

Cantor, N., & Norem, J. K. (1989). Defensive pessimism and stress and coping. *Social Cognition, 7,* 92–112.

Cantor, N., Norem, J. K., Niedenthal, P. M., Langston, C. A. & Brower, A. M. (1987). Life tasks, self-concept ideals, and cognitive strategies in a life transition. *Journal of Personality and Social Psychology, 53,* 1178–1191.

Emmons, R. A. (1986). Personal strivings: An approach to personality and subjective well-being. *Journal of Personality and Social Psychology, 51,* 1058–1068.

Folkman, S., & Lazarus, D. S. (1985). If it changes it must be a process: Study of emotion and coping during three stages of a college examination. *Journal of Personality and Social Psychology, 48,* 150–170.

Frese, M., Stewart, J., & Hannover, B. (1987). Goal orientation and planfulness: Action styles as personality concepts. *Journal of Personality and Social Psychology, 52,* 1182–1194.

Higgins, E. T., Klein, R., & Strauman, T. (1985). Self-concept discrepancy theory: A psychological model for distinguishing among different aspects of depression and anxiety. *Social Cognition, 3,* 51–76.

Kuhl, J. (1985). From cognition to behavior: Perspectives for future research on action control. In J. Kuhl & J. Beckmann (Eds.), *Action control from cognition to behavior.* New York: Springer.

Langston, C. A., & Cantor, N. (1989). Social anxiety and social constraint: When "making friends" is hard. *Journal of Personality and Social Psychology.*

Miller, S. M. (1987). Monitoring and blunting: Validation of a questionnaire to assess styles of information seeking under threat. *Journal of Personality and Social Psychology, 52(2),* 345–353.

Norem, J. K. (1987) *Strategic realities: Optimism and defensive pessimism.* Unpublished doctoral dissertation. University of Michigan.

Norem, J. K. (1988). *Negativity, specifity and stability of strategies and self-knowledge.* Unpublished manuscript. Northeastern University.

Norem, J. K. (1989) *Changing tasks and changing strategies during adaptation to a life transition.* Manuscript in preparation.

Norem, J. K. & Cantor, N. (1986a). Anticipatory and post hoc cushioning strategies: Optimism and defensive pessimism in "risky" situations. *Cognitive Therapy and Research, 10(3),* 347–362.

Norem, J. K., & Cantor, N. (1986b). Defensive pessimism: "Harnessing" anxiety as motivation. *Journal of Personality and Social Psychology, 51(6),* 1208–1217.

Norem, J. K., & Cantor, N. (1990). Cognitive strategies, coping and perceptions of competence. In R. J. Sternberg & J. Kolligan, Jr. (Eds.), *Perceptions of competence and incompetence across the lifespan* (pp. 190–204). New Haven, CT: Yale University Press.

Norem, J. K., & Illingworth, S. (1989). *Social vs. academic defensive pessimism: Issues of strategy-situation fit.* Unpublished manuscript. Northeastern University.

Palys, T. S., & Little, B. R. (1983). Perceived life satisfaction and the organization of personal project systems. *Journal of Personality and Social Psychology, 44,* 1221–1230.

Paulhus, D. L., & Martin, C. L. (1987). The structure of personality capabilities. *Journal of Personality and Social Psychology, 52(2),* 345–365.

Peterson, C., & Seligman, M. (1984). Causal explanation as a risk factor for depression: Theory and evidence. *Psychological Review, 91(3),* 347–374.

Pyszczynski, T., & Greenberg, J. (1987). Self-regulatory preservation and the depressive self-focusing style: A self-awareness theory of reactive depression. *Psychological Bulletin, 102(1),* 122–138.

Self, E. A. (1988). *Defensive pessimism: A strategy for energization?* Unpublished master's thesis. University of Kansas.

Showers, C. (1986). *Anticipatory cognitive strategies: The positive side of negative thinking.* Unpublished doctoral dissertation. University of Michigan.

Showers, C., & Cantor, N. (1985). Social cognition: A look at motivated strategies. In M. Rosenzweig & L. W. Porter (Eds.), *Annual Review of Psychology, 36,* 275–306.

Showers, C., & Ruben, C. (1988). *Distinguishing defensive pessimism from depression: Negative expectations and positive coping mechanisms.* Manuscript under review.

Snyder, C. R. & Smith, T. W. (1986). On being "shy like a fox.": A self-handicapping analysis. In W. H. Jones, J. M. Cheek, & S. R. Briggs (Eds.), *Shyness: Perspectives in research and treatment* (pp. 161–172). New York: Plenum Press.

Stewart, A. J. & Healy, J. M., Jr. (1985). Personality as adaptation to change. In R. Hogan & W. Jones (Eds.). *Perspectives on personality: Theory, measurement, and interpersonal dynamics* (pp. 117–144). Greenwich, CT: JAI Press.

Taylor, S. E. & Brown, J. (1988). Illusion and well being: A social psychological perspective on mental health. *Psychological Bulletin., 103(2),* 193–210.

Winter, D. G. (1988). The power-motive in women—and men. *Journal of Personality and Social Psychology, 54(3),* 510–519.

Zirkel, S. & Cantor, N. (1988). *Independence and identity in the transition to college life.* Paper presented at the Annual Meeting of the American Psychological Association, Atlanta, Georgia.

A Social Cognitive Approach to Motivation and Personality

Carol S. Dweck and Ellen L. Leggett

The last selection in this section, by the psychologist Carol Dweck and her for-mer student Ellen Leggett, describes the differences between people who follow "mastery-oriented" and "helpless" behavioral patterns. This emphasis on patterns of goal-related behavior resembles in many ways the research on opti-mistic and pessimistic strategies presented by Norem in the previous chapter. But while Norem emphasizes that both optimism and pessimism can be adaptive, Dweck and Leggett clearly state that a mastery strategy is better than a helpless one. Furthermore, Dweck and Leggett tie the patterns they study to both moti-vation and cognition.

Relevant to motivation, Dweck and Leggett's mastery-oriented subjects seem to be pursuing different goals than their helpless subjects. Mastery-oriented sub-jects have the goal of improving their abilities and performance, whereas helpless subjects wish merely to demonstrate that they are not incompetent. These goals are tied to different cognitions, according to Dweck and Leggett. Mastery-oriented subjects believe that intelligence (and other personal attributes) are "malleable," and can be changed through experience. Helpless subjects, on the other hand, believe that such personal qualities are fixed and cannot be changed.

The interrelation of these three levels of analysis can be seen clearly when they are rearranged. First, a person has a belief about the world, specifically that his or her personal attributes are changeable or fixed. Second, these beliefs lead him or her to have different goals, specifically either to improve oneself (if one believes that personal qualities are changeable) or to prove one has desirable at-tributes (if one believes these qualities are fixed). Third and finally, these differ-ing goals lead to different behavioral responses to failure. The improvement goal produces a mastery response, and the performance goal produces a helpless re-sponse. In this way Dweck and Leggett's theory ties together cognition, motiva-tion, and behavior—no small achievement.

However, their theory also includes at least one gap and one irony. The gap is that the theory is silent about how these orientations affect reactions to suc-cess. It would seem to predict that because success implies there is no more to learn, mastery-oriented subjects would become less motivated and deteriorate in their performance relative to "helpless" subjects. The latter subjects would still be motivated to prove their competence in further situations, and probably encouraged to think they can do so.

The irony is that although Dweck and Leggett's theory clearly implies that it is better to be what they call an "incremental" than an "entity" theorist, their own theory is an entity theory. That is, the degree to which one is an entity or incremental theorist is regarded as a personal attribute that apparently does not change much over time.

The task for investigators of motivation and personality is to identify major patterns of behavior and link them to underlying psychological processes. In this article we (a) describe a research-based model that accounts for major patterns of behavior, (b) examine the generality of this model—its utility for understanding domains beyond the ones in which it was originally developed, and (c) explore the broader implications of the model for motivational and personality processes.

Toward this end, we begin by describing two major patterns of cognition-affect-behavior: the maladaptive "helpless" response and the more adaptive "mastery-oriented" response (Diener & Dweck, 1978, 1980; Dweck, 1975; Dweck & Reppucci, 1973). The helpless pattern, as will be seen, is characterized by an avoidance of challenge and a deterioration of performance in the face of obstacles. The mastery-oriented pattern, in contrast, involves the seeking of challenging tasks and the maintenance of effective striving under failure.

Most interesting, our research with children has demonstrated that those who avoid challenge and show impairment in the face of difficulty are initially equal in ability to those who seek challenge and show persistence. Indeed some of the brightest, most skilled individuals exhibit the maladaptive pattern. Thus it cannot be said that it is simply those with weak skills or histories of failure who (appropriately) avoid difficult tasks or whose skills prove fragile in the face of difficulty. The puzzle, then, was why individuals of equal ability would show such marked performance differences in response to challenge. Even more puzzling was the fact that those most concerned with their ability, as the helpless children seemed to be, behaved in ways that impaired its functioning and limited its growth.

Our efforts to explain this phenomenon led us to the more general conceptualization of *goals* (Dweck & Elliott, 1983). We proposed that the goals individuals are pursuing create the framework within which they interpret and react to events. Specifically, in the domain of intellectual achievement, we identified two classes of goals: *performance* goals (in which individuals are concerned with gaining favorable judgments of their competence) and *learning* goals (in which individuals are concerned with increasing their competence). We then tested and supported the hypothesis that these different goals foster the different response patterns—that a focus on performance goals (competence judgments) creates a vulnerability to the helpless pattern, whereas the pursuit of learning goals (competence enhancement) in the same situation promotes the mastery-oriented pattern (Elliott & Dweck, 1988; Farrell & Dweck, 1985; Leggett & Dweck, 1986).

The question that remained, however, was why individuals in the same situation would pursue such different goals. This led us to the more general conceptualization of individuals' *implicit theories*. Here, we tested the hypothesis that different theories about oneself, by generating different concerns, would orient individuals toward the different goals. Specifically, we showed that conceiving of one's intelligence as a fixed entity was associated with adopting the performance goal of documenting that entity, whereas conceiving of intelligence as a malleable quality was associated with the learning goal of developing that quality (Bandura & Dweck, 1985; Dweck, Tenney, & Dinces, 1982; Leggett, 1985). Thus we will present a model in which individuals' goals set up their pattern of responding, and these goals, in turn, are fostered by individuals' self-conceptions.

The model represents an approach to motivation in that it is built around goals and goal-oriented behavior. At the same time, it represents an approach to personality in that it identifies individual differences in beliefs and values that appear to generate individual differences in behavior. The model may also be said to represent a social-cognitive approach to motivation and personality in that it (a) seeks to illuminate specific, moment-to-moment psychological mediators of behavior and (b) assigns a central role to interpretive processes in the generation of affect and the mediation of behavior.

Having arrived at this more general conceptualization, we asked a number of questions about the range of phenomena that the model could potentially explain. In this article we examine the degree to which the model can be used to organize and illuminate a variety of phenomena beyond those it was developed to explain, to generate new hypotheses about personality-motivational phenomena, and to shed light on more general issues in the study of personality and motivation.

In these next sections, for clarity, we start with the response patterns and work up to the goals and implicit theories that appear to foster them. We also begin with the domain of intellectual achievement, where the patterns were established

and the model has been most extensively researched, and then move to the domain of social interactions, where evidence for the model is growing.

Maladaptive Versus Adaptive Patterns: Cognitive, Affective, and Behavioral Components

Why are the helpless and the mastery-oriented patterns considered to be maladaptive and adaptive, respectively, and why are they important? The helpless response as a characteristic style can be considered maladaptive because challenge and obstacles are inherent in most important pursuits. Indeed, one might ask, what valued long-term goal (e.g., pertaining to one's work, one's relationships, or one's moral strivings) does not at some point pose risks, throw up barriers, present dilemmas? A response pattern that deters individuals from confronting obstacles or that prevents them from functioning effectively in the face of difficulty must ultimately limit their attainments.

The mastery-oriented pattern involves the seeking of challenging tasks and the generation of effective strategies in the face of obstacles. As a characteristic style, this enjoyment of challenge and willingness to sustain engagement with difficult tasks appears to be an adaptive stance toward valued goals. Of course, individuals need to be able to gauge when tasks *should* be avoided or abandoned (see Janoff-Bulman & Brickman, 1981); nonetheless, the ability to maintain a commitment to valued goals through periods of difficulty must maximize attainments in the long run.

As we have noted, the helpless and the mastery-oriented patterns are two distinct, coherent patterns, with striking differences in the cognitions, affect, and behavior that characterize each. Because these patterns lie at the heart of our model, we shall describe them in some detail. In doing so we draw primarily on a series of studies conducted by Diener and Dweck (1978, 1980), in which the patterns were first extensively analyzed and in which the cognitive, affective, and behavioral components of the pattern were first conceptualized as interrelated aspects of a continuous process. A brief outline of their basic method will provide a context for the findings. In these studies, participants (late grade-school age children) who were likely to display the helpless or mastery-oriented patterns were identified by their responses to an attributional measure. They worked on a concept formation task, successfully solving the first eight problems but failing to solve the next four problems (which were somewhat too difficult for children their age to solve in the allotted number of trials). Of interest here were the changes in cognition, affect, and behavior as the subjects went from success to failure.

To capture the timing and the nature of these changes, several procedures were used. First, after the sixth success problem, subjects were requested to verbalize aloud what they were thinking and feeling as they worked on the problems (Diener & Dweck, 1978, Study 2). They were given license to hold forth on any topic they wished—relevant or irrelevant to the task—and they did so at length. Second, the problems were constructed so that children's hypothesis-testing strategies could be continuously monitored, and thus changes in the sophistication of the strategies could be detected (Diener & Dweck, 1978, Studies 1 & 2; 1980). Third, specific measures, such as predictions of future performance, were taken before and after failure (Diener & Dweck, 1980).

All children attained effective problem-solving strategies on the success problems, with training aids being given when necessary. Moreover, there was no difference in the strategy level attained by the helpless and mastery-oriented children on the success problems or in the ease with which they attained that level. (Indeed, whenever any difference emerged, it was the helpless children who appeared slightly more proficient.) In addition, the verbalizations of both groups on the success problems showed them to be equally interested in and engaged with the task. However, with the onset of failure, two distinct patterns rapidly emerged.

First, helpless children quickly began to report negative self-cognitions. Specifically, they began to attribute their failures to personal inadequacy, spontaneously citing deficient intelligence, memory, or problem-solving ability as the reasons for their failure. This was accompanied by a striking absence of any positive prognosis and occurred despite the fact that only moments before, their ability had yielded consistent success.

Second, helpless children began to express pronounced negative affect. Specifically, they reported such things as an aversion to the task, boredom with the problems, or anxiety over their performance—again, despite the fact that shortly before they had been quite pleased with the task and situation.

Third, more than two thirds of the helpless children (but virtually none of the mastery-oriented ones) engaged in task-irrelevant verbalizations, usually of diversionary or self-aggrandizing nature. For example, some attempted to alter the rules of the task, some spoke of talents in other domains, and some boasted of unusual wealth and possessions, presumably in an attempt to direct attention away from their present performance and toward more successful endeavors or praiseworthy attributes. Thus, instead of concentrating their resources on attaining success they attempted to bolster their image in other ways.

And finally, also in line with the negative cognitions and negative affect, the helpless children showed marked decrements in performance across the failure trials. Specifically, more than two thirds of them showed a clear decline in the level of their problem-solving strategy under failure and over 60% lapsed into ineffective strategies—strategies that were characteristic of preschoolers and that would never yield a solution (even if sufficient trials for solution had been permitted on those problems). Thus although all of the helpless children had demonstrated their ability to employ mature and useful strategies on the task, a sizable number were no longer doing so.

In short, helpless children viewed their difficulties as failures, as indicative of low ability, and as insurmountable. They appeared to view further effort as futile and, perhaps, as their defensive maneuvers suggest, as further documentation of their inadequate ability.

In striking contrast, the mastery-oriented children, when confronted with the difficult problems, did not begin to offer attributions for their failure. Indeed, they did not appear to think they were failing. Rather than viewing unsolved problems as failures that reflected on their ability, they appeared to view the unsolved problems as challenges to be mastered through effort. Toward that end, they engaged in extensive solution-oriented self-instruction and self-monitoring. Interestingly, their self-instructions and self-monitoring referred to both the cognitive and motivational aspects of the task at hand. That is, in addition to planning specific hypothesis-testing strategies and monitoring their outcomes, they also instructed themselves to exert effort or to concentrate and then monitored their level of effort or attention.

Also in contrast to the helpless children, the mastery-oriented children appeared to maintain an unflagging optimism that their efforts would be fruitful. For example, the mastery-oriented children said such things as "I did it before, I can do it again" or even "I'm sure I have it now." Nearly two thirds of them spontaneously offered statements of positive prognosis.

In keeping with their optimistic stance, the mastery-oriented children maintained their positive affect toward the task, and some even showed heightened positive affect with the advent of the difficult problems. As noted by Diener and Dweck (1978), one boy, soon after the failure problems began, pulled up his chair, rubbed his hands together, smacked his lips, and exclaimed, "I love a challenge!" Another boy, also upon confronting the failure problems, regarded the experimenter and stated in a pleased tone of voice, "You know, I was *hoping* this would be informative." Thus, the mastery-oriented children not only believed they could surmount obstacles and reach a solution, but some even relished the opportunity to do so.

Finally, the positive cognitions and affect were reflected in the problem-solving performance of the mastery-oriented children. In contrast to the helpless children, who showed marked decrements in their level of problem-solving strategy, 80% of the mastery-oriented children succeeded in maintaining their problem-solving strategies at or above prefailure levels, with over 25% increasing the level of their strategy. That is, these children actually taught themselves new, more sophisticated hypothesis-testing strategies over the four failure trials.

In short, in the face of failure, helpless children exhibited negative self-cognitions, negative affect, and impaired performance, whereas mastery-oriented children exhibited constructive self-instructions and self-monitoring, a positive prognosis, positive affect, and effective problem-solving strategies. Despite the fact that they had received identical tasks and earned identical task outcomes, helpless and mastery-oriented children processed and responded to the situation in entirely different ways.

Although these patterns were first identified in research with children, they have been well documented in adults as well (see, e.g., Brunson & Matthews, 1981). Moreover, although the patterns were first investigated in laboratory settings, they have been shown to operate in natural settings. A study by Licht and Dweck (1984) provides a clear demonstration. In this study, children were taught new material (the principles of operant conditioning) in their classrooms by means of programmed instruction booklets. For all children, an irrelevant passage (on imitation) was inserted near the beginning of their instructional booklet. For half of the children, this passage, although irrelevant to the principles to be learned, was clear and straightforward. For the other half, the passage was rather tortuous and confusing. The question was whether helpless and mastery-oriented children (as defined in this study by their attributional tendencies) would show differential mastery of the material in the no-confusion and confusion conditions; that is, whether difficulty in the irrelevant passage would impair helpless children's subsequent learning.

Mastery of the material was assessed by means

of a seven-question mastery test that asked subjects to employ the principles they had just learned. Any child who failed to answer the seven questions correctly was given a review booklet followed by another mastery test. In all, children were given as many as four opportunities to demonstrate mastery.

The results showed that in the no-confusion condition, the mastery-oriented and helpless children were equally likely to master the material: 68.4% of the mastery-oriented children and 76.6% of the helpless ones reached the mastery criterion, again demonstrating no difference in ability between the groups. However, in the confusion condition a clear difference emerged. As before, most of the mastery-oriented children, 71.9%, reached the learning criterion. In contrast, only 34.6% of the helpless children in the confusion condition ever mastered the material. Thus with "real" material in a real-world setting, the mastery-oriented and helpless patterns were shown to be associated with effective versus ineffective functioning in the face of difficulty.

To conclude, the Diener and Dweck research suggests that whereas helpless individuals appear to focus on their ability and its adequacy (or inadequacy), mastery-oriented ones appear to focus on mastery through strategy and effort; whereas helpless individuals appear to view challenging problems as a threat to their self-esteem, mastery-oriented ones appear to view them as opportunities for learning something new.

GOALS   In view of these entirely different ways of perceiving identical situations, Elliott and Dweck (1988) hypothesized that helpless and mastery-oriented individuals might be pursuing very different goals. That is, their different perceptions and reactions might be a result of their different aims or purposes in the situation. Helpless children, they suggested, might be pursuing *performance* goals, in which they seek to establish the adequacy of their ability and to avoid giving evidence of its inadequacy. In other words, they may view achievement situations as tests or measures of competence and may seek, in these situations,

to be judged competent and not incompetent. Mastery-oriented individuals, in contrast, might be pursuing *learning* goals. They may tend to view achievement situations as opportunities to increase their competence and may pursue, in these situations, the goal of acquiring new skills or extending their mastery. Thus, in challenging achievement situations, helpless children might be pursuing the performance goal of *proving* their ability, whereas the mastery-oriented children might be pursuing the learning goal of *improving* their ability. It might be these different goals, Elliott and Dweck reasoned, that set up the patterns of cognition, affect, and behavior.

To test the hypothesis that goals generate the helpless and mastery-oriented responses, Elliott and Dweck experimentally induced performance or learning goals and examined the pattern of cognition, affect, and behavior that followed from each goal. The question of interest was whether the performance goal, with its emphasis on measuring ability, would create a greater vulnerability to the helpless pattern, whereas the learning goal, with its emphasis on acquiring ability, would create a greater tendency to display the mastery-oriented pattern. More specifically, as shown in Table 53.1, they hypothesized that when individuals held a performance goal and had a low assessment of their present ability level, they would display the helpless pattern in the face of failure. That is, concern with one's ability combined with doubts about its adequacy should create the negative ability attributions, negative affect, and performance deterioration characteristic of helplessness.

In contrast, it was hypothesized that when individuals held a learning goal, they would display the mastery-oriented pattern, even when they assessed their present ability level to be low. That is, when individuals are seeking to increase their ability, the adequacy of their present level of ability should not be a deterrent to their pursuit of their goal and could even be seen as providing an additional reason to pursue the goal.

Briefly then, Elliott and Dweck simultaneously manipulated subjects' (a) goals (by orienting them

TABLE 53.1

THEORIES, GOALS, AND BEHAVIOR PATTERNS IN ACHIEVEMENT SITUATIONS

Theory of intelligence	Goal orientation	Perceived present ability	Behavior pattern
Entity (Intelligence is fixed)	Performance (Goal is to gain positive judgments/avoid negative judgments of competence)	High	Mastery oriented (Seek challenge; high persistence)
		Low	Helpless (Avoid challenge; low persistence)
Incremental (Intelligence is malleable)	Learning (Goal is to increase competence)	High or low	Mastery-oriented (Seek challenge that fosters learning; high persistence)

more toward evaluations of ability or more toward the value of the skill to be learned) and (b) assessments of their present ability level (via feedback on a pretest). To test the effect of the goal-orienting manipulation on subjects' actual goal choices, children were then asked to choose one task from an array of tasks that embodied either a learning or a performance goal. The learning goal task was described as enabling skill acquisition, but as entailing a high risk of a negative ability judgment. In contrast, the performance goal options allowed children to obtain a favorable ability judgment (by succeeding on a difficult task) or to avoid an unfavorable judgment (by succeeding on an easier task), but did not afford any opportunity for learning. Following this choice, all children were given the Diener and Dweck concept-formation task. (Children had in fact been asked to make several task selections so that the Diener and Dweck task—described as moderately difficult—could be presented to them as consonant with their choice. Thus it would not appear that the wishes of some children were granted and others denied.) As in the Diener and Dweck research, children were requested to verbalize as they worked on the problems, and verbalizations and strategies were monitored and categorized.

The results showed the predicted relations. When children were oriented toward skill acquisition, their assessment of their present ability was largely irrelevant: They chose the challenging learning task and displayed a mastery-oriented pattern. In contrast, when children were oriented toward evaluation, the task they adopted and the achievement pattern they displayed (mastery-oriented or helpless) were highly dependent on their perceived ability. Children who perceived their ability to be high selected the challenging performance tasks that would allow them to obtain judgments of competence, whereas children who perceived their ability to be low selected easier tasks that would permit them to avoid judgments of incompetence. Note that the great majority of children in the evaluation-oriented condition sacrificed altogether the opportunity for new learning that involved a display of errors or confusion.

What was most striking was the degree to which the manipulations created the entire constellation of performance, cognition, and affect characteristic of the naturally occurring achievement patterns. For example, children who were given a performance orientation and low ability pretest feedback showed the same attributions, negative affect, and strategy deterioration that characterized the helpless children in our earlier studies (Diener & Dweck, 1978, 1980).

*　*　*

Although we have been emphasizing the vulnerability created by an orientation toward performance goals over learning goals, it is essential to note that there are also adaptive performance concerns. It is often important for individuals to evaluate their abilities or to gain positive judgments of their competence. Indeed, sometimes this may be a prerequisite to the successful pursuit of learning goals: Obtaining an objective diagnosis of strengths and weaknesses may be a necessary step in the learning process, and earning the positive judgment of those who control important resources may be a necessary step in one's pursuit of skills and knowledge. Thus adaptive individuals effectively coordinate performance and learning goals. It is when an overconcern with proving their adequacy (to themselves or others) leads individuals to ignore, avoid, or abandon potentially valuable learning opportunities that problems arise.

It is also important to reiterate that when confidence in ability is high, performance goals can produce mastery-oriented behavior, and they have undoubtedly fueled many great achievements. However, it is equally important to reiterate that high confidence is necessary within a performance goal to support a mastery orientation but, as we will show, high confidence may be difficult to sustain within a performance goal. Learning goals, as the research indicates, tend to make individuals less vulnerable to the effects of fluctuations in confidence.

HOW GOALS CREATE PATTERNS What are the mechanisms through which the different goals produce their associated patterns of cognition, affect, and behavior? Why and how do they lead to such different patterns? Evidence increasingly suggests that the goal an individual is pursuing creates a framework for interpreting and responding to events that occur. Thus the same event may have an entirely different meaning and impact if it oc-

curs within the context of a learning versus a performance goal. In this section, we propose what the different frameworks established by the two goals might be and build a case for how the observed cognitive, affective, and behavioral patterns follow from these frameworks.

Cognitions. How might the different goal frameworks set up the different cognitions in the face of failure? Individuals adopting different goals can be seen as approaching a situation with different concerns, asking different questions, and seeking different information (see, e.g., Dweck & Elliott, 1983). For each individual, the data in the situation are interpreted in light of their focal concern and provide information relevant to their question.

Within a performance goal, individuals are concerned with measuring their ability and with answering the question, Is my ability adequate or inadequate? Within such a framework, outcomes will be a chief source of information relevant to this concern and thus failure outcomes may readily elicit the helpless attribution that ability is inadequate.

In contrast, learning goals create a concern with increasing one's ability and extending one's mastery and would lead individuals to pose the question, What is the best way to increase my ability or achieve mastery? Here, then, outcomes would provide information about whether one is pursuing an optimal course and, if not, what else might be necessary. Failure would simply mean that the current strategy may be insufficient to the task and may require upgrading or revision. The self-instructions and self-monitoring of the mastery-oriented children can therefore be seen as a direct implementation of this information in pursuit of future goal success. Thus the attributions of the helpless children and the self-instructions of the mastery-oriented children in response to failure may be viewed as natural outgrowths of their goals.

Recent research (Leggett & Dweck, 1986) has shown that another potentially informative event

—one's input or effort expenditure—will also be interpreted in line with the differing goal concerns: as an indicant of ability versus a means of achieving learning or mastery. Leggett and Dweck measured eighth graders' goal preferences and devised a questionnaire to assess their interpretation of effort information. The results clearly indicated that those with performance goals used effort as an index of high or low ability. Specifically, they viewed effort and ability as inversely related: High effort (resulting in either success or failure) implies low ability, and low effort (resulting in success) implies high ability. These children endorsed items such as "If you have to work hard at some problems, you're probably not very good at them" or "You only know you're good at something when it comes easily to you." In essence then, children with performance goals use an inference rule that says effort per se—even when it accompanies success—signifies a lack of ability.

In contrast, those with learning goals were more likely to view effort as a means or strategy for activating or manifesting their ability for mastery. Here effort and ability are seen as *positively related*: Greater effort activates and makes manifest more ability. These children endorsed items such as "[Even] when you're very good at something, working hard allows you to really understand it" or "When something comes easily to you, you don't know how good you are at it." Thus, within a learning goal, high effort would represent a mastery strategy and would signify that one was harnessing one's resources for mastery.

In short, children with different goals appear to use very different inference rules to process effort information (cf. Jagacinski & Nicholls, 1983; Surber, 1984). This research suggests how use of the *inverse* rule by individuals with performance goals can contribute to their helpless pattern of attributing high-effort failures to low ability (and of doubting their ability after high effort *success*; see Diener & Dweck, 1980). It also shows, in contrast, how use of the *positive* rule by those with learning goals can contribute to their mastery-oriented tendency to focus on effort when challenged.

In summary, performance goals create a context in which outcomes (such as failures) and input (such as high effort) are interpreted in terms of their implications for ability and its adequacy. In contrast, learning goals create a context in which the same outcomes and input provide information about the effectiveness of one's learning and mastery strategies.

Affect. How would the different goal frameworks result in different affective reactions to challenge or setbacks? Within a performance goal, experiencing failure or effort exertion warns of a low-ability judgment and thus poses a threat to self-esteem. Such a threat might first engender anxiety (Sarason, 1975; Wine, 1971), and then, if the negative judgment appears increasingly likely, depressed affect (Seligman, Abramson, Semmel, & von Baeyer, 1979) and a sense of shame (Sohn, 1977; Weiner & Graham, 1984) may set in. Alternatively, individuals could adopt a more defensive, self-protective posture, devaluing the task and expressing boredom or disdain toward it (Tesser & Campbell, 1983; cf. Berglas & Jones, 1978). All of these emotions—anxiety, depressed affect, boredom, defiance—were apparent among the helpless subjects in the Diener and Dweck (1978, 1980) studies as failures accrued.

Within a learning goal, however, the occurrence of failure simply signals that the task will require more effort and ingenuity for mastery. This creates, for some, the opportunity for a more satisfying mastery experience, producing the heightened positive affect noted earlier. In addition, the continued belief that success can occur through effort will engender determination—and indeed in many of our studies, mastery-oriented children (whether instructed to verbalize or not) have issued battle cries or vows of victory.

Finally for individuals with learning goals, exerting effort in the service of learning or mastery may bring intrinsic rewards, pleasure, or pride (Deci & Ryan, 1980; Lepper, 1981). Whereas within performance goals high effort may engender anxiety, and high-effort progress or mastery is a mixed blessing, within a learning goal high-effort mastery may often be precisely what is sought. Indeed, in the study by Bandura and Dweck (1985), children with learning goals reported that they would feel bored or disappointed with a low-effort success. (Children with performance goals reported that they would feel proud or relieved about a low-effort success.) Similarly, Ames, Ames, and Felker (1977) found that within an individualistic (learning goal) structure, children's pride in their performance was related to the degree of effort they perceived themselves to have exerted. This was true in both the success and the failure conditions, indicating that within a learning goal, effort per se can be a source of pride.

In summary, because of their different meanings in the context of the two goals, events that produce negative or depressed affect within one goal may produce positive affect and heightened engagement within the other.

Behavior. How would the goal-related differences in cognition and affect create different behavior? First, they would influence task choices. The ideal task within each goal would be a task that maximized goal success and positive affect or minimized goal failure and negative affect, or both (see Dweck & Elliott, 1983).

Within a performance goal the ideal task would be one that maximized positive judgments and pride in ability, while minimizing negative judgments, anxiety, and shame. For performance-oriented individuals with low confidence in their ability, challenging tasks (those requiring high effort and having uncertain outcome) would promise aversive experiences: high anxiety, expected negative judgments, and loss of esteem. These individuals would thus orient themselves toward easy tasks, ones that minimized negative outcomes and affect, even though such tasks would preclude the possibility of positive judgments.

Performance-oriented individuals with high confidence, although more challenge seeking, would nonetheless avoid challenge when the threat of performance failure existed. And indeed, these individuals are found to sacrifice learning opportunities that pose the risk of errors and difficulty

(Bandura & Dweck, 1985; Elliott & Dweck, 1988).

The ideal task within a learning goal, however, would be one that maximized the growth of ability and the pride and pleasure of mastery, quite apart from how one's abilities are showing up at any given moment. Indeed, Bandura and Dweck (1985) found that their learning-oriented children with low confidence were the most likely of any group to seek a challenging learning opportunity even though it carried the risk of negative ability judgments. Moreover, within a learning goal, there is no need to withdraw from a task that proves to be unexpectedly difficult, because a failure episode or the exertion of high effort does not engender cognitive or affective distress. Instead one would expect withdrawal from a task that became useless or boring, even if it continued to promise favorable ability judgments (see Bandura & Dweck, 1985).

* * *

Implicit Theories of Intelligence

What leads individuals to favor performance goals over learning goals or vice versa? Why do some individuals focus on the adequacy of their ability whereas others focus on the development of their ability? Our recent work shows that a consistent predictor of children's goal orientation is their "theory of intelligence," that is, their implicit conception about the nature of ability (cf. Goodnow, 1980; Nicholls, 1984; Sternberg, Conway, Ketron, & Bernstein, 1981; Wellman, 1985; Yussen & Kane, 1985). Some children favor what we have termed an *incremental* theory of intelligence: They believe that intelligence is a malleable, increasable, controllable quality. Others lean more toward an *entity* theory of intelligence: They believe that intelligence is a fixed or uncontrollable trait. Our research consistently indicates that children who believe intelligence is increasable pursue the learning goal of increasing their competence, whereas those who believe intelligence is a fixed entity are more likely to pursue the performance goal of securing positive judgments of that entity or preventing negative judgments of it (see Table 53.1).

TABLE 53.2

PERCENTAGE OF SUBJECTS WITH EACH THEORY OF INTELLIGENCE
SELECTING EACH ACHIEVEMENT GOAL

| | Goal choice | | |
Theory of intelligence	Performance goal (avoid challenge)	Performance goal (seek challenge)	Learning goal (seek challenge)
Entity theory ($n = 22$)	50.0	31.8	18.2
Incremental theory ($n = 41$)	9.8	29.3	60.9

For example, in a study with late grade-school-age children, Bandura and Dweck (1985) found that children who endorsed the incremental theory (e.g., "Smartness is something you can increase as much as you want to") were significantly more likely to adopt learning goals on an experimental task than were children who endorsed the entity theory (e.g., "You can learn new things, but how smart you are stays pretty much the same"). Similar findings were obtained in a classroom setting (see Dweck & Bempechat, 1983): Incremental theorists were significantly more likely than entity theorists to report a preference for classroom tasks that embodied learning goals ("Hard, new, and different so I could try to learn from them") versus performance goals ("Fun and easy to do, so I wouldn't have to worry about mistakes"; "Like things I'm good at so I can feel smart").

In a recent study, Leggett (1985) revised the theories of intelligence assessment and examined the relation between theories of intelligence and goal choice in a junior high school sample. As shown in Table 53.2, children's theories of intelligence were again reliable predictors of their goal choice. The challenge-seeking performance goal ("I'd like problems that are hard enough to show that I'm smart") and the challenge-avoidant performance goal ("I'd like problems that aren't too hard, so I don't get many wrong" or "I'd like problems that are fairly easy, so I'll do well") are presented separately in Table 53.2 to emphasize the degree to which the incremental and entity theories are differentially associated with challenge seeking versus challenge avoidance.

To illuminate the casual relationship between implicit theories and goal choice, Dweck, Tenney, and Dinces (1982) experimentally manipulated children's theories of intelligence and then assessed their goal choice on an upcoming task. In their study, children were oriented toward either an entity or incremental theory by means of reading passages that portrayed the intelligence of notable individuals (Albert Einstein, Helen Keller, and the child Rubik's Cube champion) as either a fixed, inborn trait or an acquirable quality. The structure, content, tone, and interest value of the two passages were highly similar, except that they presented and illustrated different definitions of smartness. Great care was taken to avoid attaching any goals to these theories, that is, to avoid any mention or implication of learning versus performance goals.

The passage on intelligence was embedded in a series of three short, interesting reading passages, all concerning "things that psychologists study" (imprinting, intelligence, dreams). As a rationale for reading these passages, children were asked to indicate after each one whether they would like to know more about this topic. As a rationale for their subsequent goal choice, children were told that psychologists also study how people think, form concepts, and solve intellectual problems. They were then asked to select from a list of different types of problems (each embodying a different goal choice) the type of problem they would like to work on when the experimenters returned. The results showed that the experimental manipulation of theory affected children's goal choices in the predicted direction: Subjects who had read the incremental passage were significantly more likely to adopt learning goals for the upcoming task than were those who had read the entity passage. This study, then, by (temporarily) orienting children toward a particular theory of intelligence, provided support for a causal relationship between implicit theories and goal choice.

Taken together, the research indicates that an incremental theory of intelligence is more consistently associated with adaptive motivational patterns. In this context, it is interesting to note (along with Covington, 1983, and Gould, 1981) that Alfred Binet, the inventor of the IQ test, was clearly an incremental theorist. He believed that not only specific skills, but also basic capacity for learning, were enhanced through his training procedures:

> It is in this practical sense, the only one accessible to us, that we say that the intelligence of these children has been increased. We have increased what constitutes the intelligence of a pupil: the capacity to learn and to assimilate instruction. (Binet 1909/1973, p. 104)

It is therefore a particular irony that the assessment tool he developed within an incremental theory and learning goal framework has been widely interpreted within an entity theory and performance goal framework as a measure of a stable quality. As Dweck and Elliott (1983) pointed out, perhaps the most appropriate view represents an integration of both entity and incremental theories, that is, a recognition of present differences in relative ability but an emphasis on individual growth in ability (see also Nicholls, 1984).

In summary, implicit beliefs about ability predict whether individuals will be oriented toward developing their ability or toward documenting the adequacy of their ability. As such, these theories may be at the root of adaptive and maladaptive patterns. Indeed it may be the adherence to an underlying entity theory that makes performance goals potentially maladaptive, for within an entity theory individuals are not simply judging a momentary level of ability. Rather, they may be judging what they perceive to be an important and permanent personal attribute. Thus, an entity theory may place one's intelligence on the line in evaluative situations, magnifying the meaning and impact of negative judgments.

Summary and Conclusion

We began by documenting patterns of cognition-affect-behavior that have profound effects on adaptive functioning. We then asked questions about the underlying motivational and personality variables that give rise to these response patterns, first demonstrating the role of learning and performance goals in producing the patterns and then linking these goals to individuals' implicit theories of their attributes.

*   *   *

In closing, we would like to highlight what we believe to be the central aspect of our model: its depiction of the manner in which underlying personality variables can translate into dynamic motivational processes to produce major patterns of cognition, affect, and behavior. Although much model-testing and model-building research remains to be done, the existing work lends encouraging support to the present model. It suggests that this model may be useful for both tying together existing lines of research and generating new lines of research in the future.

References

Ames, C., Ames, R., & Felker, D. W. (1977). Effects of competitive reward structure and valence of outcome on children's achievement attributions. *Journal of Educational Psychology, 69,* 1–8.

Bandura, M., & Dweck, C. S. (1985). *The relationship of conceptions of intelligence and achievement goals to achievement-related cognition, affect and behavior.* Manuscript submitted for publication.

Berglas, S., & Jones, E. (1978). Drug choice as a self-handicapping strategy in response to non-contingent success. *Journal of Personality and Social Psychology*, 36, 405–417.

Binet, A. (1973). *Les idees modernes sur les enfants* [Modern ideas on children]. Paris: Flamarion. (Original work published 1909).

Brunson, B., & Matthews, K. (1981). The Type-A coronary-prone behavior pattern and reactions to uncontrollable stress: An analysis of performance strategies, affect, and attributions during failure. *Journal of Personality and Social Psychology*, 40, 906–918.

Covington, M. V. (1983). Strategic thinking and the fear of failure. In J. Sigal, S. Chipman, & R. Glaser (Eds.), *Thinking and learning skills: Relating instruction to research* (Vol. 2, pp. 389–416). Hillsdale, NJ: Erlbaum.

Deci, E. L., & Ryan, R. M. (1980). The empirical exploration of intrinsic motivational processes. In L. Berkowitz, (Ed.), *Advances in experimental social psychology* (Vol. 13, pp. 39–80). New York: Academic Press.

Diener, C. I., & Dweck, C. S. (1978). An analysis of learned helplessness: Continuous changes in performance, strategy and achievement cognitions following failure. *Journal of Personality and Social Psychology*, 36, 451–462.

Diener, C. I., & Dweck, C. S. (1980). An analysis of learned helplessness: II. The processing of success. *Journal of Personality and Social Psychology*, 39, 940–952.

Dweck, C. S. (1975). The role of expectations and attributions in the alleviation of learned helplessness. *Journal of Personality and Social Psychology*, 31, 674–685.

Dweck, C. S., & Bempechat, J. (1983). Children's theories of intelligence. In S. Paris, G. Olsen, & H. Stevenson (Eds.), *Learning and motivation in the classroom* (pp. 239–256). Hillsdale, NJ: Erlbaum.

Dweck, C. S., & Elliott, E. S. (1983). Achievement motivation. In P. H. Mussen (Gen. Ed.) & E. M. Hetherington (Vol. Ed.), *Handbook of child psychology: Vol. IV. Social and personality development* (pp. 643–691). New York: Wiley.

Dweck, C. S., & Reppucci, N. D. (1973). Learned helplessness and reinforcement responsibility in children. *Journal of Personality and Social Psychology*, 25, 109–116.

Dweck, C. S., Tenney, Y., & Dinces, N. (1982). [Implicit theories of intelligence as determinants of achievement goal choice]. Unpublished raw data.

Elliott, E. S., & Dweck, C. S. (1988). Goals: An approach to motivation and achievement. *Journal of Personality and Social Psychology*, 54, 5–12.

Farrell, E., & Dweck, C. S. (1985). *The role of motivational processes in transfer of learning.* Manuscript submitted for publication.

Goodnow, J. J. (1980). Everyday concepts of intelligence and its development. In N. Warren (Ed.), *Studies in cross-cultural psychology* (Vol. 2, pp. 191–219). Oxford, England: Pergamon Press.

Gould, S. J. (1981). *The mismeasure of man.* New York: W. W. Norton.

Jagacinski, C., & Nicholls, J. (1983, March). *Concepts of ability.*

Paper presented at the annual meeting of the American Educational Research Association, New York, NY.

Janoff-Bulman, R., & Brickman, P. (1981). Expectations and what people learn from failure. In N. T. Feather (Ed.), *Expectancy, incentive, and action* (pp. 207–237). Hillsdale, NJ: Erlbaum.

Leggett, E. L. (1985, March). *Children's entity and incremental theories of intelligence: Relationships to achievement behavior.* Paper presented at the annual meeting of the Eastern Psychological Association, Boston.

Leggett, E. L., & Dweck, C. S. (1986). *Goals and inference rules: Sources of casual judgments.* Manuscript submitted for publication.

Lepper, M. (1981). Intrinsic and extrinsic motivation in children: Detrimental effects of superfluous social controls. In W. W. Collins (Ed.), *Minnesota Symposium on Child Psychology* (Vol. 14, pp. 155–214). Hillsdale, NJ: Erlbaum.

Licht, B. G., & Dweck, C. S. (1984). Determinants of academic achievement: The interaction of children's achievement orientations with skill area. *Developmental Psychology*, 20, 628–636.

Nicholls, J. G. (1984). Achievement motivation: Conceptions of ability, subjective experience, task choice, and performance. *Psychological Review*, 91, 328–346.

Sarason, I. G. (1975). Anxiety and self-preoccupation. In I. G. Sarason & C. D. Spielberger (Eds.), *Stress and anxiety* (Vol. 2, pp. 27–44). Washington, DC: Hemisphere.

Seligman, M. E. P., Abramson, L. Y., Semmel, A., & von Baeyer, C. (1979). Depressive attributional style. *Journal of Abnormal Psychology*, 88, 242–247.

Sohn, D. (1977). Affect generating powers of effort and ability self-attributions of academic success and failure. *Journal of Educational Psychology*, 69, 500–505.

Sternberg, R., Conway, B. E., Ketron, J. L., & Bernstein, M. (1981). People's conceptions of intelligence. *Journal of Personality and Social Psychology*, 41, 37–55.

Surber, C. (1984). Inferences of ability and effort: Evidence for two different processes. *Journal of Personality and Social Psychology*, 46, 249–268.

Tesser, A., & Campbell, J. (1983). Self-definition and self-evaluation maintenance. In J. Suls & A. Greenwald (Eds.), *Social psychological perspectives on the self* (Vol. 2, pp. 123–149). Hillsdale, NJ: Erlbaum.

Weiner, B., & Graham, S. (1984). An attributional approach to emotional development. In C. Izard, J. Kagan, & R. Zajonc (Eds.), *Emotions, cognition, and behavior* (pp. 167–191). New York: Cambridge University Press.

Wellman, H. M. (1985). The child's theory of mind: The development of conceptions of cognition. In S. R. Yussen (Ed.), *The growth of reflection in children* (pp. 169–206). New York: Academic Press.

Wine, J. (1971). Test anxiety and direction of attention. *Psychological Bulletin*, 76, 92–104.

Yussen, S. R., & Kane, D. T. (1985). Children's conceptions of intelligence. In S. R. Yussen (Ed.), *The growth of reflection in children* (pp. 207–241). New York: Academic Press.

Afterword

The 50- to 80-year history of personality psychology is one of theorists sharpening distinctions and highlighting differences between their approaches. The attempt to show that one's own theory is (a) different and (b) better than anybody else's seems almost obligatory, and examples of such attempts are seen throughout the preceding selections in this reader.

Although it may be necessary to show how theories differ from one another, and irresistible to make invidious comparisons, too tight a focus on differences can produce a misleading view. Many of the theoretical approaches within personality psychology are not really in competition with each other, because they are theories about different things. The trait approach's interest in individual differences is not better, worse, or even in competition with the psychoanalytic interpretation of dreams; it is about something else entirely. By the same token, the different approaches are not really commensurate either, because they are couched in different languages, make different assumptions and, as we have just observed, are about different phenomena.

Your editors believe it is time for an integrative phase in the development of personality psychology. The very first piece in this reader (by McAdams) had the explicit goal of integrating different approaches to and levels of personality description. Some approaches may be more similar and less contradictory to each other than they are sometimes portrayed. For example, writers in the social-cognitive tradition, as we have seen, often set themselves in explicit opposition to the trait approach. They typically argue that trait concepts are too broad, and that their own, more narrow units of analysis are preferable. Yet they not infrequently use self-report questionnaires in their assessments, and more fundamentally their research often addresses individual differences in personality and psychological processes that translate motivation and cognition into behavior. These are concerns that are shared by some researchers within the trait approach.

The final selection in this reader, by one of your editors, is an exposition of a particular approach—a version of modern trait theory—that has as its goal a broader and more encompassing view than is traditional. Its "neo-Allportian" approach to personality stems in part from Allport's comment that traits have the capacity to render different situations functionally equivalent. For some the world seems a bright and cheery place, full of opportunities; for others the world offers only danger and obligation. This observation—that people with different traits have different views of the world—opens a door to the potential, eventual integration of phenomenological, cognitive, and trait conceptions of personality.

Of course, such a rapprochement is a long way off. And even it would be incomplete—psychoanalytic issues remain neglected, for example. But both this article and the one earlier by McAdams exemplify what may be the beginning of an effort to reunite some of the historically opposing camps within personality psychology.

GLOBAL TRAITS: A NEO-ALLPORTIAN APPROACH TO PERSONALITY

David C. Funder

But let us not join the camp of skeptics who say an individual's personality is "a mere construct tied together with a name"—that there is nothing outer and objectively structured to be assessed. No scientist, I think, could survive for long if he heeded this siren song of doubt, for it leads to shipwreck. (Allport, 1958, p. 246)

One of the most widely used concepts of intuitive psychology is the global personality trait. Almost everyone is accustomed to thinking about and describing the people one knows using terms like "conscientious," "sociable," and "aggressive." Traits like these are *global* because each refers not just to one or a few specific behaviors, but to *patterns* of behavior presumed to transcend time and specific situations. Historically, the global trait used to be an important part of formal psychological theory as well. Gordon Allport (1931, 1937) wrote extensively about traits more than a half century ago, and for a time many research programs either developed general trait theories (Cattell, 1946), or investigated in detail specific traits (Witkin et al., 1954).

In recent years, however, theorizing about dispositional constructs such as global traits has been at a relative standstill. As Buss and Craik (1983) pointed out, "the field of personality appears to have set its theoretical gears into neutral" (p. 105). One cause of this inactivity may have been the field's two decades of immersion in a distracting debate over whether significant individual differ-

ences in social behavior exist at all (Mischel, 1968). Although, in the end, the existence of important individual regularities was reaffirmed (Kenrick & Funder, 1988), a lingering effect of the controversy seems to be an image of traits—most especially global ones—as old-fashioned, rather quaint ideas not relevant for modern research in personality. Indeed, when global traits do appear in the literature nowadays, it is usually to play the role of straw man. The recent literature has seen a plethora of "reconceptualizations" of personality each of which begins, typically, by announcing its intention to replace global traits.

Modern reconceptualizations differ from global traits in at least three ways. First and most obviously, many constructs of the new personality psychology go out of their way *not* to be global. The range of life contexts to which they are relevant is specified narrowly and specifically, and this narrowness is touted as an important virtue. For instance, the recently promulgated "social intelligence" view of personality "guides one away from generalized assessments . . . towards more particular conclusions about the individual's profile of expertise in the life-task domains of central concern at that point in time" (Cantor & Kihlstrom, 1987, p. 241).

Second, and just as importantly, many modern personality variables are relatively *esoteric*—they are deliberately nonintuitive or even counterintuitive. For instance, in the place of trait terms found in ordinary language, one prominent investigator has offered person variables such as "self-regulatory systems," "encoding strategies," and the like (Mischel, 1973).

Third, some modern reconceptualizations go so far as to eschew an explanatory role for personality variables altogether. For instance, the act frequency approach treats personality dispositions as little more than frequency counts of "topographically" (i.e., superficially) similar acts (Buss & Craik, 1983).

The intent of these reconceptualizations is laudable. Each is designed to correct one or more of the problems of overgenerality, vagueness, and even philosophical confusion to which trait psychology has sometimes been prone. The present article, however, is motivated by a belief that the movement away from global traits, however fashionable it may be, entails several dangers that are not usually acknowledged.

Briefly, the dangers are these. First, when we use dispositional terms that are framed *narrowly*, we discard any possibility of generating statements about individual differences that have real explanatory power. Second, when we use dispositional terms that are *esoteric*, we fail to make contact with traits as used in everyday social discourse, lose any basis for understanding and evaluating lay trait judgments, and discard the vast lore of common sense and wisdom that they embody. And third, when we are content to define traits as *frequencies* of superficially similar behaviors, we run the risk of being fundamentally deceived when, as often happens, the causes of behavior turn out to be complex. Each of these points will be expanded later in this article.

What follows is a brief outline of a modern, *neo-Allportian* theory of global traits, presented in the form of 17 assertions. The term "neo-Allportian" is meant to emphasize that this approach to personality is fundamentally based on the seminal writings of Gordon Allport (especially Allport, 1937), but also to acknowledge that his basic theory was published more than a half-century ago and so is ripe for updating and reinvigoration (Zuroff, 1986). As it turns out, Allport's basic

ideas look remarkably sound even with 53 years of hindsight, and yield a large number of implications for conceptualization and research in modern personality psychology.

Definitional Assertions

TRAITS ARE REAL This assertion is the most fundamental of Allport's assumptions, one he believed was essential for subsequent research to be meaningful. He held this position in the face of objections that it was philosophically naive and arguments (still heard today) that traits should be regarded not as entities that have objective reality, but merely as hypothetical constructs (Carr & Kingsbury, 1938). Allport believed that this idea made about as much sense as astronomers regarding stars as hypothetical constructs rather than astronomical objects. He failed to see how any science, including personality psychology, could proceed without assuming its subject of study to be real.

More specifically, Allport (1931, 1966) said traits are "neurodynamic structures" (1966, p. 3) that have "more than nominal existence" (1966, p. 1). If it is obvious that all behavior originates in the neurons of the brain, and that does seem obvious, then it follows that stable individual differences in behavior—to the extent they exist—must similarly be based on stable individual differences in neural organization.

Unfortunately, a method to assess the neural basis of personality is not yet in sight. The presence of a trait can only be *inferred* on the basis of overt behavior. For all practical purposes, therefore, a global trait must refer to two things at the same time: (a) a complex pattern of behavior from which the trait is inferred, and (b) the psychological structures and processes that are the source of the pattern. When we call someone "friendly" or "aggressive" or "generous," we are saying something both about how the person behaves (or would behave) in certain kinds of situations *and* about the functioning of his or her mind. The next assertion follows as a consequence.

TRAITS ARE MORE THAN JUST SUMMARIES A viewpoint prominently expressed in recent years is that "dispositions" (a.k.a. traits) should be considered as no more than summaries of behavioral frequencies, or "act trends" (Buss & Craik, 1983). An individual's generosity then becomes the frequency, over a specified unit of time, of his or her superficially generous acts.

This definition deliberately abdicates any explanatory role. Dispositions are treated as circular constructs in which a generous act implies generosity, and the attribution of generosity is used to predict future generous acts solely "on actuarial grounds" (Buss & Craik, 1983, p. 106).

However, the appearance of behavior can be misleading (Block, 1988). As Allport pointed out:

> A bearer of gifts may not be, in spite of all appearances, a truly generous person: he may be trying to buy favor. . . . Pseudo-traits, then, are errors of inference, misjudgments that come from fixing attention solely upon appearances. The best way to avoid such errors is to find the genotype that underlies the conduct in question. What is the individual trying to do when he brings his gifts? (Allport, 1937, p. 326)

THE MEANING OF A BEHAVIOR DEPENDS ON TWO KINDS OF CONTEXT A single behavior, considered out of context, is frequently ambiguous. Depending on the intention with which the act was performed, there may be multiple possible and plausible alternatives for the traits that might be relevant. This is not to deny that there are interpretational defaults. The act of gift-giving might be interpreted as generous, all other things being equal. All other things are seldom equal, however, so the gift-giving might also reflect insecurity, Machiavellianism, or even anger, depending on the situational circumstances, the gift-giver's behavior in other situations, and what together they imply about the gift-giver's inner state and motives.

Two kinds of context help disambiguate an act. The first is the immediate situation. The giving of a gift becomes more interpretable if one knows whether it was given to a subordinate who performed a job well, or to a superior considering the promotion of the gift-giver. The usefulness of this kind of situational information has been discussed in detail by attribution theorists within social psychology (Heider, 1958; Kelley, 1967), but has been taken into account less often by personality psychologists.

The other kind of context is just as important, but is mentioned even more rarely. Acts become less ambiguous to the extent they fit into a pattern of the individual's other acts. A consistent pattern of generous behavior provides a more plausible context in which to infer that generosity is the trait underlying the gift-giving than does a consistent pattern of mean, nasty, and sneaky behavior. (Indeed, an act that seems inconsistent with the actor's past patterns of behavior is commonly called suspicious.) A pattern of sneaky behavior might lead to an attribution of Machiavellianism that would explain, in turn, why the person gave a lavish gift to his worst enemy.

Developmental Assertions

TRAITS ARE LEARNED Global traits are manifest by patterns of perception and action in the social world; therefore, they must be a product of how one has learned to interact with that world. The process of learning that produces a trait almost certainly involves an interaction between one's experience (in one's particular social environment) and one's genetic endowment (Scarr & McCartney, 1983). Thus, two people with identical environments, or two people with identical genes, could and often do have very different traits.

Because traits are learned, they are not necessarily immutable. Anything learned can in principle be unlearned. Global trait theory is not necessarily pessimistic about possibilities for either personal or social change.

However, traits are relatively stable. Presumably, the difficulty in unlearning a trait (the amount of retraining or new experience required) will be proportional to the amount and salience of the experience through which it was learned in the first place. Genetic predispositions, and perhaps even species-specific characteristics, may also make some traits easier to learn and harder to unlearn than others (Buss, 1984). But the present analysis asserts that because all traits are, in the final analysis, learned, all traits can, in theory if not always in practice, be unlearned.

THE PROCESS OF LEARNING A TRAIT IS COMPLEX Such learning is far more than a simple matter of reward and punishment or S and R. That simple kind of learning can produce, at most, the narrow patterns of behavior that Allport (1931) called "habits." Traits are the result of complex patterns of experience and of higher-order inductions the person makes from that experience. Kelly (1955) believed that *any* pattern of experience could lead a person to any of at least a large number of behavioral outcomes (just as any pattern of data can always lead a scientist to more than one interpretation). Kelly believed that the ability to choose between these alternative outcomes provided a basis for free will. The comedian Bill Cosby has described his childhood neighborhood as a place where adolescents were all on the verge of deciding whether to be killers or priests. The point is that similar patterns of past experience do not necessarily produce similar outcomes.

When *fully* analyzed, every person's pattern of behavior will be every bit as complex as the unique pattern of endowment and experience that produced it. Again, in Allport's (1937, p. 295) words: "Strictly speaking, no two persons ever have precisely the same trait. . . . What else could be expected in the view of the unique hereditary endowment, the different developmental history, and the never-repeated external influences that determine each personality?"

But there are commonalities among people that are useful for characterizing individual differences. A trait like sociability is relevant to behavior in a set of situations regarded as functionally equivalent by people in general: specifically, situations with other people in them. Hence, it is *generally* meaningful to rank-order people on their overall sociability. Allport acknowledged this point as well: "The case for the ultimate individuality of

every trait is indeed invincible, but . . . for all their ultimate differences, normal persons within a given culture-area tend to develop a limited number of roughly comparable modes of adjustment" (1937, pp. 297–298).

Still, the list of social situations that are functionally equivalent for people in general is unlikely to fully capture the situations that are regarded as functionally equivalent by any *single* individual. To capture general trends or gists, and to detect things that are true of people in general, one always loses the details of each individual case. This trade-off between nomothetic and idiographic analyses can be and often has been lamented, but it is inevitable.

Functional Assertions

A BEHAVIOR MAY BE AFFECTED BY SEVERAL TRAITS AT ONCE

The chief danger in the concept of trait is that, through habitual and careless use, it may come to stand for an assembly of separate and self-active faculties, thought to govern behavior all by themselves, without interference. We must cast out this lazy interpretation of the concept. . . . The basic principle of behavior is its continuous flow, each successive act representing a convergent mobilization of all energy available at the moment. (Allport, 1937, pp. 312–313)

The fact that every behavior is the product of multiple traits implies that disentangling the relationship between a given trait and a given behavior is extremely difficult. It also implies that the ability of any particular trait to predict behavior by itself is limited. Ahadi and Diener (1989) showed that if a behavior is totally caused by only four traits whose influence combines additively, the maximum correlation between any one trait and behavior that could be expected is .45. If different traits combine multiplicatively, which seems plausible, the ceiling is even lower.

A third implication is that modern research on traits should conduct a renewed examination of the way traits combine in the determination of behavior. Investigators should more often look beyond the traditional research question of how single traits affect single behaviors, to how multiple traits interact within persons (Carlson, 1971).

TRAITS ARE SITUATIONAL EQUIVALENCE CLASSES
In a trenchant phrase, Allport wrote that traits have the capacity "to render many stimuli functionally equivalent" (1937, p. 295). The tendency to view different situations as similar causes a person to respond to them in a like manner, and the patterns of behavior that result are the overt manifestations of traits.

The template-matching technique (Bem & Funder, 1978) provides one empirical approach to the study of situational equivalence classes. The technique looks for empirical ties between behavior in real-life situations that subjects' acquaintances have viewed and interpreted, and laboratory situations in which subjects' behavior is measured directly. To the extent higher-order similarity or functional equivalence exists, correlations will be found. The experimental situations are then interpreted, or in Bem and Funder's words, the subjects' "personalities assessed," based on the equivalence classes thus established.

For instance, in one of Bem and Funder's first studies (1978), the parents of nursery school children provided judgments of the degree to which their children were cooperative with adults. These ratings of cooperativeness turned out to correlate highly with minutes and seconds of delay time measured directly in our delay-of-gratification experiment. We inferred that our experimental situation must have been in some way functionally equivalent to the situations at home from which the parents had judged cooperativeness. Our final conclusion was that delay time in our experiment was a symptom of such cooperativeness as much as it was of self control or anything like it. The equivalence class to which the delay experiment seemed to belong consisted of other cooperation situations, not necessarily other self-control situations.

ACCESS TO ONE'S OWN TRAITS IS INDIRECT The interpretation of a trait as a subjective, situational-equivalence class offers an idea about phenomenology—about what it feels like to have a trait, to the person who has it. It doesn't feel like anything, directly. Rather, the only subjective manifestation of a trait *within* a person will be his or her tendency to react and feel similarly across the situations to which the trait is relevant. As Allport wrote, "For some the world is a hostile place where men are evil and dangerous: for others it is a stage for fun and frolic. It may appear as a place to do one's duty grimly; or a pasture for cultivating friendship and love" (1961, p. 266).

Certainly a friendly person (ordinarily) does nothing like say to him- or herself, "I am a friendly person; therefore, I shall be friendly now." Rather, he or she responds in a natural way to the situation as he or she perceives it. Similarly, a bigoted person does not decide, "I'm going to acted bigoted now." Rather, his or her bigoted behavior is the result of his or her perception of a targeted group as threatening, inferior, or both (Geis, 1978).

But on reflection one can indeed begin to come to opinions about one's own traits (Bem, 1972; Thorne, 1989). One might realize that one is always happy when there are other people around, or always feels threatened, and therefore conclude that one must be "sociable" or "shy," respectively. But again, this can only happen retrospectively, and probably under unusual circumstances. Psychotherapy might be one of these: when "on the couch," one is encouraged to relate past experiences, and the client and therapist together come up with interpretations. Whether called that or not, these interpretations often involve the discovery of the client's situational equivalence classes, or traits. Certain profound life experiences might also stimulate conscious introspection.

In rare cases, explicit, volitional self-direction toward a trait-relevant behavior might take place. For example, one might say to oneself (before going to an obligatory party attended by people one detests), "now, I'm going to be *friendly* tonight," or, before asking one's boss for a raise, self-instruct "be *assertive*." As a matter of interesting psychological fact, however, in such circumstances the resulting behavior is *not* authentically a product of the trait from which it might superficially appear to emanate. The other people at the party, or the boss, probably would interpret the behavior very differently if they knew about the individual's more general behavior patterns and certainly would interpret it differently if they knew about the self-instruction.

Traits Influence Perceptions of Situations Through Dynamic Mechanisms Different situations may be rendered functionally equivalent through at least three kinds of mechanism. One kind is *motivational*. A person who is hungry arranges situations along a continuum defined by the degree to which food is offered. A person who is dispositionally fearful sees situations in terms of potential threat. A person with a high degree of sociability approaches most situations where other people are present in a positive frame of mind. Another way to say this is that one's perception of the world is partially structured by one's goals (Cantor & Kihlstrom, 1987).

A second kind of mechanism concerns *capacities* and *tendencies*. A person with great physical strength will respond to the world in terms of situational equivalence classes that are different than those experienced by one who is weak. Situations containing physical obstacles may appear interesting and challenging rather than discouraging. Similarly, a person with a tendency to overcontrol motivational impulses will behave differently across a variety of motivationally involving situations than a person whose tendency is towards undercontrol. The overcontroller will restrain his or her impulses, whereas the undercontroller will tend to express them (Funder & Block, 1989).

A third kind of mechanism is *learning*. Perhaps one has been rewarded consistently in athletic settings. Then one will approach most new athletic-like settings with an expectation of reward, with direct consequences for behavior. (This learning experience might itself be a function of one's physical prowess, an example of how these mechanisms can interact.) Perhaps one has been consistently punished for risk-taking. Such an individual is likely to perceive situations involving risk as threatening, and behave across them in a consistently cautious manner.

An important direction for future research is to specify further the dynamic mechanisms through which global traits influence behavior. Several modern approaches bypass trait concepts on the way to examining goals, perceptions, or abilities. Instead, or at least additionally, it might be helpful to ascertain how people with different traits perceive and categorize situations. In turn, it might be useful to explore how these perceptions and categorizations can be explained through motivational mechanisms, abilities and capacities, and learning.

Assessment Assertions

Self-report Is a Limited Tool for Personality Assessment Because people are not directly aware of the operation of their own traits, their self-reports cannot always be taken at face value. Such reports might be wrong because of errors in retrospective behavioral analysis—including failures of memory and failures of insight. Both kinds of failure are very common. Self-reports are also subject to self-presentation effects, the desire to portray oneself in the most favorable possible light.

This is one point where the present analysis diverges from previous and traditional presentations of trait theory. Self-reports have been and continue to be the most widely used tool for trait measurement (see McClelland, 1984, and Block & Block, 1980, for notable exceptions). This is unfortunate because, according to the present analysis, the person is in a relatively poor position to observe and report accurately his or her own traits, except under exceptional circumstances. Indeed, certain important traits may be almost invisible to the persons who have them. Imagine a chronic repressor asked to rate him- or herself on the item, "tends to deny one's own shortcomings."

This analysis helps account for one of the best

known findings of attribution research. Observers of a person's behavior are more likely to report that it was influenced by traits than is the person him- or herself. Traditional accounts of this finding have assumed this is because the observers are, simply, wrong (Jones & Nisbett, 1972). The present analysis views the actor-observer effect as a natural result of the person being in a relatively poor position to observe his or her own traits. A more objective, external point of view is necessary. This leads to the next assertion.

THE SINGLE BEST METHOD OF TRAIT ASSESSMENT IS PEER REPORT As was discussed above, traits are manifest by complex patterns of behavior the precise nature of which have by and large gone unspecified, as personality psychologists focused their attention elsewhere. However, our intuitions daily utilize complex *implicit* models of how traits are manifest in behavior. Making explicit these implicit understandings is an important but almost untouched area for further research. In the meantime, such intuitions are there to be used.

The intuitions available are those of the person being assessed, and those of the people who know him or her in daily life. Self-judgments of personality are easy to gather, and research suggests that by and large they agree well with judgments by peers (Funder & Colvin, in press). Nonetheless, self-reports are also suspect for a number of reasons, as was discussed earlier.

The impressions a person makes on those around him or her may provide a more reliable guide for how he or she can be accurately characterized. Peers' judgments have the advantage of being based on large numbers of behaviors viewed in realistic daily contexts, and on the filtering of these behavioral observations through an intuitive system capable of adjusting for both immediate situational and long-term individual contexts (Funder, 1987). Moreover, as Hogan and Hogan (1991) have observed, "personality has its social impact in terms of the qualities that are ascribed to individuals by their friends, neighbors, employers, and colleagues" (p. 12). For social traits at least, it is hard to imagine a higher court of evidential appeal that could over-rule peers' judgments, *assuming the peers have had ample opportunity to observe the target's behavior in daily life.* If everyone you meet decides you are sociable, for instance, then you *are* (Allport & Allport, 1921).

This assertion implies that an important direction for future research is to find out more about how judges of personality perform (Neisser, 1980). A better understanding of the cues that are used by everyday acquaintances in judging personality, and the circumstances under which those cues are accurate, will lead to progress regarding two important issues: (a) how personality is manifest in behavior, and (b) how personality can most accurately be judged. My own current research focuses on these topics (Funder, 1987, 1989).

Epistemological Assertions

FOR PURPOSES OF EXPLANATION, THE MOST IMPORTANT TRAITS ARE GLOBAL (BUT FOR PURPOSES OF PREDICTION, THE NARROWER THE BETTER) It appears to have become fashionable in the personality literature to eschew generality by constructing individual difference variables that are as narrow as possible. Cantor and Kihlstrom (1987) espouse a theory of "social intelligence" that regards the attribute as central to personality but *not* a general individual difference. Rather, it is viewed as a collection of relatively discrete, independent, and narrow social capacities, each relevant to performance only within a specific domain of life. A related viewpoint is that of Sternberg and Smith (1985), who suggest that different kinds of social skill are relevant only to extremely narrow classes of behavior, and that as a general construct "social skill" has little or no validity (but see Funder & Harris, 1986).

The use of narrow constructs may well increase correlations when predicting single behaviors, just as at the same time (and equivalently) it decreases the range of behaviors that can be predicted (Fishbein & Ajzen, 1974). But beyond whatever predictive advantages narrowly construed variables may have, they are often presented as if they were somehow *conceptually* superior as well. They are not. Indeed, explaining behavior in terms of a narrow trait relevant to it and little else represents an extreme case of the circularity problem sometimes (unfairly) ascribed to trait psychology in general. If "social skill at parties" is a trait detected by measuring social skill at parties, and is then seen as a *predictor* or even *cause* of social skill at parties, it is obvious that psychological understanding is not getting anywhere.

Global traits, by contrast, have real explanatory power. The recognition of a pattern of behavior is a *bona fide* explanation of each of the behaviors that comprise it.[1] Indeed, the more global a trait is, the more explanatory power it has. Connections between apparently distal phenomena are the most revealing of the deep structure of nature. For instance, if a general trait of social skill exists (see Funder & Harris, 1986), then to explain each of various, diverse behavioral outcomes with that trait is not circular at all. Instead, such an explanation relates a specific behavioral observation to a complex and general pattern of behavior. Such movement from the specific to the general is what explanation is all about.

This is not to say the explanatory task is then finished—it never is. These general patterns called traits should be the targets of further explanatory effort. One might want to investigate the developmental history of a trait, or its dynamic mechanisms, or its relationships with other traits, or the way it derives from even more general personality variables. But traits remain important stopping points in the explanatory regress. To *any* expla-

nation, one can always ask "why?" (as every 4-year-old knows). Still, between each "why" is a legitimate step towards understanding.

THE SOURCE OF TRAIT CONSTRUCTS SHOULD BE LIFE AND CLINICAL EXPERIENCE, AS FILTERED BY INSIGHTFUL OBSERVERS It has often been argued that personality constructs should be formulated independently of, or even in explicit avoidance of, the constructs used by ordinary intuition. Indeed, this is one point upon which investigators as diverse as R.B. Cattell and Walter Mischel have found common ground. Often, mechanical procedures (e.g., factor analysis, behavioral analysis) have been touted as ways to construct personality variables uncontaminated by erroneous preconceptions. The results can be quite esoteric, having ranged from Cattell's (1946) favored variables of "alexia," "praxernia," and the like, to Mischel's (1973) cognitive social-learning variables of "subjective expected values," "encoding strategies," and so forth.

However, the theory of global traits asserts that trait constructs *should* be intuitively meaningful, for three reasons. First, intuitively discernible traits are likely to have greater social utility. Many global traits describe directly the kinds of relationships people have or the impacts they have on each other. More esoteric variables, by and large, do not.

Second, psychology's direct empirical knowledge of human social behavior incorporates only a small number of behaviors, and those only under certain specific and usually artificial circumstances. Restricting the derivation of individual difference variables to the small number of behaviors that have been measured in the laboratory (or the even smaller number that have been measured in field settings) adds precision to their meaning, to be sure, but inevitably fails to incorporate the broader patterns of behaviors and contexts that make up daily life. Our intuitions, by contrast, leapfrog ahead of painstaking research. The range of behaviors and contexts immediately brought to mind by a trait like "sociable" goes far beyond anything research could directly address in the

---

[1]A reviewer of this paper expressed concern that it fails to distinguish sufficiently "between trait words as descriptions of regularities in others' behavior, and trait words as explanations of those regularities." My position is that the identification of a regularity in a person's behavior *is* an explanation of the specific instances that comprise the regularity, albeit an incomplete explanation (i.e., the next question will always be, What is the source of the regularity?). Thus, rather than confounding the two meanings of trait, the present analysis does not regard them as truly distinct.—Author

foreseeable future. Of course, our intuitions are unlikely to be completely accurate, so traits as we think of them informally and as they actually exist in nature may not be identical. However, to be useful in daily life our intuitions must provide at least roughly accurate organizations of behavior, and provide a logical starting point for research (Clark, 1987). Corrections and refinements can come later, but to begin analysis of individual differences by eschewing intuitive insight seems a little like beginning a race before the starting line.

Third, the omission of intuitively meaningful concepts from personality psychology makes study of the *accuracy* of human judgments of personality almost meaningless. People make global trait judgments of each other all the time, and the accuracy of such judgments is obviously important (Funder, 1987). However, unless one wishes to finesse the issue by studying only agreement between *perceptions* of personality (Kenny & Albright, 1987), research on accuracy requires a psychology of personality assessment to which informal, intuitive judgments can be compared. Gibson (1979) has persuasively argued that the study of perception cannot proceed without knowledge about the stimulus array and, ultimately, the reality that confronts the perceiver. This point applies equally to person perception. A theory of personality will be helpful in understanding judgments of people for the same reason that a theory of the physics of light is helpful in understanding judgments of color.

Empirical Assertions

GLOBAL TRAITS INTERACT WITH SITUATIONS IN SEVERAL WAYS Every global trait is situation specific, in the sense that it is relevant to behavior in some (perhaps many), but not all, life situations. Sociability is relevant only to behavior in situations with other people present, aggressiveness when there is the potential for interpersonal confrontation, friendliness when positive interaction is possible, and so forth. Our intuitions handle this sort of situational delimitation routinely and easily.

The delimitation of the situational relevance of a trait is sometimes called a "person-situation interaction." The empirical and conceptual development of this idea is an important achievement of the past two decades of personality research, and a valuable byproduct of the consistency controversy (Kenrick & Funder, 1988). The kind of interaction just described has been called the ANOVA or "passive" form (Buss, 1977). All that is meant is that different traits are relevant to the prediction of behavior in different situations. A child whose cooperativeness leads her to delay gratification in a situation with an adult present may be the first to quit if left alone (Bem & Funder, 1978).

At least two other, more active kinds of interaction are also important. The first is situation selection. Personality traits affect how people choose what situations to enter (Snyder & Ickes, 1985). A party might contain strong, general pressures to socialize, pressures that affect the behavior of nearly everyone who attends. But sociable people are more likely to have chosen to go the party in the first place. Thus, the trait of sociability influences behavior in part by affecting the situational influences to which the individual is exposed.

Traits can also magnify their influence on behavior through another kind of interaction. Most situations are changed to some extent by the behavior of the people in it. The presence of a sociable person can cause a situation to become more sociability-inducing. An aggressive child can turn a previously peaceful playground into a scene of general mayhem.

However, certain situations are *not* freely chosen, being imposed arbitrarily, and some situations will *not* change, no matter what the people in them may do. By short-circuiting the two kinds of person-situation interactions just discussed, such situations limit severely the influence traits can have on behavior. A prototypic example is the psychological experiment. Experiments assign subjects to conditions randomly, and the experimenter works from a set script. The subject's personality then cannot influence which situation he or she is exposed to, nor can his or her actions change the nature of the situation into which he or she is thrust (Wachtel, 1973).

But even in experiments like this, the influence of global traits is frequently detected; many examples could be cited. Consider the delay-of-gratification experiment already discussed (Bem & Funder, 1978). Nearly all the children who happened to be enrolled in a certain nursery school class entered this situation, and the experimenter worked from a set script that did not vary as a function of what the child did. Even so, the children's delay-of-gratification behavior had many and meaningful ties to their global personality traits, as assessed by their parents.

EVIDENCE CONCERNING PERSONALITY CORRELATES OF BEHAVIOR SUPPORTS THE EXISTENCE OF GLOBAL TRAITS Findings such as those summarized in the preceding paragraph have been obtained again and again. Numerous studies report correlations between behavior in arbitrarily imposed, implacable situations, and personality traits judged on the basis of behavior observed in real life. These correlations constitute powerful evidence of the important influence of personality traits on behavior, even under circumstances where one would expect their influence to be weakened.

Most of this evidence has accumulated since 1937, and so was not available to Allport, but has been summarized many times in the course of the person-situation debate. Reviews can be found in articles by Funder (1987), Kenrick and Funder (1988), and many others.

EVIDENCE CONCERNING INTERJUDGE AGREEMENT SUPPORTS THE EXISTENCE OF GLOBAL TRAITS Another form of evidence for the existence of global traits is the good agreement that can be obtained between judgments of traits rendered by peers who know the subject in diverse life situations, and between such judgments and the subject's own self-judgments. Allport regarded evidence of this sort as especially persuasive:

What is most noteworthy in research on personality is that different observers should agree as well as they do in judging any one person. This fact alone proves that there must be something really there, something objective in the nature of the individual himself that compels observers, in spite of their own prejudices, to view him in essentially the same way. (Allport, 1937, p. 288)

Fifty-three years later, the evidence is even stronger. Acquaintances who are well-acquainted with the people they judge can provide personality ratings that agree with ratings provided by other acquaintances as well as by the targets themselves (see Funder & Colvin, in press, for a review). This issue being settled, more recent work has focused on the circumstances that make interjudge agreement higher and lower, including level of acquaintanceship and the nature of the specific trait being judged (Funder, 1989).

EVIDENCE CONCERNING THE STABILITY OF PERSONALITY ACROSS THE LIFE SPAN SUPPORTS THE EXISTENCE OF GLOBAL TRAITS Allport lacked access to well-designed longitudinal studies that examined the stability of personality over time. Today, a vast body of research convincingly demonstrates that general traits of personality can be highly stable across many years. Data showing how behaviors can be predicted from measures of traits taken years before, or "post-dicted" by measures taken years later, have been reported by Funder, Block, and Block (1983), Funder and Block (1989), and Shedler and Block (1990). Similar findings from other longitudinal studies have been reported by Block (1971), Caspi (1987), McCrae and Costa (1984), and others.

Directions for Research

As a fruitful theory should, the theory of global traits raises a host of unanswered questions that deserve to be the focus of future research. They include matters of definition, origin, function, and implication.

Definition. How many global traits are there? Allport (1937, p. 305) reported finding 17,953 terms in an unabridged dictionary. Fortunately, these can be partially subsumed by more *general* constructs. Personality psychology seems to be achieving a consensus that most trait lists boil down to about five overarching terms (Digman, 1990). This does not mean there are "only" five traits, but rather that five broad concepts can serve as convenient, if very general, summaries of a wide range of the trait domain. They are Surgency (extraversion), Neuroticism, Openness (or culture), Agreeableness, and Conscientiousness.

Global traits may also be partially reducible to more narrow constructs. Perhaps friendliness is a blend of social potency and positive affect, for instance. The reduction of global traits into more specific (and possibly more factorially pure) constructs is a worthwhile direction for research. But the position taken here is that the appropriate level of analysis at which investigation should *begin*, and which more specific investigations should always remember to *inform*, is the level of intuitively accessible, global traits.

Origin. Developmental psychology has been dominated in recent years by studies of cognitive development, with the term "cognitive" sometimes construed rather narrowly. The theory of global traits draws renewed attention to the importance of investigations, especially longitudinal investigations, into the genetic and environmental origins of personality traits.

Function. The dynamic mechanisms through which global traits influence behavior remain poorly understood. As Allport hinted, they seem to involve the way individuals perceive situations and group them into equivalence classes. But the exact learning, motivational, and perceptual mechanisms involved, the way that different traits interact within individuals, and the circumstances under which a person can become consciously aware of his or her own traits are all issues needing further empirical examination.

Implication. Given that a person has a given level of a global trait, what kinds of behavioral predictions can be made accurately, into what kinds of situations? This *deductive* question will require further and more detailed examination of person-situation interactions. And, given that a person has performed a certain pattern of behavior across a certain set of situations, what can we conclude about his or her global traits? This *inductive* question will require close attention to the behavioral cues that laypersons use in their intuitive judgments of personality, and an empirical examination of the validity of these cues. Progress toward answering this question will help to provide a valid basis by which human social judgment can be evaluated and, therefore, improved (Funder, 1987).

In the current literature, these issues receive much less attention than they deserve. A neo-Allportian perspective may lead not only to a renewed examination of these central issues, but to progress in the study of personality's historic mission of integrating the various subfields of psychology into an understanding of whole, functioning individuals.

References

Ahadi, S., & Diener, E. (1989). Multiple determinants and effect size. *Journal of Personality and Social Psychology, 56*, 398–406.

Allport, F. H., & Allport, G. W. (1921). Personality traits: Their classification and measurement. *Journal of Abnormal and Social Psychology, 16*, 6–40.

Allport, G. W. (1931). What is a trait of personality? *Journal of Abnormal and Social Psychology, 25*, 368–372.

Allport, G. W. (1937). *Personality: A psychological interpretation.* New York: Henry Holt & Co.

Allport, G. W. (1958). What units shall we employ? In G. Lindzey (Ed.), *Assessment of human motives* (pp. 239–260). New York: Rinehart.

Allport, G. W. (1961). *Pattern and growth in personality.* New York: Henry Holt.

Allport, G. W. (1966). Traits revisited. *American Psychologist, 21*, 1–10.

Bem, D. J. (1972). Self-perception theory. In L. Berkowitz (Ed.), *Advances in experimental social psychology* (Vol. 6). New York: Academic Press.

Bem, D. J., & Funder, D. C. (1978). Predicting more of the people more of the time: Assessing the personality of situations. *Psychological Review, 85*, 485–501.

Block, J. (1971). *Lives through time*. Berkeley, CA: Bancroft Books.

Block, J. (1988). Critique of the act frequency approach to personality. *Journal of Personality and Social Psychology, 56*, 234–245.

Block, J. H., & Block, J. (1980). The role of ego-control and ego-resiliency in the organization of behavior. In W. A. Collins (Ed.), *Minnesota symposium on child psychology* (Vol. 13). Hillsdale, NJ: Erlbaum.

Buss, A. R. (1977). The trait-situation controversy and the concept of interaction. *Personality and Social Psychology Bulletin, 3*, 196–201.

Buss, D. M. (1984). Evolutionary biology and personality psychology: Toward a conception of human nature and individual differences. *American Psychologist, 39*, 1135–1147.

Buss, D. M., & Craik, K. H. (1983). The act frequency approach to personality. *Psychological Review, 90*, 105–126.

Cantor, N., & Kihlstrom, J. F. (1987). *Personality and social intelligence*. Englewood Cliffs, NJ: Prentice-Hall.

Carlson, R. (1971). Where is the person in personality research? *Psychological Bulletin, 75*, 203–219.

Carr, H. A., & Kingsbury, F. A. (1938). The concept of trait. *Psychological Review, 45*, 497–524.

Caspi, A. (1987). Personality in the life course. *Journal of Personality and Social Psychology, 6*, 1203–1213.

Cattell, R. B. (1946). *Description and measurement of personality*. Yonkers, NY: World Book.

Clark, A. 91987). From folk psychology to naive psychology. *Cognitive Psychology, 11*, 139–154.

Digman, J. M. (1990). Personality structure: Emergence of the five-factor model. In M. R. Rosenzweig & L. W. Porter (Eds.), *Annual Review of Psychology* (pp. 417–440). Palo Alto, CA: Annual Reviews.

Fishbein, M., & Ajzen, I. (1974). Attitudes toward objects as predictors of single and multiple behavioral criteria. *Psychological Review, 81*, 59–74.

Funder, D. C. (1987). Errors and mistakes: Evaluating the accuracy of social judgment. *Psychological Bulletin, 101*, 75–90.

Funder, D. C. (1989). Accuracy in personality judgment and the dancing bear. In D. M. Buss & N. Cantor (Eds.), *Personality psychology: Recent trends and emerging directions* (pp. 210–223). New York: Springer-Verlag.

Funder, D. C., & Block, J. (1989). The role of ego-control, ego-resiliency, and IQ in delay of gratification in adolescence. *Journal of Personality and Social Psychology, 57*, 1041–1050.

Funder, D. C., Block, J. H., & Block, J. (1983). Delay of gratification: Some longitudinal personality correlates. *Journal of Personality and Social Psychology, 44*, 1198–1213.

Funder, D. C., & Colvin, C. R. (1997). Congruence of self and others' judgments of personality. In R. Hogan, J. Johnson, & S. Briggs (Eds.), *Handbook of personality psychology*. Orlando, FL: Academic Press.

Funder, D. C., & Harris, M. J. (1986). On the several facets of personality assessment: The case of social acuity. *Journal of Personality, 54*, 528–550.

Geis, F. L. (1978). The psychological situation and personality traits in behavior. In H. London (Ed.), *Personality: A new look at metatheories*. Washington, DC: Hemisphere Publishing.

Gibson, J. J. (1979). *The ecological approach to visual perception*. New York: Harper & Row.

Heider, F. (1958). *The psychology of interpersonal relations*. New York: Wiley.

Hogan, R., & Hogan, J. (1991). Personality and status. In D. G. Gilbert & J. J. Conley (Eds.), *Personality, social skills, and psychopathology: An individual differences approach* (pp. 137–154). New York: Plenum.

Jones, E. E., & Nisbett, R. E. (1972). The actor and the observer: Divergent perceptions of the cause of behavior. In E. E. Jones, D. Kanouse, H. H. Kelley, R. E. Nisbett, S. Valins, & B. Weiner (Eds.), *Attribution: Perceiving the causes of behavior*. Morristown, NJ: General Learning Press.

Kelley, H. H. (1967). Attribution theory in social psychology. In D. Levin (Ed.), *Nebraska symposium on motivation* (pp. 192–241). Lincoln: University of Nebraska Press.

Kelly, G. A. (1955). *The psychology of personal constructs* (Vols. 1 and 2). New York: Norton.

Kenny, D. A., & Albright, L. (1987). Accuracy in interpersonal perception: A social relations analysis. *Psychological Bulletin, 102*, 390–402.

Kenrick, D. T., & Funder, D. C. (1988). Profiting from controversy: Lessons from the person-situation debate. *American Psychologist, 43*, 23–34.

McClelland, D. C. (1984). *Motives, personality and society*. New York: Praeger.

McCrae, R. R., & Costa, P. C., Jr. (1984). *Emerging lives, enduring dispositions*. Boston: Little, Brown.

Mischel, W. (1968). *Personality and assessment*. New York: Wiley.

Mischel, W. (1973). Toward a cognitive social learning reconceptualization of personality. *Psychological Review, 80*, 252–283.

Neisser, U. (1980). On "social knowing." *Personality and Social Psychology Bulletin, 6*, 601–605.

Scarr, S., & McCartney, K. (1983). How people make their own environments: A theory of genotype –> environment effects. *Child Development, 54*, 424–435.

Shedler, J., & Block, J. (1990). Adolescent drug use and psychological health. *American Psychologist, 45*, 612–630.

Snyder, M., & Ickes, W. (1985). Personality and social behavior. In G. Lindzey & E. Aronson (Eds.), *The handbook of social psychology* (3rd ed., pp. 883–948). New York: Random House.

Sternberg, R. J., & Smith, C. (1985). Social intelligence and decoding skills in nonverbal communication. *Social Cognition, 3*, 168–192.

Thorne, A. (1989). Conditional patterns, transference, and the coherence of personality across time. In D. Buss & N. Cantor (Eds.), *Personality: Recent trends and emerging directions*. New York: Springer-Verlag.

Wachtel, P. (1973). Psychodynamics, behavior therapy, and the implacable experimenter: An inquiry into the consistency of personality. *Journal of Abnormal Psychology, 82*, 324–334.

Witkin, H. A. Lewis, H. B., Hertzman, M., Machover, K., Meissner, P., & Wapner, S. (1954). *Personality through perception*. New York: Harper.

Zuroff, D. C. (1986). Was Gordon Allport a trait theorist? *Journal of Personality and Social Psychology, 51*, 993–1000.

REFERENCES FOR EDITORS'
INTRODUCTORY NOTES

Allport, G. W., & Odbert, H. S. (1936). Trait-names: A psycho-lexical study. *Psychological Monographs: General and Applied, 47*, 171. (1, Whole No. 211).

Barocas, R. Seifer, R., & Sameroff, A. J. (1985). Defining environmental risk: Multiple dimensions of psychological vulnerability. *American Journal of Community Psychology, 13*, 443–447.

Bem, D. J., & Allen, A. (1974). On predicting some of the people some of the time: The search for cross-situational consistencies in behavior. *Psychological Review, 81*, 506–520.

Bem, D. J., & Funder, D. C. (1978). Predicting more of the people more of the time: Assessing the personality of situations. *Psychological Review, 85*, 485–501.

Block, J. (1965). *The challenge of response sets*. New York: Appleton-Century-Crofts.

Block, J. (1995). A contrarian view of the five-factor approach to personality description. *Psychological Bulletin, 117*, 187–215.

Booth-Kewley, S., & Friedman, H. S. (1987). Psychological predictors of heart disease: A quantitative review. *Psychological Bulletin, 101*, 343–362.

Briggs, S. R., & Cheek, J. M. (1986). The role of factor analysis in the development and evaluation of personality scales. *Journal of Personality, 54*, 106–148.

Briggs, S. R., & Cheek, J. M. (1988). On the nature of self-monitoring: Problems with assessment, problems with validity. *Journal of Personality and Social Psychology, 54*, 663–678.

Franz, C. E., & White, K. M. (1985). Individuation and attachment in personality development: Extending Erikson's theory. *Journal of Personality, 53*, 224–256.

Freud, S. (1965). *New introductory lectures on psychoanalysis*. (J. Strachey, Ed. & Transl.) New York: Norton. (Original work published 1933.)

Freud, S. (1989). *The psychopathology of everyday life.* (J. Strachey, Ed. & Transl.) New York: Norton. (Original work published 1920.)

Funder, D. C. (1997). *The personality puzzle.* New York: Norton.

Funder, D. C., & Colvin, C. R. (1991). Explorations in behavioral consistency: Properties of persons, situations, and behaviors. *Journal of Personality and Social Psychology, 60,* 773–794.

Gay, P. (1988). *Freud: A life for our time.* New York: Norton.

Mischel, W. (1968). *Personality and assessment.* New York: Wiley.

Mischel, W., & Peake, P. K. (1982). Beyond *déjà vu* in the search for cross-situational consistency. *Psychological Review, 90,* 730–755.

Mischel, W., & Shoda, Y. (1995). A cognitive-affective system theory of personality: Reconceptualizing situations, dispositions, dynamics, and invariance in personality structure. *Psychological Review, 102,* 246–268.

Murray, H. A. (1938). *Explorations in personality.* New York: Oxford University Press.

Myers, I. B., & McCaulley, M. H. (1985). *Manual: A guide to the development and use of the Myers-Briggs Type Indicator.* Palo Alto, CA: Consulting Psychologists Press.

Ozer, D. J. (1989). Construct validity in personality assessment. In D. M. Buss & N. Cantor (Eds.), *Personality psychology: Recent trends and emerging directions* (pp. 224–234). New York: Springer-Verlag.

Ozer, D. J., & Reise, S. P. (1994). Personality assessment. *Annual Review of Psychology, 45,* 357–388.

Ross, L. (1977). The intuitive psychologist and his shortcomings. In L. Berkowitz (Ed.), *Advances in experimental social psychology* (Vol. 10, pp. 174–214). New York: Academic Press.

Sameroff, A. J., & Seifer, R. (1995). Accumulation of environmental risk and child mental health. In H. E. Fitzgerald, B. M. Lester, & B. S. Zuckerman (Eds.), *Children of poverty: Research, health, and policy issues.* New York: Garland.

Snyder, M., & Gangestad, S. (1986). On the nature of self-monitoring: Matters of assessment, matters of validity. *Journal of Personality and Social Psychology, 51,* 125–139.

Westen, D. (1990). Psychoanalytic approaches to personality. In L. Pervin (Ed.), *Handbook of personality: Theory and research* (pp. 21–65). New York: Guilford Press.